The Encyclopedia
of
Practical Christianity

The Encyclopedia
of
Practical Christianity

Dr. Robert Morey

Christian Scholars Press
1350 E. Flamingo Road, Suite 97
Las Vegas, Nevada, 88119

Copyright ©2003 by Robert A. Morey
Published by Christian Scholars Press
1350 E. Flamingo Rd., Suite 97
Las Vegas, Nevada, 88119

ISBN No. 931230-11-0

About the Author

D r. Robert Morey is the executive director of Faith Defenders and the author of more than forty books, some of which have been translated into French, German, Indonesian, Italian, Polish, Finnish, Dutch, Spanish, Norwegian, Swedish, Farsi and Mandarin Chinese. Dr. Morey is an internationally recognized scholar in the fields of philosophy, theology, comparative religion, the cults and the occult. He earned a bachelor of arts degree in philosophy, a master of divinity degree in theology, a doctor of ministry degree in cult apologetics and was awarded a doctor of divinity degree for his outstanding research on the origins of Islam. For more information on his books, audiotapes and videotapes, write to Faith Defenders, P.O. Box 7447, Orange, California, 92863; call 1-800-41-TRUTH; or visit the Faith Defenders website at www.faithdefenders.com

Other books by Dr. Robert Morey

An Analysis of the Hadith
Battle of the Gods
Common Logical Fallacies Made by Muslims
Death and the Afterlife
A Defense of Original Sin
An Examination of Exclusive Psalmody
The Dooyeweerdian Concept of the Word of God
Exploring the Attributes of God
Fearing God
The Giving of Offerings and Tithes
Here Is Your God
Horoscopes and the Christian
How the Old & New Testaments Relate to
    Each Other
How to Answer a Jehovah's Witness
How to Answer a Mormon
How to Keep Your Faith While in College
How to Keep Your Kids Drug-Free
An Introduction to Defending the Faith
Is Allah Just Another Name for God?
Is the Sabbath for Today?
The Islamic Invasion

Jesus in the Mishnah and Talmud
Jewish Apocalypticism and Biblical Prophecy
Jihad According to the Qur'an
Men's Discipleship Manual
The Moon God Allah in the Archeology of the
    Middle East
The Nature and Extent of God's Knowledge
The New Atheism and the Erosion of
    Freedom
The Reformation View of Roman Catholicism
A Refutation of Roman Catholicism
Reincarnation and Christianity
A Reply to Shabir Ally
Responding With Reason
Satan's Devices
Studies in the Atonement
The Trinity: Evidence and Issues
The Truth About Masons
When Is It Right to Fight?
Will Islam Cause World War III?
Winning the War Against Radical Islam
Worship: It's Not Just Sunday Morning

Special thanks to Matthew Meiser, Rae Boeving, Tom Hanson, and, most of all, my son, John Morey, whose enthusiasm for this project encouraged me to complete it.

My Personal Statement of Faith

I BELIEVE that I exist to glorify God and to enjoy Him forever; nothing in life has a higher purpose than this grand goal; in this great truth I find comfort as well as purpose.

I BELIEVE that God has revealed in the Bible how I should glorify and enjoy Him; the Bible is the infallible Word of God; it comes from the inspiration of the Holy Spirit; it is inerrant in all that it affirms as true; it tells us what to believe and how to live; our confidence in life and death is based on the certitude of God's Word.

I BELIEVE that God is Spirit in nature, infinite in all His attributes, and incomparable in all that He is; He is one God in Three Persons: the Father, the Son, and the Holy Spirit; our Creator, Redeemer, and Sanctifier; in whose power and wisdom, righteousness, goodness, mercy, and grace we trust.

I BELIEVE that in the beginning God created the heavens and the earth, and that He sustains and guides all things in accordance with His divine will; in His wisdom and kind Providence I safely trust.

I BELIEVE that God created man in His own image, thus I am not an animal or a machine produced by a chance-driven evolutionary process; as God's image bearer, I have intrinsic worth, significance, and meaning; I have an immortal soul, which will depart my body at death and will go either to heaven or hell; my dignity comes from being created in the image of God, which dignity I share with all other men and women regardless of race or creed.

I BELIEVE that I fell into sin and guilt with Adam and Eve in the garden of Eden; the results of Adam's Fall are so cosmic in scope and so radical in nature that only God Himself could restore Paradise to man; by virtue of our sinful nature inherited from Adam, I am incapable of meriting the grace or favor of God; I am entirely dependent upon His mercy and grace for my salvation and I do not trust in my own works or goodness.

I BELIEVE that the Father sent the Son to redeem a lost and erring mankind; Jesus of Nazareth actually existed in history and that He was the Christ, i.e. the long-awaited Jewish Messiah; He is the eternal pre-existent Word of God; He is God of very God as well as man of very man, two natures but one person; He willingly died on the cross for my sins; He arose bodily on the third day for my justification; He ascended into heaven for my sanctification; and He is now at the right of the Father to intercede on my behalf.

I BELIEVE that the Father and the Son sent the Holy Spirit to apply to me what Christ accomplished according to the plan of the Father; my only hope for heaven is based on the fact that I am chosen by the Father, purchased by the Son, and sealed by the Spirit, blessed God Three in One!

I BELIEVE that salvation is by grace alone, through faith alone, in Christ alone, apart from works; justification is that act of God in which the imputed righteousness of Christ is credited to my account; all my hopes for heaven rest solely on the divinity of His person and the sufficiency and finality of His work of atonement.

I BELIEVE that the Christian Church, both universal and local, was set up by the Lord Jesus Christ to be His Body on earth; God has given to the Church the glorious privilege of preaching the gospel in all the world; all those who have placed their faith in Jesus Christ for salvation are our brothers and sisters in Christ regardless of denominational distinctions.

I BELIEVE that Jesus Christ is the only way to the Father; His name is the only name under heaven whereby I might be saved; there is only one true God, Maker of heaven and earth; all the gods of the heathen are false gods; repentance toward God and faith in Jesus Christ are essential to salvation; the gospel is the only message of salvation for a lost and erring mankind.

I BELIEVE in the resurrection of the body and life everlasting; Jesus Christ is going to return visibly and physically to this world at the end of the ages; He will come to judge the living and the dead; history will reach its appointed end; the earth will be purified and redeemed; the saints will inherit a new earth; and eternal conscious torment awaits all those who do not know God through faith in Jesus Christ. Amen!

My Personal Testimony

While I was visiting my grandmother in Orlando, Florida, she asked me to visit her church, North Park Baptist Church (Southern Baptist Convention). I did not believe in anything at the time—as my father was an agnostic when sober and an atheist when drunk. But on Oct. 29, 1962, a Mr. Mobley witnessed to me. That night, I saw my need of salvation and asked the Lord to save me.

My father became so upset that he gave me an ultimatum to either give up Jesus or leave the family. So, I packed my bags and left home at the age of 16.

Various Christians have helped me along the way and fulfilled Jesus' promise that if you have to give up mother and father in this life, He would send you many mothers and fathers to take their place.

I was called to preach the same day I was saved and began preaching from the pulpit two weeks after my conversion. I minister today in eternal gratitude to God for saving me. On Oct. 27, 1963, I was baptized at and joined Calvary Baptist Church in New York City, where I remained for eight years under Dr. Stephen Olford.

Table of Contents

Part One — The Individual

Part Two — The Family

Part Three — The Church

Part Four — The Nation

Introduction

The Encyclopedia of Practical Christianity is a chronicle of what was taught at New Life Bible Church for nearly twenty years and then at Faith Community Church. When New Life Bible Church was first established, it was decided that if we failed to plan what we were going to do as a church, we were actually planning to fail. Instead of aimlessly wandering around in our study of the Scriptures, we decided to develop a comprehensive plan that would give us the scope of the biblical topics that we should cover. This volume of material represents our attempt to fulfill our original goal.

Vision

Your vision is composed of the goals that you set before yourself. These goals provide you with the reasons why you must do or not do certain things. They also provide you with the motivation to persevere in the face of trials and suffering. The desire to reach your goals will enable you to sacrifice willingly to see your "vision" fulfilled. You will gladly spend your time, energy and money in order to see your goals realized.

I. The Nature of Our Goals

Various kinds of goals make up a person's vision. We must understand what our goals are.

A. Short-range or long-range goals: We must be careful not to expect the immediate fulfillment of all our goals. Instant gratification is not the Christian way. Some goals are fulfilled only after a long time of hard work or suffering. We often experience failed expectations because we wrongly identified long-range goals as short-range goals.

B. Consistent or inconsistent goals: If we fail to identify what our goals are, then we will be inconsistent in our goals. One goal may actually cancel out another goal. Thus we will experience failure and frustration as our goals fight against each other.

C. Material or immaterial goals: The child of God gives the greatest priority to the immaterial goals of spirituality such as love, humility, kindness, etc. The goal of material wealth is proper as long as it is secondary (1 Tim. 6:6-10, 17-19). Your character is more important than your possessions.

D. Comprehensive or incomplete goals: The Lordship of Christ is over all of life. No aspect of life is neutral or secular. Everything should be ordered according to the truths, values and priorities of Scripture.

E. Yourself or others as goals: We must not be self-centered or selfish in our goals. We must keep in mind that we exist to serve God and others (1 Cor. 6:19-20).

F. This life or eternity as goals: This life is so short that the priority of preparing for eternity must influence every decision (James 4:13-17).

> *Only one life,*
> *'Twill soon be past;*
> *and only what's done,*
> *for Christ shall last!*

II. The Origins of Your Goals

Your goals come from somewhere. They do not just pop into existence without an origin or source. We must ask ourselves from where do our goals come? Why do we desire them? There are only four possible origins of goals.

A. The WORLD around us may squeeze us into its own mold. Thus we find ourselves with worldly goals that are unbecoming of a child of God (Rom. 12:1-2; Eph. 2:1-2).

B. The FLESH (i.e., our sinful side) will provide us with all kinds of selfish goals (Gal. 5:17-21; Eph. 2:3).

C. The DEVIL is more than willing to give us harmful goals that destroy the soul (Eph. 2:1-2; 6:11-18).

D. The LORD has revealed our goals in Scripture so that the youngest and weakest of His people can know His will (Rom. 12:2).

III. God's Goals for Your Life

When we desire to establish our goals in life, we must turn to the Scriptures as the place where God has revealed His vision for our lives. The Bible is to be our rule in faith and practice (Isa. 8:20; 2 Tim. 3:16-17).

IV. The Comprehensive Vision

The Lordship of Christ in All of Life

We must reject the idea that life is divided into secular and sacred sections. All of life is sacred. Christ's Lordship extends into every area of life. There are no neutral or secular areas for "the earth is the Lord's and the fullness thereof and they that dwell therein" (Psa. 24:1). We must do all things for the glory of God (1 Cor. 10:31).

V. The Comprehensive Vision From God As Given in Scripture

God wants us to KNOW, BE and DO certain things as:

A. Individuals

B. Families

C. Churches

D. Nations

Note: KNOW means the acquisition of biblical knowledge.

BE refers to the development of a godly character.

DO means putting God's Word into action.

A. God's Vision for Us as Individuals

KNOW	BE	DO
The inspiration and origin of Scripture	knowledgeable	think
hermeneutics	saved	read the Bible
doctrine of God	confident	seek salvation
doctrine of man	consistent	obtain assurance
doctrine of salvation	dependent on God	pray
assurance	trustworthy	resist temptation
devotions	Spirit-filled	seek the Spirit
how to pray	obedient	make right decisions
obedience	disciplined	give to God
temptation	godly	worship God
the filling / baptism of the Spirit	charitable	exercise gifts
guidance	God-fearing	witness
discipline	zealous	manage time well
how to develop godly habits	hopeful	attend church
stewardship / money	loving	join the church
worship	faithful	seek to minister
the fear of God	kind	accept responsibility
the priesthood of the believer	considerate	practice
spiritual gifts	sensitive	one-anothering
how to witness	respectful	live for Christ
how to manage your time and energy	moral	have right priorities
how to testify	honest	seek knowledge
how to counsel	careful	obtain wisdom and understanding
apologetics	aggressive	persevere
the Christian world and life view	submissive	cooperate
cults / occult	persistent	cope with things
how to develop a good conscience	hard-working	handle emotions
fasting	healthy in mind, body and soul	resist the devil
chastisement: its nature / our response	successful	grow in grace / knowledge
good works	prosperous	use all means of grace
the Law of God in the life of the believer	responsible	keep eternity in view
prophecy	content	seek godly counsel
	humble	admit weaknesses
	patient	confess sin and ask for help and prayer
	joyful	win converts
	peaceful	etc.
	balanced	
	stable	
	mature	
	etc.	

Know	Be	Do
how to handle suffering and pain death, Hell and Heaven devices of Satan Christian hospitality church involvement survey of the Bible the Christian life how to handle / solve depression Bible doctrines backsliding: its causes and cures apostasy basic books to read etc.		

B. God's Vision for Us as Families

KNOW	BE	DO
the origin, nature and structure of the family dating sexuality youthful lusts premarital counseling planning a Christian wedding how to create harmony in marriage how to create a theistic atmosphere home standards family devotions and worship how to train children for Christ the needs of men and women why marriages fall apart how to sweeten a sour marriage singleness divorce remarriage death in family religious education in the home parental authority abortion birth control mercy killing euthanasia suicide cults / occult drugs Christian schools etc.	a Christian home harmonious peaceful loving restful content hospitable evangelistic mission-minded stable healthy joyful prosperous obedient productive consistent disciplined friendly open etc.	think read the Bible practice the principles accept roles given in Scripture have family devotions create a theistic atmosphere have family night resolve problems avoid divorce seek counseling date and marry only Christians flee immorality communicate with mate and children be united and consistent in discipline control anger and bitterness have right priorities be pro-life do not neglect parents provide for children etc.

C. God's Vision for Us as a Church

KNOW	BE	DO
the origin, nature and structure of church the offices of the church responsibility of members Body Life concept worship social action discipleship programs missions house churches political action church goals financial freedom etc.	Biblically based and structured Christ-centered charismatic joyful dynamic stable balanced in form / freedom evangelistic involved in ministering to other churches friendly etc.	think read the Bible join the church get involved minister to others through your gifts seek the purity of life and doctrine avoid causing divisions learn to cooperate with others submit to the elders aspire to leadership etc.

D. God's Vision for Us as a Nation

KNOW	BE	DO
the origin, nature, functions and authority of the state the right use of force the just war theory how to overcome tyranny taxes church / state issues social action justice and the poor communism / socialism God's civil law the origin of the free enterprise system and democracy etc.	free righteous just faithful aggressive compassionate lawful constitutional capitalistic etc.	think read the Bible understand the issues vote intelligently get involved speak out and protest be Christian first and American second run for office etc.

VI. The Church's Responsibility

The leaders of the church have the God-given responsibility to teach the whole counsel of God as given in Scripture (Acts 20:27). Thus their teaching ministry should cover all the topics in the above chart. To see how you have been taught, go through the chart and see how much of the material has been dealt with in your church. Pastors should review the chart to see how they are doing.

At one pastors conference I asked the following questions:

> If you were to take a pair of scissors and go through the Church Epistles and cut out and pile together all the verses dealing with a call to salvation, how many verses would there be in that pile? Then if you went back and cut out all the verses dealing with doctrine, how many verses would be piled up? And if you went back yet again and piled up all the verses on how to live the Christian life, how many verses would you have piled up? Now, which of these piles would be the biggest?

> Did the Apostle Paul spend the majority of his time telling the churches "to be saved" or did he teach them sound doctrine and how to live the Christian life? Since the Church Epistles major on what to believe and how to live and minor on how to be saved, does this indicate how we should structure our preaching?

Some of the pastors were deeply convicted that their preaching ministry did not reflect the priorities found in Scripture. The major responsibility of pastors according to Eph. 4:11-12 is to "equip the saints," not to get people "saved." What is so sad today is far too many evangelical churches spend so much time trying to "save" sinners that they never teach the saints anything! The sermons are often shallow and filled with jokes, stories and tearful calls to "come down to the altar." The only problem is that 99.9 percent of those hearing the sermon are already "saved" and in desperate need of sound doctrine and practical teaching. The Christian life does not end when someone is saved. It has just begun!

What is equally sad is that in the few churches that understand that their job is to minister to God's people, they focus only on one of the "know," "be" or "do" categories. Thus while some churches are good at teaching doctrine, they utterly fail when it comes to character building or putting God's Word into practice. Then there are those churches that emphasize character building but never teach doctrine or call for action. And there are those churches that are filled with a whirlwind of activities but never teach doctrine or focus on character building. God never intended His church to be lopsided. This is why the whole counsel of God should be taught to His people.

One helpful thing to remember is that since every Christian is a minister, every church is a seminary. The purpose of church is not to run down or dance in the aisle! The church is not a circus or an evangelistic crusade! It is the place where the Lordship of Christ over all of life is put into practice by teaching God's people what to believe and how to live.

VII. The Order of the Topics

A pastor should be careful not to overemphasize one aspect of the whole counsel of God. He cannot just teach doctrine or character qualities. People need all the truth found in Scripture. For example, after preaching on the family, he should deal with the church or the nation. If he has just finished a how to series, he should do an expository series on some book of the Bible or expound on some great doctrine. If he has been doing some heavy teaching, he should next do a light series of sermons. He needs to teach from the O.T. as well as the N.T. He must preach on the Gospels as well as the Epistles. He must strike a balance between Law and Gospel. He must be careful not to become lopsided, for "as goes the priest, so go the people."

The exact order in which the topics on the chart should be dealt with is left up to the individual needs and circumstances of each congregation. The Holy Spirit will guide the elders or the pastor in this regard. We have attempted to arrange the topics in a logical order, not a homiletical order. Thus we did not hesitate to skip from section to section and topic to topic depending on what our needs were at that time.

VIII. The Chart Is Not Complete

The chart is by no means complete. When New Life Bible Church started, I asked the congregation to write down all the subjects in the Bible that they wanted to know about. Then I wrote down topics I had always wished some pastor would have taught me. Then the lists were placed together. The results were humbling to say the least! I could no longer say, "I don't know what to preach," for here was a list of topics from God's Word which demanded my attention.

I have always heard that the Bible was an "inexhaustible barrel," but now I know that this is true! As the years have gone by, more topics have been added to the list. New topics and insights are constantly being added. There is no end in sight! The Scriptures are as infinite as the Mind that inspired them.

IX. The Need Dictates the Style

Since these studies were given in the context of a real-life church and not a seminary classroom, they will vary in style from a simple sermon outline to a detailed theological statement. Some subjects naturally require a deeper treatment due to the difficulty of the topic. Thus, the uneven treatment of the topics covered in this book reflects the normal preaching ministry of any local church. The needs of the people of God should always dictate the form as well as the content of sermons.

Chapter One
Salvation

An understanding of God's wonderful plan of redemption from eternity to eternity reveals the magnitude of the love He has bestowed upon us.

1) Salvation from God's viewpoint
   a) Salvation began as a divine plan or blueprint God made in eternity past, before the world was created (Eph. 1:4-5; 3:11; 2 Tim. 1:9-10; Titus 1:2; 1 Pet. 1:20; 2 Thess. 2:13; Rev. 13:8).
   b) Basic truths concerning God's plan of salvation
      i) God was not taken by surprise when man fell into sin and guilt. He knows all things before they come to pass.

Note: Some modern theologians teach that God is finite in His knowledge; i.e., He does not know the future. This heresy is refuted by the simple fact that the Bible argues that God is God because He does, indeed, know the future. Prophecy is the revelation of what God knows will happen according to His predetermined plan. See Isa. 41:21-29; 42:8-9; 44:7-8; 45:11-13, 21-22; 46:8-11; 48:5-6, 14.

      ii) Salvation is not something God concocted on the spur of the moment out of panic when man fell. God never panics! The plan of salvation is rooted in the eternal decrees of God (Acts 13:48; Eph. 1:4-11; Rev. 13:8). The atonement was not something that happened by chance. It was planned by God before the world was created. (For further details see Robert Morey's book, *Battle of the Gods*.)
      iii) God's plan reveals four things:
         (1) God's decision (purpose and decree)
         (2) God's choice (election and predestination)
         (3) God's commitment (love)

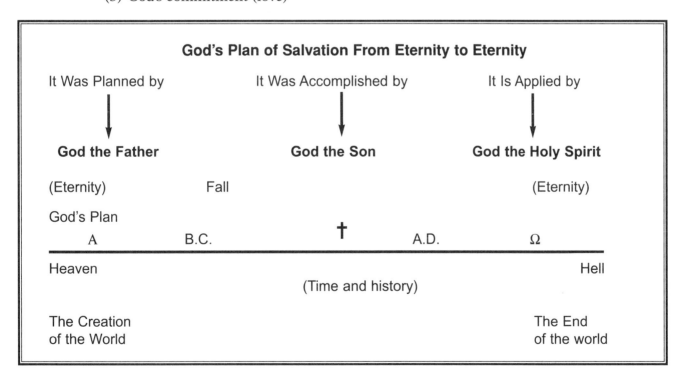

(4) God's covenant (the death of Christ)

iv) Salvation involves the Triune God:

(1) It was planned by the Father in eternity (Eph. 1:3-6).

(2) It was accomplished by the Son in history (Eph. 1:7-12).

(3) It is applied by the Spirit in the present (Eph. 1:12-13).

> We are chosen by the Father,
> Purchased by the Son,
> Sealed by the Spirit,
> Blessed God three in one!

v) Salvation is all of God 100 percent (Jonah 2:9). He saves us all by Himself. Salvation is of the Lord (Eph. 2:1-10; Rom. 9:15-16).

(1) This means there is always hope for salvation for anyone as long as they are alive. There is no point of no return in the Gospel. Sinners can be saved even on their deathbed. Keep on praying and witnessing (2 Tim. 2:10, 24-25).

Note: Some thinkers (such as Charles Finney) have believed that salvation is a work of man and not a sovereign work or act of God. This led them to teach that some men are too hardened to change themselves. Thus some people are savable and others are not. They say there is no hope for those who are no longer capable of self-reformation. This leaves hardened sinners with no way out. This is one of the most depressing as well as damning heresies ever invented.

(2) This means that God should receive all the glory for salvation (1 Cor. 1:26-31). All Christians on their knees praying, or on their feet praising God, know and acknowledge that they owe everything to Jesus. God will not share His glory with man (Isa. 42:8). Any theology that gives any man the glory is not of God.

The humble child of God rightfully sings:

> Thank you, Lord, for saving my soul.
> Thank you, Lord, for making me whole.
> Thank you, Lord, for giving to me
> Thy great salvation, so rich, so free.

2) Salvation from man's viewpoint

a) The fact that God saves sinners does not negate or lessen the fact that man is responsible to repent and to believe the Gospel. Unless you repent of your sins and turn to Christ in faith, you shall most surely perish.

b) We are commanded to repent and to believe the Gospel (Acts 17:30; Matt. 11:28-30; Acts 16:30-31). This truth complements Divine Sovereignty. It does not contradict it.

John 6:37		John 6:28-29
God's Sovereignty		Human Responsibility

c) The fact that man is spiritually dead and helpless does not negate or lessen his responsibility to believe the Gospel or repent of his sins.

John 6:44, 45		John 6:40
Human Inability		Human Responsibility

d) Therefore, as far as you are concerned, election and human inability are issues that belong to God—not you!

So, don't worry about election.
Don't worry about inability.
Trust Christ instead!

e) From man's viewpoint, what is his responsibility?

Answer: To receive Jesus Christ as his personal Lord and Savior. This commitment involves the whole being of a person.

Chart No. 1: Commitment of the Total Man		
I. Intellect	II. Emotion	III. Will
1. Know the Gospel (John 8:32; Rom. 10:17)	1. Sorrow for sin (2 Cor. 7:9-11) (Acts 20:21)	1. Turn from sin (Acts 20:21)
2. Accept the Gospel as truth (Matt. 16:13-18)	2. Awareness of needs (Mk. 10:46-52)	2. Receive Christ as Lord & Savior (John 1:12)
	Christ Only **Faith Only** **Grace Only**	

II. The Emotions
  1) In order to experience God's salvation, there must be true, heartfelt sorrow for sin.
    a) Sorrow is absolutely necessary for salvation (Pro. 15:13; cf. Psa. 51:17 and Psa. 38:18).
    b) We must be careful to distinguish between true sorrow and false sorrow (2 Cor. 7:10).
Definition: Godly sorrow is Godward sorrow. True sorrow is mental grief and inward pain caused by an overwhelming awareness of one's sin against such a good God and a wonderful Savior. The fact of one's sin causes regret and grief (Lk. 15:17-19).
(Note: There will be various degrees of sorrow because of personality differences).
Definition: Worldly sorrow is manward sorrow. It is grief and regret over the results and penalty of sin. It is sorrow for getting caught. It is self-pity for the mess into which sin brings us. (Example: unwed teenage mother, Heb. 12:16-17.)
    c) True sorrow will lead to repentance. Repentance is a change of mind in which you turn away from sin to walk in the way of righteousness (2 Cor. 7:9-11).

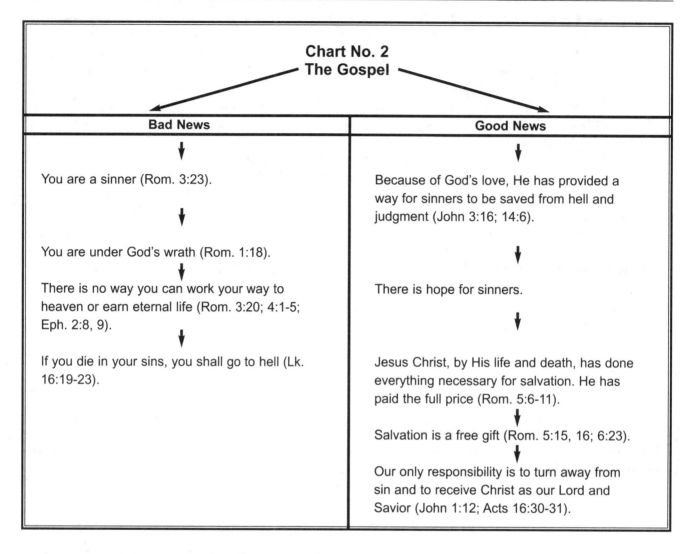

Chart No. 2
The Gospel

Bad News	Good News
You are a sinner (Rom. 3:23).	Because of God's love, He has provided a way for sinners to be saved from hell and judgment (John 3:16; 14:6).
You are under God's wrath (Rom. 1:18).	There is hope for sinners.
There is no way you can work your way to heaven or earn eternal life (Rom. 3:20; 4:1-5; Eph. 2:8, 9).	
If you die in your sins, you shall go to hell (Lk. 16:19-23).	Jesus Christ, by His life and death, has done everything necessary for salvation. He has paid the full price (Rom. 5:6-11).
	Salvation is a free gift (Rom. 5:15, 16; 6:23).
	Our only responsibility is to turn away from sin and to receive Christ as our Lord and Savior (John 1:12; Acts 16:30-31).

Have you ever experienced godly sorrow—for sin—unto repentance?
If you have, then you have felt your need of salvation.
Do you have an overwhelming sense of your need for salvation?

Your need:
1. To be saved from hell.
2. To be forgiven of your sins.
3. To be a child of God.
4. To be given power to change your life and break evil habits.

SORROW + NEED = SEEKING CHRIST

III. The Will
1) Repentance is a change of mind in which you turn away from sin. You do this as a deliberate willful choice on your part. Repentance was preached by Christ (Matt. 4:17) and the apostles (Acts 2:38; 20:21; 26:20).

2) Faith is an active receiving of Christ as your personal Lord and Savior (John 1:12).

Forsaking		Forsaking
All		All
I	or	I
Take		Trust
Him		Him

3) Salvation is: By grace alone as the foundation and basis of salvation,
   Through faith alone as the means of salvation,
   In Christ alone as the object of faith

SALVATION: LEADING SOMEONE TO CHRIST

Problems to be avoided

In dealing with a person concerning his spiritual needs, several pitfalls must be avoided in order to ensure that the person truly understands the Gospel.

Problems to Be Avoided	
Problems	**Solutions**
A. "Easy believism"	Stress repentance and commitment (Mk. 12:30-31; Mk. 8:34-38)
B. Earning salvation by good works	Salvation by God's works. Grace alone. (Eph. 2:8-9)
C. Peer pressure — "everyone does it"	Stress personal commitment (John 6:60-69)
D. Emotionalism	Stress content (1 Cor. 15:3-4)
E. Perfectionism	Sin will always be a problem in this life (Rom. 7:21-24)

1) General guidelines for witnessing
   a) Use your Bible.
   b) Take the time required to communicate the message.
   c) Avoid the many pitfalls that distort the Gospel, such as quick decisions, trickery or bribery, etc.
   d) Make it personal, i.e. avoid treating the person as a number.
   e) Stress the Gospel essentials.
2) Gospel essentials
   a) Man's desperate need of the sovereign grace of God because of his sin and guilt.

b) The sufficiency of Christ's work on the cross. He did it all for us.

c) Man's need for repentance (turning from sin) and faith (trusting in Christ).

d) Man's need for personal commitment to the Living Christ.

Conclusion

We must strive to present the Gospel as clearly as possible. If our message is distorted we will give a false hope and a false assurance of salvation to those who hear us.

Chapter Two
Assurance of Salvation

Introduction

"How can I know that I am a true child of God?" is one of the most practical questions a human being can ask. After all, to face an unknown eternity is a burden that most people do not wish to bear throughout their life. Yet, many people do not know that if they were to die today that they would be in Heaven with Christ. Do you know that you have eternal life? Are you sure that you have been saved? Have you been born again?

I. The History of the Doctrine of Assurance

The history of the doctrine of assurance is filled with many false views on the subject, and the believer must be willing to cast off his or her previous views and look to the Scriptures alone for light on the subject. A brief review of the history of the doctrine of assurance will help us to clear the air of the false views that have robbed the people of God of enjoying the wondrous gift of assurance.

    A. The Roman Catholic Church denied the possibility of assurance at the Council of Trent. This is understandable because they taught that their salvation depended on:

    1. Their works—not Christ's works alone.
    2. Their life—not Christ's life alone.
    3. Their holding on—not Christ's holding on alone.
    4. The circumstances of their death—not Christ's death alone.

Biblical answer

The Bible clearly teaches that we can have assurance of salvation. This is clear from 1 John 5:13; 2 Pet. 1:10; Rom. 6:23, 2 Tim. 4:18; etc. We are saved on the basis of the work of another, namely the work of Jesus Christ (Rom. 5:6-10, Eph. 2:8-10; Titus 3:5). Christ has done it all for us.

Note: Assurance of salvation is one of the most powerful ways to witness to Roman Catholics. Not even the Pope has assurance of salvation!

When we come to the age in which we live, we find the Catholic view resurfacing in the Arminian holiness movement, which teaches that you are saved if YOU live right. You lose or gain your salvation depending on your works. For many years, my grandmother believed that whenever she lost her temper, she lost her salvation as well! She could be saved and lost several times a day! Thankfully, she came to a biblical understanding of her security in Christ.

    B. Some of the Protestant Reformers swung to the opposite extreme and demanded that a person must have absolute assurance or he was not saved. This was understandable because they taught that assurance was a part of the essence of true saving faith. Salvation included the assurance of salvation.

Biblical answer

The Bible teaches that a Christian can be in need of assurance. That this is true can be seen from the fact that believers are commanded in the New Testament to seek a full assurance of faith (2 Pet. 1:19; 1 John 5:13). If all believers had assurance as a part of saving faith, such commands would be meaningless.

The Reformer's view has resurfaced in some Fundamentalist circles, which teach: "If you are saved, you will know it. If you do not know it, you are not saved." If you do not know the exact time of your salvation, you are made to feel that you are either not saved or are unspiritual.

C. A new view of assurance has been developed as a by-product of mass evangelism through large crusades. The counselor is said to be the one who gives assurance to new converts by taking them through this syllogism:

> Whoever believes is saved.
> *You now believe.*
> Therefore you are saved.

Assurance is gained by endlessly repeating the syllogism. I have met some very ungodly people who never darken the door of any church whose claim to salvation rests entirely on what was once told them by a counselor.

Biblical answer

Assurance is not a syllogism and neither is it something given by one human being to another human being. It is a work and gift of the Holy Spirit (Rom. 8:16; 1 John 3:24, 4:13). While a counselor can give you human assurance, only God the Holy Spirit can give you divine assurance. This view actually produces a cheap and counterfeit assurance.

II. The Scriptural Doctrine of Assurance

The Foundation of Assurance: Jesus Christ in His life and death is the only foundation of salvation in all of its aspects including assurance (1 Cor. 3:11). Our assurance does not rest on our own righteousness, because God justifies the ungodly—not the righteous (Rom. 4:5; 5:6-10).

What is our only hope in this life and in the life to come? Jesus Christ. What is the only basis of our hope for Heaven? Jesus Christ. Jesus and His work alone is all we need or desire. We must not look to our works or to our piety or to our persevering as the basis of our hope for Heaven. When our piety falters and we sin, we should look to Christ for grace and forgiveness. In this life we will always be sinners whom Jesus must save. The moment we trust in our own righteousness and when our piety becomes our security, we have fallen from grace into a works-salvation mentality (Gal. 5:4). While we will fail to live a perfect life, Jesus never failed!

A. The Source of Assurance: It is the Holy Spirit who makes us dynamically aware of our salvation. It is His joy and peace that flood our souls with that inner conviction that our sins have been washed away by the precious blood of Jesus (Rom. 8:16; 1 John 3:24, 4:13). When we grieve the Spirit, He will, at times, remove the joyous awareness of our salvation. Did not David cry out to God, "Return to me the joy of Thy salvation" (Psa. 51:12)? Thus, assurance is not something we believe, and neither is it something we have. It is not the power of positive thinking. Assurance is a work of the Spirit of God. In this sense, it is experiential as opposed to being merely theoretical. It is a dynamic "happening." It is joy, peace, power and love in the Holy Ghost (Rom. 5:5). The Holy Spirit imparts assurance of salvation as an immediate knowledge or inward intuition (1 John 3:24).

B. The Awareness of Assurance: How does the Spirit make us aware objectively of our union with Christ? First, He does so by making us aware that we do have the biblical evidences of true conversion that are laid out in Scripture. While such evidence is not the basis or foundation of assurance, they are the test of salvation that renders our profession of faith valid or invalid. This is why John could say, "We *know* that we know Him *if...*" certain things are true of us. He also points out that if certain negative things are true of us, this means that we do not know Him (1 John 2:3; 3:19, 24; etc.).

John's call to self-examination can be structured in the following way:

1. Examine your faith.
   a) The content of your faith (objective: others can judge you)
      (1) positive beliefs: 1 John 2:23, 4:2, 15; 5:1
      (2) negative denials: 1 John 2:22, 23; 4:1, 3
2. The commitment of your faith (subjective: you judge yourself)
   a) present tense faith: 1 John 5:1; cf. John 3:16
   b) decisionism and easy-believism condemned
3. Examine your life.
   a) Outward walk (objective: others can judge you)
      (1) positive obedience: 1 John 2:3, 5-6, 29; 3:3, 24
      (2) negative disobedience: 1 John 2:4; 3:6-10
   b) Inward emotions (subjective: you judge yourself)
      (1) positive feelings: 1 John 2:10; 3:11-14, 17-19
      (2) negative feelings: 1 John 2:9, 11, 15-17; 3:15; 4:20

C. The Fruit of Assurance
   1. It gives meaning to life.
   2. It gives joy to living.
   3. It produces confidence in prayer.
   4. It puts boldness into witnessing.
   5. It gives strength under trial.
   6. It imparts stability in following one's calling.

D. Applications
   1. Make sure that God has called you unto salvation (2 Pet. 1:10). How? Read through 1 John and ask God the Holy Spirit to show you whether you have the biblical evidences of salvation. Write out the evidences in your life that prove to you that you are a real Christian.
   2. Share with a godly friend why you believe that you are a Christian.
   3. When a person requests membership in the church, the elders should ask, "What evidences do you now see in your life that indicate to you that you are saved?" Too many people have had a false conversion experience in the past that their present life reveals to be false.

Conclusion

One of the greatest blessings in life is to know that our sins are forgiven and that we are on our way to heaven by the grace of the Lord Jesus Christ.

Chapter Three

How Do We Know the Bible Is the Word of God?

Introduction

Our presentation of "Why I Believe the Bible Is God's Word" begins with the internal foundation of our faith and then slowly builds the whole picture.

I. The Inner Witness of the Holy Spirit (Lk. 24:32; John 16:13-14)

Our assurance that the Bible is God's Word begins with an inner conviction that what we are reading is God's Word. The Bible authenticates itself as you read it with an open mind and heart. This is the work of the Holy Spirit who bears witness to the Word. This subjective witness is not sufficient in and of itself to "prove" the inspiration of the Bible. Yet, without it, the Bible would never be received as inspired. It is something that the Bible tells us will happened if we read it. This is the position of historic Christianity.

The Westminster Confession of Faith

"Our full persuasion and assurance of the infallible truth and divine authority thereof, is from the inward work of the Holy Spirit, bearing witness by and with the word in our hearts." (I, V)

The Westminster Larger Catechism

Q.4 How doth it appear that the Scriptures are the Word of God?
A. "The Spirit of God, bearing witness by and with the Scriptures in the heart of man is alone able to persuade it that they are the very Word of God."

A.A. Hodge, *The Confession of Faith* (pp. 36-37): "The highest and most influential faith in the truth and authority of the Scriptures is the direct work of the Holy Spirit in our hearts. The Holy Spirit opens the blinded eyes and gives due sensibility to the diseased heart; and thus assurance comes with the evidence of spiritual experience."

II. Lest someone think that "feelings" are the only basis for accepting Scripture, we must go on to set forth the evidences that confirm this faith. Historic Christianity goes on to state the evidential confirmation of faith.

A.A. Hodge, *The Confession of Faith*, p. 37: "When first regenerated, he first begins to set Scripture to the test of experience; and the more he advances, the more he proves them true and the more he discovers of their limitless breadth and fullness, and of their evidently designed adaptation to all human wants under all conditions."

The Evidences

I. The Scriptures claim to be the inspired Word of God. While this does not in and of itself "prove" the Bible to be God's Word, without this claim, there is no reason to view the Bible as God's Word. Its claim to inspiration is what we would expect to find if it is God's Word. What do we mean when we say that the Bible is inspired? Theologians refer to the doctrine of the verbal, plenary inspiration of the infallible and inerrant Word of God.

    A. "Verbal": every letter and word in the original manuscript.
        1. Matt. 5:18; cf. Matt. 22:31-32
        2. 1 Cor. 2:13
    B. "Plenary": all 66 books of the Bible.
        1. O.T.: Matt. 5:17; cf. 2 Tim. 3:16
        2. N.T.: 2 Pet. 3:15-16; 2 Tim. 3:16; 1 Cor. 14:37
    C. "Infallible": without error in all matters of faith and morals.
    D. "Inerrant": without error in all that it says about anything including scientific matters.
        1. Num. 23:19; cf. Heb. 6:18
        2. John 10:35
        3. John 17:17

Note: This is not "arguing in a circle" because the Bible is not one book. The Bible is a library of 66 books written by more than 40 authors over several thousand years. To quote one book to document another is the soul and substance of all scientific research.

With the Bible we have an experiment over a period of several thousand years. The data from such documentary evidence cannot be swept aside by a wave of a hand.

This is in opposition to the "Bibles" of other religions such as the Koran or the Book of Mormon. They are one book with no historic documents to substantiate them.

II. Personal Experience Confirms It.
    A. Conversion experiences confirm it.
      (Convinced—Convicted—Converted)
    B. The Christian life confirms it.
        1. Everything that happens is exactly what the Bible said would happen.
        2. We can live what we believe and believe what we live.
        3. The Bible is constantly validated by all the facts at my disposal.
    C. Witnessing experiences confirm it.

Non-Christians react and believe exactly the way the Bible said they would. Example: When an arrogant atheist in New York City demanded to know how I knew that the Bible was true, I responded by telling her that she proved the Bible to be true every time she opened her mouth! She was shocked and asked how is this true.

I asked her, "Do you fear God?"

She said, "No."

"Well, then you just proved that Rom. 3:18 is true. Is the Gospel foolishness to you?"

"Yes!"

"Well, you just proved that 1 Cor. 1:18 is true. Do you want your own way instead of living according to God's way?"

"I don't want God's way. I will do as I please."

"Well, you just proved that Isa. 53:6 is true. Every time you open your mouth you confirm the

Bible by saying what it said you would say. Thank you for making me a stronger Christian."

III. Scientific Facts Support It.
  A. We are talking about "facts" and not theories.
  B. All the "facts" so far validated support the teachings of the Bible. No "facts" disprove the Bible.
  C. Archaeology proves much of Scripture to be true.
    1. Sir William Ramsey's conversion and his vindicating of Luke's and Acts' historicity.
    2. Verifying fulfilled prophecies: Tyre (Ezk. 26-27).
    3. Resolving apparent contradictions
    4. Clarifying biblical words
IV. The Bible teaches a completely satisfying philosophy and way of Life.

Conclusion

"There is more than enough evidence on every hand from every department of human experience and knowledge to demonstrate that Christianity is true.

"The light is shining and the music is playing but the non-Christian shuts his eyes and plugs his ears and then pretends that there is neither light nor sound" (*An Introduction to Defending the Faith*, p. 12).

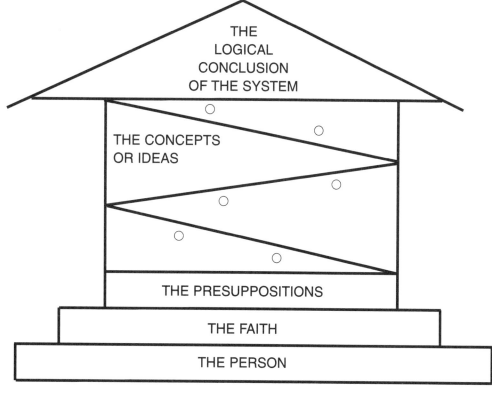

(1) The person is the foundation of any system, for the nature of the person determines the precepts. Who and what we are determines who and what we can know or understand. Too often we forget that we are dealing with a person and not just with a position. The nature of the person determines our methods in apologetics.

(2) The faith which underlies the presuppositions needs to be examined, for at the bottom of every system there is faith.

(3) We must examine the presuppositions which underlie a system and from which the concepts are developed.

(4) Next comes the individual concepts or ideas which make up the bulk or substance of the system.

(5) In the last section we come to the logical conclusion of the system, for if we are consistent, the system will take us somewhere. Where it will take us is the crucial question.

For more details see Robert Morey's book, *An Introduction to Defending the Faith.*

Chapter Four
Many Infallible Proofs

He showed himself alive after His passion by many infallible proofs (Luke 1:3).

Introduction

As a physician, Dr. Luke was a trained scientific mind. This is why he did not base the resurrection of Jesus on an existential leap of faith. Instead, he talks in terms of overwhelming evidence that demonstrates that Jesus had been physically raised from the dead. He calls these evidences "infallible proofs."

The word "infallible" is not the best translation of the Greek word τεκμηπιος. This is why most modern versions do not render the word that way.

> New American Standard: "convincing proofs"
> Amplified Bible: "convincing demonstrations"

The whole point of Dr. Luke is that to his scientific mind, the evidence that Christ arose is very convincing to anyone open-minded enough to look at it honestly. Let us review some of these convincing evidences.

Today, all modern biblical scholars, conservative or liberal, Christian or Jewish, are in general agreement about 12 historical facts surrounding the resurrection story of Jesus. After a century of arguing over the resurrection of Christ, a consensus has finally appeared in our day. While there are radical differences when it comes to explaining these 12 facts, there is no disagreement that these 12 things are historical facts.

Twelve Facts That Demand an Explanation

1. Jesus died due to crucifixion.
2. He was buried.
3. His disciples became depressed, lost all hope, and scattered in fear of their lives.
4. His tomb was empty three days after his death.
5. A large number of disciples individually and in groups claimed to have seen, touched, ate with, drunk with, and openly talked with the risen Jesus.
6. The disciples were psychologically transformed from:

fear to faith	timidity to boldness
doubters to believers	scattered to unified
cowards to martyrs	depressed to joyous

7. The resurrected Christ was central to the Early Church's message.
8. This was especially true in Jerusalem, where many eyewitnesses lived.
9. As a result of the message of the resurrected Christ, the Christian Church was born and grew.
10. The Church switched from Saturday to Sunday as its day of worship because it believed that Christ arose on the first day of the week.
11. The half-brothers of Jesus such as James did not believe in Jesus as the Messiah until he appeared to them after his resurrection.
12. Saul of Tarshish became the Apostle Paul after he claimed that the resurrected Christ confronted him on the road to Damascus. The results of his conversion to Christianity cannot be underestimated.

These twelve things demand an explanation. The key is to discover who has the best explanation in terms of history, psychology, etc.

I. Naturalistic Explanations:

German Rationalists during the 19th century tried to dismiss these 12 facts as frauds, myths, etc. The amazing thing is that these same liberal scholars refuted each other so successfully that no scholars today take their ideas seriously.

    a. Albert Schweitzer refuted Reimarus' fraud theory so successfully that no scholar since 1768 has proposed it.

    b. David Strauss' refutation of Paulus' swoon theory is still the classic in the field and no scholar today takes the swoon theory seriously.

    c. On the other hand, Friedrich Schleiermacher tore Strauss' hallucination theory to pieces. Later, Theodor Keim forever nailed the coffin on the hallucination theory.

    d. Otto Pfleider did away with the mythological and legendary explanation.

    e. Dr. J. Gresham Machen's two outstanding books, *The Virgin Birth* and *The Origin of Paul's Religion,* summarized the failure of all naturalistic theories.

    f. Today, such modern liberals as Karl Barth, Paul Tillich, Raymond Brown, Pannenberg, A.T. Robinson, etc., have all rejected the 19th century naturalistic explanations as hopelessly inadequate. They simply do not fit the historical facts.

II. The Conservative Explanation:

The conservative scholars' explanation is the only one that makes any historical, logical or psychological sense. Jesus arose from the grave in the same body that hung on the cross three days earlier. His resurrection was a physical and literal event in space/time history, and not some dream or fraud. No other explanation fits the facts. Jesus is alive!

Conclusion

The resurrection of Christ is thus a historical event for which there is abundant proof today.

Chapter Five
How We Got Our Bible

Because of the modern attacks on the integrity of the text of the Old and New Testaments, Christians should have a basic understanding of the historical process which began with the original manuscripts and ends with the Bible in the English language.

I. The Original Manuscripts
   A. These refer to the actual animal skins or papyri which the authors of the various books of the Bible used.
   B. Theologians refer to the original manuscripts when they speak of the infallible, inerrant, verbal, plenary inspiration of the Bible. These original manuscripts were perfect because the authors were inspired of God.
   C. As far as we know, all the original manuscripts have been lost.
      1. Some have argued that these original manuscripts still exist because: (1) Would God inspire them and then lose them? (2) God's sovereignty guaranteed their preservation. (3) Do not such verses as Psalm 119:89; Isa. 40:8; Matt. 5:17-18; John 10:34 prove that these inspired manuscripts would be preserved for us?
      2. The only problem with the above arguments is that there are no original manuscripts which exist today. All these arguments mean nothing if you cannot produce an original manuscript.
      3. There is a good reason why God would purposely see to the destruction of these original manuscripts: to prevent us from worshiping them as idols. Remember what happened to the brazen serpent pole which Moses made? It was destroyed because it had become an idol (2 Kings 18:1-4). The idolatrous heart of man would have enshrined the originals long ago.
      4. The importance of these manuscripts lies in what was written on them and not the manuscripts themselves. Through textual criticism we are about 99 percent sure of what was written on these originals.
II. The Copies of the Original Manuscripts
   A. While the originals were perfect because the authors were inspired, we must state that no copy is perfect because no copyist was inspired. While there are no errors in the originals, there are errors in the copies.
   B. The errors in the copies are generally easily detected and are the result of honest mistakes such as:
      1. Wrong division of letters. Early copies do not have any word divisions.
         Example: "GODISNOWHERE." How should we divide the words in this sentence?

         God is now here.
         God is no where.

      2. Mistakes during dictation. Some words are pronounced the same but are spelled differently.
         Example: Rom. 5:1: ομεν or ωμεν?
         Example: English: blue or blew?

3. Skipping lines because a word begins or ends several sentences.

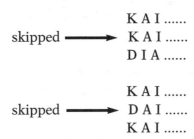

4. Dropping a word
   Example: The "wicked Bible," which dropped the word *not* out of the seventh commandment.
5. Misinterpreting a copyist's comment as being part of the text.
   Example: 1 John 5:7
C. There are deliberate insertions or deletions in some copies.
   Example: 1 John 5:7

III. Old Testament Manuscripts
A. Only 1,700 exist.
B. Nearly all are quite late and date from the Middle Ages (A.D. 1000).
C. The Jews were very meticulous in their copying of the manuscripts.
   1. Only the scribes were allowed to do this as an occupation.
   2. They counted words, destroyed any defective manuscripts, etc.
D. The accuracy of the Masoretic text has been verified by a comparison between the Dead Sea Scroll of Isaiah with the Masoretic text of Isaiah. After 1,200 years of copying and recopying, only 13 errors happened. These were simply errors like the switching of letters.
E. When we have a conflict, we can compare the Dead Sea Scrolls, the Septuagint, the Masoretic text and other versions.
F. The only controversy in O.T. textual criticism is the question of the priority of the Masoretic text or the Septuagint. The N.T. quotations of the Septuagint in passages where the Hebrew is different are problematic to this day.

IV. New Testament Manuscripts
A. There are 5,000 Greek manuscripts, 8,000 Latin and 1,000 ancient versions of the N.T. or parts of the N.T.
B. Nearly all are quite late and date from the Middle Ages (A.D. 1000).
C. The N.T. copyists were not meticulous.
   1. Lay people did the copying.
   2. No strict rules were followed.
D. More than 200,000 variant readings have resulted from the "lay" copying. Out of them all, only about 50 readings are problematic and all of them would fit on one page. The other mistakes are obvious and are easily corrected.
E. When in doubt about a text, we have a wealth of resources to consult.
   1. Greek manuscripts (skins, papyri)
   2. Latin manuscripts
   3. Ancient versions
   4. Early Fathers
   5. Early Heretics
F. How do we decide what variant reading is correct?

1. Are the majority of manuscripts always right? Not necessarily. What if the majority are copies of a poor ancestral manuscript? And they are the majority because they were geographically, politically, culturally or ecclesiastically favored? A simple majority may be wrong in manuscripts as well as in politics.

2. Is the oldest manuscript always right? Not necessarily. There are too few of them to compare. What do we do when they disagree? Could an early manuscript come from a poor ancestral copy?

3. Do we exalt one particular manuscript as being perfect? We should not. There is not a perfect one around. This is an easy way out and appeals only to those who want a "simple" and quick answer.
   Example: Lamsda and the Peshitta (Fifth Century)

4. We should take all the evidence into account and make an eclectic choice.
   a. Internal evidence: the literary context, the author's vocabulary and style, parallel passages, etc.
   b. External evidence: papyri, uncials, Fathers, ancient versions, minuscules, Latin, etc.

G. Constructed Greek texts of the New Testament

1. A Catholic Cardinal, Ximenes, decided to put out a Greek text of the N.T. which he would construct by examining several Greek manuscripts and making a compromise text.

2. When the humanist scholar Erasmus heard of the Cardinal's plans, he rushed into print a constructed Greek text of his own. He only took six to 10 months to produce this text! He used only six very late and quite poor manuscripts. His four editions are filled with a multitude of corrections. Since none of his manuscripts had the last of Rev. 22, he translated the ending from the Latin into the Greek. Although none of his manuscripts had 1 John 5:7, he put it into his later editions because of the Pope's dogmatism. His work is marked by hastiness and a multitude of mistakes, some of which he tried to correct with each new edition.

3. Robert Stephanus (1546) put out his own text. It was basically Erasmus' text. He continued the tradition of putting such verses as 1 John 5:7 into the text. He was the first to separate the text into chapters and verses.

4. The Elzevirs put out a text in 1633. In their second edition they claimed that their text was "the text received by all." It has been called the Textus Receptus since that time.

5. Bengel (1687-1752) was "the father of textual criticism." He taught that the manuscripts should be "weighed" instead of just being counted.

6. The period from 1831-1881 was filled with a host of men who spent their lifetime studying the manuscripts. Much progress was made by Lachmann, Tischendorf, Tregelles, Alford, etc.

7. The climax was reached by Westcott and Hort (1825). They did the following:
   a. Designated "families" in manuscripts
   b. Proclaimed the superiority of the Vaticanus manuscript and the Neutral Family
   c. Codified the general rules for textual criticism
   d. Dismissed the Textus Receptus as unimportant and mistaken
   e. Became the position on the N.T. for the next 50 years

8. A radical reaction rose up to defend the Textus Receptus. Such scholars as Burgon refuted the exaltation of the Vaticanus and the superiority of the Neutral Family. Others went to the extreme of exalting the Textus Receptus and the Byzantine family.

9. These two positions took the same approach but violently disagreed with the end result.

Position	Westcott & Hort	Scrivener
One Family	Neutral	Byzantine
One Text	Vaticanus	Textus Receptus

Both assumed that we needed one family and one text to act as the ultimate standard to decide all variant readings. Both positions have gradually given way to a more balanced approach.

   10. The present eclectic position:
   a. No one family, text or manuscript is to be viewed as perfect.
   b. All the internal and external evidence should be consulted.
   c. There will be a few readings where we will never know for sure with 100 percent certainty.
   d. Variant readings should be rated in terms of degrees of certainty.
   A - B - C - D

V. The English Bible
A. Various partial translations were made by such men as Bede (A.D. 674-735).
B. Wycliffe's Bible (A.D. 1382) was the first complete translation. It was translated from the Latin, not from the Hebrew or Greek.
C. Tyndale's Bible (1534) was the first printed English Bible. Although it was incomplete, he went from the Hebrew and Greek.
D. Coverdale's Bible (1535) was the first complete printed English Bible.
E. The Geneva Bible (1560) was translated by the Calvinist Reformers in exile in Geneva. It was the Bible of the Puritans and Pilgrims. It contained Calvin's notes on various verses. It was the Bible of the English people for almost 100 years.
F. The King James Version (1611).
   1. One of England's most wicked kings, King James, had a particular hatred of the Geneva Bible because of its Calvinistic footnotes. He disliked the Puritans and supported the Anglo-Catholic religion instead.
   2. At the Hampton Court, 1604, the King was presented with a Puritan petition that the Geneva Bible become the Bible of the English Church. He chose to have a new translation issued which would not have the Calvinism of the Geneva Bible in it.
   3. The Puritans did not appreciate the new translation but continued to use the Geneva Bible. One of the reasons the Pilgrims left England was to get away from the KJV and to freely use the Geneva Bible. The Geneva Bible was the Bible of early Colonial America.
G. Ultimately the KJV became the most widely used Bible by English-speaking people. Its beauty has never been surpassed.
H. Major revisions began to appear as the study of the manuscripts uncovered the mistakes that Erasmus and other early scholars had made. The KJV was based basically on Erasmus via Stephanus' Greek text and not on the Textus Receptus. The KJV was translated in 1611 and the Textus Receptus did not come out until 1633. The Textus Receptus and the text of Stephanus disagree in 287 places. They are not the same text.

Conclusion

To decide which translation you should use, the following things should be taken into account:

1. Faithfulness to the Hebrew and Greek.
2. Clarity in vocabulary and sentence structure.
3. Readability, i.e., it can be read without labor or difficulty.
4. Beauty in style.
5. Purpose of reading it: casual, study, etc.

Chapter Six
Hermeneutics

Introduction

The importance of rightly interpreting Scripture cannot be underestimated. If the people of God do not know how to read the Bible, false teaching will easily deceive them.

I. What is Hermeneutics?

Hermeneutics is the discovery, understanding and use of those linguistic and literary principles and rules of interpretation which should be followed when interpreting the Bible. Exegesis is the application of hermeneutics to a particular text of Scripture to discern the intent and mind of the author. It is the opposite of eisegesis which is the reading into a text your own ideas with little or no concern for what the author was saying.

Exegesis—Superstructure (application)

Hermeneutics—Foundation (principles)

II. Why Bother with Hermeneutics?

A. The Bible comes to us as literature: (prose, poetry, historical narrative, apocalyptic literature, letters, dialogue, theological treatise, biography, etc.)

B. Hermeneutics is simply the mind's reflection on the valid ways people read and interpret any piece of literature.

1. We must observe grammar and syntax.

2. We must observe literary units such as paragraphs and chapters.

3. We must seek to discern what the author was saying.

C. There are right ways and wrong ways to interpret the Bible.

1. The right way: 2 Tim. 2:15, cf. Matt. 22:29-32

2. The wrong way: 2 Pet. 3:16

   a. Partial quotation: "There is no God" (Psa. 14:1).

   b. Not observing who said it: "You shall be as God" (Gen. 3:5).

   c. Stringing together unrelated proof texts.

   d. Taking a verse out of context: example Col. 2:21.

   e. A mystical approach, where you let the Bible fall open at random and pick a verse by "chance."

D. This means that it is erroneous to say, "The Bible can be validly interpreted in many different ways." Except for a few difficult places, the Bible will have only one valid interpretation if the principles of hermeneutics are consistently followed. We should interpret the Bible following objective rules. The reason we are not consistent in this is that we often allow religious and personal prejudices and a denominational bias to influence our interpretation. We approach the Bible to make it say what we want instead of letting it speak for itself. Hermeneutics is an attempt to curb inconsistent and biased interpretation.

III. Where Should We Obtain Our Hermeneutical Principles?

A. The foundational principle of approach: The same basic linguistic and literary rules which we use when interpreting any historic or contemporary literature should be used when reading the Bible. Since the Bible does not contain any unique literary forms, our hermeneutics should not be unique only to Scripture.

B. This principle reveals the basic error of liberal and neo-orthodox hermeneutics. They have developed hermeneutical principles which cannot be applied to any historic or contemporary literature, but which they applied to the Bible to discredit it.

    1. The J.E.P.D. Higher Critical Theory cannot be applied to Homer, Plato, Shakespeare or contemporary works.

    2. A computer analysis of vocabulary cannot be applied to literature in general.

C. This basic principle also reveals the error of Medieval or Roman Catholic hermeneutics. It was taught that a text had three meanings:

    1. A literal meaning which ignorant and uneducated people could discern.

    2. A moral meaning which educated and cultured people could discern.

    3. A spiritual meaning which only the clergy could discern.

D. This basic principle also reveals the fallacy of cultic and occultic hermeneutics. Each cultic or occultic leader or group gives an "inner" or "secret" meaning which is not discernible from the text. Their interpretation ignores grammar, syntax, context, etc.

    Examples: Christian Science

    The Church of Bible Understanding

    The Watchtower

    The Metaphysical Bible Dictionary

E. The fact that the Bible was written in everyday language for normal people dispels all "secret" and "mystical" interpretations. A "plain" Bible written for "plain" people needs a "plain" interpretation. There are no "secret keys" to interpreting the Bible because it does not come to us as a locked book waiting for some special mystical interpreter to arrive on the scene.

IV. How Should We Approach the Bible?

A. In an Attitude of Worship: Isaiah 66:1-2; Psa. 119:97; Psa. 138:2; John 1:1-2

    1. Spirit of dependence: Psa. 119:18, 24; 1 Cor. 2:11-12; Lk. 24:25-32.

    2. Spirit of submission: John 7:17; Psa. 119:4, 5, 11; Heb. 11:6.

B. It involves our Whole Being:

    1. Mind—Call to believe: Jn. 20:31; Acts 17:10-12.

    2. Will—Call to obey: Rev. 2:5; Psa. 119:33-35; Matt. 7:24.

    3. Emotions—Call to feel: Phil. 3:1; Jn. 15:11-12.

V. Who Should Interpret the Bible?

The Basic Qualifications of the Interpreters of Scripture:

A. We must have a heart regenerated by the Holy Spirit (John 3:3-5). Why? Because the natural man cannot understand the things of God (1 Cor. 2:11-12; Rom. 3:11).

    1. The sinful nature of man renders him incapable of understanding the truth (Rom. 8: 3-9).

    2. Man's love of darkness renders him unwilling to understand the truth (John 3:19-21; John 5:40).

    3. Man's allegiance to Satan and to sin renders him rebellious against understanding the truth (John 8:43-47).

B. We need a mind illuminated by the Holy Spirit.

Example: Paul's prayers on behalf of the saints (Eph. 1:17)

C. We must have an impartial and seeking spirit. We must come to the Bible totally convinced that we want nothing but the truth. Some use the Bible to prove their pet ideas or to defend their denominational doctrines. We should come realizing that the truth

    1. liberates (John 8:32)

    2. sanctifies (John 17:17)

The Spirit renders man capable of worshiping the true God (John 4:23-24).

    D. We must have a humble spirit. Why?
        1. God resists the proud (James 4:6).
        2. God reveals to the humble (Matt. 11:25).
        3. Man knows so little (1 Cor. 8:2; 13:9-12).
    E. We must have a praying heart (Psa. 119:18, 34, 73, 125, 144 and 169).
    F. We must have a pious motive (Psa. 119:34, 73; Col. 1:9-12).

   VI. Basic Principles of Interpretation

    A. The Absolute Inspiration of the Scriptures
       The Orthodox position: the verbal, plenary, inspiration of the infallible, inerrant Bible which is the Word of God.
       1. **Verbal:** Every single letter and word of Scripture as put down in the original autographs were inspired of God (Matt. 5:18; 22:32).
       2. **Plenary:** All of the Bible, in all of its parts, is equally inspired. No part is more inspired than the other parts. The 66 books comprising the Old and New Testaments are all equally inspired (Matt. 5:17-18; 2 Tim. 3:16).
       3. **Inspiration:** God sovereignly prepared the authors of Scripture from birth in all things. He stirred them up to write. He guided them so they wrote down everything He wanted them to write. They wrote down the very words of God. God's sovereign control of the authors did not remove the characteristics and personalities of the authors, but such things were ordered by God to be a better vehicle of expression.
       4. **Infallible:** In principle, the Bible is infallible, i.e., incapable of error or mistake. Why? God cannot lie (Titus 1:2), and the Bible is His Word; therefore, the Bible cannot be a lie (John 17:17).
       5. **Inerrant:** This is biblical infallibility stressed in the area where it touches on matters of science and on any observations and explanations of the natural world. Example: Creation, the Flood, miracles, history, etc. The Bible is scientifically correct wherever it speaks in those areas.
       6. **Bible:** The books in the Protestant Bible. There are no "lost" books. The Apocrypha is not inspired.
       7. **Word of God:** The Word of God expressed in human words. It is human and Divine, with the Divine so controlling the human element, that nothing is expressed but the thoughts and Will of God.

    B. The Unity of the Bible

Although it was written by more than 40 different authors from many different walks of life over a period of 2,000 years, with no collaboration between authors, the Bible is a harmonious unit. It contains no contradictions. The New Testament does not contradict the Old Testament. Paul does not contradict Jesus or James. All the teachings of the Bible dovetail into each other. The Bible presents one, consistent, cohesive, coherent view of truth throughout all its parts. Liberals say that the Old Testament and the New Testament contradict each other and even present different gods. This comes from ignorance, both spiritual and scriptural. The following chart reveals how the New Testament completes the Old Testament.

Old Testament	**New Testament**
Unexplained Ceremonies	Ceremonies Explained
Unfulfilled Prophecies	Prophecies Fulfilled
Unsatisfied Longings	Longings Satisfied
Incomplete Destiny	Destiny Completed

Some liberal theologians have claimed that Jesus contradicted the Old Testament in His Sermon on the Mount. Look at Matthew 5 where they say Christ contradicts the Old Testament and throws out the "eye for eye and tooth for tooth" doctrine of the primitive and uncivilized Jews who believed in a bloody and savage tribal war-god named Jehovah. In its place, Jesus teaches the Fatherhood of God, the brotherhood of man, pacifism and other teachings shared by all the great religious leaders of all religions.

The Liberal misinterprets Matthew 5 completely, for

1. Christ came to fulfill, not to contradict or destroy (Matt. 5:17-19).
2. Christ was contradicting the Pharisees' interpretation of the Law which had externalized it.
   a. He did not say "As it is written."
   b. He did not quote Scriptures but the Rabbis (Matt. 5:21, 27, 33, 38, 43).
   c. He was establishing a "New" Covenant with greater laws.

C. Diversity of Clearness
   While all Scripture is equally inspired, it is not equally clear (2 Pet. 3:16). Thus we must interpret the
   1. Unclear in the light of the clear.
   2. Difficult in light of simple.
      Example: John 14:28 must be interpreted in the light of John 1:1, 18; 5:18, 23; 20:28.

VII. Basic Method of Interpretation
   A. The example of Christ and the Apostles: They dogmatically appealed to the Scriptures as the sole source of their authoritative teaching (Matt. 4:3-10; cf. 1 Cor. 15:3-4).
   B. The method used by Christ and the Apostles in their interpretation of Scripture should be our method (1 John 2:6).
   C. The writers of Scripture treated the text of Scripture in terms of grammar and syntax.
      1. Example: Galatians 3:16-17: Observation of the difference between singular and plural nouns.
      2. Example: Matthew 22:32: Observation of the difference between the present and past tense of verbs.
   D. The writers of Scripture treat the text of Scripture as being a reliable historical account from which they can draw doctrinal conclusions.
      Example: Romans 4:9-12: Two doctrines are drawn from the historical fact that Abraham was justified before he was circumcised.
      1. Justification is by faith alone, apart from works.
      2. Gentiles are now included in Abraham's Covenant.
   E. The writers of Scripture treat the text of Scripture as being a reliable historical account from which they can draw ethical and moral imperatives and prohibitions.
      1. 1 Corinthians 10:1-12
      2. 1 Timothy 5:19
      3. Matthew 12:1-8

F. Why did Christ and the Apostles treat the Scriptures the way they did? They had a primary assumption concerning the nature and use of the Bible (2 Tim. 3:16-17).
   1. All Scripture:
      a. Is inspired
      b. Its purpose is to perfect and to protect the elect.
      c. Its method or use:
         (1) Doctrine—Theology and Philosophy
         (2) Reproof
         (3) Correction

VIII. The Canon
   A. The canon was not a product of human invention or ingenuity, but it everywhere manifests itself to be the product of Divine design.
   B. Justification of the canon of Old Testament and New Testament:
      1. The historical roots of the canon end in mystery.
      2. The arrangement is not according to chance, size, chronology, date of composition or authorship.
      3. The arrangement is according to subject matter. See diagrams No. 1 and No. 2 on page 43.
      4. The arrangement manifests a Divine hand.
   C. The significance of canonical observations in studying a book of the Bible: We can find a clue as to the theme of a book and its importance in the whole counsel of God by observing where it is placed in the canon.

IX. How to Study a Particular Book of the Bible

Seek to answer these basic introductory questions.
   A. What is its place in the canon?
   B. Who wrote it?
   C. What were the circumstances of the author?
   D. To whom was the book written?
   E. What do we know about them and their relationship to the author?
   F. What is the tone and theme of the book?
   G. What is the outline of the book?

X. How to Study a Particular Verse of the Bible

Basic questions to ask yourself
   A. Who spoke or wrote it?
   B. To whom was it spoken or written?
   C. What is the context?
   D. Are there any parallel passages?
   E. Is it an Old Testament quotation or allusion?
   F. Is there a clearer or fuller passage which explains this verse?
   G. Is this a passage of full mention?
   H. Are there any historical observations which throw light on the verse?
   I. What is the grammatical significance of the verse?

XI. How to Study a Word in the Bible

Basic principles

   A. Find the definition of the word in a Bible dictionary or encyclopedia.
   B. Find out all the places in the Bible where the word occurs. Be careful to observe the principle of progressive revelation. The meaning of biblical words deepened as God revealed more truth.
   C. If there are different meanings to the word, classify them into groups.
   D. From the context, determine the meaning of the studied word.
   E. Check commentaries.

XII. Special Principles

   A. Analogy of faith (Rom. 12:6): Any interpretation of any particular verse in the Bible must not contradict but be in harmony with the teaching of the whole of Scripture.
   B. A simple positive implies a negative and a simple negative implies a positive (Psa. 40:9, 10; Eph. 4:25, 28).
   C. Rhetorical questions are expressed for emphasis sake (Matt. 6:27; 16:26; 22:42; John 5:44; Rom. 9:14).
   D. Do not absolutize general statements and promises (Prov. 17:6; 18:22; 23:1, 2).
   E. Observe non-literal language (Matt. 15:11; 16:6, 7; John 4:32, 33).
      1. Metaphor: John 6:35; 15:1
      2. Ironic language: 1 Cor. 4:8
      3. Hyperbole—exaggeration for emphasis sake (Josh. 11:4; Judges 7:12; John 21:25)
   F. Observe the significance of types. Various people, places, actions and things in the Old Testament were instituted by God for the express purpose of prefiguring the person and work of Jesus in the New Testament (John 1:29; Heb. 12:22).
   G. Seek out the passage of full mention. There is usually one central passage in which a particular doctrine is expounded. All other scattered references should be interpreted in the light of the passage where it is discussed in full.
   Example: Isa. 40 (the transcendence of God); John 3 (regeneration); Matt. 24-25 (the return of Christ); 1 Cor. 15 (the resurrection), etc.

   H. Remember that divine revelation was progressive in nature (Heb. 1:1-2). This means that the New Testament interprets the Old Testament. The New Testament has the priority over the Old Testament.

   I. Principles for interpreting parables:
      1. Parables are not to be regarded or used as a proof of truth but only as an illustration of truth.
      2. As illustrations, they never expressed the whole truth but only part of the truth.
      3. They emphasize one major lesson or truth: the details are only part of the study, i.e., "filler" and, as such, cannot be viewed as teaching anything significant.
      4. They are always in subjection to doctrinal passages.
      5. The context determines the scope or purpose and the point of the parable (Lk. 15:2).
      6. The best interpretation is the one which Christ or the Apostles supply.

Old Testament — Diagram No. 1

History (17)			Experience	Prophecy (17)		
Basic Law	Pre-Exile History	Post-Exile History	Inner Life	Basic Prophecy	Pre-Exile Prophets	Post-Exile Prophets
5	9	3	5	5	9	3

New Testament — Diagram No. 2

History	Doctrine	Doctrine	Experience
Historic Foundation 5	Church Epistles 9	Pastoral Epistles 4	General Epistles 9

Chapter Seven
Christian Maturity

Introduction

Three biblical themes form the focus of our study:

> Putting Off
>> Putting On
>>> Going On

There are things we must put off and put on before we can go on. May this year be the year when you take off in the Christian life. But this can only be done in the right order. The negative must be dealt with first. Then a positive base must be laid before you can go on to deeper maturity in your life.

PART 1:

Putting Off/Putting On

Romans 13:11-14

I. Paul says to "put off the deeds of darkness."

II. Then he lists six sins in three groups of two each. The sins are related to each other in terms of cause and effect.

revelings/drunkennesses	(social)
immoralities/lusts	(secret)
dissension/jealousy	(seditious)

Cause ———⟶ effect

III. Then he says to "put on the armor of light."

The deeds of darkness	The armor of light

IV. We are told to "put on the Lord Jesus Christ" because His character qualities are the opposite of the deeds of darkness. We must seek to be like Him in all that we do. Our behavior will become "decent" and transparent (Ephesians 4:22-5:7)

I. Paul tells us to "put off the old self."

II. The "old self" is defined in terms of the sins of that day:
falsehood
sinful (i.e. lingering) anger
stealing
unedifying speech
grieving the Spirit
bitterness/rage
anger/brawling
slander/malice
immorality
impurity
greed
obscenity
foolish talk
coarse joking

III. Paul then says to "put on the new self"—the old self vs. the new self.

IV. He illustrates what he means by the "new self"—Ephesians 6:11-18.
speaking the truth
resolving anger
hard working
giving to others
edifying speech
kindness
compassion
forgiveness
imitating God
living a life of love

I. We are told to "put on the full armor of God."

II. The armor is defined as
truth
prayer
righteousness
readiness to preach
faith
salvation
the Spirit

The Armor of God

1. The armor comes from God.

2. We are to "put it on" in the sense of using it in our battles with the devil. Paul assumes that we have already put it on. Notice the tenses of the verbs.

He uses four aorist middle participles:

1. having belted yourself
2. having clothed yourself
3. having shod yourself
4. having shielded yourself

We put these on at conversion when we became soldiers in Christ's army. These four things refer to what we received at salvation.

3. The primary focus of these four things is objective and not subjective.
   a. "the truth" refers to what we believe—not just to sincerity.
   b. "righteousness" refers to justification—not to our goodness.
   c. "the shoes" refer to the Gospel.
   d. "the shield" is the Faith.
4. He assumes that we already have been given our helmet and sword. He commands us to "take them up" in the aorist imperative tense.
   a. "take up the helmet": Salvation
   b. "take up the sword": the Bible
5. Our armor is perfect and eternal. Our character is not our armor. Our armor is Christ in His person and work (Rom. 13:14).
6. Paul adds one item to our armor:

   v. 18 "Praying in the Spirit"—Colossians 3:1-17

   He uses the present participle tense to emphasize our utter dependence on the power of the Holy Spirit. We are to pray constantly by the power and guidance of the Spirit. Prayer gives us the energy to fight the devil and win. It gives us the drive and motivation to fight. It heals our wounds, lessens our pains and keeps us from bitterness and depression.

I. Paul tells us to "put off the old self."
II. The old self is defined in the terms of our "earthly nature."
III. He lists the sins which were problems in that culture. He groups them in twos to show them as cause and effect.
    immorality/impurity
    lust/evil desires
    greed/idolatry
    anger/rage
    malice/slander
    filthy/lying language
    cause ⟶ effect
IV. Paul once again pits the "old man" against the "new man."
V. The "new man" is heavenly, while the "old man" is earthly.
VI. Since we became "new" when we came into union with Christ (2 Cor. 5:17), we should "put on" virtue. He groups them in twos to show cause and effect.
    compassion/kindness
    humility/gentleness
    patience/forbearance
    forgiveness/love
    cause ⟶ effect
VII. He concludes with an exhortation to let the Peace and the Word of Christ rule/dwell.

PART 2: Going On

Hebrews 6:1-3

I. "Let us leave the elementary teachings about Christ":
repentance
laying on of hands
faith
the resurrection
baptism
eternal judgment

II. "Let us go on to maturity." The goal of the means of grace both public and private is:

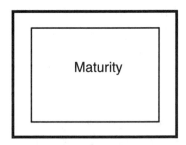

Special Note on Spiritual Maturity

The second goal of the church is to promote spiritual maturity in the members. After personal salvation, spiritual maturity is second in importance. Let us study the New Testament concept of spiritual maturity in order to understand God's goal and vision for our lives.

I. Basic Word Study
   A. The basic Greek word for maturity is teleios.
   B. This word and its derivations appear 50 times in the New Testament.
   C. In the plant realm, the word refers to a plant or fruit reaching its ripe or mature stage in which it is ready to be used (Lk. 8:14). In this sense, the plant or fruit has finally reached its goal or end. The process is completed. It has gone from the potential of a seed or bud to the actual plant or ripened fruit. It is fully developed.
   D. In the human realm, the word is used to describe the opposite of being childish in attitude and action. It means to be fully grown, grown up and mature. It means that you have passed from childhood to adulthood (Heb. 5:14).

II. New Testament Teaching on Spiritual Maturity
   A. It is the will of God (Rom. 12:2; Matt. 5:48).
   B. It is the burden of the prayers of Christ (Jn. 17:23).
   C. It is the second great goal in life (Heb. 6:1).
   D. It is the goal of the elders' ministry (Eph. 4:12-13; Col. 1:28; 4:12).
   E. It should be your concern in prayer (Col. 4:12).
   F. It means to act as an adult and not as a child (1 Cor. 2:6; 14:20; Eph. 4:14; Col. 4:12; Heb. 5:14).
   G. It consists of adult thinking, attitudes and priorities (1 Cor. 14:20; Phil. 3:13-15).

H. It refers to discernment (Heb. 5:14).

I. It is produced by endurance under trials and testing (Jas. 1:3, 4).

J. It means to control yourself, especially your tongue (Jas. 3:1-6).

K. It arises out of ministering through your spiritual gift in the context of the local church (Eph. 4:13).

III. The Essence of Spiritual Maturity

A. The heart or essence of spiritual maturity is responsibility.

B. The main characteristic of children is that they are irresponsible. They must be told what to do. They must be constantly corrected and guided. They are dependent upon others. They do not take responsibility upon themselves.

C. The main characteristic of maturity is responsibility. What is it? Responsibility is an attitude in which one keeps in mind the fact that he will be accountable to God on the Judgment Day for what he thinks, says and does. Obedience to God's Law is important. Why? Future accountability means present responsibility. It means responding to life with the recognition of one's accountability to God. When you "grow up," you shoulder your responsibility. You do not childishly fritter away the time in childish and selfish squabbling with others. You get things done because they are your responsibility. A child thinks of his feelings while an adult thinks of his responsibility. A mature person does not have to be constantly told, scolded and corrected about his responsibility.

IV. The Focus of Responsibility (Spiritual Maturity)

A. We should respond to each situation in life according to the teaching of Scripture and the inward prompting of the Holy Spirit.

B. This maturity, or responsible thinking and living, will develop many important character traits in one's life. To be conformed to the character of Christ is the ultimate goal of the entire process of God's plan of salvation (Rom. 8:29).

C. List the character traits which develop out of spiritual maturity and responsible living.

1. Obedience

2. Stability, not tossed to and fro by everything

3. Ability to stand alone

4. Understanding

5. Wisdom

6. Sensitive to Spirit's prompting

7. Discernment

8. Spirit-filled

9. Boldness

10. Walking by faith, not by sight

11. Assurance

12. Experiencing God's love

13. Forgiveness, etc.

V. The Standard of Measurement for Spiritual Maturity

A. Spiritual maturity should not be measured by looking at what we do or do not do. A spiritually immature person may be very active in church work.

B. Spiritual maturity is measured by the degree of faith, hope and love which manifest themselves in the life of a Christian (1 Cor. 13; Eph. 1:15-16, 18; Col. 1:3-6; 1 Thess. 1:2, 3; 2 Thess. 1:3-4; 1 Tim. 1:5; 1 Pet. 1:21-22).

Spiritual maturity is the basis of stability in the Christian life. It involves a responsible lifestyle that manifests faith, hope and love. It is the first qualification for leadership because it is foundational to spirituality.

I. The Bible contains concepts that stretch the mind: deep, lofty and mysterious. Heb. 5:11 contains "hard to explain" and 2 Pet. 3:16 has "hard to understand." "Difficult" does not mean impossible.

II. They were "dull of hearing" (Heb. 5:11).
   1. "dull," not hard or slow
   2. when "hearing" the Word preached
   3. they did not pay attention (Heb. 2:1-4).

III. The problem: Immaturity
   A. They were still "infants" (Heb. 5:13).
      1. They were still pupils when they should be teachers (Heb. 5:12).
      2. They could only handle "milk" and could not digest "meat" (Heb 5:12, 13).
         a. simple vs. complex ideas
         b. shallow vs. deep concepts
         c. elementary vs. advanced
         d. ignorant vs. informed
   B. The Goal: Mature Saints
   They love to think through deep concepts and wrestle with the tough issues (Heb. 5:14a).
   C. The Means: Exercising the mind
      1. "constant use" of the mind (Heb. 5: 14b)
      2. "trained themselves"
      3. "to distinguish": discerning, not gullible or naive
         a. ethical issues: good from evil
         b. doctrinal issues: the teaching about righteousness (Heb. 5: 13).
   D. The Path: Heb. 6:1-2
      1. Master the basics
         a. "elementary truths of God's Word" (Heb. 5:12)
         b. "elementary teachings about Christ" (Heb. 6:1)
         c. "milk" (Heb. 5:12)
      2. Some of the basics:
         a. "repentance from useless acts"
         b. faith in God
         c. baptisms
         d. laying on of hands
         e. the resurrection of the dead
         f. eternal judgment
      3. The Text
         a. "therefore": the logical link
         b. negative: "let us leave the elementary doctrines"
         c. positive: "let us go on" (NIV) literal Greek: "let us be carried"
            1) You cannot go it alone.
            2) Sometimes you need to be carried by others.
         d. We must go on to build a superstructure on the foundation. Beware of "foundationalism."

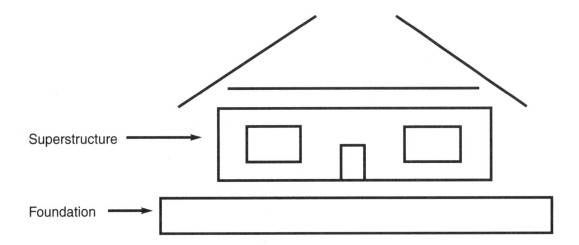

Superstructure ⟶

Foundation ⟶

e. the goal: "to mature"
  1) Its nature: intellectual.
     a) Thayer: "more intelligent"
     Note: Intellectual maturity leads to emotional maturity that leads to volitional maturity.
     Understanding ⟶ Character ⟶ Action
     b) Knowledge of the truth saves and sanctifies: John 8:32; 17:17.
     c) We must grow in knowledge to have our minds renewed so that our lives may be transformed: 2 Pet. 3:18; Rom. 12:1-2.

  2) There are degrees of maturity.
     a) Children-youths-adults: 1 John 2:12-14
     b) We never reach perfection in this life: Phil. 3:12-14; 1 John 1:8-10

  3) Significant Passages on Maturity. The usage of the word "maturity" determines its meaning.

Maturity	Immaturity
1. 1 Cor. 2:6-3:5	
ready for philosophy	not ready
spiritual	carnal/worldly
adults	infants
meat	milk
able to take it	not able
godly living	envying, strife, divisions, false teachers

Maturity	Immaturity
2. 1 Cor. 14:20	
thinking like adults	thinking like children
3. Eph. 4:11-14	
unity	disunity
knowledge	ignorance
adults	infants
stable	unstable
grown up	still a child
4. Col. 1:28-29	
the means	the hindrance
admonition	reject
instruction	reject
the goal of the ministry	reject
5. Col. 4:12	
prayer	no prayer
standing firm in the will of God	vacillating in the will of man
fully assured	doubting
6. James 1:2-8	
Handling trials right brings maturity	Blowing it reveals immaturity.

Conclusion

The goal of the Christian life and the Christian ministry are the same:

MATURITY

Chapter Eight
The Attributes of God

Introduction

Why did Jesus come to earth and die for our sins? What was His goal or mission? In John 17:2-3 Jesus stated that the goal of salvation ("eternal life") is to know God. Indeed, the entire process of redemption can be summed up in the words: to know God (Gal. 4:8-9). Christians are people who have come to know God (1 John 5:20-21).

Do You Know God?

Now, "knowing God" involves three things:
1. Knowledge about God
2. Intellectual assent to God
3. Personal trust in God

True saving faith begins with an intellectual faith in the head and ends with a personal faith in the heart. The only way to reach the heart is through the mind.

It is not surprising in the least to find that modern unbelief centers its main attack on knowing God. They deny that God can be "known" intellectually. They claim that no one can know anything about God. This is the very soul of unbelief and is a device of Satan to keep people from saving faith. While they agree that people can experience God, this experience is non-rational. No one can talk about God in an objective or rational way.

The modern attitude of up-playing experience and down-playing theology has found its way into the church. People do not sense the value and importance of an intellectual knowledge of God. All they want is a "happy" time in church, i.e., experience! They do not want to think deeply about the existence, nature and being of God. They want their "heart" filled but their "mind" empty. They want "fun" but not "facts."

But the Bible does not go along with the existential spirit of the age. It calls us to a three-fold knowledge of God:

The Mind (understanding)
The Heart (assent)
The Will (trust/choose)

In this light, when we say, "God has attributes and we can talk about them," we are saying something truly profound.

While modern theologians and philosophers admit they know nothing about God, the humblest saint knows through Scripture all there is to know about God! The key is divine revelation. If God has revealed Himself to man in words which we understand, then we can know God. But if there is no revelation from God, there can be no knowledge of God.

1) "God has attributes"
   a) What do we mean when we say attributes?
      i) A characteristic or quality of God's existence, being or nature
      ii) Not something we attribute to God but something He has revealed about Himself:

    (1) Revealed (not "reasoned")

    (2) Objective (not "subjective")

    (3) Immutable (not "cultural")

    (4) True (not "mythological")

  iii) God is not just the sum of His attributes any more than we are the sum of our attributes.

  iv) God's attributes/qualities are "invisible" (Rom. 1:20). Since God is invisible, having no body, His attributes cannot be perceived by the senses.

2) "And We Can Talk About Them"

  a) Jesus (John 4:24) and the Apostles (Rom. 1:20) had no difficulty in talking about God's attributes. All the names and titles of God are actually ways of talking about God's attributes (1 Tim. 1:17; 6:13-16).

  b) As long as we limit our understanding about God to the Bible, our knowledge of God will be:

    i) Objective

    ii) Immutable

    iii) True

  c) If we go beyond Scripture and mold our understanding of God by what we "think," "feel" or "experience," then we are engaged in idolatry and our knowledge of God becomes:

    i) Subjective

    ii) Mutable

    iii) False

Summary

The God who is truly there has not been silent. He has revealed Himself and facts about Himself in Scripture (the Written Word) and in Christ (the Living Word). We can know true facts about God as well as personally knowing God. This knowledge is only possible because salvation was planned by the Father in eternity, accomplished by the Son in history and applied by the Spirit in the present. To the Triune God of Father, Son and Holy Spirit be all the glory forever and ever. Amen!

1) We Can Talk About God in a Meaningful Way

Christian Theology	Modern Unbelief
God ⟶ Man	Man ⟶ God
Revealed by God	Projection of Man
Objective	Subjective
Immutable	Mutable
Transcendent	Cultural
Absolute	Relative
Universal	Particular
Knowledge	No Knowledge
Truth	Myth/Speculation

While the Christian God gives us a sufficient basis for truth, morals, justice and beauty, modern unbelief has ended in total skepticism (no truth possible) and relativism (no morals possible): God, morals, science, history, etc.

Of course, both relativism and skepticism are self-refuting.

"There is no absolute truth."

"No one knows anything about God."
"There are no absolutes."
"Everything is relative."
"Truth/morals are subjective."

Attribute No. 1

Maker of Heaven and Earth

When we open the Bible, we are at once confronted with the first attribute of God that He wants us to understand about Him.

1) God Is the Maker of Heaven and Earth.

"In the beginning God created the Heavens and the earth" (Gen. 1:1).

a) The early church saw this in a really profound way and placed it in the forefront of all their creeds.

The Apostles' Creed: "I believe in God the Father Almighty, Maker of Heaven and earth."

b) The implications of God as creator are stupendous! They formed the basis of Western culture and made science possible.

   i) God exists prior to, apart from and independent of the space/time world which He created out of nothing for His own glory. This "demystified" the world.

   ii) The world is not eternal.

   iii) It had a beginning and will have an end.

   iv) It is not a part of God but a separate creation of God.

   v) The reality and goodness of matter is established and spiritualism is refuted.

   vi) The reality and goodness of spirit is established and materialism refuted.

   vii) The world reflects God's law and power and not chaos and confusion.

   viii) It began with the personal and rational God and not with non-personal and irrational chance.

   ix) Man has dignity, worth, significance and meaning. He is not a "fluke" of evolution.

   x) All people are "human" because we all came from Adam and Eve. Racism is not true.

   xi) History follows a divine plan and has meaning and significance.

   xii) We can make moral judgments.

   xiii) We can know the truth.

   xiv) We can make the distinction between:

Creator/Creation	Truth/Error
God/Man	Right/wrong
Eternal/Temporal	Male/Female
Infinite/Finite	Justice/Injustice
Man/Animal or thing	Order/Chaos

c) If one accepts God as Maker of Heaven and earth, then he will not have any difficulty in accepting the rest of the Bible. All the other attributes of God modify the Creator. They are understandable only in the context of creation *ex nihilo*.

d) This is why unbelief attacks the creator-hood of God with so much rage. They say:

   i) "The world is eternal."

   ii) "It does not have a beginning or an end."

   iii) "Chaos, chance and luck rule this world."

   iv) "Man is only ooze that oozed out of ooze and is returning to ooze."

e) King Solomon said: "Remember now Thy Creator" (Ecc. 12:1).

f) The Prophet Amos said: "Prepare to meet your God" (Amos 4:12).

Attribute No. 2

The Incomprehensibility of God

Introduction

2) The early church began the attributes of God with "Maker of Heaven and earth." The doctrine of creation is the foundation of everything else in the rest of the Bible. Nothing else in the Bible is true if Gen. 1:1 is not true. But if Gen. 1:1 is true, then everything else in the Bible is true. The early Christians wisely chose incomprehensibility as the second attribute of God. Definition of "Incomprehensibility":

The finite mind of man cannot exhaustively or completely grasp, understand, explain or define the infinite nature of God.

a) "Incomprehensibility" tells us that God is beyond our capacity to grasp for four reasons.
   i)   God is infinite. Thus only God understands God infinitely (1 Cor. 2:11).
   ii) Since man is finite, his mind cannot fully comprehend the Almighty. This is not evil but good, for God made man finite (Eph. 3:19).
   iii) Since man is sinful, he has a moral aversion to God (John 1:10; cf 3:19-20).
   iv) The confines of revelation limit man's understanding of God to what is found in Scripture (1 Cor. 4:6).

b) "Incomprehensibility" does not mean:
   i)   God is unknowable (John 17:3).
   ii) God is illogical or irrational. He is a-rational, i.e., beyond reason/logic.
   iii) Beware of the hidden assumption of modern philosophy: Either man knows all there is about God or he knows nothing at all about Him.

c) Because God has revealed Himself, our knowledge of Him is finite, true and certain (1 John 5:20).

d) Biblical basis of incomprehensibility
   i)   O.T. passage of full mention: The Book of Job
      (1) The incomprehensibility of God is revealed as God's "answer" to the problem of evil as found in the evils inflicted on poor Job.
      (2) The context: The evils which came upon Job
      (3) The source: Did the evils come from God? or Satan? or evil people? or all of them at the same time? Is God the author of evil?
      (4) Job's position
         (a) God was in control of all things.
         (b) No evil could come upon Job unless God approved.
         (c) God was not the agent or cause of the evil. The devil and evil people were to blame—not God.

Note: God's sovereignty and man's responsibility are both true!

Man's failure to reconcile these two truths does not negate their truthfulness.

Faith swims when reason can no longer feel the bottom!

         (d) Job trusted in God that He had sent these evils for God's glory and Job's good.
         (e) While Job could not understand why God allowed these evil things to happen, he could still worship God!

(f) The basic texts
    (i) A contest in Heaven led to a conflict on earth: 1:6-12
    (ii) Job's godly attitude: 1:20-22
    (iii) Another evil comes upon Job: 2:1-9
    (iv) Job's godly attitude: 2:10
    (v) God's incomprehensibility: 5:9; 9:10-12; 11:7-10; 38:1-5; 42:1-6

Attribute No. 3

God Is Infinite

Introduction

Ever since Francis Schaeffer pointed out that we can have truth, justice, morals and beauty because God is the infinite reference point which gives meaning and significance to all things, the infinite nature of God has come under a mounting attack. If God can be reduced to a finite being, then there is no infinite or universal standard which can form a sufficient basis for truth or morals. Relativism can win if God is not infinite.

Once God is reduced to finiteness, then He is just another particular in search of a universal means to explain Him!

The denial of God's infinite nature is a master stroke of Satan because by attacking this one attribute, he has attacked all the other attributes of God. If God is not infinite, then no "omni" attributes (example: omnipotence) are true, and the distinction between God and His creation is erased.

The Christian God is different from angels and man by virtue of being infinite. While God, men and angels possess Person, Power, Presence and Perception, they are not the same.

1) Definition: The word "infinite" does not describe an independent attribute of God. It is an adjective which when applied to all the other attributes of God make God who He is—"GOD."
    INFINITE Person
    INFINITE Power
    INFINITE Presence
    INFINITE Perception

  a) The Hebrew word itself means "unlimited," "boundless," "without a cutting off place."
  b) God is present everywhere in the totality of His person, i.e., we cannot find a "cutting off place" for God. He has no "limitations" or "boundary" after which we can say, "God stops here." There is "no end" to God's presence.
  c) God's love, mercy and grace must be infinite or all is lost. Prayer depends on God's infinity! (Psa. 139).
  d) Biblical Support—O.T. passage of full mention: Psa. 147
    i) God's omniscience (v. 4): The stars may be "without number" to man, but God knows their "number" and "name."
    ii) Verse 5 is a poetic contrast to verse 4.

THE STARS	GOD'S KNOWLEDGE
"have a limit"	"is infinite" (NASV)
"can be numbered"	"without limit"
stars … no more stars	God … (no limit)

    iii) God's infinite nature is what makes Him superior to the stars. He is "great" and "mighty" because He is infinite.

Attribute No. 4

The Existence of God

Introduction

We have already seen that God is infinite in His existence, being, nature and attributes. The word "infinite" simply means that for God there are:

No limitations
No boundaries
No "cutting off point"
No beginning or end

1) God's existence is infinite.
   a) It is self-existent (John 5:26; Exo. 3:14).
   b) It is independent (Acts 17:24-25).
   c) It is eternal (Deut. 33:27; Isa. 57:15).
   d) It is immortal (1 Tim. 1:17).
   e) It is perfect (Job 37:16; Psa. 19:7; Rom. 12:2).
   f) It is immutable (Psa. 102:24-27; Psa. 42:2).

2) Man's existence is finite.
   a) It is dependent (Job 12:10; Dan. 5:25; Acts 17:25).
   b) It is temporal (Acts 17:26).
   c) It is mortal (Psa. 90:9-12).
   d) It is imperfect (Phil. 3:12; cf. Heb. 12:23).
   e) It is mutable (Job 14:1-6).

3) Applications
   a) What a glorious God!
   b) What an amazing Gospel!
   c) What a terrifying prospect if we reject such a God and His Gospel!

Attribute No. 5

The Eternity of God

When we say, "God is infinite," we mean that He is infinite in respect to something. Infinitude is not an independent attribute, but it is that element which when applied to all the attributes of God makes God who He is—"GOD."

God is infinite in respect to:
    ● Time, i.e., ETERNAL
    ● Space, i.e., OMNIPRESENT
    ● Knowledge, i.e., OMNISCIENT
    ● Power, i.e., OMNIPOTENT
    ● Will, i.e., SOVEREIGN
    ● Goodness, i.e., HOLY

1) What do we mean when we say that God is "eternal"?
   a) This tells us that God is:
      i) Self-existent

   ii) Beginningless
   iii) Endless
   iv) Uncreated
   v) Uncaused
   vi) Timeless
  b) This tells us that the world:
   i) Is Dependent
   ii) Has a Beginning
   iii) Will Have an End
   iv) Was Created
   v) Is Caused
   vi) Is Limited by Time, i.e., "in" Time
  c) This tells us that "time":
   i) Is Dependent
   ii) Has a Beginning
   iii) Will Have an End
   iv) Was Created
   v) Is Caused
   vi) Is Limited by God

2) Modern theologians reject the eternity of God in three ways:
  a) God is merged into the world and takes on all the attributes of the world.
  b) Time is moved up to take God's place and attributes.
  c) Time becomes the God in whom and by whom God exists! This is the Greek god "Kronos"!

3) What is shocking is that some modern evangelical/Reformed theologians (Davis, Pinnock, Rice, etc.) are now teaching this heresy!

4) What does Scripture teach?
  a) Gen. 1:1 does not say, "In the beginning TIME." It says, "In the beginning GOD."
  b) Gen. 1:1 says that God created the space/time world. It does not say, "God and time created the world" or "Time created God and the world."
  c) God alone is said to be "eternal" in the Bible (Gen. 21:33; Rom. 1:20). Not once is "time" said to be "eternal."
  d) God is the creator of all things, time included. They are "in" Him (Col. 1:16-17; Acts 17:28; Rom. 11:36).
  e) God is said to be "eternal," i.e., timeless (Psa. 41:13; 90:1-4; 106:48; Isa. 57:15; Isa. 43:13).
  f) Time is a process (Gen. 4:3; 38:12) which God "sets" (Acts 1:7), "appoints" (Gen. 18:14; Dan. 8:19; 11:27, 29, 35) and "determines" (Acts 17:26). Nowhere in the Bible does time control or limit God!

5) The philosophic arguments against God's eternity are foolish (see Morey, *Battle of the Gods*).

Application

What a strong foundation for our hope and security in God. Because He is eternal, He has, is and will take care of us (Deut. 33:26-29)!

Attribute No. 6

The Omnipresence of God

When God's infinitude is applied to time, we say that God is eternal. When it is applied to space, we say that God is omnipresent.

1) Definition: God is present everywhere at the same time. God is present in the totality of His personhood "in," "throughout," "beyond," "above," "beneath," "before," "after" and "beside" all things. There is no place where God is not.

   a) What a comfort to the saints! No matter where you are at any time, God is there. At morning, noon or night, He is there. In times of plenty or want, He is there. In times of joy or sorrow, sickness or health, in riches or poverty, God is there.

   b) What an encouragement to awakened sinners. God is there and He is ready, willing and able to receive sinners who come to Him through Christ alone, by grace alone, through faith alone.

   c) What a terror to rebel sinners! You have no place to hide! Where can you go to escape God? His arm of justice is long, His wrath may seem to tarry, but it is only delayed in mercy. Fear God and live!

2) Biblical support

   a) Gen. 1:1 tells us that God is greater than the space/time world.

   b) God cannot be contained or confined by space (1 Kings 8:27; Acts 17:24-25).

   c) He "fills" Heaven and earth (Jer. 23:23-24).

   d) Earth is His "footstool" (Isa. 66:1-2).

   e) Psa. 139:7-13 is the O.T. passage of full mention:

      i) v. 7a—"Were can I go from Your Spirit (within)"; v. 7b—"Where can I flee from Your Presence?" (without) (lit. "FACE").

WE CANNOT ESCAPE FROM GOD MENTALLY,
PHYSICALLY, INTERNALLY OR EXTERNALLY!

      ii) v. 8-12—Possible places to hide from God
         (1) "Up" (the Heavens) (height)
         (2) "Down" (Sheol) (depth)
         (3) "Sideways" (the wings of dawn) (speed)
             (East or West) (the far side of the sea) (distance)
         (4) "Darkness" (the darkness will hide me) (cover)

3) Prayer presupposes God is everywhere (Psa. 65:2).

4) Salvation presupposes God is everywhere (Acts 17:27-28).

Attribute No. 7

The Omniscience of God

Just as we applied God's infinitude to God's relationship to space and time and found Him omnipresent and eternal, we will now apply it to His knowledge. Once we do this, we must say that God is omniscient.

1) Definition: God knows everything about everything only as God can know it. His knowledge is infinite and has no "cutting off point" or limitations (Psa. 147:5). It is not only infinite, but:

   a) Eternal (Acts 15:18).

   b) Self-Existent (Rom. 11:33-35).

   c) Perfect (Job 37:16; 11:11).

2) Biblical foundation
   a) The plain statement of Scripture
       i) "The Lord is a God of knowledge" (1 Sam. 2:3)
       ii) "He knows everything" (1 John 3:20)
       iii) "His understanding is infinite" (Psa. 147:5)
       iv) He is "perfect in knowledge" (Job 37:16)
       v) "All things are open and laid bare" to Him (Heb. 4:13)
       vi) "God knoweth!" (2 Cor. 12:2-3)
   b) The vocabulary used to describe God's knowledge
       i) "Foreknows" (Acts 2:23)
       ii) "Foresees" (Gal. 3:8)
       iii) "Nothing hid" from God (Heb. 4:13)
   c) The chief attribute of God is his Prescience, i.e., foreknowledge of the future (Isa. 41:21-26; 44:6, 7, 26, 28; 45:11-13, 21; 46:9-11)

Special Note: Isa. 46:10: "Declaring the End from the Beginning."
   Human knowledge must progress from the beginning to the end.
   Divine knowledge already knows the end from the beginning.

Application
   i) What a comfort to the believer! (Psa. 138:1-6)
   ii) What a terror to the unbeliever! (Rom. 4:4-16)

Attribute No. 8

The Omnipotence of God

When we apply God's infinitude to His power, we say that God is omnipotent or "all-powerful." This is one of the most misunderstood attributes of God and we need to define what it means carefully.

1) What "omnipotence" does not mean:
   a) That God can do anything and everything!
       i) Can God sin? No!
       ii) Can God lie? No!
       iii) Can God become non-God? No!
       iv) Can God make a rock so big He cannot move it? No!

The key to remember is that God cannot do or be anything which contradicts His Divine nature (2 Tim. 2:13; Tit. 1:2; Heb. 6:18).

   b) That God is now doing all He can or could do.
2) What "omnipotence" means:
   a) God's Power is Infinite
       i) Eternal
       ii) Self-Existent
       iii) Inexhaustible
   b) God's Power is exercised only in conformity to:
       i) His immutable nature
       ii) His sovereign will
   c) Nothing and no one can hinder God in the execution of His will, i.e., nothing outside of God can frustrate Him.

3) Biblical basis
   a) Gen. 18:14
   b) Job 42:2
   c) Psa. 115:3
   d) Jer. 32:17, 27
   e) Dan. 4:35
   f) Zech. 8:6
   g) Matt. 19:26
   h) Lk. 1:37

Application

God's omnipotence means that our salvation is eternally secure (Heb. 9:12), and the Judgment of the wicked is inescapable (Acts 17:31) .

Attribute No. 9

The Sovereignty of God

Introduction

When we apply God's infinitude to His control of the universe He has made, it means that God's control is infinite, i.e., nothing and no one can limit God's control.

God's Omnipotence = Infinite Potential Power

God's Sovereignty = Infinite Actual Control

God's omnipotence supplies the will of God with all the power it needs to control all that exists so that everything in Heaven and earth will bring glory to God.

1) God's sovereignty is an attribute of God
   a) It is not just an attribute but the chief attribute of God. A.W. Pink, following the Puritans, called God's sovereignty "The Godhood of God" because it is God's sovereignty that makes all the attributes of God work together to accomplish God's will.
   b) This means that we cannot strip God of His sovereignty without destroying His deity.
   c) God's sovereignty amplifies and magnifies all the other attributes of God.
        Example: God's love becomes God's sovereign love. (Jer. 31:3 KJV).
             God's grace becomes God's sovereign grace (Eph. 2:8-9).
        Note: What hope of salvation would we have if God were not sovereign?
        Note: What assurance would we have that the good will ultimately triumph over the evil? that history is His-story? that it will reach its climax as predicted in Scripture? if God were not sovereign?

2) The basis of the doctrine of divine sovereignty
   a) Biblical basis
      i)   General statements of Scripture

O.T.	N.T.
a. Gen. 1:1	f. Rom. 8:28
b. Job 42:2	g. Rom. 11:33-36
c. Psa. 103:19	h. Eph. 1:11
d. Psa. 115:2-8	i. Acts 17:24-28
e. Dan. 4:34-35	j. Rev. 4:11

    ii) Specific Scriptures
        (1) 1 Chron. 29:10-13
        (2) 1 Sam. 1:6, 10; 2:1-10
        (3) Pro. 16:33
        (4) Col. 1:16, 17
        (5) James 4:13-15
    iii) The Names of God reveal that He is sovereign.
        (1) Lord (Adonai): Sovereign Upholder of the universe
        (2) Most High: Ruler over all things
        (3) Ruler Over All: Blessed Controller
        (4) King of Kings: Nations in His control
        (5) Lord of Lords: Rulers in His control
  b) Historical basis

The sovereignty of God is what the Christian faith has believed for nearly 2,000 years. Modern denial of God's sovereignty reduces God to a finite god who sits with man in the back seat of a driver-less car rushing to possible oblivion in a chance-based universe where nothing is secure! And they expect us to worship such a divine wimp? No way!

  3) Illustrations of God's sovereignty
    a) Biblical illustrations
      i) Animals: birds: 1 Kings 17:2-4
                    cattle: 1 Sam. 6:7-12
                    colt: Mk. 11:1-10
                    fish: Matt. 17:24-27
      ii) Man: Joseph: Gen. 27:17-31; 39:6-20; 45:4-9; 50:19-20
                    Christ: Rev. 13:8; Lk. 22:22; Acts 2:23; 4:24-30

Conclusion

No discussion of the attributes of God can be complete without reference to the "Godhood of God," which is His divine sovereignty over all things. It is only by His sovereignty over all things that we know that our God is GOD!

This then is the God we love and serve. He is a mighty God! He is a God who is worthy of our worship, a God before whom we should bow in wonder, awe and praise. To Him belongs all the glory both in this world and in the next. Amen!

Chapter Nine
The Fear of the Lord

Introduction

Both David and Solomon tell us that "the fear of the Lord is the *beginning* of wisdom."

In Psa. 111:10, David uses the Hebrew word "Re-sheet" when he says, "The fear of the Lord is the *beginning* of wisdom." "Re-sheet" is translated elsewhere as:

"The best" (1 Sam. 15:21)

"The supreme" (Pro. 4:7)

This word emphasizes that the chief, the best and the supreme part of the worship of God is the fear of the Lord.

In Proverbs 9:10, Solomon uses the word "Te-Chil-Lah" when he says, "The fear of the Lord is the *beginning* of wisdom." "Te-Chil-Lah" emphasizes that the first thing one must do to obtain wisdom is to fear God.

It is clear that the fear of God is the first step to wisdom as well as the chief part of wisdom. Without the fear of God, there can be no true wisdom.

Therefore, it is essential for us to understand what it means to fear God. Its nature, attributes and consequences must be grasped if wisdom is to be obtained.

1) The Nature of the Fear of God
   a) The first problem we face is the poverty of the English language. We have only one English word ("fear") which is used as the translation of 18 Hebrew words and of two Greek words.
   b) The fear of God means many different things depending on the word used and the context where it is found.

Objective vs. Subjective	Temporary vs. Permanent
Positive vs. Negative	Saving vs. Non-saving
Particular vs. General	Individual vs. Group
Action vs. Attitude	Spiritual vs. Carnal
Sincere vs. Hypocritical	Character vs. Episode
Inward vs. Outward	Attract vs. Repulse
Mobilize vs. Paralyze	True vs. False
Active vs. Passive	Joy vs. Sadness
Awe vs. Terror	

Each occurrence of the term, "the fear of God," combines different aspects of the above list. Example: The repentance of Nineveh was a temporary, negative, non-saving, particular group action which was a carnal, hypocritical, outward, false terror of God's judgment. After the judgment passed, they returned to their paganism!

2) The Structure of the Fear of God

In the following diagram, the fear of God is first divided into objective and subjective meanings. These distinctions are further broken down into positive/negative and then permanent/temporary. In this way, we can structure a logical outline for the fear of God.

The Fear of God

Objective Meanings		Subjective Meanings	
Positive	Negative	Positive	Negative
Temporary	Permanent	Temporary	Permanent

With this logical structure, a comprehensive survey of the biblical teaching on the fear of God is possible.

3) Objective Meanings of the "Fear of God"

a) God's name is "Fear" (Gen. 31:42, 53)

b) The Word of God is "The Fear of the Lord" (Psa. 19:9)

c) God's nature is "awesome," i.e., "fearful" (Deut. 7:21)

d) God's works are "awesome," i.e., "fearful" (2 Sam. 7:23)

e) Revealed religion (Psa. 34:11)

f) Believers in general (Psa. 22:23)

g) Gentile converts (Acts 13:26)

h) The public worship of God (Rev. 15:4)

4) Subjective Meanings of the Fear of God

a) Because of the vast amount of biblical material on the fear of God, perhaps the best way of arranging things in a logical order is to make a basic distinction between the positive and negative aspects of the fear of God.

b) The second basic division under both of the above subtitles is the distinction between temporary and permanent aspects of the fear of God.

c) All the other distinctions on the list will be developed under the temporary and permanent aspects of the positive and negative points under the subjective meanings of the fear of God.

5) Subjective Positive Meanings

a) The positive meanings of the fear of God encompass a wide range of emotions. These emotions are positive in that they uplift, encourage and motivate a person to respect, revere, stand in awe of, esteem, love, worship, tremble before, delight in, rejoice, obey, serve, honor, etc., the Lord.

b) These positive feelings can be temporary or permanent. Just because a feeling is temporary does not mean it is not positive. Some good things do not last very long.

c) Examples of a positive temporary fear of God

i) There is a positive temporary awe or reverence associated with the worship of God either private or public which one experiences when in the presence of God (Psa. 33:8, 9; 96:8-9; Rev. 14:7).

ii) There is a positive temporary awe which is provided by witnessing a miracle (Matt. 9:8).

iii) There is a positive temporary respect for God, His Law, Word and Worship (2 Chron. 26:5, 16).

iv) There is a positive temporary national fear of God (Exo. 14:31; Jonah 3:6-10).

v) There is a positive temporary awe of God connected with a religious revival (Acts 9:31).

d) Examples of a positive permanent fear of God.

i) When God takes first place in someone's life in terms of priorities, Scripture describes him as a "God-fearing" person. This reverence for God, His Law, Word and Kingdom pervades his entire life. In this sense, "the fear of God" is a permanent character trait (Gen. 42:13; cf. 39:6-13; Exo. 1:17, 21).

Note: One can be "God-fearing" yet unsaved (Acts 10:1-2, 11:14).

ii) "The Fear of God" can be the ethical and moral pressure to keep politicians and judges just and fair. Without the fear of God (i.e., their accountability to God), leaders become corrupted by bribes and favors (Exo. 18:17-23; 2 Chron. 19:4-10).

iii) There is a permanent positive subjective fear of God in Heaven (Rev. 15:3-4).

iv) In the N.T., the fear of God and Christ is a motivation to obedience (2 Cor. 7:1; Eph. 5:21; Col. 3:22).

6) Subjective Negative Fear of God

a) It may come as a surprise to many today, but the N.T. is about 42 percent "negative" in content and thrust: "negative" in the sense of being "bad" news. The Bible is faithful in telling us the bad news as well as the good news about God, man, sin and salvation. Any preaching or teaching ministry which is either wholly positive or entirely negative must be viewed as unscriptural.

b) What Does "Negative" Mean?

sadness not gladness	tears not cheers
downer not upper	depression not happiness
bad news not good news	conviction not peace of mind
guilt not innocence	terror not joy
repulsion not attraction	dread not hope
apprehension not anticipation	

c) An example of negative fear on the human level of man-to-man relationship (Deut. 2:24-25).

d) This negative fear can be temporary or permanent.

e) Examples of a temporary negative fear of God.

i) The fear of God which causes you to hide from Him (Gen. 3:10).

ii) The fear that the Bible is true after all and there really is a Hell (Lk. 21:25-27; Rev. 6:12-17).

iii) A feeling of despondency because you know you are fighting a losing battle against God (Exo. 15:11-16; 23:27).

iv) A fear of Christ that He was who He claimed to be because you just witnessed a miracle (Lk. 8:37).

v) Fear in the midst of divine judgment upon sinners (Acts 5:5, 11). Maybe you are next.

vi) Fear felt when seeing Christ in His glory—spiritually (Lk. 5:6-10) or physically (Rev. 1:17-18).

f) A Permanent Negative Fear of God.

i) A fear of the Judgment Day when we will be held accountable for our thoughts, words and deeds.

(1) This judgment will be in two stages. There is a judgment after death (Heb. 9:27), and there is a judgment at Christ's return (Matt. 25:31-46).

(2) Those who accept this prepare themselves to meet God (Lk. 23: 39-43). Those who do not fear God do not expect to be held accountable for their actions (Lk. 18:1-8).

(3) Many Christians think there is no Day of Judgment for them. They arrive at this error by:

(a) Misapplying Rom. 8:1 and Heb. 10:17.

(b) Confusing Justification with Sanctification.

(c) Denying the Day of Judgment at the resurrection.

(4) "The Resurrection" is referred to 29 times in the N.T. (example: John 11:24; Acts 23:6-8; Heb. 6-2, etc.). The N.T. never speaks of "Resurrections."

(5) This resurrection involves all men (John 5:28-29; 1 Cor. 15-20-22; Rev. 20:11-13).

(6) This resurrection takes place when Christ returns on the "Last Day" (John 11:24; 1 Cor. 15:22, 24).

(7) "The Judgment" is referred to 21 times in the N.T. It takes place on "The Great Day of

Judgment" (Jude 6) and involves all men (Matt. 12:36-37; Acts 17:30-31; 24:25; Rev. 20:1-15).

    (8) Since all judgment has been given to Christ (John 5:22), He sits as judge over all men (Matt. 25:31; 2 Tim. 4:1).

    (9) The N.T. always pictures the righteous and the wicked standing under judgment (Matt. 25:31-32; 2 Cor. 5:10; Rev. 20:13).

  (10) The wicked will be sent into an eternal Hell (Rev. 20:15; 14:9-11) while the righteous will inherit a new earth (Rev. 21:1-4).

  (11) Some men will be resurrected unto life (John 5:29), others unto condemnation (John 5:29).

  (12) The righteous are judged in terms of "rewards" (Matt. 16:27; 1 Cor. 3:8-15; Rev. 22:12) based on their lives (Rom. 14:9-12; 2 Cor. 5:10; 2 Pet. 3:11-14).

  ii) A fear of God's chastening rod (Heb. 12: 3-13; Psa. 38; David; Peter).

 iii) A fear that God will throw you into an eternal Hell (Lk. 12:4-5).

 iv) A fear of apostasy which leads to God's wrath (Heb. 4:1-2).

Conclusion

The fear of God should be greater in your life than the fear of poverty, sickness, loneliness, failure or rejection. God alone is worthy of your trust, love and service.

Chapter Ten

How to Hear the Word With Profit

To understand how to hear the Word requires us to study the Parable of the Sower. We must first review a basic introduction to the Gospel of Matthew as a whole. Its purpose, message and place in the Bible forms the context of Christ's parables.

MATTHEW
I. Author: The Apostle Matthew (Matt. 9:9-12)
II. Date: A.D. 60
III. Setting: Chapters 1-18 Ministry in Galilee (4:12)
                             Chapters 19-21 Ministry in Judea (19:1)
IV. Structure: Not chronological but thematical. Matthew groups together Christ's sermons, miracles, parables, reactions, etc. in clusters.

V. Relationship to the Old Testament
   A. General relation of Gospels to Old Testament
      Old Testament—Preparation   Gospels—Manifestation
   B. Special relation of Matthew to Old Testament
      1. Matthew quotes or paraphrases the Old Testament 120 times, which is more than any other Gospel. This is more than the total of Mark (63) and John (43) combined!
      2. More than any other Gospel, Matthew says that things happened "that [O.T.] Scripture might be fulfilled," at least 15 times.
      3. Matthew's genealogy picks up where the Old Testament left off and brings it down to Christ.
      4. Matthew is thus the historical bridge between the Old and New Testaments.
VI. Matthew's relationship to the other Gospels
   A. Different Audiences
      Matthew to the Jew
      Mark to the Roman
      Luke to the Greek
      John to the Christian
   B. Different Questions
      1. Matthew answers: "What did Jesus say?"
         Out of 1,068 verses in Matthew, 644 verses record the words of Christ. This is three fifths of the Gospel! He records more sermons, parables, sayings and words than any other Gospel. He always gives the full text of a sermon or parable, whereas the other Gospels abridge or omit them. Out of 1,068 verses, 410 verses contain material unique to Matthew. This is one third of the Gospel.

    2. Mark answers: "What did Jesus do?"

    3. Luke answers: "Who followed Jesus?"

    4. John answers: "Who is Jesus?"

Note: This observation solves the so-called "contradictions" in the Gospels. The Liberal assumes whenever Matthew records more of the words of Christ than the other Gospels, this means that Matthew fictionalized those words and put them into the mouth of Christ when He never actually said them.

Examples: 1. Matthew's Sermon on the Mount contains 109 verses. Luke's account has only 18 verses.

          2. Compare Matthew and Luke on the Lord's Prayer (Matt. 6:9-13, cf. Lk. 11:2-4).

          3. Compare Matthew 19:9 and Mark 10:11-12 on divorce and remarriage.

            The Gospels complement each other. They do not contradict each other.

The Parable of the Sower

Given the emphasis of Matthew on Christ's words, it is no surprise that although both Mark 4:3-20 and Lk. 8:5-15 record the Parable of the Sower, Matthew 13:3-23 gives us the fullest account of Christ's words. Matthew is thus the "passage of full mention."

I. A General Introduction to the Parable

  A. In the context, people had begun to ignore or reject Jesus.

    1. The people would not repent (11:20-24).

    2. The Pharisees decided to kill Him (12:14). They claimed He was demon-possessed (12:22-45).

    3. Even His own family rejected Him and thought He was crazy (12:46-50; cf. Mk. 3:20, 21, 31-35).

    4. The crowds followed Him only for what they could get out of Him. They wanted healing or food (John 6:25, 26).

  B. In this parable three things are mentioned.

    1. The Sower, who is Christ Himself

    2. The Seed, which is the Word of God

    3. The Grounds, which are the hearers

  C. The focus is not on the Sower or the seed but on the grounds. The problem in Christ's day was not the preacher or His sermon, but the hearers. They were not responding to the Word of God as they ought.

    Application: Christ speaks through every true elder (pastor) (Rom. 10:14). When you reject the biblical teaching or counsel of pastors, you are rejecting Christ (Lk. 10:16; 1 Cor. 14:37, 38).

  D. The four different grounds represent four different ways people respond to hearing the Word of God.

    ● The wayside hearer (Matt. 13:4)

    ● The stony ground hearer (vs. 5, 6)

    ● The thorny ground hearer (v. 7)

    ● The good ground hearer (v. 8)

  E. The first, second and third hearers reveal the ways people respond.

F. The first three hearers have certain common errors that sealed their fate.
1. Diligent hearers, but negligent doers (vs. 19, 20, 22; James 1:22-25)
2. No true understanding (v. 19): They did not understand their sinful state before God and the urgency of their salvation.
   a. First hearer—no understanding (v. 19)
   b. Second hearer—superficial understanding (v. 21)
   c. Third hearer—incomplete understanding (v. 22)
3. No root, i.e., no true heart work (v. 21)
4. No fruit, i.e., no repentance, faith and love

II. The Stony Ground Hearer
A. A Physical Description of the Ground (v. 4)
1. The "path" was the hard footpath used by men and animals as they went to and from the fields.
   It was hard for two reasons.
   (1) It had never been plowed.
   (2) It was hardened by constant use.
2. Because of its hardness, the seed, which fell on it, remained on top of it. The birds saw the seed and ate it. The seed was gone in a short time.
B. A Spiritual Description of the Heart (v. 19)
1. The success or failure of the Sower and his seed depends on the condition of the heart of the hearer.
2. The basic problem of this hearer is that he never responds to the Word of God. Preaching does not stir him to do anything. He sits with a blank mind during the sermon. There is no anger or joy; no faith or repentance. Nothing happens to change his life! The Word falls on deaf ears. His mind is in neutral during the sermon. He daydreams or sleeps during the message. No one ever sees any change in him.
3. He has a hard heart.
   a. Like Pharaoh, who was determined to have his own way, he hardened his heart by determining in his mind that he would not give in to God's command regardless of what God said (Ex. 7:10-13).
   b. Like Pharaoh's army, who determined not to fear God or His wrath (Ex. 14:17).
   c. An insensitive heart that refuses to allow its feelings to be stirred (Deut. 15:7-8).
   d. A heart that refuses to repent (2 Chron. 36:11-14)
   e. An obstinate heart, which is not willing to listen (Ezk. 3:7).
   f. A heart which has no understanding of the Word (Matt. 13:19).

How to Avoid a Hard Heart
1. Listen to God and His Word (Heb. 3:8, 15; 4:7).
2. Do not harden your heart (Heb. 3:8, 15; 4:7).
3. Get involved in one-anothering (Heb. 3:12, 13; 10:25).
4. Seek understanding (Prov. 4:5).
5. Be warned of sudden judgment (Pro. 29:1).

4. He has a dry heart.
   a. Just as the seed found no moisture in the ground, the Word touched no emotion in the heart.

      b. He never watered the Word by thinking about what he heard. It is "in one ear and out the other" for this hearer.

      c. Because of his hard heart, nothing developed.

    5. He has an unplowed heart.

      a. He has never allowed God's Law to plow up his conscience. Thus he is insensitive to his sin and guilt (Jer. 4:3, 4; Hos. 10:12; Rom. 7:7-13).

      b. He has never allowed the Gospel to plow up his conscience. He is insensitive to the sufferings of the Son of God (Isa. 53:3).

C. A Description of Satan's Work (Matt. 13:19)

    1. Satan is "the evil one."

    2. He always seeks to neutralize the Word.

    3. In this case, he causes the hearer to forget the Word as soon as possible.

    4. He is always ready to provide "reasons" for ignoring the Word of God.

- I don't care what God says.
- That is just the pastor's opinion.
- I don't have to obey him.
- This refers to someone else.
- The pastor is attacking me!
- I'll not listen to this!
- Why is he getting so worked up?
- Why get so excited about it?
- Religion is boring anyway.
- He is a fanatic!
- I'd better be careful here.

D. Some Remedies to Satan's Devices

    1. Realize that Satan aims at the damnation of your immortal soul.

    2. Your own sinful heart is by nature in league with the prince of darkness.

    3. The world gives its full support to any plan to oppose the Word of God.

    4. Your case is hopeless on the human level because you are helpless to change your heart.

But God can intervene

    1. His Word, like a hammer, can break the hardest heart (Jer. 23:29).

    2. His Word can make the driest heart burst forth in streams of water (Isa. 35:1-7).

    3. His Word can make the dead live (Ezk. 37:1-14).

III. The Rocky Ground Hearer

A. A Physical Description of the Ground (Matt. 13:5)

    1. Outward Softness

      a. A shallow one- or two-inch layer of soil.

      b. A deceptive appearance! The ground looked promising to the eye.

    2. Inward Hardness

      a. A shelf or ledge of rock lay beneath the soil.

      b. No deep plowing could be done. Only a shallow work was accomplished.

B. A Spiritual Description of the Heart

    1. He heard the Word (v. 20a).

    2. He received the Word (v. 20b).

      a. Immediately: quickly, without hesitation

      b. With joy: happiness, excitement

3. He encountered problems because of the Word.
   a. "Trouble" comes into his life (v. 21).
      examples (1) His conscience troubles him about things he wants to continue to do.
             (2) His wife does not like it.
             (3) His business is troubled with the problem of honesty.
   b. "Persecution," i.e., laughter, scorn, ridicule, threats, intimidation dries up any zeal for the Word of God (v. 21). When the implication of Christ's Lordship over all of life begins to pinch, he is tested.
4. He abandoned the Word (v. 21).
   a. Immediately: quickly, without hesitation.
   b. He lasted only a short time.
C. The Causes of His Destruction
   1. He was shallow in his thoughts and character.
      a. He was too easily influenced by others.
      b. He did not think things through but acted on the impulse of the moment.
      c. He was too quick to jump into things, start a new hobby or business but never completed things.
      d. He was always on the lookout for "get rich quick" plans and did not think of the cost.
   2. He was deceived by emotionalism.
      a. He thought he could have Jesus as Savior without obeying Him as Lord. ("Fire escape insurance")
      b. He did not realize that his joy over the good news of the Word meant nothing to his true spiritual state.
      c. Emotions can be produced by many things.
         (1) High blood sugar or hormone levels
         (2) Peer pressure
         (3) Mob psychology
         (4) Psychological manipulation by music, sad stories, gimmicks, etc.
   3. He deceived others by his immediate zeal.
   4. He had the mistaken idea that once he "accepted Christ," life would be a bowl of cherries. His assurance was based on the "magic words" theory.
   5. He "accepted Christ" for what he could get out of Him, not for what he could give to Him.
   6. He actually had a very hard heart beneath all the surface emotion. God delights in a broken and contrite heart, a heart soft toward God and His Word (Psa. 51:16-17).

Note: You must be troubled by your sin before you can be calmed by the Savior.
You must be lost before you can be found.
You must be wounded by the Law before you can be healed by the Gospel.
You must be cast down before you can be lifted up.
You must be broken by the cross before you can be mended by the Christ.
You must be stripped of the rags of your righteousness before you can be robed with Christ's righteousness.
You must be emptied of self before you can be filled with the Savior.

7. In short, no true heart work was accomplished in this hearer. There was no staying power because there was no saving power.

8. He or she promised much but delivered nothing.
9. Churches are filled with such people: once persecution comes, millions of them will abandon Christianity.
   Example: The Third Century Church.

IV. The Thorny Ground Hearer
  A. A Physical Description of the Ground
    1. An outward deceptiveness. It has been cleared of weeds, thorns and bushes.
    2. An inward problem. The roots of the weeds and thorns were still there. They had not been removed.
  B. The Fate of the Seed
    1. The seed germinated.
    2. The thorns sprouted.
    3. Since the thorns already had their root systems, they quickly grew and overshadowed, starved and strangled the new sprouts.
  C. A Spiritual Description of the Heart
    1. He was a hearer of the Word (Matt. 13:22). (Gk. word for "hears" means he habitually heard the word, i.e., he was and remained a church "member.")
    2. Even though he was "in church," he was never "in Christ." Religion and morality are not enough. He thought he was a Christian because of external things such as baptism, confirmation, church membership, etc.
    3. He makes a public profession of faith that he has believed in Christ; that he is now saved.
    4. There is a visible change in his life. His involvement in scandalous sins ceases. A moral reformation is accomplished.
    5. There is visible growth and interest in the things of God. Things look hopeful. People think he or she is truly converted.
    6. Slowly—almost imperceptibly—his interest in the things of God begins to die.
       Step No. 1: He loses interest in theology and books on religious issues.
       Step No. 2: He stops reading the Bible, praying, etc.
       Step No. 3: He avoids discussing religious issues.
       Step No. 4: He begins to lose interest in the preached Word. It becomes boring and too long.
       Step No. 5: He seeks silly excuses for not going to church.
               "It's too hot, too cold."
               "Well, you see, the weather is too wet, too dry."
               "I am too busy, too tired."
               "It's too late, too long."
               "The church is too beautiful, too ugly."
               "My wife, husband, children, etc."
    7. He begins to think, "What is the absolute minimum I have to do to still be called a Christian?"
  D. The Causes of His Downfall
    1. The thorns destroyed the seed in three ways:
       a. Robbed it of sunlight by overshadowing it
       b. Robbed it of nutrition by starving it
       c. Strangled it by their overwhelming number
    2. The things of this world destroyed the seed by robbing the things of God of:
       a. the sunlight of attention
       b. the nutrition of time and energy

3. The things of the world strangled the seed by their number.
4. The specific things in this world that choke the Word of God:
   a. "The worries of this life" (v . 22)
      The anxiety, worry and fretfulness of providing for one's self or family
      (Antidote: Matt. 6:24, 25, 31, 34)
   b. "The deceitfulness of wealth" (v. 22)
      The trust in wealth, which needs no God
      (Antidote: Mk. 10:17-26)
   c. "The desire for things" (Mk. 4:18)
      Covetousness, which is idolatry (Col. 3:5)
      (Antidote: 1 Jn. 2:15-17; Heb. 11:24-26)
   d. "The pleasures of this life" (Lk. 8:14)
      The pursuit of pleasure
      (Antidote: 1 Cor. 10:6-13)

5. The Inner Problem: While outward sins were removed, the root of the sinful nature was not dealt with. Sin was not dealt with by regeneration. Only an external moral reformation was accomplished (2 Pet. 2:20-22).

V. The Good Ground Hearer
   A. A Physical Description of the Soil
      1. It was good (Matt. 13:8).
      2. It was soft instead of hard (v. 4).
      3. It was deep instead of shallow (v. 5).
      4. It was clean instead of corrupt (v. 7).
   B. A Spiritual Description of the Heart
      1. He had a "noble and good heart" (Lk. 8:15).
         a. By nature our heart or soul is hopelessly corrupt and wicked (Gen. 6:5; 8:21; Jer. 17:9; Matt. 15:19).
         b. Only God can give us a good heart: (Ezk. 11:19- 20; Acts 16:14; Psa. 119:25).
      2. He persevered in the Word (Lk. 8:15). He did not gradually lose interest like the thorny ground hearer.
      3. He bore fruit (Matt. 13:23).
         a. None of the others bore fruit.
         b. The "fruit" simply means faith, repentance, peace, joy, etc. (true conversion).
         c. There are various degrees of fruit bearing.
            30/60/100
         d. Fruit bearing is either increasing or decreasing.
            Matthew: 100 60 30
            Mark: 30 60 100
      4. He really heard the Word (Matt. 13:23). His hearing was not defective like in the others. He was attentive (Heb. 2:1-3).
      5. He really understood the Word (Matt. 13:23). This is in contrast to the others who had either no understanding, superficial understanding or selective understanding.
      6. He really accepted the Word (Mk. 4:20). His acceptance was not superficial or hypocritical.
      7. He retained the Word (Lk. 8:15). He did not abandon it when trials came. He did not let Satan take it away.

Closing Applications

I. The fate of the seed depends on the condition of the ground. One may preach like an angel, but it is the heart that determines if salvation is accomplished.

II. The only hope is that God will intervene and give a new heart.

III. A portrait was painted during this study on the Parable of the Sower. Which hearer are you?

Chapter Eleven

The Priesthood of Every Believer

I. Basic Theological Definition

Under the New Covenant, every Christian is a priest of the most High God (Isa. 61:1-6; 1 Pet. 2:5, 9; Rev. 1:6; 5:10). All Christians have immediate access to God's presence through Christ and thus have no need for human priests or mediators. There is now only one High Priest who is the mediator of the New Covenant, Jesus Christ our Lord (1 Tim. 2:5).

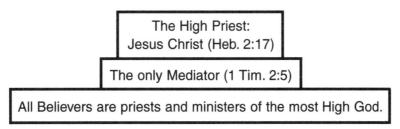

```
┌─────────────────────────┐
│     The High Priest:     │
│  Jesus Christ (Heb. 2:17)│
└─────────────────────────┘
┌──────────────────────────────┐
│  The only Mediator (1 Tim. 2:5)│
└──────────────────────────────┘
┌────────────────────────────────────────────────┐
│ All Believers are priests and ministers of the most High God. │
└────────────────────────────────────────────────┘
```

II. The Basic New Testament Principle

All the privileges and responsibilities of the Old Testament priests now belong to all believers—except those privileges and responsibilities fulfilled or abrogated by Christ or delegated to the officers of the New Testament Church or explicitly denied them by the New Testament itself.

III. The Old Testament Priesthood
  A. The Privileges of Being a Priest
    1. Immediate access to God (2 Chron. 26:16-21)
    2. Enjoying the dignity of the office (2 Chron. 26:16-21)
    3. Exercising the authority of the office (Lev. 13:1-8)
  B. The Responsibilities of Being a Priest
    1. Offering up sacrifices (Lev. 1-7)
    2. Worshiping God (Heb. 9:6)
    3. Interceding on behalf of others (Lev. 16:17)
    4. Church discipline (Neh. 8:13-18)
    5. The ministry of the Word (Neh. 8:1-8)
    6. Seeing to it that the ceremonies were properly observed (Neh. 8:13-18)

IV. The Priesthood of the Believer in the New Testament
  A. Our Privileges as Priests
    1 Immediate access to God's presence (Matt. 27:51; Heb. 10:19-22)
    2. Enjoying the dignity of our office (1 Pet. 2:5, 9)

   3. Exercising our authority over:
     a. Sin (Matt. 16:19; cf. Jn. 20:23; Acts 8:20-23)
     b. Satan (Lk. 10:17; Rom. 16:20; Acts 16:18)
  B. Our Responsibilities as Priests
    1. Offering up sacrifices to God: "Spiritual" not animal sacrifices (1 Pet. 2:5)
     a. The sacrifice of obedience (Psa. 4:5)
     b. The sacrifice of thanksgiving (Psa. 50:14, 23)
     c. The sacrifice of a broken spirit, a broken and contrite heart (Psa. 51:16-17)
     d. The sacrifice of our body and mind (Rom. 12:1-2)
     e. The sacrifice of the people we have won to Christ (Rom. 15:16)
     f. The sacrifice of our gifts to support the Gospel Ministry (Phil. 4:18)
     g. The sacrifice of praise and thanksgiving (Heb. 13:15)
     h. The sacrifice of good works such as sharing with others in need (Heb. 13:16)
    2. Worshiping God (Jn. 4:23, 24; Phil. 3:3)
    3. Interceding for others (1 Tim. 2:1; James 5:16)
    4. Church discipline (Matt. 18:15-17; 1 Cor. 5:4, 7, 11; 2 Thess. 3:14; Rom. 15:14)
    5. The ministry of the Word
     a. To the Unsaved: Matt. 28:19, 20; Acts 8:4
     b. To the Saved: Col. 3:16; Rom. 14:19
    6. Participation in the New Testament ordinances
     a. Baptism: Receiving: Acts 2:41; Giving: Acts 8:12; 36-38
     b. Lord's Supper: Receiving: Acts 2:46; 20:7; Giving: Acts 2:46; 20:7

Note: In the following chart, numbers 4, 5, 6, are controversial and all require great care that a proper balance be maintained. The difference between traditional and biblical practice can be seen by the following charts.

I. Church Discipline

	Scripture	Tradition
Who is involved in discipline?	All believers should be disciplining one another as individuals (Matt. 18:15; Heb. 10:24) and as a congregation (1 Cor. 5:4, 5, 11; 2 Thess. 3:14, 15; Rom. 16:17; 1 Thess. 5:14).	The Clergy is "paid" to do all the disciplining in the church. All private discipline is his job. The denomination (clergy) does all public discipline.
Why is discipline done?	To cause repentance; to stimulate growth; to keep the sin from infecting others; to prevent evil as well as to cure it (1 Cor. 5:5; Heb. 10:24; 1 Cor. 5:6, 7; 2 Cor. 2:6, 7).	To punish those who politically or morally transgress. It is hoped that they go away quietly.
Who has official responsibility to to see discipline done?	The elders of the church (Acts 20:28). They are to equip the saints to discipline each other (Eph. 4:11-12).	Only the clergy can do this. The other elders (if any) do not have any real authority or responsibility to discipline.

II. The Ministry of the Word

	Scripture	Tradition
Who is involved?	All believers are to minister the Word to the lost (evangelism) Matt. 28:19, 20; Acts 8:4 and to the saved (nurture) Col. 3:16.	Only the clergy should minister the Word, particularly from the pulpit. No real concern for "lay evangelism."
The goal of the ministry	To make disciples (Acts 2:37-42). To mature disciples (Heb. 6:1).	To get as many decisions as possible.
The place	Everywhere (Acts 8:4).	At the altar in church.
Who has responsibility?	The elders are to encourage and equip the saints for this (Eph. 4:11-16).	Only the clergy.

III. The Lord's Supper

	Scripture	Tradition
Who can administer communion?	All believers have this privilege. The general principles of doing things properly and in order would apply (Acts 2:46; 20:7; 1 Cor. 10:16).	Only ordained clergy. If there are no clergy present, there can be no Lord's Supper.
Where can communion be observed?	At home (Acts 2:46) or at church (1 Cor. 11:20). Any time Christians meet together for fellowship is appropriate. The sick, imprisoned, etc. can have communion as long as two or three gather in Christ's name (Matt. 18:20).	Only at the congregational service. No "private" communion. Sick, imprisoned, and nursing home patients cannot observe the Lord's Supper without a congregation or clergy.
How often is communion to be observed?	"As often" as the believers wish (1 Cor. 11:26; Acts 2:46).	Only at stated times on the church calendar, usually determined by the clergy according to tradition.

IV. Baptism

	Scripture	Tradition
Who is to baptize new converts?	All believers can baptize. Matt. 28:19, 20 is clear that those who (1) evangelize are (2) to baptize and (3) to teach their converts. Acts 8:4 reveals that all who "preach" can also baptize (cf. vs. 5, 12, 38). There is not one verse in the New Testament that forbids "laymen" from baptizing new converts.	The legitimacy of the rite is tied to it being done by the clergy. All others are forbidden to baptize.
When should new converts be baptized?	At once, upon profession of faith (Acts 2:41; 8:12, 38; 10:47, etc.).	After a long waiting period to make sure they are true believers.
Where are people to be baptized?	Anywhere there is enough water. It can be public or private (Acts 2:41; 8:36-38).	Only in church building or at a special church service. Only public baptism allowed.

C. The Characteristics of Our Priesthood
    1. Ours is to be a "holy" priesthood (1 Pet. 2:5)
        a. Holy in being separated from
            (1) Sinners: 2 Cor. 6:14-18
            (2) Sin: 2 Cor. 7:1
        b. Holy in striving to grow in grace and in the knowledge of Christ (2 Cor. 7:1; 2 Pet. 3:18)
           Note: Heb. 12:14
    2. Ours is to be a "royal" priesthood
        a. "Royal" in our subduing sin and Satan (Rom. 6:12-16; James 4:7; Rom. 16:20)
        b. "Royal" in conquering the world for Christ (Matt. 28:19, 20; Acts 1:8)
D. The Significance of Our Priesthood
    1. The universal priesthood of the believer is foundational to the New Testament concept of worship and practice of the church.
    2. The priesthood of the believer is foundational to a New Testament understanding of the church.

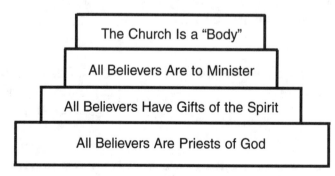

E. Application Drawn From Our Priesthood
1. An understanding of the priesthood of the believer is crucial to our self-image and self-acceptance.
2. It provides a motivation for holy living.
3. It is the basis of our entering into private and public worship.
4. It helps us to be independent of men and dependent upon God.
5. It overthrows the Romish doctrines of prayers to the "saints" (and Mary) and the priest being our mediator before God. It establishes once and for all the believer's right to read and interpret the Bible and to pray directly to God through Christ as the only mediator between God and man.

Chapter Twelve
The Baptism of the Holy Spirit

Introduction

This subject is one of great controversy because of extreme positions and emotions. We need to develop biblical balance on this issue in order to escape all the false teaching of our day.

I. The Person of the Holy Spirit
  A. The Deity of the Spirit: He is God.
    1. He is called "God" (Acts 5:3, 4; 2 Cor. 3:17).
    2. He has the attributes of God (Heb. 9:14).
  B. He is a "Person" and not an impersonal force.
    1. He has the attributes and the names of a person (John 14:16-17; 15:26; 16:7-15).
    2. He can be lied to (Acts 5:3-4).
    3. He has a "will" (1 Cor. 12:7-11).
    4. He can be grieved and quenched (Eph. 4:30; 1 Thess. 5:19).
  C. He is distinct from the Father and the Son. We must reject two growing heresies:
    1. Sabellianism: The "Jesus Only" cult and heresy.
    2. Modalism: One God in three forms or faces.

II. The Work of the Holy Spirit
  A. In the Old Testament and New Testament (before Pentecost)
    1. He indwelt the saints (Gen. 41:38; Num. 27:18; cf. Deut. 34:9; Dan. 4:8, 9, 18; 5:11, 14; 6:3; 1 Pet. 1:11; 2 Cor. 4:13; Lk. 1:15; John 3:3, 5; John 14:17; John 20:22; Rom. 8:9-11; 1 Cor. 2:10-16; 1 Cor. 12:3).
    2. He came "upon" and "filled" the saints.
      a. "Upon": Judges 3:10; 15:14, etc.
      b. "Filled": Deut. 34:9; etc.
    3. "The Filling of the Spirit" meant the desire and power to do God's will.
    4. A special outpouring of the Holy Spirit was prophesied in the Old Testament (Joel 2:28-32): No racial, sexist, age or social discrimination in this outpouring (no race, rank, sex, age).
      a. Isa. 32:15-20: It will bring peace and prosperity to God's people.
      b. Ezk. 39:25-29: It will mean an end of God's judgment and the beginning of World Missions.

  B. In the New Testament
    1. Before Pentecost
      a. He indwelt pre-Pentecost New Testament saints (John 3:3, 5; 14:17, NAS).
      b. He filled pre-Pentecost saints (Luke 2:25-27).
      c. He came "upon" pre-Pentecost saints (Luke 2:25-27).
      d. He was "breathed" on pre-Pentecost saints (John 20:22).

e. John the Baptist prophesied that Jesus would "baptize with the Spirit" (Matt. 3:11).
   (1) The agent is Jesus.
   (2) The means is the Spirit.
   (3) This was a future experience that Jesus was to give to His people.
   (4) It was to be opposite and different from John's baptism.

C. The teaching of Christ

1. He prophesied that a special outpouring of the Spirit would occur when He was glorified at the right hand of the Father (John 7:37-39). At that time He would give them the promise of the Father that was the outpouring of the Spirit in fulfillment of the New Covenant prophecies in the Old Testament. This promised outpouring would mean power (Lk 24:49).

2. When this outpouring took place, the Spirit would begin to function in new ways. He would take the place of Christ as the Paraclete (John 14:16-26; 15:26-27; 16:5-15).

3. While Jesus referred to a future outpouring of the Spirit, He also referred to a regular infusion of the Spirit's power and guidance whenever the believers needed it (Lk. 11:13). Just ask the Father for it.

4. Just before He ascended, Jesus prophesied that the outpouring of the Spirit or "baptism with the Spirit" would mean *power*. The particular focus or purpose of this power is missions and evangelism (Acts 1:5-8). This echoed Christ's teaching in Lk. 24:46-49.

5. The promise of power for proclamation is part of the Old Testament prophecy that all racial, rank, sex and age barriers would be undone by the universal work of the Spirit in the New Kingdom age (Joel 2:28-32). All God's people would be anointed evangel-priests.

6. Jesus never spoke of this outpouring as "indwelling" or "salvation." It had reference to something that would happen to people already indwelt and saved.

D. The Outpouring at Pentecost

1. The disciples waited in prayer for Jesus to "pour out" the Spirit or "baptize" them "with the Holy Spirit" (Acts 1:5-8, 12-14; 2:1-4).

2. The "outpouring" or "baptism with the Spirit" took place as Jesus was glorified.
   a. Jesus glorified by the Father (Acts 2:33).
   b. The Spirit poured out by Jesus (Acts 2:33).
   c. This outpouring was the promise of the Father (Acts 2:33).

3. It was a fulfillment of the Old Testament prophecies (Acts 2:33).

4. It is said that the disciples were "filled" with the Spirit (Acts 2:4). "Baptism with the Spirit" up to this point always refers to the "filling of the Spirit." The "filling of the Spirit" refers to Pentecost, and Pentecost means *power* for evangelism.

5. Thus, "baptism" and "filling" are at this point the same.
   prophecy: "baptized with the Holy Spirit"
   fulfillment: "filled with the Holy Spirit"

6. Is there any indication that this was a once for all event, i.e., the only fulfillment of the Old and New Testament prophecies? Answer: No. The Old Testament and New Testament prophecies clearly marked out the entire age of "the last days" as the age of the Spirit. The Spirit would function the same throughout the time from Christ's glorification to the return of Christ. Who would limit John 14, 15, 16 to Pentecost? Why then do they limit Matt. 3:11 or John 7:37-39 only to Pentecost?

7. Pentecost was not conversion, salvation or indwelling. It was *power* for *proclamation*. "Filling leads to speaking" sequence.
   a. Old Testament background: Num. 11:25

b. New Testament pattern: Acts 2:4; 4:8, 31; Eph. 5:18

8. The proclamation was here in Spirit-given, unknown languages (tongues) (Acts 2:4).

9. Peter did not believe that he and the others were the only ones who could receive the promise of the Spirit. He offers this same experience to all who believe (Acts 2:5, 8, 38, 39). Thus the "promise" of the Holy Spirit (i.e., the "baptism," "filling" or "outpouring" of the Spirit) is something for everyone and cannot be limited to Pentecost. Pentecost was the first baptism with the Spirit but not the final one.

E. After Pentecost in the Acts

Note: That Pentecost was the first baptism of the Spirit and not the final one is irrefutable. Why?

1. Peter himself describes what happened to Cornelius and his family as a fulfillment of Matt. 3:11 (Acts 10:44-46; 11:15-17; 15:7-11). Thus we cannot limit the Old Testament and New Testament prophecies of a future "outpouring" or "baptism" to Pentecost.

2. Since the "filling of the Spirit" is what the "baptism with the Spirit" is all about, it is important to point out that this experience happened again and again throughout Acts to individuals and churches (Acts 1:5, 8; 2:4; 4:8, 31; 9:17; 13:9, 52).

3. Some people were marked out as being especially filled with the Holy Spirit (Acts 6:3, 5; 13:52).

4. The predominant effect of being filled with the Spirit (baptized with the Spirit) is proclamation. Sometimes tongues appeared, other times they did not.

Acts 2:4 — Tongues	8:16-17 — Tongues
Acts 4:8 — No Tongues	10:44-46 — Tongues
Acts 4:31 — No Tongues	19:6 — Tongues

5. It has been suggested by some that we need to view the prophecy of Acts 1:8 as predicting four different Pentecosts.

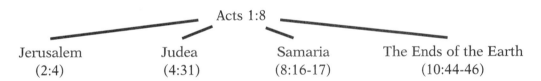

	Acts 1:8		
Jerusalem	Judea	Samaria	The Ends of the Earth
(2:4)	(4:31)	(8:16-17)	(10:44-46)

6. But can we say that there were only four baptisms or outpourings? One for each race or rank of mankind? Answer: No. We have all the other baptisms with the Spirit or fillings with the Spirit throughout Acts (Acts 2:4; 4:8, 31; 19:6). They often involved the same people again.

7. The "baptism with the Spirit" or "filling with the Spirit" is repeatable and normative for this entire age (Acts 13:52).

8. It is something that is experienced after conversion (Acts 2:4) or simultaneously with conversion (Acts 10:44-46). No rule can be made either way. It is to be repeated all the time.

9. Its primary effect or evidence is bold proclamation (with or without tongues): (Acts 2:4; 4:31).

10. No distinction was made between "baptism" and "filling" with the Spirit in the book of Acts.

11. The "filling" or "baptism with the Spirit" is an experience or blessing that all believers are commanded to seek (Eph. 5:18). It is also called "walking in the Spirit" and is recommended in Gal. 5:16-26 for all believers. Those who are "Spirit-filled" are called "spiritual" in Gal. 6:1 as a way to distinguish between believers.

12. The "filling" or "baptism with the Spirit" is needed for:

a. prayer: Jude 20

b. worship: Phil. 3:3

c. mortification of sin: Rom. 8:13

d. daily living: Eph. 5:18; 6:18

13. In distinction from Jesus baptizing us with the Spirit, Paul mentions that the Spirit baptizes us into the Body of Christ at the new birth and, at that time, equips all believers with at least one spiritual gift: (1 Cor. 12:3-13; Rom. 12:3-8).

The Baptism *with* the Spirit (Matt. 3:11)	The Baptism *by* the Spirit (1 Cor. 12:3; 8-13)
Agent: Jesus	Agent: Holy Spirit
Medium: Holy Spirit	Medium: Power of the Spirit
Goal: The desire and power to do God's will: "filling with the Spirit."	Goal: Incorporation into the Body and equipping with gifts.
Result: Bold proclamation, missions, evangelism, practical living.	Result: The unity and functioning of the Body of Christ.

14. In 1 Cor. 12:3-11, Paul is describing what the Spirit does. The Spirit gives gifts (4-11) and unity to the church (v. 13). Paul is not referring to the filling or baptism of the Spirit, which is only true of some Christians some of the time (a repeatable experience). Paul is talking about a non-repeatable experience, once for all time in the life of every Christian, when he or she was engrafted into the Body and gifted for ministry within the Body.

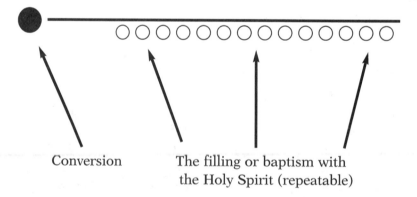

"The Baptism by the Spirit" into the Body of Christ (non-repeatable, final)

Conversion

The filling or baptism with the Holy Spirit (repeatable)

15. 1 Cor. 12:13
   a. Some think it refers to water baptism.
   b. Some think it refers to Matt. 3:11 or Acts 2:4.
   c. But it is describing something spiritual, not carnal such as water (See Hodge's commentary).

16. The baptism by the Spirit in 1 Cor. 12:13 finds its parallel in the "sealing" by the Spirit (Eph. 1:13; 4:30; 2 Cor. 1:21-22) and the "anointing" by the Spirit (1 John 2:20, 27; 2 Cor. 1:21).

1 Cor. 12:13 Baptized by the Spirit		Acts 1:8; Eph. 5:18 Baptized by Jesus with the Spirit
at conversion		daily
engrafted into the body	gifted for ministry	power for witnessing and power for living the Christian life
once for all time		repeatable
all Christians have it		some Christians have it
don't seek it		seek it
position		power
salvation		sanctification

Conclusion

1. Historic Pentecostal theology is in error when it states:
   a. Old Testament saints were not indwelt by the Holy Spirit.
   b. 1 Cor. 12:13 is not an experience of all Christians.
   c. There is a "Second Work of Grace" called "the Baptism of the Holy Spirit" (non-repeatable) and the only sign of it is speaking in tongues.
2. Historic anti-Pentecostal theology is in error when it states:
   a. The 1 Cor. 12:13 experience is all there is to the Christian life. There is nothing more.
   b. The "baptism with the Holy Spirit" was fulfilled in its entirety at Pentecost.
   c. We don't need to seek any deeper experiences with God. We got all we will ever need at regeneration.

Chapter Thirteen
The Filling of the Holy Spirit

Introduction

What is the Normal Christian Life?

1) Some people are afraid of anything having to do with the filling of the Spirit.

    a) They are content to live what they call "the normal Christian life" and leave the "Spirit-filled life" to super Christians who are "fanatic" and "extreme" in their religion.

    b) What they do not realize is that the Bible pictures the Spirit-filled life as the normal Christian life. Thus, many modern Christians are actually living subnormal Christian lives.

THE BIBLE NORMAL LIFE?	vs.	TRADITION NORMAL LIFE?
Love		Hate
Joy		Sadness
Peace		Guilt
Patience		Anger
Gentleness		Rudeness
Kindness		Unkindness
Faith		Unbelief
Humility		Pride
Self-Control		Lust

    c) The real shock is that the devil causes people to attack the normal Spirit-filled life as being:

        1 Fake   4. A Passing Phase

        2. Immaturity   5. For New Christians Only

        3. Ignorance   6. Dangerous

    d) The Issue: Did Jesus commend or condemn the Ephesians for losing their "first love" (Rev. 2:1-7)? Were they only "normal" or were they disobedient?

    e) We must reject the myth that we cannot experience the same Christian life as the early Christians did. Why? Hebrews 13:8 says:

        "Jesus is the same yesterday, today, and forever."

The Basic Truths About the Filling of the Spirit

1) There is much confusion about the filling of the Holy Spirit, but...

2) We are commanded to seek this experience (Eph. 5:18). Therefore, we must understand what the Bible teaches and obey what the Bible commands.

3) The filling of the Spirit is a key to a dynamic Christian life. To the degree we are consciously depending upon and crying out to the Holy Spirit, to that degree the fruit of the Spirit will be developed in our lives (Gal. 5:22-25).

Note: Show me a Christian who is concerned with having the power of the Spirit in his life and, generally, I will show you a Christian who is filled with the joy of the Lord and is bold in his witnessing. He prays for the filling of the Spirit because he is conscious of his need for grace. A person who has no conscious need of the Spirit and thus does not think about or pray for the Spirit should question his salvation.

4) We must be careful to avoid the two extremes on the subject:
   The new birth is everything.
   The new birth is nothing.
5) The new birth is important and essential, but we must go on to deeper experiences with God. We must grow in grace and in the knowledge of the Lord Jesus Christ (2 Pet. 3:18).

The New Birth	Deeper Experiences With God
Lk. 24:49	Eph. 6:11-13
Acts 1:8	Phil. 3:10
Acts 2:4	Phil. 4:7
Acts 4:31	Col. 1:9-10
Acts 13:48-52	Col. 3:12-15
Eph. 1:16-19	2 Pet. 3:18
Eph. 5:18	Rom. 12:1-2

6) The filling of the Spirit is, at times, an unsolicited sovereign act of God. But, since we are commanded to see to it that we are filled with the Spirit and we are given a divine promise that if we ask for the Spirit, we will receive Him; then the filling, fullness, guidance and power of the Spirit is our responsibility.

THE FILLING OF THE SPIRIT	
TEXT	**FOCUS**
Eph. 5:18	Individual, family, career
Rom. 8:13	Putting sin to death
Phil. 3:3	Worship
1 Pet. 1:22	Obedience
Jude 20	Prayer
Luke 11:13	Ask for His fullness

7) Why Do We Need the Filling of the Holy Spirit?
   a) The filling of the Spirit meets our greatest problems in the Christian life. What are the greatest problems in your Christian life?

   Our Greatest Problems in the Christian Life

   i) We often lack the desire to do and to be what God wants (1 Kings 8:57, 58; Psa. 119:36; Phil. 2:13).
   ii) Even when we desire to do and to be what God commands, we often find that we do not have the power to accomplish it (Rom. 7:18, 19, 22-24).
   iii) Sometimes we are keenly aware that we lack both desire and power to do God's will. Now, if a lack of desire and power is our greatest problem in the Christian life, then our greatest need is to obtain biblical desire and power. But to where can we turn to obtain the desire and the power to do and to be what God commands?

   The Biblical Answer Is: 'The Filling of the Spirit'

   Definition: "The Filling of the Spirit" is simply God working in you the desire and the power to do and to be what He commands. It is only by the filling of the Spirit that we can do the work of Christ and develop the character of Christ.

   The filling of the Spirit = Desire   To do the work of Christ.
                        and Power   To develop the character of Christ.

b) The Law of God can only command and condemn. It cannot give you the desire or the power to do the will of God.

   i) Knowing what we ought to do and then doing it are two different things. Mere hearers of the Word vs. doers of the Word (James 1:22-25).

   ii) When the Law of God is preached and taught without an emphasis on the filling of the Spirit as the means whereby we can obtain the desire and the power to obey God, the People of God will suffer greatly.

Preaching the Law of God without the message of the Spirit

↓

reveals our duty to God and man

↓

points out all our failures

↓

brings condemnation to our conscience

↓

produces guilty feelings

↓

causes discouragement (no vision)

↓

all hope for living a Christian life is given up

↓

develops despair

↓

sadness and gloominess characterizes the life

↓

sin-centeredness develops

↓

legalism is the end result

c) The filling of the Spirit is never to be viewed as the goal but as the means unto other goals.

   i) One biblical goal is to minister to the Body of Christ through the gift or gifts which the Holy Spirit has given to us.

The means	The goal
The filling of the Spirit	Ministry through the gifts of the Spirit

  (1) Every Christian has at least one gift (Rom. 12:3-8).

     Prophecy   Service   Teaching   Exhortation   Giving   Ruling   Mercy

  (2) In order to minister to the Body through our gift, we must be filled with the Spirit.

The Bible and the Filling of the Spirit

The Means	The Goal
The Filling of the Spirit	The Ministry Through Gifts
Ex. 28:3 (first mention)	Service
Ex. 31:3-6	Service

Ex. 35:20-22	Giving
Ex. 35:30-35	Service
Num. 11:17	Ruling
Num. 11:25-29	Prophecy (1 Cor. 14:1-5)
Num. 24:2	Prophecy
Deut. 34:9	Ruling
Judges 3:10	Ruling
Judges 6:34	Ruling
Judges 11:29	Ruling
Judges 13:25; 14:6, 19	Ruling (Miracles)
Judges 15:14	?
1 Sam. 10:6-13	Ruling + Sign/prophecy
1 Sam. 11:6	Ruling
1 Sam. 16:13	Ruling
1 Sam. 19:20-24	Prophecy
2 Sam. 23:2	Prophecy
2 Kings 2:9-15	Prophecy
2 Chron. 15:1	Prophecy
2 Chron. 20:14-15	Prophecy
2 Chron. 24:20	Prophecy
Isa. 11:42, 61	Prophecy (Christ)
Ezek. 11:5	Prophecy
Joel 2:28-29	Prophecy
Micah 3:8	Prophecy (Power)
Lk. 1:15, 41, 67	Prophecy
Lk. 2:25-26	Prophecy
Lk. 4:1, 14, 18	Prophecy
Acts 2:4, 16-18	Prophecy (other tongues)
Acts 4:8	Prophecy
Acts 4:31	Prophecy
Acts 6:3	Service + Mercy
Acts 7:55	Prophecy
Acts 11:21-24	Exhortation
Acts 13:9	Prophecy
Acts 13:52	?
Acts 19:6	Prophecy (other tongues)

(3) When people seek to use their gifts without the filling of the Spirit, there arise confusion, division, pride and conflicts within the Body. This is clear in the sad example of the Corinthian Church.

ii) We need the filling of the Spirit for everyday living as well as for ministering to the Body through our gift.

'Be Being Filled With the Spirit' (Lit. Gk.) Eph. 5:18

Eph. 5:19-20	Private fellowship with God
5:19-20	Christian fellowship with others
5:21	Submission to each other

5:22-24	Submissive wives
5:25-33	Loving husbands
6:1-3	Obedient children
6:4	Faithful fathers
6:5-8	Good employees
6:9	Good employers
6:10-18	Whole armor of God for spiritual warfare

iii) We need the filling of the Spirit in order to overcome the lusts of the flesh (Gal. 5:16-26).

(1) True Christian freedom is found in the desire and ability to serve one another in love (5:1-15).

(2) True freedom can be experienced only by the power of the Holy Spirit (16-26).

Notice the number of times the Holy Spirit is referred to in Gal. 5:16-6:1:

    v. 16 "walk in the Spirit"

    v. 17 "The Spirit" vs. "the Flesh"

    v. 18 "Led of the Spirit"

    v. 22 "The fruit of the Spirit"

    v. 25 "Live in the Spirit"

          "Walk in the Spirit"

    6:1 "Ye which are spiritual"

iv) Paul says, "If you walk in the Spirit, you shall not fulfill the lusts of the flesh"; i.e., liberty from the power of sin comes from the power of the Holy Spirit unleashed through the filling of the Spirit (v. 16).

v) The works of the flesh reveal that you are not living the Spirit-filled life (vs. 19-21).

ADULTERY—Moral impurity involving a married person

FORNICATION—Moral impurity involving unmarried people

UNCLEANNESS—Unnatural sex

LASCIVIOUSNESS—Preoccupation with sensuality

IDOLATRY—Having someone or something other than God as the terminal focus of your affections

WITCHCRAFT—Drug abuse and the occult

HATRED—Murderous anger at someone

VARIANCE—Out of step, rebellious, divisive

EMULATIONS—Jealousy

WRATH—Fits of rage and anger

STRIFE—Quick to fight with others

SEDITIONS—Joining/making a group of malcontents

HERESIES—False doctrines that lead to ungodliness

MURDERS—Killing yourself or others

DRUNKENNESS—The abuse of alcoholic beverages

REVELINGS—Attending wild parties

vi) The test and evidence of "walking in the Spirit" or the "Spirit-filled life" is the fruit of the Spirit (Matt. 7:16).

LOVE—Giving to other's needs without having as my motive personal reward

JOY—Exultation of my inner being that results from genuine harmony with God and others

PEACE—Inward harmony arising from a clear conscience

LONGSUFFERING (PATIENCE)—Accepting a difficult situation from others without giving them a deadline to remove it

GENTLENESS—Expressing personal care appropriate to another's emotional need.

GOODNESS (KINDNESS)—Expressing concern for others through deeds of love.

FAITH—Visualizing what God intends to do in a given situation and acting in harmony with it.

MEEKNESS (HUMILITY)—Recognizing that God and others are actually responsible for the achievements in my life.

TEMPERANCE (SELF-CONTROL)—Instant obedience to the Spirit's promptings.

vii) How can we become "filled with the Spirit?" How can we live a "Spirit-filled life?"

Step No. 1. You must approach the filling of the Spirit in the right attitude of the heart.

(1) You must believe that you can be filled. You must be convinced this is possible even in your case (Heb. 11:6).

The Attitude of the Heart

FAITH	vs.	UNBELIEF	If you fail
HOPE	vs.	DESPAIR	here, you will
CONVINCED	vs.	DOUBTS	not be filled (James 1:6-7)

(2) You must desire the filling of the Spirit. You must thirst and hunger for the Spirit's power in your life (Matt. 5:6; Lk. 11:9-13).

(3) You must count the cost. Every sin in every area of your life will be dealt with by the Holy Spirit.

(a) Some want to be filled, but, at the same time, keep certain favorite sins and lusts. You cannot pick and choose with God (Psa. 66:18).

(b) Some want the filling of the Spirit but they refuse to deal with unresolved conflicts with others (Matt. 5:23-24).

(c) The filling vs. an offended relative: Some want the filling of the Spirit, but there is a basic area of disobedience in their life.

(d) The filling vs. not taking headship in the home.

> The Point Is:
> We must be emptied of self and sin
> before we can be filled with the Spirit of God (Psa. 24:3-5).

Step No. 2. Confess your sins and receive forgiveness by faith (Prov. 28:13; 1 John 1:9).

Step No. 3. Submit yourself to God (Romans 12:1-2).

Step No. 4. Ask God for the filling of the Spirit as a definite request (Lk. 11:13; James 4:2).

Step No. 5. Obey God in terms of definite action (Acts 5:32).

Step No. 6. Believe God and His Word by a definite act of trust and thanksgiving (James 1:6-7).

Step No. 7. Abide in the Spirit by avoiding quenching or grieving Him (Psa. 51:11; 1 Thess. 5:19; Eph. 4:30).

Note: We quench the Spirit when we turn a deaf ear to His instructions and refuse to obey His promptings and guidance (1 Thess. 5:19).

We grieve the Spirit when we fail to be loving, kind and forgiving to others and allow bitterness, wrath, anger, clamor, evil speaking and malice to develop in our hearts (Eph. 4:30).

Conclusion

The filling of the Spirit is for all Christians and should not be viewed as a private experience for a few super saints. The Spirit of God is our point-guide in the Christian life.

Chapter Fourteen
Spiritual Gifts

Introduction

One of the most dynamic truths of God's Word is that He has equipped all His people for the work of ministry through the gifts of the Spirit (Eph. 4:12). No one is to view himself or herself as giftless or ministry-less. We are all part of the Body of Christ. Is it any wonder then that God wants us to understand spiritual gifts (1 Cor. 12:1)?

Part I

I. Foundational Facts
  A. Every Christian has a spiritual gift.
    1. "Every," i.e.:
      a. Not just a select few.
      b. All Christians without exception.
      c. We must all seek to discover and use our gifts.
      d. Our basic gift is given at regeneration.
      e. Our basic gift does not await:
        "a second work of grace"
        "the baptism of the Spirit"
        "a higher-life experience"
      f. Since we already have our basic gift, we do not need to pray or fast to obtain it.
      g. Our basic gift is important to our self-image as Christians. We are important to and in the Body.
      h. All Christians have been:
        (1) Indwelt by the Spirit (John 3:6; Rom. 8:9; 1 Cor. 12:3).
        (2) Sealed by the Spirit (Eph. 1:13; 4:30).
        (3) Baptized by the Spirit into the Body of Christ (1 Cor. 12:13).
        (4) Anointed by the Spirit with saving knowledge (2 Cor. 1:21, 22; 1 John 2:27).
        (5) Gifted by the Spirit to minister to the Body (Rom. 12:3-8; 1 Cor. 12:1-30; 1 Pet. 4:10).
    2. "Christian," i.e., someone regenerated by the Spirit. Every Christian has as a present possession one basic spiritual gift. There is no such thing as a "giftless" Christian. This gift was received at the moment of regeneration.
    3. "Has," i.e., right now as a present possession.
    4. "A," i.e., at least one basic gift (Rom. 12:6-8; 1 Pet. 4:10).
    5. "Spiritual," i.e., having to do with the work of the Spirit of God. The Spirit is sovereign in the giving of your basic gift and in determining manifestation gifts (1 Cor. 12:4-11).
    6. "Gift," i.e., not a reward for anything in us or done by us. The "gifts" cannot be earned by praying, fasting, etc. The Greek word for "gift" comes from the word "grace." The gifts were earned by Christ through His obedience in life and in death (Acts 2:33; Eph. 4:7-13; Phil. 2:5-11).
  B. Joy comes into our lives as we understand and use our gifts.
  C. Personal fulfillment is experienced as we find our place in the ministry of the Church.
    1. We discover our "niche" in the Church and in the world, i.e., our function in life.

2. We can develop a meaningful ministry.

3. We begin to play a significant role in the life of the Body of Christ.

D. Every gift has the good of the Church as its goal (Eph. 4:8, 12, 13; 1 Cor. 12:7; 14:12).

E. We should not be ignorant of gifts (1 Cor. 12:1).

II. The Kinds of Gifts

A. There are three different kinds of gifts.

1 COR. 12:4-6

"GIFTS" v. 4	"ADMINISTRATIONS" v. 5	"OPERATIONS" v. 6
1. MOTIVATIONS	2. MINISTRIES	3. MANIFESTATIONS
Basic drive, ability and motivation to minister to others in a certain way	Opportunities of Christian service that allow us to exercise our basic motivational gift	The actual results in the lives of those to whom we minister as determined by the sovereign "Spirit of God"

B. Most of the confusion over spiritual gifts is a direct result of not realizing that there are different kinds of gifts divided according to their place and their function in the life of an individual believer and the church to which he belongs. As the Head of the Church, Christ endows each church with certain gifts which focus the ministry of that congregation. No two congregations are the same. One church may be gifted in a ministry of mercy and have great social works. Another church may be gifted in a teaching ministry and have a great educational ministry. The key is not to judge other churches by what your church is doing. God equips each church to do a special calling. The gifts that are given within the church are for that grand end. Every church should understand its own focus of ministry.

C. Three kinds of gifts can be understood in terms of motive, means and end.

1. MOTIVE	2. MEANS	3. RESULTS
MOTIVATIONAL GIFTS	MINISTRY GIFTS	MANIFESTATION GIFTS
given at new birth	offices, occasions and opportunities in which or by which you can minister to the Body through the developing of your basic motivational gift	things which the Holy Spirit does in the lives of those to whom you minister
sovereign choice of God		
basic place and ministry in Body	you can seek these gifts	you have no control over this
accountability at judgment seat of Christ (Matt. 25:19, 2 Cor. 5:10)		the sovereignty of the Spirit determines these things
main focus of life		

D. Three different lists of gifts correspond to the three kinds of gifts.

MOTIVATIONAL GIFTS	MINISTRY GIFTS	MANIFESTATION GIFTS
Rom. 12:3-8	Eph. 4:1, 11	1 Cor. 12:28-31; 1 Cor. 12:7-11
1. Prophecy 2. Service 3. Teaching 4. Exhortation 5. Giving 6. Ruling 7. Mercy	1. Apostle 2. Prophet 3. Evangelist 4. Pastor 5. Teacher 6. Miracles 7. Healings 8. Helps 9. Government 10. Tongues	1. Word of wisdom 2. Word of knowledge 3. Faith 4. Healing 5. Miracles 6. Prophecy 7. Discerning of spirits 8. Tongues 9. Interpretation of tongues

E. That Paul speaks of three different kinds of gifts in 1 Cor. 12:4-11 is something that the classic commentaries stated many years ago before there was any controversy over the issue of spiritual gifts.

   1. *Lange's Commentary on The Holy Scriptures,* vol. 10, pp. 249, 263
      "This expression is repeated three times in connection with three different classes of objects —rendered gifts, ministries, operation."

      "gifts are qualifications or capabilities peculiar to Christianity."

      "ministries are the manifold offices or functions in the church ... in which those gifts were employed."

      "Operations are the various effects resulting from the exercise of the 'gifts' in their particular 'ministries.' "

      "By means of gifts, offices and powers, the Spirit commits Himself to the church for the common endowment of the saints, for the edifying of the body of Christ, and these things stand related to each other and help toward the attainment of a common end."

   2. F. Godet, *Commentary on the First Epistle to the Corinthians,* vol. II, p. 189f
      "the difference between the divine gifts, ministries and operations. More than this: in each of these principal classes there is seen to be a subordinate variety of kinds of species."

      "gifts are the creative power which God communicates to believers."

      "ministries ... denotes, not like the preceding, inward attitudes, but external offices."

      "Manifold operations due to the exercise of both of those gifts and those offices ... the real effects Divinely produced either in the world of body or of mind as often as the gift or the office comes into action."

3. H. Alford, *The Greek New Testament*, vol. II, p. 577
   "gifts (eminent endowments of individuals, in and by which the Spirit dwelling in them manifests Himself."

   "ministries (appointed services in the church, in which as their channels of manifestation the 'gifts' would work)."

   "operations (effects of divine energy): not to be limited to miraculous effects but understood again commensurately with the gifts of whose working they are the results."

4. Ellicott, *Ellicott's Commentary*, vol. VIX, p. 335
   "Although conversion is identical in every case, yet afterwards there are spiritual gifts which vary according to individual capacity and character, but they all come from the one Spirit. Those spiritual gifts are employed ... there are varieties of operations resulting from those gifts and ministrations."

5. M. Henry, *Matthew Henry's Commentary*, vol. VI, p. 568
   "These spiritual gifts, though proceeding from the same Spirit, are yet various. They have one author and originator, but are themselves of various kinds... There are various gifts, administrations and operations."

6. M. Vincent, *Word Studies in the New Testament*, vol. III, p. 256
   "operations ... outward manifestations and results of spiritual gifts."

7. A. Bittlinger, *Gifts and Graces*, pp. 20-21
   "there are varieties of gifts, varieties of service, varieties of working."
   "The term *diaponial*, i.e., ministries or services, points to the way in which the gifts become real in practice."
   "The gifts bring about definite effects. They are "energemata" i.e., outworkings."

Summary

Individuals and churches fall into the sin of covetousness when they set their eyes on the gifts and ministries of others. Just as each believer is called to a certain task in life, each congregation is called to a certain ministry. We must not blindly try to make our church a copy of some other church that we respect. Remember, copies are never as good as the original. Instead, each individual and each church must discover its own ministry to a sick and dying world. The way to begin is to find what gifts Christ has placed in you and in your church. These gifts will determine what ministry God has called you to do.

Part II

Motivational Gifts

I. The Motivational Gifts
   A. There are seven basic motivational gifts. They are listed in Romans 12:6-8.
      1. Prophecy
      2. Ministry
      3. Teaching

    4. Exhortation

    5. Giving

    6. Ruling

    7. Mercy

B. It must be pointed out that these seven activities are "graces" as well as "gifts." As a "grace" or "virtue," every Christian is expected to perform all of these activities to some degree. Having one of these as a motivational gift does not negate your responsibility to do the other six as virtues.

    1. All should prophesy—1 Cor. 14:1, 5, 31

    2. All should serve—Gal. 5:13

    3. All should teach—Col. 3:16

    4. All should exhort—Heb. 3:13; 10:25

    5. All should rule—Prov. 16:32; 1 Tim. 3:4

    6. All should give—Rom. 12:13

    7. All should show mercy—Col. 3:12, 13

C. At regeneration, God gives one of these seven basic gifts to all believers. This is your basic and permanent gift. You have no control over this. You cannot get rid of your gift or exchange it for another one (Rom. 12:3-8; 1 Pet. 4:10).

D. We experience minimum weariness and maximum effectiveness as we minister to others when we are ministering to them through or by our basic gift.

E. Frustration, tiredness and ineffectiveness result from trying to minister to others through a gift which is not your basic gift.

F. One important reason for identifying and using your basic gift is to free others to exercise their gift.

G. There are several stages to discovering what your basic gift is:

    No. 1. Keep the three kinds of gifts distinct. Do not confuse them.

    No. 2. Do not confuse general Christian maturity in all seven activities with the one special activity which acts as the underlying motivation in your life.

    No. 3. Listen carefully as we define all seven activities. Do not ask, "Do I do this activity?" Rather ask, "Is this my DESIRE, my MOTIVATION and my JOY? Do I experience minimum weariness when doing this? Could I be content knowing that I am ministering to others in this way? Am I 'uptight' when I see this activity missing or misused?"

    No. 4. When in doubt, ask those to whom you minister what they think your gift is (Prov. 11:14).

    No. 5. If you cannot identify your gift, one of the following things may be the cause.

        a. You still do not understand the biblical teaching on gifts.

        b. There may be a root problem of unconfessed sin in your life.

        c. You are not involved in ministering to others (Pew-warmers). You need to try out the seven activities to see where your gift is. No involvement means no experience. No experience means nothing to draw on to determine your gift.

I. The Motivational Gift of Prophecy

I. A basic meaning

    A. There are three essential ideas in the root meaning of prophecy:

        1. A proclaimer of God's Truth to believers

        2. Concerning the past, the present and the future

        3. To reveal sin, to convict of sin and to lead to repentance

    B. That this is the biblical meaning is seen from the following facts:

        1. The basic thrust and emphasis of a Prophet's ministry (1 Sam. 3:10-14; Lk. 3:3, 7-14)

        2. The usage of the word "prophecy" in such places as 1 Cor. 14:24, 25

C. Given these facts, we come to this definition of prophecy:

An inner desire and motivation to minister to God's people by revealing their sins to lead them to repentance. God's truth is proclaimed with an eye to correcting the sins of the people of God.

II. Three elements in prophesying

1 The ability to see sin in the lives of others: A prophet's glasses	2. The desire and motivation to help others to deal with the sin in their lives. A prophet's heart	3. The ability to confront people directly but lovingly about their sin: a prophet's strength and boldness

III. Characteristics
  A. They have an inner desire and need to denounce sin (Jer. 20:7-9).
  B. They have a supernatural ability to discern the evil in the character, motive or spirit of others (Acts 8:18-23).
  C. They have an unusual ability and desire to identify, expose, root out, hate and denounce evil (Isa. 1:2-20).
  D. They experience brokenness over their own sin. They deal with their own heart as ruthlessly as they deal with others (Psa. 139:19-24).
  E. They have to use Scripture to back up their denunciation of sin (Isa. 8:20; 2 Cor. 13:3, 4).
  F. They will not accept any empty profession of repentance and faith. They must see clear evidences of true repentance before they are willing to accept people (Lk. 3:7-14).
  G. They are very persuasive, frank and direct in their speech when dealing with sin (2 Sam. 12:1-7).
  H. They are deeply stirred when God's reputation or work is blasphemed because of sin in the people of God (2 Sam. 12:14).
  I. They feel, sympathize and weep with those who are burdened with sin because they know the wickedness of their heart (Lam. 3:48, 49).
  J. They desire that others will point out the evil in their character, motives or spirit (Psa. 141:5).
  K. They can fall into pride over their ability to persuade people to repent of their sins.
  L. They deal with society in terms of groups instead of seeing people as individuals with personal needs (Tit. 1:12-14).
  M. They face the constant temptation to depend on their own persuasiveness instead of relying on the Holy Spirit (1 Cor. 2:1-5).
  N. They can experience deep depression when their message is rejected (example: Jeremiah).
IV. Dangers
  A. Their direct and frank speech is seen as harshness.
  B. Their emphasis on sin seems negative, and it is assumed that it will produce morbid introspection.
  C. The demand for evidences seems to lack compassion or understanding.
  D. Their cut and dry ethics—"right" or "wrong"—seem to neglect gray areas of personal liberty.
  E. Their drive to deal ruthlessly with sin seems to be sin-centered instead of Christ-centered.
  F. They seem overbearing, super-aggressive, dogmatic, narrow-minded and insensitive to the feelings and needs of others.

II. The Gift of Service

  I. A basic definition
  A. An inner drive and desire to demonstrate true Christian love by meeting the practical needs of others

B. Biblical illustrations of the meaning of service
1. Lk. 7:36-46
2. Lk. 10:38-42

II. Three essential ideas in the root meaning of service

1. The ability to see the practical needs of others: a servant's glasses	2. The desire and motivation to meet the practical needs of others: a servant's heart	3. The ability to serve others in practical ways—tirelessly, joyfully and selflessly: a servant's power and strength

III. Characteristics
1. The ability to recall specific likes and dislikes of people.
2. Alertness to detect and meet practical needs. Especially enjoys manual projects.
3. Motivation to meet needs at once even if it means acting on your own.
4. Amazing physical stamina to fulfill needs without weariness.
5. Willingness to use your own money to get needs met and to avoid delays.
6. Ability to sense true vs. false appreciation for work done.
7. Desire to get the job done with extra uncalled-for service.
8. Getting involved in too many things. Cannot say "no" to people's needs.
9. Joy over short-term goals/jobs. Frustration over long-term goals/jobs.
10. Frustration when time limits are given. "Rush jobs" are not enjoyed.

IV. Dangers
1. May appear pushy by being so quick to meet needs.
2. Avoiding red tape and doing it yourself may get the job done quickly but it excludes others from the opportunity of serving.
3. Disregard for personal needs may lead to a failure to meet the needs of your family.
4. Eagerness in serving may prompt others to be suspicious that you are seeking self-glory and self-advancement.
5. Bitterness toward those who do not see what are to you obvious needs is sometimes thought to be pride. We must let our love cover those special "sins" and "infirmities" of servants.
6. Insistence on serving may appear as being too proud to be served.
7. You get hurt easily when you sense that people are not really appreciating your work.
8. Quickness in meeting needs may interfere with spiritual lessons God is trying to teach those in need.
9. Others may think that you are not spiritual because your "love" and "joy" is found in serving instead of doctrine, etc.
10. Your ability to "work circles around others" or to push others to keep on working when you are not tired but they are, will be interpreted as insensitivity and impatience with others.
11. You may be elected to a church office that creates frustration because you must go through all sorts of red tape to get anything done.
12. You may fail to follow an employer's directions by being sidetracked to help others.

V. The glory of being a servant
A. It manifests Christ's likeness in a practical way (Matt. 20:20-28).
B. It is a demonstration of love of which the world takes notice (John 13:35).

C. It requires self-sacrifice (Phil. 2:5-8).

D. True service for Christ shall be rewarded (Matt. 23:11-12; 1 Cor. 15:58).

E. It is through this gift that the Body is called upon to meet the material needs of believers and unbelievers (James 2:15, 16).

VI. The temptations

A. Pride over good works (Romans 3:12)

B. Being pushy or premature in meeting the needs of others before they realize their needs

C. Bitterness when not appreciated or recognized for work done (Lk. 10:40)

D. Tendency to overlook spiritual or doctrinal things by over-emphasizing practical needs (Lk. 10:42)

E. Difficulty in maintaining consistent private devotions (Lk. 10:42)

F. "Workaholic" (Lk. 10:41)

G. Doing too much and worrying as a result (Lk. 10:40- 42)

III. The Gift of Teaching

I. A basic definition

The motivation and inward drive or desire to clarify God's Word in order to present God's truth to others and to search out and validate truth which has been presented.

II. Three essential elements in teaching

1. The ability to discern error quickly and to grasp the Truth firmly: a teacher's glasses	2. The desire and motivation to discover the Truth and share it with God's people: a teacher's heart.	3. The ability to research and study until the Truth is discovered: a teacher's perseverance and labor.

III. Requirements for teaching

1. Diligent in the details of his study (example: doing exhaustive word studies)

2. Fervent and joyful in spirit while engaged in research

3. Does his work unto the Lord

IV. Dangers

1. Pride over his knowledge

2. Boasting before others

3. Neglect love and sensitivity to the feelings of others

4. Concentrate on accuracy of details instead of presenting the basic life principles which arise out of God's truth

5. Temptation to major in being "mighty in intellect" and to minor in being "mighty in spirit"

6. More concerned about research than people's response

7. Trying to correct everyone's theology

V. Characteristics

1. The conviction that the gift of teaching is foundational to all the other gifts.

2. An emphasis on obtaining an exact and accurate definition of biblical words.

3. You will test the knowledge of those who are to be your teachers. If you know more than they do, you cannot respect them.

4. A delight in doing research in order to discover or demonstrate Bible truths, particularly when it is for others.

5. New information is validated by seeing if it fits into established truths.
6. Truth is presented in a systematic and logical sequence.
7. Avoidance of using illustrations from non-biblical sources to define biblical words. Scripture should define Scripture.
8. Resistance to the use of Scripture out of context.
9. Greater joy in research than in presentation.
10. A love of books and a desire to put your research into writing.

VI. Misunderstandings
   1. Emphasis on accuracy of scriptural interpretations and definitions may appear to neglect the practical side of truth.
   2. Emphasis on commentaries and the research of others may appear to some to neglect the Holy Spirit.
   3. Testing people's knowledge may appear to be pride.
   4. The concern to impart to others:
       How they discovered truth
       All the verses which teach the truth
       All the details of research
       All the authorities on their side, etc.
       May appear to be unnecessary to those listening
   5. The inner need to be utterly factual and truthful in research may appear to lack warmth and feelings when the research is presented.

VII. The Gift of Exhortation

I. A basic definition
   A. The inner drive or desire to stimulate spiritual growth in others by motivating them to grow in faith, hope and love. The ultimate goal is to see people develop into mature Christians who respond to trials with Christ-like action and attitudes.
   B. Biblical examples: Acts 11:23, 14:22; Rom. 12:1-2; Eph. 4:1-3

II. The three elements in exhorting

1. The ability to see how sin can be overcome in people's lives: an exhorter's glasses	2. The desire to help people overcome evil by taking steps of action: an exhorter's heart	3. The ability to give positive steps of action to correct or avoid evil: an exhorter's strength and boldness

III. Word study
   1. Root meaning of Greek word:
      "To call to the side to urge one to pursue a course of conduct."
   2. Exhorting involves the use of personal counseling to help others.
   3. An exhorter must:
      a. Rejoice in hope for others (Rom. 12:12)
      b. Be patient (Rom. 12:12)
      c. Be persistent in prayer (Rom. 12:12)
      d. Have love without hypocrisy (Rom 12:9)
      e. Have faith in the steps of action he gives (James 1:6, 7)

IV. Dangers
   1. Pride and boasting about results in changing people's lives
   2. Discouragement when slow progress or failure is seen in people whom you are counseling
   3. Sometimes motivated by self and ego
   4. Wasting time with people who really do not want help (Matt. 7:6; Rev. 22:11)

V. Characteristics
   1. The desire and ability to visualize what things are lacking in a person's life. They "see" character defects just like a servant "sees" practical needs.
   2. The desire and ability to give precise steps of action to overcome a defect or problem in others.
   3. A tendency to avoid systems of information or theology or kinds of preaching which lack practical application.
   4. The ability to see how trials or problems can be used to build character if they are handled and resolved using biblical steps or principles.
   5. A dependence on "body language," i.e., the visible response of people.
   6. A tendency to go from human experience to the Bible. They "see" an insight on how to or how not to live. This is seen in people's lives; then they turn to the Bible for validation of their insights.
   7. Joy over those who eagerly follow steps of action.
   8. Grief when sin is preached against but no steps of action are given on how to overcome sin.
   9. Delight in personal conferences when new insights are gained.
   10. A drive or desire to find steps of action which are universally valid for all who want to overcome any particular sin or problem.

VI. Misunderstandings
   1. Giving precise steps of action may appear to oversimplify problems.
   2. Some may suspect that there is too much confidence in these simple rules or steps of actions.
   3. A lack of zeal for verbal witnessing may appear to reveal a lack of concern for the lost and their evangelism.
   4. The abstracting of "principles" out of Scripture may appear to be taking Scripture out of context.
   5. The urgency and firmness which accompany steps of action may appear to ignore the feelings of others.
   6. The steps of action may appear too hard or the exhortation too harsh.

VIII. How to give an exhortation
   A. The qualifications to administer exhortations (Gal. 6:1)
      1. You must be "spiritual" i.e.
         a. "Living by the Spirit" daily (Gal. 5:16)
         b. Bearing "the fruit of the Spirit" (Gal. 5:22-25)
         c. "Walking in the Spirit" (Gal. 5:25)
      2. This means that you must be Spirit-filled and Spirit-led (Eph. 5:18; Rom. 8:14).
   B. The manner in which you give an exhortation (Gal. 6:1).
      1. You must be gentle, i.e., patient in giving loving rebukes.
      2. You must be cautious and not proud because you yourself can be tempted to fall into the same sin. Pride comes before a fall into sin. Do not have a smug spirit of self-superiority or self-sufficiency.
   C. Give positive steps to correct the problem. Do not just rebuke people; instruct them how to overcome evil.

IX. How to receive an exhortation
   A. Because exhortation is a ministry sent from God, desire that someone would love you enough to exhort you when you need it (Psa. 141:5).
   B. Because it is a blessing like oil upon the head, let the exhorter exhort you (Psa. 141:5).
   C. Respond in love to exhortations (Prov. 9:8).
   D. Receive them (Prov. 10:8).
   E. Seek to gain a clearer knowledge of your sins and weaknesses (Prov. 19:25).
   F. Look upon an exhortation as something beautiful and valuable (Prov. 25:12).
   G. Realize that when an exhorter rebukes you, he reveals that he is a true friend who is dealing with you faithfully (Prov. 27:6).
   H. Immediately follow his steps of action. Do not rationalize or cover up your sins (Prov. 28:13).

V. The Gift of Giving

 I. A basic definition
An inward drive or motivation to see the work of God supplied with the necessary funds to minister to the Church and to the world. A desire to see the financial needs of people supplied even if it means a giving of one's own personal assets.

II. The three elements in giving

1.The ability to see the financial needs of others, a sensitivity to financial problems: a giver's glasses	2.The ability to make quick decisions to give away money unselfishly, to assess true needs from wants, not tied to the things of this world: a giver's heart	3.The ability to make and to to retain money, being thrifty and amassing a large amount of assets: a giver's financial record

III. Evidences of this gift
   1. A giver must have shown the ability to give freely and lovingly to the material needs of people and organizations.
   2. There must be a sensitivity to the problems of strangers, orphans, widows, i.e., the poor and the oppressed.
   3. A giver cannot be materialistic. He knows that God owns everything. Thus Christ's Kingdom is more important than personal pleasure.

IV. Temptations
   1. Pride over his ability to make and manage large sums of money
   2. Pride over his giving to the Lord's work
   3. Equating financial success with spirituality; judging himself and others' spirituality on the basis of financial prosperity
   4. A danger of giving to immediate needs without a regard for long-term needs

 V. Characteristics
   1. An uncanny ability always to find the lowest prices when buying and the highest prices when selling.

2. A "Midas Touch" when it comes to making good returns from investments. A giver knows where to put his money to make the greatest profit. Example: A giver would not have a large amount of money in a savings account.
3. A giver can "sense" through the Holy Spirit when someone or an organization needs money. He can be thousands of miles away and yet know to send money even though no request was made.
4. He can "see" through religious rackets. He is cautious when pressure is put upon him to give.
5. He desires to give in a quiet way without fanfare.
6. He gives to Christian works which are effective in producing results.
7. He loves to see his giving motivate others to give.
8. Joy comes when his gift goes to someone who had prayed specifically for a certain amount and waited on God in faith instead of asking others for it.
9. He looks to his spouse to confirm the amount of the gift.
10. He must feel that he is a part of whatever ministry he supports.
11. He detects overlooked needs.
12. He does not want to give all the money needed. Neither does he want to give all his money to one organization.

VI. Misunderstandings
1. Their "buy low/sell high" practice looks like they are "cheap."
2. Their concern to gain high profits and to retain large amounts of money looks like materialism.
3. Their resistance to pressure seems to indicate a hard heart.
4. Their thriftiness is interpreted as stinginess.
5. Their concern to give to ministries which produce highly visible results looks like a carnal attitude instead of being spiritually minded.
6. Their refusal to give everyone what they claim is a "need" is viewed as selfishness and a lack of generosity.
7. The fact that they have a nice home, a new car and money in the bank seems unspiritual to those less fortunate or less industrious. Some think that all Christians should take "a vow of poverty" in which they give everything away.

VI. The Gift of Ruling

I. A basic definition

A. Instead of calling it "ruling," it would be better to call it the gift of "organization" or "administration."
B. It is that inner drive, desire or motivation to organize, to administer, to arrange and to rule over the activities and things in one's own life and in the lives of others, particularly of those who are under your authority or those for whom you feel responsible.

II. There are three elements in ruling

1. The ability to see where organization is needed: an organizer's glasses (example Neh. 1:3)	2. The desire to straighten up and organize what is disorderly: an organizer's heart (example Neh. 1:4; 2:5)	3. The ability to organize things and then to keep them in order: an organizer's strength (example Neh. 7:1-3)

III. Characteristics
    A. They can lead, organize, set up and preside over a group (Neh. 2:17).
    B. When they find themselves in an unorganized group, they will step in and take over. They cannot stand confusion and disorderly groups (Neh. 2:17).
    C. They can visualize the goals of a group, how to achieve them and the asset needs (Neh. 2:11-17).
    D. Their enthusiastic zeal for their vision inspires others (Neh. 3).
    E. They see the overall picture and the long-range goals by means of charts and graphs. They mentally love to visualize the goals, structure and results of their group.
    F. They "know" what can be delegated and what cannot. Then they delegate as much as possible. They would rather supervise than do it themselves (Neh. 3).
    G. They like to be under authority and want others to be under authority and disciplined (Neh. 2:7).
    H. They do not like doing routine jobs which should be delegated to others.
    I. They experience real joy when people and things are efficiently organized to realize a common goal (Neh. 8:10).
    J. They realize that criticism always comes to those in authority and thus expect people to be critical and unkind at times.
    K. They want things and people organized to achieve goals in the shortest time with the least expense or energy.
    L. They will set new goals after completing previous ones. "Forward" is their motto, not "rest" (Neh. 13:30-31).
    M. They are impatient with red tape which hinders success (Neh. 2:7-9).

IV. Misunderstandings
    A. Their aggressive leadership and the way they order people and things around may be called pride, self-appointed, "popery," bossy, etc. (Neh. 2:17-19).
    B. When they step in and organize an unstructured group, people respond, "Well, who do they think they are?"
    C. Their charts of long-range goals and of the structure of a group, seem to be "pushy" and "insensitive."
    D. Their delegating and supervising work looks like they are "lazy."
    E. When people are viewed as "sources," "useful" or "in the way," it seems to mark an unloving, insensitive heart.
    F. They are accused of being "loud-mouthed show-offs" because they dominate the group discussions, lead them to achieve goals and reject tangents.

V. Dangers
    A. Pride over ability to lead, rule, organize, delegate and supervise others (Dan. 4:30)
    B. Projects becoming more important than people
    C. Neglect the needs of their own family
    D. Impatience with red tape, officials, rebellious people and "stupid" people who cannot follow simple directions and, as a result, mess up things
    E. "Using" people to accomplish goals
    F. Using people who have valuable skills but major character defects as well
    G. Pushing plans down people's throats
    H. Gets on too many committees at one time

I. Not flexible or spontaneous.

J. Cannot stand meetings which do not begin or end at the appointed time.

K. Think ill of people if they are too tired to do their work.

VII. The Gift of Mercy

I. A basic definition

   A. That inner drive or motivation to empathize with the emotional states of others, particularly when others are in pain or misery.

   B. Empathizing is not the same thing as sympathizing. When we empathize with people, we actually feel with them whatever pain or misery that they are experiencing at that time. We feel what that they feel personally and subjectively. In contrast, we sympathize with people when we feel sorry for their misery. Our sorrow is objective and while we have pity or compassion for them, we do not feel with them.

II. Three elements in showing mercy

1. The ability to sense when someone is in pain or misery. You feel drawn to such people: Merciful glasses.	2. The desire to empathize with those who are hurting. You feel fulfilled after you empathize with someone: A merciful heart.	3. The ability to empathize with others even for long periods of time: Merciful strength.

III. Characteristics

   A. You want to relieve mental distress. Physical distress does not prompt you to action.

   B. You are concerned to bring reconciliation among everyone. You cannot take unresolved conflicts in your own life or in others.

   C. You are careful not to hurt people's feelings. Somehow you feel that to hurt someone's feelings is not right.

   D. You can spot insincerity quickly.

   E. You can sense the true emotional state of people.

   F. You enjoy other compassionate people.

   G. You close your spirit to all insensitive or insincere people.

   H. You are not usually a "hard" or "firm" person unless you see how it will help someone.

   I. You can sense the atmosphere of a group.

IV. Misunderstandings

   A. They are "too emotional" and are not "logical" or "rational." Therefore they should never be allowed leadership.

   B. They appear proud when they say they can sense the true motives of others.

   C. Their indecisiveness looks like immaturity or stupidness.

   D. Their desire and ability to "tune" into the emotional states of others instead of being involved in theology or good works looks like they are not spiritual.

  E. Their dealing with a person's mental distress instead of working on the physical needs of people makes it appear that they are lazy.

V. Dangers

   A. Pride over your ability to empathize

B. Indecisiveness because you depend too much on feelings in making decisions

C. Your feelings lead you more than your reason

D. Touchy, super-sensitive and easily hurt

E. Easily offended without a real cause

F. Taking up offense easily and quickly

G. Could mislead opposite sex with compassion

H. Resentful of those who only sympathize

Summary

Your job is to discern what basic gift God has given to you and then to give yourself to that ministry. You must not be ignorant of spiritual gifts.

PART III

Ministry Gifts

We now come to the ministry gifts which refer to those offices and opportunities that God gives us to minister to each other and to a world lost in sin. Perhaps the best place to begin is with Eph. 4:11 where the Apostle Paul sets forth some of the ministry "gifts" which the risen Christ gave to His Church. Other minstry gifts such as "healing" will be dealt with in separate studies.

I. APOSTLESHIP (Eph. 4:11)

A. Old Testament Background: In its verb and noun forms, the word "apostle" is used in the Septuagint about 800 times. When used of an office, it referred to people sent forth with delegated authority to teach or govern the people (example: 2 Chron 17:7-9).

B. Intertestamental Judaism: Between Malachi and Matthew, "apostles" were Jewish missionaries who traveled in the gentile world to teach Jews and convert gentiles.

C. Basic Meaning of "Apostle": Someone "sent out" to be a traveling teacher/missionary.

D. Four Groups of "Apostles" in the New Testament

1. "The Twelve Apostles" (Matt. 10:2-4)

a. A unique group always separated from other disciples, including Paul (1 Cor. 15:5).

b. Handpicked by Christ at the beginning of his ministry (Matt. 10:1).

c. When Judas fell out of office, it would seem that Matthias took his place (Acts 1:26).

d. After Matthias, no more individuals were chosen to be part of "The Twelve" (Acts 12:2). There were Old Testament directions for filling Judas' empty office.

e. The requirements set forth in Acts 1:21-22 forbid anyone today from claiming the office.

f. "The Twelve" refer to a unique group of men (Lk. 22:29, 30; Rev. 21:14).

g. They formed part of the historic foundation of the Church (Eph. 2:20).

h. They were given special power to do miracles (Heb. 2:3-4).

i. When "The Twelve" died, their office died with them.

2. Other "apostles" at Jerusalem

a. James, son of Alphaeus, was one of "The Twelve." He was killed by Herod (Acts 12:2). Since this is true, we must ask who is the Apostle James mentioned after Acts 12. He cannot be the son of Alphaeus. The James who was an "apostle" in the Jerusalem Church (Acts 12:17; 15:13; 21:18; Gal. 2:9) and who wrote the New Testament book called "James" was a son of Joseph and Mary (Matt. 13:55), who became a believer after Christ arose (1 Cor. 15:7). He along with "The Twelve" pastored the Jerusalem Church.

b. Judas and Silas were also called "apostles," i.e., "sent ones" (Acts 15:22-23, 40; 1 Thess. 2:6).

3. The "apostles" at Antioch
   a. Paul was an apostle, i.e., missionary (Gal. 1:1), but he is not one of "The Twelve." He never claimed to be part of "The Twelve" and clearly spoke of them as a separate group (1 Cor. 15:5).
   b. Barnabas and all those "sent forth" to minister were called "apostles" (Acts 13:1-3; 14:14).
4. There were other "apostles" who ministered in a local church context.
   a. Andronicus and Junia (Rom. 16:7).
   b. Titus and Timothy (2 Cor. 8:23; 1 Thess. 1:1; 2:6).
   c. An "apostle" was an office in the Corinthian church (1 Cor. 12:28-29).
E. "Apostles" in the early church were church planters/missionaries (Didache 11:3-6).
F. Since no provision was made for the continuance of this office in Scripture, it passed away in a few generations.
G. We can recognize gifted church planters, missionaries and apologists as "apostles" today (Schaff, vol. 1, pp. 488-489). Example: Francis Schaeffer's work among 20th century pagans.

II. PROPHET (Eph. 4:11)

Much confusion has arisen because of the failure to distinguish three different issues.
1. The Office/Position of Prophet
2. The Motivational Gift of Prophecy
3. The Ministry Gift of Prophecy

A. The Office/Position of Prophet
   1. It was an office/position like apostleship (1 Cor. 12:28).
   2. It formed part of the historic foundation of the Church (Eph. 2:20).
   3. It was second in influence to the apostles (Eph. 2:20; 4:11; 1 Cor. 12:28).
   4. Prophets are not to be confused with teachers. Prophets and teachers were viewed as two different positions (Eph. 4:11; Acts 13:1).
   5. Some of these prophets were named in the New Testament.
      Agabus (Acts 11:27-30; 21:10)
      Barnabas, Simeon and Lucius (Acts 13:1)
      Judas and Silas (Acts 15:32)
   6. There were women prophets in the New Testament Church:

      a. Old Testament background: Miriam (Exo. 15:20)
                                    Deborah (Judges 4:4)
                                    Huldah (2 Kings 22:14)

      b. New Testament passages: Anna (Lk. 2:36)
                                    Acts 2:17
                                    Acts 21:9
                                    1 Cor. 11:5

   7. Prophets mainly edified believers by proclaiming God's Word (Acts 15:32). But they could foretell the future at times (Acts 11:27-30).

      8. Prophets could travel as "apostles" (Silas, Paul, etc.) or settle down in one church (Acts 13:1; 1 Cor. 12:28-29).

      9. The early church recognized "prophets" as well as "apostles" as valid positions for their day (Didache 11:3-13:4).

    10. While not all who had the gift of prophecy were given the office of prophet, it was assumed that all who had the office possessed the gift.

B. The Motivational Gift of Prophecy

It was one of the basic motivational gifts (Rom. 12:6). (See discussion of motivational gifts)

C. The Ministry Gift of Prophecy

      1. While the position of prophet and the gift of prophecy are clearly not given to all (1 Cor. 12:29), yet all are exhorted to prophesy (1 Cor. 14:31, 39; Num. 11:25-29; Acts 2:17).

      2. Women as well as men "prophesied" in church meetings (1 Cor. 11:4, 5; 14:31).

      3. These "prophecies" were not primarily fore-telling but forth-telling. They discerned evil in people's hearts and called them to repentance (1 Cor. 14:22-25). What was said was not viewed as an inspired message but was scripturally judged by all the people (1 Cor. 14:29, 37, 38; 1 Thess. 5:20, 21; 1 John 4:1-3).

      4. We are not to despise prophesyings but instead to desire them (1 Thess. 5:20; 1 Cor. 14:39).

      5. All Christians should seek opportunities to prophesy.

Special Note

The passage of full mention on the ministry of prophesying is 1 Cor. 11, 12, 13, 14. A brief analysis of this passage would be helpful.

1 Cor. 11:3-10

    1. The "prophesying" and "prayer" are in the context of the worship service.

    2. Both men and women participated in the worship service.

    3. Paul desires that they conform to the surrounding cultural customs for dignified worship and avoid adopting offending clothing or habits.

1 Cor. 12

    1. Prophesying is one of the gifts of the Spirit (vs. 4, 10).

    2. The Spirit gives the ability to prophesy as He wills (v. 11) for the building up of the Church (v. 7).

    3. In the New Testament Church, the Spirit gave "prophets" as well as "apostles" (v. 28). (Note: No definite article before "apostles or "prophets.")

    4. Not everyone is given the ministry or the position of prophet (v. 29).

1 Cor. 13

    1. Without love, the gift of prophecy is nothing (v. 2).

    2. We prophesy "in part," i.e., imperfectly (v. 9).

    3. When Christ returns, we will be able to prophesy "in whole" (v. 10).

1 Cor. 14

    1. There are "greater" and "lesser" gifts (12:31).

    2. We should seek to prophesy (v. 1).

    3. The primary function of prophecy is to "strengthen, encourage and comfort" believers (v. 3). (Note: not foretell the future).

    4. Prophecy exists for edifying the Church (v. 4).

    5. Prophecy is "greater" or "better" than speaking in tongues (vs. 4-23).

6. Prophesying has as its focus the sin that is in people's hearts, i.e., inner motives. It calls people to repentance and results in conviction and conversion (vs. 24-25).
7. In a normal service, only two or three prophecies should be given (v. 29).
8. All should scripturally judge what is prophesied (v. 29).
9. Those who are prophesying should:
   a. Not monopolize the time (v. 30).
   b. Take turns (v. 31).
   c. Not interrupt or cause confusion (v. 32).
   d. Be orderly (v. 33).
10. Those who feel they are prophets must be under the authority of Scriptures (vs. 37-38).
11. We should all be eager to prophesy in the service in order to edify one another (v. 39). As long as it is done in a fitting and proper way (vs. 39-40) under the authority of Scripture and the elders of the church, it may be accepted.

D. While the office of "prophet" gradually passed away because no provision for its continuance was made in Scripture, we can recognize gifted theologians, preachers and counselors and "prophets" for today (See Schaff, Vol. 1, p. 489).

III. EVANGELIST (Eph. 4:11)
   I. The Office
      A. The word "evangelist" is found only three times in the New Testament.
         1. In Eph. 4:11, the office of "evangelist" is mentioned.
         2. Philip is called an "evangelist" in Acts 21:8.
         3. Timothy is told to do the work of an "evangelist" (2 Tim. 4:5).
      B. While only Philip is directly called an "evangelist," it is clear that many others were called to this ministry. Example: The Seventy (Lk. 10:1), Paul, Timothy, Luke, Titus, Silas, Apollos, Tychicus, Trophimus, Mark, etc.
      C. Deacons (Philip), apostles (Paul) or elders (Timothy) could also be evangelists.
      D. The task of an evangelist is to preach churches into existence by converting unbelievers (Acts 8:4-8).
      E. Once the churches are established, the evangelist appoints elders (Tit. 1:5), then moves on to plant new churches (Acts 8:26-30).
      F. We still recognize evangelists today. There is always the need for evangelists, from George Whitefield to Billy Graham, .

   II. The Ministry
      A. While not all are called to the office of evangelist, all are called to evangelize their relatives friends, fellow-workers, etc. (Matt. 28:19; Acts 8:4).
      B. Conducting Bible studies and house churches is one way of exercising the ministry of evangelist.
      C. For the contrasts between tradition and Scripture on evangelism, consult the chart in the study on the subject in the church section.

IV. PASTORS AND TEACHERS (Eph. 4.11)
      A. Paul uses two words to describe one office in the church.
         1. The grammar of the Greek text reveals that "teachers" cannot be separated from pastors.

2. The New Testament and early church history do not speak of an office of "teacher" as separate from "pastor."
3. All pastors must teach (1 Tim 3:2).

B. The New Testament uses different terms to describe the office of "pastor."

1. "Elder": a Greek term originally from the synagogue. It reflected a position of dignity and respect in the congregation (Exo. 3:16-18). Elders were to be appointed in every church (Tit. 1:5).

2. "Bishop": a term which emphasized that this person had the rule and oversight over the congregation (Acts 20:28).

3. "Pastor" or "Shepherd": an Old Testament term which indicated that this person was responsible to guide, feed and discipline the congregation (Psa. 23). Used of "elders" (Acts 20:28; 1 Pet. 5:2).

4. "Teacher" or "Preacher": an Old Testament term which emphasizes that this person will instruct the congregation (Ecc. 12:9-11; 1 Tim. 5:17-18).

C. The terms elder, bishop, pastor and teacher are used interchangeably in the New Testament. Example: Acts 20:17, cf. 20:28

ELDERS = OVERSEERS (BISHOPS) = SHEPHERDS

D. Summary diagram

OFFICE	FUNCTION
Elder	Overseer, bishop, ruler, shepherd, guide, protector, teacher, preacher, exhorter

E. The qualifications: 1 Tim. 3:1-7
                               Titus 1:5-9
                               1 Pet. 5:1-4

Conclusion

Those offices that God wanted to continue in the church were given a permanent place by His setting forth their requirements and duties in Scripture. While temporary offices come and go as the needs of the church dictate, the offices of elder and deacon must continue as they are the only offices with biblical provisions for their continuance.

Chapter Fifteen
Healing in the Bible

Introduction

One of the areas of biblical truth which directly applies to everyone is the subject of healing. All of us get sick now and then and some of us more often than others. We even marry promising to love each other "in sickness and in health." Parents take care of their sick children when young and the grown children must take care of their sick parents when old. There is that final sickness which will usher us into the presence of the Lord.

In this light, we should answer such questions as: Does God always heal us if we pray for it? Is all healing of God? Is sickness always a punishment for sin? Is there healing in the atonement?

The first step to understand healing is to make the distinction between natural and miraculous healing.

I. Natural Healing
    A. This refers to the normal healing process that God has placed in the human body. Examples:
        1. The antibodies that fight infections
        2. The natural process of the tissue and skin rebuilding flesh
        3. Broken bones mending over time
    B. It is called a "blessing" of God in Scripture. In Psa. 103:3, David thanks God for the daily blessings of natural healing.
    C. Natural healing is never called a "miracle." That which is normal to everyday living is not a miracle.

II. Miraculous Healing
    A. This kind of healing has nothing to do with the natural process of healing. It refers to healing which comes from a supernatural source and is accomplished by supernatural power. Such healing can come from the devil or from the Lord. Thus all healing is not of God. Satan can heal, too.
    B. Satanic Miraculous Healings
        1. Various cultic groups practice what they call "divine" healing. They appeal to such healings as proof of the truth of their teachings. Yet, Deut. 13:1-5 tells us that such miracles and signs do not prove anything. If the teachings are in error, then the miracles are from Satan.
            a. Catholic healings
            b. Christian Science healings
            c. Jim Jones' healings
            d. Mormon healings
        2. Occultic healings have been documented in various forms of white and black witchcraft.
            a. potions, charms, etc.
            b. powwows
            c. demonic healings
            d. Satanism, Church of Satan
            e. Church of Wicca
            f. Voodoo, root magic, etc.

3. Modern psychic healings seem to be the rage today. These healings supposedly come from people who have "powers." Most of the time they claim that God gave them the gift to heal.
   a. the "Inner Healing" movement
   b. psychic surgery (Filipino, Brazilian, etc.)
   c. "religious" faith healers
   d. non-religious psychic healers
   e. "name it, claim it" healing
   f. positive thinking healing
   g. imaging healing
   h. healing through hypnosis
   i. all "New Age" methods of healing.
   j. acupuncture

C. Divine Miraculous Healing
   1. This is healing that takes place when God heals directly by His sovereign power with no secondary agent used. There are 35 incidents in Scripture of direct healing.
   Examples:
   a. Gen. 17 and 21: Abraham and Sarah
   b. Isaiah 38:1-6: Hezekiah
   c. Luke 7:1-10: the centurion's servant
   2. Indirect healing, which takes place when God heals through a secondary agent
   a. The majority of the healings recorded in Scripture refer to secondary agents
      1. 1 Kings 13:1-6: Jeroboam healed by the prayer of the man of God
      2. Acts 3:1-16: the lame man healed through the ministry of Peter and John
      3. Acts 28:8: Publius' father healed through the prayer and laying on of hands of Paul
      4. James 5:14-16: the Elders commanded to anoint with oil and pray for the sick
   3. Healing through prayer alone (five incidents in Scripture)
   4. Healing through prayer and laying on of hands (12 incidents in Scripture)
   5. Healing through prayer and anointing with oil (two incidents in Scripture)

III. The Gift of Healing in Scripture

Important Principles of Approach

A. Beware of being "gift centered" instead of being "character centered." It is not what you do in the Christian life or the gifts that you have that determine the level of your sanctification. It is what you are in your character that determines your spiritual condition. Example: The Corinthian Church was a "carnal" church but had a great abundance of spiritual gifts at the same time. The exercise of the gifts did not indicate true spirituality.
B. Beware of extreme positions on this subject: "God always heals." "God does not heal today." "He stopped healing when the last Apostle died."
C. Unscriptural positions will often reveal themselves by producing depression and despair in the lives of those who hold to those positions. Francis Schaeffer said, "If you have biblical Truth, you can live what you believe and believe what you live."
D. Human experience is a test of doctrine, but never the proof of it. Let Scripture interpret experience. Never let experience interpret Scripture.

IV. The Major Issues

   A. Does God heal today?

      Answer: Yes, of course, God heals today.

      1. There is nothing in Scripture that says He will not or cannot heal today.

      2. There are too many cases of healing to be ignored.

      3. Jesus is still the same (Heb. 13:8).

   B. Does God always heal?

      Answer: No, God does not always heal.

      1. There is no promise in Scripture that He will always heal.

      2. It is appointed for all men to die (Heb. 9:27). Those who teach that a Christian should never be sick or get sick and die are living in a fantasy world. They all die in the end.

      3. The Apostles who had the gift of healing got sick themselves. Those who worked with them also got sick. There is no record of a sickness-free ministry in the New Testament (Phil. 2:26, 27; 2 Tim. 4:20; 2 Cor. 12:7-10).

      4. There are too many illnesses among God's people for this to be true.

      5. God never promised in Scripture to deliver us from those common ills which beset mankind.

   C. Is the failure of healing due to a lack of faith or of positive confession?

      Answer: No, God has never made healing or anything else depend on man's will or faith (Rom. 9:14-18).

      1. It is God's will which determines who is healed and who is not healed (1 John 5:14).

      2. Two equally good Christians can be sick; both ask for healing with the same amount of faith, yet, one is healed and the other is not. The sovereignty of God is ultimate.

      3. False teaching puts poor sick saints on a "guilt trip" by blaming their illness on a supposed lack of faith.

   D. Is there healing in the Atonement?

      Answer: Yes, there is healing in the atonement.

      1. Isa. 53:5: "by His wounds we are healed."

      2. In Matt. 8:14-17, Jesus is the Messiah because of the physical healings He did.

      3. In 1 Peter 2:24, Peter speaks of spiritual healing through Christ's death.

   E. When are we to receive the healing in Christ's Atonement?

      Answer: At the second coming of Christ.

      1. There is no logical reason or scriptural basis for the assumption that the healing that we have in the Atonement is something we get NOW by an act of faith.

      2. We will receive our physical healing at the Resurrection and it will be final, perfect and complete when Jesus returns (1 Thess. 5:23).

      3. Any miraculous healing which is given today is incomplete and does not render anyone immortal.

   F. Are the gifts of healings mentioned in 1 Cor. 12:9, 28, 30 still in operation today?

      1. Preliminary remarks.

         a. Beware of approaching this subject with unproven assumptions, distinctions or ideas in your mind which you never got out of Scripture but which you bring to the Scriptures. Such distinctions as:

            (1) natural/supernatural gifts

            (2) permanent/temporary gifts

            (3) sign/church gifts

         b. Beware of such arbitrary interpretations as:

            (1) some gifts for today/some for first century

(2) some necessary now/some not needed

2. Either all the gifts stay or all the gifts go. To go through the various lists of gifts given in Scripture and choose the ones you like as being still present today and to leave the ones you do not like as no longer present is the height of hypocrisy.

3. God wants us to understand the nature and purpose of spiritual gifts (1 Cor. 12:1).

4. Beware of a "scissors and paste" approach to the New Testament in which various sections are arbitrarily set aside as having relevance only to the Jews or to a supposed "Apostolic Age." Example: C.I. Scofield stated that the four Gospels and the first 10 chapters of Acts are for the Jews and do not relate to the Church.

Biblical Answer:

   a. Just as the entire Old Testament was for Israel, the entire New Testament is for the Church.

   b. Scofield's position is impossible to carry to its logical conclusion and is disastrous to the unity of the New Testament.

   c. Scofield's position would take the Lord's Prayer, the Lord's Supper and the Great Commission from the Church and give them to the Jews because they were instituted in the Gospels.

5. The classic example of an arbitrary interpretation is what the anti-gift people have done with 1 Cor. 13:8-12.

   a. This is the only text in the New Testament which supposedly speaks of the cessation of spiritual gifts. It has become the basic text for doing away with certain gifts such as healing and tongues. It is claimed that all spiritual gifts would be withdrawn once the New Testament canon was complete.

   b. A survey of the classic commentators on 1 Cor. 13 reveals that in 2,000 years of church history, none of them states the closing of the canon in 1 Cor. 13. Without exception, they saw that Paul was saying that the gifts would change when Jesus returned.

   c. Most biblical translations with parallel references on this text point to such places as 1 John 3:1-3 as being the scriptural parallel to 1 Cor. 13:8-12. Thus the context is the return of Christ and not the closing of the canon.

   d. A detailed examination of 1 Cor. 13 reveals that Christ's return is the subject in Paul's mind.

   e. The point of 1 Cor. 13:8-12 is not that prophecy, tongues and knowledge shall be done away with as soon as the New Testament is finished. The point is that "perfection" will be ushered in when Jesus comes back.

   f. Paul is saying that imperfect tongues, prophecy and knowledge will be supplanted by perfect tongues, prophecy and knowledge. There is a transition from part to whole, from imperfect to perfect. The emphasis is not on cessation but on a transition from the lesser to the greater. It emphasizes completion and fulfillment, not cessation.

G. Is sickness ever God's will?

Answer: Yes, of course, it is.

1. There is a sickness unto death, for God has determined when we are to die (Job 14:5). Even those who say that sickness is never God's will die like everyone else.

2. There is a sickness unto chastisement as God punishes us for our sins. This is true both for unbelievers (Exo. 8-12) and God's people (Num. 12:4-10; 1 Cor. 11:30).

3. There is a sickness unto God's glory (John 9:3).

4. There is a sickness unto humility (2 Cor. 12:7-10).

H. What are the gifts of healings?

   1. Remember that there are three basic kinds of gifts.

      a. Motivational gifts

         (1) Your basic gift and responsibility.

         (2) Given by the Spirit as He wills.

         (3) Given at the time of rebirth.

         (4) Each Christian has one and only one.

         (5) The list of gifts is in Rom. 12:6-8.

      b. Ministry gifts

         (1) May be offices in the Church (elders, deacons, etc.).

         (2) Opportunities of service.

         (3) You may minister in more than one gift.

         (4) The list of gifts is in 1 Cor. 12:28-31.

      c. Manifestation gifts

         (1) What happens to the people as you minister.

         (2) The end result of your ministry.

         (3) The list of gifts is in 1 Cor. 12: 7-11.

   2. The gifts of healings may be a ministry or a manifestation gift. Paul refers to "gifts" instead of "gift" for this reason.

      a. The ministry gift of healings is not a basic gift but a temporary ministry. It comes and goes according to the Spirit.

         (1) Examples of healings (Acts 14:8-10; 19:11-12; 20:9, 10)

         (2) Examples of not being healed (Phil. 2:25-27; 1 Tim. 5:23; 2 Tim. 4:20)

         (3) Examples of times when Paul was sick himself (1 Cor. 2:3; 2 Cor. 11:30; 12:5, 9-10)

      b. It is rarely mentioned in the New Testament and does not seem to be frequently given by the Spirit.

      c. You can seek this ministry through prayer.

      d. You may pray for the sick to be healed and/or lay hands on the sick if desired (Jas. 5:16).

      e. You should call for the Elders of the Church to anoint with oil and pray for the sick (Jas. 5:14-15).

      f. If you are sick because of divine punishment, healing will come only after confession of sin is made (Jas. 5:16).

      g. Healing depends on God's will (1 Jn. 5:14; Jas. 4:15).

   3. The manifestation gift of healings

      a. Paul says "healings" because there are different kinds of healing.

         (1) healing for the body

         (2) healing for the mind

         (3) healing your relationship with God

         (4) healing your relationship with others

I. Why does God not always heal?

   1. He does not want to (Rom. 9:15-18).

   2. For greater glory.

   3. For growth in grace.

   4. For lessons in humility.

   5. To make Heaven sweeter.

   6. As a punishment for sin.

Conclusion

We should pray when sick that if it is His will, God would heal us in order for us to serve Him here on earth. If He does not heal us, we should realize that He has opened a new path of service for us in which we can still praise Him for all things. God accomplishes His sovereign will through pain and suffering as well as by pleasure and health (2 Cor. 4:16-18).

Chapter Sixteen
Satan's Devices

Introduction

While the Church of the 21st century prides itself on being knowledgeable about spiritual and worldly things, there is one great area of ignorance which plagues the Church today. Sadly, this area of ignorance is essential to living a scripturally victorious life.

By "victorious life," I am not referring to the myth that God will deliver us out of all our internal trials, temptations and struggles. I am referring to the truth that God will enable us to persevere in the midst of trials, temptations and inner struggles.

The key to perseverance is knowledge (Rom. 5:3-4). Knowledge of the "ins" and "outs" and "ups" and "downs" of the Christian life is essential to maintaining a balanced Christian life. Even though it is not usually done, the first instruction a new Christian should have is an understanding of the Christian life.

So many new Christians are disillusioned about the Christian life because no one ever told them what to expect, or they were told a pack of lies about "everything becoming beautiful" and life becoming a "bowl of cherries" once we receive Jesus as our personal Savior.

Among the most important things relating to the Christian life which we should know are the devices or schemes which Satan uses to keep people from being saved and to keep Christians in a depressed and discouraged condition.

Paul said in his day,

> "If you forgive anyone, I also forgive him. And what I have forgiven—if there was anything to forgive—I have forgiven in the sight of Christ for your sake, in order that Satan might not outwit us. For we are not unaware of his schemes" (2 Cor. 2:10-11).

In his letter, Paul encouraged the Corinthians to forgive and not to retain a spirit of bitterness because it is a device or method which Satan uses to disturb the Church. In this context he states, "We are not ignorant of Satan's schemes or devices."

While the early Christians evidently were taught to recognize the schemes of Satan, today we are quite ignorant of them. For this reason, we need to study the devices of Satan.

One word of warning: We must first deal with any unresolved sin in our lives before studying this subject. We must examine ourselves (2 Cor. 13:5), judge ourselves (1 Cor. 11:31-34), cleanse ourselves (2 Cor. 7:1), and put on the armor of God to withstand the schemes of Satan (Eph. 6:10-20).

PART I

1) Foundational Principle No. 1

   We must understand what the Bible says about the person and work of Satan.

   a) Obtaining a biblical understanding of Satan will bring many positive results.

      i) It will remove our ignorance of Satan.

      ii) It will counter false ideas about Satan.

      iii) It will release us from any fear of Satan.

      iv) It will inform us as to Satan's methods.

      v) It will enable us to recognize and defeat his plans for us and for others.

   b) Ignorance of or false ideas about Satan are deadly.

2) Foundational Principle No. 2

The atoning work of Christ has secured the ultimate defeat of Satan.

Thus the Christian is not fighting for victory but from a position of victory.

a) Christ came to defeat Satan (Gen. 3:15; Heb. 2:14-15; 1 Jn. 3:8).

b) He bound Satan while on earth (Matt. 12:28-29; Jn. 12:31; 16:11; Acts 10:38).

c) By His death and resurrection He has accomplished the ultimate defeat of Satan (Col. 2:15).

d) Because of their union with Christ, the weakest Christians can be victorious over Satan (Rom. 16:20).

e) Satan is now "bound," i.e. limited in his power to blind entire nations to the Gospel (Matt. 12:22-29).

3) The Person and Nature of Satan

a) The first thing which must be done is to remove the mental image from your mind that Satan is a man, dressed up in a red suit, with horns on his head, a pitchfork in his hand, and a long, pointed tail, who lives in hell where he torments people. This is nothing more than the childish drivel found in comic books and cartoons.

  i) Because of "comic book theology," Satan's first device is to cause people to assume that Satan does not really exist.

> DEVICE No. 1: "Satan does not really exist. He is just a childish fear.
> He is only the projection of man's fear of the unknown."

  ii) This device results in too low a view of Satan and his work.

  iii) Because most people have in mind the comic book devil when they ask, "Do you really believe in a personal Satan?" never answer until they define what they mean by the word "devil" or "Satan."

> Do you believe that the devil really exists? | It all depends on what you are talking about. What do you mean by the word "devil?"

b) What is the nature of Satan?

Satan is an angel or spirit creature. He or "it" is a supra-dimensional energy-being composed only of "mind" or mental energy.

  i) Satan is a creation of God. He is not to be viewed as a deity equal to God but as a creature created by God.

> DEVICE No. 2: Some people have too high a view of Satan.
> He is godlike to them.

  ii) Since he is created, Satan is not:

    (1) eternal (He had a beginning)

    (2) omniscient (He does not know all things)

    (3) omnipotent (He is limited in what he can do)

    (4) omnipresent (He can be only at one place at one time. He is not everywhere.)

iii) Being composed only of "spirit" or "mind" (Eph. 2:2), Satan is undetectable by the five senses. He is usually invisible to the eye (Lk. 22:3).

iv) As with any angel, he can appear in various forms:

    (1) animal forms (Gen. 3:1; Rev. 20:2)

    (2) angelic forms (2 Cor. 11:14; Gal. 1:8)

    (3) human forms (1 Sam. 28:4-25)

    (4) natural forms (Lk. l0:18; Job 1:19)

c) Important Questions About Satan

  i) How, when, where, and why did Satan become evil?

    (1) Since the Bible was written for man, it does not go into great detail concerning the fall of Satan, yet, there are passages which deal with this issue.

    (2) Satan was originally created good, and some have speculated that he was an archangel because he is compared to Michael in Jude 9 and Rev. 12:7-12.

    (3) The original sin of Satan was pride (1 Tim. 3:6). This sin is exemplified in "the king of Babylon" (Isa. l4:12-17) and "the king of Tyre" (Ezk. 28:11-19).

    (4) Once he sinned, he was cast down to this planet (Lk. 10:18), where he tempted Adam and Eve into joining his rebellion against God (Gen. 3:1-6). He sinned before man was created.

    (5) He still has access to Heaven (Job 1:6) to accuse us before God (Rev. 12:10) until the final battle comes (Rev. 12:7-13).

  ii) What are the names and titles of this fallen angel?

    (1) Satan (53 times): O.T. (1 Chron 21:1; Job. 1:6; Zech. 3:1-27), N.T. (Matt. 4:10; Acts 26:18; Rom. 16:20; Rev. 12:9)

    (2) The devil (31 times) Matt 4:1; Acts 10:38; Eph. 6:11; 1 Pet. 5:8; Rev. 20:10

    (3) The dragon (13 times): Rev. 12:1-17; 13:1-11; 16:13; 20:2

    (4) The evil one (12 times): Matt. 5:37; 6:13; 13:19, 38; 1 Jn. 2:13, 14; 3:12; 5:18, 19

    (5) Beelzebub (11 times): O.T. (2 Kings 1:2, 3, 6, 16), N.T. (Matt. 10:25; 12:24, 27; Mk. 3:22; Lk. 11:15, 18, 19)

    (6) The serpent (snake) (10 times): O.T. (Gen. 3:1-14), N.T. (2 Cor. 11:3; Rev. 12:9, 14, 15; 20:2)

    (7) The prince of this world (three times): Jn. 12:31; 14:30; 16:11

    (8) The adversary (two times): 1 Tim. 5:14; 1 Pet. 5:8

    (9) The prince of demons (three times): Matt. 9:34; 12:24; Lk. 11:15

    (10) The prince of the power of the air: Eph. 2:2

    (11) The god of this age: 2 Cor. 4:4

    (12) The accuser of the brethren: Rev. 12:10

    (13) The spirit which works disobedience: Eph. 2:2

    (14) The deceiver of the whole world: Rev. 12:9

    (15) A ruler: Eph. 6:12

    (16) An authority: Eph. 6:12

    (17) A power of darkness in this world: Eph. 6:12

    (18) A spiritual force of evil in heavenly places: Eph. 6:12

    (19) Abaddon or Apollyon: Rev. 9:11

    (20) The father of lies: John 8:44

    (21) King over the demons: Rev. 9:11

    (22) The tempter: 1 Thess. 3:5

    (23) Lucifer (?): Isa. 14:12

    (24) A murderer: Jn. 8:44

iii) What are Satan's powers or abilities?
    (1) We are referring to Satan's present powers.
    (2) There are various ways Christian theologians approach this subject today. Much confusion has resulted from false teaching on this subject and much care must be taken to avoid extreme positions.
    (3) Some theologians teach that Satan's power stopped when the "apostolic age" came to a close. Thus, no one can be demon-possessed today. Satan cannot do any "miracles." What can we say to such a position?

Some Crucial Objections to This Position

      (a) Scripture knows nothing of this "Apostolic Age." There are the old and new covenants, but no middle age.
      (b) No Scripture says that the death of the last apostle would stop all miracles.
      (c) Church history continues with Divine and Satanic miracles. The evidence is overwhelming.
      (d) Some "psychic experiments" are real.
      (e) Satan is active today.
      (f) Demon possession does occur.
    (4) What can Satan do?
      (a) He is a very powerful angel. As such, his strength and intelligence are far superior to man's.
      (b) He is capable of:

          (i) Inter-dimensional teleportation (Job 1:6, 7)
          (ii) Visual materialization in various forms (2 Cor. 11:14)
          (iii) Apporting objects and people from place to place (Matt. 4:5, 8)
          (iv) Molecular transformation of matter (Ex. 7:12, 22)
          (v) Counterfeit miracles (Ex. 8:7; 2 Thess. 2:9; Rev. 13:13-15)
          (vi) Spontaneous human combustion (Job 1:16; Rev. 13:13)
          (vii) Possession of the minds of non-Christians (2 Tim. 2:24-26)
         (viii) Thought transference/implantation (1 Chron. 21:1; Matt. 16:22-23)
          (ix) Death (Heb. 2:14)
          (x) Hindering man's ability to comprehend the Gospel (2 Cor. 4:3-4)
          (xi) Producing bodily illness (Lk. 13:11-17)
          (xii) Producing mental illness (Mk. 5:1-13)
          (xiii) Inciting opposition to God (Acts 13:6-12)
          (xiv) Removing the Word of God from the mind (Matt. 13:19)
          (xv) Manipulating the weather (Job 1:19; Mk. 4:35-39)
          (xvi) Hindering answers to prayer (Dan. 10:12-14, 20-21)
          (xvii) Tempting people to sin (1 Thess. 3:5)
        (xviii) Inventing false religions/ideas (2 Cor. 11:3-4; 1 Tim.4:1-3; 1 Jn. 4:1-3)
          (xix) Manipulating things to bring financial disaster or wealth to individuals (Job 1:3, 13-19; Matt. 4:8-9; 1 Tim. 6:9-10)
          (xx) Disrupting the assembly of the saints by his presence or by inciting disunity, lies, divisions, etc. (Acts 5:1-10; 6:1)
          (xxi) Guiding the spirit/actions of nations (Dan. 10:13; Rev. 16:14; 20:7-9)
          (xxii) Keeping believers in a constant state of depression and discouragement (1 Pet. 5:8-9)

(xxiii) Sending a messenger to be "a thorn in the flesh" in a believer, to vex his or her spirit as long as they live (2 Cor. 12:7-10)

Note: God uses this Satanic device to keep believers humble, revealing their weakness and absolute dependence on God's grace.

(xxiv) Killing the body of excommunicated believers (1 Cor. 5:5)

(xxv) Communicating with people during seances and other occultic rites (Deut. 18:9-11)

(d) In the light of what has been said about Satan, why should we be concerned about him or his activity? After all, he is finite and can be only in one place at a time. So, why worry about it?

   i) Satan is not alone. He has a kingdom and a vast army to help him to oppose God and us.

     (1) Satan has a kingdom and he is its king (Matt. 12:26; Rev. 9:11).

     (2) He rules over an immense army of demons (evil spirits) who, like himself, are fallen angels (supra-dimensional energy-beings, Rev. 9:11). How many angels followed Satan in his revolt against God? Many commentators think that up to one third of the angels followed Satan (Rev. 8:12). They probably number in the billions.

   ii) Some of the demons were confined to "Tartarus" at the time of the revolt (2 Pet. 2:4). Others were allowed to migrate to this planet.

   iii) We must dismiss some false ideas about demons.

     (1) Demon possession is not a superstitious explanation of physical and mental illnesses. It actually happened in biblical times and happens today.

     (2) Demons are not the disincarnate spirits/souls/minds of people who have died. There are no "ghosts" haunting places or people. You may "adopt" a demon who pretends to be the "ghost" of a dead person, but the spirit/soul/mind of that dead person is either in Heaven or Hell.

     (3) Demons are not the spirit/soul/mind of a pre-Adamic race.

     (4) Demons are not creatures from another planet, time period, parallel universe, the center of the earth, UFOs, etc. They are angels who rebelled against God.

     (5) Demons are not man's thought projection, psychic powers or telekinesis. They are self-existent apart from the belief or wishes of man.

   iv) What is demon possession?

Device No. 3: Demon possession occurs when Satan himself or one or more demons enter the body of a non-Christian and take control of it and forces the person's mind into an unconscious state. In effect, an alien "mind" takes over the person. This "mind" will do the thinking, speaking, etc. When the demon or demons leave the person, that person does not generally remember anything that happened during the time of their possession.

---

     (1) In many cases, there are no outward signs until confronted by possible exorcism (Mk. 1:21-28).

     (2) When there are outward manifestations of demon possession, the most significant sign is that of an altered personality, which is usually evil and malicious (Mk. 5:2-15).

Some of the following may be signs of possession:

(a) Dual or multiple personalities (Mk. 5:2-5, 15).

(b) Different voices, genders, even languages (Mk. 5:7).

(c) The "voice" talks about the person it possesses (Mk. 5:9-12).

(d) You can talk with the demon directly (Mk. 5:8-10).

(e) Sudden suicidal or homicidal desires (Mk. 5:5).

(f) The demon will give you its name (Mk. 5:9).

(g) The evil "personality" leaves when commanded in Jesus' name and the person's normal personality resurfaces (Mk. 5:18).

(h) Long-term depression or sudden ecstatic state.

(3) Demon possession may manifest itself in bodily afflictions. Some sicknesses, handicaps, sudden illnesses, etc., are the result of demonic activity.

Device No. 4: The demon may cloak his possession of a person by mimicking the symptoms of true physical ills. This will avoid detection and will allow the demon to deceive people.

---

(4) How can we tell the difference?

If "the problem" goes away through the casting out of the demon(s), it was demon possession. If prayer, fasting and exorcism have no effect, it is a physical or mental illness.

(5) Demon-possessed people are capable of super-human strength (Mk. 5:3-4).

(6) Demon-possessed people often have "psychic" powers. They exercise occultic powers and have occultic knowledge (Mk. 3:11; James 2:19; Acts 16:16-19).

(7) Demon-possessed people are capable of the most vile and inhuman acts. They are capable of the lowest moral depravity known to man (Mk. 5:2).

v) When confronted with a demon possessed person:

(1) Do not run away out of fear. You are a priest of the Most High God and have authority over Satan and his demons by virtue of your union with Christ (Matt. 10:1; Lk. 10:1, 17-20; Eph. 1:18-22; 2:6; James 4:7; 1 Pet. 5:8-9).

(2) Get right with God. Confess all known sin to God. Pray for the filling of the Spirit and the protection of the blood of Jesus (James 4:6-10; 1 Pet. 5:5-9).

(3) If you are not a Spirit-filled Christian or you are not saved, "run for the hills" and do not even try to exorcise the demons (Acts 19:13-20).

(4) Get one or more Spirit-filled Christians to go with you (Lk. 10:1).

(5) Speak directly to the demon (not to the person possessed) (Mk. 1:25; Acts 16:18, etc.).

(6) Ask the demon(s) for its name (Mk. 5:9-10).

(7) Using its name, command it in the name of Jesus Christ to leave the person (Acts 16:18).

(8) Be prepared for resistance, lies, pleas, threats, faked leavings, more than one demon, arguments, cursing, blasphemy, accusations, evasions, etc.

(9) Some people have so many demons and such powerful ones that days of prayer, commands and fasting may be required (Mk. 9:17-18, 28-29).

(10) Once they are exorcised, warn them that the only safe position to be in to avoid being possessed again is to receive Christ at once. If they are not saved, a worse form of possession will take place (Matt. 12:43-45).

(11) Do not touch a demoniac. Jesus always only spoke to them.

PART II

1) Satan's devices are first directed to keeping people from a saving knowledge of Jesus Christ. He has various methods which he uses to hinder the salvation of sinners. What are these devices?

> **Device No. 1:** Satan does all in his power to keep people from ever hearing the Gospel. He knows that ignorance of the Gospel means eternal damnation (Rom. 10:13-17).

How does he keep people from hearing the gospel?

a) Political persecution and suppression.

b) Control of mass media to omit Christian shows.

c) Jamming radio waves and TV shows.

d) Outlawing Christian literature.

e) Destruction of Christian schools.

f) Stopping missions in the name of "cultural anthropology."

g) Getting the church to neglect her mission by materialism and cold-heartedness.

h) Making Christians feel too embarrassed, inferior, ashamed, afraid, etc., to witness to the lost. Using their pride and fear to silence their witness.

> **Device No. 2:** Satan creates false religions and philosophies to satisfy the religious desires of man. Then he ties these false religions to the culture to make it very difficult for someone to receive Christianity.

How Does God View Other Religions?

a) Man is not searching for God, but running from God (Gen. 3:10; Rom. 3:11).

b) Pagan religions are not the result of man's accepting light, but they are the result of man's rejection of light (Rom. 1:18-25).

c) Worship in pagan religions is not really worship of the true God, different names for God being used, but all pagan worship is demon worship (Deut. 32:16-17; 1 Cor. 10:20).

d) All other religions are Satanic in origin and power. They are the devices of Satan to blind whole cultures to the Gospel (2 Cor. 4:3-4; Exo. 20:3-4; Jn. 14:6; Acts 4:12; Rom. 1:25; 2 Cor. 11:3-4; Gal. 1:6-9; 1 Tim. 2:5; etc.).

> **Device No. 3:** Once a person has heard the Gospel, Satan will give him all the "reasons" or "rationalizations" why the Gospel should be ignored (Matt. 13:19-22).

Popular Excuses

1. "All religions are the same. They all worship the same God. As long as you are sincere, it does not matter what you believe." Answer: Jn. 3:16; 14:6; Acts 4:12; 16:30-31; 1 Tim. 2:5.

2. "There is no hell. Everyone goes to Heaven when they die. There are people who died and came back and said that there is no Hell." Answer: Rev. 20:15; Matt. 25:34, 41, 46.

3. "There is no God, no life after death and no moral absolutes. Eat, drink, be merry because we all die and pass into nothingness." Answer: Psa. 14:1; Heb. 9:27.

4. "People are basically good. I am not a sinner. I am not as bad as some people and better than most. I will take my chances with God. After all, He is a good God and will take into

account the good things I have done." Answer: Rom. 3:10-23; Lk. 18:9-14.

5. "I plan to repent just before I die. You see, I want to have some fun first. I have to get it out of my system first. Then I will settle down and become a Christian." Answer: Lk. 12:13-21.

6. "The wicked have more happiness in life than do the righteous. Look around you. Who are the rich, the powerful and the beautiful people? The wicked!" Answer: Psa. 73.

7. "I know some churchgoers who are hypocrites. My uncle is a Christian and a low-down skunk. He stole three hundred dollars from me. So, do not talk to me about becoming a Christian. I know all I want to know about them." Answer: John 3:16; Acts 16:30-31; Matt. 13:26-43.

8. "My family would disown me if I became a Christian." Answer: Matt. 10:32-39.

9. "My parents are Christians, and I have heard the Gospel all my life. I know I can be saved when I want to, but I am not ready for it yet." Answer: 2 Cor. 6:2; Heb. 2:3; 3:7-12.

10. "Why should I become a Christian? I have things under control. I do not need a savior. I can handle things all right. I do not feel any need, desire or alarm. I am happy the way I am. If Christianity makes you feel good, great! But do not push it on me." Answer: Rev. 3:17-18; Acts 17:30-31.

11. "Oh, I am saved, but, you see, I am a carnal Christian. I received Christ as my Savior years ago. I may not be one of those super-duper Christians, but I am saved anyway." Answer: 1 Jn. 2:4, 9, etc.

12. "I am a Christian. I was brought up as a Christian and have been baptized and I am a church member. I am a good person. What else would God demand?" Answer: Eph. 2:8-10; Rom. 6:23; Tit. 3:5.

Note: Do not be intimidated by dogmatic false excuses. Stand up and speak the truth!

Part III

Once a person is regenerated by the Spirit of God, Satan knows that he has forever lost that soul to God and that there is nothing he can do to retrieve that soul (Rom. 8:38, 39). So, he spends his time organizing his demonic army to utilize various devices or schemes which will keep believers in a defeated and depressed condition. While he cannot regain the believer, he can pain the believer. Satan's devices focus on individuals, families, churches and nations.

1) Devices against individual Christians

> No. 1: Satan will inspire false teachings concerning the Christian life in order to confuse believers, to make the Christian life unlivable and to bring them into bondage and defeat.

Popular False Teachings
1. Legalism (under the Law) Answer: Rom. 3:20, 28; 7:1-6; Gal. 3:1-5; 4:4-5
2. Antinomianism (without the Law) Answer: John 14:15; Rom. 3:31; 6:14-15; 1 Cor. 9:21
3. Perfectionism (above the Law) Answer: 1 John 1:8-10; James 3:2; Rom. 3:23
4. Positionalism (no holiness of life) Answer: Heb. 12:14; 1 John 2:4, 6
5. Passivism (let go, let God) Answer: Phil. 2:12; Col. 1:29; Gal. 2:20
6. Mysticism (over-emphasis on Holy Spirit). Answer: Isa. 8:20; John 16:7-15
7. Rationalism (under-emphasis on Holy Spirit). Answer: 1 Cor. 2:14; Eph. 5:18
8. Carnal Christianity (heresy) Answer: Gal. 5:19-21; Eph. 5:5-7; 1 John 3:7-8

> No. 2: Satan has certain favorite devices which he uses often because they are so effective in neutralizing the life and testimony of believers. We must not be ignorant of these well-used devices.

1. He inspires us to be sin-centered instead of Christ-centered. Answer: Phil. 2:21.
2. He reminds us of our besetting sins over which we have frequently wept and repented. He tells us that we cannot be saved if we cannot gain the victory over them. Answer: James 3:2; Phil. 3:12-14; 1 John 1:9.
3. He encourages us to live by sight and feelings instead of by faith. Answer: 2 Cor. 5:7; Heb. 11:1.
4. He magnifies the prosperity of the wicked and the poverty of the righteous. Answer: Psa. 73.
5. He tells us to "retire" from being active in the Lord's work. Answer: 1 Cor. 15:58; 2 Tim. 4:6-8.
6. He injects doubts into our minds to disturb our faith and zeal. Answer: 2 Cor. 10:4-5.
7. He promotes worldliness, carnality, selfishness and immaturity (acting like spoiled brats). Answer: Eph. 4:11-16.
8. He tempts us at the weakest points of our personality and constitution. He sets up situations which will tempt us to fall. Answer: 1 Pet. 5:8-9.
9. He leads us to associate with people who will drag us into sin by social pressure. Answer: 1 Cor. 15:33.
10. He emphasizes the fleeting pleasures of the present and encourages us not to think in terms of eternity. Answer: 2 Cor. 5:10; Heb. 11:24-27.

2) Devices Against Christian Families

Satan will seek to destroy the Christian family. He has certain well-used and highly effective devices for neutralizing a Christian family.

a) Satan encourages husbands/fathers not to take loving leadership in the family, especially in the things of God. Answer: Eph. 5:25; 6:4.
b) He encourages wives/mothers not to be godly examples of a submissive attitude and responsible leadership in setting the atmosphere of the home. Answer: Prov. 31:10-31; Eph. 5:22.
c) He fights against family devotions and worship. Answer: Deut. 6:5-9; Eph. 6:4.
d) He encourages sinful words, deeds, attitudes and music in the home in order to create an ungodly atmosphere which smothers a spiritual thirst for God but encourages a thirst for the things of this world. Answer: Josh. 24:14-15; 1 John 2:15-17.
e) He inspired the idea that the Sunday School and the church have the obligation of the religious instruction of children. Answer: Eph. 6:4.

3) Devices Against Churches

Satan is afraid of churches that are full of zeal and good works. He seeks to put to sleep churches where dedication and sacrifice are stressed and where sin and repentance are preached. While he cannot destroy a true Church, he can nullify its testimony and blunt its effectiveness.

a) Satan inspires false views of the church in order to get churches on the wrong track. Answer: 1 Tim. 3:14-15; Matt. 16:18.
b) He encourages disloyalty and an independent attitude among the people. Answer: Heb 13:17; Acts 20:28.

c) He disrupts the unity of the church by lies, gossip and slander. Answer: Eph. 4:29-5:2.

d) He creates division in the church by false teaching and power struggles. Answer: 1 Thess. 5:12-25.

e) He sends people to churches who will cause disunity and controversy. Answer: Acts 20:29-31.

f) He inspires people to be married to the church building instead of to Christ. Answer: 1 Cor. 3:16.

g) He encourages attitudes of compromise (peace at any price), carnality, superficiality and personality worship in the church. Answer: Jude 3; Rev. 2:2, 6; 1 Cor. 1:10-18; 3:1-9.

h) He provides false ministers and false churches where Christianity is only a nominal and ritualistic thing. Answer: 2 Cor 11:3, 4; 13-15; 2 Tim. 3:1-9.

i) He promotes entertainment as the chief goal of church services. Answer: Acts 20:26-27; Eph. 4:11-16.

j) He always strives to cause us to seek comfortable lives in comfortable churches where no dedication or sacrifice is required. Answer: Rom. 13:11-14.

4) Devices Against Nations

Satan will use the political and cultural forces of a nation to suppress the people of God in order to bring about the downfall of that nation. He seeks to overthrow any nation which punishes wickedness and rewards righteousness.

a) Satan corrupts the culture and lifestyle of a nation to the point where a godly person is out of place and feels uncomfortable. The saint is grieved by all the sin and wickedness which surround him. Answer: 2 Pet. 2:7-8; 3:11-12.

b) He encourages the mass media to ridicule the righteous and to exalt the wicked. Answer: Jn. 15:18-25; Lk. 6:26.

c) He incites politicians and people to persecute believers. Answer: 2 Tim. 3:12.

d) He has the believers put to death. Answer: Matt. 10:16-33.

e) He desires to be worshiped by all men and will one day kill all who refuse to do so. Answer: Rev. 13:11-17; 20:7-15.

Conclusion

These are some of the many devices of Satan which he uses against the saints. They are powerful, yet the armor of God and our spiritual weapons enable us to overcome Satan and all his works (1 Jn. 2:13; Rev. 12:11). We can rejoice for we stand in Christ's victory and march in His triumphant army (Col. 2:15).

Chapter Seventeen
Stewardship

Foundational Principles

I. Every Christian must look upon himself as a steward of the things of God (1 Pet. 4:7-11)
Definition: A steward is a person who has the responsibility of managing the money and possessions which belong to someone else (Lk. 16:1-12).

II. Stewardship is based on the fact that God owns everything and that we do not own anything, not even ourselves (Psa. 24:1, 2; Lev. 25:23; 1 Cor. 6:19, 20).

III. Stewardship involves a threefold managing of the money God has given to us.

SPENDING	GIVING	SAVING
Prov. 21:20 Luke 15:13	Luke 6:38 Acts 20:35	Prov. 6:6-11 2 Cor. 12:14 Prov.11:24-26, 28 Matt. 6:19-21

The point is that God is so concerned with what we do with his money that He has put in Scripture clear-cut financial principles which are to regulate our spending, giving and saving.

Are you a faithful steward? (1 Cor. 4:2)

The Book of Proverbs on Money

I. Principles of Earning Money
  1. Do not profit through crimes such as theft (1:10-19).
  2. The hard-working ants show lazy people the right path (6:6-11).
  3. Ill-gotten money will not ultimately profit (10:2).
  4. Negligence leads to poverty (10:4).
  5. Diligence leads to wealth (10:4).
  6. Employers hate lazy workers (10:26).
  7. God hates cheating (11:1, 20:10, 23).
  8. God loves honesty (11:1).
  9. Hard work pays off (12:11; 14:23).
  10. Daydreamers will fail in life (12:11; 28:19).
  11. Lazy people are always greedy and covetous (13:4).
  12. Hard work is good for mental health (13:4).
  13. Wealth obtained through fraud is spent quickly (13:11).
  14. Wealth obtained by hard work accumulates (13:11).
  15. Those who merely talk instead of work, become poor (14:23).
  16. Lazy people live in constant frustration (15:19).
  17. To destroy your family, seek profit through crime (15:27).

18. If you hate bribes and kickbacks, you love life (15:27).
19. God is vitally interested in honest weights and work (16:11).
20. Lazy people are always sleepy (19:15).
21. When you are idle, you get hungry (19:15).
22. A lazy person is too lazy even to feed himself (19:24).
23. Lazy people do not plan ahead and thus end up begging (20:4).
24. Poverty comes to those who love to sleep (20:13).
25. Although wealth obtained by theft brings immediate joy, it will bring ultimate destruction (20:17).
26. Wealth obtained through "get rich quick" schemes can be lost just as quickly (20:21).
27. Be careful and diligent by planning ahead. Do not try "get rich quick" schemes (21:5; 28:20, 22).
28. Wealth obtained through lying does not last long (21:6).
29. Lazy people do not give to others because they are greedy (21:26).
30. Lazy people refuse to work and this will lead to their death (21:25).
31. Hard-working people give to others and do not hold back (21:26).
32. Lazy people can always make up some ridiculous excuse to get out of work (22:13).
33. Poverty comes to those who try to impress the rich (22:16).
34. God will punish those who oppress the poor (22:22-23).
35. Do not falsify property lines to steal land (22:28; 23:10).
36. Obtain a skill and be good at it. You will be honored for it (22:29; 18:16).
37. Do not wear yourself out in trying to obtain riches. Why? They are quickly spent and soon disappear (23:4-5).
38. Establish yourself financially before building your own house (24:27).
39. Laziness will end in poverty (24:30-34).
40. Lazy people are full of fear and insecurity. It cripples them (26:13).
41. Lazy people love sleep (26:14).
42. Lazy people are often too "tired" to eat (26:15).
43. Lazy people really think that they are the wisest people around. They love to give advice (26:16).
44. Manage your finances correctly and you will prosper (27:23-27).
45. A rich person will think he is wise, but a wise poor person can see the foolishness of the rich (28:11).
46. Government officials who oppress the people by unfair taxation are fools (28:16).
47. The official who rejects dirty money will stay in office (28:16).
48. Do not rob your parents (28:24).
49. Since poverty can lead to stealing, and riches can lead to indifference toward God, it is better to be in the middle (30:7-9).
50. A wise woman shows her wisdom by hard work and good investments (31:13-19).

II. Principles of Spending Money
 1. Do not get involved in immoral activities. Such things as prostitution, pornography, etc., will ultimately take all your money (5:3-10; 6:24-28; 29:3).
 2. Poverty comes to those who live for the pleasures of this life (21:17).
 3. Do not associate with drunkards or gluttons. To do so will reduce you to poverty (23:20, 21).
 4. Always seek advice from several wise counselors before making financial decisions (24:6).

III. Principles of Borrowing and Loaning Money
 1. If you have already co-signed a note, do whatever you have to do, but get out of it. Do not rest until you are free of that note (6:1-5).

    2. If you co-sign a note for a stranger, you will have to pay it. So, do not co-sign any notes. Hate the very idea of it and you will be safe (11:15).

    3. Only a fool would co-sign a note for his neighbors (17:18).

    4. You are a slave to the one who loans you money. The rich rule over the poor by loaning them money (22:7).

    5. Do not pledge or sign any notes. If you cannot pay, they can take your bed from you (22:26-27).

    6. When foolish people co-sign a note for a stranger, do not hesitate to collect from them what they owe you (27:12-13).

IV. Principles on Saving Money

    1. The ants teach us to prepare for the future. Only lazy people neglect to do this (6:6-11).

    2. A wise son is known by his careful preparation for the future. Only a lazy son lives day to day (10:5).

    3. A man's savings are a fortress of protection (10:15).

    4. Do not put your ultimate trust in wealth (11:28).

    5. A good man leaves an inheritance to his grandchildren (13:22).

    6. The righteous should have wealth stored up (15:6; 21:20).

    7. Wealth is like a strong city and a high wall (18:11).

    8. The more wealth you have, the more friends you will have (19:4).

    9. A father should leave his wealth to his children (19:14).

   10. Only a fool does not prepare for future evils. The wise foresee it and deliver themselves (22:3; 27:12).

V. Principles on Giving Money

    1. We must honor the Lord with our wealth by giving from the first part of our income (3:9).

    2. Do not refuse to give to those in need if you have the means (3:27-28).

    3. The way to increase your wealth is by giving it away (3:10; 11:24-25).

    4. The person who refuses to sell basic products such as food will be cursed by the people. But if he sells, they will bless him (11:26).

    5. The person who gives to the poor is gracious (14:31).

    6. Everyone wants to be a friend of a generous person (19:6).

    7. If you refuse to give to others, they will refuse to give to you when you are in trouble (21:13).

    8. A gift often patches up a quarrel (21:14).

    9. God blesses the generous (22:9).

   10. Give to the needs of your enemies as well as to your friends (25:21, 22).

   11. If you give to the poor, you will never end up in need (28:27).

   12. If you close your eyes to the needs of others you will be cursed (28:27).

   13. A wise woman gives to the poor (31:20).

Special Note on Giving

I. God has commanded in Scripture that the ministries and ministers of the church should be supported through the giving of believers.

    Old Testament — Num. 18:20-24   New Testament — 1 Cor. 9:4-10, 13-14

II. Giving has always been regulated by God and is to be done according to biblical principles. God never said that giving should be regulated by emotionalism or sentimentality.

III. One basic biblical principle envisions every believer as giving tithes and offerings.
    Definition: A tithe is 10 percent of one's gross income.
    Definition: Offerings refer to anything beyond the tithe.

Tithing

TAUGHT BY	PRACTICED
Example: Gen. 14:20	Before the Law: Gen. 28:22
Precept: Lev. 27:30 Matt. 23:23	Under the Law: Mal. 3:10
Command: Mal. 3:10	Under the Gospel: 1 Cor. 9:13-14

IV. Not to give is to rob God of what belongs to Him.
    (1) Example: Ex. 20:15: "You shall not steal"
        Definition: Stealing is the taking and using as your own that which belongs to another without his permission.
    (2) We are stealing from God when we fail to give God what we owe Him and what belongs to Him (Mal. 3:7-10; Mk. 12:17).
    (3) To return to God, we must repent and give restitution to God (Mal. 3:7; Lk. 2:8,10-14; Ex. 22:1-15; cf. Lk. 19:8, 9).

V. Our attitude in giving should be regulated by Scripture. 2 Cor. 9:7 says that we are to give cheerfully, not grudgingly, or out of necessity.

VI. The secret of cheerful giving is to see that giving is not losing but gaining, because giving is sowing (2 Cor. 9:6; Gal. 6:6-9).

VII. As you sow through your giving, you shall reap if you do not faint.

SPIRITUAL REAPING	MATERIAL REAPING
2 Cor. 8:1-7 2 Cor. 9:7-8 Gal. 6:6-7	Mal. 3:7-11; Phil. 4:14-19 Prov. 3:9-10 Prov. 11:24-25

Questions

Must all giving be to or through the local church?
or
Should all giving be to or through the local church?

Answer: These are complicated questions and a simple "yes" or "no" will not be sufficient. To arrive at the biblical answer several steps must be taken first.

Step 1: Recognize that this question is crucial today because there are so many Christian organizations asking for money.
A. Para-church organizations did not exist in the early church because the church was fulfilling its biblical responsibilities.
   (1) The ministry of the Word—Col. 1:28
   (2) The ministry of mercy—Acts 6:1-3
   (3) The ministry of evangelism—Acts 4:31; 8:4
   (4) The ministry of missions—Acts 13:1-4, etc.
B. These organizations arose when the church failed to fulfill its responsibilities.
   Example: Independent missionary organizations arose because the established churches were not concerned with missions.
C. The modern Christian is torn between giving everything to his church and splitting up his giving between the church and worthy Christian organizations.

Step 2: Gather the Biblical data.
A. Old Testament picture
   (1) All giving was generally to the church, but there were exceptions to this general practice (Num. 18:21; Deut. 12:5-6, 11; 26:12-14).
   (2) No absolute rule was given.

B. New Testament picture
   (1) Since the church was doing its job and had competent spiritual leaders, all giving was generally to or through the church (Acts 4:32-37; 5:2; 6:1-7; 2 Cor. 8:1-4; 9:7; Phil. 4:14-18).
   (2) No absolute rule was given.

The biblical answer is that while we cannot say that all giving *must* be to or through the local church, we must say that all giving *should* be to or through the local church.

Why should all giving should be to or through the local church?

   (1) This was the general practice of the people of God throughout the ages.
   (2) This is the general practice of giving which best fulfills the biblical vision of the ideal church.
   (3) The church is the center of God's plan of salvation (Matt. 16:18).
   (4) Organizations come and go but the institution of the local church will always remain (Matt. 16:18).
   (5) Without sufficient funds, the local church will never be able to take up its biblical responsibilities.
   (6) This is God's method of training the leaders of the church to be good stewards of God's money. This puts the pressure on them (Acts 6:1-6).

Now what about the "What if ..." questions?
1. Make sure that you are not trying to rationalize your disobedience.
2. If you ask honest questions, you will get honest answers.

Question: "What if I belong to a liberal church or denomination?"
Answer: Leave at once and join a Bible-believing church (2 Cor. 6:14-18).

Question: "What if I feel that my church has all the money it needs?"
Answer: Seek the advice of the pastors or church leaders as to worthy projects which you can support.
    (1) We are told to seek godly advice in Prov. 11:14; 12:15; 19:20; 20:18; 24:6.
    (2) There are dangers in giving your money without first seeking godly advice.
        (a) Pride (wise in own eyes).
        (b) You will give on emotion.
        (c) You may support unsound works.

Question: "What if a Christian organization is doing something that the church is failing to do?"
Answer: Until the church begins to fulfill its biblical responsibilities, we must support these para-church organizations which "fill in the gap." But give to such groups after seeking advice from your elders.

Conclusion

God will hold us responsible for all the things He has given us. The money we have is to be used to His glory as well as to support ourselves and our families.

Chapter Eighteen

The Origin of Giving Offerings to God

Introduction

Have you ever wondered when, where, and why did people begin the practice of giving offerings to God? Why do we give an offering to God during the worship service? Can we omit this practice and just put a box at the door and let people drop in whatever they want? Instead of looking inside ourselves to human reason, emotions or experience, let us go to the Bible and find out what God says about offerings.

I. Giving to God Was a Creation Ordinance

God came down to man in human form in the Garden of Eden and taught man about all things including how to worship Him (Gen. 3:8). From the New Testament we learn that it was the eternal Son of God who came in the form of a man and walked and talked with them in the Garden. This is why the conversations between God, Adam and Eve are causal and quite normal. They were talking to the God/man standing in front of them. (See my book on the Trinity for the documentation.)

II. Giving To God Was Part of the Worship of God Before and After the Fall

A. After the Fall, God still came to man in human form (Gen. 3:8). This is why the conversations between God, Adam and Eve recorded in Gen. 3:8-19 and between God and Cain recorded in Gen. 4:3-16 are casual and quite normal as one man talks to another. God was visibly in front of them in the form of a man.

B. Notice that the giving of offerings was not something new or novel invented by Cain or Abel. The Hebrew text indicates that the giving of offerings is something that they had been doing all their lives. Luther commented:

"The custom of offering sacrifices was not a later innovation, but dates back to the beginning of the world ... the practice of offering sacrifices was handed down from Adam..."

C. In his classic commentary on Genesis, Candlish states that the phrase "in the process of time" (Gen. 4:3) in the Hebrew text meant that God came to visit Adam and his family at specific times, and they gave Him offerings to show their gratitude for all of His blessings. Thus, God himself instituted the worship service as the time and place for man to worship Him.
The text tells us that Cain and Abel came into the presence of the God/man at the appointed time and place to engage in public worship by the giving of their offerings. As Leupold points out in his commentary on Genesis:

"The brothers had many times before brought their sacrifices after the example of what they had seen their father do."

D. Both Jewish and Christian commentators point out that Adam and Eve taught their children to attend the stated worship service and give an offering to God. This is why Cain and Abel gave their offerings to the God/man who stood before them. From the story of Cain and Abel, it is clear that Adam and Eve clearly taught their children:
1. You do not come into the presence of God empty-handed.
2. You don't give to God what costs you nothing.
3. You give of your best to the Lord—not the least; the first fruits of your labor and not the dregs of what is left over at the end.
4. Your offering should be act of faith in the Lord.
5. If your offering is not given in faith, God will not accept your gift.

III. The Story of Cain and Abel

A. It is amazing that the very first story given in the Bible after the Fall concerns the giving of offerings to God. Of all the spiritual truths to illustrate, God chose the issue of giving offerings to Him. This indicates the high priority He places on this issue. But is the giving of an offering to God a high priority in your life? Does His kingdom have first priority in your life? Or have you thought little or nothing of the giving of offerings?

B. The story given in Gen. 4:3-16 underscores the principle that God looks at what is in the heart as well as what is in the hand. If the heart is not right, He will reject the gift no matter how large or costly. Mere formalistic worship is not acceptable to God. As Leupold, points out:

"It is evident that one [Cain] gave because it was time and custom to give—pure formalism; whereas the other [Abel] gave the best—pure, devout worship... With characteristic spiritual discernment the Scripture goes to the heart of things. Formalistic worship is of no value in God's eyes; it is an abomination in the sight of the Lord."

C. Since Cain's countenance fell when he saw that his gift was not acceptable to God but Abel's gift was accepted, how did Cain know that his offering was not accepted? What did he see? Let us ask the following questions:
1. Are there other times in biblical history when God appeared in human form?
2. When he was worshiped by offerings?
3. When there was some kind of visible sign to indicate if the offering was accepted or rejected?

To all three questions we must answer, "Yes" (example Judges 6:11-24; 13:1-23). The God/man would consume with divine fire those offerings that were acceptable to Him. Evidently, Cain's gift was not consumed by the divine fire. It was left on the rock or altar as a testimony to his selfishness. It was obvious to him, his father, mother, brothers and sisters that God had rejected his offering. Thus it was the public shame in front of his family that enraged Cain.

F. Why was Cain's offering rejected? There has been much speculation by both Jewish and Christian commentators. But Gen. 4 and Heb. 11 give us the specific reasons why Cain's offering was rejected.

The Story Given in Gen. 4:3-16

1. Throughout biblical history God has always demanded that we give Him the "first fruits" of our labor because this means that we have put God first in our priorities. It did not matter if this meant the first fruit, vegetables or grains or the first born of the flock or herd. The

first fruit belongs to God. This even applied to the first born of our children. We are to dedicate them to God.

2. Thus when we read that Abel gave "the first born of his flock" to God, this meant he gave the first fruit of his labor to God. He did not take the first born for himself. No, he put God first and himself second.

3. But the text also says that he gave "the first born … of their fat" to God. This is the Jewish way of saying that he offered to God the best of the first born of his flock. They were fat and healthy animals without any physical defects. Instead of giving to God the worst animals he could find, he gave the best.

Oh, that we might learn the principle of giving only the best to God. Christians today ask: "What is the least I have to give to God? What is the cheapest way to serve God? What is the absolute minimum I have to do and still be considered a Christian?"

4. What a contrast between righteous Abel and wicked Cain. The text emphasizes that Cain only gave "an offering" of vegetables to God. There are two contrasts that should be pointed out:

   a. Cain did not give the "first fruits" of his garden to God. The ancient Jews noted that Cain ate the first fruit of his harvest. And now he brings some later fruit to offer to God. This shows that God was not first in his priorities.

   b. Cain did not bring the "fat" of the harvest to God, i.e. he did not offer the best vegetables he had. No, what he offered was some old, withered vegetables that he was not interested in eating. He gave the dregs of his labor to God.

      1. These sins so controlled Cain that he thought he could offer trash to God and get away with it. No wonder God rebuked him and told him to master these sins (Gen. 4:7).

      2. But Cain did not repent. Instead he murdered his brother in a fit of jealousy and rage. He buried the body and thought that no one saw what he had done. He did not see the God/man anywhere around and thus he concluded that even He did not know about the murder.

      3. Then it was time once again for the worship service. Adam and Eve and all their children came before the Lord to give their offerings. Cain showed up with some vegetables. But Abel did not show up. So, God asked Cain, "Where is Abel, your brother?"

      4. Cain pretended not to know where his brother was. But the Lord standing there revealed the murder and how Cain had buried his brother in the ground. Then God pronounced a curse upon Cain and sent him into exile.

      5. Notice, that the conversation between God and Cain took place in the presence of Adam, Eve and their other children. It is recorded in the Bible because it was not a secret conversation but a public one. One can only imagine the pain and grief of

Adam and Eve when they heard of the murder of Abel by their son Cain.

6. When we read that Cain was sent away "from the presence" of God (Gen. 4:16), this meant that the God/man would never appear before him again. Cain would never again be invited to the public worship of God. He lost his soul, his God and his family.

7. Genesis 4 goes on to record how Cain's descendants went into idolatry and such wickedness as polygamy and murder. The sins of their father were upon them, and they did as he did.

8. Lastly, notice that all these terrible events happened as a direct result of Cain's failure to honor the Lord with the best offerings he could give. By cheating God he cheated himself and brought divine judgment upon himself and his family.

9. Alas, there are some reading this who have the curse of God upon them because, like Cain, they offer only the dregs of their income to God! They do not give the first fruits of their labor to God but spend it on themselves. Will a man rob God? Yes, we can rob God by failing to give him the offerings that are due to Him. What we give to God is an indication of the depth of our love for Him (Lk. 7:37-50).

The Commentary of Heb. 11:4-6

The foundational principle is set forth in verse 6: "Without faith it is impossible to please God." This is illustrated at the beginning of the chapter by contrasting the offering of Abel to the offering of Cain.

First, notice that Abel gave a "more excellent sacrifice than Cain," i.e. he offered the first fruits of his labor and the best of his flock. He had his priority right. The Lord had first place in his heart and in his life.

Second, Abel's offering was a witness or testimony that he was a righteous and godly man. What you put into the offering basket is a witness to your character and spirituality.

Third, God Himself publicly testified that He accepted the offering of Abel. This divine testimony happened when the divine fire consumed the offering.

Fourth, Abel's sacrifice was accepted because he offered it "by faith." What he gave with his hand was acceptable because of what he had in his heart.

Fifth, Cain offered his sacrifice without faith. Thus Cain's offering did not please God for without faith it is impossible to please Him.

IV. The Story of Abraham and Melchizedek (Gen. 14:18-20)

A. The giving of 10 percent or a tithe to God also seems to go back to the Garden of Eden. It is mentioned in this story in such a nonchalant manner that all commentators, Jewish and Christian, acknowledge that the principle of tithing had been established long before Abraham.

B. That it was later made mandatory by Moses should not be used as a reason to reject it today. Tithing was practiced before the Old Covenant was given on Mt. Sinai. It was practiced by Jesus and the apostles.

C. To a new Christian, 10 percent seems almost an impossible amount to give to God. They do not see how they can possibly give a tithe and support themselves or their family. So they give to God the dregs of their income. They open their wallet to see what they have left after they have first spent their money on themselves. Their priorities are "Me first—God last." Jesus warned us about having "me first" priorities in Lk. 9:59-62.

D. But as they grow in grace and knowledge, they begin to see that God wants the first fruits of their labors and not just the dregs. The first thing they should do with their paycheck is to take 10 percent off the top and give it to God before they start spending their money on other things. Thus their priorities change to "God first, me last" (Matt. 6:33).

E. Then a miracle happens, they discover that when they tithe to God with the first fruits of their labor, they did not go bankrupt. Somehow God provided for their needs better than when they took the first fruits for themselves. Their trust in what Jesus said in Lk. 6:38 begins to grow. And as they grow in grace and knowledge of Christ, they learn that you cannot out-give God.

F. But then another miracle happens, they begin giving more than 10 percent to God, and, instead of ending up in the poor house, God blesses them even more. The tithe is the bare bones minimum of 10 percent. When you give above 10 percent that is called an offering.

G. Now by grace, they discover that when they give to God out of faith, hope and love, they begin to prosper as never before. This has been the testimony of saints down through the centuries and has been proven over and over again.

To this we must add that 2 Cor. 8:1-15; 9:6-15 give us other general principles that determine whether our giving is acceptable to God.

Chapter Nineteen

A Christian View of Time and Eternity

Introduction

Why bother studying the subject of time? Why think about it?

First, the ignorance and abuse of time leads to:

Ineffectiveness	Boredom
Depression	Poor organization
A Wasted Life	Frustration
Wrong Priorities	Indecision
Failure	Unnecessary Delays
Crisis	Lack of Preparation
Procrastination	Poverty

Second, America had at one time the highest standard of living in the world. This was the direct result of the Calvinistic view of time held by our Puritan forefathers. The reason why America is now losing its prosperity is the direct result of the loss of its Puritan or Calvinistic view of time. We need to regain the biblical view of time which was developed by the Reformers in order to make America great once again.

Example: 1. A biblical view of time sees work as the purpose of life. We live to work.

2. A humanist view of time sees leisure or pleasure as the purpose of life. We work to live.

CHRISTIAN	HUMANIST
"I live to work. God has a work for me to do. Leisure is good because it helps me do my work better. What I do during the week is very important to me. I want to do the best job I can."	"I work to live and to afford a nice vacation and retirement. I can hardly wait until the weekend. I want a job that gives me the most money for the least work in the shortest time. I get out of work whenever I can. Why should I work my tail off?"

CHRISTIAN	HUMANIST
"A penny saved is a penny earned."	"You cannot take it with you."
"A day's wages for a day's work."	"Life begins on Fridays."
"Only the best for God."	"Everybody else cheats."

PART I

Different Views of Time

I. The Liberal or Neo-Orthodox View:

God is transcendent but not immanent.

GOD

CREATION   The Space/Time Continuum (History)   THE END

ETERNITY	HISTORY	ETERNITY

Space/Time

Most modern liberal theologians believe that God is so transcendent above time that He cannot act in time. God is trapped outside of the space/time continuum and cannot act in history as a real agent. Therefore no supernatural events (i.e., miracles, prophecy, etc.) are possible in history.

Answer: The God who made this world is not limited by what He made.

In the Scriptures, God does act as a real agent in changing the course of history according to His will. In personal revelation God revealed His existence to men such as Abraham. By miracles of mercy, such as healings, or miracles of judgment, such as the Flood, God revealed His mercy and holiness. By sending His Son to redeem us in history, God revealed His love.

II. The Socinian View

God is immanent but not transcendent.

CREATION   THE END

ETERNITY	GOD HISTORY	ETERNITY

Space/Time

According to some people, God is not sovereign over or in time. History is not predetermined by God. What happens is a matter of "chance" or "luck." This means for some that "prophecy" is God's looking into the future to see how things turn out. He knows what man will do and then He plans around it.

For others, God is finite in His knowledge because he does not know what will happen in the future. They have made God finite because they want to make "luck" the ultimate force in the universe in order to make the freedom of man absolute. They know that there is not enough room in the universe for two ultimate forces. Either God or "luck" will be ultimate over history. So, they make "luck" infinite and God finite.

They not only make God finite in knowledge but also in power. God cannot interfere with man's absolute free will. God is trapped in the space/time continuum where man is the "god" of history.

Answer: This issue touches on the very godhood of God. In the Scriptures, God is revealed as being sovereign over history because He is infinite in knowledge and power. Thus He knows the beginning from the end. He is not ignorant or impotent like the dumb idols of the heathen. His knowledge of the future is true and certain for He has ordained whatsoever will come to pass.

The passage of full mention on the transcendence of God's sovereign power and knowledge over history is the book of Isaiah. See Isa. 40:10-31; 41:1-4, 21-29; 42:8-9; 43:9-13; 44:7-8; 45:1-13, 20-23; 46:5-13; 48:1-16, etc.

III. The Biblical View of Time

God is transcendent and immanent.

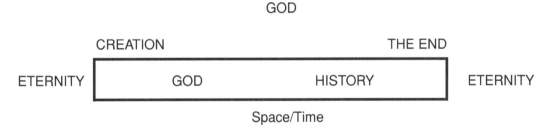

God is sovereign over and in time. History is His-Story. He has ordained all things. Prophecy is God telling us what will happen according to His plan. God is the ultimate force in the universe. His will is the ultimate power. There is no such thing as the pagan Greek gods' "chance," "luck" or "fate." God acts in history as a real agent. Miracles do happen.

PART II

The Biblical View of History

I. Reality is divided into two levels of being (Gen. 1:1).

GOD ⟷ THE CREATION

II. Being eternal, God is transcendent ABOVE time. He is not bound by time (2 Pet. 3:8).

III. Being sovereign, God is immanent IN time (Eph. 1:11). God is both transcendent above and immanent in time in a sovereign way.

The Sovereignty of God Over Time

I. General statements in Scripture (Job 14:5; Psa. 31:15; Prov. 16:4; Eccl. 3:1, 17; Dan. 4:34-37; Acts 1:7; 17:26, 31; Rom. 8:28; 11:36; Eph. 1:9-11; etc.)

II. Biblical examples of God's predetermined plan.
   A. The birth of Isaac (Gen. 18:14; 21:2).
   B. Joseph in Egypt (Gen. 45:4-8; 50:19).
   C The Exodus (Gen. 15:12-16; Exo. 9:5-6).
   D. The end of the world (Dan. 8:19; 11:27, 29, 35).
   E. Christ's incarnation and death (Gal. 4:4; Acts 2:23; Acts 4:27-28).

III. The universe is measured by space and time.

IV. Both space and time came into existence when God created the universe out of nothing (Gen. 1:1).

V. Time has a beginning, a middle and an end.

	The Beginning	Christ's	The End	
Eternity ←		Coming		→ Eternity
	(Gen. 1:1)	(Gal. 4:4)	(1 Cor. 15:24)	

Space/Time Continuum

VI. Time flows along a predetermined plan set by God from eternity. Thus time has meaning and significance.

VII. Since man was created in God's image, he is accountable to God for how he uses the time allotted to him (Job 14:5; Psa. 31:15; 2 Cor. 5:10).

VIII. To waste time is to sin (Matt. 20:6; Eph. 5:16).

PART III

The Eastern View of Time

America is now being swamped with an Eastern view of time. Time has no beginning, middle or end because it is eternal. Time repeats itself in endless cycles which have no ultimate purpose. It does not matter what you do with time. "Wasting" time is not a sin. There is no infinite/personal God to whom you are accountable. Only finite deities exist. Luck is the ultimate force in the universe.

PART IV

A Practical Understanding of Time

A. God gives us usually 70 to 80 years to complete the work assigned to us (Psa. 90:10).
B. We are accountable to God for all the time we spend on earth (2 Cor. 5:10).
C. Our lifetime can be divided into work and leisure.

D. The average person will spend over 100,000 hours in work.

E. The dignity and worth of work must be upheld (Gen. 2:15, 19; Prov. 10:4, 5; 13:4; 2 Thess. 3:6-15; Eph. 4:28).

F. The goodness of leisure must be guarded (Mk. 6:31; Sabbath; Holidays; Fourth commandment, etc.).

G. The evilness of slothfulness must be rebuked as sin. (The evilness of a welfare state) (Eph. 5:16).

SLUGGARD	SLOTHFULNESS	IDLENESS
Prov. 6:6-11	Prov. 12:24, 27	Prov. 21:27
10:26	15:19	Eccl. 10:18
13:4	18:9	Matt. 12:36
20:4	19:15, 24	20:3, 6
26:16	21:25	1 Tim. 5:13
	22:13	
	24:30, 33	
	26:13-15	
	Matt. 25:26	
	Rom. 12:11	
	Heb. 6:12	

I. Priorities and Time

A. Our priorities arise out of our values.

B. Our values are those things in life which we view as important.

C. A Christian looks to Scripture for his values and priorities and not to his own reason, feelings or experience.

D. What are our priorities as Christians?
   1. God: Matt. 6:33
   2. Your own soul: 1 Tim. 4:16
   3. Your family: 1 Tim. 5:8
   4. Your Church: Heb. 10:25
   5. Your job: Eph. 6:5-8
   6. Your community: Gal. 6:10
   7. Your nation: 1 Tim. 2:1-2
   8. Your world: Matt. 28:20-21

II. Practical Steps
    A. Memorize and display wise sayings:
        You never "find" time to do what is right, you must "make" time for it.
        Plan your work and work your plan.
        If you fail to plan, you plan to fail.
        Time like money must be spent wisely.
        If you aim at nothing, you are bound to hit it.
        Only one life, it will soon be past and only what is done for Christ shall last.
        Urgent things are seldom important, just as important things are seldom urgent.
    B. Get your priorities in line with Scripture.
    C. Make a list each day or once a week of the things you must do that day or week.
    D. Assign priorities to what you have listed.

        EXAMPLE: Has to be done today.
                          It would be nice if done.
                          Should be done but not urgent today.

    E. Allow no interruptions as much as possible.
    F. Start and finish one item before going on. Do one thing at a time.

III. Pitfalls
    A. Workaholic:
        1. Description: guilt feelings if idle
                      never lies around
                      always busy
                      too nervous to sit still
                      no day off or vacation
                      cannot rest or enjoy free time
                      tyranny of the "urgent"
                      cannot say "no"
                      type "A" heart attack

        2. Cure   realize it is alright to enjoy life and its pleasures
                      understand God gave us rest, recreation and leisure
                      humility to see that they are not indispensable
                      plan leisure
                      learn to say "no"

    B. The Slothful Person:
        1. Description: avoids work at all cost
                      loves sleep
                      loves to sit back and criticize others
                      has unfounded fears
                      poverty
                      thinks himself wiser than all
                      victim of "get rich quick" schemes
                      daydreams of wealth but does not labor for it

in debt all the time
takes the course of least resistance

2. Cure: emphasize responsibilities instead of rights
remember that we will all stand before Christ's Throne in Judgment
Take the rebukes of Scripture seriously
Ask others to help you learn to be accountable and active
Begin an exercise program
Seek the filling of the Spirit

Conclusion

God has given each of us only so many years on earth. All preparations for eternity must be made in this life. What we will be and do forever is determined by what we are and do now. Our time is shorter than we think (Rom. 13:11-14).

Chapter Twenty

How to Control Your Anger

Introduction

We are dealing with those who have the character defect of an angry personality.
Such a person:
(1) has a weakness or propensity to get angry easily
(2) has a bad habit of outbursts of anger
(3) has developed an angry spirit
(4) causes constant grief to those around him

The Biblical Material

I. His Nature
   A. Proverbs 12:16 "easily annoyed"
      1. reacts instead of acts
      2. speaks before thinks
      3. does not consider others
      4. does not overlook offenses
   B. Proverbs 14:16 "hotheaded"
   C. Proverbs 14:16 "reckless"
   D. Proverbs 14:17 "quick-tempered"
   E. Proverbs 15:18 "hot-tempered"
   F. Proverbs 21:9 "quarrelsome"
   G. Proverbs 21:19 "ill-tempered"
   H. Proverbs 22:24 "easily angered"
   I. Proverbs 27:3 "burdensome"
   J. Proverbs 27:4 "cruel"
   K. Proverbs 27:4 "overwhelming"
   L. Proverbs 29:11 "gives full vent to his anger"
   M. Ecclesiastes 7:9 "quickly provoked"

II. The Results of His Anger
   A. Proverbs 14:17 "does foolish things"
   B. Proverbs 17:17 "displays folly"
   C. Proverbs 15:1 "stirs up anger"
   D. Proverbs 15:18 "stirs up dissension"
   E. Proverbs 19:19 "gets in trouble repeatedly"
   F. Proverbs 29:22 "commits many sins"
   G. Proverbs 30:33 "produces strife"

III. Biblical Condemnation of Anger
  A. It is forbidden: Ephesians 4:31.
  B. It does not lead to righteousness: James 1:20.
  C. It leads to greater evils: 2 Corinthians 12:20; Colossians 3:8.
  D. It can reveal an unconverted heart: Galatians 5:19-21.

IV. How to Deal With It
  A. Accept biblical condemnation.
  B. Confess it to God and others.
  C. Identify it as a besetting sin.
  D. Realize you can only hope to control it, not vanquish it: Psalm 37:8.
  E. Cease from giving in to it: Psalm 37:8.
  F. Replace the vice with the virtue: Proverbs 12:16; 15:1, 18; 17:14; 19:11; 29:11; Ephesians 4:31-32.
  G. Ninety-nine percent of all anger is totally unjustifiable and leads to evil. We get angry when we make mistakes about moral issues or when we attack the motives of others. The following charts help us to make the distinction between mistakes and moral issues.

Mistakes/Accidents	
← ——————————— Responses ——————————— →	
godly	ungodly
accept it and go on	anger/evil speaking
overlook it	blames to hide the guilt
don't waste time/energy on it	justifies anger by: 1. bringing up past offenses 2. exaggerating the issue 3. impugning evil motives
don't let things bother you	leads to bitterness and self-centeredness

  H. Understanding the difference

Mistakes	vs.	Lying
non-moral		moral
ignorance or faulty memory		deliberate falsehood

Accidents	vs.	Offenses
non-moral		moral
did not intend or plan evil		deliberate evildoing
no forgiveness required		forgiveness needed

Sin	vs.	Culture
moral		manners
forgiveness needed		no forgiveness needed

Sin	vs.	Common Sense
Scripture		custom
morals		maturity
wickedness		stupidity or foolishness
forgiveness needed		no forgiveness needed

I. Anger is often related to the failure of someone to meet our needs. This is usually rooted in ignorance or misinformation.
   1. We confuse wants with needs.
      Needs: real necessities of life.
      Wants: what we think we need: real/imagined, true/false, etc.
   2. We forget men and women are different.
      Men usually have their physical needs in mind: good food, clean clothes, decent house, good love life, etc.
      Women have their emotional needs in mind: communication, togetherness, security, appreciation, etc.
         When a wife tells her husband, "You are not meeting my needs," he often says, "What do you mean? You have a roof over your head, food to eat and clothes to wear!"
   3. Meeting the needs of someone does not mean pampering to their wants. You can spoil a child/spouse by meeting their wants. Sometimes saying "No!" is the way to meet someone's true needs.
   4. Try to understand your spouse in terms of his/her needs, not yours.

J. Wrong expectations can lead to anger. We make invalid demands on others and cause strife.

A Special Note on Sensitivity:

One of the great errors of our day is the idea that our feelings are the most important thing in life.

Happy feelings = the greatest good

Hurt feelings = the greatest evil

If someone hurts our feelings, we take it for granted that they have "sinned" against us. They were not "sensitive." But what does the Bible say about "sensitivity?"

1. The Bible never mentions it. It is never referred to as a virtue or a vice! Evidently, God does not rate sensitivity as high as some do today. Insensitivity is not listed as a sin.

2. The "sensitivity" training that we have all received comes from a humanistic psychologism and is in clear conflict with Scripture.

Scripture	Psychologism
God-centered	man-centered
objective	subjective
sin = violation of God's Law	sin = hurt feelings
hurt feelings necessary sometimes	hurt feelings always wrong
no moral offense	moral offense
no forgiveness	forgiveness needed

3. Sensitivity is not usually defined as a virtue in dictionaries.

a. Britannica Dictionary: "1. Easily affected by outside operation or influence; touchy; easily offended."

b. Webster's Dictionary: "Irritability: capacity of being easily hurt; awareness of ... the emotions of others."

Summary

Christians look to Scripture to define "sin." Thus we reject the modern feeling-centered psychologism. God's Law and not our feelings is the only path to holiness and maturity.

1. If someone offends me, must he ask for my forgiveness?

Not necessarily! Offenses must be real/not imagined, true/not false, biblical/not opinion, important/not trivial. Someone can be offended for no good reason.

Biblical examples where no forgiveness was needed:

David: Psalm 35:7

Nehemiah: Nehemiah 4:7-8

Jesus: Matthew 15:12-14

Paul: Acts 21:27-32

The Gospel: Galatians 5:11

If we know we have truly sinned against someone according to the Bible, then go ask for forgiveness (Matthew 5:23).

2. Should not a husband and wife always agree?

   Two adults are going to see things differently at times. They should be able to disagree without being disagreeable or attacking each other's character. The man must make the final decision as he must answer to God for it. Beware of trying to manipulate your mate.

   "If you really understood me, you would agree with me."

   "If you really loved me, you would agree with me."

   "You are not listening! If you did, you would agree with me."

   "I will stop nagging when you agree!"

3. Godly advice from Proverbs:

   a. Virtues to seek: wisdom, understanding, patience and prudence simply mean maturity.

   b. Things to do:

      Overlook most offenses: 12:16; 19:11

      Do not snap back: 15:1; 26:4

      Calm things down: 15:18

      Control your temper: 16:32

      Drop trivial issues: 17:14

      Avoid angry people: 22:24-25

      Do not try to reason with an angry person: 29:8-9

Conclusion

To control the "demon" of anger is a lifelong task for those who must bear the burden of this besetting sin. While it remains, it must not reign but be continually put to death by the Spirit.

Chapter Twenty-One

The Biblical Concept of Guidance

Introduction

The issue of divine guidance is important for two reasons.

First, the person who does not seek divine guidance for life-changing decisions is, no doubt, unconverted and on his way to a Christless eternity (Rom. 3:18).

This Man is "ungodly" because:
1. God is missing.
2. God's Word is missing.

It does not matter how wisely you have made decisions. If you do not seek divine guidance, you are not saved (Rom. 3:18).

I. Foundational Principles
   A. We are not to seek God's secret and sovereign will. Moses declared that the secret things belong to God and not to us (Deut. 29:29). Nowhere in Scripture are we promised that God will tell what He has decreed concerning the future. Since God's sovereign plan will come to pass whether we know about it or not, it is a waste of time to seek it.
   1. You can never get out of God's sovereign will (Eph. 1:11; Rom. 8:28).
   2. God's sovereign will may be different from His revealed will.
      Example: While Abraham's sacrifice of Isaac was God's revealed will, it was not His secret plan (Gen. 22:22; 10-12).

3. Beware of occult attempts to discern God's secret will (Deut. 18:9-13).

B. We must avoid extreme positions on guidance.

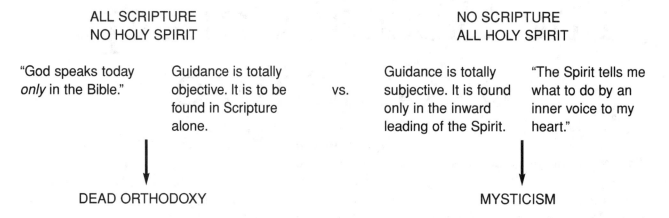

ALL SCRIPTURE
NO HOLY SPIRIT

NO SCRIPTURE
ALL HOLY SPIRIT

"God speaks today *only* in the Bible."   Guidance is totally objective. It is to be found in Scripture alone.   vs.   Guidance is totally subjective. It is found only in the inward leading of the Spirit.   "The Spirit tells me what to do by an inner voice to my heart."

DEAD ORTHODOXY   MYSTICISM

C. We should never pray for guidance when Scripture is clear.

Objective clear guidance given in Scripture should not even be prayed about. The Laws and doctrines of the Bible are to be obeyed.

Example: It is not right to pray and ask about the following things:

1. A Christian girl prays about a non-Christian boy, "Lord, is he the one I should marry?" (2 Cor. 6:14-18).
2. "Lord, should I give money to the Church?" (Mal. 3:7-10).
3. "Lord, should I go to church?" (Heb. 10:24-25).
4. "Lord, should I read my Bible?" (1 Pet. 2:1-2).
5. "Lord, should I pray?" (Luke 18:1).

Note: Some people will talk about seeking guidance in order to escape obedience!

II. The Means By Which God Guides His People

A. Scripture is to decide all issues of doctrine and morals (2 Tim. 3:16, 17; Gal. 1:6-9). This is why we reject the Mormons, Jehovah's Witnesses, Seventh-day Adventists, Moonies and all other various cults which have prophets or prophetesses who give "new" revelations. The canon of the Bible is closed. This also means that when it comes to doctrine and morals, you do not just "pray" about it to see if you "feel" the doctrine is true or false. You must study the **Bible** and believe what it says. Do not let your feelings be the ultimate judge of truth in the place of Scripture.

B. When you are faced with a choice involving several good options, there are several things which you should take into account before deciding. The order is not absolute.

1. Biblical principles.

Are there any principles in Scripture which bear on the issue? Find them and apply them to the question.

2. Sanctified reason and common sense.

God expects you to use the mind that He has given you. Why do you think that He gave us the book of Proverbs? Most of guidance is resolved by good old common sense. Instead of the present day "voodoo" guidance of "voices," "spirits" and "prophesyings," make a pro and con list and make the wisest choice after asking God to guide your mind.

PRO	CON

3. Check out Providence, i.e. the situation (James 4:13-15).
   Do not count your chickens before they hatch! Deal with reality and not with fears of what might happen.
4. Ask yourself how you feel about the choices, for God may have placed His desire in your heart (Phil. 2:13).
5. Seek the advice of your Elders and godly friends (Prov. 12:15). In the counsel of the many, there is safety.

III. What is Needed to Receive Normal Guidance?

"Get right with God."
Psa. 24:3-5

1. You need ears to hear and eyes to see (Matt. 13:9; Rev. 2:7; Eph. 1:18; Psa. 66:18).

"Pray for wisdom."

2. You need wisdom from God (James 1:5-8).

"Rededicate your life to the Lord."

3. You must be surrendered to Christ and be transformed (Rom. 12:1-2).

"Trust in the Lord."

4. You must trust in the Lord. Trusting is an act of your will (Prov. 3:5-6; Psa. 37:3-7; 55:22).

"Ask for the filling of the Spirit.

5. You must be filled with the Spirit (Eph. 5:18; Acts 6:2-4; Lk. 11:13).

Pray: "Ask"
      "Seek"
      "Knock"
      (Luke 11:9-10)

6 You must pray to God and listen to God while you pray.

"Be submissive to those over you."
Rom. 13:1-3: State
Heb. 13:17: Church
Eph. 6:1: Parents
Eph. 5:21-22: Home
Eph. 6:5-8: Business

7. You must be under authority for God may tell those over you what you should do without telling you. This is to test your spirit for submission.

IV. There are several questions which you must ask when faced with life-changing decisions.
    A. Will this course of action or decision:
        1. Make me a more dedicated and spiritual Christian?
           Is it "unto edification?" (1 Cor. 14:26)
        2. Develop the qualities of Christ's moral character in my life? (Rom. 8:29; Gal. 5:22-23)
        3. Harm the spiritual health of my family? (Josh. 24:15)
        4. Shame the name and church of Christ? (2 Sam. 12:14)
        5. Glorify God? (1 Cor. 10:31)
        6. Demonstrate to the world that God exists and is powerful? (Matt. 5:16)
        7. Hinder or enable me to minister to others by my spiritual gift? (1 Pet. 4:10)
        8. Is this decision "decent" and "in order"? (1 Cor. 14:40)
    B. What would Jesus do in this situation? (1 John 2:6)
V. At times, you will have to fast and pray (Ezra 8:21-23).

Conclusion

Guidance is practical. Do not make mountains out of molehills! Insignificant issues should not involve a great deal of time. So, do not waste time on non-moral or non-doctrinal issues. If it is between equally good choices, use the mind that God gave you. You can even flip a coin in such cases (Pro. 16:33). There is no moral issue involved in choosing blue over brown socks! Guidance simply means that we should make the most rational and wise choice possible.

Chapter Twenty-Two

The Biblical Concept of Fasting

1) Foundational Principles
   a) Fasting is the deliberate foregoing of food and water. It can last for hours, days or weeks.
   b) Fasting, in and of itself, does not merit God's grace. It is an empty work. It is what you do while fasting that determines whether you grow in grace.
   c) While fasting, you should spend your time in prayer, Bible reading and meditation. The mere foregoing of food without prayer, Bible reading or meditation is dieting and is not to be viewed as biblical fasting.

2) Old Testament Fasting
   Individuals, congregations and entire nations fasted in Old Testament times (Psa. 35:13; Neh. 9:1; Jonah 3:4-10).

3) New Testament Fasting
   a) Jesus, the apostles and the early church fasted (Matt. 4:2; Acts 14:23; 13:2-3).
   b) Jesus assumed that all who followed Him would fast as well as pray (Matt. 6:16; 9:14-15).
   c) Jesus gave rules to govern our fasting (Matt. 6:16-18).

4) Why People Fast
   a) The purpose of fasting is to spend time alone with God and to deal with spiritual issues without the normal distractions of life.

THE KEY CONCEPT:
GIVING TOTAL, UNDIVIDED CONCENTRATION AND
ATTENTION TO SPIRITUAL ISSUES

   b) Some specific reasons for fasting:
      i)   to discern God's will in a specific matter (Judges 20:26; Acts 14:23)
      ii) repentance for sin (Neh. 9:1; 1 Sam. 7:6; 2 Sam. 12:16-22)
      iii) out of concern for the work of God (Neh. 1:4)
      iv) to gain spiritual alertness to overcome temptation and satanic attacks (Matt. 4:2)
      v)   for deliverance and protection (2 Chron 20:3; Ezra 8:21-23)
      vi) to humble yourself before God (Psa. 69:10-11, 13)
      vii) as part of worship (public and private) (Luke 2:37; Acts 13:2-3)
      viii) because of deep sorrow (1 Sam. 31:13; 2 Sam. 12:16)
      ix) to exorcise stubborn demons (Matt. 17:21)

5) Defining God's Purpose for Your Life
  a) God's will for all Christians is:
    i) Their sanctification (1 Thess. 4:3)
    ii) Their spiritual maturity (Gal. 4:19; Col. 1:28)
    iii) Their conformity to the moral character of Christ (Rom. 8:28, 29)
  b) Everything which happens to you, good and evil, is part of this overall or ultimate will of God to recreate you in the image of Christ (Rom. 8:28).
  c) Thus the success or failure of your life as a man, woman or young person does not depend on:
    i) The money or possessions you have
    ii) The honor or fame you receive
    iii) The power or influence you wield
    iv) The pleasures you enjoy

"Success is determined by checking to see if you have built the principles of God's Word in your life so that you are equipped to understand and follow the promptings of the Holy Spirit in knowing how to respond to any situation with Christ-like attitudes."—Bill Gothard

Chapter Twenty-Three
Spiritual Dryness

One of the most frustrating problems for the Christian is when he becomes spiritually dry. This means that he has run out of spiritual joy, zeal and power. Even when he reads the Bible or prays, it is like pumping a dry well. Nothing happens! What can be done about it?

Principles of Recovery

I. The first thing to do about spiritual dryness is to admit to yourself that you are dry. Do not try to cover it up by ignoring it (Pro. 28:13). If you ignore it, it will only get worse (Psa. 32:3-4).

II. The second thing to do is to go to God and tell Him that you are dry (Pro. 28:13; Psa. 32:5-7; 1 John 1:9).

III. The third thing to do is to realize that spiritual dryness is a normal problem in the Christian life. Every Christian experiences it (1 Cor. 10:13; Psa. 38; 42; 63; 69:1-3; 119:131, 176; 143:1, 4, 6-11).

IV. Resolve to correct the problem by following biblical directives.

A. Generate hope by believing the promises of God (Psa. 42:5, 11; Isa. 55:1-3; Rev. 22:17).

B. If you are dry because a particular sin has plugged up your well and the water cannot get through, repent of it and forsake it (Pro. 28:13; Psa. 38:18; 119:133).

C. Wait upon the Lord (Psa. 38:15). Do not give God a deadline. Realize He is more concerned with developing your character than making your life easy (Rom. 5:3-5).

D. Remember God (Psa. 42:6; 63:6). Do not leave Him out of the problem. If you remember how big He is, your problems will become smaller.

E. Earnestly seek God day and night (Psa. 63:1). Do not give up so quickly.

F. Praise God (Psa. 63:4).

G. Sing to God (Psa. 63:5, 7; 69:30-31).

H. Remember the days of old (Psa. 143:5). Review God's mighty acts in your life (Psa. 42:4; Rev. 2:5) and in the lives of other saints (Psa. 145).

I. Confess your problem to others who can pray with you and for you (James 5:16).

J. Attend all church meetings, particularly prayer meetings and small group studies or fellowship (Heb. 10:25).

K. Read exciting biographies of famous Christians to stir up your desire to live for Christ (Hebrews 11).

L. Go to a rescue mission, nursing home, Christian coffee house or get on a visitation team where you can witness to the lost. As you witness to them, you will once again get excited about the Gospel (Acts 1:8).

M. Listen to good Christian music such as Bach, Handel, Mendelssohn, etc., or black Gospel music. Be stirred in your emotions by such rich music (1 Sam. 16:14-23).

N. Read much in the Psalms, for David was often dry in his spiritual life.

O. Have a physical checkup, take vitamins, begin to exercise, take a vacation, get some extra sleep, etc. Beware that at times our "dryness" is due to fatigue or other physical problems (Matt. 9:12).

P. Finally, remember that the soul has seasons as does nature. There is the winter of the soul as well as the bright summer. We usually experience a "low" after a "high" (1 Kings 18-19). Expect to have dry periods as part of the cycle of spiritual life.

Conclusion

When feeling down, keep looking up by repeating to yourself the biblical phrase, "And it came to pass." Your dry spell will pass away one day. Your weeping may endure for the night, but joy cometh in the morning. The darkness will give way to the light and the refreshing rains of blessing will be yours once again.

Chapter Twenty-Four

How to Renew Your Love for Christ

Introduction

One of the greatest problems in the Christian life is losing our fervent love for Jesus Christ. We can gradually drift away from the wholehearted and fervent love commitment to Christ without consciously realizing what is happening. This is why the author of Hebrews warned us:

> "Encourage one another day after day, as long as it is still 'today,' lest any one of you be hardened by the deceitfulness of sin" (Heb. 3:13).

Losing your love for Christ can be a slow and silent process which goes on unnoticed until the bitter fruits "suddenly" appear. It would be better to set up an "early warning system" which would reveal the process to us than to wake up with the problem upon us.

I. The Problem: A Lost Love (Rev. 2:1-4)

A. You may be very active in church work but still lose your love for Christ (v. 2a).

B. You may live a separated life and have Christian friends but still lose your love for Christ (v. 2b).

C. You may be zealous in defending the truth against all heresies but still lose your love for Christ (v. 2c).

D. You may "keep the faith" in spite of persecution but still lose your love for Christ (v.3).

Conclusion

Everything externally is properly in place.	Internally your love for Christ is gone or weak.
TRUE √	TRUE √

II. How to Discern the Problem: Discern the process by learning the signs of losing your love for Christ. Identify it early and deal with it seriously.

Twenty-Five Signs of a Lost Love

1. When you lack concern for the problem.
2. When you switch primary and secondary motives.

PRIMARY MOTIVE	SECONDARY MOTIVE
Love to Christ	Love for people
John 14:15	Duty to God
John 14:23	Dedication to church
	Fear of shame/embarrassment
	Guilt feelings
	Keeping up appearances

3. When you no longer yearn for or delight in private times of communion with Christ.
4. When your thoughts no longer fly to spiritual things when your mind is free but they fly instead to self or sin.
5. When you begin to excuse "little sins" as a matter of personality or situation.
6. When you regret giving your tithes and offerings and begin to cut back due to greed.
7. When you allow bitterness to arise through failed expectations and violated rights.
8. When you gossip or slander and ignore Matthew 18:15-20.
9. When you begin to let witnessing opportunities slip by due to feeling embarrassed or "funny."
10. When you hold grudges and "cannot" forgive others.
11. When you feel uncomfortable around spiritual Christians and cannot look them in the eyes.
12. When you associate with "carnal Christians" who, like you, avoid spiritual discussions which search the conscience.
13. When you compete with other Christians for power or recognition.
14. When you "cannot" be transparently honest with others but wear a "mask" of spirituality.
15. When you no longer "feel" God's love (Rom. 5:5; Jude 21).
16. When you do not see specific answers to your prayers.
17. When you pray in generalities instead of praying specifically.
18. When you experience general moodiness, anxiety, depression and insecurity.
19. When you are quick to seek advice from people instead of going to Christ.
20. When you start losing your temper and are impatient with others.
21. When you placate your conscience by "feeling bad" about your lack of spirituality but do not go on to take positive steps of repentance.
22. When you return to the sins of preconversion days.
23. When you feel no compassion or concern for others.
24. When you complain and murmur.
25. When you are defensive when others exhort you about your backsliding.

III. How to Cure the Problem: Twelve Cures
   1. Get right with God by confession and repentance (Prov. 28:13; 1 John 1:9).
   2. Recommit yourself to Christ (Rom. 12:1-2).
   3. Get right with those against whom you have sinned or toward whom you have been unforgiving and bitter (Matt. 5:23-24; 18:15-17; Eph. 4:31-32).

4. Get alone and meditate on the kind of Christian life you used to experience when your love for Christ was fervent: "Remember from where you have fallen" (Rev. 2:5a).
5. Repent of what you have become (Rev. 2:5b).
6. Repeat the activities which grew out of your first love (Rev. 2:5c).
7. Read exciting and inspiring Christian books, particularly biographies (Jude 20).
8. Confess the problem to the church and ask for prayer (James 5:16).
9. Associate with spiritual people.
10. Fast and pray.
11. Spend time in private worship by listening to Christian music which both inspires and humbles you (1 Sam. 16:14-23; cf. Col. 3:15-16).
12. Go and witness to non-Christians (Rescue missions, door-to-door visitation, neighbors, etc.).

Conclusion

Our love to the Lord Jesus must be constantly reaffirmed as the main motivation in the Christian life. We should love Him, for He first loved us!

Chapter Twenty-Five
Vows

The subject of vows has received much attention in the last few years due to various family life conferences where the making of vows has been stressed.

While the emphasis on vows is proper, the majority of people do not understand what the Bible says about the making and keeping of vows. Thus, much harm and confusion have resulted from people making foolish and invalid vows. Indeed, some current ideas on vows result in bondage and not liberty. This bondage is not of God's Spirit, for where the Spirit is, there is liberty (2 Cor. 3:17).

1) What is a vow?
   A vow is a voluntary contract or covenant between two persons in which the one who makes the vow promises to give or do certain things for the one to whom the vow is given if certain conditions are met by him.
2) What are the ingredients of a vow?
   Observe "the principle of first mention" in Jacob's vow (Gen. 28:20-22).
   a) Vower: Jacob
   b) Conditions: divine protection, provision, guidance and a safe return home.
   c) Promises: make YHWH his only God, build a house for YHWH at Bethel, give YHWH a special tithe of all he owns.
   d) The one to whom the vow is made: God.
3) What points should be remembered about vows?
   a) Vows are voluntary. Not to vow is not a sin (Deut. 23:22).
   b) In order to be valid, a vow must be accepted by both parties.
   c) Vows are specific and not vague. They usually concern a definite time period which has a beginning and an end.
   d) Vows concern what you are going to give to God if He meets your condition. A mere prayer to God for Him to enable you to do some task is not a vow.
4) Does God ever reject vows made to Him? Yes. God automatically rejects vows which concern:
   a) Things forbidden by Scripture (Deut. 18:10; Judges 11:30)
   b) Things which are impossible by nature
   c) Sins of the spirit or attitude and besetting sins
      Example: While you may vow not to commit adultery physically with your body, never vow that you will never again commit adultery in your mind. Such vows are doomed to failure.
   d) Ill-gotten money (Deut. 24:18)
   e) Promises which do not cost you anything in terms of sacrifice or price (Lev. 22:21-25)
5) What kind of things did biblical characters promise to give God?
   a) To make God their only God (Gen. 28:22)
   b) To give themselves to full-time divine service (Num. 6:2-21)
   c) To dedicate members of their family to full-time divine service (Lev. 27:2; 1 Sam. 1:11)
   d) Special animal sacrifices (Lev. 7:16; Num. 15:3, 8)
   e) Destruction of enemies (Num. 21:2-3)
   f) Special tithe offerings (Deut. 12:11)
   g) Public testimony in the congregation (Psa. 22:22; 56:12; 61:8; 66:13-20; 116:14)

6) What did these people want from God?
   a) A baby (1 Sam. 1:11)
   b) Military victory (Judges 11:30)
   c) Divine protection, provision and guidance (Gen. 28:20-22), etc.
7) Are all vows binding? No.
   a) All vows are rejected by God if they are either foolish or wicked.
   b) All vows which those in authority over you feel are wrong are not binding. Example: Vows can be nullified by parents or husbands (Num. 30:2-16).
8) Are valid vows binding? Yes.
   You must fulfill your promises if God meets your conditions (Deut. 23:21; Ecc. 5:4-7).
9) Are vows only related to Moses' law, and thus no longer valid to make?
   Vows were made to God before the Patriarchs (Job 22:27), by the Patriarchs before Moses (Gen. 28:20-22), under Moses (Psa. 22:25), and by the Apostle Paul after Moses (Acts 18:18; 21:23-24, 26). Vows are still valid today.
10) But, did not Jesus condemn all vows in Matt. 5:34-36; 23:16-22?
    In the N.T. the Greek word for "vow" is *euche*. The Greek word for "swear" in Matt. 5 and Matt. 23 is *omnuo* Thus, Jesus is not referring to vows but to swearing by the temple, gold or other valuable things to emphasize the truthfulness of a statement. Today people say, "May God strike me dead if I am not telling the truth." Jesus was condemning all exaggerated and blasphemous oaths and swearings that invoked the name of God.
11) Can Hebrew Christians make Jewish vows like Paul did in Acts? No/Yes
    No, if they place themselves under bondage to Moses' law or view the ceremonial laws still valid. Christ has fulfilled all such things and we cannot return to the beggarly elements of the Old Covenant (Hebrews and Galatians).
    Yes, if it is for cultural conformity, not for spiritual profit. Cutting your hair or being circumcised will not spiritually profit anyone anything (1 Cor. 7:19; Gal. 6:13; Phil. 3:3). A Christian can observe any cultural norm which does not violate N.T. principles or involve one in demonic rites.

Conclusion

We are warned in Ecc. 5:4-7 not to make vows quickly or foolishly. A New Testament believer can vow unto God things which will bring glory to God and spiritual profit to man. But let all beware of foolish vows which God rejects.

Chapter Twenty-Six
Divine Forgiveness

We need to understand God's forgiveness in order to maintain a clear conscience before God and to be able to forgive others (1 John 1:9). Judicial forgiveness refers to that once for all act of forgiveness which takes place in justification. By it we escape hell. Parental forgiveness refers to the need for daily cleansing. By it we escape chastisement. Our focus is parental forgiveness.

I. The Condition of Forgiveness (1 John 1:9a)
   A. A word of condition: "If"—You must take the initiative to seek divine forgiveness.
   B. A word of contrition: "If we confess."
      1. We are not to conceal our sins but to reveal our sins (Prov. 28:13; Psa. 32:5).
      2. We must take full responsibility for our sins and refuse to shift the blame to others (Psa. 32:5; Prov. 28:13).
      3. We must repent of our sins.
   C. A word of conviction: "If we confess our sins." The word "sins" means specific sins.

II. The Basis of Forgiveness (1 John 1:9b)
   A. The basis for forgiveness is found in God and not in man. "He is"
   B. God's faithfulness to His Covenant is a basis of forgiveness (Heb. 8:8, 12). "He is faithful"
   C. God's righteousness before the Law is a basis of forgiveness (1 John 2:1-2). "He is faithful and righteous"

III. The Nature of Forgiveness (1 John 1:9c)
   A. Removal of guilt (position) — "to forgive us"
   B. Removal of pollution (condition) — "to cleanse us"

IV. The Perfection of Forgiveness (1 John 1:9d)
   A. God forgives us for the "sins" we have confessed.
      1. Sins of commission: when we do what we are not supposed to do (1 John 3:4).
      2. Sins of omission: when we fail to do what we are supposed to do (James 4:17).
   B. God also forgives us for all the other sins which we do not know of or have forgotten (Psa. 19:12-14). He cleanses us from "all unrighteousness."

Conclusion

We can obtain daily forgiveness from God because of His faithfulness to the covenantal promise of forgiveness which He proclaimed in the New Covenant and because Christ has fulfilled all the demands of the Law and has thereby provided a righteousness for us (Phil. 3:9).

Chapter Twenty-Seven
Biblical Obedience

I. What is obedience?

    A. Obedience involves a proper attitude toward God's Law.
        1. We are to love, respect and delight in the Law of God (Psa. 119:97; Rom. 7:22). In other words, be positive and not negative toward God's Law.
        2. The key to a proper attitude: to see that the Law is for man's sake. It is the setting forth of the principles of successful living and moral freedom (Josh. 1:7- 8; Psa. 119:9).

    B. Obedience is not optional but essential for assurance of salvation.
        1. Jesus taught this (Matt. 7:21-22; Mk. 10:17-22).
        2. The Apostles taught this (Heb. 5:9; James 1:22-25; Acts 5:22).

    C. Obedience is one of the clearest tests of salvation because it is the greatest evidence of love to Jesus (John 14:15, 21; 1 John 2:3, 4; Luke 6:46).

LOVE   ⟶   OBEDIENCE

II. Why should we obey God?

    A. Biblical obedience is based on the fact that we are the servants (slaves) of God and that He is our Master and Lord (1 Cor. 6:19-20; Psa. 119:124, 125).

    B. Threefold purpose of obedience:
        1. To grow in wisdom and character (Proverbs).
        2. To gain protection from Satan (1 Sam. 15:23).
        3. To get clear guidance from God (Prov. 3:5-6).

    C. Ten facts on obedience:
        1. It is the goal of election (1 Pet. 1:2).
        2. It is better than sacrifice (1 Sam. 15:22).
        3. It reveals commitment to God (Exo. 24:7).
        4. It brings God's blessing (Deut. 11:26-28).
        5. It proves your love to God (Deut. 13:1-4).
        6. It is something we "ought" to do (Acts 5:29).
        7. It is what Christ learned (Heb. 5:8).
        8. It brings the power of the Spirit (Acts 5:32).
        9. It reveals whose servant you are (Rom. 6:16).
      10. It purifies the soul (1 Pet. 1:22).

III. How do we obey God?
    Step 1: We must distinguish between the demands of tradition and the commands of God's Law

if we are to focus our obedience correctly and to experience a conscience free from unnecessary guilt feelings (Mk. 7:1-13; Col. 2:16; Gal. 5:1).

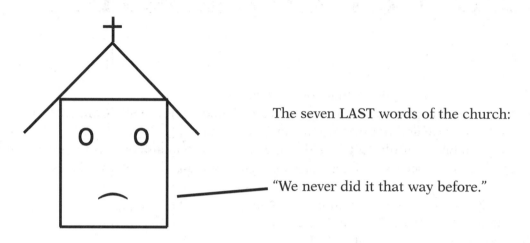

The seven LAST words of the church:

"We never did it that way before."

WHAT ARE YOU?		
TRADITION CENTERED QUESTIONS	vs.	BIBLE CENTERED QUESTIONS
What do I FEEL about it?		Is it SCRIPTURAL?
Did I ever do it BEFORE?		Is it unto EDIFICATION?
Are OTHERS DOING IT?		Does it GLORIFY GOD?
Is this something NEW?		Is it CHRIST CENTERED?
Why CHANGE?		Is it EFFECTIVE in COMMUNICATION?
Cannot we REMAIN the same?		Are sinners CONVERTED?
What will others THINK?		Are saints BLESSED?

Step 2: Draw upon God's power for your obedience by seeking and experiencing the filling of the Spirit (Eph. 5:18).
Step 3: OBEY IN FAITH. If you doubt what you are about to do, do not do it (Rom. 14:22-23).
Step 4: Obey God regardless of your feelings (1 Pet. 1:14).
Step 5: Obey God and leave the consequences to Him (Acts 4:19).
Step 6: Learn how to resist the Devil and to overcome temptation (James 4:7; Matt. 26:41; 1 Cor. 10:13).
    a. Submit to God
    b. Resist Satan by Scripture
    c. Take God's way to escape

Conclusion

Obedience cannot be ignored in the name of "grace." God's grace leads us toward obedience, not away from it (Eph. 2:10).

Chapter Twenty-Eight

A Christian View of Values

I. The Nature of Values:
   A. Definition: Your "values" refer to those things in life which you feel are so important to you that you are willing to sacrifice time, money and energy in the pursuit of them.
   B. Your values are of two kinds:
      1. Secular values: Those values shared with all people: physical health, marriage, children, career, money, cars, clothing, land, a house, etc.
      2. Spiritual values: Those values shared with all Christians: the Bible, prayer, church attendance, Christian books, the salvation of your children, a Christian home, missions, revival, etc.
II. The Origin of Values: There are four possible sources for your values
   A. The World: the culture around you (Rom. 12:2)
   B. The Flesh: your feelings and tastes (Eph. 2:2)
   C. The Devil: Satanic influences (Eph. 2:2)
   D. The Lord: the Bible (2 Tim. 3:15-16)
III. The Wrong Values Can Destroy You (Gal. 5:19-21; 1 Tim. 6:6-12)
IV. The Priority of Values
   A. You will unconsciously or consciously rate your values in the order of their importance to you at this time in your life.
   B. The Bible demands that you value the things of God as more important than anything else in life: Matt. 6:24-34; 10:24-42; 11:28-29; 16:24-26; 19:16-30; 22:36-40; 28:19-20; Lk. 6:46-49; 9:57-62; Rom. 12:1-2; 13:11-14; 1 Cor. 10:31; Gal. 5:22-23; Eph. 5:18f; 1 Tim. 2:15; 1 Pet. 3:15; Jude 20-21, etc.
   C. You are spiritually healthy when you have your values in the right order.

      Jesus first
      Others second
      Yourself last
   D. You are spiritually unhealthy when you have your values in the wrong order.

      Yourself first   Others first
      Others second   Yourself second
      Jesus last   Jesus last
V. The Importance of Values
   Your values reveal what is really in your heart. The way you rate your values reveals what is really in your heart. For example, someone may say he believes in the local church, evangelism, apologetics, etc., but what do his actions reveal?

Chapter Twenty-Nine

How to Deal With Temptation

I. What Is a Temptation?

Definition: A person is tempted when one or both of the following is true:

No. 1. The lusts and corruptions in the heart rise up and seek to capture the mind with rationalizations or blindness, the emotions with cravings for pleasure-sins and the will with urgings to act at once for sin (James 1:13-15; Gal. 5:17-21; Matt. 15:18-20).
Note: This kind of temptation involves us in sin. We must confess it as such.
No. 2. A person is tempted when he finds himself in a situation which provokes his lusts or in which he is actually solicited to sin by sources outside of his own heart.
A. This kind of temptation is not sin at first. We live in a sinful world exposed to all kinds of evil influences (Matt. 4:1; 2 Tim. 2:22).
B. You cannot keep the birds from flying over your head, but you can keep them from building a nest on it.
C. The first look is not sin. It is the second, third, fourth, etc., look!

II. Why Are Christians Tempted?
A. We are tempted as Christians because no Christian is rendered perfect or sinless in his nature at his new birth or at any time during his life. Every Christian is still a sinner by nature and by his acts, words and deeds until he dies or until Christ returns (1 Thess. 5:23).
   1. "Sinless perfection" is a myth as well as unscriptural (Rom. 3:23b; Rom. 7:14-25; Phil. 3:12-14; Gal. 5:17; 1 John 1:8 (nature), 9 (confession), 10 (practice).
   2. "Sinless perfection" actually means that some Christians no longer need the blood of Jesus or the Holy Spirit!
   3. "Sinless perfection" does not square with the experience of the best saints in the Bible or history. (Noah, Abraham, David, Peter, Paul, Barnabas, Augustine, Luther, Calvin, Whitefield, Edwards, etc.)
   4. The filling of the Spirit does not make anyone sinless. The Spirit can give us victory over this or that particular sin—He does not enable us to have victory over all sin all of the time.
   5. Entire sanctification awaits the second coming of Christ (1 Thess. 5:23).
B. Christians are tempted because Satan uses all his schemes to get Christians to sin. By this he hinders God's work and promotes his own (Matt. 4:1-3; 1 Thess. 3:5). Sometimes we forget that we are involved in a spiritual battle (Eph. 6:10-18).
C. Christians are tempted because the world (i.e., the evil within human society or culture) tries to draw and to squeeze the Christian into sinful patterns of living (Rom. 12:1-2).
   1. We once lived according to the fashions and fads of the world (Eph. 2:1-3).

2. Now that we are converted, we must not "love the world" (1 John 2:15-16) or allow the world to squeeze us into its own mold (Rom. 12:1-2).

3. Nowhere more visible does the world squeeze many Christians into a worldly mold than in the area of clothing. Yet, God is concerned how and with what we clothe ourselves. God's vision includes the way a Christian is to dress.

   Fact No. 1: God has been concerned with clothing ever since man fell into sin.

   a. After the fall: Gen. 3:21

   b. Under the Law: Num. 15:37-41

   c. Under the Gospel: 1 Tim. 2:9-10

   Fact No. 2: God has set forth two basic guidelines for clothing.

   a. Your clothing must clearly reveal the distinction between male and female (Deut. 22:5).

   b. Your clothing must be modest; i.e., not seductive or provocative (1 Tim. 2:9-10). Do your clothes draw attention to your face or to your reproductive parts?

III. How Should One Deal With Temptation?

   A. Realize that you must always remember the following biblical facts when you are tempted.

   Fact No. 1: Remember that this temptation does not come from God (James 1:13-15).

   Fact No. 2: Remember that self-pity because of temptation is inexcusable in a Christian. The same holds true for despair, doubt and hopelessness.

   We should not be discouraged by our temptations for the following reasons:

   a. Other Christians are experiencing the same, exact temptation which bothers you. You are not alone. You have joined a club (1 Cor. 10:13). All Christians have besetting sins, marriage problems, etc.

   b. God never promised in the Bible that you would be free from being tempted by any particular sin. Neither did He ever promise complete victory over your besetting sin. You will be tempted and tried. Accept this and go on in the Christian life.

   Fact No. 3: Remember that because God is faithful, He will always intervene on our behalf in two ways.

God's Faithfulness to Us

1 Cor. 10:13	Guarantees	1 Cor. 10:13
We will never be confronted with a temptation too strong for us. We can never be forced into sinning by the world, the flesh or the devil. We can never say, "I could not help myself."		There is always a way to escape the temptation. We are never in a situation where we have to sin. We are never forced to break one Law of God in order to keep another Law of God. We can never say, "There was no way out but to sin."
Thus when you sin, you do it deliberately.		Thus when you sin, it is because you did not use God's way of escape.

B. Ten steps to take to avoid or escape temptation.
   1. Be alert and watch out for temptations (Matt. 26:41; 1 Thess. 5:6-11; 1 Pet. 5:8).
   2. Live a Spirit-filled life (Eph. 5:18).
   3. Pray that you will not be tempted (Matt. 6:13).
   4. Be quick in dealing with the first signs of temptation (James 1:14-15).
   5. Know biblical escapes (1 Cor. 10:13).
      a. Moral impurity: 2 Tim. 2:22
      b. Satanic doubts: Matt. 4:1-11
      c. Demonic attack: James 4:7
   6. Pray to God for victory (Psa. 25, etc.).
   7. Obey God by using His way of escape (1 Cor. 10:13).
   8. Be afraid of where this temptation wants to take you, what it wants to do to others and that God will make you reap what you sow (Prov. 3:7; Heb. 11:24-26; Gal. 6:7-8).
   9. When you do sin, do not give up the war. In any war, you win some battles and you lose some battles. Be assured, your war with the world, the flesh and the devil will end with you as the victor. You may lose many battles, yet you will win the war.
   10. Always remember that God's grace is greater than all our sin.

Conclusion

While we cannot stop the birds from flying over our roof or even landing on it, we can stop them from building a nest on it. If we do not want to hear the bell ring, we should not play with the rope!

Chapter Thirty

The Sovereignty of God and Prayer

One of the most difficult biblical topics with which I have ever wrestled is the subject of prayer. Why? Prayer is so difficult to deal with because, in the final analysis, only the Holy Spirit Himself can teach us what it is really to pray. We may read all the books written on prayer and hear great sermons on prayer and yet these things will never teach any believer the secrets of true prevailing prayer. The Holy Spirit and the Holy Spirit alone, can teach us what it is to pray truly.

Men of prayer in ages past all point to the absolute necessity of the Spirit's assistance and guidance in prayer. Listen to some of their testimonies:

C.H. Spurgeon:
Prayer is an art which only the Holy Spirit can teach us. He is the giver of all prayer.

John Bunyan
There is no man, nor church in the world, that can come to God in prayer but by the assistance of the Holy Spirit.

Octavius Winslow
It must be acknowledged by the spiritual mind that all true prayer is of the leading of the Spirit; that He is the author of all real approach of the soul to God. All true prayer is put into words by the Spirit. He is the Author of prayer in the soul.

Edwin Palmer
Without the Spirit, prayer is impossible. To pray acceptably to God, to pray with power, one must pray in the Spirit. Without the Holy Spirit, there can be no true prayer.

John Calvin
God gives us the Spirit as our teacher in prayer, to tell us what is right and to temper our emotions. We should seek such aid of the Spirit.

C.H. Spurgeon
Pray for prayer—pray till you can pray; pray to be helped to pray and give not up praying because you cannot pray, for it is when you think you cannot pray that you are most praying.

When we study the person and work of the Sovereign Spirit of God, we soon discover that He is called "the Spirit of grace and supplication" (Zech. 12:10). The apostle Paul tells us in Eph. 2:18 that it is only by the Spirit's assistance that we can have access through Christ to the Father. And again, in Eph. 6:18, he commands us to be continually "praying in the Spirit" as part of the armor of God which protects us from the schemes of the Devil. Jude also tells us in his little epistle that one of the keys to keeping ourselves in a living awareness of God's love is to pray "in the Spirit" (v. 20). Thus, in Rom. 8:26-27, we are told that it is the distinct ministry of the Holy Spirit to help us overcome our infirmities in our prayer life. It is His ministry to teach us what to pray for and to stir us up to groan our infirmities to God.

The Several Aspects of Prayer to Be Considered

Now the subject of prayer involves many different things and, therefore, we cannot hope to plumb the depths nor scale the heights of this aspect of the unsearchable knowledge and wisdom of God. But I do wish to emphasize those aspects of biblical praying which should be most searching to our consciences and most helpful in our daily lives.

I. The first question we need to answer is: "What is prayer?" Prayer is the soul's automatic response to the Spirit's work of regeneration; or to put it in other words, all true Christians are characterized by a life of prayer.

According to the Word of God in Gal. 4:6, once a man, woman or child has been born again, regenerated by the power of the Holy Spirit, they become children of God. The Spirit then functions as the Spirit of adoption and causes the believer to cry, "Abba, Father" from the very depths of his heart. As the indwelling Spirit of adoption, He bears witness to our spirit that we are the children of God and leads us to seek the things of the Spirit (Rom. 8:5, 13-16). Thus John Bunyan comments:

> If the grace of God be in him, it will be as natural for him to groan out his condition as it
> is for a sucking child to cry for the breast. Prayer is one of the first things that discovers a man
> to be a Christian.

And, along this same line, Richard Hooker adds, "Prayer is the first thing wherewith a righteous life begins and the last wherewith it ends."

This leads us to several questions. Are you living a life of prayer? Do you find yourself constantly at prayer throughout the day? Is prayer something natural for you or is it something forced? Let no one fool himself, even if you have all the theological knowledge in the world, if you are a prayerless man, woman or child, you are not a Christian. I did not ask you if you were a church-going person. I asked, "Are you a praying man?" How did Ananias know that the violent persecutor of the church, Saul of Tarsus, had now become a Christian? "Behold, he prays" (Acts 9:11). Listen to some men of old on this important point:

Timothy Dwight
He who does not habitually pray to God, cannot be a Christian.

Charles Hodge
A prayerless man is, of necessity and thoroughly, irreligious. There can be no life without activity. As the body is dead when it ceases to act, so the soul that goes not forth in its actions towards God, that lives as though there were no God, is spiritually dead.

John Bunyan
You then are not a Christian if you are not a praying person. The promise is "that everyone that is righteous will pray." You then are a wicked wretch if you do not pray.

In the light of these things we would be fools to assume that prayerless people have been regenerated by the Holy Spirit. If the subject of prayer is of little interest to you and your mind would rather dwell on the attempts to cut the Gordian knots of the Calvinist-Arminian debate, then you have grounds to question your salvation. The true Christian is vitally interested in prayer. Is your life characterized by prayer?

II. Evangelical and experiential motives comprise the only proper basis for prayer.

Having established that all true Christians pray by virtue of the indwelling of the Spirit of supplication, we need to examine the inner motives which prompt us to pray. What are these evangelical motives?

First of all, there must be an awareness of our absolute dependence upon the grace and mercy of God as given to us through the redemptive work of Christ. We must pray as those who trust in Christ's righteousness alone. This is the essence of what it means to pray "in the name of Christ."

Secondly, we should pray because we want to, because we love to and because it is as natural as our breathing. Our love to God, Christ and neighbor, which arises from our hearts in response to God's prior love to us (1 John 4:10), should constrain us to prayer.

Therefore, we must beware of legal motives for prayer because they indicate an unregenerate heart. The children of God cry, "Abba, Father" through freedom in Christ, not as those in bondage to the elements of the world (Rom. 8:14-16).

Questions for your conscience: Why do you pray? Do you pray because you are supposed to? Is it merely a habit with you? Do you pray because you cannot do otherwise? Do you love to pray? Does the love of Christ constrain you to pray?

III. We should conform and construct our prayers according to God's revealed will in Holy Scripture. We should never attempt to conform our prayers to the ultimate purposes of God, which are unknown to us (Deut. 29:29).

John Bunyan and John Cotton commented on this point as follows:

John Bunyan

Prayer is a pouring out of the heart to God, through Christ, in the strength of the Spirit, for such things as God has promised. Prayer must be within the compass of God's Word; it is blasphemy or at best babbling, when the petition is beside the Book. David therefore in his prayers kept his eye on the Word of God: "My soul cleaves to the dust; quicken me according to your Word'; "Remember Your Word to Your servant, on which you have caused me to hope." Indeed the Holy Spirit does not immediately quicken and stir up the heart of the Christian without, but by, in and through the Word. The Spirit by the Word directs the manner as well as the matter of praying.

John Cotton

What is it to pray according to God's will? When we pray for things which are agreeable to God's will, i.e. His revealed will; we should ask for nothing but what He commands us ... for those things we have warrant to pray.

Realizing that we should have biblical warrant for our petitions should cause us to be more careful and serious in making our requests to God. It should cause us to prepare for prayer. But on the other hand, if we foolishly try to conform our prayers according to God's secret will, then we will soon cease to pray for anyone or anything. Thus, some have abandoned believing prayer as being unprofitable. They sneer at days of prayer and know little of agonizing in prayer because they think that the doctrine of God's sovereignty is opposed to effectual, believing prayer. In their minds they view prayer as the enemy of divine sovereignty.

It is no wonder that some people complain that if God is sovereign and if everything is preordained, then prayer is useless at its best and blasphemous at its worst, for if we pray for something which ultimately is not God's decreed will, we appear to be fighting against God. We seem to be sinning against God by rebelling against His sovereign will.

Timothy Dwight dealt with the exact problem in a sermon on Job 21:15, "What profit should we have if we pray to Him?" In this sermon, he quotes those who hold to the false theory that the doctrines of grace are opposed to believing prayer and then he goes on to tear this theory to pieces. I would like to quote part of a statement in which he quotes the objections raised against prayer.

Prayer is fruitless or in the language of the text, unprofitable, because all things are determined from everlasting by an immutable God and will, therefore, take place according to His determination. Hence our prayers, making no alteration in anything, must be an idle, perhaps an impious, service; idle, because they can effect nothing; impious, because they are expressions of our desires for blessings, which God has not chosen to give. If God has determined to give us these blessings, we shall receive them without prayer. If He has determined not to give them, we shall not receive them, however fervently we may pray. So far, then, as we pray for things which God has determined to give, our prayers are useless. So far as we pray for those which He has determined not to give, our prayers are directly opposed to His pleasure.

I think that all of us have either thought of these objections in our minds or have had Arminians hurl them at us as objections against the doctrines of grace. But there are several solid biblical arguments which refute this position.

1. Since the Christian is to do whatever the Bible commands him, he must pray because he is commanded to pray (1 Thess. 5:17). And since God commands us to pray, it is obvious that it is not useless or stupid, but of great profit and efficacious in procuring the blessings of God. For example, God revealed His purpose to send rain, yet Elijah prayed and his prayer stopped and started the rain (1 Kings 18:1, 42). Thus, James 5:16 says, "The effectual fervent prayer of a righteous man avails much." Prayer cannot be unprofitable for it avails much.

2. All prayer is to be exercised in an attitude of submissiveness to God, in which you really desire God's will as to what is best and good: "Your will be done." (Matt 6:10b) Thus, there is no impiety in prayer because we are not demanding that God do what we ask. We want His will to be done on earth as it is in Heaven.

3. This objection, if true, would apply equally to all activities of life. It would mean not only no more praying, but also no more preaching, witnessing, working, eating, no more anything. All activity would be paralyzed because all is determined.

4. This objection is based on ignorance of the fact that God ordains the means as well as the end. Prayer plays a part of the outworking of God's decree. God has decreed that we have not if we ask not. He has predetermined to hear our prayers and answer them. He has decreed that His eternal plan of salvation be worked out through the effectual, fervent prayers of righteous men, women and children.

5. The doctrines of grace should strengthen and provoke believing prayer because they point us to the absolutely sovereign God who can do what we ask. The God addressed in prayer is mighty to save, mighty to deliver, and mighty to sanctify. Pray for God to save sinners and to revive saints. On the other hand, it is actually the Arminian who should give up prayer, for his god is too small, too weak and too flabby to answer prayer. If God is not sovereign and man has a "free will" which even God

cannot tamper with, why pray (a) for the lost or (b) for protection from enemies, either human or demonic? What comfort can be derived from a Deity who is biting his fingernails over whether or not men will "let" him do something?

6. Historically, the doctrines of grace, rightly understood and applied to the Christian life, have always produced men of prayer, as any honest survey of church history would reveal. In days gone by, most men of prayer were thorough-going Calvinists.

7. Therefore, if your theology has led you to abandon prayer and to sneer at the concept that prayer is vital and necessary, then your theology is not biblical.

IV. A close examination of the prayers recorded in Scriptures reveals that the saints of old filled their mouths with arguments when presenting their petitions to God. They buttressed their requests with biblical arguments. They pleaded with God in terms of His Word, His glorious names, His covenants of promise, and His plan of redemption. In short, they presented their prayer requests like a lawyer who skillfully presents his arguments to judge and jury.

Pleading with God in prayer and presenting reasons to God why He should grant our requests is a lost art today. It was even a lost art in George Mueller's day, as his biographer points out:

> At this time of need ... this man who had determined to risk everything upon God's word of promise, turned from doubtful devices and questionable methods of relief to pleading with God. And it may be well to mark his manner of pleading. He used argument in prayer and at this time he piles up eleven reasons why God should and would send help.... He was one of the elect few to whom it had been given to revive and restore this lost art of pleading with God.

In his sermon on Job 23:3-4, C.H. Spurgeon commented:

> The ancient saints were given, with Job, to ordering their cause before God. Not filling the mouth with words nor good phrases, not pretty expressions, but filling the mouth with arguments.... When we come to the gate of mercy, forcible arguments are the knocks of the rapper by which the gate is opened.... When a man searches for arguments for a thing it is because he attaches importance to that which he is seeking.

Now, to be sure, we are not to suppose that the arguments we present in prayer are given to convince or to inform God as to what course He should take in His administration of the universe. Rather, the arguments focus on the strengthening of our faith. Mueller's biographer goes on to point out:

> Of course God does not need to be convinced; no argument can make any plainer to Him the claims of trusting souls to His intervention, claims based upon His own Word, confirmed by His oath. And yet He will be inquired of and argued with. That is His way of blessing.... We are to argue our case with God, not indeed to convince Him, but to convince ourselves.

To this Ezekiel Hopkins adds:

> Now, although it be true that all the arguments that we can urge and all the reasons we can allege, cannot alter the purposes and determinations of God, as to any event that He has ordained, yet there is this twofold use and necessity of pleasing them. First, because by considering the reasons we have to pray for such mercies, our desires will be the more earnest and fervent in the obtaining of them.... Secondly, because reasons in prayer do mightily conduce to the strengthening of our faith and give us great encouragement to believe that we shall certainly obtain what we have so much reason to ask....

Or again, as C.H. Spurgeon put it:

Why are arguments to be used at all? The reply is, certainly not because God is slow to give, not because we can change the divine purpose, not because God needs to be informed of any circumstance with regard to ourselves.... The arguments to be used are for our own bene-fit, not for His. Our use of arguments teaches us the ground upon which we obtain the bless-ing.... Besides, the use of arguments is intended to stir up our fervency....

Now, it is important to ask, from what shall we construct our arguments? Where can we find weighty reasons to lay before God? Where can we derive arguments from which we can present weighty reasons along with our petitions?

1. God's attributes. Spurgeon put it like this:

You and I may take hold at any time upon the justice, the mercy, the faithfulness, the wis-dom, the long-suffering, the tenderness of God and we shall find every attribute of the Most High to be, as it were, a great battering-ram with which we may open the gates of Heaven.

For example, we can argue from 1 John 1:9 that God's faithfulness and justice are grounds for for-giveness (cf. Psa. 51:1-3).

2. The promises of God. Spurgeon observes, "If you have a divine promise, you need not plead that with an "if" in it; you may plead with a certainty" (cf. 1 Kings 8:56; 1 Thess. 5:23-24).

3. The names of God. When in need of strength, should we not cry out to Elohim, the God of power and strength? When seeking a blessing from the New Covenant, should we not argue from the name Yahweh, which is God's covenantal name? When appealing to God's sovereignty, Adonai should be upon our lips. When confronting satanic forces, the Lord of Hosts should be our shield and high tower.

4. The sorrows of God's people. The present condition of the church is a weighty argument for our need of revival (cf. Psa. 80:4-7; Psa. 12:1). We should also plead our own unworthiness, weakness and poverty of spirit (cf. Psa. 25:16; Luke 15:18-19).

5. The history of redemption. God's mighty acts in past history provide a foundation for our trust in God (cf. Psa. 30:11; 143:1-6).

6. The atoning life, death and intercession of Christ.

Spurgeon observes:

When you plead the name of Christ, you plead that which shakes the gates of Hell and which the hosts of Heaven obey and God Himself feels the sacred power of that divine plea. You would do better if you sometimes thought more in your prayers of Christ's griefs and groans.... Speak out and tell the Lord that with such griefs and cries and groans to plead, you cannot take a denial.

The end result of using argument in prayer shall be a strengthened and energized prayer life. Faith will be emboldened to go to God's throne and secure the petitions inquired of God. Thus we will rejoice in seeing our prayers avail much.

If the Holy Spirit shall teach us how to order our cause and how to fill our mouth with ar-guments, the result shall be that we shall have our mouth filled with praises. The man who has his mouth full of arguments in prayer shall soon have his mouth full of benedictions in answer to prayer. (Spurgeon)

At this point, we must apply the principle of argumentation in prayer to our own lives. Do we have much of a prayer life? Do we agonize before God, groaning out our requests? Has our understanding of the doctrines of grace revolutionized our prayer life for the better or for the worse?

V. A study of the prayers in the Bible reveals that the saints of old—and even our Master—set apart whole days or nights dedicated to prayer. When something great was requested from God or whenever the situation was desperate and important decisions were soon to be made, the saints of old would give themselves to fasting and prayer.

When we examine the lives of men of prayer in every generation, we find that they too would set apart whole days for prayer and fasting. Is it any wonder that they often witnessed the power of God in their own day? Is it any surprise that they attained to great measures of holiness in their lives? Perhaps one reason why we are not seeing a mighty revival of the doctrines of grace moving in this country is because we do not desire it enough. We really do not believe that God can do it in our own day. We study much and pray little to our shame and confusion.

As an aid to organizing a day of prayer and fasting, I would like to share the following suggestions (not rules). Of course, I would point out that fasting is not a virtue in and of itself; it simply means that we engage ourselves in prayer instead of eating and drinking.

1. In setting up a day of prayer, be very selective about whom you ask to join you. An Achan in the midst can destroy the spirit of the day. Choose a few men or women who you know can abandon themselves in true fervent prayer and who are more concerned with God and His glory than with their impression on others.

2. Do not talk about prayer or boast around others that you are having a day of prayer. Be secretive about this as Christ commands in Matt. 6:5-18.

3. When you gather together for a day of prayer, do not waste time talking with one another, for you are there to talk to God. A day of prayer is not a Bible study or testimony meeting. Foolish jesting and too much talk can ruin the day because this grieves the Author of prayer, the Holy Spirit.

4. Structure your day carefully to make sure that you do not wander aimlessly in your prayers or repeat yourself. There are enough issues in life to pray about. I suggest the following divisions, not as the only way or even the best way, to structure a day of prayer. You may arrange your day in any way you please, but it should be orderly. However, the following basic procedure has been a source of great blessing:

    1. Invocation—Call upon God to hear you.
    2. Confession—Confess your sins to God.
    3. Worship—Praise and worship God.
    4. Petition for your own needs.
    5. Intercession and supplication for others.
    6. Thanksgiving.

If you allow 30 minutes for each section, three hours will be required for your day of prayer. But you may spend an hour or more in each section if you are so led. The essential thing is to pray effectual, believing prayer, patterned after the prayers recorded in God's Word.

Conclusion

Obviously, volumes have been written on the subject of prayer. I heartily recommend John Bunyan's book, *Prayer*, as an excellent treatise on this topic. I trust that the aspects covered in this study will stimulate you to "pray without ceasing."

Chapter Thirty-One

Three Kinds of Faith

Introduction

A misunderstanding of what the Bible means when it speaks of faith can lead to immense guilt and frustration in the Christian life. This understanding is usually rooted in a failure to see that the Bible speaks of three distinct kinds of faith.

The Grace of Faith	The Fruit of Faith	The Gift of Faith
1. This is saving faith which is given to all Christians (Acts 18:27; Phil. 1:29).	2. This is sanctifying faith which is developed only by those who are "filled by the Spirit" and thus "walk in the Spirit" (Gal. 5:16, 18, 22, 25).	3. This is a special faith rooted in a unique call of God to develop a distinct life-message centered in proving God to the world by His meeting "impossible" needs (1 Cor. 12:9).
All of us have this kind of faith.	Some of us have this kind of faith.	A few of us may have this kind of faith.
Without it, you are not saved.	Without it, you are not a Spirit-filled Christian.	

Principles

1. While God grants to us all the Grace of Faith and commands us all to develop the fruit of faith, He does not give the gift of faith to all (1 Cor. 12:29-30).

2. It is wrong to call all Christians to live a life solely based on developing a special life-message through the gift of faith. God does not call us all to live by faith alone apart from a job, insurance policies, retirement funds, etc.

3. God does not call us all to be George Muellers, i.e., to develop a life-message centered in the exercise of the gift of faith. Each of us is called to develop our own special life message. (Example: Job—patience in the midst of failure and defeat).

4. Do not get hung up on a "guilt-trip" because you do not experience what George Mueller or other Christians have experienced. Accept yourself and your own life-message.

Chapter Thirty-Two
Death, Sheol and Hades

Introduction

Unless the Lord returns in our lifetime, we will all experience death. Thus, we need to understand it and to face it with peace instead of fear.

Part I

I. The Fact of Death

    A. The inescapable reality of death removes all the vain hopes of physical immortality.

        1. Science will never conquer death.

        2. The occult cannot avoid it.

        3. The cults may deny it as a teaching, but they experience it as a reality.
           Example: Mary Baker Eddy (Christian Science)

    B. God has ordained that each of us shall die once and then pass on to judgment (Heb. 9:27; Eccl. 3:1-2; Job 14:1-5).

II. The Origin of Death

    A. Death is the punishment placed upon man because of Adam's sin and our sin (Gen. 2:16-17; Rom. 5:12, 17, 6:23; James 1:14-15).

    B. This means that death is not "natural," "normal" or "human." It is unnatural and sub-normal. All the humanistic concepts about death being "natural"or part of human nature are false. Death is the terrible and unnatural ripping of the soul out of man's body. Death tears man in half. Man was made to live, not to die.

Christian Attitude	Humanist Attitude
1. Death is unnatural. 2. Death flows from sin. 3. Death is a time of sorrow (Jn. 11:33-38). 4. Death will be done away with when Jesus returns (Rev. 21:4).	1. Death is natural. 2. Death is part of life. 3. Death should mean little or nothing to us. 4. Death will always be here.

III. The Nature of Death

    A. Death takes place when the spirit/soul leaves the body (James 2:26). Thus death means separation, not unconsciousness, annihilation or soul sleep.

    B. The proof that death means the separation of the spirit/soul from the body is as follows:

        1. At the first occurrence of the word "death," it cannot mean unconsciousness, annihilation or soul sleep (Gen. 2:17; 3:8, 24). Adam and Eve "died" when they ate the fruit, i.e. they were separated from God.

2. What death means on the spiritual level is what it means on the physical level.

Spiritual Death	Physical Death
Gen. 2:17 Eph. 2:1-3 1 Tim. 5:6	1. The soul leaves the body at death (Gen. 35:18; I Kings 17:21-22; Eccl. 12:6-7; Acts 7:59; James 2:26)
	2. At death, a person is gathered to where other people exist (Gen. 25:8, 17; 49:29, 33).

3. The plain statements of Scripture show that death is the separation of the spirit/soul from the body with the conscious life continuing.
   a. Matt. 22:32
   b. Luke 16:19-31
   c. Luke 9:30; cf. Deut. 34:5
   d. Luke 23:43; cf. 2 Cor. 12:2, 4
   e. Phil. 1:21-24
   f. 2 Cor. 5:1-9
   g. 1 Thess. 5:10
   h. Heb. 12:22-23
   i. Rev. 6:9-11; cf. 4:1

IV. The Character of Death
   A. It is the last enemy to be destroyed (1 Cor. 15:26, 54-56; Heb. 2:14-18).
   B. It is gain for the Christian (Phil. 1:21; 2 Cor. 5:8; Rev. 14:13).

V. Application
   A. Are you ready for death?
   B. Have you wisely provided for your family in the case of your death?
   C. We can face death with peace if we have Christ.

Part II

I. Sheol
   A. This word is found 65 times in the Old Testament. It is mistranslated every time by the KJV. It translates sheol as "grave" 31 times, "hell" 31 times and "pit" three times.
   B. The etymology or root of sheol is still debatable. Some scholars feel it is from the word Sha-al which means "inquiry." Thus sheol would refer to the land of inquiry where the heathen seek to communicate with the spirits of the dead through necromancy. Others feel sheol comes from Sha-al, which originally meant "hollow." Sheol would then refer to the hollow place where the spirits of the dead exist.
   C. The basic meaning of the word in extra-biblical literature during the age of the Old Testament is clear. Sheol always meant "underworld," "the land of the dead," "the shadowy place of the dead." This is the meaning of the word in all the nations of the Fertile Crescent. No

one has ever found any literature in this time period where sheol was understood as "non-existence" or "annihilation." All archaeological finds point to sheol as referring to the nether world. That this is taught in the Old Testament will be demonstrated (Brown, Driver & Briggs, *A Hebrew and English Lexicon of the Old Testament*, p. 982).

D. Taking the principle of progressive revelation from Heb. 1:1-2, we do not expect to find in the Old Testament a complete picture of what happens to the soul of man after death. The complete picture awaited the fuller revelation of the New Testament. Thus, we will find that the Old Testament does not give us all the answers to the many questions we have concerning the "other side."

E. We can start by pointing out what sheol cannot mean.

    1. Sheol does not mean death, because the word *Moth* signifies death.

    2. Sheol does not mean the grave, for the word *Kever* means grave or sepulchre (Gen. 50:5). Indeed, in such places as Gen. 37:35, sheol cannot mean grave. Graves can be purchased, dug, uncovered, sold, defiled, opened and closed by man, while sheol is never spoken of in such ways. Only God puts man into sheol.

    3. Sheol does not mean the corruption of the body because *shachath* means this.

F. What *Kever* and *shachath* are to the body, sheol is to the soul. It is the soul of man which enters sheol, not his body (Psa. 16:10; 30:3; 49:14; 86:13; 89:48; Prov. 23:14, etc.). The Old Testament people desired that their soul be delivered from sheol. They never spoke that way of their body.

G. That the Old Testament people and prophets did not believe that sheol meant non-existence or soul-sleep or unconsciousness is clear from the continual problem of necromancy, i.e. seeking to contact the spirits of the dead through mediums. The people constantly fell into the sin of necromancy throughout Israel's history (2 Kings 17:7-23; 1 Sam. 28:7-25). If they believed that the dead were unconscious or non-existent, they would not have practiced necromancy, which assumes the dead can listen and respond to inquiry. That the prophets did not believe that the dead were unconscious is seen from the fact that they never used such an idea to correct the people's necromancy. They condemned it as forbidden, not as impossible (Deut. 18:9-14).

H. Sheol has gates by which one enters, and bars which keep one in (Isa. 38:10; Job 17:16).

I. After death, one enters sheol through its gates. What is on the other side of those gates is not clearly stated. The following things are mentioned in the Old Testament as describing sheol.

    1. Sheol is a shadowy place or place of darkness (Job 10:21-22, Psa. 143:3).

    2. It is beneath the world, in the lowest parts of the earth (Isa. 44:23; 57:9; Ezk. 26:20; Amos 9:2).

    3. It is the place where one's ancestors (fathers) dwell. You go to be with them in sheol. This cannot refer to a common grave but to going to the underworld where the souls of your ancestors dwell (Gen. 15:15; 25:8; 35:29; 37:35; 49:33; Num. 20:24; 31:2; Deut. 32:50; 34:5; 2 Sam. 12:23).

    4. Because sheol is exposed to God's sight, his anger burns in the deepest sheol (Job 26:6; Deut. 32:22). Evidently there are divisions within sheol (higher vs. lower).

J. The condition of those in sheol is not clearly defined in the Old Testament. The following things can be stated, with the caution that while the Old Testament may state something about those in sheol, it never explained what was stated.

    1. Once in sheol, all earthly pursuits such as the planning and executing of works are no longer possible. No earthly pleasures can be enjoyed, such as the giving of thanks or

praise in public worship, eating, drinking, etc. Those in sheol do not have any knowledge or wisdom about what is happening in the land of the living (Eccl. 9:10; Psa. 6:5, etc.).

2. Those in sheol may converse with one another (Isa 14:9-20; 44:23; Ezk. 32:21). This hardly fits the soul-sleep theory.

3. Because God's anger burns in sheol against His enemies (Deut. 32:22), pain and sorrow are experienced by some in sheol (Psa. 116:3; 2 Sam. 22:6; Psa. 18:5). The expressions, "the pains of sheol," "the sorrows of sheol," demonstrate that sheol does not mean unconscious non-existence. How can non-existence or unconsciousness feel pain or sorrow?

K. The Old Testament does not develop a concept of "Hell," except to state that after the resurrection, the wicked will suffer eternal shame (Dan. 12:1-2). Neither does the Old Testament develop the concept of Heaven except to hint that believers dwell there after death (Psa. 73:24-25), awaiting the eternal bliss which would come after the resurrection (Dan. 12:1-2). What is clear is that both believer and unbeliever enter sheol at death. They may separate after entering, but both go through the gates of sheol.

II. Hades

A. This word is found 11 times in the New Testament. The KJV mistranslates the word 10 times as "Hell" and once as "grave." In 1 Cor. 15:55, it translates Hades as "grave." But better manuscripts have a different word than Hades. Thus, the New Testament text actually has the word Hades only 10 times.

B. Hades was consistently used in the Greek version of the Old Testament as the Greek equivalent for the Hebrew word sheol. This does not mean that the New Testament picks up where the Old Testament left off by progressively developing the concept of what happens to the soul of man after death. We will expect that the fuller revelation of Christ and the Apostles will clarify what was vague in the Old Testament (Heb. 1:1-3).

C. The basic meaning of Hades in contemporary extra-biblical literature is "the underworld" or "the place where the soul of man goes after death." No one has ever found places where Hades meant unconsciousness or non-existence. All Greek lexicons record this basic meaning of Hades.

D. We can start by pointing out what Hades cannot mean.

1. Hades is not death because the Greek word *thanatos* means death.

2. Hades is not the grave because *mneema* means grave or sepulchre.

3. Hades is not "Hell"—the final place of eternal judgment—because *gehenna* and the lake of fire refer to this place.

4. Hades is not Heaven—the place believers go at death—because *ouranos* is the Greek word for Heaven.

5. Hades is not the place of eternal bliss which the righteous will enjoy after the resurrection—because the New Earth is the name of that place.

E. Hades can be entered only by death (Lk. 16:23). Thus "death" is always placed before Hades (Rev. 1:18; 6:8; 20:13-14).

F. The wicked enter Hades at death and are in conscious torment, being continually punished (Lk. 16:23; cf. 2 Pet. 2:9).

Note: 2 Pet. 2:9 is clear that the wicked are under continuous punishment or torture.

1. The wicked are being "held." Present active infinitive: "are continuously held" (literal Greek).

2. They are "being punished." Present passive participle: "are continuously being punished or tortured" (literal Greek).

G. Before Christ's ascension, believers as well as unbelievers were said to enter into sheol. With Christ's death on the cross, the New Testament pictures believers after death as entering paradise (Lk. 23:43), which is the third Heaven (2 Cor. 12:2, 4), to be with Christ (Phil. 1:23), which is far better than Hades. They are present with the Lord (2 Cor. 5:6-8), worshiping with the angelic hosts of Heaven (Heb. 12:22-23) at the altar of God (Rev. 6:9-11). Thus, believers do not now enter Hades.

H. Hades is the temporary, intermediate state between death and the resurrection where the wicked suffer. Hades will be emptied at the resurrection and then the wicked will be cast into "Hell" (gehenna).

III. Gehenna

A. This word is found 12 times in the New Testament.
It is correctly translated in each case as "Hell" by the KJV.

B. It originally referred to the Valley of Hinnom, which was just outside the city of Jerusalem (Josh. 15:8). It became the place where idolatrous Jews gave human sacrifices to pagan deities (2 Kings 23:10; 2 Chron. 28:3; 33:6, etc). Because of these horrible idolatrous practices, the Valley of Hinnom was hated and considered "unclean" by pious Jews. In Christ's day, this hatred of the Valley of Hinnom caused the Valley to become the town dump, where all the garbage of Jerusalem could be thrown. Any unclean bodies were thrown into it as well. Because garbage was constantly thrown into the Valley, the fires never stopped burning and the worms never stopped eating. This picture of an unclean garbage dump where the fire and worms never died out became to the Jewish mind an appropriate description of what fate awaited all the pagans. Gehenna came to be understood as the final, eternal garbage dump where all the idolaters would be thrown. The wicked would suffer in Gehenna forever, because the fires would never stop burning them and the worms never stop gnawing them.

C. Jesus Christ agreed with and taught the above contemporary view of the final or ultimate fate awaiting the wicked.

1. He used the word Gehenna, which could only mean "Hell" to the minds of his hearers.
2. He taught that Gehenna was a place of condemnation (Matt. 23:33).
3. Gehenna was connected with the Day of Judgment (Matt. 5:22; 23:33; cf. Rev. 20:14).
4. Gehenna was a place where the body as well as the soul could be tormented (Matt. 5:22; Matt. 10:28; Mk. 9:43-48).
5. Only God can cast someone body and soul into Gehenna (Matt. 10:28; Lk. 12:5). This proves that Gehenna cannot be the grave, for men can cast bodies into graves, while only God can cast body/soul into Gehenna.
6. The fires of Gehenna never die out and the worms keep on gnawing (Mk. 9:47-48).
7. Gehenna is a place of eternal shame, grief and torment (Dan. 12:1-2; Matt. 8:12; 22:13; 24:51; 25:41, 46; Mk. 9:48; Rev. 14:10-11; 19:20; 20:10, 15).
8. The wicked are "cast" into Gehenna and "destroyed" (Matt. 5:29-30; 10:28). That the word "destroyed" does not mean "annihilate" or "pass into non-existence" is clear from the usage of the word in the New Testament (example: Matt. 9:17; Lk. 15:4, 6, 8, 9; John 6:12, 27; 2 Cor. 4:9, etc). All Greek lexicons establish that *apolluo* means to "render something useless, good for nothing, lost, etc." When it is used in connection with gehenna it emphasizes the picture that the wicked are "good for nothing." Thus they should be thrown on the garbage dump of eternity—Gehenna. (See Robert Morey, *Death and the Afterlife*, for greater detail.)

Special Note on the Book of Ecclesiastes and Death

I. The problem before us:
Those cults which teach "soul sleep" or annihilationism use Ecclesiastes as the main source of biblical proof for their position. (See: Eccl. 3:18-22; 9:5-6). Example: Seventh-day Adventists, Jehovah's Witnesses.

II. The Real Problem
The underlying problem with the cultists' misuse of Ecclesiastes is an ignorance of the basic rules of hermeneutics. They misinterpret verses because they do not know how to interpret anything in the Bible.
  A. They depend upon the O.T. almost to the exclusion of the N.T. They fail to see the nature of progressive revelation, the vagueness of the O.T. or the priority of the N.T. over the O.T.
  B. They ignore the contexts of a verse:
    1. The immediate paragraph.
    2. The chapter.
    3. The section of the book (the outline of a book).
    4. The book as a whole.
    5. The book's place in the canon.
    6. Its stage or place in the unfolding drama of redemptive history.
    7. The historical, cultural and linguistic background of the words, phrases, idiomatic expressions and figurative language.

III. Ecclesiastes is a case in point.
  A. In terms of its historical, cultural and linguistic context, Ecclesiastes falls into the genre of ancient literature which posed one speaker against another. There are ancient parallels to Ecclesiastes where two opposing philosophies dialogue. The Hebrew grammar is clear on this point.

   Speaker No. 1 vs. Speaker No. 2

  B. Ecclesiastes is in the "wisdom" section of the O.T.
  C. It teaches us about life and how to live it in a way different from Proverbs. Proverbs tells us what happens if we begin with God, while Ecclesiastes tells what happens if we begin without God (*Death and the Afterlife*, p. 216).
  D. Speaker No. 1 is a man devoid of God's grace, who looks at life from a humanist view. He is "under the sun," i.e. naturalistic.

  E. The humanist viewpoint is given from chapter one to chapter 11. The theist answers in chapter 12. There are two different speakers representing two opposite ways of looking at life.

  F. That we are dealing with humanist man in chapters one to 11 is clear.
   "Everything is meaningless" (1:2)
   "I hate life" (2:17, 18)
   "I am nothing but an animal" (3:18)
   "I will die like an animal" (3:19-20)
   "Pleasure and money answer everything" (10:19)

G. The humanist objects to the common religious beliefs of his day.
1. Wisdom and knowledge bring joy and comfort (1:18) vs. wisdom and knowledge bring grief and pain
2. The spirit or soul of man ascends up to Heaven at death, while animals expire downward (3:21) vs. Who knows if this really happens?
H. The theist answers in 12:1, 6-7, 13-14

Premise No. 1: Death does not end all.

Premise No 2: You will be held accountable after death for how you lived.

Conclusion: Fear God and Keep His Commandments

Conclusion

The old Gospel story of Jesus and His love who came to save us from an eternal Hell and to give us a home in Heaven is still the same Gospel we preach today. Those who deny a conscious afterlife are preaching "another" gospel and fall under the condemnation of Gal. 1:8.

Chapter Thirty-Three

The Biblical Doctrine of Heaven

Introduction

Natural theologians and philosophers are utterly blind, mute, and dumb when it comes to the afterlife. The can try to use their human reason, experience, and feelings, but in the end they will have to bow before the edict of 1 Cor. 2:9:

> No human eye has ever seen,
> No human ear has ever heard,
> No human mind has ever conceived—
> What God has prepared for those who love Him.

Paul stresses the futility of natural theology because of the impossibility of man being the Origin of truth, justice, morals and beauty in things mundane or divine. He then proceeds to point us to Scripture as the only means whereby we can have knowledge of such things.

> But God has revealed it to us by His Spirit.

Once again the contest is between human reason and divine revelation. Humanists can speculate all they want, but we will not settle for anything less than the chapter and verse of Holy Writ.

Part I

I. Three different "heavens" are mentioned in the Bible (2 Cor. 12:2).
  A. The first heaven: air (where birds fly) Matt. 6:26
  B. The second heaven: space (where stars shine) Acts 7:42
  C. The third heaven: Paradise (where God rules) Matt. 6:9-10

II. The third heaven is a physical place where physical bodies as well as spirit creatures and human souls dwell.
  A. Christ's resurrection body is now in heaven: John 2:19-22; Heb. 1:3; Phil. 3:20-21.
  B. Enoch (Gen. 5:24) and Elijah (2 Kings 2:11) were translated to heaven with their bodies.
  C. Various creatures such as angels (Heb. 12:22), cherubim (Ezk. 10:1-25) and seraphim (Isa. 6:2, 6), etc. dwell in the third heaven.
  D. The souls/spirits of believers are now in heaven (Heb. 12:23; Rev. 6:9).

III. What awaits you in heaven?
  A. Reunion with loved ones who have gone ahead to heaven (Gen. 25:8, 17; 35:29; 37:35; 49:33; Num. 31:2; Deut. 32:50).
  B. Dwelling in the house of Yahweh forever (Psa. 23:6).

C. Glory (Psa. 73:23-24).

D. The presence of God (Ecc. 12:5-7).

E. Divine comfort (Lk. 16:25).

F. Entering Paradise where we eat of the Tree of life (Lk. 23:43; cf. 2 Cor. 12:4; Rev. 2:7).

G. The beatific vision (Matt 5:8; Heb. 12:14; 1 John 3:2-3; Rev. 22:4).

H. Communion with God (Matt. 22:32).

I. Coming into possession of the treasures you sent to heaven while on earth (Matt 6:19-21; Lk. 12:21, 33-34; 1 Tim. 6:17-19).

J. The Father's heavenly house (John 14:1-3; 2 Cor. 5:1-3).

K. Being at home with the Lord (2 Cor. 5:8).

L. Opportunities to please God (2 Cor. 5:9).

M. Gain (Phil. 1:21).

N. Being with Christ, which is far better (Phil. 1:23).

O. Living with Jesus (1 Thess 5:10).

P. Perfection (Heb. 12:23).

Q. Joining in the worship in heaven (Heb. 12:22-24; Rev. 4:9-11; 5:8-14; 7:9-12; 11:16-18; 19:1-7).

R. Safety from the second death (Rev. 2:11).

S. Hidden manna, a white stone, and a new name known only to you (Rev. 2:17).

T. Authority over the nations, and the morning star (Rev. 2:26-28).

U. White garments; your name will not be erased from the book of life; Christ will confess your name before the Father and the angels (Rev. 3:5; Matt. 10:32-33).

V. You will be made a pillar in the temple; you will not go out anymore; Christ will write on you the name of God, the name of the city of God, and His new name (Rev. 3:12).

W. Sitting down with Jesus on His throne (Rev. 3:21).

X. Being before the throne of God to serve Him day and night in His Temple; God will spread his tabernacle over you; you will no longer hunger or thirst; the sun will not burn you nor any heat bother you; The Lamb will shepherd you and guide you to the waters of life and God will wipe away every tear from your eyes (Rev. 7:16-17).

Y. Rest from your labors, for your works will follow you to heaven (Rev. 14:13).

Z. No more tears, death, mourning, crying, pain, or any curse; you will serve God; you will see His face; the sun is no longer needed; His name will be written on your forehead; you will reign forever (Rev. 21:4; 22:3-5).

IV. When Christ returns to earth from heaven, God will bring our souls "with Him," so that we may receive our resurrection body (1 Thess. 4:14).

V. The earth will be purged with fire and emerge as a "new earth" where no evil dwells (2 Pet. 3:3-13).

VI. "Heaven" will come down to the new earth. We will inherit it and fulfill the cultural mandate originally given to Adam (Rev. 21:1-2; Matt. 5:5; Gen. 1:28).

Conclusion

Between death and the return of the Lord, we will dwell in heaven. Then heaven will descend to the earth where we will forever serve the Lord.

Chapter Thirty-Four

The Biblical Doctrine of Hell

Introduction

The doctrines of the immortality of the soul, a conscious afterlife with bliss for believers and torment for unbelievers, the Resurrection, the Judgment Day, and eternal conscious punishment were progressively revealed in the Old Testament.

Orthodox Jews developed these same doctrines further during the period between Malachi and Matthew. Thus, it is no surprise that these developments form the doctrinal background of the New Testament and supply us with an explanation of crucial passages such as Lk. 12:4-5, 16:19-31, etc.

I. The Old Testament Evidence
   A. The time between your death and your resurrection is called the "intermediate period."

   Death ——————————————— Resurrection ——— Eternal state
                Intermediate state

   B. Sheol had two compartments (Psa. 32:22).
      1. a "lower" section where unbelievers experience terror and suffering (Psa. 116:3).
      2. a "higher" section where the saints experience happiness (Psa. 73:23-25; 23:6).

   C. There is going to be a resurrection of the wicked and the righteous at the end of history (Dan. 12:2).
      1. The saints will enjoy eternal bliss.
      2. The wicked will experience eternal shame and contempt.

II. The Period Between the Old and New Testaments
   A. The 400 years between Malachi and Matthew is called the "intertestamental period."
   B. Before archaeologists unearthed literature from that period, Christians called it "400 years of silence." But now that hundreds of scrolls from that period have been found, this gives us the theological context in which the New Testament and the Church were born.
   C. Before the literature was discovered, liberal theologians taught that the Jews did not believe in a conscious afterlife. This erroneous idea still pops up in cultic and liberal circles. It reveals a total ignorance of the intertestamental Jewish literature.
   D. The Jewish literature demonstrates that orthodox Jews believed in the immortality of the soul, a conscious afterlife with bliss for the righteous and torment for the wicked, a day of Judgment, the Resurrection of all human beings, and eternal bliss or torment.

E. The conscious torment of the wicked in the eternal state is clearly taught in this literature. The attempt of cultists and liberals to wiggle out of this fact has utterly failed in the face of overwhelming evidence documented in Robert Morey's book, *Death and the Afterlife* (pgs. 119-128).

Conclusion

We thank the Lord that the truth that there is hell to shun and a heaven to gain is firmly founded on the rock of Scripture and cannot be moved. Liberals and cultists have not be able to refute the evidence and arguments set forth in *Death and the Afterlife*.

Chapter Thirty-Five
Biblical Doctrine

Preliminary Remarks

I. Doctrine divides and that is exactly what God intends it to do (1 Cor. 1:18-24). The function of doctrine is to separate:

truth from error
light from darkness
righteousness from wickedness
orthodoxy from heresy
good from evil
the saved from the lost
the Church from the world

Principle: Never be ashamed or intimidated because you are willing to obey God (Rom. 3:4).

II. All church leaders should be champions of doctrine. This is part of the qualifications for their office and an essential aspect of their ministry.

See elders: Tit. 1:9; 1 Tim. 1:3-11; 1 Tim. 4:16
    deacons: 1 Tim. 3:9

Problem: Very few church leaders know anything about doctrine or are willing to defend the faith against heresy. Why? Only two possible reasons exist:

1. They are ignorant of God's Word.
2. They are disobedient to God's Word.
   Why do they disobey God?
   a. They were never really called by God.
   b. They are not shepherds but hirelings.
   c. Popularity is their goal.
   d. They want to be positive and not negative.

III. When the leaders fail to obey God, He will raise up someone else to do it. God raised up the prophets and the apostles because the priests failed to obey God's Word (example: Jeremiah 1:17-19).

IV. All Christians are called upon to defend the faith (Jude 3; 1 Pet. 3:15). When the apostles failed to obey (Acts 1:8), God raised up other people to do it (Acts 8:1-4).

The Source of All Doctrines

Principle No. 1: There can be only one ultimate final authority.

The attempt to have two, three or more "final" authorities is impossible. Ultimately one will win out over the others. Just as there can be only one captain of the ship or one head of the home, even so there is only enough room in this universe for one final authority (Matt. 6:24).

Principle No. 2: God is this one, ultimate, final authority.

He is Lord of all because He is the Creator and Sustainer of all things (Matt. 28:18).

Principle No. 3: God has revealed His mind and will in Scripture and, thus, Scripture is the ultimate, final authority.

The Bible is not to be viewed as a collection of funny, religious ideas from thousands of years ago. It is the present revelation of the heart and mind of the Creator toward man, His image-bearer. It is the last court of appeal, the final judge, the ultimate arbitrator, the absolute standard of truth, justice, morals and beauty:

      a. Isa. 8:20; 66:2
      b. Acts 17:2, 10-12
      c. 2 Tim. 3:16
      d. 2 Pet. 1:19-21

Principle No. 4: Nothing can override the authority of Scripture.

Churches, popes, bishops, pastors, priests, human traditions, kings, presidents, congresses, civil judges, supreme courts and all human authorities must bow before the eternal Word of the Almighty. Nothing is to be added to or subtracted from the Word of our God.

      a. Deut. 4:2; 12:32
      b. Pro. 30:5-6
      c. John 10:35
      d. Rev. 22:18-19

Principle No. 5: Beware of all attempts to derive doctrine from:

      a. Rationalism (reason)
      b. Empiricism (experience)
      c. Mysticism (feelings)

Conclusion

God did not put any razor blades in the apples of His revelation in Scripture. Everything that He has chosen to reveal is for us and for our children (Deut. 29:29).

Chapter Thirty-Six

The Role of Human Reason in Scripture & Theology

Introduction

From the very beginning, whenever the Church has confronted the world with the Gospel message of repentance toward God and faith in our Lord Jesus Christ, unbelief has always responded in three basic ways.

When the Apostle Paul preached on Mars Hill, some of the Greeks believed and were baptized. Those who did not believe were divided into two groups (Acts 17:32-34).

The first group was composed of those who said that they were open-minded and thus they were willing to think about and to discuss these issues again. They were willing to consider the possibility that Christianity was the true religion.

The second group was composed of those who were not open-minded at all. They were not willing to hear the Gospel or to examine its claims. They chose instead to mock and ridicule Paul and his message. They were the bold skeptics and sophists of their age. Any idea that did not first arise in their own minds was dismissed as sheer foolishness.

The taunt and ridicule of the skeptic has always accompanied the proclamation of the Gospel. In every age they have mocked and attacked the Gospel with the fury of savage, wild dogs. Now that they have come into power through Marxism, they have taken over entire nations and have engulfed millions of Christians in a tidal wave of inhuman violence, torture and murder. Their hatred of the Gospel knows no bounds and there is no compassion or pity with them.

As the Church of the 21st century faces the greatest onslaught of persecution and ridicule since the first three centuries of her beginning, she must respond with vigor and boldness to all the attacks made against the Gospel (Jude 3).

The weapons of her warfare are mighty through God to the pulling down of strongholds (2 Cor. 10:4). In every age she has to cast down all the vain and pretentious philosophies which exalt themselves against the knowledge of God (2 Cor. 10:5a). Every philosophy must be brought into obedience to Christ (2 Cor. 10:5b).

One of the greatest challenges the church faces today is the philosophy of rationalism which was an outgrowth of the humanism of the Renaissance during the 15th and 16th centuries in Western Europe.

Descartes is usually designated as the Father of Rationalism. He believed that while he could doubt the existence of God, the world, other people and even his own body, there was one thing that he could not doubt: that he existed—because he was the one doubting! *Cogito ergo sum* meant "I think —therefore I am."

Descartes said that we must, therefore, begin with man and not God. Man was the measure of all things. Man was the origin of meaning and morals. Man was the source and judge of all truth.

Descartes was following the same path that unbelief has always taken. Some aspect of man was abstracted from his being and made into the Origin and Source of Truth. Man's feelings, experience, or reason took the place of God.

The Mystics took human feelings and turned them into an abstract concept of "Emotion" which was their guide to all truth. The Empiricists took human experience and made "Experience" the origin of all knowledge. The Rationalists took human reason and turned it into the idea of an abstract, absolute, transcendent "Reason" which was the the basis and judge of all truth.

To the Rationalist, "reality" is limited to what he thinks it to be in his own mind. Whatever is unthinkable to him cannot exist. He can simply sit down in a dark room and, through "Reason" alone, come to understand everything without having to go and see it with his own eyes.

The Rationalists developed various phrases and slogans which expressed the supremacy of reason. All ideas must be "in accord with Reason." They must be "tried before the bar of Reason." Any idea that does not "satisfy the demands of Reason" must be rejected. All things, including religion, must "justify themselves before Reason." Philosophy begins and ends with the "first principles of Reason."

They did not hesitate to demand that such things as the existence of God or the inspiration of the Bible must be "justified before the bar of Reason." They would accept the Bible only in so far as it is "in agreement with Reason." Christian doctrines such as the Trinity, the imputation of Adam's sin or Christ's substitutionary atonement were denounced as "not in accord with Reason." Human Reason had become the Alpha and the Omega, the beginning and the end of all knowledge.

We who live in the 21st century must endure modern Rationalists who mock us for being "irrational" because we cannot justify our beliefs before their particular brand of reason. What should be our response to modern rationalism?

Some Christians have given in and simply become Religious Rationalists. They create their own idea of the nature of God according to what they think is in accord with reason. They accept only those Christian doctrines that appeal to them as being "reasonable." They begin with themselves and defend man at every point. If they must choose between the supremacy of man or the supremacy of God, they exalt man and dethrone God. Man is the measure of all things including religious ideas. This is the heart and soul of religious humanism.

The majority of Christians have always seen that human reason was not as trustworthy as the Rationalists claimed. Each Rationalist had his own puny mind in view when he spoke of "Reason" with hushed tones. They disagreed among themselves as to whose "Reason" was the ultimate Arbitrator of all Truth. Each one, in turn, tried to claim the honor for himself and refute all the Rationalists who went before him. The Rationalist movement fell into disgrace as they endlessly squabbled among themselves as to whose "Reason" was the greatest.

I wish that I could tell you that the Rationalists perished from off the face of the earth many years ago. But I am sad to report that I have encountered more Rationalists in the Christian Church than I have found in the world. If I had a dollar for every time someone rejected Revealed Truth because he did not think it "Reasonable," I could retire today. As the people of God we need to understand the role of human reason in Scripture and in theology in order to pick our way safely through the minefields of heresy that abound on every hand today. This is part of the whole counsel of God as given in Scripture and is thus part of the elders' teaching responsibility to equip the saints unto the work of ministry (Acts 20:27).

PART ONE

The Role of Human Reason in Scripture

A. The first thing that strikes the reader of the Bible is the conspicuous absence of any reference to any abstract concept of "Reason." The authors of Scripture never claimed that their doctrines were true because they were "reasonable." They never referred to or viewed human reason as "the ultimate court of appeal." They never demanded belief or obedience "in the name of Reason," and at no time did they ever justify their teachings "before the bar of Reason."

B. The various Hebrew and Greek words which are translated as "reason" in our English versions always refer either to sanity or to common sense (Dan.4:36; Acts 6:2). Since the abstract concept of "Reason" was not developed until the Renaissance, this is to be expected.

C. Instead of seeking to justify Divine Revelation before human reason, the authors of Scripture always demanded that human reason justify itself before Revelation! Human reason was correct to the degree that it agreed with Revelation.

Moses is a good example of the way biblical writers viewed human reason. He began the Bible with the existence of God (Gen. 1:1). He did not justify the existence of God before man's reason. Moses did the exact opposite. He justified the existence of man on the basis of the existence of God!

When Moses gave the Law to Israel he never said, "Do this because it is reasonable." He said, "Do this because God said so." The supremacy was always given to Revealed Truth.

D. That the authors of Scripture viewed Divine Revelation as the Ultimate Court of Appeal and the Origin and Judge of all Truth is clearly seen from the way they handled all conflicts between human reason and Revelation. Whenever there was a conflict between human reason and Revelation, human reason was rebuked as rebellious (example Rom. 9:10-21).

Even if all of mankind were to rise up and call a certain Revealed Truth "irrational," "not in accord with Reason," "unjust" or even "wicked," the Apostle Paul said, "Let God be true and every man a liar" (Rom. 3:4).

It is interesting to note in passing that when Paul, in the book of Romans, had to deal with the conflict between sinful human reason and Revealed Truth, the focus of controversy was always the doctrine of God's sovereignty in predestination and condemnation (Rom. 3:1-19; 9:1-33; 11:1-36). The rejection of the Doctrines of Grace is ultimately rooted in man's rebellion against God.

E. Throughout Scripture, man is viewed as the receiver of Truth, not its creator. God is the Author of all Truth and the Source of all wisdom and knowledge (2 Chron. 1:10-12; Pro. 1:1-7; Dan. 1:17; John 1:17; Rom. 1:25; James 1:5, etc.).

F. Human reason is not viewed in Scripture as the Origin or Judge of Truth on the basis of two inescapable realities.

1. Human reason is finite. Thus, it is incapable of an exhaustive understanding of the Truth. The intrinsic limitations of human reason forever disqualify it as the Origin or Judge of Truth.

Since it is finite, it is not surprising in the least to find that Revealed Truth goes beyond the ability of the human mind to understand and reconcile. Indeed, if the human mind could understand and reconcile all the doctrines of Scripture, this would prove that Scripture was of human origin and not inspired by God! The seeming contradictions and irreconcilable truths found in Scripture only point to us the Infinite Mind who gave it.

The person committed to the supremacy and sufficiency of Scripture is not bothered by the fact that he cannot completely understand or explain the doctrine of the Trinity, the decrees of God, creation, original sin, predestination or the atonement. They are called "mysteries" in Scripture because they are Truths which the mind of man did not create and which he cannot fully understand.

In the O.T., the passage of full mention is found in chapters 38-40 in the book of Job. (See also Job 5:9 and 11:7-9.) In the N.T., the passage of full mention is found in Romans 11:33-36. (See also Eph. 3:8, 19; Phil. 4:7.)

The Christian is not under any biblical constraint whatsoever to justify Revealed Truth before the bar of a mythological "Reason" created by the Rationalists. The doctrine of the Trinity is true because it is a revealed truth. It is not true because it is "reasonable." It is reasonable because it is true!

St. Augustine put it beautifully when he said: "I believe that I might understand. I do not wait until I understand before I believe."

2. Human reason is not only finite but it is also corrupted and twisted by sin. Thus the human mind or heart is morally incapable of submitting to or understanding Revealed Truth.

As soon as Adam and Eve fell into sin, their reason became darkened and they thought and did the most wicked and stupid things (Gen. 3:8-12).

In Scripture the reason or heart of man is described in the following ways:

evil (Gen. 6:5; 8:21)
corrupt and vile (Psa. 14:1-3)
futile (Psa. 94:11)
senseless (Jer. 10:14)
deceptive above all things (Jer. 17:9)
beyond cure (Jer. 17:9)
hostile to the Light (John 3:19-20)
carnal (Rom. 8:6)
death (Rom. 8:6)
rebellious and hostile to God and His Law (Rom. 8:7)
incapable of pleasing God (Rom. 8:8)
blinded by Satan (2 Cor. 4:3-4)
corrupted (2 Cor. 11:3; 1 Tim. 6:5; 2 Tim. 3:8)
futile and darkened (Eph. 4:17-19)
unspiritual (Col. 2:18)
defiled (Tit. 1:15)

The passage of full mention concerning the total depravity of human reason is found in Rom. 1:18-32 where the mind of man is said to suppress the truth revealed by God in general and special revelation. Man's reason is said to be without excuse, futile, foolish, darkened, idolatrous, sinful, immoral, depraved, hateful of God, etc. In Rom. 1, the Apostle Paul describes what man is really like if God does not intervene by his Revelation and by His Sovereign Grace.

Summary

Since human reason is finite and has been corrupted by sin, we must not "lean on our own understanding" or " be wise in our own eyes" (Prov. 3:5-7). Human reason must bow before Scripture and admit that some things revealed in it "transcend all understanding" (Phil. 4:7). God's Revelation is "unsearchable" and it "surpasses all understanding" (Eph. 3:8, 19). We must confess with the Psalmist that such knowledge is "too wonderful" and "too lofty" and "cannot be fathomed" by the mind of man (Psa. 139:6; 145:3). Both the old and new testamtents remind us:

> "Who has understood the mind of the Lord,
> or instructed Him as His counselor?"
> (Isa. 40:13; 1 Cor. 2:16)

PART TWO

The Role of Human Reason in Theology

Having seen that human reason is not the abstract and absolute "Reason" that the Rationalists invented, we must emphasize that one can be rational without being a Rationalist. We can use reason without absolutizing it into the Origin and Judge of all Truth.

Human reason is to function as the servant of Revelation and not its judge. Once man's reason bows to the supremacy of God's Reason, it is set free to be what God intended it to be.

In God's wondrous work of salvation, He illuminates, regenerates and renews the corrupt mind of man which has been darkened by sin and blinded by Satan (2 Cor. 4:4-6; Matt. 16:17; Eph. 1:18; John 3:3, 5; Rom. 12:2).

Once the mind is set free from its bondage to sin and guilt, it is ready to fulfill its role in God's world. The role of human reason is to study God's Revelation, to plumb its depths and scale its heights, to clarify and refine its concepts, to apply its principles, to obey its commands, and to defend its truthfulness.

Now, as Calvin warns us, we must always be conforming and reforming our reason to God's Revelation because, although our minds have been renewed, the power of the sin that "so easily besets us" will twist Scripture to devious ends.

Human Logic

One can use logic without being a Rationalist. In terms of its nature, a particular principle of human logic is valid if it reflects the Mind of God as Revealed in Scripture.

Man was made in the image of God, and part of this image is his capacity for logical thought, which is simply thinking God's thoughts after Him. Thus, while man's understanding is finite, it is true, nevertheless, because it comes from the image of God within him.

A close study of Scripture reveals that logic is used to convey, clarify and defend Revealed Truth. For example, the "law of contradiction" is rooted in the very Being of the God who cannot lie (Tit. 1:2). God cannot both be God and a lying God at the same time.

The truthfulness of the rule of logic which says that the denial of the consequence is always valid is found in such places as Gal. 5:18-21; 1 Cor. 6:9-11; 2 Cor. 5:17, etc. In such places Paul did not hesitate to argue:

> If someone is in union with Christ,
> ∴ then he is a new creature.
> _____
> If someone is not a new creature,
> ∴ then he is not in union with Christ.

The Apostle Paul had no problem whatsoever "reasoning" from the Scriptures (Acts 17:2; 18:4, 19, etc.). In all his writings, Paul constantly used logically valid forms of argumentation which demonstrated from the Old Testament that Jesus was the Messiah.

We must also remember that human logic only tells us if the structure of an argument is valid, and it cannot tell us if it is true. Indeed, an argument can be logically valid and materially false at the same time! Observe the following example.

Premise: Something which is correct part of the time is better than something which is never correct.

Premise: A stopped watch is correct twice a day, while a fast or slow watch is never correct.

Conclusion: It is better to wear a stopped watch than one that is fast or slow.

The above argument is logically valid but false! While something that is true will always be logically valid, the converse is not true.

Conclusion

Logic is the servant of the Lord. It does not sit in judgment of Divine Truth but seeks to serve it with reverence and humility. This is the true role of human reason.

Chapter Thirty-Seven

The Role of Emotion in Scripture & Theology

Introduction

One of the most perplexing problems we face today is the resurgence of Mysticism in the Church of the 21st century. We encounter more people every day who mold their views of God and His salvation solely on the basis of their "feelings." Indeed, it can be said without contradiction, that we are living in a generation of Christians who practice the maxim, "If an idea feels good, believe it."

The History of Mysticism

As a distinct philosophy, Mysticism arose out of the humanism of the Renaissance. In Mysticism, the emotions or the feelings of man are isolated from the rest of his being and then absolutized into the Origin of all meaning and the basis and judge of all Truth. Thus the "feelings" of man become the measure of all things including truth, justice, morals and beauty.

Mysticism has always been attractive to people who have already tried Rationalism and Empiricism but found them cold and sterile. Most Mystics had come to the depressing conclusion that a rational understanding of the universe was not really possible. Neither could the universe be understood by experimentation as the Empiricists claimed. There had to be some other way of knowing the Truth besides human reason or experience.

One would have hoped that having seen the futility of beginning with man's reason or experience as the measure of all things, they would have realized that the root problem was beginning with man in the first place. When we begin with finite man, we always end in skepticism (we cannot know truth from error) and relativism (we cannot know good from evil).

The Scriptures begin with God (Gen. 1:1). They do not begin with man. We must begin with God if we are to obtain true wisdom and knowledge (Prov. 1:7). The humanists have always begun with man as a self-sufficient being who does not need God's grace or revelation.

Christians have always believed that God is the Measure of All Things. Only His infinite nature can provide a sufficient basis for Truth or morals. All the finite gods of Greece and India put together cannot give a sufficient basis for truth or morals because they are finite. This is why modern attempts to finitize God by saying he is not omniscient, i.e. he does not know all things including the future, have always ended in skepticism and relativism. God is infinite in being, knowledge and power. The attempts to limit God have always led to disaster.

Instead of looking away from themselves to the God who made them, people turned to what they thought was a "new way" of knowing. This new way was to look within themselves for the Truth.

This, of course, had already served as the basis of Eastern religions for thousands of years. But to the Western Europeans of the 16th century, the idea that Truth could be found by simply looking within themselves to their emotions was quite new. This meant that they did not need a great intellect or vast scientific experience to understand the universe. Their heart, i.e. their feelings, was the best guide to what was good, just and true.

To the biblically informed Christian, the idea that he should trust his own heart is foolish, for God has warned us:

"The heart is deceitful above all things and desperately wicked. Who can understand it?" (Jer. 17:9).

The question as to how one went about looking within himself proved to be a tricky problem. Some said that Truth could be found only after various ceremonies such as fasting or prayer. Others said that they instantly knew the Truth when they heard it because their hearts felt a certain chill when the Truth was being expressed. Still others required people to go into trances before the Truth could be found.

The twin facts that the Mystics could never agree upon, namely, how to "look within" yourself, and what was good, just or true, proved to be insurmountable problems. The philosophy of Mysticism fell into disrepute as the Mystics fought among themselves as to whose feelings were the ultimate judge of Truth.

While Mysticism is no longer a popular philosophy in the world, it is alive and well in the Christian Church. Indeed, it has become a dominant force in some Christian circles. Christian Mystics identify themselves by their dependence on feelings for their doctrines and morals; and this is where the problem lies.

The Bible clearly teaches that our doctrines and morals should arise from a careful study of the Scriptures (2 Tim. 2:15; 3:16-17). Instead of studying the Bible to see what it says, however, the Mystic will try to "feel" his way to the Truth. He is not interested in a careful study of the text of Scripture.

As a matter of record, he is only interested in how he "feels." He assumes that Truth will conform itself to what his feelings tell him is true or false, right or wrong.

When confronted with a doctrine he does not like, such as predestination, a Mystic will usually say something like: "Well, I feel it is false. Therefore I cannot accept it."

The Mystic is not saying that he will examine Scripture and let Scripture alone decide his doctrines. In reality, his doctrines come from those mysterious "feelings" of his which supposedly tell him truth from error and right from wrong.

Whenever you hear someone saying that he will "pray about it" in order for him to "feel" what the Lord "says to him in his heart," you are dealing with a Mystic. Truth is discovered not by "feeling" the heart but by reading the Scriptures. As a way of obtaining doctrine, morals or guidance, Mysticism has a poor track record. If the Truth can be known through feelings, then all Mystics should perceive the same Truth. However, there is nothing more fickle than human emotion. Thus the Mystics disagree among themselves and the same Mystic will change his mind as many times as his feelings change.

Human Emotion in Scripture and Theology

In Scripture, human emotion plays no role whatsoever in determining doctrine or morals. Not once did God ask people how they felt about His Laws. They were to obey regardless of feelings. Revealed Truth was never said to be true because someone felt good about it. As a matter of fact, the history of the people of God as given in Scripture reveals that people did not generally like God's laws at all, and they certainly had some very bad feelings about the judgment of God on their sin.

Human emotion cannot be the measure of all things because it is finite. It is therefore insufficient as a basis for Truth. It is not only finite, but it is also sinful according to Scripture (Gen. 6:5; Rom. 3:10-18). Our emotions are hostile to God and our hearts actually hate God (Rom. 8:7; 1:30). Our hearts are deceitful and cannot be trusted (Jer. 17:9). We do not want the light of Truth, but rather the darkness of error, because our deeds are evil (John 3:19-21). No one seeks after or understands the true God (Rom. 3:11).

Whenever there was a conflict between human emotion and Revealed Truth, the authors of Scripture rebuked that emotion as rebellion against God (Rom.9:14-23). It also comes as no surprise to find that it was over such man-humbling doctrines as election that sinful emotions rose up against God (Psa. 2:1-12; Rom. 4:4-8; 9:14-23).

Just because we do not "like" a doctrine does not mean that it is not true. Most of the doctrines of Scripture are very hard on the emotions of man. We are told that we are wicked sinners on our way to a Hell which we justly deserve. Our pride is trampled to the dust, and the Holy Spirit makes us feel guilty and afraid. Nevertheless, the doctrines of the sinfulness of man and the justice of Hell are clearly taught in the Bible.

Does this mean that there is no place for human emotion in the Christian life? Of course not! We can state that human emotion has a role to play without becoming a Mystic.

Human emotions such as guilt and fear are the means God uses to bring us to true repentance (2 Cor. 7:10). The joy of His salvation comes to us at conversion (Psa. 51:12). Emotion has a very powerful role to play in the salvation of lost sinners. Until they feel as well as understand their need of salvation, they will not seek the Lord.

Emotion plays a powerful role in the Christian life. In the Book of Psalms we find human emotion in all its forms, from the heights of joy to the depths of depression (Psa.6; cf. Psa.8). There are "songs in the night" as well as "joy in the morning." There is an appropriate Psalm for every occasion and condition of the human heart. This is why it is the favorite prayer book and hymn book of true Christians.

Throughout the Scriptures, "happiness depends on happenings," i.e. our emotional state usually depends on the circumstances around us. There are times and situations where we should sorrow and weep (1 Cor. 12:26; James 4:9-10). Even Jesus wept at the grave of Lazarus (John 11:35).

The idea that Christians have to be happy all the time violates Scripture as well as sound, human psychology. It burdens the people of God with an impossible task. It leads to a kind of hypocrisy that drives the unsaved away from the Gospel. We must not wear a mask of happiness when we are sick, sinful or sorrowful.

While "happiness" comes and goes with the ebb tide of daily events and can be affected by such things as the level of sugar, iron or calcium in the blood, monthly cycles, personal tragedy, amount of sleep, etc.; our ability to "thank God for everything" remains firm; for giving thanks is an act of the will and not an emotion. Regardless of how we feel, we are to trust God and thank Him that He knows "why" things happen. We can commit our souls to our Maker and trust His Sovereign Will (1 Thess. 5:18).

Certain emotions such as joy, peace, patience, etc., should be cultivated in the Christian life (Gal. 5:22-23). Sinful emotions such as lust, anger, envy, hate, etc., should be "put to death" or "put off" (Rom. 8:13; Col. 3:8-9).

We should express our emotions in public and private worship (Psa. 150). The idea that "emotions" are intrinsically bad and should never be expressed in the worship of God flows out of the Greek deification of the mind and not from the Scriptures.

Human emotions are never condemned in Scripture because they are human. If an emotion was sinful, it was condemned. Jesus expressed every emotion of the human heart without sin being involved at any point. We should never be ashamed of our tears or our laughter, because the Lord Jesus Christ Himself wept and rejoiced openly. (See B.B. Warfield's article "The Emotional Life of Our Lord" in *The Person and Work of Christ*, P & R.)

Conclusion

Human emotion must be made the servant of the Lord. As a humble servant, it will not try to judge Truth or to be the origin of morals. Instead of looking within ourselves, we need to look away from ourselves to God, His Word and His Grace. Instead of conforming Scripture to our feelings, we need to conform our feelings to Scripture. We need to feel as God feels and to think as He thinks. This is only possible to the degree that we learn to trust in the Lord and His Word instead of trusting in our deceitful feelings. The choice is between the depravity of our hearts and the Revelation of God.

Chapter Thirty-Eight

The Role of Human Experience in Scripture & Theology

Introduction

Humanism has always taught that man is the measure of all things. Thus man's experience has been viewed by some as the origin and basis of all Truth. We can know what is true, just and moral from human experience. Thus there is no need for divine revelation. Man can discover the Truth by himself.

This humanist view gave rise to such principles as:

"If it works, it's true."

"The end justifies the means."

That such a principle should be used by unbelievers in the world is not surprising. But when we find Christians using such principles as the basis of their doctrines and morals, it is scandalous.

Its History

Humanism has always rested on the doctrine of the human autonomy, i.e. man has everything he needs within himself. He does not need God, His Word or His Grace. Man is self-sufficient. Man is his own god.

Humanism can express itself in religious terms as easily as in secular terminology. There are those within the Church of the 21st century who boldly teach that man is his own "god." Man has all the power he needs within himself. The "free will" of man is absolute and thus he is not a helpless sinner in need of God's intervention by way of Revelation or Grace.

The only way that these Christian humanists can exalt man is by dethroning God. Instead of man being dependent on God, God is said to be dependent on man! It is said that God is helpless and impotent. He is not allowed to intervene or to interfere with the affairs of almighty man. This "God" is a poor, pathetic being who deserves our pity. Man is on the throne now and God waits to do his bidding. God has been reduced to a mere puppet with man pulling the strings.

One of the clearest expressions of humanistic pragmatism is found in the idea that truth and morals depend on one's personal experiences. Instead of studying Scripture to see what God has revealed, the Christian humanist will base his beliefs on human experience.

One example comes to mind which clearly illustrates this problem. The following is a dialogue between Sam and Bob over the issue of being "slain in the Spirit."

Sam: "Oh, what a wonderful time I had last night in church! I was 'slain in the Spirit,' and I must have lain there at least an hour. When Kathryn touched me, I felt the electricity of the Spirit and it knocked me down flat. Wasn't it wonderful?"

Bob: "I am glad that you had a wonderful time in church, but I am not altogether sure that this 'slain in the Spirit' stuff is Scriptural."

Sam: "Don't be silly! Of course it is true because I experienced it, and a lot of other people have experienced it too. And, it felt so good to be slain. Kathryn came by me and I reached out and touched the hem of her garment and down I went. What could possibly be wrong with that?"

Bob: "But where in the Bible or church history do you find this stuff? Aren't you concerned in the least if 'being slain' is true according to God's Word? We must not interpret the Bible according to our experience. Instead, we must interpret our experience according to the Bible. Wouldn't you agree?"

Sam: "I don't see what you are getting all hyper about. I know it is true because I experienced it. I don't have to run around and prove it by the Bible or church history. But I'll ask my pastor for the proof tonight, and I'll tell you tomorrow."

The Next Day.

Bob: "Well, what did your pastor say?"

Sam: "He told me that I should not talk to you anymore. He said that you are guilty of something called 'bibliolatry' because you think that the Bible is God."

Bob: "But I don't think that the Bible is God and neither do I worship it as God. But the Bible does tell us that what we believe and how we live are to come from it and not from human experience. I guess that he could not come up with any proof and just told you to avoid me."

Sam: "No, he gave me all the proof I needed. Being 'slain in the Spirit' is clearly taught in John 18:6 and Rev. 1:17. There! Does that satisfy you?"

Bob: "I don't really think that you can legitimately use those passages. First, let me ask you something. Was being 'slain in the Spirit' a blessing or a judgment of God?"

Sam: "It's a wonderful blessing! I know because I experienced it."

Bob: "But if this is so, how can you use John 18:6, when in that passage Jesus judged his enemies who were coming to kill him by knocking them down? Furthermore, they did not become unconscious. It was also a very unpleasant experience for them. Remember, this was not a worship service! Jesus did not touch them. As a matter of fact, in the Gospels whenever Jesus touched people or they touched him, no one ever got knocked down."

Sam: "Well, I must admit that John 18 doesn't exactly prove my case but Rev. 1:17 does."

Bob: "Sam, did you bother to look at the text at all? It isn't enough to quote a verse. You have to examine it. Was there a worship service going on? Did an evangelist touch him? If you read the text you will find that John actually fainted in fright. He was so frightened by the appearance of Jesus that he fainted. Are you going to say that whenever someone faints in fright that this is what 'slain in the Spirit' is all about? I thought you told me it was a pleasant experience. Did you faint in fright the other night?"

Sam: "You are doing exactly what my pastor said you would do. He warned me that you would rob me of those verses."

Bob: "But, Sam, all I did was to look at the context and the wording of those passages. Isn't this what we are supposed to do as Christians?"

Sam: "I'm not going to talk about it anymore with you. I know I am right because I experienced it, and you could show me all the verses in the Bible until you are blue in the face and I still will not believe you."

This illustration is based on an actual conversation. Sam did not know it, but he was really a humanist and not a theist. His own experience was the measure of truth. He did not need the Bible to tell him right from wrong or truth from error. It did not matter what the issue was. It could be tongues, worship, healing, salvation, etc. In all these issues his experience was ultimate—not the Bible!

Human Experience in Scripture and Theology

Human experience is never appealed to in Scripture as the basis or judge of truth or morals. Since our experiences need to be interpreted and understood, how could they serve as the basis for anything? The real issue is, "how do we interpret our experiences?"

The humanist will interpret his experiences according to what he thinks or feels that they mean to him. He does not go outside of himself for an interpretation.

For example, Saul went to the witch of Endor because others had gone there and experienced what they claimed was communication with the dead. So, he went and asked her to call up Samuel. After the seance, Saul thought that he had talked with Samuel.

Now, the theist will not trust his reason or emotions to interpret his experiences (Prov. 3:5-7). Instead, he goes outside of himself to God's Word to seek an explanation.

In the case of Saul, the theist would interpret Saul's experience at Endor in a different way. On the basis of many texts of Scripture, he would say that Saul was actually talking with a demon who pretended to be Samuel. Saul was deceived and tricked by the old witch.

Now, no one denies that Saul had an experience. The issue comes down to how do we interpret it. The humanist will look to himself for the interpretation while the theist will look to Scripture (2 Tim. 3:16-17).

Conclusion

Truth and morals cannot be decided by our experience because each experience itself must be judged as to whether it is true, just or moral according to Scripture. Just because something works, gets the job done or feels good, does not mean that it is true, just or moral (Deut. 13:1-5). The ends do not justify the means (Rom. 6:1-2).

"To the Law and to the Testimony!

If they do not speak according to this Word, they have no light" (Isa. 8:20).

Chapter Thirty-Nine

A Christian Introduction to Logic

Introduction

The ability to think through issues, evaluate arguments, weigh evidences and come to valid conclusions is essential for making rational decisions. The goal of the study of logic is what the Bible calls wisdom. This wisdom is the ability to discern truth from error, good from evil, justice from injustice and beauty from ugliness. It is the natural outgrowth of spiritual maturity (Heb. 5:12-14). Being foolish and childish in our thinking is condemned by Scripture (Eph. 4:14; 1 Cor. 13:11).

The scope of logic is universal. No area of life can escape logic. Regardless if we are dealing with religious, political, financial, social or domestic issues, the ability to think correctly and to draw valid conclusions is paramount.

The study of logic has always had a special place in Christian thought because the prophets and apostles used logic in their writing of Scripture. Indeed, the Bible is the most logical book that comes to us from ancient times. Its inspiration is revealed when it is contrasted to the mystical and irrational religious works of its own day.

The correct interpretation of the Bible depends on a careful analysis of the logic used by the authors of Scripture. The intelligibility of the Bible is based on the assumption of its logical nature. It speaks to us about life as it really is, in language that we can understand and arguments we can appreciate. Without this assumption, the interpretation of the Bible becomes a subjective word game.

Religious irrationalism reaches its apex in the theology of the absurd in which idealism triumphs over realism, sentimentality over reason and gullibility over common sense. Indeed, in some circles, gullibility and naivete have become hallmark virtues! But this was not always the case.

Our Protestant forefathers were keenly interested in logic. To them the study of logic was essential to Christian thought and life. Rational thought was viewed as a virtue while irrationalism was labeled a vice. But today the opposite has become true. While John Calvin was praised in his day as the greatest Protestant theologian because he was so logical in his arguments, he is castigated today for the very same reason! We are now living in an upside-down world where rationality is viewed as the greatest vice and irrationality as the greatest virtue! It would seem that the more irrational and absurd the religion, the greater its popularity today!

Secular humanists are more than justified when they complain that most religions today are essentially irrational. Yet, they themselves suffer from the same disease. Modern atheists have reduced logic to subjective personal preference, cultural norms and psychological data. The law of non-contradiction is assumed to have no more force than one's preference for chocolate over vanilla.

Religious humanists have come together in the New Age Movement, which is the clearest example of how far humanists are willing to go in the pursuit of the absurd. The attempt of modern philosophy to escape logic by leaping into some kind of "upper-story" irrationalism has always ended in failure because those who champion such causes cannot live what they believe or believe what they live.

The absurdity of existentialism, the bankruptcy of modern atheism and the poverty of relativism are all good examples of such self-abasing futility.

We have now arrived at that stage of history where the only champions of logic are orthodox Christians who are trying to make their way through a sea of irrationalism in the church as well as in the world.

I. The Nature of Logic:

A. There are two approaches to logic today: subjectivism vs. objectivism.

No. 1 Subjectivism

No logic
↓
culture
↓
custom
↓
preference
↓
common sense
↓
psychology
↓
skepticism
↓
relativism
↓
no truth
↓
no morals
↓
no knowledge

The Problems with Subjectivism

1. The attempt to deny logic is self-refuting because one must use logic to deny anything.

2. The belief that everything is relative and that there are no absolutes is self-refuting.

3. The belief that everything can be reduced to psychological factors, cultural norms or personal preference is self-refuting.

4. The belief that man can choose to think and communicate in some other way than logic has never been able to come up with such a system.

5. The transcultural universality of logic and its linguistic necessity for all communication reveals that logic is both objective and transcendent in nature.

No. 2 Objectivism

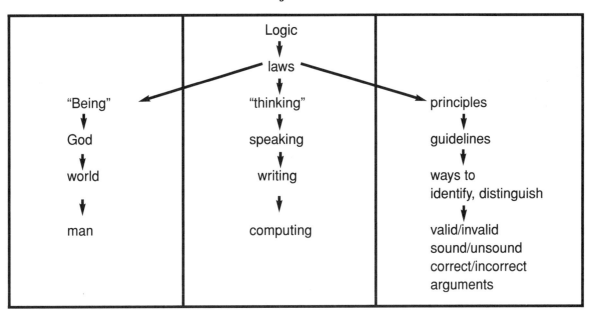

II. The Nature of Arguments

Arguments

not	declarative sentences	structure
emotive	propositions	form
exclamatory	1. Three or more	not:
expository	sentences strung	1. good/evil
explanatory	together as:	2. right/wrong
anecdotal	a. premises	3. true/false
illustrative	b. conclusion	
descriptive	2. Attempt to justify	
repetitive	belief/action as	
sentences	valid/correct.	
parables	3. Attempt to convince	
	others of correctness of	
	beliefs/actions.	

III. Two Kinds of Arguments

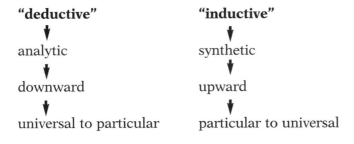

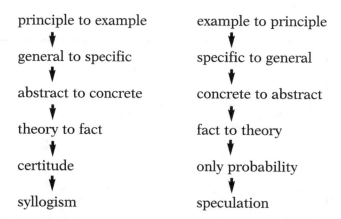

Note: The scientific method is inductive. Thus it can never come up with certain knowledge, absolute truths or universal laws. You cannot logically leap from particulars to a universal no matter how many particulars you may pile up.

$$p+p+p+p+p+= p \; [\sim U]$$

IV. Deductive Syllogisms

The use of syllogisms is essential to the study of logic. But in order to set up a syllogism, we must be able to reduce an argument to its underlying form/structure by using symbols instead of words to represent the concepts stated in the argument.

1. The use of symbols, in this case letters, will save us much time and energy. Instead of trying to determine the truth or falsehood of an argument, we must first determine whether the argument in terms of its form is valid or sound. If an argument is invalid in its form, then the argument is unsound no matter how "true" the premises may be. Thus the foundational principle of all logic is, the form of the argument has priority over its content.

2. Reducing an argument to a syllogism is a short cut to truth. Instead of arguing over the ideas stated in the argument, we must be able to use "x-ray vision" to see the bones of the argument. If the form, or bones of the argument are unsound, then the argument is invalid.

3. Logic asks, "Is the form used in this argument valid?" It does not ask, "Is the argument good/true?"

4. An argument can be valid in its form but false in its contents.

> Something right part of the time is better
> than something that is never right.
>
> A broken watch is right twice a day while
> <u>a fast or slow watch is never right.</u>
> *A broken watch is better.*

5. We substitute symbols for words every day.
   a. letters for ideas/sounds/words: a, b, c, etc.

b. numbers for words.

One plus one equals two or 1+1=2

c. letters for numbers: a+b=c

6. In logic, we use letters to represent the ideas found in arguments.

If you believe in Jesus, you will be saved.

<u>If you are saved, you will go to Heaven.</u>

Then if you believe in Jesus, you will go to Heaven.

$$a>b$$
$$\underline{b>c}$$
$$a>c$$

If you are saved, you will be godly.

if you are not godly,

Then you are not saved.

$$a>b$$
$$\underline{\overline{b}}$$
$$\overline{a}$$

V. Rules for Valid Syllogisms

1. If the premises are unclear in their meaning, no conclusion can be drawn.

2. There may be only three terms, i.e., two premises and a conclusion.

(No conclusion can be drawn from one premise.)

3. The middle term must be distributed.

$$a>b$$
$$\underline{b>c}\quad \text{b=middle term}$$
$$a>c$$

(If the middle term is not distributed, no conclusion can be drawn.)

4. If both premises are positive, the conclusion will be positive.

$$p$$
$$\underline{p}$$
$$p$$

(You cannot draw a negative conclusion from two positive premises.)

5. If one premise is negative, the conclusion will be negative.

$$p$$
$$\underline{n}$$
$$n$$

(You cannot draw a positive conclusion if one of the premises is negative.)

6. If both premises are negative, no positive conclusion can be drawn.

n
n̲
?

(You cannot draw a positive conclusion from two negative premises.)

7. If all-inclusive terms are switched, no conclusion can be drawn.

all   all
a̲l̲l̲   s̲o̲m̲e̲
all   ?

8. If there is no universal in the premises, no universal can appear in the conclusion.

p   p
p̲   p̲
p   U

(If you want a universal in the conclusion, you must have one in the premises.)

U
p̲
U

9. If a term does not appear in a premise, it cannot appear in the conclusion.

a>b
b̲>̲c̲
a>x

10. If there is a particular in the conclusion, there must be a particular in the premises.

U   u
p̲   u̲
p   u

(You cannot draw a particular from two universals.)

Conclusion

This brief introduction to logic is enough to encourage any Christian to study the laws of logic which are in reality the laws of the divine Logos, the Logic or Wisdom of God (John 1:1).

Chapter Forty

Just How Old Is the Universe?

Some Puzzling Scientific Facts

Have you ever wondered about the origin of the universe? Did it start with a whimper or a big bang? How old is the universe? Is it eternal or was it created out of nothing by nothing, and for good measure, how old is the planet on which we live?

Questions such as these are valid and demand careful attention because they provide important solutions to the great riddle of life. What is important is that these questions should be approached with an open mind instead of a predetermined judgment. We should follow the evidence wherever it leads.

Since the present, popular, evolutionary position is that the universe is 15 to 25 billion years old, we should check the evidence to see if this position is true. The following is a brief and partial list of some puzzling scientific facts that indicate the universe and the earth may not be billions of years old. The evidence seems to indicate that we should think in terms of thousands of years instead of billions of years.

I. The Topsoil Factor

It takes around a thousand years to produce one inch of topsoil by the forces of erosion, such as wind and rain. If the earth is billions of years old and the process by which topsoil is created has been functioning all the time, there should be a thick layer of topsoil on the earth's crust. However there is only an average depth of six to nine inches of topsoil on the earth! This amount can only explain thousands of years of erosion. Where is the topsoil created by billions of years of erosion? Where did it go?

Sources: Mickey, Karl, "Man and the Soil," International Harvester Co., 1946, pp. 17, 22; Orr, Lord, Broadcast, Canadian Broadcasting Corp., June 6, 1948; "Lawns." A pamphlet. Ontario Department of Agriculture. Bulletin 48, April 1947. Shoemaker and Taylor.

II. The Ocean Floor

Perhaps the vast amount of topsoil created by billions of years of erosion has simply washed into the ocean and can be found in sedimentary deposits on its floor. If the earth is billions of years old and the erosion rate has been steady and of such a degree as to explain where all the topsoil went, the sediment at the bottom of the ocean should be miles deep. However the sediment on the ocean floor only has 0.56 mile average thickness! This depth can only explain thousands of years, and cannot represent billions of years of erosion. Where is the sediment created by billions of years of erosion? Where did it go?

Ewing, M., Carpenter, G., Windisch, C., Ewing, J., "Sediment Distribution in the Oceans: The Atlantic," January 1973, *Geological Society of America Bulletin,* Vol. 84, p. 83; Holeman, John N., "The Sediment Yield of Major Rivers of the World," August 1968, *Water Resources Research,* Vol. 4, p. 737.

III. Meteor Dust

When meteors collide with the earth's atmosphere they disintegrate into dust that settles on the earth's surface. Given the present rate at which meteor dust is settling on the earth, if the earth is billion years old there should be at least 54 feet of meteor dust on the surface of the planet. Since the depth of topsoil and ocean sediment do not contain billions of years of meteor dust, what happened to this dust? Where did it go?

Scientific American, February 1960, p. 132; "Dust," *Encyclopedia Britannica*, 1958, Vol. 7, p. 766; Wilder-Smith, Arthur E., 1985, *Origins*, F.F.C. Mesa, Ariz., pp. 12-13; Kofahi and Segraves, 1975, *The Creation Explanation*, p. 190.

IV. The Helium Factor

As radioactive materials disintegrate, helium is released as a by-product into the atmosphere. Given the present rate at which helium is released into the atmosphere, if the earth is billions of years old, there should be enough helium in the atmosphere to make us all talk like Donald Duck. There is only enough helium in the atmosphere to explain thousands of years. Where did the helium produced by billions of years go?

Encyclopedia Britannica, 1958, Vol. 11, p. 400; Cook, Melvin, 1985, "Radiogenic Helium," Salt Lake City.

V. The Salty Sea

Given the present rate at which salt and other minerals are being washed into the ocean, if the earth is billions of years old, what should be the concentration of salt in the earth's oceans? There is only enough salt in the ocean to explain thousands of years of erosion. The concentration of such minerals as nickel, as well as salt, in the earth's oceans would be many times greater if the earth were billions of years old. Where have all the billions of years of salt and other minerals gone?

Scientific Studies in Special Creation, ed. Lamments Co., Pres. & Ref. Pub., 1971; A Symposium on Creation, Grand Rapids, Mich.: Baker Book House, 1975, ed. by Donald Patten; Dillow, J., *The Waters Above*, Chicago: Moody Press.

VI. The Earth's Magnetic Field

The scientific evidence clearly indicates that the earth's magnetic field is decaying. With an understanding of the second law of thermodynamics, this should be expected. Given the present rate of decay, if the earth were billions of years old, the earth's magnetic field would have passed into nonexistence long ago. If the earth is billions of years old, why does it still have a magnetic field?

Barnes, Thomas G., July 21, 1980, "Satellite Observations Confirm the Decline of the Earth's Magnetic Field," University of Texas, El Paso, Texas; Chapman, Sidney, 1951, "The Earth's Magnetism," Methuen & Co. Ltd., London, John Wiley & Sons, Inc., New York, p. 15; McDonald, Keith L. and Guust, Robert H., 1967, "An Analysis of the Earth's Magnetic Field From 1835 to 1965," ESSA Technical Rept. IER 46-IES. I. U.S. Government Printing Office, Washington, D.C., p. 1.

VII. Moon Dust

The vehicles prepared for landing on the moon were equipped with special snowshoes because it was assumed that if the moon is billions of years old, there should be an incredibly thick layer of dust on the moon created by such things as meteor impact. They discovered only one-fourth of an inch of dust on the moon! This amount of dust can account for only thousands of years. If the moon is billions of years old, where did all the dust that accumulated during this time go?

Wilder-Smith, Arthur E., 1985, *Origins*, F.F.C. Mesa, Ariz., pp. 12-13; *Scientific American*, February 1960, p. 132; Lewis, Richard, *Appointment on the Moon*, pp. 234, 249, 254.

VIII. The Shrinking Sun

The sun is shrinking as its energy is flung into the galaxy. Given the present rate of shrinkage, if the sun is billions of years old, it should have disappeared by now. Or if the sun is billions of years old, in order for it to have shrunk down to the size it is now, it would have engulfed the space now occupied by most of the planets in this galaxy. If this is true, where did the planets come from?

Eddy, John A. and Boomazian, Aram A., 1979, "Secular Decrease in the Solar Diameter, 1836-1953," *Bulletin of the American Astronomical Society,* Vol. 11, p. 437; "Analyses of Historical Data Suggest Sun Is Shrinking," 1979, *Physics Today* 32(9): pp. 17-19; "New Test for Solar Neutrinos Proposed," 1976, *Sky and Telescope* 52(5): pp. 324-325.

IX. Active Volcanoes

Since the earth's moon is a dead world with no active volcanoes, it was assumed that this meant that the moon was billions of years old. It was also assumed that no moons would have active volcanoes. The evidence is now clear that at least one of the moons of Jupiter has active volcanoes. Does this fact not indicate that the assumption of the necessity of billions of years for the age of the universe is erroneous? As a matter of fact, if the universe is billions of years old, why and how should any planet or moon have active volcanoes?

Smith, Bradford A., et al, 1979, "The Jupiter System Through the Eyes of Voyage 1," *Science* 204 (4396):95 1-972, see especially table 3, p. 967; Voyager 1 Encounter With the Jovial System," 1979, *Science* 204 (4396):951-972, see especially table 2, p. 947; Akridge, Garth Russell, March 1980, "Jupiter's Galilean Moons," *Creation Research Society Quarterly,* Vol. 16, No. 4, p. 207.

X. The Rings of Saturn

If the universe is billions of years old, we must assume that the rings of Saturn are of this age. Given the rate of orbital and structural decay, if the rings are billions of years old, they should have collapsed and blurred into one vast confusion. Yet, the evidence is clear that the rings are so distinct that they can be counted, and some of them look as if they were braided. Given the laws of physics, the rings must be viewed as young and not old. If the rings are billions of years old, why are they clear and distinct?

Conclusion

These are 10 puzzling scientific facts that will lead any open-minded person to the conclusion that the universe is a lot younger than billions of years old. We should not let the religious prejudice of the evolutionists force us to accept their doctrines by a blind leap of faith, when the scientific evidence does not correspond to their theories. Perhaps it is time for modern man to reconsider the words of a man who was one of the most educated scholars that Egyptian education ever produced: "In the beginning God created the heavens and the earth" Gen. 1:1 (Moses).

Postscript

"The age of our globe is presently thought to be some 4.5 billion years, based on radio decay rates of uranium and thorium. Such 'confirmation' may be short-lived, as nature is not to be discovered quite so easily. There has been in recent years the horrible realization that radio decay rates are not as constant as previously thought, nor are they immune to environmental influences.

"And this could mean that the atomic clocks are reset during some global disaster, and events which brought the Mesozoic to a close may not be 65 million years ago but, rather, within the age and memory of man."

Frederic B. Jueneman, FAIC, "Secular Catastrophism," *Industrial Research and Development,* June 1982, p. 21.

"Evolutionism is a fairy tale for grown-ups. This theory has helped nothing in the progress of science. It is useless."

Prof. Louis Bounoure (former president of the Biological Society of Strasbourg and director of the Strasbourg Zoological Museum, later director of research at the French National Centre of Scientific Research) as quoted in *The Advocate,* Thursday, March 8, 1984, p. 17.

Chapter Forty-One

Must We Tie Into a System?

When God created man in His own image, He gave man a holistic outlook on life. This world-and-life view was a system of thought in which Adam and Eve were able to see all of life from God's perspective. They could interpret all of reality in its proper meaning and significance. This original creation world-and-life view was internally and externally consistent, harmonious, satisfying and complete. Since it was internally satisfying, Adam and Eve experienced intellectual and aesthetic pleasure as they interpreted the world around them. From the standpoint of this comprehensive world-and-life view, Adam was able to name all the animals (Gen. 2:20). Prior to the fall, then, Adam had an "answer" for everything he experienced in life.

The fall of man into sin must be interpreted as involving, initially, a radical change in his perspective on life. What Satan offered man was a different system of thought in which the significance of the Tree of Knowledge of Good and Evil was interpreted from Satan's viewpoint instead of God's. Satan's perspective also reinterpreted God's motives and character and man's potential. Man was faced with two conflicting systems of thought which interpreted reality from two different outlooks.

Once man began to see the tree, God's person and his own place in creation from Satan's viewpoint, man fell. His eating the fruit was merely the outward sign of the inward change of his perspective.

As a result of sin's entrance into the world, the holistic, consistent, harmonious, satisfying and complete world-and-life view that man had at the beginning was lost. Instead of the ability to view all of life in its proper context, man's view of life was shattered, twisted and distorted. Satan had offered to man another system of thought, but one which could not match the Wisdom of God.

Though man had lost his initial, God-given view of life, there remained in him a desire and need for an intellectually and aesthetically pleasing system of thought in which all of life could be interpreted. This inward drive came from God's image within man and called him to search for a perfect system. This need and desire has indeed prevailed throughout the history of mankind.

The history of philosophy is the greatest testimony to man's search for a perfect system. In this light we can understand why so much hope was placed in the systems of the classical Greek philosophers. Plato's system was initially thought to be the "answer." Then along came Aristotle, who refuted Plato and gave his system in its place. After Aristotle came Plotinus, who refuted Aristotle. One successor upon another, the modern philosophers such as Kant, Hegel and Dooyeweerd bring us up to the present. Each of these philosophers in his own generation developed what he thought was a perfect and complete system of thought by which all of life could be interpreted.

The scientists have followed in the same path. It had been hoped that Newton had articulated the perfect scientific system. Then Einstein developed his system of thought, which refuted Newton's, and a new way of interpreting reality was posited. Now we have the emergence of quantum mechanics and the introduction of Eastern philosophy into physics in order to give us a new system beyond that of Einstein's theory of relativity.

Perhaps we can make the general observation that the main problem came in viewing systems as fixed instead of viewing the extension of human knowledge as a process.

When we examine the history of theology, we must admit that nearly all the theologians seem to be on the same path that the philosophers and scientists have taken. Most theologians assume that there is a perfect theological system which is complete and answers all the problems. Just as the philosophers sought a perfect philosophical system and the scientists a perfect scientific system, so most theologians went in search of a perfect theological system by which all of life and Scripture should be interpreted.

In this search for a perfect system, Augustine ended up importing neo-Platonist philosophy into Christian theology. Aquinas rejected neo-Platonism but imported Aristotle's system. When we deal with the Reformation we discover that Calvin, and later the Puritans, developed another system by which they could interpret Scripture and life. This has come to be called covenant theology. Charles Hodge in his systematic theology imported Scottish Realism by way of McCosh. W.G.T. Shedd introduced Kant's philosophy in his theology.

Since many feel uncomfortable with both dispensationalism and covenant theology, the question arises, do we need a system? Must we carry on the quest which has been followed for centuries? Several considerations should cause us to hesitate in producing another theological system.

First, there is no warrant in Scripture itself for the assumption that there is a perfect system to be found and set forth by men. There is no indication in the Word of God that it was given to provide us with such a system or that seeking a system is in harmony with its inspired purpose.

Second, when we begin to search the Scriptures to find the system, we end up ignoring many texts and avoiding detailed exegesis. We are drawn toward speculative theology instead of exegetical theology.

Third, once we have artificially constructed a system, it becomes ultimately more authoritative than Scripture itself. Doctrine need not be based on any text, but only on what we think can be "deduced therefrom." Church confessions and creeds begin to carry more weight than Scripture.

Fourth, Scripture in no longer regarded as the substance or focus of revelation, but only as the package in which the system arrives.

Fifth, it is assumed that a system is needed in order to provide "the key" to unlock the many parts of Scripture. A "key" methodology functionally denies the perspicuity or clearness of Scripture.

Sixth, all "key" systems are reductionist methodologies. Contemporary theologians often pick one theme in Scripture, abstract it out of its context, absolutize it as the "key" and reduce all other ideas in Scripture to that theme. The popular "keys" include hope, promise, reconciliation, Kingdom of God, remnant, dispensations, covenant, Pauline eschatology, people of God, etc. It is assumed that unless we choose one of these "keys," it will be impossible to interpret Scripture.

Seventh, the "key" theologians fail to recognize is that Scripture is multi-thematical, multi-dimensional and, in everything, focused on Christ. A close exegesis of Scripture reveals that a number of themes which begin in Genesis are developed throughout Scripture. Just as a rope has many strands which stretch from beginning to end, so the Bible develops a number of themes. To choose one theme and reduce all of Scripture to it flattens the Bible as if it were a single-dimensional revelation.

Eighth, our natural fixation on one system has the tragic, practical effect of cutting us off from learning from other traditions. When we view one system as "it," we look down our nose at what others are saying.

Conclusion

Considering the current theological systems vying for our allegiance, we should be cautious about any "key" system which is one-dimensional and reductionist. We will have to be content to live with many loose ends; that is, insoluble problems and unanswered questions. The antinomies, mysteries and paradoxes of Scripture must be accepted for what they are. Yet we must never use our "finiteness" as an excuse to skirt discovering all of God's truth that we can. To opt for dispensational or covenant hermeneutics is often an escape from honest exegesis. Let us speak where Scripture speaks and remain silent where it is silent.

Chapter Forty-Two
Calvinism and Arminianism

Introduction

Due to an aggressive revival of Calvinism in the 20th century, many Christians in the United States are hearing the word "Calvinism" for the first time. They are vaguely aware that there is a theological battle between Calvinism and Arminianism today.

It is obvious that the battle is going to heat up as Calvinism is gaining strength among serious-minded Christians who desire to be exegetical in their approach to Scripture and are tired of the shallow sermons of the typical Arminian evangelical pastor.

There is also a revival of interest in the Reformation and its theology because this is where the Protestant Church began. Such modern leaders as Francis Schaeffer, J. I. Packer, Jay Adams, Gordon Clark, R.C. Sproul, James Boice and James Kennedy are openly Calvinistic in their theology. A new day seems to be dawning for the Reformed Faith as people are discovering that their roots lie in the theology of the Reformation.

It is important for the modern Christian to understand that the present battle between Calvinism and Arminianism is not a new or recent development. The issues that are being fought over have been points of controversy for two thousand years. It is thus essential to place the present controversy in the context of two thousand years of Christian research and conclusions.

Part One

I. "Calvinism" is a label that was placed on those who basically agreed with the theology of John Calvin (1509-1564). Calvin was the greatest theologian of the Reformation in that he was the one who first developed a systematic Protestant theology. What he taught concerning the nature of salvation and the nature of man was in union with what the other Reformers taught. Even his doctrine of predestination and his denial of the Catholic teaching of "free will" were the accepted Protestant position. For example, see Luther's book *The Bondage of the Will*, where Luther gave his full weight to what was appropriately called "the doctrines of grace."

Calvin's position on salvation was officially accepted by representatives of all Protestant Churches at the Synod of Dort in 1619. Let there be no mistake on this point. The Protestant theology of the Reformation was what we now call Calvinism.

II. Arminianism is a label that was put on those who followed the theology of James Hermann (1560-1609), whose Latin name was Jacob Arminius. Although he was raised in the Reformed Church of Holland, through reading the works of the Socinian cult, whose most famous member was Servetus, he came to embrace their brand of Pelagianism.

His followers waged a battle to change the creeds of the Church to reflect their views instead of keeping the theology of the Reformation as the official position of the Church. This controversy reached its climax at the Synod of Dort, where the issues were debated by representatives from all of Protestantism.

The views of Arminius were condemned as heresy and as a veiled attempt to return to Roman Catholicism. It was also pointed out that Arminius was only reviving the doctrine of semi-Pelagianism that had already been condemned as heresy by the Council of Orange in A.D. 529.

The issues that Arminius was now raising were the same issues that were involved in the controversy between Augustine and Pelagius in the early church.

III. Augustinianism is a label placed on those who follow the theology of St. Augustine (A.D. 354-430), who was the greatest theologian of the Early Fathers. His position on the nature of salvation and the nature of man reflected, for the most part, the views of the orthodox Fathers before him.

He was the one who was called upon to refute the teachings of the monk Pelagius. Augustine believed that salvation was all of grace and that man does not contribute anything toward his own salvation. He taught that man is totally unable to seek after God or do any good works that could merit salvation.

All men are born with the guilt and depravity of Adam upon them and, by nature, we are spiritually dead and incapable of saving ourselves. Thus God must initiate salvation, faith and repentance, which are the good gifts of God. His views were accepted as the official position of the Christian Church and ratified as such by various councils.

After several centuries, the Roman Church embraced a semi-Pelagian view that promoted good works for salvation and the necessity of earning merit for salvation.

At the time of the Reformation, the Reformers were simply reviving Augustinianism. They proclaimed that salvation was all of grace. Justification was by grace alone, through faith alone, in Christ alone. The Roman Church officially condemned the "doctrines of grace" at the Council of Trent. The Roman Church today shows itself to be heretical by teaching that which was condemned by the councils of the early church.

IV. Pelagianism is a label placed on those who follow the teachings of the Monk Pelagius (A.D. 411-431). Following the teachings of the heretical Origen, who attempted to combine Christianity and Greek philosophy, Pelagius came to believe that each human soul was placed in the infant by a creative act of God. Each soul was therefore perfect and sinless at birth in the same way that Adam and Eve were at the original creation. Thus the fall of Adam and Eve did not in any way affect their children. We have perfect free wills and can be sinless if we so decide. Salvation is not all of grace because we are perfectly able to be saved by an act of our own free wills. Faith and repentance are not the gifts of God. Man can initiate his own salvation. We are free to be sinless or sinful. We are not helpless. We do not need God to intervene for salvation.

Pelagius' teachings were first discovered through his disciple Coelestius, who preached this boldly in Carthage. After much debate, Pelagius' doctrines were condemned as heresy by the Church of Carthage in A.D. 412. Later, more churches got involved in condemning Pelagianism at the Synod of Mileum in A.D. 416. It reached its climax in A.D. 431, when the Ecumenical Council of Ephesus condemned Pelagianism as heresy. There were seven such Ecumenical Councils where representatives of all the churches of Christianity met to decide such issues.

With the triumph of Augustinianism at the Council of Ephesus, the followers of Pelagius modified their views at certain points and put forth what was called semi-Pelagianism. This was condemned by the Council of Orange in A.D. 529. Twenty-five articles were developed against semi-Pelagianism. Some of these articles are as follows:

1. We condemn those who maintain that the sin of Adam has affected only the body of man by rendering it mortal and has not affected the soul also.

2. We condemn those who maintain that the sin of Adam injured only himself or that the death of the body is the only effect of his transgression which has descended to his posterity.

3. We condemn those who teach that grace is given in answer to the prayer of man and who deny that it is through grace that he is brought to pray at all.

4. We condemn those who teach that God waits for our wish before purifying us from sin and that he does not by His Spirit give us the wish to be purified.

5. We condemn those who maintain that the act of faith, by which we believe in Him who justifieth, is not the work of grace but that we are capable of doing so of ourselves.

6. We condemn those who maintain that man can think or do anything good, as far as his salvation is concerned, without grace.

Part Two

The Present Situation

Pelagianism appeals to unregenerate man because it exalts man and downgrades the need for divine grace. It eventually supplanted Augustinianism in the Roman Church by the time of the Reformation. The Protestant churches revived Augustinianism and proclaimed the doctrines of grace. Arminius was the first to officially desire a return to the semi-Pelagianism of the Roman Church. It was hoped that the Synod of Dort would be able to stop the spread of this ancient heresy. But within two centuries, Arminianism supplanted Calvinism in the mainline churches.

It has come full circle once again. There are those who exalt man and his supposed free will and who maintain that man has all he needs in his own powers to acquire salvation. No divine grace is needed to repent or believe. They speak of children as "innocent" and have invented the unscriptural concept of an "age of accountability." Any attempt to view man as a helpless sinner is resisted. God is viewed as responding to what we do. He chooses us if we choose him. Man is the ultimate arbitrator of his salvation. The needs of man and not the glory of God is the goal of salvation.

Today, there is a revival of what is called Calvinism, Protestant Theology, Reformed Theology or Augustinianism. There is a New Reformation beginning in which the old doctrines of grace are being boldly proclaimed for the first time in a long time. People sense that the time has come to exalt God as the Lord of all of life and to dash to the ground the pretended autonomy of men who see themselves as the center of the universe.

The churches need to be reformed according to the Word of God. For too long God has been pictured as a helpless old man or as a puppet whose strings man controls. God is treated like a servant who waits on man's commands.

Serious Christians can no longer abide the downgrading of God and the exalting of man. God is sovereign and His salvation is all of grace from beginning to end. We are helpless sinners who are in need of God to intervene in our lives to bring us to Himself. This is the only answer to the teachings of secular and religious humanism. The reason that the Fundamentalists cannot answer humanism is that their Arminianism is itself a form of humanism. This is why they must depend on Calvinists such as Francis Schaeffer.

Just as humanism finds its logical climax in atheism, even so theism finds its logical climax in Calvinism. It alone gives to God all the glory and calls sinners to fall down and serve Him who is their Creator and Redeemer.

Part Three

25 Crucial Questions

1. What was the original spiritual condition of man at his creation? Did he have a free will? In what sense?
2. What happened to Adam and Eve when they sinned against God? What effect did their sin have on their mind, emotions and will?
3. Did the sin of Adam affect his posterity? In what way?
4. When and how do people receive their soul?
5. What is the spiritual condition and standing of man at conception? Did Adam pass on his guilt and depravity to all of his posterity?

6. Is human nature perfectible by its own abilities? Is it possible to be sinless in this life?

7. Are we capable of pleasing God by our own actions, words or deeds?

8. Do we have the ability to produce good works and our own righteousness before God that merits our salvation?

9. Does man need God to intervene in grace to save him or does man just need another chance?

10. What is grace and why does the Bible refer to it so much?

11. Was Christ's life and death necessary for our salvation or was there an infinite number of ways that salvation could be given?

12. Is the work of the Holy Spirit necessary for salvation? Does He interfere with the heart and will of sinners to cause them to turn to God?

13 Are faith and repentance the gifts of God to helpless sinners or the gifts of man to God?

14. Can we say that men have free wills? In what sense?

15. Who initiates salvation? God or man?

16. Is the goal of the plan of salvation the glory of God or the needs of man?

17. Who completes the salvation process? God or man?

18. Is salvation a 50/50 deal between God and man with each doing their parts, or is salvation wholly of God's grace or man's work?

19. What is the basis of justification?

20. Was Christ's active obedience in life vicarious in nature, that is, in our place?

21. Is divine election and predestination based on anything we will do or have done? Does God choose us because we chose Him or do we choose Him because He first chose us?

22. Did Christ come to make salvation merely possible or did He come to secure the actual salvation of sinners? Was the atonement only hypothetical or was it actually vicarious in nature? Did Christ die in the place of only the elect, securing their eternal salvation? Or, was His death a hypothetical situation in which He did not actually die for anyone at all? Thus did He actually die in the place of all men or of the elect? Did He make salvation possible only if men will use their free will to seek it?

23. Does regeneration (i.e., the new birth) precede or follow the act of faith?

24. Is man totally passive in regeneration? Can man regenerate himself by an act of his own will?

25. What is man's true spiritual condition and standing before God?

The above issues must be honestly dealt with because they involve the essence of the Gospel of the unmerited grace of God. The Christian Church was founded on the doctrines of grace and had her greatest growth in that period. She has always triumphed over paganism and humanism when these same doctrines are preached. These wonderful doctrines of grace returned to Europe in the Reformation. They were revived in America by the Great Awakening under the great Calvinist Jonathan Edwards. They formed the basis of the Evangelical revivals under Whitefield and were the guiding force behind the great missionary efforts of Carey and Judson.

The Church has had her darkest hours when she turned to Pelagianism and its various formulations. The Church today is sunk in extreme ignorance and spiritual poverty. Man-centered preaching abounds on all hands. Secular humanism is triumphing in our culture because religious humanism has been the norm in our churches for generations. We are back to "square-one" with most "religious" people believing that they are going to Heaven on the basis of the good life they are trying to lead. It is as if the Reformation never happened!

Let us therefore understand the grace of God and the power that it has in saving helpless sinners. Let us cleanse ourselves from the errors of Pelagianism and Arminianism, its modern expression. And let us boldly proclaim that salvation is totally by the sovereign, unmerited grace of Almighty God (Eph. 2:8-10).

Part Four

The Foundation of Calvinism

The basis of Calvinism is its commitment to the absolute supremacy of Scripture above all other things. The Reformers rejected the humanism of the Renaissance that taught that man was the origin and basis of all things including religious truth. Humanism has always deified some aspect of human nature and turned it into the origin of truth, morals, justice and beauty. Three general philosophical views have developed from humanism's commitment to the idea that "man is the measure of all things."

1. The Rationalists claim that human reason is the basis and judge of truth.
2. The Empiricists point to human experience as the source of all knowledge.
3. The Mystics look within themselves and claim that their emotions can tell them right from wrong, truth from error.

The objections we hear today against the doctrines of God's sovereign grace usually arise from someone's commitment to Rationalism, Empiricism or Mysticism. The Doctrines of Grace are rejected before the Bible is even opened. The Calvinist is usually not given the benefit of the doubt nor allowed to present his case because of a prior commitment to humanistic thought.

The Rationalist: "It is unreasonable to believe in God's sovereignty. As I see it, Reason demands that man has a free will. As to limited atonement, it is unthinkable! Who can reconcile the free offer of the Gospel with election? If I cannot understand it, I reject it. Our beliefs should be justified before the bar of Reason. Why waste time looking in the Bible to see if such irrational ideas as Calvinism are true?"

The Calvinist: "I do not pretend to understand everything. I admit that I do not know how to reconcile God's sovereignty and human responsibility. But, that I cannot does not bother me in the least. The issue is, what does the Bible teach? I reject human reason as the final court of appeal. The Scriptures alone decide what I believe and how I live. I do not understand the Trinity, but I do not reject it because I do not understand it. Faith swims when reason can no longer touch the bottom."

The Empiricist: "I think that Arminianism is true because it works. Look at all the money they have! Look at their big churches! Hey, you cannot argue with success. If it works, do not knock it. I do not need to look in the Bible when I see the answer in front of me."

The Calvinist: "Human experience should not be viewed as the origin of truth and morals. We must interpret our experience according to Scripture and not the other way around. The Scriptures clearly teach that just because something works, this does not mean that it is true. The end does not justify the means. I do not care what success some evangelist or pastor has had. The only question I am interested in is whether his message and his methods are Scriptural."

The Mystic: "I do not like that awful doctrine of election. It makes me so mad! It is unkind and not loving at all! I prayed about it and the Lord told me in my heart it cannot be true. I know what he told me because I feel it deep inside me. Well, anyway, my feelings tell me that election is not true. That is how I feel about it. You can show me all the verses in the Bible until you are blue in the face, but I know how I feel."

The Calvinist: "Our emotions should not be put in the place of God's Word. Instead of looking within yourself to your feelings, you should be looking away from yourself to the Scriptures. Feelings do not and cannot determine Truth. Scripture alone is the origin and judge of truth."

Nearly every objection to Calvinism that we have ever read or heard comes down to three basic arguments:

Rationalism: "It is not reasonable."

Empiricism: "It will not work."

Mysticism: "My feelings reject it."

The Calvinist knows from Scripture that he cannot trust in human reason, experience or feelings (Prov. 3:5-7). What then does he trust? He trusts in the Infinite Mind of God as revealed in Scripture. The Calvinist is willing to bow in humility before the infinite wisdom of God which transcends man's finite and sinful mind (Rom. 11:33-36; Eph. 3:9, 19; Phil. 4:7). He knows that he is not under any biblical constraint to justify Revealed Truth before man's reason, experience or feelings. To do so would be sinful.

The Calvinist stands on the shore of God's infinite wisdom and knows that he will never plumb its depths, scale its heights or search out all its riches. He is content to believe in Revealed Truths even if they seem to be contradictory. While his reason cannot understand it, he knows that there is no conflict in the mind of God over such things (Isaiah 55:8, 9).

Experience or feelings do not fluster the Calvinist. Scripture must interpret them. What if some sinner does not like God's sovereignty? What if he objects to God's decrees? Both the O.T. and the N.T. rebuke such attitudes and objections as rebellion against God (Psa. 2; Rom. 9:10-23; Ezek. 18:25, 29).

What if all men were to raise up and condemn a certain teaching of Scripture as "wicked," "irrational," "unreasonable," "useless," "unloving" or "unkind?" The Calvinist would answer in the words of the Apostle Paul: "Let God be true and every man a liar" (Rom. 3:4).

What man thinks or feels about Revealed Truth has no bearing whatsoever on the Truth. We must humbly bow before the Infinite Mind of God and accept whatever He has revealed and leave the secret counsels of God alone (1 Cor. 4:6; Isa. 8:20; Deut. 29:29).

Any religion that is completely understood by man is of human origin and not the true religion. The religion that comes from the Infinite Mind who created the universe will surpass the feeble mind of man. Its mysteries prove its divine origin.

Since Scripture reveals the Infinite Mind of God, the Calvinist expects to find ideas in it that surpass all understanding. Thus he does not get "shook up" when he runs across things he cannot understand. His beliefs do not rest on his ability to understand but on God's faithfulness to reveal. As Augustine said: "I do not understand to believe. I believe to understand."

Once someone decides that the Bible is really trustworthy and that he will believe whatever it teaches regardless of the fact that he cannot understand it or reconcile it or that his feelings rebel against it, he will become a Calvinist in the end. Thus, the number of Calvinists in any generation is directly related to the number of those who really accept the Bible as the final authority in all matters of doctrine and life.

Conclusion

Calvinism was the religion of our Puritan and Pilgrim fathers who started this country. They were committed to the absolute authority of Scripture over all of life. When liberalism arose in New England, the authority of the Bible was rejected and Calvinism fell on hard times. During the last fifty years, two things have happened. The full authority of Scripture has been revived and Calvinism has begun to flourish once again. The two are interrelated and stand or fall together. You cannot have a Bible fully inspired and free from error unless God is sovereign over all things, including the will of man.

Chapter Forty-Three
The Sovereignty of God

I. Opening Principles of Approach:
   A. Approach the Sovereignty of God in terms of God's attributes.
   B. Approach the Sovereignty of God always remembering that the Sovereignty of God magnifies human responsibility.
   C. Approach the Sovereignty of God as the solution to problems.
   D. Approach the Sovereignty of God in a simple worshiping faith realizing that we are studying the Godhood of God.

II. Two Methods of Approach:
   A. The "J.I. Packer Approach" as found in his book, *Evangelism and the Sovereignty of God.* He assumes that all Christians believe in God's Sovereignty when they pray or worship.
   B. The "A.W. Pink Approach" as found in his book, *The Sovereignty of God.* He goes through the Bible and proves the Sovereignty of God by hundreds of verses from the Old and New Testaments.

III. Passages on Sovereignty
   1. God sits on His Throne ruling over all things: 2 Chron. 18:18; Psa. 9:4; Isa. 6:1; Mat. 5:34; Acts 7:49f; Heb. 4:16; Rev. 4:10; 20:11-12.
   2. God reigns over all things: 1 Chron. 16:31; Psa. 47:8; 93:1; 96:10; 97:1; 99:1; Isa. 52:7; Rev. 19:6.
   3. His kingdom rules over all things: Psa. 47:2; Dan. 4:3, 34; 6:26; Mat. 6:33.
   4. His dominion is over all: 1 Chron. 29:11; Psa. 145:13; Dan. 4:34; 1 Tim. 6:16; 1 Pet. 4:11; 5:11; Jude 25; Rev. 1:6; 5:13.
   5. He is sovereign over all things: Psa. 103:19; 1 Tim. 6:15.
   6. He is "over all things": Rom. 9:5; Eph. 4:6.
   7. All things are from, through, and to Him: Eph. 4:6; 11:36.
   8. He works all things together: Rom. 8:28; Eph. 1:11.
   9. God orders our steps: Pro. 16:9; 20:24
   10. Only if God sovereignly wills, we can do things: James 4:13-15; Acts 18:21; Rom. 1:10; 15:32; 1 Cor. 4:19; 16:7; Heb. 3; 1 Pet. 3:17.

Note: Even what we consider to be chance or luck is under the sovereign control of God (Pro. 16:33). Some translators slip the word "chance" into the English Bible when it never appears in the original text (example 1 Sam. 6:9).

Hebrew scholars point out:
   a. The classical words for "chance" and "luck" never appear in the Bible. Why? The pagan worldview of a universe based on chance and luck was never part of the Jewish worldview. God was sovereign and thus there is no such thing as luck and chance.
   b. The Hebrew word found in 1 Sam. 6:9 is found elsewhere and is translated "fate" (Ecc. 2:14, 15; 3:19; 9:2), which is the opposite of chance!
   The *International Standard Bible Encyclopedia's* comment on the word "chance" is most instructive.
   c. This situation reveals why an educated ministry is needed now more than ever.

IV. Names of God
   Lord — Adonai
   LORD of Hosts
   El Shaddai

V. Closing Principles
   A. Accept the simple statement of Scripture.
   B. Defend God at all costs (Rom. 3:4).
   C. Remember that any truth of God is subject to abuse.
   D. Take the simple step of faith.

The clincher verse for the doctrine of the Sovereignty of God is Psalm 97:1:
   "The LORD reigns; let the earth rejoice."

Chapter Forty-Four

Original Sin, the Atonement and Justification

Introduction

Most Christians understand that Adam is the "Father" of the human race in the sense that he was the first human being from which all other human beings originated. For this reason, Adam is called the "first" man in such places as 1 Cor. 15:45.

What most modern Christians do not seem to understand is that we are related to Adam in more ways than simply by genetics. In Rom. 5 and 1 Cor. 15, the Apostle Paul draws several parallels between Adam and Christ. Jesus is described as the "last Adam" just as Adam is described as the "first man" (1 Cor. 15:45).

Adam and Christ

In these passages it is clear that Adam's fall into sin was substitutionary and vicarious in nature just like Christ's atoning obedience. In fact, as we shall we see, Rom. 5 says that we are condemned by virtue of Adam's disobedience just as surely as we are justified by virtue of Christ's obedience. While the imputation of Adam's sin is the problem confronting all men (Rom. 5:12), the imputation of Christ's righteousness is the remedy to that problem (Rom. 5:17).

Bound Together

Our participation in Adam's disobedience and our participation in Christ's obedience are linked together in such a way that if one rejects the doctrine of the imputation of Adam's sin—the basis of the doctrine of original sin—he must also logically reject the imputation of Christ's righteousness, the basis of the doctrine of forensic justification.

Throughout church history, intelligent heretics have always seen that the doctrines of original sin, a substitutionary atonement, and forensic justification stand or fall together as a unit. This is why Socinus and Finney in the past and others in the present feel logically compelled to deny all three doctrines.

The Same Terms

Our relationship to Adam is spoken of in the same terms that are used to speak of our relationship to Christ. For example, we are "in Adam" just as we are "in Christ." Thus, union with Adam and union with Christ are two realities that share mutual meanings. All those "in Adam," i.e. in union with Adam, receive certain things by virtue of that union just as all those "in Christ," i.e. in union with Christ, receive certain things by virtue of that union.

Part I

Inconsistent Denials

Because the Evangelical world is filled with teachers, pastors, and evangelists who have very little theological knowledge, no grasp of church history and absolutely no training in logic, it is not surprising to find some people objecting to the doctrine of original sin on the grounds that it would be "unjust" if God were to punish us on the basis of the evil done by someone else. The very idea that God would view and treat us on the basis of what someone else did or did not do is "absurd" according to them.

Yet, at the same time, these same people when pressed will admit that God viewed and treated Jesus on the basis of their sin! If "Jesus died for our sins according to the Scriptures" (1 Cor. 15:4), then how can it be unjust for us to die for Adam's sin?

Church History

Church history demonstrates that a rejection of the doctrine of original sin will, in time, lead to a rejection of the vicarious atonement and forensic justification. This is exactly what happened in 18th century Liberal Theology.

Liberal theologians began with a rejection of the doctrine of original sin and its resulting depravity. This led them to reject the doctrine of Christ's substitutionary atonement. On the basis of "reason," they then concluded that if it is unjust to be condemned on the basis of the work of another, then it is equally unjust to be saved on the basis of the work of another. Their rationalism eventually led them to deny the blood atonement of Christ.

This is why the doctrine of original sin is absolutely essential to Christian theology and why the Christian Church has always condemned as heretical all Pelagian and semi-Pelagian views of man which in some way deny or weaken the doctrine of original sin and its resulting depravity. The validity of a substitutionary atonement and forensic justification is based on the validity of the imputation of Adam's sin to us.

Three Essential Concepts

Three essential concepts form the basis of the doctrines of original sin, vicarious atonement, and forensic justification:

No. 1: Solidarity

The Bible teaches a concept of solidarity in which an individual is viewed and treated in terms of his relationship to a group, be it a tribe, a nation or mankind as a whole, while the "group" is viewed and treated in terms of its relationship to its original head.

Man as Image Bearer

This is why the Bible can speak of each individual human being as having dignity and worth by virtue of his or her participation in the solidarity of the human race. Each individual person is important because mankind as a whole is important. We can view each person we meet as being in the image of God by virtue of mankind's relationship to Adam, who was created in the image of God (Gen. 1:26-27; James 3:9).

Corporate and Individual Election

An individual Jew was viewed as "chosen" by virtue of his participation in the solidarity of the "chosen" nation. Yet, at the same time, the nation was viewed as "chosen" because of its relationship to Abraham, who was individually chosen by God (Gen. 12:1-7).

The Levitical Priesthood

An individual could be blessed by virtue of his participation in the solidarity of his tribe. For example, an individual Levite could be a priest by virtue of his participation in the solidarity of the Tribe of Levi, while the Tribe of Levi was viewed as the priesthood by virtue of its relationship to Levi, who was individually chosen to be the high priest (Num. 18:6-24).

The Ninevites

Each individual Ninevite was delivered from judgment by virtue of his participation in the solidarity of the nation of Nineveh, whose king repented before God (Jonah 3; 4:11). He could just as easily have been punished for the corporate guilt he bore, but the nation as a whole was delivered on a corporate basis when its head repented in sackcloth and ashes. It did not matter if he, as an individual, had sinned or repented. The destiny of his nation was his destiny.

Corporate Guilt and Punishment

The suffering experienced by individual Egyptians during the plagues, by individual Canaanites, Philistines, Amorites, Hittites, etc., during the conquest, by individual Jews in the Assyrian and Babylonian captivities, and all the other judgments sent against nations, was justified by God on the basis of their participation in the solidarity of their nation.

For example, even though a certain individual Egyptian may not have harmed or mistreated the Jews in any way, yet because he was an Egyptian, he suffered under the ten plagues. His individual actions did not negate his corporate guilt that arose out of his participation in the solidarity of the nation of Egypt.

Even the Righteous

A righteous man can view himself guilty in a corporate sense by virtue of the solidarity of his tribe's or nation's sin. Thus Nehemiah confessed the corporate sins of his nation (Neh. 1:5-11).

In this passage, it is clear that an individual can be viewed and treated by God as being guilty of sins for which his nation was guilty. That he himself had not done the particular sins in question did not negate the corporate guilt he bore.

It is on this basis that the punishment for certain sins was visited on entire cities such as Sodom or nations such as Egypt. Because of the solidarity of the family unit, the punishment for certain sins could rest on several generations (Exo. 20:5; Josh. 7:24-26; Jer. 22:28-30; 36:31).

God's corporate blessing or judgment on tribes, cities, nations, and mankind as a whole is possible only on the basis of the concept of solidarity. Such judgments as the Flood or the Conquest can only be understood and justified in this way.

In Our Secular Life

The concept of solidarity is also a necessary part of secular life as well as being a biblical principle. When the leadership of a nation declares war on another nation, each individual citizen is at war whether he knows about it or agrees with it. He can be killed or his goods seized simply on the basis of his being a part of his nation. He must bear the corporate guilt and punishment due to the sins of his nation. Thus, human government itself is based on the concept of solidarity.

No. 2: Representation

The Bible teaches a concept of representation in which the acts and decisions of one's representative are viewed and treated as being one's own acts and decisions.

In its secular sense, this concept serves as the basis for representative government. If our representatives in Congress declare war, it means that we are viewed and treated as having declared war.

If our representatives vote in a new tax, we have to pay it because we are viewed and treated as if we voted it into law. It does not matter if you disagree with or are ignorant of the actions of your representative. You are responsible legally and morally for the acts and decisions of your representatives.

Examples in Scripture

We find this same principle at work in Scripture. Individuals are viewed and treated by God according to the actions and decisions of their representatives. This worked for either cursing or for blessing.

For Cursing

In terms of cursing, Pharaoh's stubbornness led to God's judgment on the entire nation (Exo. 7-11). Those who followed Korah, Dathan, Abiram, and On suffered their fate (Num. 16). Each evil king of Israel or Judah brought judgment on the entire nation. For example, Israel had no rain because of the evil deeds of King Ahab (1 Kings 17f).

For Blessing

In its positive sense, the actions and decisions of good kings brought blessing to the entire nation. For example, the nation was delivered because godly King Hezekiah sought the Lord (2 Kings 19).

The Atonement

The greatest illustration of the principle of representation is the substitutionary and vicarious atonement of Christ (1 Cor. 15:3-4). We are saved on the basis of the actions and decisions of Christ our representative. He is our mediator, advocate, and great high priest (1 Tim. 2:5; 1 John 2:1; Heb. 2:17). The atonement and justification as well as original sin are all based on the principle of representation.

No. 3: Imputation

The Bible teaches a concept of imputation in which God takes the life and works of someone and applies them to the record of another who is then treated on that basis. Christian theology has always taught that there are three great acts of imputation:

> 1. Adam's sin is imputed to us at conception.
> 2. Our sin was imputed to Christ in the atonement.
> 3. Christ's righteousness is imputed to us in justification.

The Logic of It

That Adam's sin is imputed to us should not bother us any more than that our sins were imputed to Christ. That we should suffer for Adam's sin is just as acceptable as Christ suffering for our sins. That death came to us through Adam is just as acceptable as life coming to us through Christ. Divine justice is as equally satisfied with the imputation of Adam's sin as it is with the imputation of Christ's righteousness. The justice of all three acts of imputation rises or falls together.

Biblical Examples

That God can choose to "impute" sin or not to "impute" sin is clear from Psa. 32:2 and Rom. 4:6. That it is God who determines what sins are to be placed on one's record is clear from the usage of the word in Scripture: Lev. 7:18; 17:3-4; 1 Sam. 22:15; Rom. 4:8, 11, 22, 23, 24; 5:13; 2 Cor. 5:19; James 2:23

That Christ suffered and died for our sins which were imputed to His account by the Father is the very heart and soul of the Christian Gospel (1 Cor. 15:3-4). Our sins were imputed to Christ and He was viewed and treated by God accordingly. Such passages as Isa. 53:4-6; John 1:29; 1 Cor. 15:3-4; 2 Cor. 5:21; 1 Pet. 2:24, etc., are so clear that only a deranged mind could miss this point.

Once a person accepts the justice of Christ bearing his sin, guilt, and punishment, then he cannot logically or exegetically reject the justice of his bearing the sin, guilt, and punishment of Adam.

Forensic Justification

In the biblical doctrine of justification, the righteousness of Christ is "imputed" to us, i.e., God places it on our record and then views and treats us in terms of that righteousness (Rom. 5:1-21; Phil. 3:9).

Righteousness can be imputed to us because Christ is our representative (Heb. 9:11-28) and because of the solidarity of His people for whom He came (Matt. 1:21). Justification is based on the concept of imputation just as much as the doctrines of original sin and the atonement.

Part II

Our Relationship to Adam

In what ways are we related to Adam?

No. 1. We are related to Adam in terms of a genetic solidarity.

In Scripture, genetic solidarity in and of itself can serve as a sufficient basis for moral and spiritual implications. Thus the superiority of Christ's priesthood over against the Levitical priesthood is based solely on the fact that Abraham, the genetic source of Levi, paid tithes to Melchizedek (Heb. 5:6; 7:4-10).

That all men participate in a genetic solidarity with Adam is the basis for the doctrine that all men are created in the image of God. Thus if you deny the justice of genetic solidarity when it comes to original sin, you have also in principle denied that man is God's image bearer.

Ideas are not like taxi cabs, which you can get out of when you want. You have to ride in that cab until you get to the end of your journey. The attempt to deny the principle of solidarity when it comes to the Fall, but accept it when it comes to the Creation, is sheer hypocrisy.

No. 2. We are related to Adam in terms of a spiritual solidarity.

Adam procreated his descendants "in his own image," which had been corrupted by his fall into sin and guilt (Gen. 5:3). That Adam's depravity was passed on to his children is manifested by the universality and totality of man's sinfulness that reveals itself "from the womb" and even "in the womb" (Gen. 6:5; 8:21; 25:22-26; Psa. 14:1-6; 51:5; 58:3; Rom. 3:23; Eph. 2:1-3).

No. 3. We are related to Adam in terms of representation.

In Rom 5:12-21, Paul clearly draws several parallels between the representative nature of Christ's actions and the representative nature of Adam's actions.

In 1 Cor. 15, Paul tells us that by virtue of our being "in Adam," i.e. in union with Adam as our head and representative, we are all spiritually dead. He sets forth a parallel between being "in Adam" and being "in Christ."

What Adam or Christ did is viewed by God as what we did. When Adam sinned, we sinned (Rom. 5:12). When he died spiritually, we died spiritually (1 Cor. 15:22). When Christ was crucified, we were crucified (Gal. 2:20). We died, were buried and rose when Christ our Head and Representative died, was buried and rose from the dead (Rom. 6:1-6; Eph. 2:6).

No. 4. We are related to Adam by way of imputation.

Rom. 5 clearly teaches that Adam's sin and condemnation were imputed to his descendants. Thus the universality of death is traced to the solidarity of mankind's participation in the sin of Adam (vs. 12-17).

The universality of condemnation is also traced back to man's solidarity in Adam (v. 18). Paul also tells us that all men are "constituted" or "made" sinners by virtue of their union with Adam (v. 19).

Part III

Eden and Calvary

What Christ did on Mount Calvary is viewed in Scripture as the opposite of what Adam did in the Garden. Thus, as our legal representative and substitute, Christ lived and died in our place. In other words, what He did was credited to our account as if we did it. His life and death are substitutionary in the same way that Adam's life and death were substitutionary.

Christ's atoning work also provided the remedy to undo the consequences of Adam's fall into sin and guilt. Thus forensic justification is designed to remove the imputation of Adam's guilt, while progressive sanctification is designed to remove the impartation of Adam's depravity.

The atonement of Christ is structured to be the reverse parallel to the imputation and impartation of Adam's sin and guilt. To claim that it is unjust for us to share in Adam's sin and yet, at the same time, to claim that is just to share in Christ's righteousness is irrational as well as anti-scriptural. You cannot have your cake and eat it too!

The Temptation

The obvious parallel between Christ's temptation in the wilderness (Matt. 4) and Adam's temptation in the Garden (Gen. 3:1-7) cannot be denied. But whereas Adam was defeated by the devil, Christ was now victorious.

Why did Christ have to go through the Temptation at the outset of His public ministry? Jesus begins at the beginning of man's sin, the Fall of Adam in the Garden. He must begin by passing the same temptation that foiled the first Adam.

The Parallels

The following chart reveals some of the parallels between Adam and Christ:

The First Adam	The Second Adam
The Son of God (Lk. 3:38) Temptation (Gen. 3) Disobedience (Gen. 3) Condemnation (Rom. 5) Death (Rom. 5; 1 Cor. 15)	The Son of God (Mk. 1:1) Temptation (Matt. 4) Obedience (Matt. 4) Justification (Rom. 5) Life (Rom. 5; 1 Cor. 15)

Obedience vs. Disobedience

The chart above reveals that it is the "obedience" of Christ which removes the "disobedience" of Adam (Rom. 5:19; Phil. 2:5-11; Heb. 5:8). We are saved by His active and passive obedience and not just by His death on the cross alone.

Creation

All men are viewed as being in the image of God because of their solidarity with Adam, who as their representative, was created in the image of God. Although this image is marred by sin, man is still the image-bearer of God and has intrinsic worth and dignity (Gen. 1:26-27; cf. James 3:9).

The Cultural Mandate

Because of man's solidarity with Adam, when he was given the task of taking dominion over the earth, all his descendants were given the responsibility to be good stewards of the earth and its resources. Thus mankind as a whole was given the Cultural Mandate through Adam their representative (Gen. 1:27-30; 2:1-17).

The Radical Fall

The imputation of Adam's sin, guilt, and condemnation to his descendants and the resulting universality of death and totality of depravity are clearly revealed in Scripture. In Rom. 5:12-21, we are said to receive the following things from our solidarity with Adam our representative:

> sin (v. 12a)—legal and personal
> physical death (v. 12b)—consequence
> spiritual death (v. 15)—depravity
> judgment/condemnation (v. 16)—guilt
> the reign of death (v. 17)—bondage
> condemnation for all (v. 18)—guilt
> all made sinners (v. 19)—depravity

In 1 Cor. 15, our union with Adam means:

> death (v. 21)—consequence
> all "in Adam" died when he spiritually died (v. 22)—consequence
> we bear his image and likeness, which is sinful, mortal and corrupt (v. 45-49)—nature

Redemption

The results of Adam's disobedience and Christ's obedience are parallel to each other in Scripture.

Adam	Christ
condemnation (position)	justification (position)
depravity (condition)	sanctification (condition)
death (future)	life (future)

Conclusion

The doctrine of original sin is based on the same essential principles that underlie the doctrines of man as the image-bearer of God, the atonement and justification. We are viewed and treated by God as sinners on the basis of the imputation of Adam's sin, guilt, and condemnation to our account and the impartation of Adam's depravity and death to our natures. In short, we sin because we are sinners by nature from conception. Thus it is no surprise that sin and death are both universal and total.

All of humanity is in solidarity with Adam in his creation and his fall. Just as man's dignity is based on his solidarity with Adam in his creation, man's depravity is based on his solidarity with Adam in his fall. Both begin at conception. To reject one is to reject the other.

Christ's work of atonement is based on the same kind of solidarity and representation that are found in our relationship to Adam. They are both substitutionary and vicarious in nature. To reject one is to reject the other.

The imputation of Christ's righteousness in justification is structured in Scripture to be the remedy to the imputation of Adam's unrighteousness in original sin. To reject one is to reject the other.

The impartation of Christ's righteousness to our natures in sanctification is structured in Scripture to be the remedy to the impartation of Adam's depravity and death to our natures. To reject one is to reject the other.

In short, the decisions and actions of Adam and Christ are so intertwined in Scripture that they cannot be separated. To deny one is to deny the other. Thus any denial of the doctrines of original sin, substitutionary atonement and forensic justification must be deemed as serious heresy and as sufficient grounds for excommunication.

Chapter Forty-Five

Doctrine of Effectual Atonement: Problem Passages

I. Principles of Approach

    A. Every doctrine of Scripture has problem passages. Thus, it is no surprise to find that the doctrine of Effectual Atonement has verses that on the surface seem to contradict it. No big deal!

    B. It is the only position that is in harmony with the nature of the atonement.

    C. It is the only position that is logically in line with the work of the entire Trinity. Those chosen by the Father are purchased by the Son and sealed by the Spirit.

Person	Work	Subjects
The Father	election	the elect
The Son	atonement	the elect
The Spirit	application	the elect

    D. It is the only position that harmonizes the work of Christ. He prays for those for whom he died.

Christ's work	the subjects
atonement	the elect
intercession	the elect

II. The Problem Passages

The so-called problem passages arise only if you fail to accurately interpret the Scriptures according to the rules of historical-grammatical exegesis.

A. Partial quotation: 2 Pet. 3:9
B. Misquotation: Matt. 23:37
C. Failure to check the context: 1 Tim. 2:4, 6
D. Failure to check the Greek: Heb. 2:9
E. Failure to do a basic word study:
    1. "world": John 3:16
    2. "all": 1 Tim. 2:5

Chapter Forty-Six

The Question of Man's Free Will

I. You must define your terms. What does free will mean?
   A. Human Responsibility? Yes, man is responsible.
   B. Objective Choice? Yes, man has a choice set before him in the Gospel.
   C. Is man a machine? No, he is God's image bearer.
   D. Is man's will a slave to sin? Yes.
   E. Is man's will under God's control? Yes.
   F. Does man have the ability to do spiritual good before God? No.

II. What is "freedom"?
   A. We must begin with a contrast between biblicism and humanism.

The Bible	Humanism
True freedom is the desire and the ability to do what is right., i.e. the freedom to do what you ought to do.	Man is neutral and his will has the ability to do evil or good. True freedom is the ability to do what you ought not to do.

   B. Important questions to answer:
      1. Is God free? Yes. (Dan. 4:34-35; Job 42:2; Psa. 115:3)
      2. Can God sin? No. (James 1:13)
      3. Did Christ have a free will? Yes. (Matt. 26:39)
      4. Could He sin? No. (Heb. 4:15)
      5. Do the saints in Heaven have a free will? Yes. (Heb. 12:23)
      6. Can they sin in Heaven? No. (Heb. 12:23)
      7. Will they be able to sin in the eternal state? No. (1 John 3:2-3)

III. Deal with one issue at a time.
   A. Is man a slave to sin? Yes! (Rom. 3:10-18; 6:17)
   B. Does God's Sovereignty control man's will? Yes!
      1. General statements (Dan. 4:34-35; Eph. 1:11)
      2. Specific statements (Pro. 21:1; Acts 4:27-28)

Special Note: Without God's sovereign control of the will of man, the concept of a verbal, plenary, infallible, inspired Bible is impossible.

IV. Does the natural man have the ability to do spiritual good before God? No! (Rom. 3:10-18; 8:7-8; 1 Cor. 2:14; 12:3; John 6:44, 65)

V. Remember that this question has four different answers.

Four-Fold State of Man			
Pre-Fall	Lost	Regenerate	Eternal State
total ability perfection of the will	no ability bondage of the will	growing ability partial freedom of the will	total ability perfected free will for all eternity

VI. The Bible and "Free Will"

The issue of man's supposed "free will" is more philosophical than biblical due to several facts:

1. The Bible never refers to "free will" in the Arminian sense.
2. It became relevant during the Reformation only as it related to the issue of good works.
3. It is usually framed today in the context of faculty psychology that teaches that man has a will, a mind, and emotions.

VII. Free Will in Modern Philosophy

A. "Free will" in some modern philosophies means that the universe is based not on divine Providence but on pure chance, luck and ultimate contingency. This is actually a form of atheism and no Christian should support it.

B. "Free will" in some modern philosophies means that man is not fatalistically determined in his thoughts, words and deeds by irrational forces such as genetics or environmental factors. This is in agreement with the biblical view of man in which man has dominion over the world instead of the world having dominion over man.

Conclusion

Man lost his ability to please God when Adam and Eve fell into sin and guilt. Thus we do not have the ability to do good works or merit our salvation. The Reformers were absolutely right on this issue.

Chapter Forty-Seven
Apostasy

Introduction

We have all experienced grief and sorrow over loved ones and friends who have fallen away from the Gospel. At one time, they were faithful and zealous Christians, but they gradually or suddenly left the church and now live without any concern for their soul. They are missing from the church and now live only for this world and the pleasures it offers. We miss them and wonder why they, like Judas, have betrayed the Lord. The doctrine of apostasy answers all our questions.

I. The Nature of Apostasy
   A. The Meaning of the Word "Apostasy"
      "To fall away from; to leave, abandon or desert something."
   B. Biblical Usage and Meaning
      "To fall away from God, His word and His people. To abandon the true worship of God."
      Example: Num. 31:16; Heb. 3:12; 6:4-6
   C. Its Scope to Abandon

1. Biblical Doctrine	2. Biblical Holiness	3. Biblical Worship
Gal. 1:6-9;	2 Pet. 2:20-22	1 John 2:19
4:2-6; 5:4;	2 Tim. 4-10	1 Kings 4:1-10
2 Tim. 2:17-19		

   D. Apostasy Can Be
      1. Temporary or permanent
      2. Partial or total
         Example. David: Temporary and partial.
                  Judas: Permanent and total.
   E. Passage of full mention: Hebrews
      Under persecution, Jewish Christians left the church and returned to temple worship. This is the focus of the Book of Hebrews.
   F. Apostasy Concerns Professing Christians.
      Professors vs. Possessors
      (Lips)   (Heart)
II. The Causes of Apostasy
   A. In the Gospels:
      1. Ignorance (Matt. 13:19; Hos. 4:6)
      2. Trouble/Persecution (Matt. 13:20-21)
      3. Worries of this life (Matt. 13:22)
      4. The deceitfulness of wealth (Matt. 13:22)
      5. Hard Teaching (John 6:60-66)
         Example: Young Man (Mk. 10:17:27)
                  Judas (John 12:4-6; Matt. 26:14-15; John 13:27,30)
   B. In the Church Epistles
      1. Satan's devices (2 Cor. 11:3-4, 13-15)
      2. Hurt feelings (Gal. 4:12-16)

    3. The desire to be rich (1 Tim. 6:6-10; 17-19)

    4. Love of this world (1 John 2:15-17)

       Example: Demas (2 Tim. 4:10)

  C. In the Book of Hebrews

    1. Not paying careful attention to sermons (2:1)

    2. Ignoring salvation (2:3)

    3. Not holding on (3:6, 14; cf. 1 Cor. 15:1-2)

    4. A sinful heart (3:12)

    5. An unbelieving heart (3:12)

    6. A hardened heart (3:7-8, 15; 4:7)

    7. Rebellion (3:15-16)

    8. Unbelief (3:19)

    9. Falling short of entering God's rest (4:12)

   10. Did not combine faith with the word (4:2)

   11. Disobedience (4:6; cf. 3:18)

   12. Lazy (6:12)

   13. No one-anothering (10:24-25)

   14. Not attending church (10:25)

   15. Deliberate sin (10:26)

   16. Lack of perseverance (10:35-36)

   17. Shrinking back (10:38-39)

   18. Bitterness (12:15)

   19. Sexual immorality (12:16)

   20. Refusing God (12:25)

   21. Love of money (13:5)

   22. Disrespect of leaders (3:7, 17)

   23. False doctrine (13:9)

   24. Public disgrace (13:12-13)

III. The Consequence of Apostasy

  A. NO ESCAPE! (Heb. 2:3)

  B. NO REST! (Heb. 4:3)

  C. NO HOPE! (Heb. 10:26-31)

IV. The Prevention of Apostasy

  A. "Prevention" is always better than "Cure."

  B. We need to guard our hearts (Pro. 4:23).

  C. We must take care we do not fall (1 Cor. 10:11-13).

  D. We should examine ourselves (2 Cor. 13:5).

  E. The message of Hebrews concerns preventing apostasy.

  F. The positive exhortations focus on what to do to ensure spiritual health.

  G. These exhortations have five centers of focus: the Word, God, Salvation, the Church and the Heart.

  H. Our response to these five centers determines our future.

    1. Your response to God's Word will reveal the true condition of your heart (Heb. 2:1-4).

    2. Your response to God is the ultimate issue.

      a. In the last analysis, it is the Lord who will keep you from falling (Jude 24) or pick you up after you have fallen and set you back on the path of righteousness (Psa. 145:14; Pro. 24:16). He is the one who must keep us from apostasy and watch over us night and day (Psa. 121).

  b. We must keep close to God. This is spoken of in many different ways:

Abide in Him (John 15:4)
Believe in Him (Heb. 11:6)
Come to Him (Matt. 11:28)
Delight yourself in Him (Psa. 37:4)
Enter His Presence (Psa. 100:4)
Follow Him (1 Kings 18:21)
Give thanks to Him (Psa. 106:1)
Hold on to the End (Heb. 3:14)
Keep His Way (Gen. 18:11)
Love Him (Matt. 22:37)
Obey Him (Acts 5:29)
Pray to Him (1 Thess. 5:17)
Receive Him (John 1:12)
Seek Him (Isa. 55:6)
Trust Him (Pro. 3:5-6)
Walk with Him (Gen. 5:22)

3. Your response to God's offer of salvation determines your eternal destiny (Heb. 2:3).

4. Your response to His church reveals your relationship to Christ.

5. To avoid apostasy, keep your heart full of the graces mentioned by the author of Hebrews.

Conclusion

Every human heart has the seeds of apostasy within it. Nothing in this life can remove these seeds. It is only the power of God that keeps us until we reach Heaven's shore. This preservation of God is part of the blessings of the New Covenant and is ours through our union with Christ (Jer. 32:38-40).

Chapter Forty-Eight

Eschatology: the Study of the Future

Part One

The following outline surveys the ongoing issues in Bible prophecy. An overview of these issues will safeguard us from the heresies and errors of the age in which we live.

I. Personal Eschatology
  A. What is Your future?
  B. Your Death
    1. Its nature: the fact of it
    2. Its cause: the origin of it
    3. Its time: the timing of it
  C. The intermediate state between death and the resurrection
    1. Issues
      a. the soul:
      (1) Its nature: Is it immortal?
      (2) Its destiny: Does it leave the body at death?
      (3) Is it conscious or unconscious after death?
      (4) Does it experience bliss or torment?
    2. False Ideas
      a. materialism
      b. soul sleep
      c. occultism
  D. Your resurrection
    1. Why needed?
    2. Its nature
    3. Its time
    4. Why at the end of the world?
    5. False ideas
      a. annihilationism
      b. spiritualism
  E. The eternal state
    1. eternal bliss
      a. Its nature
      b. Its degrees
      c. Its duration
      d. Its location
    2. eternal torment
      a. Its nature

        b. Its degrees

        c. Its duration

        d. Its location

II. Ecclesiastical Eschatology

    A. What is the future of the Church?

    B. Is there a "church age" with a beginning and an end?

    C. Key elements

        1. "the last days" or "end times"

        2. the anti-christ and the false prophet

        3. the "Great Tribulation"

        4. the Great Apostasy

        5. the Second Coming of Christ

        6. resurrection of the dead

        7. translation of the living

        8. judgment of the believers

        9. "end of the world" vs "end of the age"

    D. Arranging the Elements

        1. Scripture is not precise in the details (Acts 1:7).

        2. Beware of those who know too much (Matt. 24:23-27, 36).

        3. Christians have disagreed about the details down through the ages.

        4. The fundamental truths are shared by all Christians.

        5. Dogmatism in prophecy is not the way to go.

        6. Beware of wild speculators who are deliberately sensational in their approach to prophecy.

        7. Always keep in mind the threefold test for all doctrine:

            a. Where in the Bible is this clearly stated?

            b. Where in church history can this belief be found?

            c. Where do the best scholars stand on this issue?

    E. The hermeneutical differences

        1. A literary or literal approach?

        2. Is speculation or fulfillment the best guide?

    F. The different views

        1. On the Rapture Issue

            a. pre-trib.

            b. mid-trib.

            c. post-trib.

        2. On the Millennium Issue

            a. Premillenniumism

                (1) historic

                (2) dispensational

            b. Postmillenniumism

                (1) historical

                (2) dominionism

            c. Amillenniumism

III. Cosmic Eschatology

    A. What is the future of the world?

    B. What about the judgment of the wicked?

C. Are the wicked resurrected?

D. What happens to this planet?

E. Do we look forward to eternity in Heaven or do we return to live on this earth?

F. What will we do for all eternity?

Conclusion

All these issues should humble us to realize that no one should be ugly toward other Christians who hold to different views. We all see through a glass darkly until the day Jesus comes back. After all, the fulfillment of a prophecy is its only infallible interpretation.

Chapter Forty-Nine

Jewish Apocalypticism and Biblical Prophecy

Introduction

When you begin to read the Bible for the first time, you soon run across bizarre passages that use weird images. Cosmic battles will take place in heaven and on earth. Is this sci-fi stuff, or is it for real? A huge red dragon with seven heads, 10 horns, and seven crowns comes out of the sea. Is the Bible saying that Godzilla is for real? What about those weird creatures with body parts from insects, animals, and man? Are they real? An angel grabs a dragon, puts a chain on him, opens a hole in the ground, and then throws him in it. Is the Bible talking about literal chains, dragons and holes in the ground? Or, are all those things symbolic images of something else? How do we interpret those kinds of passages?

Part I

The following propositions are meant to give us a bird's-eye view of the issues involved in interpreting prophetic passages in the Bible.

1. The failure to begin with the Bible as literature is the chief source of most of the nonsense and heresy that is passed off today as "Bible prophecy." Too many people assume that the Bible is one book that can be interpreted by one hermeneutical principle, such as literalism. This false assumption has spawned thousands of apocalyptic cults (such as the Jehovah's Witnesses), and has misled sincere Christians.

The "Bible" is a collection of 66 ancient Jewish scrolls written by more than 40 men during a 2,000 year process. It is composed of many different kinds or genres of literature. There are historical narratives, poetry, hymns, theological discourses, and prophetic passages that talk about the near and distant future of men and nations, and even about the end of the world.

2. Each type or genre of literature found in the Bible must be interpreted according to its own unique historical, cultural, religious, and literary context. The failure to do so results in *eisegesis* (i.e., the reading of one's own subjective ideas into the text of Scripture), instead of *exegesis* (the digging out of the text the objective ideas that the author of that text was trying to convey to his readers).

3. The goal of biblical studies is to discover what the authors of the Bible were saying to the people of their day. The reason why this is important is that they were not simply giving their own private opinion on things, but instead they spoke from Divine inspiration (2 Pet. 1:20-21). In other words, their opinion was God's opinion! This is why it is wrong to obscure their message by inserting your own ideas into their documents.

4. The last book in the Bible is titled by its author as "The Apocalypse of Jesus Christ" (1:1). When the King James Version changed the title to "The Revelation of St. John the Divine," it obscured the nature of the book.

5. The Greek word "apocalypse" at that time meant the "unveiling" of hidden mysteries

concerning the future as it relates to the ultimate outcome of the final battle between good and evil at the end of the world.

6. The word "apocalyptic" became a literary and theological term to describe any literature that "unveiled" the end of the world. Hence, the word "apocalyptic" is applied to other biblical books and passages. The following is a list of some of the books and passages found in the Bible.

Old Testament Material							
Isaiah	65-66	Ezekiel	38-42	Daniel		Zechariah	12-14
New Testament Material							
Matthew	3:7-10	Matthew	13:24-30	Matthew	22:29-31	Luke	1:32-33
	5:17		13:36-43		24-25		10:12-15
	6:10		13:47-50	Mark	1:15		12:4-5
	7:21-22		16:27-28		9:10-13		12:35-53
	11-15		19:28-30		12:18-24	John	5:25-29
	12:36-37	22-24	13				
Acts	1:11	Phil.	3:20-21	1 Tim.	6:14-16	1 John	3:2-3
	3:19-20	1 Thess.	4:13-18	Titus	2:13	Jude	
Rom.	11		5:1-11	Heb.	9:28	Revelation	
1 Cor.	15	2 Thess.	2	2 Pet	3		

7. In the last 50 years, an enormous amount of ancient documents have been discovered in Israel that date from 250 B.C. to A.D. 200. Some of these documents are written in the same genre as the books of Daniel and Revelation, and are clearly "apocalyptic" in nature. While we do not consider them inspired or part of the canon of Scripture, they do have great historical and literary value.

The following is a list of some of these works that in part or in whole have been classified as "apocalyptic." We also add to the list below The Dead Sea Qumran Community's Commentaries on Isaiah, Hosea, Micah, Nahum, Habakkuk, Zephaniah, and Psalm 37. While they are not apocalyptic per se, they do have sections that are clearly apocalyptic in nature.

1 Enoch
The Testament of the 12 Patriarchs
The Assumption of Moses
The Book of Jubilees
The Apocalypse of Moses
The Sibyline Oracles III, IV, V
2 Baruch
The Zadokite Document
The Rule of the Congregation
The Messianic Anthology
The War Scroll

2 Enoch
The Psalms of Solomon
The Martyrdom of Isaiah
The Testament of Abraham
The Apocalypse of Abraham
2 Esdra (or 4 Ezra)
3 Baruch
The Manual of Discipline
A Scroll of Benedictions
Hymns of Thanksgiving
The Book of Mysteries

A Midrash on the Last Days   The New Jerusalem
An Angelic Liturgy   The Prayer of Nabonidus
Pseudo-Daniel Apocalypse   A Genesis Apocryphon
The Testament of Levi

These ancient documents reveal aspects of the religious context in which Christianity arose and prospered. Jesus and the Apostles did not step off a UFO one day. They spoke in the context of the religious, political, and cultural situation of their day.

9. When we interpret the "apocalyptic" sections of the New Testament, we must take into account the extra-biblical "apocalyptic" books that came into existence before, during, and after the New Testament was written. These books form the religious, political, and cultural context in which the New Testament was produced. They give us clear indications as to how and why Christianity was transformed from being a minor Jewish sect called "The Way" (Acts 19:9, 23) to a major world religion.

10. Almost without exception, "prophecy experts" ignore the Jewish apocalyptic context of the New Testament. As a result, they insert modern Gentile, European, and American ideas into the first century Jewish documents called the New Testament. They assume that prophetic passages should be interpreted the same way as historical narratives, i.e., literally.

11. This is why most "prophecy experts" arbitrarily identify contemporary events, individuals, and nations as the fulfillment of end-time prophecies. For example, during World War II, Hitler was frequently identified as the Antichrist. The fact that he did not turn out to be the Antichrist and that World War II did not turn out to be Armageddon has not deterred them from going on to name new individuals such as Henry Kissinger, John Rockefeller, Prince Charles, Ronald Reagan, Saddam Hussein, or Bill Clinton as the Antichrist. The identity of the Antichrist changes so often that an Antichrist-of-the-Month Club should be started to see who is on the hit list this month.

12. If Church history after the New Testament is important to our understanding of the apocalyptic sections of the New Testament, then Jewish history before and during the formation of the New Testament is even more important. We are not aware of any pre-, post-, or a- millennial books that begin with a discussion of the nature and significance of apocalyptic literature as it bears on interpreting prophetic sections in the Bible.

13. If it is objected that Christians should ignore the apocalyptic literature because it is Jewish, it must be pointed out that:
  a. It was the early Christian Church that preserved these works. They were quoted universally throughout the Early Church. We would not have these works except that the early Christians copied, read, and cherished them.
  b. The early Christians went on to write their own distinctively "Christian" apocalyptic works. The following is a list of the apocalyptic works that appeared early in the history of the Church. They reveal that the average Christian was apocalyptic in his views of the future.

The Didache (16)   The Shepherd of Hermes
The Ascension of Isaiah   The Fifth and Sixth Books of Ezra
The Christian Sibylines   The Book of Elchasai
The Apocalypse of Peter   Apocalypse of Sophonias
Apocalypse of Elijah   Apocalypse of Zechariah
Apocalypse of John   Apocalypse of Mary
Apocalypse of Stephen   Apocalypse of Bartholomew
Apocalypse of Paul   Apocalypse of Thomas

14. **The following questions must be answered:**
   a. Why did Jewish rabbis abandon apocalypticism after A.D. 70?
      That they did abandon it is clear from three things:
      (1) They did not preserve the pre-Christian apocalyptic literature.
      (2) They did not write any more literature in that style.
      (3) Even though elements of apocalypticism can be found in the Talmuds, there is a general hostility toward it.
   b. Why did the early Church take over the apocalyptic movement from Judaism?
      That the Church did so is clear from three things:
      (1) The Church preserved the Jewish apocalyptic literature.
      (2) It went on to write more books in that genre.
      (3) Down through the centuries, apocalypticism has been kept alive mainly by Christians. Without the undercurrent of apocalypticism in the Church, the so-called "prophecy experts" would have gone out of business long ago.

15. **The two questions above are answered as follows:**
   First-century Judaism had many sects or denominations. Within Jewish orthodoxy there were two major movements:
   a. Legalistic groups promoted the idea that it is through the keeping of the Torah that salvation will come. They assumed that all revelation ceased since Malachi, and that external conformity to the laws of Moses was all that God required. The Pharisees are singled out in the Gospels and in Galatians as examples of this school.
      After the Temple was destroyed in A.D. 70, the Pharisees took over the guardianship of Judaism, and they were the ones who wrote the Midrash, the Mishnah, and the Talmuds. Contemporary Orthodox Judaism is a modern version of the Pharisees.
   b. The second movement within Orthodox Judaism was the apocalyptic movement. They, like the legalists, held the Torah in high regard. But, unlike them, they were open to new revelations. They were expecting the Messiah to come and then return to Glory. They felt that they were in the "last days" foretold by the prophets.

16. **The apocalyptic movement was characterized by the following beliefs:**
   a. All things are predestined by God and will happen according to His eternal plan. History is thus linear, and has a beginning and an end. There is no such thing as chance or luck.
   b. The world is doomed to get worse and worse.
   c. The wicked will become bolder in persecuting the saints in the last days.
   d. At the last moment, God will intervene through sending the Messiah, the "Son of Man" referred to in Daniel, to defeat the forces of evil.
   e. There will be a final battle in heaven between the Devil and his angels and Michael and his angels. The elect angels will win.
   f. There will also be a final battle on earth between Israel and the Gentile nations. The chosen people will win.
   g. There will be a bodily Resurrection of all men.
   h. All men will be judged by King Messiah.
   i. The reprobate will be thrown in eternal fire where they will be tormented forever.
   j. The earth will be cleansed by fire.
   k. A new earth and a new heaven will be created.
   l. Messiah's kingdom shall be eternal.

17. The main source of converts in the Palestinian Church came from those Jews involved in the apocalyptic movement. While the Pharisees, Sadducees, Herodians, Zealots, etc., were all enemies of Jesus and the Church, the apocalyptic-minded Jews were open to the idea that the Messiah had come because they believed that they were living in the "last days." They were open to new revelations, and thus had no problem accepting the New Testament being inspired.

18. The Pharisees saw the apocalyptic movement flowing into the Church and this is why they decided to abandon apocalyptic literature as a genre and to repudiate the apocalyptic movement that produced them. To this day, modern Judaism is still hostile to its own tradition of Messianic expectations. Many rabbis now pretend that Judaism never interpreted the OT verses identified by the NT as Messianic in nature that way before. This is either complete ignorance or willful deception on their part. I document this in the book, *The Trinity: Evidence and Issues* (World Pub.).

19. Given the above facts, we must still resist the temptation to reduce Christianity to mere Jewish apocalypticism. Christianity influenced apocalypticism more than apocalypticism influenced Christianity. Christianity took the apocalyptic movement and radically transformed it by rooting it in such historical events as the incarnation, death, burial and resurrection of the Messiah. These historical events became the basis of their expectation of final victory at the end of history. The Gospel message looks back to the cross as well as forward to the crown. Salvation is not earned by observing the Torah. It is a free gift of God's grace by virtue of the atonement that Jesus paid on the cross.

20. The future victory over evil was now secure because Jesus conquered Satan. He took the keys of hell and death away from the Devil and now wears them on his belt. The kingdom of the Messiah is both now a present spiritual reality and later a physical manifestation on a new earth. His present kingdom is the rule of God in the hearts of men and, after the end, it will be the realm where His rule is universal, complete, final, and eternal for "of his kingdom there shall be no end" (Luke 1:33).

Part II

We will now set forth those hermeneutical principles that should be used when interpreting apocalyptic literature.

1. There are times when a biblical prophet was not talking about end-time events, but about future events that would transpire during this age. Yet, because these events are so significant and important, he borrows apocalyptic language to describe them. For example, the passage may have in view a coming invasion of Israel or some other great moment in redemptive history (Isa. 13; 24:1-4, 19-23; 30:27-33; Ezek. 32:2-8; Joel 2:10-11, 28-32; 3:4, 14-17; Amos 5:18-20; 8:9; Zeph. 1:7, 14-15; Matt. 24-25; Acts 2:14-21). The book of Joel is an excellent example of this.

    a. A coming invasion of the nation is described with vivid apocalyptic imagery. In the "last days," the "day of the Lord" would come and "destruction will come upon them" (Joel 1:15). An army of weird locusts will descend upon the nation and strip it clean. While this invasion was not the literal "Day of the LORD" at the end of history, yet, it was so much "like" that Day that it was described as if it were.

    b. Joel predicted that "in the last days" the Holy Spirit would be poured out in a dramatic manner not heretofore seen (Joel 2). He used apocalyptic imagery to underscore the importance of this event in the history of redemption.

"And I will show wonders in the heavens and in the earth. The sun will be turned into darkness; and the moon into blood, before the great and terrible day of the LORD comes" (Joel 2:30-31).

When Peter stated that this prophecy was fulfilled on the day of Pentecost (Acts 2:14-21), he was not saying that the above apocalyptic imagery was literally fulfilled on that day. The sun did not literally turn to darkness and the moon into blood on that day. Pentecost was not literally the "Day of the LORD." The apocalyptic imagery was used to underscore the significance of that day.

2. **Jesus used the same technique in Matt. 24 when He compared the end to Noah's flood, the destruction of Sodom, and the destruction of the temple.** While these events did not literally constitute the "end" of the world, yet they were described as if they were in order to emphasize the catastrophic nature of those events.

Events in history that prefigure the end: Flood, Sodom, Canaan, Egypt, Assyria, Babylon, Pentecost, Temple.

3. **The failure to understand the use of apocalyptic language to emphasize important non-apocalyptic events in history has led to errors.**

   a. Literalists are left with a host of prophecies that were not literally fulfilled. Faced with this fact, some become delusional and pretend that the sun and moon were destroyed at Pentecost! Others invent convoluted principles such as "double" fulfillment. If a prophecy could have more than one fulfillment, then why not three fulfillments or three thousand fulfillments? If a prophecy can mean different things at different times in different places to different people, it means nothing.

   b. Preterists fail to understand that just because a future event is described in Scripture with apocalyptic end-time imagery, this does not mean that it is the end. Something can be an "end" (example of a city, nation, empire, age, etc.) without being the end. In this way they confuse Pentecost or the destruction of the temple in A.D. 70 with the end of the world and the return of Christ. The presence of apocalyptic language does not logically or hermeneutically imply that the end is in view. The event may foreshadow the end without being the end itself.

   Those Preterists who deny a future Second Coming of Christ and the resurrection of the dead by reducing them to some event in history, such as Pentecost or the destruction of the Temple, clearly contradict the Seven Ecumenical Creeds of the early church and the great creeds of the Reformation, such as the Westminster Confession. They are thus not part of Christian orthodoxy and must be deemed heretical. They should be excluded from membership in all orthodox communions. The anathema found in 2 Tim. 2:14-19 is applicable to any form of preterism that denies a future bodily Resurrection of the dead at the end.

4. **Two things follow from the above observations:**

   a. The mere presence of apocalyptic imagery does not automatically mean that the end time is being described.

   b. We should not automatically assume that a literal fulfillment of apocalyptic images will take place. The imagery could be used to underscore important events not related to the end of history.

5. **Do not fall for the silly notion that the issue is whether you take a "literal" or "spiritual" method of interpretation.** It is a false distinction that no one really observes.

   a. Those who teach the dichotomy have never been able to define the words "literal" or "spiritual." Does "literal" mean a real, live dragon, or is the dragon a symbol for something else? Then we must take a symbolic interpretation. But if it is a symbol for some literal person or event, then is it a literal symbol? The definitions end up being absurd.

   b. The word "literal" establishes a direct correspondence between a word and physical reality. For example, do we interpret the word "dragon" literally or symbolically? A literal interpretation would posit the existence of some kind of huge reptile, perhaps a dinosaur. A symbolic interpretation would deny the existence of this reptile and, instead, would say that the word "dragon" is a symbol for the devil.

    c. Literalists, such as the Dispensationalists, do not really believe in literal dragons or a literal Whore riding upon a literal Beast. They often give bizarre typological interpretations of such things as the furniture of the tabernacle and generally are as quick to take a non-literal approach as anyone else. Until I see them with one eye gouged out and one hand chopped off, they are full of hot air when they boast that they "take the Bible literally."

    d. Since I have never met anyone who takes a "spiritual" approach to interpreting the Bible, I must assume that this is a straw man invented by literalists as a boogeyman to frighten lay Christians.

6. It is impossible to decide ahead of time how a passage is going to be fulfilled. We did a detailed study of all the OT citations in the NT to see if there was any way to determine ahead of time how a particular prophecy would be fulfilled. We found no such way.

7. Each passage must be interpreted in the light of its own layers of context:

    a word in terms of its grammar, syntax, and vocabulary

     a verse in the context of the paragraph

      the paragraph in the context of that section of the chapter

       that section in the context of the entire chapter

        that chapter in the context of that section of the book

         that section in the context of the book as a whole

          that book in the context of its place in the canon

           the historical, cultural, political, and religious context of

            the author and the people to whom he is writing

8. Apocalyptic literature is not the rewriting of past events in order to give them a supernatural twist. The liberals are hopelessly trapped in a circular argument that since miracles cannot happen, then predictive prophecies cannot happen. Their anti-supernatural bias is a leap in the dark. It is an example of the psychological phenomenon known as "wish fulfillment." They do not wish miracles to happen, so they don't.

9. Apocalyptic literature is not a historical narrative of the future. Read the book of Acts and then the book of Revelation. If you cannot see the difference between historical narrative and apocalyptic writing, you need to take a course in English literature! Apocalyptic literature is not historical in nature for the following reasons:

    a. It does not attempt to give the exact names, dates, places, or numbers of end-time events, symbols, or images. This is why there are as many interpretations of such things as there are interpreters!

    b. We are told only a few of the events to transpire at the end. Thus, we do not have the whole picture. Without the entire picture, it is difficult to interpret the parts.

    c. Apocalyptic literature is progressive in nature, with each prophet adding only a few parts of the puzzle. This progress can be seen by comparing Daniel to Revelation. You cannot "stop the clock" by freezing one apocalyptic work such as Daniel, and then think that you got the whole story.

10. In apocalyptic literature, the authors used images and symbols from their own personal history and the experience of others to describe the end. God always revealed His Word to people using their language and their experience so that they could understand what He was saying.

11. Dress styles (robes, dresses, military uniforms, etc.), modes of transportation (camels, horses, etc.) and military hardware (swords, spears, etc.), are not used in apocalyptic literature as literal predictions that wars at the end will be limited to the clothing, transportation, and military hardware of Ezekiel's day. Apocalyptic visions such as Ezek. 38-40 do not mean that the final battle at the end will be done on horseback with swords waving over our heads! It is assumed that the final battle between good and evil at the end will use whatever clothing, modes of transportation, and weapons that are current at that time.

12. Since the end would usher in a new form of worship that has yet to be experienced on earth, the authors used contemporary symbols of worship such as temples, priests, and sacrifices, because that is all they knew about worship. It was understood that the use of temple images did not predict that the old Mosaic temple worship would be reestablished on earth in the eternal kingdom after the end. Some literalists have gone so far as to teach that the temple, the Levitical priests and the sacrificial system would be established once again. But the book of Hebrews reveals that the temple sacrifices were fulfilled in Christ's death and were done away with. He is now the temple and the tabernacle as well as the Lamb.

13. Apocalyptic literature used idealized situations from the life experience of the author to paint a beautiful picture of what a wonderful life it will be in the eternal kingdom after the end. The imagery of everyone sitting under his own tree and just reaching up and picking fruit off his tree whenever he was hungry was not to be taken literally. Neither was the imagery of children playing with poisonous snakes or lions lying down with lambs. The point of such apocalyptic imagery was to emphasize the safe and bounteous life in the eternal kingdom.

14. In the NT, some of the symbols and images of the eternal conscious torment that awaits the wicked at the end were drawn from earlier apocalyptic literature such as 1 Enoch. It was understood that the fire, the worms, the bottomless pit, the darkness, the dragon, etc., were all symbols of something that was so awful that human words could not convey it. No symbol is as real as what it symbolizes. See my book, *Death and the Afterlife* (Bethany House Publishers) for the documentation for this. To make literal what was originally metaphorical is to make the final hell less than what it will be.

15. Apocalyptic literature was free to mix metaphors and symbols because it was assumed that no imagery was to be literally fulfilled.

    a. The final hell, Gehenna, could be imagined as a lake of fire and as wandering around in the mist of darkness at the same time because both were understood to be symbols of the indescribable torment of the damned.

    b. In Matt. 25:31, the earth still exists on the Day of Judgment, while in Rev. 20:11 the earth no longer exists. Were the authors contradicting each other? No. It did not matter in apocalyptic literature what symbols or imagery were used, because none of them were intended to be interpreted literally.

16. Apocalyptic literature was free to use conflicting chronologies of future events at the end because it was assumed that no chronology was to be taken literally. It is thus multi-chronological. The attempt to reduce all the different chronologies down to one chronology is nothing more than the old error of reductionism. That this is true is seen from the following illustrations drawn from Scripture.

    a. In the apocalyptic parables of the kingdom found in Matt. 13, Jesus gave the chronology that the wicked would be taken first and the righteous left behind on the Judgment Day (vs. 24-30, 36-43). But in His apocalyptic sermon found in Matt. 24-25, Jesus said that the righteous would be taken first and the wicked left behind (vs. 31). Obviously, the wicked can't be first and the righteous first at the same time. One can be first and the other second, but they can't both be first.

    Was Jesus contradicting Himself? This apparent contradiction can be resolved by the fact that in apocalyptic literature you can have as many conflicting chronologies as you want, because none of them should be taken as a literal schedule of future events.

    b. According to 1 Cor. 15:50-57, the end-time events, such as the resurrection, take place "in a moment, in the twinkling of an eye." The words imply that everything will happen instantaneously in a fraction of a second. In other words, it will all be done in an instant. No waiting in line.

Yet, in other apocalyptic passages such as Matt. 25:31-46; 2 Cor. 5:10; Rev. 20:11-15; etc., the scene is drawn out with Christ coming to earth, setting up His throne, resurrecting all men, assembling them before His throne for judgment, everyone standing in line until his/her turn to be brought before Christ. Then everything we ever thought, said or did is publicly revealed and judged. Christ then pronounces judgment upon us and we are either ushered into the eternal kingdom or thrown into the eternal fire.

Now, there is no way this long, drawn out apocalyptic vision can be reduced to "in a moment, in the twinkling of an eye." But once it is understood that we are dealing with different apocalyptic visions of the end, then there is no contradiction. None of these things are to be interpreted as a literal calendar of events.

c. In John 5:25-29, Jesus spoke of the "hour" when "all who are in the grave will hear His voice" and come forth, some to life and some to damnation. The passage is straightforward, and there is no time space between the resurrection of believers and nonbelievers. The resurrection is pictured as a single universal event embracing all of humanity. A-millennialists love this passage and use it to refute Pre-millennialism.

On the other hand, in Rev. 20:4-15, two resurrections with a thousand-year interval between them are pictured. There will be a "first" and a "second" resurrection. The Pre-millennialists, of course, love this passage and use it to refute A-millennialism.

Now, it is obvious that John 5 and Rev. 20 confront us with two different chronologies of the resurrection. Is it one event or two events? Are all or only some resurrected? They cannot both be literally true!

The choice is clear. If we give a literalistic interpretation of John 5 and Rev. 20, the Bible ends up contradicting itself! But if we approach John 5 and Rev. 20 as being apocalyptic, then there is no contradiction, because neither passage is to be taken as a literal chronology. According to Dan. 12, John 5, 1 Cor. 15, Rev. 20, etc., all the dead will be bodily raised and judged by Christ at the end. This much is clear. But when we try to find out the details of how and in what order such things will happen, we are rebuked in Acts 1:6-7:

> "So when they had come together, they were asking Him, saying, 'Lord is it at this time You are restoring the kingdom to Israel?' He said to them, 'It is not for you to know the times or epochs which the Father has fixed by His own authority.'"

The tense of the verb translated "asking" in verse 6 indicates that they had repeatedly asked Jesus about the details of future events. Since this was His last discussion with them before He ascended into heaven, He answered them by pointing that when it came to the details of the future, they were not allowed to know the *chronous* or the *kairos*. Prof. F.F. Bruce, in his commentary on Acts, states:

> "*Chronous* refers to the time that must elapse before the final establishment of the Kingdom, *kairos* to the critical events accompanying its establishment" (p. 70).

Only the Father knows the details of such things, and He has decided not to tell us. We must also point out that in the Greek text, the word "not" is taken out of its normal word order in the sentence and put first to reveal that Jesus stressed this word. "It is NOT for you to know..." This grammatical observation underscores the importance of His rebuke.

If we took this passage to heart, there would be no pre-, post-, or a-millennialism. We would be content with the Apostles' Creed:

> He ascended into heaven,
> and is seated at the right hand of God
> the Father Almighty;
> From there he shall come to judge the
> living and the dead.
> I believe in the Resurrection of the body,
> and the life everlasting. Amen.

17. The failure to understand this is the main error of present day millennial schemes.
They run through the Bible trying to find chronologies to fit their prophetic views.

a. The Pre-millennialists seize upon the chronology found in Rev. 20 as the basis for their view. Despite the twin facts that this is the ONLY place in the Bible that refers to a thousand-year kingdom and it is in a highly symbolic passage with a dragon, an angel, a chain, and a hole in the ground, none of which they view as literal, they demand a literal fulfillment for this chronology.

   It never dawns on them that the chronology found in Rev. 20 is only one of several different chronologies found in the Bible. Thus, we can admit that Rev. 20 does have a chronology that fits the Pre-millennial scheme, but, at the same time, point out that apocalyptic chronologies are not to be taken literally.

b. The A-millennialists are just as guilty of this error. They grab hold of the chronology found in 1 Cor. 15 and point out that when Christ returns, this means "the end" of His kingdom—not "the beginning" of it. He gives up His kingdom to the Father when He returns.

   Since they assume that they must reduce all other biblical chronologies to the one found in 1 Cor. 15, they end up giving weird interpretations of Rev. 20.

c. The Post-millennialists do the same thing with Psa. 22, etc. They think that they have found biblical chronologies that favor their view. In Daniel chapters 2 and 4, the kingdom grows and covers the earth before the end. But this vision is not intended to be taken as a literal calendar of events. Other passages indicate that the world will be worse at the end, not better!

   It is apparent to those who have studied all the present prophetic views that they can all find apocalyptic chronologies in the Bible to fit their views. Thus, they are all right and wrong at the same time. Their failure to understand the genre of apocalyptic literature has doomed them to endlessly squabbling over each other's chronologies.

18. The use of Hebrew parallelism and synchronism, in which events and things during the same time period are described by several different sets of symbols, is a feature of apocalyptic literature that is not well-known today. Imagine one wave of fireworks exploding in the air and then another wave of fireworks shooting up in the same sky. Then another wave and yet another wave of fireworks exploding in the same sky with different colors and symbols. Each wave produced a different pattern in the same space.

a. This is a good description of what we find in Scripture. For example, in Daniel, the same time period is first described in Nebuchadnezzar's dream of a giant statue in chapter 2 and then described again by the imagery of the four beasts in chapter 7. The imagery changes, but not the time period in focus.

b. The book of Revelation is divided into seven sections that cover the same time period, but with different symbols and imagery each time. If you do not understand this, you would make the mistake of assuming that each set of symbols described a different time period that must be put end to end. For example, the seven seals, the seven trumpets, the seven vials, etc., are not consecutive time periods laid out end to end, but the same time period with different symbols being used to emphasize different aspects.

    c. Another example is the image of the 144,000 in Rev. 7:4-8. It is then replaced in verse 9 with the image of a crowd that cannot be numbered. Both images are of the same group of people seen from different perspectives.

19. If a symbol in an Apocalyptic is explained, do not contradict it or go beyond it. The symbol of the seven candlesticks in Rev. 1:20 is explained as the seven churches of Asia Minor to whom Christ was dictating letters. To claim that the seven candlesticks do not represent the seven churches, but rather that they refer to seven different consecutive ages is to contradict Christ's own explanation!

20. If a symbol is nowhere explained, then take Paul's advice to heart: "Do not go beyond what is Written" (1 Cor. 4:6). Once you enter into vain speculation as to the meaning of symbols for which you have no divine interpretation, you can easily fall into a gnostic attitude, in which you imagine that you alone have discovered the secret meaning of a symbol.

21. In apocalyptic literature, if a symbol is not explained, its meaning is hidden until it is fulfilled. The only certain and infallible interpretation of prophecy is its eventual fulfillment in God's timetable. There is no hermeneutical principle found in Scripture by which we can know ahead of time how and in what way a particular prophecy will be fulfilled.

Part III

Once we de-apocalypticize biblical prophecy, with what do we end up? We end up with all the historic creeds of Christianity. They do not go into any details when it comes to the end. They are not on the side of any modern millennial schemes. They emphasize the core of the biblical vision of the end.

1. Christ sits in His resurrected body at the right hand of the Father in heaven.
2. From there He will personally and literally return to earth.
3. All men will be resurrected on the Day He returns.
4. Christ shall judge all men and angels.
5. He will destroy the old earth by fire, and create a new earth where no evil will be allowed.
6. The elect will inherit the new earth as an everlasting kingdom.
7. All the demonic and human evildoers shall be sentenced to eternal conscious torment in Gehenna.
8. All things will happen according to God's eternal timetable.

When it comes to detailed questions such as how, in what way, and in what order will all these events happen, no one knows. What will be the exact order of events? Are the wicked or the righteous left behind? Who goes first? What kind of resurrection body will we get? Will we look like we do now? If we are radically changed, how will our relatives and friends recognize us? Will we all be young? What age? Is 18 years old a good age? What about 21? Will we all sing like opera stars? Will we all be beautiful, rich, and thin? Or, will such things no longer matter to us at that time because we will no longer care about carnal things? Who will be the servants and who will be the people getting served? Who hauls away the garbage? Who cleans the streets?

Does everything happen "in a moment, in the twinkling of an eye?" Or will things get dragged out for years? After all, if everyone is standing in line waiting to be called to judgment, there are a lot of people in front of you! Will the line be arranged alphabetically, or by your date of birth, or by your date of death?

As a young believer, I was told that I would be called up to the throne and Jesus would show my entire life on a big screen so everyone would see everything I ever thought, said or did—even things done in darkness! As a teenager, this sounded horrific to me!

The pain and the discomfort felt by the audience who is forced to watch all this stuff is probably as great as the poor person whose life is being exposed to public review! Wouldn't we see icky things that would repulse and sicken us? Who, but the most hardened voyeurist, could bear looking at all the details of every sexual thought, word and deed of billions of people? Wouldn't this be some kind of pornography?

Those who assume that prophecy is a literal record of future history must answer such questions. Thankfully, the symbols and imagery found in the apocalyptic visions of the Judgment Day are not to be taken literally. Their purpose is to emphasize that the Judgment will be complete and just. King Jesus will decide the degree of eternal bliss or torment. Our responsibility is to live each day in the light of the fact that it may be our last day on earth.

Conclusion

One of the main purposes of apocalyptic literature is to comfort the afflicted and persecuted saints with the assurance that in the end justice shall prevail, the Devil will lose, the Messiah will establish His eternal kingdom, the earth will be made into a Paradise once again, and we will be raised immortal and incorruptible.

This apocalyptic comfort gives us the strength to go on in the Christian life, even when it seems that the forces of evil are winning. At the end of his apocalyptic sermon found in 1 Cor. 15, Paul comforted the saints by saying:

"But thanks be to God who gives us the victory through our Lord Jesus Christ. Therefore, my beloved brethren, be steadfast, immovable, always abounding in the work of the Lord, because you know that your labor in the Lord is not in vain."

Knowing that we are on the winning side gives us the ability to surmount all obstacles and endure all persecution. Keep your eyes on Jesus and the fact that He is coming back one day. Be steadfast, immovable, always abounding in the work of the Lord until you meet Him in heaven at death, or in the sky at His return.

Chapter Fifty

The Structure of the Bible

Introduction

Even though the Bible is a library of 66 books written by more than 40 authors over a period of several thousand years, its internal structure reveals its divine inspiration.

The order of the books of the Bible is not a product of:

(1) chance
(2) chronology
(3) authorship
(4) size
(5) human opinion

The order of the books of the Bible is according to subject matter. The marvelous way it is structured reveals that One Mind must have directed each book to its own unique place in the canon of Scripture. This One Mind had to see all the books at the same time in order to determine the time and place of each individual book. Only One Mind could have directed the development of Scripture over thousands of years and controlled each author so completely that he wrote only what God wanted him to write. This One Mind was God Himself.

I. The Old Testament

    A. The Old Testament as a Whole: The O.T. telephone number is 593-5-593. Once you have memorized this number, you will know the theme of every book in the Old Testament.

5 Basic Law		5 Basic Prophecy
9 Pre-exile History	5 Inner Life	9 Pre-exile Prophecy
3 Post-exile History		3 Post-exile Prophecy

B. The Major Prophets

2 Pre-exile Prophets   Lamentations   2 Post-exile Prophets
(Isaiah and Jeremiah)   (Ezekiel and Daniel)

C. Isaiah: The Bible in Miniature

The Bible	Isaiah
66 books	66 chapters
Two-fold division:	Two-fold division:
O.T. 39 books	Part I: 39 chapters
N.T. 27 books	Part II: 27 chapters
Two themes:	Two themes:
O.T. Sin/judgment	Part I: Sin/Judgment
N.T. Grace/salvation	Part II: Grace/Salvation

D.   The Order of the Psalms

Psa. 22 The Cross: Jesus as Priest   Savior   "Jesus"
Psa. 23 The Crook: Jesus as Prophet   Sanctifier   "Christ"
Psa. 24 The Crown: Jesus as King   Sovereign   "Lord"

II. The New Testament

A. The New Testament as a Whole

Five-fold Division	Three-fold Division
4 Manifestation	5 Historical
1 Proclamation	13 Theological
13 Explanation	9 General
8 Application	
1 Expectation	

B. The Significance of the Four Gospels
   Matthew:
   1. Written to the Jews
   2. Answers the question: "What did Jesus say?"
   3. Emphasizes the words of Jesus
   Mark:
   1. Written to the Romans
   2. Answers the question: "What did Jesus do?"
   3. Emphasizes the works of Jesus
   Luke:
   1. Written to the Greeks
   2. Answers the question: "Who followed Jesus?"
   3. Emphasizes the followers of Jesus
   John:
   l. Written to the Christians
   2. Answers the question: "Who was Jesus?"
   3. Emphasizes the deity of Jesus

C. The Significance of Matthew, Romans, Hebrews
   1. Matthew: the first book in its section (historical).
      Romans: the first book in its section (theological).
      Hebrews: the first book in its section (practical).
   2. Matthew quotes more of the O.T. than any other book in its section.
      Romans quotes more of the O.T. than any other book in its section.
      Hebrews quotes more of the O.T. than any other book in its section.
   3. Matthew the historical bridge between the O.T. and the N.T.
      Romans the theological bridge between the O.T. and the N.T.
      Hebrews the ceremonial bridge between the O.T. and the N.T.

D. The Book of Romans
   Since it was not Paul's first epistle, why was it placed first in the Pauline Epistles? It was
   placed first because:
   1. It is the theological bridge between the O.T. and the N.T.
   2. It is the passage of full mention on God's plan of salvation.
   3. It is foundational to all the other epistles.
   4. It deals with the whole while the other epistles deal with the parts.

Romans:	The Gospel of Christ
1 & 2 Corinthians	The Body of Christ
Galatians	The Freedom in Christ
Ephesians	The Blessings of Christ
Philippians	The Humility of Christ
Colossians	The Preeminence of Christ
1 & 2 Thessalonians	The Return of Christ
1 & 2 Timothy	The Church of Christ
Philemon	The Equality in Christ

5. Romans answers the objection of the Jews that the Gospel of Christ offers a different salvation than what was taught and experienced in the O.T.

   a. The gospel comes from the Father as well as the Son. This is why he wrote "Gospel of God" in Rom. 1:1.

   b. The gospel was taught by the prophets in the O.T. (Rom. 1:2).

   c. Abraham, who lived before the Law, was justified solely by faith apart from works (Rom. 4:1-3).

   d. David, who lived after the Law and thus under it, was justified solely by faith apart from works (Rom. 4:4-8).

   e. Even Moses, who gave the Law, taught the same thing (Rom. 10:1-10).

   f. Since there is only one God, there can be only one way of salvation (Rom. 3:29-30).

   g Paul quotes from the entire O.T.:

the Law	Rom. 4: 1-5
the Writings	Rom. 4:6-8
the Prophets	Rom. 1:17

Conclusion

The inspiration of the Bible rests on its internal structure as well as such external evidences as fulfilled prophecy and archaeology. Only the sovereignty of God can explain the canon of the Bible.

Chapter Fifty-One

The Inerrancy of the Bible

Introduction

Would you call someone "reliable" who:

- ✓ was frequently mistaken on what he believed and said?
- ✓ contradicted himself many times?
- ✓ deliberately and knowingly lied to you on many occasions?
- ✓ made up stories whenever it suited him?

Would you continue to trust his word after being deceived by him again and again? I don't think so! Yet, this is what liberal theologians ask us to do with the Bible!

Liberal theologians claim:

- ✓ The authors of the Bible were often mistaken in what they believed and wrote.
- ✓ They frequently contradicted themselves and other biblical writers.
- ✓ They deliberately and knowingly tried to deceive people into thinking that their books were written by such famous men as Moses, Daniel, Matthew, Paul, etc. (1992, R.A. Morey)
- ✓ They made up details of the birth, life, sermons, miracles, death and resurrection of Jesus.
- ✓ They fabricated a new theology around their fabricated Christ and created a new religion called Christianity, which Jesus would have never recognized.

I. The Reliability of Scripture

When Christian theologians use such words as "infallibility" and "inerrancy," they are simply saying that the Bible is reliable in everything it records. Thus you can count on the Bible because it is true, factual, real and historical. The Bible is:

- ✓ A reliable record of the experiences and beliefs of the biblical authors.
  Illustration: In the book of Romans, we have a reliable record of what the Apostle Paul experienced and believed.
- ✓ A reliable record of the beliefs and experiences of other people.
  Illustration: The beliefs and practices of the Pharisees are described in the Gospels (Mark 7:3-4).
- ✓ A reliable record of the lies and false ideas of men and demons.
  Illustration: Gen. 3:4; Job 42:7
- ✓ A reliable record of the good things that people do.
  Illustration: Dorcas (Acts 9:36-39)
- ✓ A reliable record of the evil things that people do.
  Illustration: The rape of Dinah (Gen. 34:1-2)
- ✓ A reliable record of the historical events—natural and supernatural—which surrounded the rise and progress of the people of God.
  Illustration: The Creation, the Fall, the Flood, the Tower, the Patriarchs, the Exodus, the rise, fall and return of Israel, the life of Christ, and the expansion of the early church into Europe.

✓ A reliable record of biblical authorship.
  Illustration: Isaiah, Daniel, Matthew, etc.
✓ A reliable record of what God revealed to the authors of Scripture.
  Illustration: Gal. 1:1, 11-12.
✓ A reliable record which does not contradict itself.
  Illustration: 2 Pet. 2:20-21.
✓ A reliable record of what we must believe to be saved and how to live the Christian life.
  Illustration: Acts 4:12; Rom. 12:1-2.

II. Common questions about inerrancy
✓ "Should we interpret the Bible literally?"
  Answer: No. The Bible contains many different kinds of literature: history, poetry, prophecy, doctrine and ethics. Figurative language is frequently used.
✓ "If it is in the Bible, is it true?"
  Answer: No. The Bible is a reliable record of the lies and false ideas of men and demons as well as a record of the truth. A verse must be interpreted in the light of its context.
  Illustration: Ecclesiastes.
✓ "If it is in the Bible, is it good?"
  Answer: No. The Bible records many evil things, which it condemns.
  Illustration: Rape, cannibalism, murder, etc.
✓ "Is the Bible a textbook on history, science, mathematics, biology, etc.?"
  Answer: No. The writing of textbooks was not the intent of the authors of the Bible. But whenever they do touch on such areas, they are reliable.
✓ "Can we judge the Bible by today's literary standards?"
  Answer: No. Each book of the Bible must be judged by the literary standards of the age in which it was written.
  Illustration: Paul's name at the beginning of his letters. Moses' use of the third person.
✓ "Are the Gospels biographies of Christ?"
  Answer: No. The modern idea of writing a chronologically structured "biography" was unknown in the first century. It was not the intent of the gospel writers to write a "biography" of Jesus in the modern sense.

Each gospel writer selected certain things from the life of Christ to illustrate a particular theme that he wanted to convey to a specific audience he had in mind. He would arrange these things in a way to highlight his message, thus they did not try to give a precise chronology of the words or actions of Christ. For example, Matthew groups together all the kingdom parables in chapter 13 regardless of when they were given. He structured his gospel account according to certain themes—not chronology.

Book	Theme	Audience
Matthew:	What did Jesus say?	The Jews
Mark:	What did Jesus do?	The Romans
Luke:	Who followed Jesus?	The Greeks
John:	Who was Jesus?	The Christians

✓ "If two or more accounts of the same incident are different in any way, are they contradictory?"
  Answer: No. Differing accounts can be supplementary and not contradictory. Liberals assume that if two or more accounts "differ" in any details, they automatically are "contradictory." But this is a common logical fallacy. When two or more accounts of the same incident are given by

different individuals, they will always "differ" in some details. But these "differences" only supplement each other and once they are put together, they give us the whole picture. Different accounts by different people will usually differ for the following reasons:

a. The accounts are given from different viewpoints.
   Example: Four people see an accident from four different corners.
b. People are emphasizing different things.
   Example: Political, society and gossip reporters' accounts of a Washington party.
c. When one account is written after the others and it adds new information that was not available before, this is not contradictory but supplementary.
d. The intent of a person must be recognized.
   1. If he did not intend to put things in a chronological order, but to group things thematically, he cannot be faulted.
   2. If he did not intend to give a literal word for word quotation but to summarize a sermon in his own words, or to paraphrase a statement in order to emphasize its meaning, he cannot be faulted.
   3. If he did not intend to give an exact numerical count, but to round things off to the nearest whole number, he cannot be faulted.
   4. If he did not intend to use literal language, but to use figurative language in a description of something, he cannot be faulted.
e. The audience must also be taken into account. We do not speak to a child in the same way we speak to an adult. What we say in a court is more formal than a casual conversation with a friend. When one audience is Jewish and another is Gentile, different terminology may be used given the different backgrounds.
f. Leaving out those details which do not fit in with your theme is perfectly normal.
   Example: A black history course which only describes black inventors is not erroneous because it omits any references to white inventors.
g. When one account mentions one person while another account mentions more than one, there is no logical contradiction if the first account does not say "only" one person was present. The author is simply emphasizing the presence of one person without denying the presence of others.

✓ "But how about when Matthew says that two blind men were healed while Mark and Luke say that only one was healed?"
Answer: It must be pointed out that you added the word "only" to the accounts. This is a point of logic that must be emphasized. Neither Mark nor Luke said that "only" one blind man was healed. They just tell the story of the one man whose name was known as Bartimaeus. Matthew mentions in passing that there was a second blind man healed. They supplement each other. There is no logical contradiction.

✓ "Mark 10:46 says that this healing took place as Jesus approached Jericho, while Matthew 20:30 says that it took place as He was leaving Jericho. You can't be approaching and leaving a city at the same time. Isn't this a clear contradiction?"
Answer: No. Archaeology has discovered that when the Romans tried to set up a base in Jericho, the Jews rioted so much that the Romans went down the road about two miles and set up their own settlement, which they also called Jericho. Thus the word "Jericho" in New Testament times referred to two settlements: one Jewish and one Gentile. The merchants and beggars would gather between the two settlements to catch the traffic going either way. In this light, it is clear that the healing took place after Jesus had left the Jewish Jericho but before He got to

the Gentile Jericho. In other words, it took place between the Jewish and Gentile sections of Jericho. Since Matthew was writing to the Jews, he referred to the Jewish section of Jericho. And, since Mark was writing to the Gentiles, he referred to the Gentile section of Jericho, thus, there is no contradiction.

✓ "But the New Testament authors frequently misquote the Old Testament. Is this not a clear contradiction?"
Answer: No. The modern literary practice of giving an exact quotation of someone's words was not practiced in the first century. The biblical authors, like the rabbis, would paraphrase (i.e. put into their own words) an O.T. text in order to emphasize its meaning. They had just as much right to paraphrase the Bible as we do today.

✓ "But what if the wording of what Jesus or someone else said is different from one gospel to the other?"
Answer: The authors of Scripture plainly stated that they did not record the full text of what Jesus or others said (John 21:24-25). They usually summarized in their own words what people said. They did not usually quote verbatim. (Illustration: Matt. 5-7; Acts 2)

✓ "But what about all the numbers and names that contradict each other in 1 and 2 Kings and 1 and 2 Chronicles?"
Answer: Divine inspiration only covers the authors of Scripture and what they originally wrote—not all the copyists since that time. Logically speaking, the existence of simple copyist errors in numbers and names cannot negate the inspiration of the original text.

✓ "What if something or someone in the Bible is not mentioned in extra-biblical literature? Is this a contradiction?
Answer: It is illogical to say that something or someone mentioned in the Bible did not exist because we do not have extra-biblical confirmation. Archaeology has a nasty habit of crushing these kinds of arguments.
Example: No writing in Moses' day; no Hittites, etc. Some liberals claim that the town of Nazareth mentioned in the New Testament did not exist at that time because the Talmud and Josephus did not mention it. They are wrong for several reasons.
    a. This is a logical fallacy because it is an argument from silence. Did the Talmud and Josephus mention every town in Israel? No.
    b. They are evidently ignorant of the "Nazareth stone," which archaeologists found in 1878, which must be dated A.D. 45-54. The stone proves that Nazareth existed at that time.
    c. While the Talmud does not use the noun "Nazareth," it does use the adjective "Notzri" as in "Jesus ha-Notzri." The word "Notzri" comes from the word Nazareth.

Conclusion
The Bible is reliable in all it records because its authors were sovereignly guided in what they wrote by God himself, and hence infallible and inerrant. You can trust the Bible.

Chapter Fifty-Two

The Biblical Concept of Pride and Humility

One area of the Christian life that has been much misunderstood is the nature of pride and humility. Can parents be proud of the accomplishments of their children? Is it wrong to boast of what God has done in your life? Can you be proud of a job well done? Questions like these need a biblical answer instead of a cultural or emotional answer.

1. Humility is the conscious intellectual recognition, either verbally or silently, that God is the Author of all good things and that you give Him all the glory (James 1:17). Pride is the conscious attempt to claim that you are the author of all the good in your life. The revolt of Satan (Isa. 14:12-14; cf. 1 Tim. 3:6) and the boasting of Nebuchadnezzar (Dan. 4:30-32) are the preeminent examples of how pride is viewed in Scripture.

2. Since pride and humility are intellectual and conscious in nature, they cannot be reduced to unconscious personality traits, body gestures, or lack of confidence. Just because someone is bold, self-confident, aggressive, etc., does not mean he is proud any more than "Henry Milquetoast" is humble because he lacks those strong qualities.

3. The Bible teaches that there are good kinds of pride and boasting as well as evil kinds. According to the Bible, God wants you to be proud of Him, His Word and the Savior. Boasting about such things is not wrong. The Psalmist boasted about his God and His works all day long (Psa. 34:2; 44:8). As long as you are consciously boasting "in the Lord," this is fine, according to Paul in 1 Cor. 1:31. Thus, there is nothing wrong in feeling proud over your accomplishments, family, job, church, nation, etc. To boast about such things is perfectly biblical (1 Cor. 8:24; 9:2, 3, 4; 10:8, 13).

4. One of the most difficult situations we encounter in life is when someone accuses us of pride. If we object that we are not proud, this proves to them that we are! If we agree with them that we are proud, the person beats us over the head! Either way we lose. It is a classic no-win situation. But what does the Bible say about the practice of accusing people of being proud? The surprising fact is that there is not one recorded instance in all of Scripture where a prophet, apostle or Jesus ever went up to an individual and accused them saying, "You are proud" or "You are not humble!"

   The only recorded instance in all of Scripture is where David's brother, out of anger and jealousy, falsely accused David (1 Sam. 17:26-29). David rightly refused to accept the accusation. If someone tries to judge your heart and motives, you must refuse to accept the accusation as David did. No one has the biblical warrant to accuse you of pride.

Why?

First, you alone know what is in your own heart, thus, no one else can judge your inner motives. Pride and humility are issues between you and God and no one has the right to judge your heart (1 Cor. 4:1-5).

Second, we are to humble ourselves. Nowhere in Scripture do the prophets or apostles demand that people humble themselves in front of them. We are to humble ourselves before God—not before man (2 Chron. 34:27; James 4:10; 1 Pet. 5:5). Do not accept the demand that you must humble yourself before somebody. Such a desire on their part is always viewed in Scripture as evil (Esther 3:1-3).

Conclusion

Don't feel guilty because you are proud of your husband, wife, children, job, church or pastor. If you feel ashamed of them, something is wrong with you. Do not let anyone judge your heart. God alone is to be the Lord of your conscience.

Chapter Fifty-Three

Men's Discipleship Manual

Introduction

In the book of Titus, the Apostle Paul is giving pastoral advice to Titus on how to regulate the affairs of the church. When dealing with Titus' responsibilities as an elder over the congregation, Paul encourages him to teach "sound" doctrine (Tit. 2:1).

The Greek word that is translated "sound" is literally the word "healthy," i.e., true doctrine will prove to be spiritually, mentally and physically "healthy" to those who embrace it. The Truth of God leads to the fullness of life in every area of life.

In order for Titus to be able to teach "healthy" doctrine in a consistent way, Paul outlines several discipleship programs that were organized around age or social status. For example, Paul sets up a discipleship program for the women in the church in which the older women instruct the younger women in biblical principles of living.

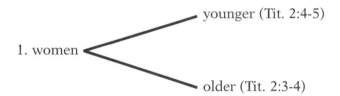

1. women
   - younger (Tit. 2:4-5)
   - older (Tit. 2:3-4)

The chapter "A Discipleship Program for Women" covers the curriculum suggested by Paul in this passage.

Paul also instructs Titus that the men in the church need to be instructed according to the particular trials and temptations that men face during the different phases of life. The men should be instructed according to their physical age and level of spiritual maturity.

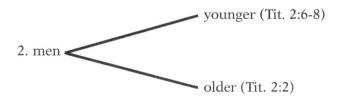

2. men
   - younger (Tit. 2:6-8)
   - older (Tit. 2:2)

This manual is an attempt to implement the discipleship program and curriculum set forth in Titus and elsewhere in Scripture. Our goal is threefold:

GOAL
- Knowing: understanding the will of God.
- Being: developing the character of God.
- Doing: obeying the Law of God.

This "knowing," "being," and "doing" encompasses all of life.

Under each heading there will be a development of those particular character qualities that God wants men to exhibit in each distinct sphere of life.

This manual is written with a certain kind of man in mind: The man who truly desires to be a better man, Christian, husband, father, employee or employer, and citizen is the kind of man for whom this manual will prove beneficial.

The man who has no desire to better himself will not find anything in this manual that will comfort or condone his sin before God. This manual is, thus, written for all those who sincerely desire to be godly and upright in all their ways.

Personal Life

Have you ever wanted to be the kind of man who is admired and respected as representing what an "ideal man" should be? The "ideal man" set forth by the world is pictured as someone who has acquired a vast amount of personal wealth, lives a life of affluence and has the sexual lifestyle of a "playboy."

The James Bond 007 lifestyle would be viewed by many as being the "best" possible life for a man. Thus, it is no surprise to find that a man's manliness is measured by Hollywood in terms of the amount of money he has, the kind of car he drives and the beauty of the woman who is with him for the night.

This is in stark contrast to the way the Bible pictures the ideal man. Instead of focusing on material standards such as personal wealth, the Scriptures focus on character traits that are manifested by the way a man deals with life. For example, how a man treats his family is a better indication of his manliness than the amount of money he provides for his family.

According to the Scriptures, the Ideal Man was Jesus Christ and not James Bond. We are called to conform our personality and character to the way that Jesus dealt with people and things. God is in the process of conforming His people to the character of Christ by the action of His sovereign power over all things (Rom. 8:28).

In various sections of the Bible, men are directly instructed to mold their personality and character to reflect the fear of God and the Lordship of Christ in all of life. There is no aspect of a man's life that is not addressed by Scripture.

The fact of sin should not negate the truth that the goal of every Christian should be total conformity to the will of God. We will never be perfect or sinless in this life, yet our goal is to find, follow and finish God's will for our lives. This over-arching goal is more important than anything else in life.

The task before us is to:

1. IDENTIFY those character traits that God wants men to manifest.
2. DEFINE these traits so we can understand what God expects of us as men.
3. ILLUSTRATE these traits by the lives of others so we have role models to follow.
4. IMPLEMENT these truths into our own lives.

This manual requires the active participation of the reader in all four steps. The time, effort and thought you put into this program will determine to a large degree what you will receive from this program.

"Be not deceived, God is not mocked; for whatever a man sows, this he will receive. For the one who sows to his own flesh shall from the flesh reap corruption. But the one who sows to the Spirit, shall from the Spirit reap eternal life" (Gal. 6:7, 8).

I. The Old Testament
   A. The passage of full mention is the entire book of Proverbs. Read through the book each day and make a list of the character traits that a man is called upon to develop. They need to be identified, defined, illustrated and implemented.
   B. We can also learn from the way that God dealt with men in O.T. history. What He desired to see developed in their lives is a good indication of what He wants us to know, be and do in our lives. Study the lives of the great men of redemptive history looking for the character traits that pleased God. Study such men as Abraham, Moses, Joshua, Elijah, David, Daniel, etc. For example, what lessons can we learn from Joshua's life? What did God say to him when Joshua was called to take Moses' place? Answer: Josh. 1:6-9.

II. The New Testament
   A. There are general passages in the N.T. that speak of the character traits that God wants his people to manifest. Example: Matt. 5:3-16; Rom. 12:8-21; Gal. 5:16-26, etc.
      These traits should be identified, defined, illustrated and implemented.
   B. The passage of full mention is Titus 2:2, 6. Identify, define, illustrate and implement the traits mentioned by Paul.
   C. There are passages that address different age groups. They need to be identified, defined, illustrated and implemented.
      1. young men: 1 Tim. 4:12; Tit. 2:6-8; 1 Pet. 5:5.
      2. adult men: Tit. 2:1-2.
   D. There are passages that address men in terms of their level of spiritual maturity. Identify, define, illustrate and implement the traits that are assigned to each group.
      1. Spiritual "Babies" still weak and unstable: 1 Tim. 3:6; 1 John 2:12-13; Eph. 4:14.
      2. Spiritual "Teenagers" beginning to develop strength and stability: 1 John 2:13-14.
      3. Spiritual "Fathers" who are strong and stable in holiness of life and doctrine: 1 John 2:13-14.
   E. Study the lives of such N.T. heroes as the Apostle Paul and discover what good character traits made him into a mighty man of God. Translate these traits into your experience.

Family Life

As the head of the family, God calls you to do certain tasks and to develop certain character traits. In order to be the kind of husband and father that you ought to be, you must identify, define, illustrate and implement the duties, roles and responsibilities for which you will be held accountable on the Day of Judgment.

I. The Old Testament
   A. Passage of Full Mention: Proverbs.
      Identify and develop those passages that describe a "good" and "wise" father and husband.
   B. Related passages: sample passages
      1. Deut. 6:1-9
      2. Joshua 24:15
      3. Exo. 20:12
      4. 1 Sam. 3:12-14
      5. Psa. 103:13, 14
II. The New Testament
   A. Passage of Full Mention: Eph. 5:25-6:4.
   B. Related passages:

1. A man's relationship to his wife: Col. 3:19; 1 Pet. 3:7-12.
2. A man's relationship to his children: Col. 3:21.

Church Life

The church, as well as the home, is to look to male leadership. This is why a woman cannot biblically be an elder over the entire congregation. To pit the headship of the home against the headship of the church would cause untold damage to the peace and unity of the people of God. We need godly men to be the heads of the home and of the church.

    I. Men need to attend church faithfully and to aspire to leadership in the church: Heb. 10:24-25; 5:12-14; 1 Tim. 3:1.

    II. Certain character traits must be manifested in the life of a man before he can be chosen to be a deacon: Acts 6:3-5; 1 Tim. 3:8-13. Develop these traits.

    III. Certain character traits are necessary before a man can be made an elder in the church: 1 Tim. 3:1-7; Tit. 1:6-11. Develop these traits.

Occupational Life

The way we view and do our work and how we treat other people in the work situation is of great concern to God. He wants men to manifest certain character traits while at work.

    I. Passage of Full Mention: Philemon
    Identify and illustrate the traits of the slave and his master and how they are to treat each other.

    II. Employees or workers are addressed:
      A. Eph. 6:5-8
      B. Col. 3:22-25
      C. 1 Tim. 6:1-2
      D. Tit. 2:9-10
      E. 1 Pet. 2:18-25

    III. Employers or management addressed:
      A. Eph. 6:9
      B. Col. 4:1
      C. 1 Tim. 6:17-19

Community Life

As men, we live in the larger context of a community. Our city, town, village or neighborhood is our community. God's Word instructs us how to live in this community.

    1. The importance of a good reputation cannot be overemphasized: Acts 6:3; 1 Tim. 3:7; 2 Cor. 8:20-21; 1 Pet. 2:12, 15, etc. Define, illustrate and implement "good reputation."
    2. It is the doing of good works that brings a good reputation: Eph. 2:8-10; Gal. 6:10; Tit. 3:8, 14. Develop these passages and any related ones on the subject of good works.

National Life

We are all citizens of a nation as well as members in a family, church and community. The Bible tells us what our attitude should be toward human government and those who are over us politically. Such issues as taxes, war, laws that violate God's Law, etc., must be decided by Scripture alone.

    I. Passage of Full Mention: Rom. 12:1-8

   II. Related Passages to develop:

      A. 1 Tim. 2:1-2

      B. Tit. 3:1-2

      C. 1 Pet. 2:13-17

Part Two
The Family

Chapter Fifty-Four
Dating and Courtship

Part One

Marriage is the institution established by God to be the only proper context of human sexuality and reproduction. It is defined in the Scriptures as a man and a woman leaving their parents and entering into a covenant relationship with each other for the rest of their lives, during which they will procreate children for the glory of God (Gen. 2:21-25). Thus, marriage is to be held in respect and honor by all mankind (Heb. 13:4).

Modern humanistic theories of marriage insist that marriage is a fluke of a mindless and purposeless evolutionary process and that it can be dispensed with if so desired. Thus, sex before marriage, i.e., fornication, and sex with partners other than one's wife or husband (i.e., adultery) are no longer viewed as immoral and offensive to God and society. Today, many people simply live together without being married.

According to the Word of God, those who engage in fornication or adultery are living in sin and will suffer the judgment of God (Heb. 13:4). The modern defense of immorality, which is based on the claim of situational ethics that as long as something is done in the name of "love" it cannot be condemned, is condemned by God Almighty. This so-called "love" is no more than animal "lust" which destroys the dignity of man who was created in the image of a holy and righteous God.

Modern humanistic views of marriage have resulted in two out of three marriages ending in divorce and 50 percent of the children in this country growing up without both of their natural parents. The children of such broken homes are the "latch key" kids who wander around after school getting into immorality, drugs and crime because they do not have a mom or a dad who love and care for them. America is now reaping the dire results of such open violations of God's Law by such things as the street gangs in the inner city which threaten the very fabric of society.

The Root Problem

The root problem of the humanistic view of marriage actually begins in its concept of sexuality and dating. So many marriages fall apart today because people get married for the wrong reasons. Their views of sexuality and dating were in error from the very beginning. Thus their marriages were doomed from the very beginning because they have been brainwashed by humanists through the sex education courses in the public school system, rock music, movies, novels and magazines. In all of these things, immorality is glorified and the biblical model of marriage ridiculed.

We need to resist the brainwashing of the world and to have our minds set on doing God's will (Rom. 12:1-2). Young people who are really Christians will not defile themselves with heathen ways. Instead, they will shine as bright lights in the midst of a perverted and wicked generation where good is called evil and evil is called good (Isa. 5:20). We are told in 2 Tim. 2:19: "Let everyone that nameth the name of Christ depart from iniquity.

I. The History of Marriage

    A. In every culture and civilization of which we have records, marriages were arranged by the family in terms of social, economic, religious and political consideration. Marriages were established in the context of the tribe or nation.

    B. There was no dating or courtship in societies where marriages were arranged. You did not need to "love" or even know the person you were to marry. When the appointed time came, you could marry someone whom you had never met. One's physical appearance or sexual appeal had nothing to do with marriage. Romantic "love," along with sex, waited until after marriage. Once you were married, you learned to love your mate and sex was a natural expression of that love. It was assumed that love and sex went together after marriage.

C. The examples set forth in Scripture were given in the context of arranged marriages. But there was a difference between the Hebrew guidelines for selecting a mate and the typical heathen guidelines. While pagan parents based their selection of mates for their children on the basis of such things as social or economic status, the Jews based their selection on primarily religious grounds. The mate must be a believer in the one true God and have godly character traits. Thus faith and character were the two most important considerations in finding a proper mate.

1. In Gen. 24, we have the story of a how a wife was chosen for Isaac.

    a. It was done in the context of prayer (vs. 12f).
    b. The first concern was that Isaac would not marry a pagan (vs. 1-9). She must be a believer.
    c. The second concern was that the girl must have godly character traits such as kindness and compassion (vs. 12-21).
    d. The girl was watched closely and tested to see if she was really godly (vs. 15-21).
    e. There was little consideration of her physical appearance or sexual appeal.
    f. She was willing to marry Isaac (vs. 57, 58). The marriage was not forced on her.
    g. When he first met Rebekah, a veil covered her face so he had no idea of how she looked. It did not matter. He loved her deeply after the marriage (vs. 65-66).
    h. They were married with the parents' blessing (v. 67).
    i. The marriage was a great success.

2. In the book of Ruth, we are given a story in which a Gentile woman is married to a Jewish man because she became a true believer in the Lord and had wonderful character qualities. The racial issue was not as important as the issue of faith and a godly character.

3. In Prov. 31:10-31, King Lemuel's mother instructed him as to the kind of woman he should choose to be his wife. He is told to choose a woman who "fears the Lord" and has godly character traits. He is warned not to choose a wife solely on the basis of physical beauty or sexual appeal. Such things fade with age and thus cannot form the basis of a godly marriage.

Summary of Biblical Pattern

D. It was during the Renaissance in Western Europe during the 15th and 16th centuries that a new concept of love, sex and marriage was developed. The Renaissance was the humanistic revival of pagan classical Greek thought and was based on the idea that "man was the measure of all things," and that he must be totally free to do whatever he desires.

This led to a new view of love, sex and marriage. Marriage was now a matter of personal choice and it did not matter what one's parents or what the Bible had to say about it. The Renaissance Man did not care what God or the Bible had to say because he was now his own god.

The picture presented in Italian operas and English plays was that marriage stood in the way of true love. Thus adultery was glorified as the example of pure love. Death was better than unfulfilled love. Fornication was glorified. Romantic "love" i.e., sexual appeal, was now to be experienced before marriage. And since sex and love go together, sex before marriage became the rule as well as the goal. The biblical pattern was turned upside-down.

    Biblical pattern: Marriage first. Then love and sex.
    Renaissance: Love first. Then sex. Then marriage.
        (or)   Sex first. Then love. Then marriage.

The pagan Greek classical ideas of physical beauty became the basis of marriage. The Renaissance invented "romantic love" as the sole foundation of marriage. You married someone if you "loved" them. It did not matter what their character was. One could be a non-Christian or a drunkard and yet "love" was all that was needed to get married. Instead of faith and character as the basis of marriage, a humanistic base was now given.

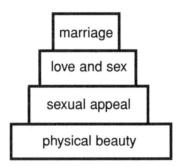

While in the past dating was viewed as the first step toward marriage, it now means a time of sexual experimentation. All the present "Teen" movies glorify the passage of young men to manhood through raw, loveless sex. The girls are viewed as sexual playthings and there is not even a mention of marriage. The downward path is as follows:

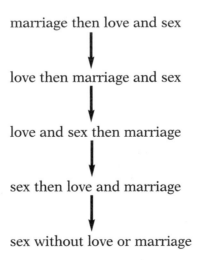

E. Consequences of the Renaissance View of Marriage
    1. Physical beauty has become the basis of personal worth as well as marriage. When a beau-

tiful person dies, it is a great shame. But if the person is fat or ugly or both, his death is ignored.

2. Those who are not physically beautiful are looked down upon when it comes to dating and marriage. They are sometimes doomed to a single life because they do not measure up to the pagan Greek ideal of physical beauty.

3. After several years of marriage and several children, the wife may lose her youthful beauty. The husband either cheats on her or dumps her for someone who is his idea of beauty. Adultery and divorce have become acceptable if your wife has become fat and ugly or old and wrinkled. The "dirty old man" syndrome sets in and the husband thinks he deserves a younger woman.

4. Christians who have been brainwashed by Renaissance thinking date and marry people on the sole basis of physical ideals instead of moral ideals. They will even date and marry people who are not Christians in the name of "love." Their marriages often end in divorce or adultery.

5. Much of child molestation is due to the demand for sexual partners who are young and beautiful.

II. What Christian Parents Should Do?

Instruct their children from the beginning that faith and character are the Christian basis of marriage. Correct the humanistic ideas given in books, television or in the movies. Do not yield to the pressure of teens who say, "Everybody else is doing it."

Ten Commandments for Parents

1. Go through the book of Proverbs in family devotions, especially when you have teenagers.
2. Illustrate from the obedience or disobedience in your own life. Is your marriage on the right basis?
3. Point out biblically based marriages and how successful and happy they are.
4. Point out all the divorces that result from humanistic marriages.
5. Give your children the biblical perspective on love, sex and marriage.
6. Do not let them date until they are emotionally mature. This is around 18 or 19 years old at the earliest. Physical maturity has nothing to do with it. Peer pressure should be rejected as ungodly.
7. The person they want to date must come to your home or call you several times before the first date is allowed so you can study his faith and character. The acid test is Mal. 3:16-18 and Matt. 5:3-16.
   Have these questions in mind:
   a. Does this person show a zeal for God?
   b. Does he talk about the Lord on his own initiative?
   c. Is he actively seeking God's will for his life?
   d. Is there a thirst and a hunger for righteousness and knowledge?
   e. Does he join enthusiastically in family worship? Hymn sings? Worshiping the Lord? Prayer?
   f. What does he believe about God, the Bible, sex, dating, petting, marriage and divorce?
   g. Does this person live for the glory of God? Is the Lord central in his life?
   h. What is his family and church background?
   i. Can he provide for his family? Does he have any skills or talents with which he can earn enough money to support a family? Is he a hard worker?
8. They may not date a non-Christian at any time for any reason whatsoever. "Love evangelism" is sinful!
9. They may not date so-called "nominal" Christians. A mere profession of faith is not enough. They must manifest the signs of regeneration in their life.
10. Only chaperoned or group dating is allowed at first. Scripture says to flee and avoid all temptations to sin.

III. What Should Young Christians Do?

A. Determine, like Daniel, that you will not defile yourself (Dan. 1:8). Virginity is a badge of moral purity and faithfulness to God (Rev. 14:4). Be proud of it and do not let the pagans brainwash you into thinking that your manhood or womanhood depends on sinning against the Savior. Be like Joseph, who would rather go to prison than sin sexually against his God (Gen. 39). It is easy to be impure today. It takes a real man or woman of character to remain pure until marriage. Learn to stand alone.

B. Do not allow the world to squeeze you into its own mold when it comes to dating and marriage. Men should study Pro. 31 for the ideal woman to marry. Women should study 1 Tim. 3:2-16; Tit. 1:6-9, etc., for the ideal man. Seek out and date only those saints who are good examples of what a Christian ought to be (1 Tim. 4:12; 2 Tim. 2:22; 2 Cor. 6:14-7:1).

Twelve Commandments for Single Christians

1. Never date non-Christians or nominal Christians.
2. Date someone who loves the Lord and lives for Him each day.
3. Before agreeing to the first date, bring him or her home so your parents can discern his or her spirit and character. If away at college, have him call your parents.
   Daughter: Your father knows best about the boy.
   Son: Your mother knows best about the girl.
4. Check to see if they talk about the Lord, or do you have to bring it up. Mal. 3:16-18 is the acid test. If they do not talk about the Lord or pray on your date, you are dealing with a non-Christian. It does not matter if they have made a thousand "professions of faith" or "decisions for Jesus" (Matt. 12:34). Try singing and worshiping the Lord with him. If he cannot do it before you marry, do you think that he will do it after you are married?
5. Do not be overly excited about sexual attraction or romantic "love at first sight" feelings. Do not marry someone simply because he stirs up your lusts. Beware: "Puppy love" usually turns into a "dog's life."
6. Never allow yourself to be alone with your date if at all possible. Date in the home or in public places such as bowling alleys or restaurants. Drive-in movies are out unless it is a group date. Keep four feet on the floor at all times.
7. If your are a woman, make sure that he has a career which can financially provide for you and your children. A man who will not provide for his family is worse than a heathen (1 Tim. 5:8).
8. Do not put your hands where you would not put them in church on Sunday morning. The moment your date attempts to do otherwise, drop the turkey.
9. Listen to your Elders for they watch over your soul. Seek their approval of the person you want to date. If they discern that he or she is not a Christian or is only a "nominal" Christian at best, obey their advice (Heb. 13:17).
10. Remember the biblical order for building a godly relationship which can serve as the basis of a Christian marriage.
    Step No. 1   Faith in Christ
    Step No. 2   Godly character
    Step No. 3   Friendship
    Step No. 4   Spiritual Oneness in Goals, Values and Priorities
    Step No. 5   Social Compatibility (same likes and dislikes in food, music, people, etc.)
    Step No. 6   Good Companionship and Communication
    Step No. 7   Pray for God's guidance and will
    Step No. 8   Seek approval of parents and godly friends

Step No. 9   Prepare for marriage by counseling with the Elders. Then announce engage-
                ment and set date.
Step No. 10 No petting, nudity or sex in any form even after engagement.
                Let kisses be as the touching of a hot iron.
                "Lust cannot wait to get, while love can always wait to give."

Step No. 11 Arrange a wedding where the Gospel is preached.
Step No. 12 After the wedding, receive the blessing of God as you experience the unspoiled
                joy of an undefiled conscience.

Conclusion

A Christian marriage does not begin in sin but in holiness. It is not carried out with lies and deceit
but with truth and honesty. It does not begin in unfaithfulness but in faithfulness. It is preceded not
by immorality, but purity. It does not bring shame but victory. Christ is the head of that home and the
unseen guest at every meal. Together they will live to the glory of God and raise their children in the
fear and admonition of the Lord.

Part Two

Dating and Marrying Non-Christians

Introduction

One of the biggest temptations young Christians face as they begin to think about marriage is to
date people who are not born-again Christians. They meet a non-Christian who is physically attractive
and quite appealing to them. This results in an inner struggle: "Do I obey God and not date this unbeliever or do I disobey God and date him?"

Very often a process of rationalization sets in and they make up all kinds of reasons as to why it
would be all right to date this non-Christian. All sorts of arguments are marshaled until their consciences are "defiled" (Tit. 1:15) and "seared" (1 Tim. 4:2), and finally silenced.

Their lust is now "free" to pursue the unbeliever despite the clear teaching of the Word of God.
Remember, a "rationalization" is a lie stuffed into the skin of an excuse and served up as the truth.

Perhaps the best way to illustrate this process is by a story. Once upon a time, in the city of "Every
town," there was a church named "St. Everywhere." In this church there was a young woman who
professed to be a Christian. She was active in the youth group and attended church regularly. For all
appearances, she was a true Christian. But during her first year in college she met a non-Christian
who wanted to date her. He was good looking and popular and she liked his personality. So, she decided to ask some people at church what they thought of dating a non-Christian.

She found that her Elders all said that she was not to date the young man for any reason whatsoever. She did not like that answer. So, she went around the church trying to find someone to tell her
what she wanted to hear. But the old "fuddy duddies" in the church warned her not to date a non-
Christian because she might end up marrying him and he would drag her away from the Lord and
from church.

Of course, she dismissed this as sheer stupidity because she was far too strong in her religion to
ever give up her faith. Her boyfriend would become a Christian anyway and they would prove all the
Elders and all the fuddy duddies they were wrong.

After dating the unbeliever, she fell "in love" with him and soon agreed to marry him. When the old fuddy duddies found out, they warned her that she was in sin. The Elders also spoke to her about the issue. Her pastor warned her that he would not marry them in the church if she went ahead with the marriage.

She became quite angry about all this and got some of the people in the church to agree with her that the Elders were being unkind and judgmental. She boldly stated: "If it were not God's will for us to marry, God would not have let us fall in love. Since we love each other, it is God's will for us to get married."

When the pastor said that he would not marry them in his church, she said: "So what! I know a lovely Methodist Church where the pastor marries anyone. I will have the marriage there."

While her boyfriend had a church background, there was no indication in his life that he had ever come to know, love and serve Jesus Christ as his personal Savior and Lord. He had never had a true conversion experience and did not claim at first to be "saved." He had not attended church for many years, but he went for her sake. She made sure that they sat up front so everyone could see them.

As time went on, the husband got tired of getting up early on Sunday mornings. He was used to sleeping in on Sundays. He also began to miss camping out for the weekend or staying out late on Saturday night. He argued with his wife until she agreed that it was all right to miss church "now and then."

They soon started to do more on the weekends. They started staying out late on Saturday nights. And, of course, they were just "too tired" to get up and drag themselves to church. They began missing a Sunday here and a Sunday there. Before long, they disappeared from church altogether.

The wife began to feel guilty for missing church, so, she got up and went to church all by herself. This failed in the end for two reasons.

First, her husband did not like her to leave him all alone. He complained that she was not there to fix him a big breakfast and dinner. He began to complain about "religious fanatics." He voiced his objections to her going to too many meetings.

Second, when she went to church all by herself, the old fuddy duddies would look at her. They had warned her about dating a non-Christian. When she claimed that she would get him saved and then they would attend church together, these old fuddy duddies had warned her that she was deceiving herself.

Now, their dire prophecies had come true. Her husband had not really become a Christian and was slowly but surely dragging her away from church. It was painful to her pride to attend church.

The woman soon got tired of sitting alone at church and coming home to an angry husband. She grew tired of pretending to be happy while at church. So, she simply stopped attending. She pacified her guilty conscience by telling herself that the fuddy duddies were to blame for the whole thing. They should have stopped her from making the biggest mistake in her life. Yes, the pastor and the fuddy duddies were to blame for everything. Her bitterness was her only comfort.

The members of the church eventually forgot about this woman until a young Christian man in the congregation started dating a non-Christian girl. The pastor and the fuddy duddies tried to warn him about the dire consequences of what he was doing. They brought up "so and so" and what happened to her.

He simply shrugged off what they had to say. After all, what do these people know? His non-Christian girlfriend will get saved and attend church with him. Everything is going to turn out great! He was far too strong a Christian to let a girl turn him away from the faith. Everything would turn out all right in the end.

I. The Problem: Mixed Dating and Mixed Marriages Between Believers and Unbelievers
  A. This problem surfaces in every Christian family and in every church. Everyone will face it at some time.
  B. Nothing causes more grief and misery in families and churches than this problem.
  C. It must be faced head on and be dealt with before the children in the church are old enough to date. The young people must be so thoroughly trained in biblical teaching during their childhood that it becomes unthinkable for them to even consider dating a non-Christian.

II. The Biblical Teaching
  A. To become involved with an unbeliever in dating or marriage is a very great wickedness. It is not a "little sin" but a great abomination in the sight of God.
    1. In Gen. 6:1-3, the cause of the judgment of the Flood is described in terms of the mixed marriages. God sent the Flood as a direct judgment on these mixed marriages.
    2. When God took the Jews and made them into a nation, He warned them that they could not marry unbelievers under any circumstances (Exo. 34:10-16; Deut. 7:3-4).
    3. When Solomon broke God's Law and married pagan women, this led to his apostasy from the faith, the introduction of idol worship in the nation and the destruction of his kingdom (1 Kings 11:1-2.).
    4. When God restored his people to the land after their captivity, the first sin to be dealt with was the sin of mixed marriages (Ezra 10:1-44; Neh. 10:28-30; 13:23-29). The church did not experience revival until this sin was confessed and dealt with.
    5. In the N.T., marriage is to be a picture of the relationship between Christ and His people (Eph. 5:22-28). Thus a believer is not to be "yoked" with an unbeliever (2 Cor. 6:14-7:1). A Christian can marry someone "only in the Lord" (1 Cor. 7:39).
  B. The only course of action that a Christian can take is to vow before the Lord that they will date and marry only someone whose faith and character meet the biblical standards of a God-fearing man or woman.

III. Rationalizations
  A. "Since she is interested in me, I will date her so I can preach the Gospel to her."
     Answer: Do not get involved in "love evangelism" (2 Cor. 6:14).
  B. "Well, he is not a 'super-Christian' if that is what you are asking, but I am sure he is saved. He is so nice that he has to be saved."
     Answer: "Nominal" Christians are not saved (John 8:31).
  C. "No, she does not go to church. But you do not have to go to church to be saved, right?
     Answer: If someone is saved they will go to church (1 John 2:19).
  D. "Do you not see that the Lord has arranged it all? Too many circumstances went together to bring us together. It must be God's will for us to marry."
     Answer: The book of Jonah reveals that God's will cannot be determined from "circumstances."
  E. "It was love at first sight. If the Lord was not in favor of it, He would not have given us love at first sight."
     Answer: This "love" is actually LUST.
  F. "Yes, I know that the church she is attending is a cult. But, what if she is a Christian who got lost in the cults and the Lord wants me to date her to bring her out of the cult?"
     Answer: An obvious rationalization.

G. "He told me that he will come to church with me after we are married."
Answer: It is foolish to believe such promises.

H. "I have to marry him. He got me pregnant."
Answer: Nothing in the N.T. says a Christian is to marry a non-Christian if they get pregnant.

Conclusion

The Bible is clear that believers and unbelievers should not date or get married. Those who disregard the warnings of Scripture will suffer the judgment of God in this life and in the life to come. You must determine to date and marry "only in the Lord."

Chapter Fifty-Five

Why Do Marriages Fall Apart?

Part One

Introduction: Almost five out of nine marriages fall apart. Why?

The first task is to define what we mean by a marriage that has "fallen apart."

I. A "dead marriage" is a marriage that has fallen apart although divorce has not taken place. There are two kinds of dead marriage.
   A. Peaceful ones: The man and woman live their own separate lives without communicating to each other.
   B. Warring ones: The man and woman constantly fight over everything.

II. When separation, desertion or divorce takes place, the marriage has fallen apart.
   A. Separation: When the couple breaks up due to legal arrangements set by the court.
   B. Desertion: When one leaves the other without legal separation.
   C. Divorce: When the marriage is legally dissolved.

III. When one partner becomes involved in adultery, the marriage is falling apart. There are two kinds of adultery.
   A. Physical adultery: moral impurity.
   B. Emotional adultery: Having your emotional needs met by someone other than the one to whom you are married.

IV. When a couple gives up all hope for reconciliation, the marriage is falling apart.

V. Why do these marriages fall apart?
   A. Wrong priorities vs. right priorities.
      1. Right priorities: Jesus first
                             Others second
                             Yourself third
      When love gives, i.e., you meet the needs of the other. Thus the fruit of the Spirit dominates.
      2. Wrong priorities: Yourself first
                            Others second
      Lust takes, i.e., it only seeks to meet your own needs. Thus the works of the flesh dominate.
   B. They were married for the wrong reasons.
      1. Sexual excitement.
      2. Financial security.

   3. Someone to keep house or to take care of your needs.
   4. Family connections.
   5. Peer pressure.
   6. Premarital sex and pregnancy.
   7. Fear that you will not get another chance.
   8. Infatuation.
   9. Social compatibility.
   10. Everyone said that you were a "perfect couple."
C. No pre-marital counseling.
D. Breakdown of communication.
E. Marriage between a Christian and non-Christian.
F. Allowing things and people to come between you.

Part Two

How to Rebuild Your Marriage

Introduction: God's Word gives all that is necessary to rebuild a marriage that has fallen apart.

I. You must admit to yourself and then to your mate that your marriage is in trouble.
   A. Many refuse to admit that problems exist. Why?
      1. Pride: it is humbling to admit it.
      2. Fear: the marriage will end in divorce.
   B. When either mate feels that the marriage is in trouble, it is in trouble.

II. Humble yourself and seek help from godly counselors.
   A. Go only to Christian marriage counselors (Psa. 1; Prov. 10:11, 13; 12:5-6, 26).
   B. Beware of ungodly counselors.

III. Things you can do at once.
   A. Confess your sins and acknowledge your failures without shifting blame (Prov. 28:13; 1 John 1:9).
   B. Receive Christ or reaffirm Christ as Lord of your life (Rom. 10:9-10; 1 Pet. 3:15).
   C. Go to your mate and ask forgiveness.
   D. Ask him or her to share with you other areas where you have offended them. Remember, the person offended is a better guide to the offenses than the one who offends.
   E. Use Hosea's method of a hedge of thorns around a wayward loved one.
      1. Build a hedge of thorns around him or her (Hosea 2:6).
      2. Allure him or her (Hosea 2:14). How?
         a. Get alone. v. 14a
         b. Speak kindly. v. 14b
         c. Give hope. v. 15
         d. They will sing. v. 15
         e. They will call you their beloved. v. 16
   F. Read helpful books on marriage renewal.
   G. Attend helpful marriage seminars.

Chapter Fifty-Six

The Ten Needs of a Husband

Introduction

It is God's will for you to understand how to love your husband by meeting his needs as a man. In Titus 2:3-4, God calls all Christian wives to learn how to love their man. This is part of God's curriculum in His discipleship program for women, to fulfill His plan for you.

I. Your Husband Needs to Be Viewed as a Human Being.
   A. He is not a robot or a machine.

He may try to be an unfeeling computer or a total rationalist. He may view himself as a machine.

ONE WAY SOME MEN VIEW THEMSELVES

He may be a blockhead.

He may be cold, mechanical, unemotional.

He may be insensitive, cruel, calculating.

He may strive to need no one and to need nothing; to be independent of others.

BUT HE IS NOT A MACHINE!

    1. He is a terribly weak creature with great weaknesses and needs.
    2. He is the pitiful victim of cultural standards which he can never meet (Rom. 12:2; Eph. 2:2).
    3. He is totally dependent upon God, his family and others (Gen. 2:18).
      B. He is not an animal.
- He may look like one.
- He may smell like one.
- He may act like one.
- He may be irrational.
- He may be irresponsible.
- He may be cruel.
- He may be only interested in sex and food.

BUT HE IS NOT AN ANIMAL!

1. He is created in the image of God (Gen. 1:26).
    a. Not physical image: "God" is not a male (Num. 23:19).
    b. But Divine capacities and capabilities:
        (1) love
        (2) communication
        (3) creativity
        (4) self-control
        (5) sovereignty over the world
2. He is important, significant and has worth because he is part of God's plan. He is not junk.

II. Your Husband Needs to Be Respected as a Man
    A. If you want a "sure-fire" way to destroy your marriage, regularly tell your husband: "You are not a man."
    B. To question your husband's "manhood" is to strike at his Achille's heel.
    C. Most men never sit down and think through what it means to be a "man." Their concepts of "manhood" often come from American culture and Hollywood instead of Scripture. Very often a husband has wrong concepts of "manhood." If you do not know what he thinks "being a man" means, grave conflicts can develop. Your sons need to hear Scriptural concepts of "manhood" as they will pattern their life according to what they think (Prov. 23:7).
    D. You must re-educate yourself and your husband concerning manhood. You need to understand God's absolutes and to have your cultural concepts corrected.
        1. After much prayer, approach your husband about reading just one book: example: *The Total Man* by Dan Benson.
        2. Support and affirm where your husband acts "manly" according to Scripture but in opposition to culture.

TO KNOW WHAT A MAN IS:
Do not look to the Marlboro Man... Look to the man Jesus Christ

III. Your Husband Needs to Be Accepted as a Leader.
    A. While you are equal to your husband in terms of creation, fall and redemption, he has been chosen by God to be the head of the family (1 Cor. 11:3).

God the Father		The Husband	
equality and submission		equality and submission	
God the Son		The Wife	

Pragmatic Economical Functional	=	Voluntary Submission	It is not Substantial Patriarchal or Essential

    B. Let him function as the decision maker.
    C. Do not be afraid of mistakes and failures.

IV. Your Husband Needs to Be Allowed to Be Alone With God and Other Men for Prayer.
    A. Jacob—Gen. 32:24
    B. Moses—Exo. 3:1
    C. Jesus—Matt. 14:23
    D. The Apostles—Matt. 17:1

V. Your Husband Needs a Loyal Wife.

What is "loyalty?"

    The protecting of another's reputation as if it were your own by not publically or privately destroying it with gossip, slander or bitterness. Loyalty is the cloak which love uses to cover a multitude of sins.

VI. Your Husband Needs a Wife Who Is Presentable in Appearance and Personality.
    A. Your husband is conscious of your acts and attitudes in the presence of others. He can be ashamed and embarrassed, or proud and pleased with your personality.
        1. Does your personality please your husband?
        2. If he is displeased with valid problems in your personality, take steps to change it.

 Bitter or Loving    Complaining or Grateful    Depressive or Optimistic   Angry or Patient

    B. Your appearance will cause your husband pride or embarrassment.
        1. This refers to things which you can change.
            ● hair
            ● teeth
            ● posture
            ● weight
            ● etc.
        2. Unchangeable things can also be dealt with.
            ● height (shoes)
            ● length of hair (wigs)
        3. Get your priorities straight (1 Pet. 3:1-6)
           No. 1 Priority—Christlike Personality
           No. 2 Priority—External Appearance

VII. Your Husband Needs a Wife Who Knows How to Appeal His Unwise Decisions.
    A. God trains men best through failure.
        1. Adam—Gen. 3:6
        2. Abraham—Gen. 12:10-20; 20:1-18
        3. Moses—Exo. 2:11-15
        4. David—2 Sam. 11
        5. Peter—Mk. 14:66-72

B. Do you not want a humble husband?

C. Rationally discuss the issue with him until he makes up his mind. Do not nag him after he has decided.

D. Tell him, "I trust you to make the wisest decision which honors God."

VIII. Your Husband Needs a Grateful Wife

A. A complaining, discontented attitude arises out of an ungrateful spirit.

B. We often fail to be grateful when people do what we expect them to do.

C. You should praise your husband for what he does more than criticize him for what he does not do.

IX. Your Husband Needs a Wife Who Is Praised by Others (Prov. 31:10, 28-31).

A. Praised for her Godliness.

B. Praised for her Faithfulness.

C. Praised for her Sacrifice. Prov. 31:10-31

D. Praised for her Labor.

E. Praised for her Kindness.

F. Praised for her Loyalty, etc.

X. Your Husband Needs a Godly Atmosphere in the Home.

A. He has to fight ungodliness all day at work. He cannot change his atmosphere at work.

B. He wants to come home to a peaceful atmosphere, which is his refuge from the battle of the day.

SOME "DON'TS"

1. Do not immediately present him with all the problems in the home.

2. Do not have him spank the children when he first comes home.

3. Do not put pressure on him as soon as he enters the house.

SOME "DO'S"

1. Present him with good news about something.

2. Make your children look forward with joy Dad's return.

3. Let him relax and unwind.

Conclusion

A wonderful thing happens when you begin to concentrate on meeting the needs of others: your own needs get fulfilled. A happy husband will share his happiness with his wife and children.

Chapter Fifty-Seven

How Can a Wife Help Her Husband to Become a Godly Man?

While there are many ways that a loving wife can help her husband, the following points give wives some concrete ideas of how to go about it.

A wife should:

1. Support his decisions and not listen to the children's complaints, but encourage them to obey their father.
2. Remind him to have family devotions.
3. Help her husband memorize Scripture.
4. Do all within her power to get her husband to come to church regularly.
5. Play Christian music when the husband comes home from work to quiet his Spirit.
6. Place a Scripture verse in her husband's lunch.
7. Refer to the Bible for solving problems and present these to her husband.
8. Place biblical pictures or verses on the walls in the home as a means of creating a godly atmosphere in the home.
9. Make wise suggestions for prayer or devotions.
10. Encourage her husband to be involved in discipleship programs.
11. Share with her husband the Scriptures that blessed her that day.
12. Pray for her husband and let him know that she prays for him regularly.
13. Pray with her husband every day.
14. Lead a godly life before her husband.
15. Encourage her husband to attend spiritual retreats or seminars for men.
16. Have special times of worship and thanksgiving to God with her husband on special occasions of the year (such as birthdays, holidays, anniversaries, etc.).
17. Encourage her husband to have his private devotions.
18. Find Scriptural ways to come to her husband with problems.
19. Search out the Scriptures and find some way to help her husband if he comes home with gripes about his job.
20. Have a good attitude toward her husband.
21. Not nag her husband.
22. Trust in her husband's judgment and leadership.
23. Be enthusiastic about building Scripture into the life of her family.
24. Be eager to have family worship and be willing to stop whatever she is doing in order to do so.
25. Be honest about her needs.

26. Share her husband's vision and support it.
27. Encourage her husband to get involved in the church leadership programs.
28. Be supportive of "family nights."
29. Lovingly point out her husband's weaknesses and humbly help him to grow in grace.
30. Be the key to her husband's enthusiasm.

Chapter Fifty-Eight
The Ten Needs of a Wife

Introduction

In order to build a solid marriage, you must learn how to meet the needs of your wife. God wants you to understand what her needs are and to strive to meet them through His power.

A wife has many needs. In fact, we stopped counting after 25 needs were recognized. We have chosen 10 needs which, to some degree, can be viewed as the "essential" or "heart" needs of a wife.

No husband can ever hope to fulfill his wife's needs by his own strength. To be the kind of husband you ought to be requires the filling of the Spirit (Eph. 5:18, 25-31). Ask God to convict you of the needs you are neglecting and to encourage you by the needs you are meeting.

I. She Needs to Feel That She Is Understood by Her Husband (1 Pet. 3:7).
   A. Understand her mind.
   B. Understand her emotions.
   C. Understand her body.

Seek to understand her, this is God's command. She needs an "understanding" husband who cares enough to try to understand her. Her self-worth depends on this.

II. She Needs to Feel That She Is Respected by Her Husband (Eph. 5:25).
   A. A good marriage is built on mutual respect. Marriage is 90 percent respect.
   B. Respect is an attitude in which you consider someone "a significant other," i.e. someone who is valuable to you and to whom you go for advice.
   C. The number one marriage problem is that the wife feels her husband does not respect her.
   D. If you want big problems in your marriage:
      1. Tell her that you do not respect her.
      2. Show her that you do not respect her.
         a. Give "put downs" all the time ("dumb," "stupid," "scatterbrain," etc.).
         b. Belittle what she does.
         c. Go to others for advice; never her.
         d. Never praise her before others.
         e. Constantly tell her what "other wives do for their husbands," or the example of some other woman; i.e. your mother, a friend of your wife's, etc.
         f. Never consider her opinions, wishes or ideas on anything.
   E. Tell and show your wife that you respect her as a:
      1. Human being created in God's image.
      2. Wife
      3. Child of God
      4. Woman
      5. Mother
      6. etc.

III. She Needs to Feel Needed by Her Husband.
   A. A wife becomes depressed if she feels that her husband does not need her and that she is only in his way, complicating and frustrating his life.
   B. Because of the "Macho Man" image of Western culture, men try to be independent and to never let their wives know how much they need them.
      Note: For God's concept of what it means to be a man, read *The Total Man,* by Dan Benson.
   C. Tell her: "Honey, I need you so much because I love you. You have helped me to grow in so many ways. I thank God I married you."
   D. Show her by opening up to her when you are insecure; by praising her, by asking her emotional support, etc.
   E. If she asks, "Do you need me?" answer, "I need you because I love you."
   F. If she asks you, "How do you need me?"
      1. Do not refer to things which any woman can do for you, i.e. cook, clean, sex, etc.
      2. Do not give her the impression that you "love" her because you "need" someone for such things as sex, housekeeping, etc.
      3. Tell her that you need her: not her services, but her as a person.

I NEED YOU BECAUSE I LOVE YOU

NOT

I LOVE YOU BECAUSE I NEED YOU

IV. She Needs to Feel Secure.
   A. Secure that you love her.
   B. Secure that you will not leave her.
   C. Secure that you will provide for her and her children.
   D. Secure that you know how to handle money.
   E. Secure that you will protect her.
   F. Secure that you will not commit adultery.

   Note: Make sure her priorities are in the right order: God first; You second!

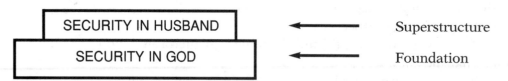

V. She Needs a Spiritual Husband.

   A. Your wife knows that a God-fearing, spiritual husband can be trusted and that an ungodly husband cannot be trusted. Her security and confidence in you is based on the level of godliness in your life.

   B. She knows that a godly husband makes the best father for her children.

   C. She knows that a godly husband will seek God's will in making decisions.

   D. She needs a godly head who will be her prophet, priest and king.

VI. She Needs an Attentive Husband.

    A. Most wives feel that their husbands do not "listen" to them. The husbands respond that they do "listen" to their wives. The problem is so hard to solve because the wife and the husband have different understandings of what constitutes "listening."

HUSBAND	**WIFE**
"I listen to her because I can repeat every word she says."	"He does not listen to me because he does not stop what he is doing, look me in the eyes and be attentive to me."

    B. Most wives want their husbands to be attentive to them, i.e. to acknowledge their existence and right to be heard. They want your undivided attention when they talk to you.

    C. If you want to have an unhappy wife, or perhaps a snapping, bitter wife:

        1. When she enters the room you are in, never acknowledge her presence. Just ignore her.

        2. Continue to do whatever you are doing. Do not stop and look at her or say anything.

        3. If she talks to you, keep your eyes on the television or newspaper or magazine or whatever you are doing. Avoid eye contact.

        4. If she asks you a question, only grunt or say "yes" or "no." Do not enter into a conversation with her.

        5. If she talks "too long," escape to the bathroom, the garage or garden. Never say anything before you leave. Just walk away as she is talking and leave her talking to the wall.

VII. She Needs a Grateful Husband.

    A. A wife needs to feel that her husband and children appreciate her and are grateful for what she does for them. She needs to be praised as well (Prov. 31:26-31).

    B. We seldom are grateful when someone does something for us if they are only doing what we expected of them. For some reason, we think, "They are doing only what they are supposed to do."

    C. Do you express gratitude for the "common things" your wife does for you?

        1. Cooking

        2. Cleaning the house

        3. Being a good mother

        4. Sex

        5. etc.

    D. The main thing is to develop a grateful attitude toward your wife.

VIII. She Needs a Loyal Husband.

    A. Being loyal to your wife means that you treat her reputation as if it were your own.

    B. This means that you will NOT:

        1. Complain about her to others who are not part of the problem or solution.

        2. Ridicule her before others.

        3. Call her names which put her down.

        4. Make her the butt of your jokes.

        5. Reveal her sins and mistakes to others.

        6. Make up lies about her to cast yourself in a better light.

    C. It means that you will cover her sins with a cloak of love, defend her to those who criticize her, and build up a good reputation for her.

IX. She Needs a Romantic Husband.

    A. A wife wants her husband to understand that she needs to feel romanced by her husband. She wants to be courted; taken out for "romantic" dinners; to be seduced by affection and sensitivity.

    B. To a woman, what happens before and after the act of sex is more important than the act itself. If her husband wants "instant sex" with no romantic prelude or goes to sleep afterward, she will feel that she is "being used" by her husband. He is only thinking of himself and his physical needs while ignoring her emotional needs.

    C. You need to spend time seeking to fill her needs for romance—time alone with her without the kids interrupting.

    D. When you take her out, concentrate on communicating with her, not just shoveling food in your mouth. Take time to dine with your wife.

X. She Needs a Stalwart Husband.

    A. To be "stalwart" means that you can take whatever she can dish out.

    B. It means that you are like a granite rock which still stands on the shoreline after hurricane force waves have crashed onto it.

    C. It means that you are not a "fair-weather" husband. He leaves when problems arise in the marriage:
      1. Money problems
      2. Fights and disagreements between husband and wife.
      3. Responsibilities
      4. Problems with the children
      5. etc.

    D. Part of the "adjustment" period with newlyweds is the wife testing the limits of her husband's patience and if he will love her no matter what she does to him. She needs to feel secure that their relationship is strong enough to take anything.

Chapter Fifty-Nine

How Can a Husband Help His Wife to Become a Godly Woman?

While there are many ways in which a loving husband can help his wife, the following 30 points give some practical ideas of how to do it.

A husband should:

1. Pray with his wife every day without fail and make sure she has had her private devotions.
2. Praise his wife.
3. Encourage his wife.
4. Lovingly exhort his wife.
5. Show love and affection toward his wife.
6. Encourage his wife to memorize Scripture, and he should also participate in it with her.
7. Listen with interest to his wife and be willing and able to discuss Scriptures studied in devotions.
8. Allow his wife to have a part in family devotions.
9. Be the supportive role in his family in helping where help is needed.
10. Discuss and decide plans and projects together.
11. Encourage his wife to get involved in church activities and seminars for women.
12. Help his wife to overcome self-centeredness, selfishness, etc.
13. Take the primary role of disciplining the children.
14. Take the leadership in a family night.
15. Pray for each person by name in his family for protection, etc.
16. Set a good atmosphere for his family, such as playing Christian music, tapes, reading books, etc.
17. Walk in the Spirit and live unto the Lord, not unto his wife or himself.
18. Find a special Scripture verse daily to give to his wife to meditate on during the day.
19. Set aside a weekly time to sit down and focus on his wife's spiritual growth.
20. Place spiritual verses around the home that could encourage his wife during the day as she labors at home or in her lunch box if she must go out to work.
21. Accept his wife's abilities and talents and accept her as she is and be supportive of her efforts.
22. Remind the wife periodically about her need of stability of being grounded in the Lord.
23. Initiate times of singing when riding in the car, working around the home, etc.
24. Help his wife out at home to give her time during the week for her personal ministry of witnessing and sharing with others.
25. Pray for his wife daily and let her know that he prays for her regularly.
26. Be sensitive to his wife's spirit (encouragement and discouragement).
27. Support his wife in her dealing with the children.

28. Encourage his wife to be faithful in church attendance.
29. Have open communication with his wife and listen to her.
30. Lovingly point out his wife's weaknesses and humbly help her deal with them.

Chapter Sixty
Christian Parenting

Introduction

Trying to please God in the way you raise your children is one of the marks of being a true Christian. Those parents who manifest no deep concern for the eternal welfare of their children demonstrate that they themselves are in need of salvation. It is inconceivable that the parents could be truly saved and yet not be deeply burdened for the salvation of their children. Such "monsters" have yet to be born.

The Greatest Goals of Christian Parenting

I. Salvation

The deepest desire of the heart of Christian parents is that their children will love and serve the Lord Jesus Christ (Eph. 6:4). This means that the salvation of their children is of the utmost priority. The eternal welfare of their children outshines all earthly concerns.

II. Godly Character Traits

The spiritual, physical and social maturity of the children in which they grow in "wisdom and stature and in favor with God and man" (Lk. 2:52) is the second most important goal of parenting. Your children must be prepared to walk with God and work with their fellow man. Their moral character should be founded on a deeply ingrained desire to please God.

III. Preparation for a Career

Children must be brought up in a way in which they look forward to finding, following and finishing God's will for their life (Acts 26:13-19; Gal.1:15-16). They must be given a sense of destiny in which they know that God has a plan for their life (Prov. 16:4). Their duty in life is to find and finish this plan (Heb. 12:1-2; 2 Tim. 4:7-8). Do not allow them to believe Satan's lie that they can be whatever they want to be (Gen. 3:1-7). They can do only what God wills them to do (James 4:13-17; Rom. 1:10). Their career should be what God wants it to be. They are his servants to obey (Josh. 24:15).

The Mechanics of Christian Parenting

1. Make sure of your own salvation (1 Pet. 1:10; 2 Cor. 13:5).

2. Seek the filling of the Spirit to raise your children in the fear and discipline of the Lord (Eph. 5:18-6:4). You will need to draw on the power and wisdom of God to cope with your children. You need all the wisdom of Solomon, the maturity of Methuselah and the patience of Job to get the job done right. In other words, you cannot do it in your own strength or by your own understanding (Pro. 3:5-7). You need to ask for divine wisdom (James 1:5-8).

3. The Scriptures should be your main manual. Beware of Dr. Spock and other humanists. The Book of Proverbs should be studied every day and the sections on child rearing marked out, thought through and applied. Gather Christian books that develop and apply biblical teaching.

4. Follow biblical principles of discipline (Eph. 6:4).
   a. aim for consistency in all things
   b. the parents must agree as to discipline and rules
   c. the second parent asked must support the first parent
   d. both parents must discipline
   e. the parent who is disobeyed is the one to administer discipline
   f. the rules cannot be ignored or changed all the time
   g. the punishment must fit the crime
   h. beware of being too strict or too lax
   i. illustrate justice and mercy
   j. be just and fair
   k. do not be afraid to spank
   l. do not play favorites
   m. do not be cruel or sadistic
   n. do not embarrass your children in front of their friends
   o. do not abuse your child with beatings
   p. fit the punishment to the age and maturity of the child
   q. involve older children in setting up rules and punishment
   r. give them a chance to explain
   s. do not discipline while angry
   t. make sure they know why they are being disciplined
   u. assure them of your love after discipline
   v. never make your love conditional on their obedience
   w. let them see your grief and hear your prayers
   x. always point to God as the One they disobeyed
   y. base your authority on God's Word
   z. remind them that you discipline for their own good

5. Protect your children from spiritual, mental, moral and physical harm.
   A. How to protect your children from spiritual harm.
      1. Their spiritual condition and destiny must be your first priority (Mark 8:36-37).
      2. You must set a good example before them (1 Tim. 4:12).
         How much do you value spiritual things?
         Are the Bible and prayer really important to you?
         Is church attendance essential or optional to you?
         Does God come first in money matters?
         When making a decision, do you pray first and seek out biblical principles and godly advice?
         Do your children hear and see you praying?
      3. Be faithful in disciplining your children (1 Cor. 4:2).
         The father has the primary responsibility as the prophet, priest and king of the home (Eph. 6:4). Children must be taught the Truth about God, the world, man and themselves (John 8:32). A child's beliefs, morals, values and priorities should come from the home (Prov. 22:6).
            The goals of discipleship: salvation, maturity, etc.
            The focus is threefold:
               1. What to believe.
               2. How to live.
               3. How to relate to others.

4. How to disciple your children.

    Recognize that this is to be done: (Deut. 6:7-9)

        all the time

        everywhere

        in all of life

        for all of the children

Beware of cheap "family devotions." For most Christians, "family devotions" means: reading a chapter of the Bible without any explanation or application and saying a general prayer. This results in: ritualism, legalism, boredom, frustration, and meaninglessness.

Note: How to Develop Good Family Devotions

1. Start where the child is. If the child is ignorant of the Bible, then emphasize Bible stories. If he knows the Bible, then teach him doctrine. If he knows doctrine, then teach him wisdom, morals and values by studying Proverbs, books on character development and biographies of Christians who illustrate godly wisdom.
2. Do not expect more than the child can give.
3. Assume each child is different.
4. Do not compete with other parents.
5. Do not be legalistic. It is not a burden, but a joy.
6. Make it a happy time. Do not spoil the fun of it by gloominess.
7. Tailor the program to the age and maturity of the child. The older the child, the more sophisticated the books you read. Prepare your child for each new phase of life. At puberty, read Christian books on sexuality, dating and marriage. When graduating from high school, study books on career choices. When starting their first job, teach them principles of finance, how to be a good worker, how to spot ripoffs, etc.
8. Do not lump children of diverse ages all together. You will bore the older or the younger kids. Fit the discipleship to the children by dividing them up between the father and the mother.
9. Smaller children love handicrafts. Buy the kits made for Vacation Bible School and use them at home. Develop plays and songs. Action is the key when the children are young while communication is the key when they are older.
10. While the children are at the home, enjoy discipleship with them. Communication, fellowship, discussion on important topics should never cease between you and your children. For example, read and discuss Schaeffer books with your college age kids.
11. After they are married, share with them biblical principles of marriage and parenting.
12. When your grandchildren arrive, disciple them when they are in your home.

---

5. Beware of ungodly influences on your children (Psa.1).

    secular humanism in the state schools (Psa. 14:1)

    ungodly friends and playmates (1 Cor. 15:33)

    games, toys, books, movies or television shows which teach your children wrong
        values and priorities (Eph. 4:17-24; 5:8-18)

    the theory of evolution (Rom.1:18-25)

    CDs or concerts of ungodly music

    wicked posters or pictures

    pornography (Matt. 5:28)

    pagan idols, symbols, statues, posters, earrings, necklaces, or ornaments (Gen. 35:2-5)

    tattoos which glorify satanic or sexual symbols (Lev.19:28)

Note: "The specific prohibition not to print any marks upon themselves evidently has reference to the custom of tattooing common among savage tribes and in vogue among both men and women of the lower orders in Arabia, Egypt and many other lands. It was intended to cultivate reverence for and a sense of the sacredness of the human body, as God's creation, known in the Christian era as the temple of the Holy Spirit" (International Standard Bible Encyclopedia, vol. III, p. 1986).

---

     symbols of rebellion or immorality
     clothing which is immoral
     clubs, societies, fraternities which promote ungodliness
     secret organizations such as the Masons
     sorcery, magic, witchcraft, good luck charms, spells, etc.

Special note: The Problem of Sorcery Today

All occult practices are detestable to the Lord (Deut. 18:9-14). Sorcery or magic of any kind is wicked. This means that all movies, books, television shows or cartoons, comic books, games and toys that magnify magic, witchcraft, sorcery, casting spells, witch doctors, Satan, demons, white magic, black magic, E.S.P., psychic powers, mind reading or levitation must not be allowed in your home. This includes all superhuman powers used by or received from witches, sorcerers, spirits, amulets, charms, swords, necklaces, rings, crystal balls, chants, dances, incantations, ram's heads, skulls, pits, pyramids, magical staffs, pentagrams, an upside down cross, goat unicorns, the rainbow, cloaks, hats, brooms, sticks, stones, bones, magical plants or brews, UFOs, other dimensions, the New Age, etc.

Anything which teaches that the way to solve problems or to defeat enemies is to use magic or sorcery is wicked. Children should be taught that problems are solved by prayer, faith, hard work, perseverance and creativity using their natural God-given talents.

It is shocking to see Christian parents allowing their children to watch shows or play games in which magic is used to solve problems, defeat enemies or to make their wishes come true. Instead of praying to God and then working at the problem, children call upon the "power" or the "force" and use incantations such as "By the power of Grayskull." We are not to have any dealings with such works of darkness (Eph. 5:11).

It is to be feared that the present generation is being prepared to accept the false prophet and the antichrist, who will use magic to win the world's belief (2 Thess. 2:9-12: Rev. 13). By such things as Saturday morning cartoons, today's children are being taught to look to sorcery for the answers, not to God. They are told to look for a "super man" who will use super powers to solve the world's problems. While Jesus is a "spiritual" savior who saves us from moral problems, a "New Christ" will arise who will be a "spectacular" savior who will save us from material problems. Do not let the witches who now control television cartoons prepare your children to accept the antichrist as the "New Christ."

The Solution

Give your children biblical heroes who solved their problems by prayer and hard work. Let them use the "sword of the Lord and of Gideon" instead of He-Man's sword. Either buy or make Christian action dolls, toys, swords and shields. Let them play with neutral toys such as cars, tanks, planes, dolls, etc.

Sit down and watch Saturday morning cartoons to see what is acceptable for your children. Then see to it that your children do not watch cartoons which feature sorcery or magic. There are still a few cartoons which do not exalt sorcery or pagan deities. The eternal destiny of your children may depend on your obedience to God.

Special Warning on New Age Mind Control in Public Schools

Superlearning and Visualization Programs

The "Visualization and Guided Imagery" program, also sometimes called "Quieting Reflex and Success Imagery" and "Superlearning," has its roots in the work of Georgi Lazanov, a Bulgarian expert in mind control, whose primary education was in the Soviet Union. His Ph.D. work in Russia focused on how to use the parapsychological techniques found in the occult and Eastern arts such as Yoga in the education of children. He discovered that the techniques used in Raja Yoga, if applied to children in their early education, enabled the state through the teacher to change, manipulate and to control the basic values, beliefs and world view of the children.

The Raja Yoga techniques penetrate the subconscious mind by bringing the child into a hypnotic trance through rhythmic breathing exercises, playing certain kinds of music, lowering the lights, having the children close their eyes and the teacher using a soft voice as she/he guides them into visualization and imagery. If practiced throughout the day before every class, Lazanov claimed that the children would be under mind control.

In *Other Ways Other Means,* one of Lazanov's books, the title reads: "Practical Teaching Strategies for the Use of Relaxation, Imagery, Dreams, Suggestology, Hypnosis, Meditation."

Lazanov states in the book that since school officials, teachers and parents would reject any program which admitted using hypnosis on the children, it would be best to call it any other name but hypnosis. He suggests calling hypnosis "suggestology," "relaxation," "visualization," etc. His disciples have been faithful in trying to deceive the public on their use of hypnosis.

Dr. Adelaide Bry, in her book, *Visualization,* comments:

If you still have trouble with the word "Meditation" when bringing this program to your children, parents, family, school administrators or board of educators, use alternative terms like Stephanie does, such as awareness training, concentration, centering, awareness games, relaxation, holistic learning, creative imagery, etc. (p. 148).

The leading books in this movement all admit that they seek to escape resistance to using hypnosis by calling it "visualization," "superlearning," "relaxation," etc. For example, Hendricks and Wills in *The Centering Book* (pp. 65-68) suggest using the term "suggestology" instead of "hypnotic induction" in order to avoid criticism.

In *Beyond Biofeedback,* in a chapter titled, "Mind Training, Hypnosis and the Development of Psychic Powers," the authors state that

Mind-training programs use a heavy dose of hypnotic programming. It may not be called hypnosis and in fact it may be vehemently denied by the instructors, but nevertheless many of the courses use hypnotic techniques that are "right out of the book."

Another author comments that the child's subconscious mind is approached through hypnotic induction or altered states of awareness techniques inducing the child into internal fantasy or mental images as directed by the counselor or teacher. The child is taken into deeper states of hypnosis to internally vision motion pictures of the mind. The program does not mention "hypnotic induction," instead it refers to the process as "entry" and "reentry."

Lazanov wants teachers to hypnotize the children in order to reach their subconscious mind. The task of the teacher is thus no longer viewed as teaching children to read, write, do math and think for themselves on a conscious level. Instead, the teacher's role is to take away the values and beliefs instilled in the children by their parents and put into their minds the religious values and beliefs found is such Eastern religions as Yoga, T.M., etc. (see quotes) No wonder Johnny cannot read!

One of the most popular commercial forms of this approach is "Silva Mind Control," which began with the idea that if the teacher is allowed to hypnotize the children, the behavior and grades of the children would improve. This explains why Jose Silva calls his material, "Mind Control." The techniques used in "visualization" programs in public education are the same ones used by Silva in his "Mind Control" classes.

Willis Harman stated in a New Age magazine called *New Times* that teachers should "focus education much more on learning to reprogram the unconscious mind" than educating the conscious mind!

In the book, *Superlearning,* hypnotic techniques are involved such as: rhythm, breathing, music, meditation, visualization and guided imagery (see p. 23 as an example). The music which is played is called "Music as Mantra" because its purpose is the same as chanting a mantra: to bring the child into a hypnotic state.

While the children are in a hypnotic trance, the teacher is free to teach them anything she/he wants. The abuse of this kind of power has been documented in court cases around the country.

Teachers have used hypnosis to "regress" children to past reincarnations, to reject their parents' religious beliefs and to accept belief in Hindu deities such as Shiva, pagan gods such as Thor, spirit guides, wise ones, ascended masters, witchcraft, Satanism, devil worship, demon possession and as a way to develop psychic powers such as levitation and psychic healings.

Hypnosis has even been used to abuse children sexually and then to tell them not to remember that they have been abused. The potential for abuse far outweighs any so called "benefits."

Teachers who use Lazanov's hypnotic techniques try to avoid criticism by referring to such secular goals as "relaxation." But the issue is not the secular goals but the fundamentally religious techniques of Raja Yoga that are used to reach those goals.

If it is illegal for the Bible and prayer to be used in the schools as a technique to relax the children and to inspire them to good behavior, then it is equally illegal for Yoga techniques to be used no matter how secular the goals. The ends do not justify the means.

In one local school district where "mind control" techniques were being done under the guise of a "relaxation" program, the parents were able to get it out of the school by using this information.

SECULAR GOALS DO NOT JUSTIFY RELIGIOUS TECHNIQUES

The techniques of "visualization" have been challenged in Arizona, Florida, New Jersey and New Mexico and have been ruled as "fundamentally religious in nature" and hence illegal in public schools. The Hatch Amendment views the use of such programs as a form of child abuse. As a parent you have the legal right to preview all materials that will be used on your child. If it is New Age material, kick it out of the school by organizing parents who care for their children.

A Sample Letter to Public School Officials
Who Are Using New Age Techniques in Their School System

Dear Principal,

In compliance with "Protection of Pupil Rights: U.S. Code 1232h," sometimes known as the "Hatch Amendment," we as concerned parents who have children as students in this School District hereby officially request access to:

All instructional material, including teachers manuals, films, tapes or other supplementary instructional material which will be used in connection with any and all existing, pilot or planned programs having to do with visualization, imagining, guided imagery, fantasizing, astroprojection, reincarnation, creative intelligence, meditation, yoga, crystals, TM, hypnosis, biofeedback, mind control, magic, autosuggestion, transpersonal psychology, music meditation, ESP, witchcraft, New Age music concepts/techniques, Eastern Religions, values clarification, the keeping of journals or diaries and any programs originating from the "human potential" movement.

This is also notification that there have possibly been several violations of the Hatch Amendment in that:

(1) concerned parents feel that they have been denied access to the materials relating to said programs even though Federal Law gives them this right.

(2) the Law states that such experimental programs must secure written permission from the parents before the material can be taught.

(3) the concepts and techniques used by any such programs may be fundamentally religious in nature and would thus be in violation of the Federal Laws which prohibit the teaching of any religion (Eastern religions, New Age concepts and the occult included). For example, all programs using "meditation" were ruled "religious" in nature by the N.J. Supreme Court and upheld by the Federal Courts. Thus it cannot be practiced or taught in public schools. "Visualization" and "Guided Imagery" programs have been declared illegal by the courts or thrown out of school systems in Arizona, New Mexico, Florida and New Jersey.

If the issues are not settled soon, the parents concerned will file a complaint according to the guidelines set forth in the Hatch Amendment and, if necessary, will take legal action against the school district, the school board and any teachers involved.

All they ask for is that the School District comply with the law.

We also request an opportunity to meet with and ask questions of all those involved in such programs.

The following documents may be of help to the administration, legal counsel, school board, teachers and the PTA.

Thank you for your prompt attention to this issue.

Concerned Parents

——————— ———————
——————— ———————
——————— ———————

The Questions You Should Ask Public School Officials

Who Is Using New Age Techniques on Their Students?

1. What are the names and addresses of the organizations, seminars, businesses, schools and people from whom you received your information and training?

2. Have you heard of, been instructed by, read material of, been trained by any of the following people? Please explain who they are and what techniques and methods they teach: Lazanov, Stroebel, Schultz, Shakti, Gawain, Holland, Bry, Galyean, Petrie, Harman, Reingold, La Berge, Silva, Ferguson, Gallwey, Ornstein, Hendricks.

3. Have you heard of, been instructed in, read material about, been trained in or know the meaning of the following terms? Explain what they mean and your involvement with them: superlearning, lucid dreaming, Quieting Reflex Training (QRT), suggestology, mind sight centering, success imagery, holistic health, Aquarian Conspiracy, New Age, astral projection, altered consciousness, ESP, meditation, creative intelligence, wise ones, ascended masters, Silva Mind Control, EST, music mantra, TM or Yoga.

4. Do you have a medical degree?

5. Do you have a degree in psychology?

6. Are you a licensed hypnotherapist? Have you ever been hypnotized? Have you ever studied hypnosis techniques?

7. Are you aware of any possible medical or psychological dangers in visualization and guided imagery techniques?

8. What percent of the students may suffer "negative behavior reactions"?

9. Is there any danger for epileptic or diabetic children? What about children taking medication? Any dangers in them using visualization? Has this question been dealt with in any medical journals?

10. What about students with psychotic problems who have difficulty maintaining contact with reality? Is visualization safe for them? Has this question been dealt with in any psychology journals?

11. Have you ever practiced meditation, Yoga, visualization, etc?

12. Can students have wise ones, ascended masters or spirit guides come to their safe place and give them advice during visualization?

13. Can you develop extra-sensory abilities through visualization techniques? What are they?

14. Have you developed any such abilities? What are they?

15. Is it possible to detect, diagnose and heal any illnesses in yourself or others through visualization?

16. Can you leave your body and travel through space and time during visualization?

17. Is it possible to be regressed to past lives during imaging?

18. How are your breathing techniques different from Yoga breathing?

19. If a professional psychologist read your material and heard a tape of what you are doing to the children and declared it psychologically dangerous and a form of mind control using hypnosis techniques, would you stop?

20. If a licensed hypnotherapist read your material and heard a tape of the techniques you are using in school and then certified that you are hypnotizing the children, would you stop?

21. Do you accept personal liability for any emotional, mental, social or physical harm that comes to any student through your program?

22. Do you accept personal liability if a parent feels that his child's values, beliefs, morals and worldview have been changed through your program? For example, what if a child's beliefs

were changed from Jewish or Christian to Hindu beliefs through this "visualization" program?

23. What would you say if a child visualizes something that he worries is wrong? What about a frightening experience during visualization? Do such things happen?

24. Do you agree with the following statements:
    "Whatever the student experiences during a guided imagery is right."
    "There are no right or wrong inner experiences."
    "There are no right or wrong imaging experiences."

25. Are you aware of any deaths, suicides, murders, rapes, assaults or any deviant behavior where it is thought that the people involved were led into these things through visualization and imaging techniques?

26. Do you know of and understand the Hatch Amendment?

---

6. Develop proper attitudes toward God's name, Word, Church and servants.

   a. All of God's names reveal different aspects of the character of God (example: Adonai). Thus they should be used only in reverence and awe. To use God's name in jesting, swearing, exclamations, blasphemy or profanity is condemned in the Ten Commandments (Exo. 20:7; cf. Lev. 19:12). God even sends a special curse upon those who take his name in vain!

   b. Try as much as possible to avoid any books, movies or television shows which use God's name in vain. Even children's magazines may contain profanity and blasphemy! You must read movie reviews and preview movies before you take your children to see them. You should scan all books before they read them. If the movie or book has blatant immorality, blasphemy or sorcery, do not take your children to see it or let them read it.

Objection No. 1: "This will take too much time."

Answer: Your children are young only once and it is during this time that you have the greatest opportunity to mold their character and beliefs. It is better to take the time to do this when they are young instead of having to take far more time to deal with a paganized rebellious teenager who is blasphemous.

Objection No. 2: "This sounds like censorship! This is too narrow-minded."

Answer: Of course it is censorship! We make no apology for it in the least. If Christian parents do not protect their children from the mental filth and garbage in the world today, who will? The humanists in the public schools? Is the mind of a child an open sewer ready to take in all the filth it can? Remember that the "narrow way" leads to life while the "broad way" leads to death (Matt. 7:14).

Objection No. 3: "My kids are strong enough to read and watch whatever they want."

Answer: 1 Cor. 10:12 warns us about such dangerous attitudes. Children and teenagers are not sophisticated enough or mature enough to avoid being influenced (Eph. 4:14).

Objection No. 4: "But if we cut out all the immoral and blasphemous movies, there will not be much we can see together as a family."

Answer: So what? So, you have to sacrifice for your children! Anyway, with a VCR, you can rent, buy or borrow all kinds of good movies that are not immoral or blasphemous. From Disney to Sherlock Holmes, there are old and modern movies worth seeing.

Objection No. 5: "But they must read dirty books in public school."

Answer: First, if at all possible, send your children to a Christian school or educate them at home. You will not have the problem of humanism to deal with in Christian education. If your children must go to the state schools, then join the PTA and run for the school board. In other words, fight for your kids! Do not let the humanists cram the religion of humanism down the throat of your children. Since state schools are supposed to be neutral and the Hatch Act forbids the teaching of humanism in the school system, object, protest and make waves. Make the school withdraw the filthy books or movies or make them willing to accept good books in the place of the trash they are assigning. Do not let your school teach Hinduism (TM, reincarnation, etc.) without a big protest from you. If they will not allow the Bible to be taught then neither can they teach pagan religions or witchcraft.

Objection No. 6: "But my kids will be labeled as rebels."

Answer: Hallelujah! Christians are rebels. Being a rebel for Christ is a badge of honor. We must fight for what we believe. The Bible tells us to overcome evil—not to let evil overcome us (Rom. 12:21).

Special Note: How to Raise Rebels for Christ
1. Your children are going to be rebels one way or the other. The question is whether they will be rebels for or against Christ. Will they conform to the pagan society around them or will they rebel against the status quo?
2. Christians are the greatest rebels the world has ever known (Acts 17:6). This is why the communists fear them so much. God has called us to obey Him even when the government or our peers tell us to do otherwise (Acts 5:29). We are not to conform to this world (Rom. 12:1-2). Even if the world took a vote and decided that we should all do something that God condemns, we are to obey God rather than man (Rom. 3:4).
3. Your children must be trained from the cradle that they are to be rebels against the status quo. They must be told to say, "NO!" to all the attempts of the world to seduce them into unbelief and sin. Using Scriptural principles teach them:
   - We must be rebels for Christ.
   - Only cowards follow the crowd.
   - Be strong and stand alone.
   - Never mind what other kids say or do. They are mindless dupes of the devil.
   - You do what God commands and ignore what your peers say.
   - Do not be so stupid as to accept blindly what your teachers or textbooks say. If you find them wrong, object in class and argue your case with respect.
   - It takes true courage and guts to refuse to do what is wrong even when you must suffer for it.
   - Never mind being popular. Jesus was not popular and he warned us against trying to be popular by giving in to sin and unbelief (Lk. 6:26).
   - Be a leader and not a follower. You set the standard and set the pace. Do not let them force you into mediocrity.
   - Do not waste your time on silly fads, your money on ugly clothing. Do not let mindless idiots pick your clothes.

- Aim for success. Go for the gold. Do not let the dumb heads and potheads stop you.
- You are here to glorify God and do His will. Find, follow and finish God's will for your life.
4. Give them godly rebels as their heroes such as Moses, Gideon and Joshua and other biblical heroes (Heb. 11). Have them read biographies of famous Christian rebels such as Augustine, Calvin, Luther, Muller, Edwards, Mildred Cable, Schaeffer, etc. Praise these brave men and women for "standing alone" and being willing to suffer and even die for what they believed.
5. Point out how stupid it is to live only for personal pleasure and material possessions (Matt. 16:26). Do not live for wealth or pleasure yourself. Teach them the meaning of Luther's mighty words:

> Let goods and kindred go,
> This mortal life also;
> The body they may kill,
> God's truth abideth still,
> His Kingdom is forever.

6. Tell your children that you are proud whenever they are brave and courageous enough to do what is right, just and true. Be proud of them when they stand up for the truth.

c. Show respect for the Bible by reading it in front of your children as well as with your children in family devotions. Show respect for the Truth by reading good books on theology and philosophy. Understand your faith and be ready to give your children solid answers when they ask questions. Show respect for the Church by your love, prayers, gifts and labor.

d. Do not show disrespect for Christ's Church or for His servants by having a bitter spirit or a complaining mouth. If you want to make your children leave the church as soon as they are old enough, criticize the pastor and the church. Demand perfection from them and when they fail to meet your expectations or violate your rights, murmur and gripe in front of your children. A steady diet of "roast preacher" will keep your children from loving or respecting the Church and her servants.

Note: How to Develop a Proper Attitude Toward the Pastor(s)

What does the Bible describe as a proper attitude?

1. According to Acts 20:28-31, the Elders are appointed by God to be "overseers" (i.e. superintendents) over the church. They fulfill this task by:
   a. "guarding," i.e. protecting the church from:
      1. evil ideas
      2. evil acts
      3. evil people
   b. "shepherding," i.e. feeding and leading the flock.
2. 1 Thess. 5 :12-13 states that the Elders:
   a. "work hard," i.e. diligently labor.
   b. "are over" the church as overseers.
   c. "admonish you," i.e. explain how to live and what to believe according to Scripture.
3. Our response as members of the church according to 1 Thess. 5:12-13 is to:
   a. "respect" and "appreciate them"
   b. "hold them in the highest regard in love"
4. 1 Tim. 5:17-20 tells us that the Elders:
   a. "direct the affairs of the church"
   b. "work in preaching and teaching"

5. Because of their labors, the Elders are to:
    a. receive "double honor"
    b. receive a salary (cf. 1 Cor. 9:13-14)
    c. be protected from slander and gossip
6. Heb. 13: 7, 9, 17, 24 tells us that Elders are to:
    a. "speak the Word of God"
    b. be "leaders"
    c. "keep watch over your soul"
    d. "give an account"
7. The members are told to:
    a. "remember"
    b. "consider the outcome of their way of life"
    c. "imitate their faith"
    d. "avoid strange doctrines"
    e. "obey"
    f. "submit"
    g. "let them watch over you with joy and not grief"
8. 1 Pet. 5:1-5 tells us that Elders should:
    a. "shepherd the flock that is under their care"
    b. "serve as overseers"
        1. "not because you must"
        2. "but because you are willing"
        3. "as God wants you to be"
        4. "not greedy for money"
        5. "but eager to serve"
        6. "not lording it over those entrusted to you"
        7. "but by being examples to the flock"
9. Remember what happened to people when they rebelled against God-ordained leadership (Num. 12:1-15; 16:1-50; Acts 5:1-11, etc.)

---

    e. Pray and work for revival in the church. Grieve over her sins instead of mocking the church. Do what you can do to make it better. Attend a church where the Word is taught in its power and purity. Look forward to going to church and your children will look forward to it as well. Attend faithfully and listen carefully (Heb. 10:25; 2:1).

Do not sleep, write personal notes, snap gum, knit, whisper, laugh or crack jokes during the sermon. Such disrespect will destroy your children's love of the Word. Taking notes on the sermon and training your children to do so as well will develop good listening habits.

    f. Enter into worship with joy. Sing your heart out. Let your children hear you sing. Do not let them just sit and draw. They are to sing as well. Give a testimony and have your children give testimonies whenever God has done something for them. Participate as a family.

Conclusion

Christian parenting is the greatest task and privilege that we can have as Christians. The next generation of missionaries and pastors depends on our obedience to raise our children in the fear and admonition of the Lord.

Chapter Sixty-One
Ten Campus Curses

Introduction
Why does the Christian Church lose 75 to 90 percent of its young people who go off to college? Even though they were raised in Christian homes, taken to church from infancy, and even sent to Christian schools, they often lose their faith after a year or two in college. Why?

1. It is not because of any intellectual or philosophical arguments against the Bible or Christianity. Such arguments have been refuted many times by competent scholars.

2. The main reason we lose so many students is to be found in the churches and Christian schools they attended. The thousands of students who lose their faith in college every year are the unpaid bills of the Christian Church and its schools.

I. The Bankruptcy of Ignorance (Hos. 4:6)

Christian young people have never been more ignorant of the Bible, theology, apologetics, and philosophy than today. They do not know what they believe or why they believe it. They do not know anything about doctrine. Why?

      a. Anti-intellectualism from the 1920s

      b. Anti-creeds/confessions/catechisms

      c. Anti-social/political concerns

      d. The search for personal peace

      e. Entertainment-centered services

      f. Baby-sitting youth ministries

      g. Stupid Sunday Schools (S.S.S.)

II. The Plague of Gullibility (1 Chron. 12:32)

Because we are sincere in our religion and tell the truth about what we believe, we assume that all other religious people have the same attitude. But Jesus warned us about religious deception (Matt. 7:15; 24:4, 5, 11, 24) and we are exhorted to be critical thinkers like the Bereans (Acts 17:11).

III. The Cowardliness of Wimpism (Eph. 6:10-18)

We have raised a generation of wimps who will not stand up for the faith when it is attacked. They "give way" to ridicule and peer pressure. They often feel inferior and helpless in the face of evil. They whine and complain, and then flee to self-centered pietism. We need young men and women with backbones who will be strong for the Lord.

IV. The Insanity of Isolationism (1 Tim. 6:12)

Instead of viewing college as a wonderful opportunity to win sinners to Christ and to take over school offices, clubs, newspapers, and activities, and then use them to teach the Christian view of things, too many Christian students retreat into isolationism.

V. The Wickedness of Mediocrity (1 Cor. 10:31)

Too many students ask, "What is the least I have to do and still get by?" instead of striving to be and do the best they can for the glory of God. We don't need any more "balanced" people. What we really need are more fanatics for Jesus.

VI. The Cult of Popularity (Lk. 6:26)

Too many of our young people want everyone to "like" them. Thus, they do not stand up for Christ when push comes to shove. But Jesus warned that if everyone likes us, this is not a blessing, but a curse!

VII. The Curse of Spiritual Apathy (Rev. 3:15-16)

We face an apathetic group of young people today. They are not interested in doing or learning anything concerning the things of God. They are neither hot nor cold, but lukewarm. They need to be on fire for God.

VIII. The Happiness Syndrome (2 Tim. 3:1-5)

One of the greatest curses today is that too many students are seeking after happiness instead of holiness. If you seek holiness, you will get happiness as a by-product. But if you seek after happiness, you will end up with neither.

IX. The Deception of Wealth (1 Tim. 6:9-10)

Everyone wants to enjoy the lifestyle of the rich and the famous. Personal peace and affluence is their god. There is no concept of sacrificial giving to the cause of Christ.

X. The Problem of False Assurance (1 John 2:19)

1 John 2:4 tells us that if someone says he is saved, but he is living a disobedient life, he is a liar. Instead of confronting young people with the truth that they are probably on their way to hell, we make far too many excuses for them.

Conclusion

Young people need to be strong in the Lord and the power of His might; to stand alone and stand up for Jesus when all around oppose them. We need to go into the world as victors—not as victims; as overcomers—not underachievers.

Chapter Sixty-Two

Teaching the Christian World and Life View

What is "Christian" education? How is it different from "public" education? What makes Christian education "Christian"?

No. 1. Is it "Christian" because the teacher is a Christian? If so, the public school system is Christian education because it has teachers who are Christians.

No. 2. Is it "Christian" because a moral message is given with the lessons (Be good; Don't fornicate; Say "No" to drugs; etc.)? If so, the public schools and the private schools of Jews, Mormons, Catholics, etc., are giving "Christian" education.

No. 3. Is it "Christian" because the class is begun in prayer? While praying at the beginning of class is good, it does not mean that the teacher is giving his students a Christian education.

No. 4. Is it "Christian" because it is evangelistic? While evangelism is good and is one of the duties of all believers, it does not mean that Christian education is going on. Being saved and getting educated are two different things.

No. 5. Is it "Christian" because it has a chapel service? Chapels are good, but what is said in chapel may have nothing to do with what is said in the classroom. Great chapels do not necessarily mean great Christian education.

No. 6. Is it "Christian" because it is funded by Christian parents? No, the parents could fund a school that fails to give a Christian education.

No. 7. Is it "Christian" because it is a church school? No, just because a school is owned by a church does not mean the students will be getting a Christian education.

What Makes 'Christian' Education Christian?

Christian education takes place when academic subjects are taught from the unique perspective of the Christian world and life view. This includes every subject, because the Christian world and life view encompasses all of life.

Just as a humanist teaches from the humanistic worldview, a Christian should teach from the Christian worldview. Thus, a Christian who teaches math should give his students a totally different view of the nature and function of math than what a humanist would give. For example, New Age teachers in the public school system use such books as *The Dancing Wu Li Masters* as textbooks for physics because it teaches quantum mechanics from the perspective of Eastern religions. The world is an illusion and does not really exist. All is ONE.

This means that Christian teachers must develop a unique Christian view of their class materials. Too many Christian teachers have taken a humanistic college education (often obtained from a so-called "Christian" college) and used it as the basis of their class material in the Christian school. They have naively assumed that academic subjects are neutral and thus free from personal value judgments and an *a priori* worldview.

The goal of Christian education is to apply the Lordship of Christ to all of life. It strives to reclaim every inch of this world for Jesus Christ. It has as its grand motto: "That in all things He might have the preeminence" (Col. 1:18).

The "all things" includes all academic subjects. For example, when teaching psychology, someone will have the preeminence in that subject. Will it be Freud, Rogers, Glasser or Jesus Christ? Whose worldview will dominate? Whose ideas will form the basis of that subject? Who will have the preeminence?

If it is Christian education, the teacher should not teach psychology from a Freudian perspective but from the Christian perspective. It will be Bible-based psychology instead of humanistic-based psychology.

What does this require of the Christian teacher? The teacher must understand that:

1. The world through its wisdom, i.e., its world and life view, cannot know God. and thus ends in foolishness (1 Cor. 1:18-29). Teachers must avoid the "enticing words of man's wisdom" (1 Cor. 2:4).

2. Christianity is a distinct system of thought in which a unique view of the world and human life is given. It is a worldview and not just a "soul saving" experience.

3. God wants to transform our minds—not just save our souls. Our minds need to be renewed (Rom. 12:2). We need to love God with all our minds (Mk. 12:30).

3. The Christian should have his own wisdom, i.e., world and life view, which is based on the Word of God (1 Cor. 2:4-10).

4. The teacher must have a comprehensive understanding of the Christian world and life view. If he doesn't, how will he teach it to his students?

5. The teacher must apply the Christian world and life view to whatever subject he is teaching.

6. The method used is deductive reasoning. For example, Gen. 1:1 tells us, "In the beginning, God created the heavens and the earth." From this statement we can deduce many things:

     a. Since the universe had a beginning, it is not eternal.
     b. Since it is not eternal, it is not infinite but finite.
     c. Since it is finite, it is not self-existent.
     d. Since it is not self-existent, it is not self-renewing.
     d. Since it is not self-renewing, it will end one day.
       etc.

This means that when a Christian and a pagan look at the same tree, they do not interpret it the same way. While the pagan sees a tree produced by a meaningless chance-driven evolutionary process, the Christian sees a tree created by God with meaning, significance, and purpose.

7. God has revealed to us in Scripture the beginning principles or *a priori* concepts that form the basis of the Christian world and life view.

8. The first principle of humanism is that man is the measure of all things. This means that man starting only with himself by himself can come to a true interpretation of the meaning of his own existence and the world around him. He does not need any revelation from God. He can do it all by himself.

9. The first principle of Christianity is that God is the measure of all things. If we begin with God we can come to a true interpretation of the meaning of our existence and of the world around us. Without the God of the Bible, all is vanity and everything ends in ultimate meaninglessness.

10. The Christian world and life view is based on three pillars:

THE CHRISTIAN WORLD AND LIFE VIEW

CREATION   FALL   REDEMPTION

11. Creation, Fall and Redemption form the basis of the biblical world and life view.

12. We develop a Christian view of something by seeing it from the perspective of Creation, Fall, and Redemption. These three *a priori* concepts are the glasses through which we view all things in life.

For example, when we look at a tree, what do we see? We see a tree CREATED by God, which is now suffering from the effects of man's FALL and which will be REDEEMED one day when Christ returns.

Conclusion

Christian educators must apply the Christian worldview to every subject they teach, because nothing in life is neutral. Since all things are to be done to the glory of God (1 Cor. 10:31), all of life is sacred, i.e., religious. Since all of life is religious, everything in life is either apostate or biblical. There is no neutral or secular realm. There are no brute facts. Either God or man is the measure of all things.

Chapter Sixty-Three

Parental Authority and Respect

Part I

America is faced with a generation of rebellious young people who behave much like the young people in Isaiah's day (Isa. 3:4, 5, 12). Not only is the public school system in shambles, but many families have given up trying to cope with their rebellious youth. What has happened? Kids act like their parents have no authority at all. Why?

We believe that the breakdown of parental authority and respect is the result of the eroding away of the religious basis of true parental authority. The parents want the authority without accepting the basis of that authority. The youth are quick to see that the parents have no objective absolute basis upon which to place their commands. The youth develop an arbitrary lifestyle because that is how they see their parents live.

The only sufficient basis for parental authority and respect is God's absolute Word. In God's Word we find that God has all authority as the Creator. Parents are given delegated authority by God. They do not have any intrinsic authority of their own.

God	Man
Intrinsic Authority	Delegated Authority
(Matt. 28:18)	(Eph. 6:1-3)

The only basis for parental authority and respect is a religious basis. No natural basis is sufficient. This is where the modern problem has its source.

THERE IS OFTEN NO RELIGIOUS BASIS IN THE HOME

The primary reason for the erosion of the religious basis of parental authority in the home is that the father does not see himself as the religious authority and leader in the home. He refuses to accept God's Word which says that he is the prophet, priest and king of his family.

√ Fathers, are you the religious leader in your home?

√ Fathers, are you a religious authority to your kids?

√ Fathers, are you a prophet, priest and king to your family?

How have some fathers who are professing Christians handled their religious responsibility in the home? They have abandoned their responsibility by giving it to:

Their wife

The Sunday School

I. Rationalization No. 1—"My wife is the religious authority in the home. Let her lead the family."
II. Rationalization No. 2—"I do my part by either sending or taking my kids to Sunday School. Let the church teach my kids."

Part II

In order to deal with these two rationalizations, observe the proper function of Sunday School as it relates to the home. Parents must take seriously the needs of their children for religious training in the home. This means regular family devotions and the creation of a theistic environment in the home.

THE RELIGIOUS EDUCATION OF CHILDREN		
PROBLEM	**TRADITION**	**SCRIPTURE**
1. Who is responsible? (Eph. 6:1-4)	The Sunday School (teacher, pastor, etc.)	The parents; particularly the father.
2. Where does it take place?	The church building	Everywhere! particularly in the home (Deut. 6:7). "A Theistic World and Life View" is necessary.
3. When does it take place?	Once a week in Sunday School, at church on Sunday.	All the time; particularly once a day at home in family devotions (Deut. 6:6-9).
4. What is to be taught?	Sunday School material; knowledge centered.	The whole counsel of God; character-centered (Eph. 6:4).
5. How is it to be taught?	Lecture by Sunday School teacher; singing, visual aids, etc.	Lecture, handcrafts, drama, singing, visual aids; personal discipleship, etc.
6. Who is responsible when kids rebel?	Sunday School teacher, pastor, church	The parents; particularly the father (Titus 1:5-6).

The biblical relationship between the Sunday School and the home.

The Sunday School applies
what is taught in the home

The foundation is the home

When parents fail to obey God's Law/Word, a chain reaction sets in which results in bitterness.

Failure	=	Guilt	=	Pride	=	Blame	=	Bitterness
to obey		sets in		takes over		is placed		grows

The Biblical Solution to the Problem

Redesign Sunday School in such a way that it helps parents to fulfill their responsibility instead of doing it for them.

A. To train parents to teach their children at home.
    1. Parents as Sunday School teachers.
    2. Special classes and seminars.
    3. Take-home literature.
    4. Role playing and drama.

B. Training in the home.
    1. Families visited in the home.
    2. Information, presentation and clarification of problems and questions.
    3. Staging of family devotions in home.
    4. Follow-up calls to check on progress.

C. Family night programs.
    1. Ideas shared (newsletters).
    2. Books recommended.

Chapter Sixty-Four

Building a Hedge Around Your Family

Introduction: We need to pray in such a way as to build a hedge of protection and thorns around ourselves, our families, church and nation.

I. There is a hedge of protection around each believer (Job 1:1, 8-11; Luke 22:31-32; John 17:12; 1 John 5:18).

II. By prayer, a hedge is built around the family of the believer (Job 1:5).

III. A special hedge of thorns can be built around a wayward loved one (Hosea 2:5-7).
   A. Hosea's wife went into adultery (2:5).
   B. A hedge of thorns was placed around her (2:6a).
   C. This hedge caused her to lose her sense of direction and purpose. She became confused and did not know which path of action to take (2:6b).
   D. This hedge drove away her lovers (2:7a). She began to feel lonely and rejected.
   E. The feelings of sadness she experienced forced her to consider returning to her husband (2:7b); cf. the prodigal son (Lk. 15:17-20).
   F. She returned to Hosea (2:14-16).

IV. A hedge needs to be built around the church by its officers and congregation.
   A. The "fathers" need to build protection around the church (2 Cor. 11:28).
   B. The "children" need to build protection around the elders and deacons.
   C. A hedge of thorns can be built around wayward church members.

V. A hedge of protection and thorns needs to be built around our nation to protect and discipline our leaders (Ezk. 22:30-31; Psa. 80:8-13; Isa. 5:5).

VI. Positive steps for hedge building.
   A. Make sure you are a Christian (2 Cor. 13:5).
   B. Pray specifically for a hedge to be built around yourself, your family, church and nation.

> O, God, I pray that you
> will now bind Satan and build
> a hedge around _____
> in the name of Jesus and by the
> power of His blood.

Chapter Sixty-Five

Christian Hospitality

One of the greatest virtues of the Christian life is hospitality. The development of this character quality is one of the most important elements of spiritual maturity.

I. What is Christian Hospitality?

Definition: It is the opening of the heart and home to entertain friends and strangers with a view to ministering to their physical and spiritual needs in the name of Christ.

A. The words, "opening of the heart," refer to your attitude about having people in your home. What is your attitude when people come into your home?

____happy or ____sad   ____gracious or ____resentful
____warm or ____cold   ____pliable or ____stiff
____joyful or ____angry   ____friendly or ____rude

Probing Questions
Do you make people feel "at home" in your home?
Do they feel welcomed?
Do your guests feel comfortable in your home?
Do you view them as invited guests or as intruders?
Do guests brighten or spoil your day?
Do you resent unexpected company?
Do you complain or murmur about people coming?
Do you feel "imposed upon" and "used"?

B. The words, "opening of the home," mean that you have an "open door" policy toward people in which the emphasis is not on the quality or condition of the furnishings or food but on creating a warm and friendly atmosphere in the home. It is better to eat beans in a home where there is an atmosphere of love and acceptance than to eat a steak dinner in a home where there is an atmosphere of bitterness and resentfulness. Feeling welcomed and accepted has little to do with whether you are in a hovel or a palace. It is your attitude which determines whether or not your guests feel welcomed (Prov. 17:1; 21:9; 25:24).

C. "With a view to ministering" means that the purpose of inviting people over to your home is to minister to them. Thus your purpose is not to impress people or show off your house or its furnishings. You should seek to be of benefit to them by providing a place, a time and an atmosphere where they can experience the joy of a Christian home and be led either to salvation or fellowship.

D. "Their physical needs" means that if someone needs a meal, provide it for them. Think of all the single adults who would love a home-cooked meal. Think of the sick or the elderly and their needs. There are those who need to "get away" from their home and could enjoy a time visiting and resting in your home. You could keep the children of a couple who need to get away as husband and wife (James 2:15-16; 1 John 3:17).

E. "In the name of Christ" means that you view your acts of hospitality as being done not only "in the name of the Lord" (Mk. 9:41) and "to the glory of God" (1 Cor. 10:31) but also "to the Lord" Himself in a personal way (Matt. 25:34-40).

Once this is understood, then a lack of hospitality or a poor attitude while engaged in hospitality must be viewed as a personal rejection of Christ Himself. How you treat the Lord's people is the surest proof of how you really feel about the Lord Himself. A consistent lack of hospitality is viewed by Christ as the clearest proof that a person is not saved but is destined for eternal punishment (Matt. 25:41-46). When you resent having people in your home, Christ takes this resentment personally.

II. Who is Supposed to be Hospitable?

A. Because hospitality is such an important virtue, the Elders must exemplify this character trait (1 Tim. 3:2; Tit. l:8). Their home must be open to the needs of people. A man who does not like people in his home or who is not able to make people feel welcomed is not suited for the office of Elder. The same holds true for any leadership position in the Church (1 Tim. 5:10). The character trait of hospitality is an essential requirement for leadership. All leaders are to be role models for the rest of the congregation to follow (1 Tim. 4:12; 1 Pet. 5:1-4).

B. All believers should develop the virtue of hospitality (Rom. 12:13; Heb. 13:2; 1 Pet. 4:9). From the Old Testament (Gen. 10) to the New Testament (Philemon), godliness and hospitality have been synonymous. All of us have been called to minister to others. Jesus has left us the example and pattern to follow (1 John 2:6; 3:16-18; Rom. 15:3; etc.).

Conclusion

The Key to Hospitality
A right attitude + consistent action = a godly habit.
A godly habit + time = a Christ-like character quality.

Chapter Sixty-Six
Christian Contentment

Introduction

One of the keys of a happy Christian life is to learn to be content with whatever lot in life God has ordained for you. One of the greatest problems today is that too many of God's people are discontented. They whine and complain as if God owed them health, wealth and popularity.

This has special relevance for the family. When the wife, husband or the children get into the habit of complaining and whining about everything, this destroys the unity and love of the family. All we should want out of life is contentment throughout it and a sense of accomplishment at the end of it because the glory of God is our all in all.

I. The Nature of Christian Contentment

An inner emotional state in which one feels at peace within himself because he is satisfied with his present lot in life regardless of the present circumstances.

II. The Focus of Christian Contentment

A. The problem of priorities.
We must all deal with three things:
The Past   The Present   The Future

B. To be content, you must have the biblical order of importance.
Which is the most important aspect of time to you?

Option No. 1	**The Past**
Result:	Discontentment (Num. 11:1-5)
Remedy:	Give the past a minor role (Phil. 3:13)

Option No. 2	**The Future**
Result:	Discontentment (Matt. 6:25-34; Pro. 22:13)
Remedy:	Give the future a minor role (Pro. 27:1; James 4:13-15)

Option No. 3   **The Present**

The major focus of your life should be on the present, for the past no longer is and the future is yet to be. You only have the present.

"Be content with the present things" (Heb. 13:5)

NOW   **TODAY**
2 Cor. 6:1-2   Heb. 3:7, 13, 15
Gal. 2:20   Heb. 4:7 and Matt. 6:28-34

III. The Independence of Christian Contentment
  A. True contentment does not depend on good circumstances for its existence (Phil. 4:11). It is "self-sufficient" in a good sense.
  B. It refers to an inner strength that depends on something other than the circumstances. Like cork which always floats on top of the water regardless if the water is calm or rough, contentment will always surface regardless of good or evil circumstances (Phil. 4:11-12).
  Note: We are not describing a stoical attitude which claims to be unaffected by anything because it cares for nothing.

IV. "The Secret of Contentment" (Phil. 4:12)
  A. You do NOT have the power in yourself to have true contentment (2 Cor. 3:5, KJV).
  B. The "secret" is something the world refuses to consider; namely, true contentment comes through Christ (Phil. 4:13). Thus, the power to be content comes from God (2 Cor. 3:5).

V. The Means of True Contentment
  A. Contentment is something you must learn by intellect and earn by experience (Phil. 4:12).
  B. It is not optional, for God commands us to be content (Heb. 13:5).
  C. It is primarily based on two things:
    1) Intellect: A clear understanding of the sovereignty of God and its application to all of life (Gen. 1:1; Psa. 103:19; Rom. 8:28; 11:36; Eph. 1:11, etc).
    2) Experience:
    Two examples
    No. 1: Job (a believer)
      a. His understanding (42:2; 14:5, 6; 1:21; 2:10).
      b. His experience (1:20-22; 2:7-10).

I will be content with my present lot in life
because my God has willed it to be for His glory and my good.
I accept the will of God for me
and give thanks to Him for all things, good and evil,
for I fear God (1 Thess. 5:18).

    No. 2: Nebuchadnezzar (an infidel)
      a. His understanding (Dan. 4:25, 27)
      b. His experience (Dan. 4:28-37)

VI. The Heart Issue of Contentment
Are you willing to accept God's will and be content with it even when He orders "evil" circumstances? Are you willing to worship God and thank Him for the evil He sends your way as well as the good (1 Thess. 5:18; cf. Eph. 5:20)?

Conclusion

How to know if you have Christian contentment.
When things do not go the way you want them to go, do you:
No. 1: View it as God's will? Accept it as God's will? Give thanks for it as God's will?

OR

No. 2: Complain? Get bitter with God and others? Angry? Sullen? Feel you deserve better? Or that you are getting a "raw" deal etc.?

Part Three
The Church

Chapter Sixty-Seven
Church Goals

As a congregation, you need to understand and to set forth specific and clear church goals. Why?

1. To know: Where you are headed. What you are aiming at.
   For what you are expected to labor, struggle and sacrifice.
   Why are you coming to church?

2. To set up clear standards that will help you to evaluate all the activities and programs of the congregation. Some old things will have to go, while some new things must come (Luke 5:37, 38).

3. To raise your vision of what God wants you to be and to do, as a congregation as well as individuals.
   Where are you going?
   By what standards do you evaluate programs?
   How can you raise your vision?

Goal No. 1

Salvation

To guide each individual to put his full faith and trust in the Lord Jesus Christ and to love Him with all his heart, soul, mind and strength (Rom. 10:9; Mk. 12:28-30)

Goal No. 2

Christian Maturity

To develop Christian maturity in individuals, families and in the corporate life of the Body of believers.

Question: When is a local church a "successful" church?

Some Traditional Answers

Some say that a successful church is:
   A theologically knowledgeable church
   An active church
   A growing church
   A soul-winning church
   A missionary-minded church
   A smooth-running church
   An exciting church
   A big church
   A politically active church
   A church with elders and deacons
   Numbers, building and money are the standards of success

Now, let us emphasize that a mature church will be active, growing, giving, etc., because a mature church will be involved in many of these things. But a church can be each of these things without being successful or mature.

For example: The Corinthian Church was active, growing, giving, "soul-winning," missionary-minded, exciting and big. But Paul clearly points out in 1 Cor. 3:1-4 that this church was "carnal," i.e., immature. It was not successful by biblical standards.

Thus, a church could be all of these things without being mature. Why? These things do not constitute the essence of Christian maturity. For the essence of Christian maturity, we must turn to the Bible. It is the Scriptures that tell us the standard of success by which we can judge our church.

The Biblical Answer

It is clear from the New Testament that the standard of Christian maturity is to be found in faith, hope and love.

> The Corinthian church: 1 Cor. 13:1-13
> The Ephesian church: Eph. 1:15, 16, 18
> The Colossian church: Col. 1:3-6
> The Thessalonian church: 1 Thess. 1:2, 3; 2 Thess. 1:3, 4
> To Timothy: 1 Tim. 1:5
> From Peter to Christians: 1 Pet. 1:21, 22

> FAITH: The trust and confidence that a local church places in Jesus Christ, the head of the church. This needs to increase.
> HOPE: The stability that arises out of clear doctrinal insight into our present and future relationship to God through Christ by the Spirit.
> LOVE: The manifestation of Christ-like attitudes and actions within the local body of Christ by members one to another. This reveals true Christian discipleship to the unbelieving world (John 13:35).

A church is successful and mature to the degree that the members are abounding in faith, hope and love. Buildings, members and money are never viewed by the New Testament as a standard of success or maturity. Yet, in most traditional churches, wall plaques are placed at the front of the sanctuary indicating:

> How many came last year _____
> How many came last week _____
> Money given last year _____
> Money given last week _____
> Building fund goal _____

These plaques constantly tell the people that they are important only in terms of their attendance and giving. There is no emphasis on growing in grace or knowledge.

Conclusion

The only times the Apostle Paul gave thanks for a church was when it was growing in faith, hope and love and manifested it to the world around them. Let us hope that the 21st century church returns to such spiritual standards of success and abandons its present carnal standards of building, numbers and money (Rom. 12:1-2).

Chapter Sixty-Eight
Faith

Introduction

One of the greatest problems which cripples the work of God and depresses the people of God is:

"O YE OF LITTLE FAITH."

We accomplish little because our faith is little. The problem of little faith is the root cause of the main ills of the church and of depression among the people of God.

We are a generation of spiritual pygmies. Since we do not attempt great things for God out of great faith in God, we do not accomplish great things through God.

If we are going to experience great things from God, we must have great faith in God. This is a spiritual law which cannot be broken. Be not deceived, "little faith" will produce very little in terms of the success and joys of a Spirit-filled life.

"ACCORDING TO YOUR FAITH SO BE IT UNTO YOU"
(Matt. 9:29)

Illustrations of the Problem

TEXT	THE OCCASION	THE PROBLEM
Matt. 6:25-34	Anxiety over the bodily necessities of life	Little faith in God's provision (v. 30)
Matt. 8:23-27	Panic in an emergency	Little faith in God's protection (v. 26)
Matt. 14:22-33	Stepping out in faith but sinking in doubt	Little faith in God's power (v. 31)
Matt. 16:5-12	Lack of spiritual understanding	Little faith in God's promise (v. 8)
Matt. 17:19-20	Inability to defeat Satan	Little faith in God's person (v. 20)

The only way that the problem will be solved is:

A. To recognize the problem of unbelief and ask Christ to help you (Mk. 9:24).

B. To ask God to increase your faith (Lk. 17:5-6).

Faith

1) The first thing we must do is to clarify what kind of faith we will be studying.
   a) Three different kinds of faith are mentioned in Scripture.

THE GRACE OF FAITH	THE FRUIT OF FAITH	THE GIFT OF FAITH
1. A gift from God (Phil. 1: 29)	A gift from God (Heb. 12:2)	A gift from God (I Cor. 12:8-9)
2. Given to all the elect in order for them to accept Christ (Acts 13:48; 18:27)	Given to all believers in order for them to live the Christian life (2 Pet. 1:5-7)	Given to some believers some of the time as a manifestation gift.
3. Primary focus: SALVATION (Eph. 2:8-9)	Primary focus: SANCTIFICATION (Rom. 1:17)	Primary focus: MINISTRY AND LIFE-MESSAGE
4. Nature of work: INSTANTANEOUS MONERGISTIC	Nature of work: PROGRESSIVE SYNERGISTIC	Nature of work: INSTANTANEOUS MONERGISTIC

2) Our focus is on a description of the fruit of faith in terms of how it functions in the believer to enable him to live the Christian life.
   a) The Scriptures do not give us a theological definition of faith. But we do find a functional description of the way faith operates in the heart of the believer. What faith does is the focus of Scripture, not what faith is.
   b) The passage of "full mention" in Scripture on faith is Hebrews 11. In this passage we have a description of how faith functions in the heart and then numerous examples are given to illustrate how faith can enable us to live the Christian life.
      i) Let us first examine the functionalistic description of faith given in Heb. 11:1.
      ii) And then let us study the examples of faith which are given to illustrate how faith enables believers to live a triumphant Christian life (Heb. 11:2-40).
3) Heb. 11:1: "Now faith is the assurance of things hoped for, the conviction of things not seen."
   a) "Faith is the assurance of things hoped for."
      i) Let us look first at the phrase "things hoped for."
         (1) Things which you hope to receive in the future because you do not have them in your present possession (Rom. 8:18-25).
         (2) Examples of "things hoped for."
            (a) Heaven at death (2 Cor. 5:8)
            (b) The resurrection (John 5:28-29)
            (c) Glorification (Rom. 8:30; Phil. 3:20-21)
            (d) A new Heavens and new earth (2 Pet. 3:13)
            (e) The ultimate victory of good over evil (Rev. 21:3-4; 22:3)

(f) Eternal happiness and fulfillment (Matt. 25:34, 46)

(g) The blessed hope of Christ's return which will bring letters a to f into reality (Titus 2:13)

(3) Our questions are these:
   ● How do we know that we will receive these things hoped for?
   ● What guarantee do we have that we will receive what we hope for?

(4) The answer is found in the word which has been translated "assurance" (NAS) or "substance" (KJV) in Heb. 11:1.

   (a) The Greek should not have been translated as "substance" or "assurance." Moulton and Milligan have shown that this word had a special meaning in the first century Koine Greek language. It referred to a title deed to a property one had not seen but was only hoped for. It was the legal guarantee that you were going to get what the deed spelled out. You knew it was yours even though you did not have it in your possession. (See *Out of the Earth*, E.M. Blaiklock, p. 64; *Word Pictures in the New Testament*, A.T. Robertson, Vol. V, p. 418.)

   (b) We now find some modern versions (K. Wuest, *The New Testament*; H. Montgomery, *The Centenary Translation*) which correctly translate the Greek word.

"Now faith is the Title Deed of things hoped for."

   (c) Thus we know for certain that we will receive those things promised to us in the future because God has given a guarantee to us by placing "faith" in our hearts as the legal title deed to these future blessings.

| A title deed in the hand to a future material property. | A title deed in the heart to future Spiritual and material blessings. |

b) Faith is "the conviction of things not seen."
   i) Let us first examine the phrase, "Things not seen."
      (1) (Literal Greek) "things which cannot be seen with the human eye, i.e., things which are invisible."

      (2) The author of Hebrews is referring to those present spiritual blessings which are invisible to the eye but which Scripture tells us are the present possession of every true believer. Biblical examples:

      (a) Calling (1 Cor. 1:9)
      (b) Regeneration (John 3:5)
      (c) Justification (Rom. 5:1)
      (d) Adoption (Rom. 8:14-17)
      (e) Forgiveness (Eph. 1:7)
      (f) Righteousness (1 Cor. 1:30)
      (g) Access to God (Eph. 2:18, 3:12)
      (h) Power (Acts 1:8)

      (3) Our questions are these:
         ● What proof do we have that we actually possess these invisible things?
         ● What evidence can convict and convince us that these unseen things are real and not just illusions?

ii) The answer is found in the Greek word which has been translated in Heb. 11:1 as "conviction" (NAS) or "evidence" (KJV).

(1) This word should not have been translated "conviction." The Greek word in its common everyday usage means the "proof" or "evidence" which produces conviction in us.

(2) Some of the newer translations have upheld the KJV's "evidence."
- Williams
- The Twentieth Century Version
- Montgomery
- Amplified New Testament

(3) The "proof" or "evidence" of the reality of unseen things is found in the fact that God has placed faith in our hearts. This faith could not have come from our own wicked hearts for we are totally incapable of faith. We all run from God as fast as we can (Rom. 3:10-18). Thus, "not all have faith" (2 Thess. 3:2). "Faith" is itself the first unseen reality which we receive from God (Eph. 2:8-9). It is God's opening the heart to cause it to receive the Gospel (Acts 16:14); God's opening the eyes of the soul to see that which is invisible (Eph. 1:18). It is through the spiritual eyes of faith that we "see" the unseen world (Heb. 11:27).

"Faith gives to things a future which as yet are only hoped for, all the reality of actual present existence and irresistibly convinces us of the reality of things unseen and brings us into their presence" (*Expositor's Greek Testament*, p. 352, V.IV).

Summary

The faith in our hearts functions as a title deed for things hoped for and as "evidence" or "proof" of things not seen.

"It is faith alone that takes believers out of this world while they are in it, that exalts them above it while they are under its rage; that enables them to live upon things future and invisible, giving such a real subsistence unto their power in them and victorious evidence of their reality and truth in themselves, as secures them from fainting under all oppositions, temptations and persecutions whatever." John Owen, *Hebrews*, Vol. VII, pp. 12-13.

"Faith apprehends as a real fact what is not revealed to the senses. It rests on the fact, acts upon it and is upheld by it in the face of all that seems to contradict it. Faith is a real seeing." Vincent, *Word Studies*, Vol. IV, pp. 509-510.

4) Having seen the function of faith, we must ask if it is possible to grow in our faith or to increase our faith so that we are enabled to live victorious Christian lives.
We have this question answered positively in the prayer of the Apostles in Lk. 17:5-6, the fruit of the Spirit in Gal. 5:22 and the admonition of Peter in 2 Pet. 1:5-11.

5) Why should we strive to increase our faith? In what ways will we spiritually profit if we do?
a) Because of their faith, God bore witness to our fathers (Heb. 11:2).
b) To please God (Heb. 11:6).
c) To accomplish great things for God (Heb. 11:32-34).
d) To witness great miracles from God (Heb. 11:35).
e) To experience deliverance by God (Heb. 11:33).
f) To endure persecutions through God (Heb. 11:35, 38).
g) To finish the race set before us (Heb. 12:1-2).
h) To be fruitful and useful in this life (2 Pet. 1:5-9).
i) To be granted a royal welcome in the life to come (2 Pet. 1:10-11).
j) To have prayers answered (Matt. 21:22).
k) To receive wisdom from God (James 1:5-7), etc.

6) To illustrate the power faith gives to enable people to become overcomers, the author of Hebrews reviews some notable examples from biblical history in chapter 11.

Person	The Focus of Faith	The Result of Faith	The Obstacle of Faith
1. We (v. 3)	creation *ex nihilo* (God's Word)	a theistic understanding of the world	the unbelief and ridicule of unbelievers
2. Abel (v. 4)	necessity of bloody sacrifice (Gen. 4:1-10)	better sacrifice, divine acceptance righteousness shown	the unbelief and wickedness of Cain
3. Enoch (v. 5)	walking with God in view of Christ's return (Jude 14-15; Gen. 5:24)	extradimensional teleportation to escape death	the unbelief and ridicule of people
4. Noah (v. 7)	coming Flood (Gen. 6:8, 13)	delivered his family; condemned the world	the unbelief and ridicule of people
5. Abraham (v. 8)	God's call to go (Gen. 12:1-4)	left homeland, family and friends	family ties; unbelief, ridicule
6. Abraham (vs. 9-10)	Promised Land (Gen. 12:6-9)	lived in land as a stranger and pilgrim	the land was not his; it was owned already by others
7. Sarah (vs. 11-12)	promised son; God's faithfulness (Gen. 17:15-21)	conceived Isaac	Abraham and Sarah were too old to have children
8. Abraham (v. 17-19)	God's commands to him; God's promises about Isaac (Gen. 17:(Gen 15-21)	sacrifice of Isaac in hope of his resurrection 22:1-19) commands	natural ties to son; seeming contradiction between God's and God's promises
9. Isaac (v. 20)	God's covenantal promises to Abraham (Gen. 27:27-40)	blessed his sons concerning their future	unbelief and doubts about the future

Person	The Focus of Faith	The Result of Faith	The Obstacle of Faith
10. Jacob (v. 21)	God's covenantal promises to Abraham and to him (Gen. 35:9-13)	blessed his sons; worshiped God (Gen. 49:1-33)	unbelief, doubts, and ridicule
11. Joseph (v. 22)	God's promise that His people would return to the Promised Land in 400 years	gave instructions to remove his body to the Promised Land (Gen. 50:22-26)	the people were in Egypt; unbelief in the revelation given to Abraham
12. Moses' parents (v. 23)	the fear of God was of greater value than the fear of man (Exo. 1:17)	did not kill Moses; disobeyed the king (Exo. 2:1-4)	the king's order, the king's wrath
13. Moses (vs. 24-26)	the present reproach and future reward of following Christ are greater in value than the pleasures of sin for a season or the treasures of Egypt	renounced sonship to Pharaoh's daughter; identified himself with the people of God; suffering ill treatment with them (Exo. 2:11-15)	loss of sinful pleasures; loss of wealth, position and power; Pharaoh angry, pain and suffering
14. Moses (v. 27)	"seeing" Him who is invisible, i.e., feared God more than he feared Pharaoh	left Egypt; did not fear Pharaoh's wrath; he endured (Exo. 2:21; 3:1)	Pharaoh's anger; possibility of death
15. Moses (v. 28)	the coming of the angel of death to kill all the first-born (Exo. 12:12)	kept the Passover and sprinkling drops of blood (Exo. 12:21-28); delivered his first-born	unbelief, ridicule
16. People of Israel (v. 30)	God's command to walk through the Red Sea (Exo. 14:10-20)	Israel delivered; Egyptian armies destroyed (Exo. 14:21-31)	fear, doubts, unbelief

Person	The Focus of Faith	The Result of Faith	The Obstacle of Faith
17. People of Israel (v. 30)	God's command to march around Jericho for seven days (Josh. 6:1-5)	the walls of Jericho fell down; city taken (Josh. 6:6-21)	unbelief, doubts; ridicule of people in Jericho, pride
18. Rahab (v. 31)	God's promise to give the land to Israel; God's power in punishing Egypt (Josh. 2:8-13)	saved herself and her family (Josh. 6:22-25); joined to the people of God (Matt. 1:5)	the anger of people in Jericho; fear, doubts
19. Gideon (v. 32)	God's command and promise to defeat the Midianites (Judges 6:1-16); God's command to reduce his army to 300 men (Judges 7:1-7)	mobilized an army; reduced it to 300; defeated Midianites (Judges 7:15-22)	cowardice, fear, doubt (Judges 6: 36-40); defeat, death
20. Barak (v. 32)	God's command and promise to defeat the Canaanites (Judges 4:6-7)	mobilized an army and defeated enemies (Judges 4:14-16)	fear, doubts (Judges 4:8)
21. Samson (v. 32)	God's mercy and forgiveness; God's power (Judges 16:23-30)	destroyed more Philistines than ever before	fear, death
22. Jephthah (v. 32)	his prayer for victory (Judges 11:29-31; cf.11: 21-24)	the Spirit's power (Judges 11:29); he defeated Amorites (Judges 11:32)	bitterness (Judges 11:1-3); fear, doubts
23. David (v. 32)	his trust in God would give him victory (1 Sam. 17:37; 45-47)	killed Goliath (1 Sam:17:41-51)	fear of others; ridicule of his brothers (1 Sam. 17:26-30); Saul's armor (1 Sam. 17:38-40)

Person	The Focus of Faith	The Result of Faith	The Obstacle of Faith
24. Samuel (v. 32)	God's command to anoint David as king (1 Sam. 16:1-13)	rejected Saul; anointed David	fear of Saul; personal reasons
25. The Prophets (vs. 32-38)	faith in God's Word	• subdued kingdoms (Joshua:10:40-42) •wrought righteousness (Josiah: 2 Chron. 34:1-7) •obtained promises (Solomon: 2 Chron. 7:11:18) •stopped the mouth of lions (Daniel: Dan. 6:19-23) •quenched the power of fire (Shadrach, Meshach, Abednego: Dan. 3:8-30) •escaped the edge of the sword (Elisha: 2 Kings 6:8-19) •went from weakness to strength (Jeremiah: Jer. 11:6-10) •became powerful in battle and routed foreign armies (Othniel: Judges 3:7-11) •women received their dead back by resurrection (Elijah: 2 Kings 4:8-37) •tortured (Jeremiah 38:6)	•jeered and flogged (Jeremiah: Jer. 20:2) •chained and imprisoned (Jeremiah: Jer. 37:14-16) •stoned (Zechariah: 2 Chron. 24:21) •sawed in half (Isaiah: Tradition) •killed by the sword (Uriah: Jer. 26:20-23) •went about in sheepskins and goatskins (Elijah: 1 Kings 19:13, 19) •destitute (Moses: Heb. 11:26) •afflicted (Jeremiah: Lam. 1:12) •ill-treated (Moses: Heb. 11:25) •wandered in deserts, mountains, caves and holes in the ground (Elijah and the prophets 1 Kings 18:4; 19:9)

Conclusion

By faith we can overcome all obstacles, endure all manner of suffering and persecution and fulfill God's plan for our lives. Faith gives us the power to turn evil into good by resting in God's Sovereignty (Rom. 8:28). We need a mighty faith which laughs at impossibilities and cries, "It shall be done through Christ who strengthens me!"

Chapter Sixty-Nine
Hope

Introduction

"Hope" is so important to a human being that when it is lost, people just lay down and die. William Frankl, the Father of Logotherapy, saw this truth while in a Nazi concentration camp. Those who lost all hope of ever getting out died. Those who kept their hope and planned on what they would do when they got out lived. When hope dies in the human heart, the mind and the will to live cease functioning. God has so created us that we must hope in order to live.

What holds for the individual also applies to a family and to a church. When people give up all hope that their family or church will succeed, that family or church will die. But as long as there is hope, there will be life. Thus faith, hope and love constitute the heartbeat of a person, a family and a church. Just as we would physically die without them, a church will spiritually die without them. The same applies to the spirit of a nation. If the "American dream," which is hope, ever dies, our nation will also die.

I. The Meaning of "Hope"

    A. Even though hope is often connected with faith and love, we must not confuse these three different things (1 Cor. 13:13).

        Hope: Concerns the Future (Rom. 8:23-24)
        Faith: Concerns the Past and Present (Rev. 1:5-6)
        Love: Concerns the Present (1 Cor. 13)

    B. While the modern meaning of the word "hope" implies uncertainty and merely wishing for something which may or may not happen, the Greek word used by the authors of the New Testament was a word which implied absolute certainty. There was no vagueness or uncertainty connected with this word.

    The New Testament meaning of the word "hope" is:

    The inner attitude of joyful and confident expectation and anticipation that everything God has promised in His Word will come to pass.

    1. "Inner Attitude": The way of mentally viewing and responding to life.

    2. "Joyful and Confident": Positive, victorious, assured, inspires joy, stability, etc.

    3. "Expectation and Anticipation": Plan on it and enjoy it now by foretaste.

    4. "That everything God has promised in His Word will come to pass": What the Bible says about our future will happen.

II. The Attributes of Hope

Text	The Attributes of Hope
Heb. 7:19	A Better Hope
1 Pet. 1:3	A Living Hope
Titus 2:13	A Blessed Hope
1 John 3:2-3	A Purifying Hope
2 Thess. 2:16	A Good Hope
1 Tim. 1:1	A Christ-Centered Hope
Rom. 5:5	A Hope Which Does Not Disappoint
Heb. 6:18	A Hope Set Before Us (In the Gospel) (Col. 1:23)
Heb. 6:19	A Sure and Steadfast Anchor of the Soul
1 Cor. 13:13	An Abiding Hope

III. The Fruit of Hope

What does "hope" do for us in terms of practical living? Of what benefit is hope? How does it help us to live the Christian life?

A. Christian hope produces perseverance and steadfastness in the face of trials, tiredness and temptation (Rom. 4:18; 1 Thess. 1:3; 2 Thess. 2:16-17; Heb. 3:6; 6:7-12; 18-20; 10:23).

Why do people stop growing and going in the Christian life?

Answer: Trials: Personal, family, church, financial, etc.
Tiredness: Physical, emotional, spiritual.
Temptation: To pursue personal pleasure, wealth, fame, acceptance of the world, etc.

Why should trials, tiredness or temptations affect us?

Answer: When we become "self-centered" and begin to dwell on present problems instead of dwelling on future blessings, and build our security and joy around temporal objects or people, the grace of hope withers within us.

Since perseverance and steadfastness depend on a strong living hope in us in which our view of the future affects the way we respond to the present, a weakened hope will weaken our dedication to persevere in the Christian life.

What is the goal of life itself? For what should I live?

Answer: The Glory of God (1 Cor. 10:31)

A. The development of Christ-like character qualities in my life (Rom. 8:29; Rom. 5:3-5; James 1:2-4; 2 Pet. 1:3-9: Matt. 5:3-16, etc.).

B. Hope is essential to the development of our character (Rom. 5:2-5).

C. The fruit of the Spirit comes from hope (joy, peace, faith: Rom. 15:13; Col. 1:4-5).

D. The ability to rejoice in the midst of trials comes from hope (Rom. 5:2-3; 12:12; James 1:2).

E. Boldness in our witness comes from hope (2 Cor. 3:12; 1 Pet. 3:15).

F. We should derive strong encouragement from our hope (Heb. 6:18).

G. Hope is our helmet in the armor of God (1 Thess. 5:8).

HOPE GIVES US THE POWER TO LIVE
THE CHRISTIAN LIFE!!

IV. The Focus of Hope

To what does hope look? Just as faith can focus on the past and love will focus on the present, hope should focus on the future.

The Future—Things Yet Unseen and Experienced

Our Future Blessings

1. Revelation (Rom. 8:19)
2. Liberation (Rom. 8:19-21)
3. Vindication (Rom. 8:23)
4. Vivification (Rom. 8:23)
   a. Our resurrection (Acts 23:6; 24:15; 26:6-7)
   b. Eternal Life (Titus 1:2; 3:7)
5. Justification (Gal. 5:5; Phil. 3:9)
6. Glorification (Col. l:27; Rom. 8:30)

THE GLORIOUS RETURN OF CHRIST

V. The Basis of Our Hopes

Upon what do we base our hopes for the future? What are the grounds of our hope? Where is the warrant for our hope?

A. It is sadly possible to have ill-founded hopes (Matt. 7:21-23).

   Ill-founded hopes
   1. "A mere profession of faith is sufficient."
   2. "My religious works will get me to Heaven."
   3. "There is no need for a personal relationship with Christ."

B. It is possible to have a firm and secure hope (Heb. 6:19).

C. We must have our hopes on the following:

   1. A reliable document: The Word of God, Scripture, the Gospel,
                               the Word of Truth (Col. 1:5, 23; Tit. 1:2-3)

   2. A Historical Guarantee: Christ's resurrection (1 Pet. 1:3, 21; Acts 17:30-31)

VI. How to Increase Your Hope

   A. Realize that God wants you to "overflow" with hope. There are degrees of hopefulness. We should strive to increase hope within us (Rom. 15:13).

   B. Recognize that all well-grounded hope comes from God. Thus you must look to the God from whom hope comes (Rom. 15:13); "The God of Hope."

   "O, God of Hope, make me to abound in hope. Increase the amount of hope within me."

   C. In faith, ask God for the filling of the Spirit (Rom. 15:13).

     1. "Fill you" (aorist tense): an act of God, not a process.
     2. "Joy and Peace": Two of the "fruits" of "walking in the Spirit" i.e., being spirit-filled (Gal. 5:16, 22, 25; Eph. 5:18).
     3. "In Believing" (present infinitive): A constant activity of exercising faith, not one act, but an abiding activity.
     4. "In order that you may overflow with hope": "Overflow" (present infinitive): A constant overflowing going on all the time. Not one act, but a continuous experience.
     5. "By the power of the Holy Spirit": Instrumental clause telling us how we overflow with hope. By the power of the Spirit, we can have this experience.

   D. As "Endurance" or "Perseverance" in the Christian life arises out of hope, your endurance of trials, tiredness and temptations will, in turn, give rise to more hope (Rom. 15:4).

   "Through endurance... We might have hope."

     1. Hope ⟶ Endurance ⟶ Hope ⟶ Endurance ⟶ Hope, etc. (Rom. 5:3).

     2. "We might have hope" (present active subjunctive): Not just one infusion of hope, but a constant increasing of hope. "We should be constantly having more hope."

   E. To "overflow" with hope, we must derive much encouragement from the Scriptures (Rom. 15:4). What does "encouragement" mean?
   To take someone aside to give them comfort or consolation.

How Can Scripture Encourage Us?

  I. By assuring us of God's faithfulness, which does not depend on our faithfulness to Him (Heb. 13:3-6; 1 Thess. 5:24; 2 Thess. 3:3; 1 John 1:9).

  II. By reminding us of man's fickleness—the best of saints had besetting sins which they never conquered. "All idols have clay feet." There is no such thing as "perfection," "victorious living," or "total sanctification" in this life.
    Abraham's Problem: Lying
    David's Problem: Lust
    Peter's Problem: Cowardice
    Paul's problem: Anger

Conclusion

Only biblical Christianity can give us a well-grounded and secure hope concerning the future. Western culture has reaped untold benefits from the Scriptural hope that good will triumph over evil in the end; the wicked will be punished and the righteous vindicated and rewarded; and that justice will triumph in the end.

The only alternative is the ugliness of existentialism, which has the evil triumphing over the good, the wicked set free and the righteous destroyed. Hopelessness and despair are the only things which humanism offers us.

As Christians, we know that we shall live "happily ever after." We look forward to a new earth wherein no evil shall dwell.

But the non-Christian does not have any well-grounded hopes for the future. He can look forward only to what Heb. 10:27, 29, 31; 12:29, describes.

We need a mighty Hope which enables us to face anything in this life because we know what the life to come will bring.

Chapter Seventy
Love

I. Six Crucial Questions:
   A. What is the greatest and most important thing in:
      1. The Heart? Matt. 22:35-40
      2. The Family? Eph. 5:1, 2, 25
      3. The Church? John 13:34, 35
      4. The World? John 3:16
   B. What is the most significant mark of maturity in a person, a family, or a church (1 Cor. 13:13)?
   C. What is foundational to all meaningful Christian living at home, work, or church (1 Cor. 12:31; 13:1-3)?
   D. What is more important than any other virtue in the Christian life (Col. 3:12-14)?
   E. What is the only motive for obedience which is acceptable to God (John 14:15, 21)?
   F. What enables us to escape from bitterness, anger, evil speaking, gossip, and slander (Matt. 5:44; Luke 23:34; Eph. 4:30-5:2)?

THE ANSWER IS LOVE

II. Love is the over-all emphasis of the New Testament
   A. "LOVE ONE ANOTHER" (John 13:34). This is given as a direct command no less than 55 times in the New Testament. It refers to the kind and level of relationship which should be developed and maintained by believers one to another.
   B. "FOLLOW THE WAY OF LOVE" (1 Cor. 14:1). Instead of following the way of selfishness and carnality by competing with each other and using their gifts to put down others and to elevate themselves, the Corinthian Christians were exhorted to live according to the way love would respond. When in a difficult situation with someone, ask yourself two questions:
      How would ANGER handle this person?
      How would LOVE handle this person?
      Then ask yourself: "Am I following the way of love or anger?"
   C. "DO EVERYTHING IN LOVE" (1 Cor. 16:14). Anything not done in love is not the will of God.
   D. "SERVE ONE ANOTHER IN LOVE" (Gal. 5:13). When Christian service is not carried out or done in love, such service destroys the person, family, job, and church.
   E. "BE PATIENT, BEARING WITH ONE ANOTHER IN LOVE" (Eph. 4:2). Some people are HARD to love! But we must love them nevertheless. Remember, love is "meeting someone's NEEDS without the motive of reward or personal gain." Love is not just a feeling but it implies action based on commitment.
   F "SPEAK THE TRUTH IN LOVE" (Eph. 4:15). Even when we speak to correct others, our speaking must not be in bitterness or anger. It must be in love, not just by saying it is in love, but by showing it by our attitude and actions (Prov. 12:18; 1 John 3:18, 19; Gal. 6:1).
   G. "PURSUE ... LOVE" (2 Tim. 2:22). Love doesn't just happen! It must be pursued. It must be a goal for every individual, family, and church. Since it is a command, it is a work, i.e., something you do, not just feel!

III. Before speaking or doing something to or for others, it is good to ask yourself:

Is what I am about to say loving?

Is love telling me to do this?

Note: The passage of Scripture which is given to us to answer these questions is:

1 Corinthians 13:4-7

In this passage, we are given 15 ATTITUDES and ACTIONS which reveal either the presence or absence of love.

We must examine our motives for what we do or say (2 Cor. 13:5). If we don't do this, we will never learn Christian humility.

1 CORINTHIANS 13:4-7: HOW LOVE ACTS

KJV	NAS
1. "suffereth long"	"patient"
2. "kind"	"kind'
3. "envieth not"	"is not jealous"
4. "vaunteth not itself"	"does not brag"
5. "is not puffed up"	"is not arrogant"
6. "does not behave itself unseemly"	"does not act unbecomingly"
7. "seeketh not her own"	"does not seek its own"
8. "is not easily provoked"	"is not provoked"
9. "thinketh no evil"	"doesn't take into account a wrong suffered"
10. "rejoiceth not in iniquity"	"does not rejoice in unrighteousness"
11. "rejoiceth in the truth"	"rejoiceth with the truth"
12. "beareth all things"	"bears all things"
13. "believeth all things"	"believes all things"
14. "hopeth all things"	"hopes all things"
15. "endureth all things"	"endures all things"

Basic Introduction

1. Paul is not DEFINING love by these terms. Rather, he is DESCRIBING the way love relates to people and to things in this evil world.

2. This hymn on love finds its greatest fulfillment as a wonderful description of the way Christ lived while on earth.

3. Since "God is love" (1 John 4:8), the central aspect of the image of God in us is that we should love as God loves. We were created and redeemed in order to develop love in our lives. Thus, we should major on this character quality above all other things in the Christian life.

Note: The Biblical Order in the Christian Life

DOING SHOULD
GROW OUT OF BEING

> TO DO what God wants YOU
> to do: ministry through gifts

> TO BE what GOD wants YOU
> to be: character development (LOVE)

BEING + DOING = MATURITY = LIFE MESSAGE

LOVE'S DESCRIPTION

1. "Love is PATIENT"

   A. This Greek word appears 25 times in the New Testament. It refers six times to God's being patient with us and 19 times to our being patient with each other.

   B. It is a word which never means to be patient with things (accidents, sickness, poverty, etc.) or even with God. Rather, it is a special word which means to be patient with evil, malicious people who are sources of irritations. This puts "LOVE" to the acid test. God wants you to respond to evil people the way Christ would respond. Now, the church at Corinth had a lot of "sources of irritation." But the Christians were not responding in love to one another. Instead of being "patient" with each other, there was BITTERNESS, WRATH, EVIL SPEAKING, FIGHTS, DIVISIONS, JEALOUSY, PARTY SPIRITS, HATRED, A SPIRIT OF UNFORGIVENESS, and FALSE DOCTRINES.

   C. The key to understanding what "patience" means for us is to see what it means for God. *God's patience with us reveals the nature of our patience with each other, for we are created and redeemed to bear His moral likeness.*

Illustration No. 1
   God's response to malicious sinners during Noah's day reveals what "patience" means (1 Pet. 3:20; cf. Gen. 6:3, 13, 14; 7:4).

GOD IS:
   ● Slow to punish or avenge
   ● Slow to anger
   ● Merciful in: Giving time and opportunity for repentance
                       Going the second mile
                       Enduring their maliciousness
   ● Calm and collected (self-restraint)
   ● Free of resentment, defensiveness, bitterness, evil speaking, and "striking back"

(GOD IS PATIENT TODAY WITH SINNERS: 2 Pet. 3:9)

The KEY concept in God's patience is "SLOW TO ANGER"

```
GOD IS "SLOW TO ANGER"; i.e., PATIENT
Neh. 9:17              With the rebels in the wilderness
Psa. 103:8-9           With believers
Psa. 145:8-9           With all men
Joel 2:12-13           With backsliders
Jonah 4:1-2            With the heathen
```

Illustration No. 2
   Matthew 18:21-35 reveals what it means for us to be "patient" with each other (vs. 26-27, 29-30).

WE SHOULD BE:
   ● Slow to punish or avenge
   ● Slow to anger
   ● Merciful in: Giving time and opportunity for repentance
                           Going the second mile
                           Enduring their maliciousness
   ● Calm and collected (self-restraint)
   ● Free of resentment, defensiveness, bitterness, evil speaking, and "striking back"

The KEY concept in OUR being patient with each other is: "SLOW TO ANGER."

To be patient (i.e., slow to anger) with someone who is a source of irritation:
   ● Arises out of and reveals GREAT UNDERSTANDING (Prov. 14:29). This is the key to over-coming anger in marriage. "Dwell with your wife according to understanding" (1 Peter 3:7).
   ● Makes one greater than the mighty who take a city (Prov. 16:32).
   ● Results in avoidance of arguments (Prov. 15:18)
   ● Keeps the unity of the Spirit in the bond of peace (Eph. 4:1-3).

THEREFORE:

   ● Be patient with all men: 1 Thess. 5:14

   ● Be patient with fellow Christians: Col. 3:1-17 (v. 12)

   D. How to develop the character quality of patience in your life

      1. Walk in the Spirit DAILY, for patience is a fruit of being filled with the Spirit (Gal. 5:16, 22). The presence of anger, bitterness, or impatience reveals the absence of the Spirit (James 1:19, 20).

      2. Remember, your responsibility is to love this person. You are not responsible for the sins of others (John 13:34, 35).

3. Remind yourself of the following things.
    ● You don't know all the facts. This person may deserve your pity, compassion and love rather than your anger. He may be the victim of gossip, false teaching or ignorance. It may be "that time of the month" for her. They may have a medical or mental problem. They may be the dupe of the Devil (Lk. 23:24).
    ● God puts up with your sin (Matt. 18:32-35).
    ● Everyone grows spiritually at their own rate (1 John 2:12, 13).
    ● It has taken you a long time to get where you are spiritually. Why do you expect others to grow up overnight?
4. Learn to respond to malicious people by acting according to SCRIPTURE instead of reacting in ANGER.
    ● In your heart: Forgive them at once. Do not wait for them to ask for forgiveness, as this will produce "gunny sacking" (Lk. 23:24; Eph. 4:32).
    ● With your mouth:
        1. Bless and curse not (Rom. 12:12). Thank God for them and pray for His blessing to come upon them.
        2. Speak soft words (Prov. 15:1); "words which minister grace" (Eph. 4:29).
        3. Be slow to speak (Jam. 1:19).
        4. Don't speak at all (John 19:9). You can't clap with only one hand.
        5. Don't argue (2 Tim. 2:24-26).
    ● With your resources:
    Meet their needs (Rom. 12:18-21).
    ● If they fail, don't rejoice, but pray for them and do what you can to help them (Proverbs 24:17-18; Psa. 35:11-14; cf. 2 Sam. 1:12).
5. Realize afresh the two main roots or causes for bitterness and anger, AND GIVE THESE THINGS TO GOD ONCE AGAIN.

6. Recognize that this evil person is under God's sovereign control and is God's tool to build Christ-like character within you. They can do nothing but make you a better Christian (Psa. 76:10; 2 Sam. 16:11; Rom. 5:3; Jam. 1:2-4).
    As long as you keep on loving, you can't lose.

7. Expect to suffer for doing what is right as a normal part of the Christian life (2 Tim. 3:12).

8. There is no other way to teach you this Christ-like virtue than by bringing evil, malicious people across your path. Just as tribulation is necessary to learn perseverance (Rom. 5:3), evil people are necessary to learn patience.

2. Love is KIND (v. 4)
    A. This Greek word appears 19 times in the New Testament. It is translated in the following ways:
    Good/Goodness: eight times
    Kind/Kindness: seven times
    Gentleness: one time
    Gracious: one time
    Better: one time
    Easy: one time

B. Both "patience" and "kindness" have in focus how LOVE deals with people even when they are sources of irritations by being evil and malicious. "Patience" tells us what not to do, while "kindness" tells us just what to do. "Patience" is the negative side of LOVE, while "kindness" is the positive side.

Note: God does not want you just to be patient with people. He wants your LOVE to do something to and for others. You may not have lost your temper—but were you kind?

C. What Does It Mean to Be Kind?

You are kind to someone when you are helpful, useful, and generous in meeting their basic needs in a gentle manner with no motive of personal reward.

GOD IS KIND
He provides for the basic physical needs of all men regardless of if they are evil, enemies, and unthankful (Lk. 6:35; Matt. 5:44, 45)
Note: All the blessings of God's kindness will either lead you to repentance or deepen your condemnation on the Judgment Day (Rom. 2:2-6).

He has provided for the basic spiritual needs of all men regardless of if they are evil, enemies, and unthankful (Tit. 2:1-11); Acts 17:30). Salvation's goal, purpose, and application are to be found in God's kindness (Eph. 2:7; 1 Pet. 2:3).

What "kindness" means for God is what it is supposed to mean for us, for we are to bear His moral image and likeness. We are to be the light of the world (Matt. 5:14-16).

THEREFORE
WE SHOULD BE KIND

Jesus illustrated what kindness means in the parable of the the Good Samaritan (Lk. 10:25-37).
Jesus is answering the questions: "What does it mean to love your neighbor? How are we to show or express this love? Who is my neighbor?" The Samaritan was kind because he went out of his way to be helpful in meeting the needs of someone who:
(1) was a Jew; i.e., an enemy (John 4:9).
(2) had no opportunity or means to repay him or render thanks.
Throughout the story, the Samaritan was gentle and generous while meeting the basic needs of this man.
The priest and Levite reveal that unkindness is not doing anything for someone in need: not getting involved; being so wrapped in yourself that you don't have time to be helpful to others. Scripture questions the profession of a Christian who is basically unkind toward those in need (Jam. 2:14-20; 1 John 3:14-19).
"Unkindness is also saying or doing things which hurt instead of help (Eph. 4:29).

D. How Do I Develop the Christ-like Character Quality of Kindness?
1. Walk in the Spirit daily, for kindness is a fruit of the filling of the Spirit (Gal. 5:22—KJV "gentleness," "kindness") (Eph. 5:18).
2. Develop the habit of seeking to do good works of kindness. Keep your eyes open to see people in need of help—physically or spiritually.

Special Note on Good Works

Since "works" have no place in salvation, and this is correctly emphasized, most Christians are so "grace-centered" that they are scared the moment anyone brings up good works in the Christian life. Most Christians live and think that good works have no real or important place in the Christian life. THEY ARE WRONG!

> Why did God save you? (Eph. 2:10; Tit. 2:13-14).
>
> Why did God give you the Bible? (2 Tim. 3:16-17).
>
> What should you be concerned about? (Tit. 3:8, 14).
>
> What special ministry has God given to godly women in general and to widows in particular? (1 Tim. 2:9-10; 5:9, 10; Acts 9:36-39).
>
> How can we cause people to glorify God? (Matt. 5:16; 1 Peter 2:12).
>
> What should we be encouraging one another to do? (Heb. 10:24-25)
>
> How will we be judged in terms of rewards on the Judgment Day?
>
> Will what I am about to say hurt or help that person?
>
> Am I being kind?

---

3. Don't Hang Around Unkind People, for "Bad Company Corrupts Kind Manners" (1 Cor. 15:33).

$$\frac{\text{BITTER}}{\text{CRITICAL}} = \frac{\text{SARCASTIC}}{\text{CYNICAL}} = \frac{\text{COMPLAINING}}{\text{CRUEL}}$$

3. Love is not ENVIOUS

Having seen the nature of Christian love with respect to the evil received from others, that it "suffers long," and also with respect to doing good to others, i.e., "is kind," we now come to the feeling and actions of LOVE with respect to the good possessed by others and that possessed by us.

The Apostle declares that in respect to the advantages, possessions and honor of others:

LOVE IS NOT ENVIOUS

A. The Greek word appears as a verb in the New Testament and is translated:

Envy: three times

Zealously affect: three times

Covet: two times

Desire: two times

Affect: one time

Zealous: one time

B. It also appears 17 times in its noun form and is translated:

Zeal: six times

Envy: six times

Indignation: two times

Fervent: one time

Jealousy: one time

Emulation: one time

C. The root meaning of the word signifies to be boiling or burning with envy and jealousy. What does it mean to be envious and jealous of others?
A painful or resentful awareness of an advantage enjoyed by another, joined with a desire to possess the same advantage.

D. There are three main ingredients in an envious spirit.
1. There is inward pain, depression, anger, resentment, or bitterness over the seeming betterment of another in riches, honor, or advantages which you feel is not right because they really deserve the opposite.
   Their happiness and prosperity just don't seem right to you (Esther 6:12; Acts 13:42-45).

2. There is discontent and dissatisfaction with what possessions, honor, or advantage you have. You deserve a better lot and station in life. What you do have and how people treat you just don't seem right to you. You deserve so much better (Esther 5:9-13).

3. There is a coveting for yourself of what another has and enjoys. You should be the one who is honored and enriched. What they have should have gone to you (Esther 6:12; Acts 13:42-45).

E. The poor have a special temptation to be envious of rich people, Christian or non-Christian. This, coupled with the fact that God didn't choose many rich people, but has filled His Kingdom with the poor, means that most Christians will be tempted with this sin (1 Cor. 1:26-29). Illustration: Psa. 73:2-4.

F. When young people see the prosperity of the wicked and the poverty of the righteous, they will be tempted to be envious of the wicked. Thus, Solomon warns young people of this trap (Pro. 23:17; 24:1, 19).

G. Envy and jealousy result in much wickedness (Jam. 3:16).
   Physical problems (Pro. 14:30)
   Strife (Rom. 13:13; 1 Cor. 3:3)
   Hatred (Tit. 3:3)
   Bitterness (Jam. 3:14)

H. How to overcome envy and jealousy
1. Since envy is a "work of the flesh" (Gal. 5:21), the fundamental way of dealing with envy is by "walking in the Spirit" (Gal. 5:16).
2. There is the negative work of "putting off" and "putting to death" this sin by the work of mortification (1 Pet. 2:1; Rom. 8:13). This is done by watching for its first stirrings and then immediately repenting and confessing to God. Get angry at it so you begin to notice when you fall into it or are tempted (Pro. 8:13).
3. There is the positive work of strengthening the opposite graces of the vice of envy. It is not enough to "put off" envy. You must "put on" Christ-like virtues when opposing envy.
4. By the work of mortification, you starve the fire by refusing to add more fuel.
5. By strengthening certain graces, you throw water on the fire and keep the fuel wet so that temptation does not easily ignite it.

THE VICE	OPPOSITE GRACES
Inner pain, anger, bitterness, depression, and resentment over the prosperity of another.	A rejoicing and a giving of thanks to God that He has once again shown that He is a God of mercy and grace, slow to anger and great in patience (Eph. 5:20; 1 Thess. 5:18).
Discontentment Dissatisfaction	Spiritual contentment (Phil. 4:11; 1 Tim. 6:6; Heb. 13:5-6). Giving your "rights" and "expectations" to God.
Coveting, which is idolatry (Col. 3:5)	Spiritual contentment (Phil. 4:11). Keeping eternity in view (Psa. 73:16-26), which means having your priorities in the right order and in a biblical value system.

Having seen how LOVE responds to the possessions and advantages of others, "love is not envious," the Apostle now tells us how love acts in respect of its own honor, possessions, or advantages.

In terms of outward behavior, "love does not brag." In terms of inward attitude, "love is not conceited."

The Outward Behavior of Love

4. "Love does not BOAST or BRAG and it is not ANXIOUS to show off or to impress others or to sound its own praises."
   A. The Greek work appears only once in the New Testament. Its root meaning is "to show oneself off in the presence of others."

   B. "Bragging" is always the outward sign of inward pride and conceit (Esther 5:11-12; Dan. 4:28-30).
   Note: There is often an underlying unity between envy, boasting and conceit (Esther 5:11-12).

   C. Stern warnings are given in Scripture against "boasting" and "bragging" (Pro. 27:1-2; Jam. 9:13-16).

The Inward Attitude of Love

5. "Love is not PROUD, CONCEITED, SELF-SATISFIED, or 'PUFFED UP' with a false sense of its own importance, authority, or superiority over others."
   A. The Greek word appears seven times in the New Testament and always carries an evil connotation (1 Cor. 4:6, 19; 5:2; 8:1; 13:4; Col. 2:18).

   B. The Corinthian Church was a disaster because they were "puffed up" about their knowledge (1 Cor. 8:1), their gifts (1 Cor. 4:18), and their liberality (1 Cor. 5:2). This is why Paul wrote 1 Cor. 13:1-3. The fighting and strife in this church illustrates the warnings of Scripture (Prov. 16:18; 28:25).

C. The root meaning of the word is "to blow up" or "to inflate yourself" with conceit. What is conceit?

Conceit is an overestimation of one's own importance, abilities, achievements, or authority joined with a desire to gain the applause of men. It is man-centered and does not desire or seek the secret approval of God.

D. Pride and conceit always lead to destruction.
   The Principle: Prov. 11:2; 15:25; 16:18; Jam. 4:6
   The Practice: Esther 7:1-10; Dan. 4:31-33

E. How to conquer the sins of bragging and conceit. The chief way to conquer these sins is by obtaining and retaining correct views of God, others, and yourself.

   1. Acknowledge that God is absolutely sovereign over all things. You owe everything to Him. In and of yourself, you are nothing, and can do nothing (Dan. 4:13-17, 28-37; 1 Cor. 4:7).

   2. Always esteem others as being better than yourself (Phil. 2:3, 4). Don't compare others with yourself as if you are the standard of measurement (2 Cor. 10:12). Realize there always are some areas in another wherein he is superior to you.

   3. Accept a sober and true view of yourself (Rom. 12:3).

   4. Seriously take note of the principle set forth in Matt. 23:12 (examples: Peter, David).

   5. Develop true Christian humility before God and before others (James 4:7, 10; Lk. 14:7-11).

      a. What is Christian Humility?
         Humility is the recognition that you owe everything to God and to others (1 Cor. 4:7).

      b. How do we develop Christian Humility?

         (1) We must have a servant's heart and attitude (Matt. 20:20-28; Gal. 5:13)

         (2) We must walk in the Spirit every day, for humility is a fruit of the filling of the Spirit (Gal. 5:16, 22-23).

         (3) We must keep our eyes on Christ and not on ourselves or others (Heb. 12:1-2)

Classic Commentaries on 1 Cor. 4:7

Ellicott's Commentary

"This is the explanation of why such 'puffing up' is absurd. Even if one possesses some gift or power, he has not attained it by his own excellence or power; it is the free gift of God."

Godet on 1 Corinthians

"Here is the standard indicated by the 'It is written.' For one of the fundamental truths of Scripture is that the creature possesses nothing which is not a gift of the Creator."

Richard Baxter

"All good gifts are of God; a fact which should exclude all boasting or self-satisfaction. Right views of ourselves will show that all we have of gifts or grace is not the result of personal merit, but through the boundless mercy of God (See John 3:27; James 1:17). 'He that glorieth, let him glory in the Lord.' 'Remember, therefore, that though thou be a vessel of mercy, it is the fountain that filleth thee, and not thyself. Whenever thou gloriest in thy graces, do it but as the beggar glorieth in his alms, that ascribes all to the giver; or as the patient glorieth in his cure, that ascribeth all to God and the physician; or as a condemned rebel doth glory in a pardon, which he ascribeth to the mercy of his prince.' "

Charles Hodge

"It is here assumed that every thing, whether natural or gracious, by which one man is favourably distinguished from another, is due to God; and being thus due to him and not to the possessor, is a cause of gratitude, but not of self-complacency or of self-applause. This is true even of those things which are acquired by great self-denial and exertion. Paul was as much self-formed as any man ever was, and yet he said, 'By the grace of God I am what I am.' "

John Calvin

"The poor man yields to the rich, the plebian to the noble, the servant to the master, the unlearned to the learned, and yet everyone inwardly cherishes some idea of his own superiority. Thus each flattering himself, sets up a kind of kingdom in his breast; the arrogant, to satisfy themselves, pass censure on the minds and manners of other men, and when contention arises, the full venom is displayed. Many bear about with them some measure of mildness so long as all things go smoothly and lovingly with them, but how few are there who, when stung and irritated, preserve the same tenor of moderation? For this there is no other remedy than to pluck up by the roots those most noxious pests, self-love and love of victory. This is the doctrine of Scripture. For it teaches us to remember, that the endowments which God has bestowed upon us are not our own, but His free gifts, and that those who plume themselves upon them betray their ingratitude. 'Who maketh thee to differ,' saith Paul, 'and what hast thou that thou didst not receive? Now if thou didst receive it, why dost thou glory, as if thou hadst not received it?' (1 Cor. 4:7). Then by a diligent examination of our faults, let us keep ourselves humble. Thus while nothing will remain to swell our pride, there will be much to subdue it…. The only way by which you can ever attain to true meekness is to have your heart imbued with a humble opinion of yourself and respect for others" (*Institutes* III 7:4).

"For while we maintain that none perish without deserving it, and that it is owing to the free goodness of God that some are delivered, enough has been said for the display of his glory; there is not the least occasion for our cavilling. The Supreme Disposer then makes way for his own predestination when depriving those whom he has reprobated of the communication of his light, he leaves them in blindness. Every day furnishes instances of the latter case, and many of them are set before us in Scripture. Among a hundred to whom the same discourse is delivered, twenty, perhaps, receive it with the prompt obedience of faith; the others set no value upon it, or deride, or spurn, or abominate it. If it is said that this diversity is owing to the malice and perversity of the latter, the answer is not satisfactory: for the same wickedness would possess the minds of the former, did not God in his goodness correct it. And hence we will always be entangled until we call in the aid of Paul's question, 'Who maketh thee to differ?' (1 Cor. 4:7), intimating that some excel others, not by their own virtue, but by the mere favour of God" (*Institutes* III 24:12).

Rev. D.W. Poor, D.D.

"Spiritual pride, self-sufficiency, vain-glory, assumption of superiority, are so unbecoming and absurd as to be the fit objects not only of severe rebuke, but also of ridicule; for they are contrary to a Christian's dependence on God for what he is and has."

Starke

"Whose is the fine plummage? Hast thou borrowed it? How then, supposing the wind should carry it away? Where is thy boasting then? Give then to God his own, and do not serve either thyself or the devil with thy gifts."

Reiger

"One chief characteristic of godliness is lowliness of mind, which gives to God all the praise, and counts man for nothing.—When we are willing to rend the bond of peace for the sake of aught we prize, we act not as if we had received it from the Lord whose gifts are to be appropriated in love, but as if we were at liberty to turn it all to our own selfish uses and advantage.—Where danger is greatest, there often-times presumption and self-confidence are at the height."

Huebner

"True humility springs from a sense of our absolute dependence on God. This guards from pride. With these there belongs also a clear recognition of God's greatness and glory; we must feel that God is every thing, and we are nothing. Only an exalted nature can be truly humble. How foolish our pride over advantages that we did not procure. The more gifts received from God, the greater the cause to be humble. Pride is not mere folly; it is wickedness also, because it robs God of his glory."

Having stated that true Christ-like love will not BOAST and it is not CONCEITED, the Apostle now describes Love by saying:

6. "Love does not ACT UNBECOMINGLY."
   The Greek word is a very powerful and dynamic word. It is very difficult to give a definition of the word in just a brief sentence. The following paraphrase or translation gives the meaning of the Greek.

   A. "Love does not act in ways which are not in line with what is accepted social behavior. It will not be disrespectful to superiors or scornful to inferiors. It will not be rude, belligerent, inconsiderate, tactless, impolite, ill-mannered, arrogant, willful, or stubborn. Love will not do or say anything which will bring shame or disgrace to itself or to others."

   B. The Greek word is found five times in the New Testament and is translated as follows:
      Rom. 1:27 "indecent act"
      1 Cor. 7:36 "unbecomingly"
      1 Cor. 12:23 "unseemly"
      1 Cor. 13:5 "unbecomingly"
      Rev. 16:15 "shame"

   C. The basic thrust of what Paul is trying to say is that Love will be careful to maintain a good testimony before believers and unbelievers by not doing or saying things which unnecessarily offend others (Rom. 12:17-18; 1 Cor. 9:19-23).

      Note: True Christian love will never flout Christian liberty before the weaker brethren because this would:
      1. Damage its testimony
      2. Place a stumbling block before the conscience of those weaker in the faith (Rom. 14:13-23)

   D. There is an underlying unity between conceit, boasting, and acting unbecomingly. Example: Haman (Esther 5:10-11).

PRIDE = BOASTING = Acting in an unbecoming way.

The Scriptures point out in a very practical and "down-to-earth" manner many of the ways in which we can act unbecomingly toward others. This is what the Book of Proverbs is all about and why we should read it every day (Prov. 1:1-7; 2:11).

Example: Prov. 27:14 (A loud voice in the morning)

A. How Should We Act Toward:
1. Our parents: 1:8, 9; 19:26
2. Criminals: 1:10-19
3. The Lord: 1:7; 3:5, 6
4. The poor: 3:27-28; 17:5
5. Your neighbor: 3:29-30; 14:21; 25:17
6. Your children: 13:24
7. Immoral people: 2:16-19; 7:1-27
8. Angry people: 15:1; 17:14
9. Scoffers: 9:7-9
10. A fool: 26:4-5
11. Animals: 12:10
12. Superiors over you: 25:6-7

B. Proverbs also points out the importance of certain things in this life.
1. A good name: 22:1
2. Giving your tithe to God: 3:9-10
3. Being a skilled laborer: 22:29
4. Not being a co-signer on a note: 6:1-5; 11:15; 17:18; 22:20-27
5. Making provision for your grandchildren in your will: 13:22
6. Seeking good advice: 15:22; 20:18
7. How to escape indigestion at mealtime: 15:17; 17:1
8. Wealth obtained through wisdom and labor: 3:16; 11:4
9. Why laziness is to be avoided: 6:1-11; 10:26
10. How to live long: 3:16; 4:16
11. Truth in weights and measures: 11:1; 16:11
12. Six things that God absolutely hates: 6:16-19

IN SHORT

The Scriptures teach us how to show our Love by our behavior before and to others.

"LOVE WILL NOT ACT UNBECOMINGLY."

Having stated how love reacts:
1. To evil people: "Love is patient and kind."
2. To the advantages of others: "Love is not jealous."
3. To its own advantages: "Love does not boast and is not conceited."
4. In its behavior before others: Love does not act unbecomingly."

Paul now points out that true Christ-like love will place a new motivation in the heart of the Christian.

LOVE

OUTWARD BEHAVIOR	INWARD MOTIVE
BEFORE OTHERS	BEFORE GOD
"love does not act	"love will not
unbecomingly"	seek its own"

Note: God wants us to be concerned about our motive and behavior. Both of them are important, and God has wedded them together.

7. "Love Does not SEEK ITS OWN."

A. A paraphrase of this statement of Paul will help us to grasp what he is seeking to emphasize.

"Love is not devoted to its own pleasure, profit, honor, or praise. It is not completely taken up with its own interests. It does not have an excessive concern for its own things to the exclusion of any concern for others."

B. The basic or root meaning is:

"LOVE IS NOT SELFISH"

or

"LOVE DOES NOT HAVE SELFISH MOTIVES"

Is your behavior motivated by selfish concerns?

C. What is "SELFISHNESS"?
An excessive and exclusive concern with oneself; i.e., a seeking of and concern for one's own advantage, welfare, pleasure, and well-being, without regard of others.

D. Selfishness is composed of two parts

SELFISHNESS

| I. You think, speak, and act with only yourself in mind. "I, myself, and me" is the terminal focus of your life. | II. You think, speak and act without any regard for the needs and feelings of others. Ministering to others is not the focus of your life (Ex. John 12:1-8). |

E. The crucial question which you must ask yourself to discover the terminal or main focus of your life is:

"To what is your happiness tied?"
Is your happiness tied to yourself? i.e., your: pleasure, wealth, security, getting your way, prosperity?

Is your happiness tied to your wealth, getting your way, pleasure, stock market, etc.?

F. To what should your happiness be tied?
    1. Your happiness should be tied to your holiness in two ways:

HOLINESS

I. The main focus, i.e., the terminal focus of your life should be:
   1. The Glory of God (1 Cor. 10:31; Phil. 2:21)
   2. Communion with God (Phil. 3:10)
   3. Growth in the Grace and Knowledge of Christ (2 Peter 3:18)

"GOD" must be your chief concern in your thoughts, words, and deeds.

II. The secondary focus of your life should be the welfare of others. You must focus on tying your happiness to your ministering to people (1 Cor. 10:24, 33)

We are "happy" to the degree that we are "useful" in being used by God to meet the needs of others. "Others" should be the secondary focus of your life.

G. How to conquer a selfish heart

    1. Recognize that selfishness is a part of our depraved nature inherited from Adam (Gen. 3:5-6).

    2. Humble yourself before God by admitting that selfish motives corrupt and pollute every "good thing" you do (Rom. 7:21).

    3. Get your priorities in the right order:
       Jesus First (Matt. 6:33)
       Others Second (Phil. 2:3-4)
       Yourself Last

    4. Practice self-examination of your motives (2 Cor. 13:5).

    5. Rededicate your life to Christ (Rom. 12:1-2).

    6. Learn to put the comfort and advantage of others above that of your own (Rom. 15:2-3).

    7. Hate even the slightest stirrings of selfishness in your spirit. Selfishness is the opposite of Christian love.

We have seen how true Christ-like love acts in many different situations. It is PATIENT and KIND. It does not ENVY, BOAST, or GET PUFFED UP WITH PRIDE. It is not RUDE or SELFISH.

The only way that we can experience and manifest this kind of love is through the power of the Holy Spirit, who is "the Spirit of love" (Rom. 5:5; 15:30). It is only through being filled with the Spirit that we can manifest the fruit of walking in the Spirit's power (Gal. 5:22-26).

The greatest danger we face as we study the character qualities of love is that we will slip into MORALISM.

MORALISM is extreme and undue attention paid to living a "good" life in external things. It is majoring on externals while ignoring CHRIST. It is assuming that you are acceptable to God because you are "nice," "loving," "kind," etc. The moment you become "character-centered" instead of "Christ-centered" you have fallen into MORALISM!

MORALISM	HOLINESS
A striving to be "nice," "moderate," "loving," "kind," "patient," simply because they are wonderful virtues which we should seek to obtain. This is done by self-effort and self-will.	A striving to be like Jesus. A desire to walk as HE walked (1 John 2:6) To be conformed to His image (Rom. 8:29). Looking to Jesus that His Spirit would love others through you A realization that you can't love anyone. Christ must fill you with His love (2 Cor. 5:14).

In our study of love, we are not studying a "virtue" and how to attain it. We are increasing our hungering and thirsting for Christ to fill us with His spirit of love so we can be like Jesus. We must be "Christ-centered" and not "virtue-centered." Only Christ in you can love others. You must look to Christ for Christ-like character qualities (2 Cor. 3:1-18; Col. 1:25-29; Gal. 4:19).

We must steer a straight path between MORALISM and ANTINOMIANISM. We need to follow the biblical balance of "PERFECTING HOLINESS IN THE FEAR OF GOD" (2 Cor. 7:1).

MORALISM	HOLINESS	ANTINOMIANISM
Looking only to building character qualities in your life. A striving to obtain all the good virtues. Thus while virtues are emphasized, Christ and the Holy Spirit are missing. It is "virtue-centered."	Looking to Christ to be like Him in our character. "Christ-centered character development" through a conscious dependence on Christ and the Holy Spirit. You look to Christ.	Looking only to our position "in Christ" while ignoring our duty to be conformed to the character of Christ. Usually "doctrine" and "position" are emphasized while "condition" and "character" are ignored.

BIBLICAL HOLINESS RIGHTLY UNDERSTOOD IS:
1. A test of salvation (Matt. 5:6)
2. A standard for sanctification (1 John 2:6)

Having stated that true Christ-like love is not selfishly caught up in its own things, the Apostle now says:

8. "Love is not EASILY PROVOKED."
    I. The first thing we must understand is the basic meaning of the Greek word which is translated "easily provoked."
        A. The root meaning of the word describes something as being so sharp that you easily cut yourself if you try to use it.
        B. Thus when used to describe an argument in Acts 15:39, it is translated "sharp disagreement," i.e., they were cutting each other with words.
        C. When used to describe a person, it has reference to the personality or disposition as being "sharp."

        "If you are loving, you will not have a 'sharp' disposition."

    II. Basic definition of the word. What does it mean to be "sharp"?

    You have a "sharp" disposition or personality when you are "irritable," i.e., cranky, crabby, quick or short tempered, touchy, grouchy, grumpy, quarrelsome or argumentative. It means that you are ready to explode in anger at the least provocation. It describes someone who is like a coiled rattlesnake, ready to strike at anything that moves (Prov. 14:17; 26:21; 29:22).

    III. Proverbs particularly points out the danger of a wife having a "sharp" or "irritable" disposition toward her husband. Just as husbands have special problems with being unloving (Eph. 5:25), wives have a special temptation to be "contentious" (Prov. 21:19; 25:24; 27:15).

    IV. There are several practical things you can do when you meet someone who is in an irritable disposition.
        A. Don't hang around them (Prov. 22:24-25).
        B. Beat it to the hills (Prov. 21:19; 25:24).
        C. Strive to give "gentle answers" (Pro. 15:1).
        D. Seek to understand why this person is irritable. Then correct it, if possible.
            1. Did you do something to set them off?
            2. Has someone else "made" them irritable?
            3. Is there a physical reason?
                a. lack of sleep, rest, proper food, etc.
                b. low blood sugar
                c. perioditus snapitus
                d. menopause
                e. etc.

    V. What should you do when you get in an irritable mood?
        A. Admit to God, yourself, and others that you are in a bad mood.
        B. Warn others that they aren't the problem. Ask their forgiveness ahead of time for your ugly disposition and for the sharp words you may say to them.

C. Look to Christ to be filled with the Spirit to overcome your disposition (Eph. 5:18).
D. Sit down and ask yourself:
   "Why do I feel so mean today?"
   "What's wrong with me?"
   "Why am I snapping at anyone?"
E. Possible areas to consider.
   1. Your body
      a. Proper rest, sleep, recreation, food, etc.
      b. Period, pregnancy, menopause, hormonal imbalance, etc.
      c. Glandular problems (thyroid)
   2. Your soul
      a. guilt-trip over failure
      b. controversy with God
      c. conviction of sin
      d. stress, worry, anxiety, tension, restlessness
      e. confusion over what to do
   3. Others
      a. unresolved conflicts
      b. bitterness from failed expectations and violated rights
      c. hatred arising from jealousy and covetousness.
F Once you have discovered why you are in a rotten mood:
   1. Confess it by faith (Prov. 28:13)
   2. Correct it by repentance (Prov. 28:13)
G. What if you can't figure out why you feel the way you do?
   1. Be alone. Don't be around people.
   2. Continue to look to Christ for deliverance.
      "Wait on God."
   3. Do something that will put you in a better mood and get your mind off your problems.
   4. Just hang on. Your mood will PASS!

The Apostle continues his dynamic description of HOW LOVE ACTS TOWARD PEOPLE IN THE REAL WORLD OF EVERYDAY LIVING.

Having stated that "love is not irritable" (v. 5), Paul now says that:

9. "LOVE THINKETH NO EVIL."
   I. The first problem to overcome in order to understand what Paul is saying is the translation found in the King James Version.
   "THINKETH NO EVIL"
      A. Commentaries and sermons based on the KJV have generally interpreted the Apostle as saying:
         1. "Love does not have evil or dirty thoughts. Love has a clean mind and pure thought life. The Apostle is talking about evil thoughts in your head."
         2. "Love does not see evil in the minds, hearts, and motives of others. It is not suspicious and it does not impugn evil motives to others. It always seeks to be positive and hopeful by thinking of others in the best possible light. Paul is talking about evil in others."

B. The only problem with the above interpretation is that the KJV completely mistranslates the Greek text. This is why new translations have arisen. They put God's Word in today's language and correct the mistakes the KJV translators made.

II. The proper translation of the Greek.

A. The Greek word in the text which the KJV translated "thinketh" is found 42 times in the New Testament. Paul uses the word 34 times in his epistles.

B. Its basic meaning is:

To take into account, compute, impute, calculate, count over, or to hold against.

C. Because of its basic meaning, it is used by Paul as a synonym for the forgiveness which arises out of God's act of justification. When God justifies us, He forgives us in the sense of not taking into account our sins against Him. He no longer computes, imputes, counts over, or holds against us our sins and transgressions (Rom. 4:3-6, 8-11, 22-24). It is used by Paul in this sense 16 times in his Epistles.

D. The primary focus of the word describes how and in what way God forgives us in the act of justification.

1. God views us and treats us as if we never sinned against him.

2. God forgives us:

a. freely (Rom. 3:24)

b. fully (Acts 13:39; Psa. 103:12; Isa. 38:17; Micah 7:19)

c. eternally (Heb. 10:16)

d. because of Christ (Eph. 4:32)

E. Having seen the primary focus of the Greek word in the Epistles of Paul, modern versions translate v. 5 as follows:

NASV—"Does not take into account a wrong suffered"

NIV—"It keeps no record of wrongs"

TGV—"It never reckons up her wrongs"

III. In 1 Cor. 13:5 the Apostle Paul is not talking about evil thoughts in our minds and neither is he talking about being suspicious of other people's motives. He is once again returning to the description of HOW THE LOVE OF CHRIST, THE FRUIT OF WALKING IN THE SPIRIT'S POWER, enables us to respond with Christ-like attitudes and actions toward those who wrong us. The real test of love is found in how we handle people who sin against us.

IV. In the light of the primary focus of the Greek word which Paul uses in v. 5, the following deductions are self-evident.

A. The Apostle is describing how and in what way we are to view and to treat those whom we have forgiven of their sins against us.

B. How and in what way God forgives us of our sins against Him becomes the pattern for our forgiveness (Eph. 4:32-5:2). We are to forgive others just as God forgives us.

C. We don't know how to forgive others until we have understood what it means when God forgives us. We must experience the forgiveness of God before we can truly forgive men.

D. God forgives us:

1. Freely

2. Fully

3. Eternally

4. Because of Christ

He views us and treats us as if we never sinned against Him.

In the same way, how we view and treat those whom we claim to forgive reveals whether or not we have truly forgiven them freely, fully, eternally, because of Christ.

    E. It is easy to give "cheap forgiveness," instead of our forgiveness being given:

        1. "Freely"—We want others to earn it;
           To lie in the dust before us;
           To feel our anger and punishment;
           To squirm awhile.

        2. "Fully"—We really hold back some forgiveness; we don't forgive them of everything.

        3. "Eternally"—We throw their sins in their face to remind them of how awful they are to us. We remember and hold their sins against them.

        4. "Because of Christ"—We forgive only because we have to in order to get some peace and quiet. We do it in our own strength when we feel they have suffered enough.

    F. "CHEAP FORGIVENESS" is manifested when we do not view and treat those whom we say we have forgiven as if they never sinned against us to begin with. The following things reveal that true forgiveness has not taken place.

- Bitterness
- Coldness
- Anger
- Impatience
- Irritability
- Gloominess
- Depression
- Self-pity

    G. God will not forgive us if we will not truly forgive others (Matt. 6:12-15). He knows when we are trying to give cheap forgiveness. We should not expect or ask of God that which we will not give to man.

    H. God does not take an unforgiving spirit in a Christian lightly. He will chastise such a believer (Matt. 18:21-35).

V. **HOW TO FORGIVE OTHERS**

    A. Keep in mind the difference between true and cheap forgiveness.

    B. Be honest with yourself, with God, and with others. If you can't forgive someone, say so. Don't be a hypocrite.

    C. Go to God and ask for the Spirit's power because you know that it is impossible to forgive others without it (John 15:5).

    D. Meditate on God's forgiveness in Christ. If you want His forgiveness, then you must surrender your unforgiveness and rebellious spirit to Him (Eph. 4:32).

    E. Regardless of feelings, by an act of your will, say to yourself:
        "I do forgive him freely, fully, and eternally because of Christ. I will now view him and treat him as if he never sinned against me."

    F. Go out of your way to be cheerful and kind to the person. Do something special for him or her. Show him your love by your works.

    G. When Satan brings up their sins to you, resist him in the Spirit's power and say:
        "Be gone, Satan! I have forgiven his sins. I will remember them no more. They are cast behind my back and thrown into the depths of the sea."

    H. If Satan keeps bringing up his sins to you, you should increase your deeds of kindness. "Overcome evil with good" (Rom. 12:17-21).

I. Give your rights and expectations to God and thank God for the "wrongs" which others have done to you. In this way, you can defeat Satan. Say to yourself when he reminds you of what someone did against you. "Yes, he did do that to me. Thank God! It has made me a better Christian. Praise the Lord!"

J. If a problem of bitterness still plagues you, then write out a contract in which you name the person, state their offense, give your rights and expectations to God. Forgive them freely, fully, eternally, because of Christ. Then give to God the punishment which justice demands. When you are tempted to get bitter, read over your contract and rededicate it to God.

K. "What shall we do about those people who wronged us but they don't ask for forgiveness? Do we forgive them or wait for their repentance?"

Inwardly, in terms of your own heart, forgive these people before they repent. In this way you escape a bitter and unforgiving spirit. Christ did this with those who crucified Him (Lk. 23:24). Stephen followed the example of Christ (Acts 7:60). We should do likewise (John 2:6).

L. Now we need to apply what we have learned about forgiveness. Who are the people who have:

> Hurt you?
> Offended you?
> Violated your rights?
> Failed your expectations?
> Etc.

The Apostle continues his description of love in the context of how love reacts to people who are sources of irritation.

He now describes the joy of love.

10. "Love does not rejoice in unrighteousness."
11. "Love rejoices with the truth."

I. The apostle first states in the negative in what true Christ-like love will not rejoice.
   A. True love will not rejoice when anyone falls into sin, not even when its enemies stumble and fall.
      1. Love is grieved at every occasion of sin (Eph. 4:30).
      2. It has pity and compassion for those who fall (Lk. 19:41, 42).
      3. We should never seek to be vindicated by the fall of our enemies into sin. When we greedily rejoice to hear that our enemies' sins have become public, we reveal that we have not obeyed Rom. 12:17-21. We are still seeking vengeance instead of leaving vengeance to God alone.

   B. True love does not rejoice when God judges and inflicts punishment on our enemies because of their sins (Prov. 24:17-18).
      1. The Great Day of Judgment is when our vindication will be accomplished by God Himself (Rom. 8:18-21).
      2. Sometimes He vindicates His servants in this life by inflicting punishment on their enemies (1 Tim. 5:24; 2 Sam. 4:8).

3. When God will punish our enemies is not our business or responsibility. Desiring the downfall of our enemies and rejoicing when we see it reveals a vengeful spirit.

A vengeful spirit is the inner desire to see one's enemies punished; this desire flows out of personal malice, hate, and bitter resentment.

4. Our duty is to follow Christ's command in Lk. 6:27-28.
   LOVE - KINDNESS - BLESSING - PRAYER

5. We should grieve for our enemies when they fall (Psa. 35:1-14; 2 Sam. 1:12; 18:33).

II. Secondly, the Apostle states in the positive, in what true love rejoices.
   "Love rejoices in the truth."
   A. The word "truth" is used in its ethical sense of "righteousness according to God's Law." It means "Right or True Living" (1 Jn. 1:6; 3 Jn. 3, 4).

   B. True love will rejoice when it sees areas of "truth" (i.e., righteousness) even in its enemies.

   C. If we are grieved to see any good character qualities in our enemies and happy when we hear of their sins, we are condemned in Scripture as having hatred and bitterness in our hearts.

III. How to Obey 1 Corinthians 13:6
   A. Recognize that this is beyond your ability.
   B. Be filled with the Spirit.
   C. Give your rights and expectations to God in order to root out bitterness.
   D. Accept the fact that your enemies are under God's sovereign rule.
   E. Understand that your enemies can only do you good for they are part of God's plan for your character development.
   F. Follow the steps of action set forth by Christ in Lk. 6:27-28.
      Love them: Their person
      Be kind to them: Their needs
      Bless them: Their spiritual state
      Pray for them: Their well-being

We now come to the climax of Paul's hymn of love. After giving us a list of negative things which true Christ-like love will not be or do, Paul concludes his poem with four positive things which form the characteristics or attributes of love.

12. "LOVE COVERS ALL THINGS."
   A. The traditional translation "bears all things" is not correct.
   B. The root meaning of the Greek word refers to protecting the reputation of others by covering over, veiling, hiding, excusing, keeping secret, etc. the sins of others as much as possible.
   C. Thus it is translated as follows:
      NIV: "It always protects"
      WEY: "She can overlook faults"
      Moffatt: "Always slow to expose"

D. Paul is still talking about how love responds to injuries received from others. In this context, he is saying that true love will give you the ability to suffer in silence when evil curses and accusations are hurled at you. Instead of loudly complaining and publicly broadcasting everything anyone does against you, you should:
1. Cover over as many sins as possible in the spirit of 1 Pet. 4:8.
2. Suffer in silence as much as is possible (Jn. 21:12-14).
3. When you cannot do Nos. 1 and 2 anymore, then go to them according to Matt. 18:15-17 in the spirit of Gal. 6:1.
4. If you must "tell it to the Church" then speak of the person and his sins objectively with as little reference to personal injuries as possible.

THE POINT IS IN REFERENCE TO PERSONAL INJURIES, LOVE WILL BE SLOW TO ANGER, SLOW TO AVENGE, AND SLOW TO EXPOSE.

13. The reason love can be slow to expose the sins of others is that "love" believes all things."
    A. Love is not quick to expose people publicly because inwardly it does not want to be suspicious of others, always seeing evil motives in everyone. Love tries hard to be optimistic about people and always look at them in the best possible light.
    B. This is not to say that love is naive or gullible. It is simply saying that a loving person wants to believe the best about people because he does not rejoice in sin but rejoices in righteousness.

14. True love can believe in people because it "hopes all things" about them.
    A. True love has no room for pessimism or despair.
    B. We can go on trusting people when we have hope that they will repent, hope that God will deal with them, hope that they will turn, hope that the conflict is due to misunderstanding, hope that the problem will not last for long, but it shall pass away soon.

15. Because love has hope, it can endure all kinds of insults and injuries. Paul now says, "Love bears or endures all things."
    A. The word "endure" is a military word which refers to a soldier's ability to resist the temptation to flee from the attack of the enemy and his ability to endure whatever is thrown against him.
    B. It is hope in God and hope in the future under the sovereignty of God that produces perseverance in the midst of persecution (Rom. 12:12; 1 Thess. 1:3).
    C. Hope is the light in the eyes of a martyr which even death cannot really destroy.

Conclusion

This last picture of love points us to Christ. He treats us in these ways. Only God's Spirit can help us to love others. It is beyond our natural strength. Let us love one another and thus fulfill the law of Christ. It is by this that all men shall know that we are His disciples.

Chapter Seventy-One

The Traditional Church vs. The New Testament Church

The following chart gives us a contrast between a traditional church and the church described in the New Testament.

Issue	Traditional Church	Biblical Church
1. Concept of church	Organization, business, club, building, etc.	Body of Christ, Kingdom of Christ, the Fellowship of the Holy Spirit
2. Believers	"Members" in a club	Disciples, ministers, brothers and sisters in the family of God
3. Involvement	Spectators, passive	Participants active in ministry
4. Ultimate authority	Tradition, constitution, etc.	The Law of Christ for His church, as set forth in the Scriptures
5. Head	The people, the board, the pastor	Jesus Christ alone is Head of the Church
6. Government	Democracy (OF and BY the people, etc.)	Theocracy (of God through the Word and Spirit)
7. Selection of	Election by "popular" vote	Appointment by eldership, recognition by people
8. Leadership	Any willing person voted in by popular vote.	Only those who meet the biblical qualifications

Issue	Traditional Church	Biblical Church
9. Basic ministry	Conducting services (Sunday, weddings, funerals, etc.)	Equipping the saints for the work of ministry, a lay seminary
10. Place of ministry	Church building at stated times	Everywhere at all times
11. Primary concern	Building, numbers, money raised	People—individuals, families, congregation
12. Objective	Build up the club	Edify the Body
13. Determining factor	What the people want (peace at any price)	What the Bible says the people NEED
14. Great goal	More club members	Develop Spirit-filled disciples who minister by the gifts of the Spirit
15. Purpose of assembling	Evangelism, pep talk, socializing, etc.	Equip the saints, stimulate to love and good works
16. Material presented	Emotion-centered (thrills & chills)	Knowledge-centered (the mind of Christ)
17. Emphasis	Meetings, decisions, moneys, etc.	God/individuals/families, quality, quality, quality
18. Resources to meet needs	Human ingenuity, available funds	Bible, prayer, Holy Spirit, faith
19. Programs	What we are USED to, feel comfortable with and demands no sacrifice	Whatever the Word indicates is needed to fulfill the mission of the church
20. Procedure to meet needs	Beg, plead, cajole and manipulate for needs	Trust God to raise up people if He wants the program to continue
21. Finances	Needs dealt with only available funds	Step out in faith and begin to meet needs, trusting God for the funds
22. Ultimate concern	What people think, "My church," "My power"	Exalt Christ and obey His Word regardless of what others think or say

Issue	Traditional Church	Biblical Church
23. End result	Rev. 3:1b "A name that you are alive, but you are dead"	A Spirit-filled church where individuals mature and families function as God intended
24. Attitude toward change	Stubborn, closed-minded tradition above Scripture	Submissive to Word, willing to change anything
25. Glory given to:	Man and his works; the "preacher"	God and His works

Summary

The 25 contrasts above reveal how far we have drifted from the purity and simplicity of New Testament Christianity. We must return to the Scriptures to reform ourselves and our churches according to the Word of God.

Chapter Seventy-Two

How to Change a Traditional Church

This is a series of lectures given at a pastors conference on the doctrine of the church. It focuses on what church leaders can do to conform their church more closely to the pattern set forth in the New Testament.

PART I

I. The Essential Role of Pastors
  A. Pastors are the gifts of Christ to His church (Eph. 4:11-12) They are sent by Christ to proclaim the Word of God in all its fullness (Acts 20:27).
  B. They have the duty of fulfilling the threefold office of:
    1. PROPHET: Proclaiming the truth as God's representative.
    2. PRIEST: Interceding on behalf of their people and leading them into worship.
    3. KING: Guiding, protecting, disciplining and providing for their people.
  C. Pastors are the "change agents" in their church, not "caretakers of tradition." You should be:

Scouts	Guides	Motivators
Pathfinders	Leaders	Instigators
Ice-breakers	Discoverers	Shock-troops

II. The Immediate Goals of the Ministry
  A. The world's goals: numbers, buildings and money.
  B. The New Testament goals: faith, hope and love (see Col. 1:3-5; 1 Thess. 1:3; 2 Thess. 1:3-4).

III. The Ultimate Goal of the Ministry
  A. To lead your people to God.
  B. This means that your focus in all you do is to lead people into the very presence of God; to encounter God; to be in awe of God; to revere Him; to exalt Him; to love Him; to obey Him joyfully; to serve Him all their days.
  C. You must strive to bring broken sinners to the cross of Christ; to the throne of grace to receive mercy and forgiveness.
  D. You must take people beyond yourself, your sermons, the rituals, the symbols and forms of the church to the reality of God, or all is in vain!
  E. In other words, you must seek to lead your people to be the true worshipers of God, who worship Him in spirit and in truth (John 4:23-24).
  F. Join your worship service to the worship going on in Heaven itself! True worship transcends all earthly limitations and blends together all the worship of men and angels into one vast hymn of praise to the Most High God (Heb. 12:18-24).
    Note: Do you seek the presence and power of God in your church service? If God died,

would your people realize it or would the service go on as usual? Would they miss God?

IV. The Centrality of Worship
A. The importance of being God-centered instead of being man-centered touches all of life: Private, Family and Church.
B. Your purpose in life, the reason for your existence, is to glorify God.
C. Everything in your church service should be viewed as an aspect of worship and have as its conscious aim to lead people into the presence of the Living God. Do you view the offering as a "necessary evil" or as an act of worship (Phil. 4:18)?

V. Hindrances to Worship
A. Manmade traditions (Mk. 7:1-13)
The seven last words of a church, "We never did it that way before."
1. God's frozen people need to become His Chosen people.
2. We must chip the barnacles off the ship of the church or it will sink! It is dirty, hard, painful work—but you must do it.
B. The "Centrality of Preaching" syndrome:
1. This always ends up as the centrality of the Preacher!
2. The only reason for going to church is to hear the sermon. Everything before or after the sermon is only a necessary evil.
a. The call to worship
b. The singing of hymns
c. The offering
Instead of viewing the hearing of the Word as one aspect of worship, worship is viewed only as a preamble to the sermon!
3. There is no "Body life" or congregational participation. People are only spectators who watch the pastor exercise his gifts.
4. Instead of coming to church to worship God, to meet Him "face to face," people come to hear the sermon. They think this is their whole duty to God and man. They come late to church because as long as they get there in time for the sermon, the other parts of the service do not matter!
5. The ministry is reduced to only one function: Preaching! Pastors are called "Preachers," as if they only worked three hours a week!
6. It opens the door to hero worship and cultic following.
7. The success of a church service is measured not by whether God manifested His presence and power, but by the sermon. The success of the sermon is not judged by the degree to which faith, hope and love are increased in the hearts of the people (1 Tim. 1:5), but by unbiblical standards:
a. Liberty, eloquence, style, etc.
b. The degree to which it inflicts pain in the hearers
c. The degree to which people are entertained and laugh
8. The Greek word "to preach" is used in the New Testament to refer to an activity usually done outside of the church. With only one possible exception, "preaching" is the work of missionaries and evangelists as they seek to convert the heathen. It is not used to describe what pastors do inside the church to those who are already converted.
9. The New Testament words which describe what pastors do in the church are teach, exhort, comfort, rebuke, disciple, equip, edify, etc.

10. The over-emphasis on "preaching" has led to an under-emphasis on teaching. The only thing people hear is "come down to the altar and get saved." They are never taught after they are caught! But is it the preaching or the teaching that is important? The goal is to usher people into the presence of God that they may fall down before Him in wonder, awe and praise.

VI. How to Deepen the Worship Experience in Your Church Without Blowing It Up
   A. The need of the Pastor to be the leader. If you are not—someone else will!
   B. A Pastor who is one step ahead of his people is a good leader. If he is three steps ahead he will be a martyr. If he is lagging behind his people, he will not be around long.
   C. Move SLOWLY — SLOWLY — SLOWLY
      Move CAREFULLY — CAREFULLY — CAREFULLY
   D. Identify the natural leaders in your church. Tell them that you have been reading some interesting books and you want them to look at them too and tell you what they think.
      Body Life (Stedman)
      The Measure of a Church (Getz)
      The Seven Last Words of the Church (Neighbour)
      All Originality Makes a Dull Church (Baumann)
      The Church That Dared to Change (Tucker)
      The Church at the End of the 20th Century (Schaeffer)
      Worship: It's Not Just Sunday Morning (Morey)
   E. Begin teaching on the biblical doctrine of the church and its worship.
   F. Where to begin? Wednesday evening prayer meeting! Why?
      1. The weakest link in the chain.
      2. Only a few people come out. They are the "spiritual" people, the core of the church, the workers, Sunday School teachers, etc.
      3. In most traditional churches, the Wednesday evening prayer meeting is:

         | Boring | Another Sermon |
         | Dull | A Spectator Sport |
         | Static | Not Biblical |

      4. People are ready to make it better.
      5. The prayer meeting is more easily changed. But when you change it, revitalize it, energize it, you have changed, revitalized and energized all the leaders in your church. They will begin to seek a change in the Sunday morning or evening service.
   G. How to Begin?
      1. Do not change anything at the beginning.
      2. Teach them how to pray. Use:
         Spurgeon: *Effectual Prayer*
         A.J. Gordon: *Life of George Muller*
         John Bunyan: *Prayer*
      3. Stress the following points:
         a. No private devotions in the prayer meeting. Thus, no "I" or "me" prayers.
         b. Pray as a body with one voice, i.e. "we" prayers.
         c. When one person prays for a request, there is no need to repeat it as if people are waiting for their turn to pray. We must join in prayer with whoever is praying.
         d. Address God directly. Do not mention Him as a "third party."
         e. Learn to praise God, to worship Him, to exalt Him together, etc.

f. Pray for specific things—not vague generalities. Your prayer requests should be measurable and verifiable. You must be accountable for them. So, do not pray for things God never promised to give us through prayer. example: holiness, humility, patience, etc.

g. Begin to give people the opportunity to "share" what their needs are, what the Lord has recently done in their lives, etc. Stress participation.

h. Break up into small groups after a time of praise. This gives everyone the chance to share their needs and pray. Put them in a circle so they can see each others' faces.

i. Phase out any "preaching" or "teaching" to give more time for praise, sharing and prayer.

j. Vary the themes for the night:

Personal needs	Missions night
Family needs	Evangelism night
Church needs	National needs

k. After the prayer meeting has become dynamic, focus attention on Sunday evening. Begin to introduce things after you have taught the concept from Scripture.
   ● Instead of two or three hymns, with only stanzas one, two and four, introduce a praise time with the people participating.
   ● Give people the opportunity to testify.

l. Sunday morning is the "sacred cow" because of all the manmade traditions. Be careful and move slowly.

m. Teach on:
   ● Why do you come to church? What is supposed to happen there?
   ● How do you prepare for worship? Entering into God's presence.

n. Develop the gifts God has placed in the church. Use them or lose them!

o. Train godly men to take traditional roles.
   examples: Leading Worship
              Group leaders
              etc.

DELEGATE - DELEGATE

Summary

Your task is to turn men from themselves and you, to look unto Jesus as the author and perfector of their faith.

Part II

Discussion Guide on Worship

Introduction

1. Are you the "change agent" or the "caretaker" in your church?

2. Do you view yourself as a "prophet/priest/king," or only as a member, deacon, elder or the "preacher"?

3. Are your constantly striving to reform your church according to the Word of God, or are you content to let things remain as they are?

4. Are you concerned about the kind of worship you are experiencing?

5. What different kinds of worship services have you experienced?

6. Do you desire to deepen your own worship experience?

7. Have would you rate your present worship service?

God-centered	Christ-centered	preacher-centered
boring	exciting	Bible-centered
passive	active	entertainment-centered
spectator	necessary evils	program-centered
participant	dynamic	sermon-centered
static	law-centered	grace-centered

8. Do you really care about the doctrines, polity, practices, programs, piety and power of the apostolic Church, or are human traditions sufficient for you?

9. Are you moving your church forward, backward or nowhere?

10. Do you consciously come to church to be in the presence of the Living God and to worship Him, or do you come for some other reason?

I. Worship Is All of Life

1. Does "worship" only refer to what happens on Sundays at 11 a.m. in church, or is worship to embrace all of life?
2. Has the secular/sacred dichotomy helped or hindered biblical religion? In what ways?
3. Do you view all of life as religion, or religion only as a "slice of the pie" of life?
4. If someone does not live all of life to the glory of God, how will this affect his private worship, family worship and church worship?
5. If people do not view worship as being all of life, what are their chances of making church worship a success?

II. Private Worship

1. How important is it for people to worship God privately?
2. Is a quick reading of the Bible and a short prayer all there is to private worship?
3. Can we have a regular Quiet Time and yet never worship God?
4. Is it possible that our emphasis on the "what" of Quiet Time has neglected the "Whom" of it?

III. Family Worship

1. Do you practice family worship?
2. Do your children delight in family worship?
3. How would you rate the following types of family worship?
   a. A chapter of the Bible is read with no comment or discussion. The father closes with a quick prayer. There is no attempt to worship God or to meet in His presence. The children do not share or ask questions. They have to "endure" the boring session.
   b. Each child is treated according to his age and maturity. Young children get Bible stories and act them out in plays or do a simple handicraft. Older children are read biographies, doctrinal books and Christian classics. High school students should read and discuss biographies, books on Christian sexuality, courtship and the Christian world-and-life view, such as books by Schaeffer.
4. Have wrong views of Sunday School harmed family worship? How?

IV. Public Worship

1. Does it matter what we do in public worship?
2. Has the pastor changed the worship service since you became a member? If so, why and how? If not, why not?
3. Have you experienced the presence of God in a worship service? Do you consciously seek it?
4. What is the difference between internal and external worship?
5. What is hypocritical worship? Relate your own experience.
6. Is "form" or "freedom" to dominate your worship service?
7. How did the Catholics and the Reformers answer this issue?
8. Explain the difference between the essentials and non-essentials of worship.
9. Did New Testament worship include the following things? Explain.

congregational	dynamic
charismatic	God-centered
kerygmatic	form and freedom
open to the Holy Spirit	physical as well as mental
edifying to all by all	Christ-glorifying

10. On the Day of Judgment, you will be held accountable for how you worshiped God in all of life. Are you ready?

Summary

The concept of the Church in the New Testament is that the church is supposed to be "alive" with the zeal and power of the Holy Spirit. It was never intended to be "dead" and boring. Its worship is to be glorious and a fulfilling experience of coming into the presence of the Living God. It is not to be reduced to entertainment. Our churches need to catch on fire once again with the vision of what a church and its worship should be. The Father is seeking such to worship Him.

Chapter Seventy-Three

The Biblical Doctrine of Worship

Introduction

Worshiping God in public is a skill that must be learned. While regeneration implants the desire to worship in the heart, it does not automatically teach us how to express that desire in public worship. But where do we find out how to worship?

Some people think that what is to be done in worship should be determined by tradition, common sense, or reason. Others think that their feelings should be the deciding factor. And still others assume that whatever "works" is fine.

There is only one place where we can learn what is to done in worship: The Scriptures alone can teach us how to worship God. God constantly told His people that if they want to worship Him they must do so in accordance with what He has revealed in His Word (Deut. 12:32).

We studied worship in great depth when our church began. In a few years we had more than doubled in size, which meant that the majority of people never heard the series. Because of this, we had drifted away from some of the principles of worship that were originally established.

Just as a ship must be dry-docked in order to chip off the barnacles, a church must from time to time review what it is doing in worship to correct any problems that have arisen.

Note: This study should be used in conjunction with the book, *Worship: It's Not Just Sunday Morning*.

I. Prelude

When the pianist or organist begins to play the prelude, this is the signal for everyone to stop talking, to get seated quickly and quietly and to prepare their hearts to worship God. In other words, shut up, sit down, close your eyes, collect your thoughts, ask God to fill you with His Spirit, ask for the service to blessed and for the pastor to be anointed from on High. Be still before the Lord (Psa. 46:10). Fix your heart to worship and sing unto the Lord (Psa. 57:7-11). Seek the filling of the Spirit (Eph. 5:18-20). If you do not prepare your heart for worship, how do you expect to be blessed?

II. Prayer

Public prayer is not the same as private prayer.

First, in private prayer it is proper to use personal pronouns such as I, me, my and mine (example: Psa. 6), but in public prayer this is not proper. Since you are leading the people of God in prayer, you should use such plural pronouns as we, us and our (Psa. 95:1-2; 124; Acts 4:24-31). This allows others to enter into your prayer and pray as you pray. It is interesting to note that all the prayers in the book of Revelation are in the plural (example: Rev. 19:6-7).

Second, in private prayer it is perfectly proper to bring up your own personal needs and requests, but this would be totally inappropriate for the public worship of God. Public prayer should address the common needs of all the people of Christ. Such things as a personal confession of sin should not have a place in public worship. You should have already confessed your sins to the Lord before you entered into the public worship of God.

III. Praise

In public worship, you should be praying and singing to God and not just about God (Psa. 30:4). You are entering into His presence when you worship (Psa. 100). The implications are many.

First, you must seek to avoid all distractions. Public worship is not the time for announcements, prayer requests, confession of sins, jokes or laughter. Requests for songs or prayers should not be unduly loud or raucous. Children are not allowed to talk, walk around, go to the bathroom or make noises during the worship service. Since they sit quietly in school five days a week, they can sit quietly in church.

Second, public worship is not a "hymn sing." Do not request a hymn or song just because you like it. Choose those hymns and songs which address the Lord directly and are conducive to a spirit of worship. Hymns which focus on man instead of God should be avoided. Songs which disturb the spirit of worship should be avoided.

Third, let there be a mixture of songs, hymns and psalms in the public worship of God (Eph. 5:19-20). But since many modern hymns are man-centered and hence not very "worshipful," it is only natural that the Psalms and Scripture songs which address God directly should comprise the bulk of material for worship.

Fourth, there should be prayer as well as praise. The prayers should be "worshipful" and not "give me" type prayers.

Fifth, public worship should be cut off before it becomes dull or boring. If it is concluded at the right time, it will always leave you wishing for more. If it drags on and on, you will feel relieved when it stops. You should sit down wanting more of it, not less.

Sixth, the leader of the worship service must keep in mind the nature and needs of ALL who are present. Since there are unconverted people as well as converted, young believers as well as mature saints, children as well as adults, he must be able to sense when the majority of people are ready to sit down.

Here is where those mature saints who are able to worship God for hours at a time need to be understanding. They are perfectly free to pray and worship God privately at home for as many hours as they desire. But they must not expect public worship to satisfy this desire.

Most people are not capable or spiritually mature enough to worship God for over an hour. We wish that this were not the case. But this fact must be taken into account when deciding how long the worship service should last.

To meet the needs of those who are spiritually ready for more prayer, you could have a regular Wednesday prayer meeting and a "half-night" of prayer once a month.

IV. Participation

If someone is truly converted, he will naturally enter into public worship. It will not be forced or unnatural to him. This holds true for children and young people as well as for adults. The Holy Spirit within them will lead them to worship the Lord.

If you do not participate in public worship, you are probably not saved. This also holds true for children and young people as well as for adults. If you daydream, sleep, look around at people, scribble on paper or do anything other than worship the Living God, you had better "wake up and smell the coffee" because you may be on your way to Hell!

God calls all mankind to worship Him (Psa. 33:8; 66:1-4). Your race, rank, age and sex do not matter (Psa. 148:1, 11-13). All men are to worship the King!

Special Note On Children

Since God calls children to worship Him (Psa. 148:12), He especially commands parents to train their children to worship the Lord (Eph. 6:4:). Children are to be trained in the art of worship at every level:

1. Children should view all of life as worship. They should be praying and singing unto the Lord everywhere throughout the day. Parents must create a theistic environment for their children, in which they live and move and have their being in God. If you train them correctly, they will automatically sing to the Lord when they are happy or sad (James 5:13). How thrilling to hear your children singing unto the Lord!

2. Children should participate in private worship. They need to trained how to read the Bible and pray on their own.

3. Children should participate in family worship. Family devotions are not to be limited to the mom or dad reading from the Bible with no participation from the children allowed. Have your children read, sing and act out biblical stories.

4. Children should participate in public worship. If you have trained your children to view all of life as worship and have taught them to participate in private and family worship they will naturally feel free to enter into public worship. It will be as natural for them to sing and pray in public as it is to breathe. In other words, it is unnatural if a child in a Christian home does not desire to participate in public worship. If a child does not naturally feel free to participate in worship, either the parents have failed somewhere to train their children properly, or the child is unconverted.

5. This explains why so many teenagers do not participate in worship. They do not pray or sing in public because they do not pray or sing in private. If you want your children to worship God when teenagers, you had better start training them for this while they are still children.

6. This also explains why some adults do not "feel" that children should be allowed to participate in public worship. Despite the fact that there is not a single verse in the Bible that forbids children from participating in public worship, they somehow "feel" it is not right. Maybe their parents never trained them to worship God. Maybe they never worshiped God when they were children. Maybe they are jealous or resentful of children who worship God because their children do not participate at all. Who knows from where such "feelings" come?

7. But the Bible is not against children at all. It has a lot to say about children. When the apostles discouraged children from coming to Christ, He rebuked them (Matt. 19:13-15). Children listened to Jesus preach, believed in Him and were saved (Matt. 14:21; 15:38: 18:1-6). Children can receive the gift of the Holy Spirit just like adults (Acts 2:39).

8. If you have followed Deut. 6:7 in training your children, they will naturally desire to participate in public worship. But does this mean that they can do whatever they want in worship? Of course not! We must avoid all extreme positions:

    Extreme No. 1: "Children cannot do anything in worship." This position, in addition to being totally without biblical support, would discourage children from actively participating in worship later on. The dead and lifeless traditional church worship service shows where this kind of idea leads.

Extreme No. 2: "Children can do anything in worship." This would lead to confusion in the worship service and cannot be tolerated. Children should not participate because it is "cute." They need to taught, not stopped.

Does this mean that we want the children to "take over" the worship service? Of course not! What it does mean is that we must channel our children's enthusiasm into proper ways of worship. Parents must decide in what ways they want their children to participate while controlling the situation.

9. Parents whose children and teenagers want to participate in worship must recognize that it will take time to teach them how to do this properly. At first they will make some natural mistakes. But how happy are those parents whose kids want to worship God! It is better to have this problem than to have a son or daughter who does not worship at all! After all, it is easier to drive a moving car than one that is parked!

A child may like a certain song and sing it at home. When he sees adults in church asking for the songs they love, he will naturally ask for his favorite song. It will take a while for him to understand that he must not ask for it every week.

This is where parents must be very careful. If they handle it the right way, their child will learn how to worship God properly. On the other hand, if they handle it the wrong way, they will kill his desire to worship. The goal is to see your children worshiping the true God. Anything that stops them from doing this is evil.

10. Mature Christians will understand this and allow children all the time they need to "grow" into proper worship. After all, the goal is to see them worshiping, not to stop them from worshiping.

If a child is doing in church what he does at home, then his worship is valid. Yes, just like the adults around him, his motives may not be right some of the time. Yet, what adult would want to be told to shut up and sit down! Do nothing to discourage little ones from worshiping Christ. They are the Church of tomorrow!

Chapter Seventy-Four
Discipleship Groups

One of the most important concepts in the New Testament concerning the nature and function of the local Church is the essential place that small groups have in the overall program of the Church.

"Small groups" or "house churches" or "discipleship groups" are not to be viewed as being a luxury which is optional. But, rather, your participation in a small group is absolutely essential for your growth and maturity as a Christian.

Let us examine the place and function of small groups in the New Testament and in history.

I. The Biblical Basis
  A. The example of the New Testament Church (Acts 2:46, 47)
  B. The theological basis in the New Testament
    1. We are called to Discipleship.
    2. Discipleship encompasses four activities.

DISCIPLESHIP	
1. To become a disciple of Christ (Matt. 11:28-30)	3. To make other disciples for Christ (Matt. 28:19, 20)
2. After conversion, to disciple yourself continuously (John 8:31)	4. After conversion, to disciple one another continuously (Col. 3:16, etc.)

    3. God has created the local Church as the context and means of discipleship (Matt. 16:18; 18:15-17).
    4. The way the local Church fulfills its God-given function is to provide the motivation, atmosphere, place, time and knowledge needed for the believers to fulfill their New Testament responsibilities to themselves, the Church and to the world.
    5. The Church does this along the lines of the four activities of discipleship.
      A. "To Become a Disciple of Christ"
        1. Motivation for personal salvation
        2. Personal counseling that leads you to salvation
      B. "To Disciple Yourself"
        1. Motivation for personal discipleship
        2. Training in discipleship
        3. Programs that provide the atmosphere, time and place for discipleship
      C. "To Make Disciples for Christ"
        1. Motivation for evangelism
        2. Training for evangelism
        3. Programs that provide the occasion, place, time and atmosphere for evangelism

D. "To Disciple One Another"

    1. Motivation for mutual discipleship.

    2. Training in discipling others.

    3. Programs which supply the place, time and atmosphere for discipleship.

6. The traditional Church has provided the place and time for the pastor and Sunday School teachers to evangelize and to disciple the congregation, but it has failed to provide the place or time for mutual discipleship. Only a small group program can enable the believers to fulfill their biblical responsibility for mutual discipleship.

7. Dynamic growth through conversions is a benefit of small groups. The groups feed into the church as the church equips the groups to do the work of ministry (Eph. 4:11-12).

II. Small Groups in Scripture and History

A. Christ and His "discipleship group," called the Apostles (Mark 3:14). The Church was born out of this small discipleship group.

B. The early church in the New Testament (Acts 2:46).

The Total Program of the Church	
CORPORATE ASSEMBLING: "In the Temple"	SMALL GROUPS: "In Houses"

C. Small Groups in Church History
    1. The Christian conquest of the Roman Empire was primarily through small groups.
    2. The Dark Ages saw knowledge survive in small groups.
    3. The Reformation advanced through small groups.
    4. The Great Evangelical Revivals always produced small groups.
    5. Christians in Communist countries exist only in small groups.
    6. Revival stirrings throughout the Church today is resulting in small groups.
    7. The Future?

III. Conclusions Drawn

A. To develop a New Testament Church today, we should meet in small groups as well as in corporate assembly.

B. To cause a mighty reformation and a revival of evangelical religion in the world today, we must return to the tried and true method of small groups.

C. This is God's way.

SMALL GROUPS	CORPORATE MEETINGS
Worship	Worship
Testimony (Give)	Testimony (Hear)
Prayer (Speak)	Prayer (Hear)
Bible study	Vital learning experience
Dialogue	Monologue
Service	Edification (General)
Revival	Equipping the Saints by the Pastors
Edification (Personal)	
Maturity (Faith, Hope, Love)	
"Community" or "Family Feelings"	
Spiritual Gifts	
Discovery	
Exercise	
Evangelism	
Discipling one another	

Conclusion

The small group setting provides the place and time for the people of God to do the work of ministry in evangelism and mutual discipleship. The importance of the small group cannot be over-emphasized.

Chapter Seventy-Five
One-Anothering

The phrase "one another" is a translation of the Greek word αλληλων. It is found 58 times in the New Testament. Of these 58 times, 40 of them are found in the writings of the Apostle Paul. The concept of the Church which this word develops is what is called "Body life." The following study develops the responsibility we have to each other as Christians.

What does this tell you about the importance of the phrase, "one another?" _____
_____

1. The first and foundational "one-anothering" to which Christ calls you is to _____
_____

(John 13:34-35; 15:12; Rom. 13:8; 1 Thess. 3:12; 4:9-10; 1 Pet. 1:22; 4:8; 1 John 3:11; 3:23; 4:7, 11; 2 John 5)

Give a definition of Christian "love." _____
_____
_____

Is love a "feeling" or something else? _____
_____

Have you ever felt "loved" by fellow Christians? _____

Explain the experience. _____
_____

How can you develop Christ-like love to others? _____
_____
_____

Does 1 Cor. 13 describe your Church experience? _____

Explain. _____
_____
_____

If you do not "love" one another, will the world ever stop and notice your testimony? (John 13:34, 35)

_____

What things in society, in your Church and in you hinder you from obeying the Scripture to "love" one another?

_____

_____

How can you overcome these hindrances? _____

_____

2. "So we who are many, are one body in Christ and individually _____

_____ " (Rom. 12:5).

The local Church is pictured in Scripture in terms of the _____

_____ (Rom. 12:5).

How many times is the word "Body" used to describe the Church in 1 Cor. 12:12-27?

_____

In 1 Cor. 12:12-27, what does "members" mean? _____

_____

What are some of Paul's main points in 1 Cor. 12:12-27? _____

_____

How does 1 Cor. 12:12-27 relate to 1 Cor. 12:1-11? _____

_____

The way you became part of the "Body" was by the _____

_____ (1 Cor. 12:13).

Have you ever felt that you were a living "member" of a real "Body" of believers? _____

Explain. _____

How does American individualism affect being a "member"? _____

_____

_____

What in your personality or background could hinder you from functioning as a full and true "member of the Body"?

_____

_____

How can you overcome these hindrances to obeying the Scriptural directive to be "members of one another"?

_____

_____

3. In brotherly love, we must be _____

_____ (Rom. 12:10).

"In many Churches today, Christians are not devoted to one another." Is this true? _____

Explain _____

_____

Being devoted to one another arises out of a special kind of love. What kind of love is this? (Rom. 12:10)

_____

This "brotherly love" arises out of the experience or feeling that you are a member of

_____ (1 Pet. 4:17).

As a member of the "family of God" we are all brothers and sisters. The term "brothers" is found approximately 230 times in the New Testament. What does this fact mean to you?

_____

_____

Have you ever felt that you were a "brother" or experienced a "family feeling" in a Church? _____

Explain. _____

Other translations of Rom. 12:10 indicate that believers are to show their love and devotion by being affectionate to one another. In the culture of the New Testament, how did believers show their affection to each other? (Rom. 16:16; 1 Cor. 16:20; 2 Cor. 13:12; 1 Pet. 5:14)

_____

_____

How can you express your affection for fellow Christians in the context of modern society?

_____

_____

Are you a "devoted family member" to others in the Church? _____

What things are holding you back from obeying Christ in this area of your life?

_____

_____

How can you overcome your hang-ups? _____

_____

4. Once we are devoted to one another, we will naturally _____ for one another (James 5:16b).

Do you pray for the other members of the Body? _____

Why or why not? _____

Do you think that anyone is regularly praying for you? _____

Explain. _____

_____

Perhaps you do not know how to pray for others. There are two ways to find out how to pray for one another. First, study Paul's prayers for others with attention to the requests for which he prayed. Read through and then discuss the prayer requests in Eph. 1:15-19; Eph. 3:14-19; Col. 1:9-12; and 2 Thess. 1:11-12.

As a group, stop right now and share with each other your prayer requests. Covenant to pray for each other every day.

Each week check each other's requests. What do you expect will happen to you and the other members of your group?

_____

_____

_____

Have you ever felt that someone really cared about you enough to pray for you daily? _____

Explain. _____

_____

Since, according to 1 Pet. 2:5, you are a priest and a minister who is supposed to exercise your spiritual gifts, do you feel it is important to have others pray for you?_____

Explain. _____

_____

5. Once you are convinced that someone loves you and is so devoted to you in brotherly

love that he or she prays for you, you will be willing to _____ (James 5:16a).

Does James 5:16 mean to describe in detail your sins? _____

What does it mean? _____

_____

Does the Bible plainly tell us the sins of biblical characters? _____

If you are burdened with a sin which is causing you problems, do you think that the prayers of others will help you? _____

Explain. _____

_____

Have you ever trusted another Christian to the degree that you actually confessed your

sins to him or her? _____

Did it help? _____ Explain. _____

_____

Is James 5:16 a command or is it an optional activity? _____

_____

What things in society, the Church and in your background could keep you from obeying God's Word in this area of your life?

_____

Do you think that your group will develop enough Christian maturity for you and others to open up and ask for prayer concerning besetting sins? _____

Explain. _____

_____

_____

6. Once we confess our sins to each other, we can _____

_____ (Heb. 3:13; 10:24-25).

To exhort someone means to encourage them to go on in the Christian life.

Has anyone ever sought to encourage you? _____

Explain. _____

_____

Have you ever made a point to encourage someone in the things of God? _____

Explain. _____

_____

In what ways do you want others to encourage (exhort) you? _____

_____

What could hinder you from receiving exhortations? _____

_____

What can prevent you from going to others to encourage them?

_____

How can you overcome these things and obey Christ's directive to you?

_____

7. When your relationship to your brothers and sisters is on the level of communication and fellowship that the Bible describes as the normal Christian Body life, you can even

_____ (Rom. 15:14; Col. 1:28; 1 Thess. 5:14; 2 Thess. 3:15).

When a brother or sister falls into sin or is losing the battle with sin, we must go to them and admonish them. To admonish is to correct someone by word.

Has anyone cared enough about your Christian life that they admonished you? _____

Explain. _____

_____

Have you gone to others and admonished them? _____

Explain. _____

_____

How do you want others to admonish you? _____

_____

How will you admonish others? _____

What would result in the Church if believers lovingly admonished each other?

_____

_____

8. When believers are experiencing normal Body life, they begin to _____
(1 Thess. 5:11; Rom. 14:19; 15:2).

Not only are we to build up (edify) one another, but we are to seek to edify _____

_____ (Eph. 4:12-13).

In small groups or in the worship service, one rule or principle which should guide us is

_____ (1 Cor. 14:26).

Have you experienced edification? _____

Describe your experience. _____

_____

Have you ever gone out of your way to edify another Christian? _____

Explain what you did _____

_____

9. One way to edify one another is to _____
(Col. 3:16; Heb. 5:11-14).

Does the Bible assume that all Christians should become teachers? _____
(Heb. 5:11-14).

Having learned the truth, what is our responsibility? _____

_____ (Tit. 2:1).

Since you must teach others, this implies that you will _____

_____ (2 Tim. 2:15).

Has anyone ever cared enough for you that they took time to teach you? _____

Explain. _____

_____

Have you ever taught others? _____

What in society, the Church or in you would hinder your obedience in this area?

_____

_____

Do you think that in an informal small group you will be able to teach others? _____

Explain. _____

_____

10. By teaching one another, we _____ (Gal. 5:13).

Do you look upon yourself as a "servant" to your fellow believers? _____

What did Jesus teach? _____

_____ (John 13:1-17).

Discuss 1 Pet. 4:10-11._____

_____

11. One way to serve one another is to _____
(1 Pet. 4:9; Matt. 25:34-40).

Do you enjoy opening your home to others? _____

Explain. _____

_____

When was the last time you had fellow Christians over to your home? _____

What in society, the Church or in you could hinder your obeying the Lord Jesus, who commands you to show hospitality?

_____

_____

12. When you show hospitality to someone, you are _____
_____ (Rom. 12:10b).

Showing honor for others requires sacrifice. Describe some of your personal experiences when you were shown hospitality and what it meant to you.

_____

_____

13. Discuss each of the following Scriptures in terms of what they command and in terms of your personal experience with each "one-anothering" activity.

Eph. 5:21 _____

1 Pet. 5:5 _____

Gal. 6:2 _____

1 Cor. 12:25 _____

Eph. 4:2 _____

Eph. 4:32 _____

Col. 3:13 _____

Rom. 15:5 _____

Rom. 15:7 _____

14. We are also told not to do certain things "one to another."
Discuss each of the following passages:

Rom. 14:13 _____

Gal. 5:15, 26 _____

Col. 3:9 _____

James 4:11; 5:9 _____

Conclusion

As a Christian, a vital part of your growth in grace depends upon your experiencing "Body life," i.e., the "one-anothering" which the New Testament commands all Christians to practice in the context of the local Church.

"One-anothering" is the basis of the orthodoxy of community which is one of the signs of a New Testament Church. Your Church experience must result in rich and deep interdependent relationships with fellow Christians. In this way, it will be by our love, manifested one to the other, that the world will know that we are Christ's disciples.

Chapter Seventy-Six

A Discipleship Program for Women

Introduction
In Titus 2:1, the focus of the teaching ministry of the local church is set forth.

"You must teach those doctrines which will promote spiritual health" (Literal Greek).

In the New Testament, "sound" doctrine refers to those doctrines which foster spiritual growth and well-being in the individual, the family, the church and the nation.

The Greek word translated as "sound" should be translated "health" for this is the meaning of the word.

Note: If this preaching guide determined all sermons, it would put an end to all useless and "novel" preaching.

The Problem
In order to fulfill their responsibility, the elders seek to disciple those under their care. But while the elders can personally and privately meet with the men in the congregation, what do they do with the women in the church?

Two Present Solutions
Solution No. 1—The women are ignored. Only the men receive personal discipling. Women are left to fend for themselves, except for public sermons on their role in the home.

Solution No. 2—The women are discipled personally and privately. This results in destroying marriage harmony and promoting moral impurity. Christian common sense revolts against this practice.

MUST WE CHOOSE ONE OF THESE?   IS THERE ANOTHER OPTION?

The Biblical Solution
The doctrine of the sufficiency of Scripture means that God has given us solutions to the problems we face in life. We will find them in His Word, the guidebook for all of life (2 Pet. 1:3).

God's solution to the problem is found in Titus 2:3-5.

God calls every mature Christian woman to be personally and privately involved in discipling the younger women in the church. On the Day of Judgment, God will hold every Christian woman responsible to be vitally involved in the discipleship program of the local church. You should be discipling or being discipled.

Notice the grammatical structure of Titus 2:3-5:

1. To Be   Four main character (v. 2) qualifications
   The Elders   The Mature

2. To teach   Their active ministry
   Are to Teach   Women (v. 4)
   (From v. 1)

3. To train   Seven subjects in
                    the discipleship
                    program for younger women

Thomas Tayler, *Titus*, p. 265.
Hendriksen, W., *Titus*, p. 365.

1) The Qualifications for This Ministry
   a) You must be a
      i) This can be translated: "elder woman," i.e., "mature woman."
      ii) Its primary meaning is not chronologically old but spiritually mature. They cannot be a new or immature believer (cf. 1 Tim. 3:6; 4:12).
      iii) Up until the end of the fourth century these women had a quasi-official position in the church. They were a vital part of the official discipleship program of the early church (*Vincent Word Studies*, p. 257).
   b) You must be reverent in your behavior.
      i) The Greek word means to be and act as a priest does when speaking or acting in the temple as part of worship. It means to be reverent about the people, places and things of God; not irreverent, superficial or giddy.
      ii) In its technical sense, it may also point to these women having a quasi-official position in the Church (*Vincent Word Studies*, p. 341).
      iii) These "women-disciplers" were viewed by the early church as "fellow-laborers in the Gospel" (Phil. 4:2-3). Euodia and Syntyche were the "Verna Birkeys" of the early church.
   c) You must not be a slanderous woman.
      i) A "slanderous woman" is one who manifests a critical spirit by harboring an unforgiving and vengeful attitude toward others. She is known for her gossipy and biting tongue.
      ii) The positive quality is that you must be a positive, forgiving and uncritical person who tries to think and to speak good of others.
   d) You must not be an alcoholic.
      i) You must manifest self-control.
      ii) You cannot be an alcoholic, foodoholic, workaholic, etc.

2) The Call to Be a Teacher in This Ministry
   a) The elders are to teach the mature women so that these women can become:

   "Teachers of those things which produce good people,
                        good homes,
                        good churches
                        and good nations."

b) God calls you to teach (Titus 2:3; cf. Heb. 5:12-14).

c) The degree of involvement depends on your situation (single, married, widow, etc.).

3) The Curriculum of this Ministry

a) These women-disciplers are to train or to school the younger women.

b) This implies a personal tutoring or training of the younger women. It means more than verbal speaking (Fairbairn, p. 273).

c) Since the Greek word is in the infinitive form, this ministry is a life-long calling.

d) Paul mentions seven basic subjects which comprise the curriculum of the discipleship program for training younger women.

e) The resource materials for teaching this curriculum are to be drawn from:

   i) The Bible

   ii) Christian books and seminars

   iii) Your experience

f) Thus you are to:

   i) Theoretical: Share what you learn from your study of the Scriptures, Christian books and seminar materials.

   ii) Practical: Draw from your personal experience illustrations of biblical principles and practical ways to implement them.

g) The Seven Subjects in the Curriculum

   i) How to love your husband by meeting his needs as a man.

   ii) How to love your children by meeting their needs.

   iii) How to be sensible and to make good judgments.

   iv) How to maintain and promote moral purity.

   v) How to be a successful homemaker.

   vi) How to demonstrate kindness to others (good works).

   vii) How to develop a submissive spirit to one's husband.

4) What Will Result if Husbands and Wives Obey God's Call to Discipleship? (The husband by releasing and encouraging his wife in this ministry and by the wife getting involved in it.)

Personal Growth	Marriage Harmony
Successful Families	Moral Purity
Right Attitudes	Happy Children
Good Works	Etc.

In other words:

"The Word of God will not be blasphemed," but people will see these things and glorify God (Titus 2:5; cf. Matt. 5:16).

Summary

Women do not have to "go it alone" in the church. God has provided a program in which they can be nurtured by one another. If the Church had kept this program going we would not be faced with the feminist rebellion today. It is not true that the only options open for Christian women are "all or nothing" when it comes to ministry.

Appendix

Women Elders in the Early Church

It is regrettable that the modern controversy over women holding church offices is structured in such a way that women are faced with two extreme positions. Either they are refused any office or position in the church or they are made the "Pastor." Neither position does justice to all the Scripture passages involved, and both ignore the dynamic solution which the Apostolic Church developed to answer this same problem.

The Apostolic Church was very creative in its approach to church offices. As different needs arose, they would set up an appropriate office or position in the church to handle the problem. For example, in Acts 6:1-6 the office or position of Deacon was created to deal with the Church's charitable work among the poor. By the time of the Epistles, this position had become a permanent part of church government (Phil. 1:1) and the responsibilities and qualifications were set forth (1 Tim. 3:8-13).

The Early Church was thus dynamic and not static in its approach to church offices. This dynamic quality has been expressed today in the 21st Century church where such positions as "Senior Pastor," "Minister of Education," "Assistant Pastor," "Youth Pastor," "Minister of Music," "Treasurer," "Board Member," etc. have been created to fulfill various cultural needs.

Although there is no biblical precedent or warrant for such offices as "Board of Trustees," yet, because the government requires such a position, churches have never felt any problem in electing individuals to such a position. Obviously, no biblical warrant is needed in such situations.

The Church's dynamic approach to positions of honor and ministry enabled it to transcend all cultural boundaries. While being careful to maintain such supra-cultural permanent offices as Elder and Deacon, the Church can set up culturally conditioned positions as a valid way to relate to every culture and civilization.

The Early Church recognized many different offices which no longer exist in modern churches. The Didache, one of the earliest Christian writings, refers to such offices as apostle and prophet (11:3-13:7) as well as bishops (elders) and deacons (15:1-2). Later, other offices such as exorcist, precentor, catechist, etc. were developed as required (see Schaff, *History of the Christian Church*, Vol. II, p. 131f).

While the Bible does mention the offices of Apostle, Prophet and Evangelist (Eph. 4:11) and possibly a host of other offices (1 Cor. 12:28-29), since no provision was made in Scripture for their permanence by the setting forth of the requirements and responsibilities of such offices, they gradually died out (see Schaff, ibid., I, pp. 484-491).

This is not to say that as the need arises, such offices cannot be revived from time to time. Calvin felt that Luther was an "Apostle" in this sense (*Institutes of the Christian Religion*, IV, III, 4).

Although most churches no longer officially recognize "Apostles," "Prophets" and "Evangelists," they are still given to the Church today in its "gifted" theologians, apologists, evangelists, missionaries and church planters, Bible teachers, etc. (Schaff, Vol. I, p. 489).

Among the offices of the Early Church was that of "widow" or "woman elder." Several things need to be spelled out about this office.

First, this office or position is described in 1 Timothy 5:9-13 in terms of the congregation electing qualified widows to a position of honor and ministry. These special widows were "put on the roll" or elected to a position and were later ordained to it by the laying on of hands (Alford, *The Greek Testament*, III, p. 347).

The requirements for joining this order of special widows were of a spiritual nature and paralleled those for male elders (1 Tim. 3:1-7). That Paul is not speaking of widows in general but a special group within such a class can hardly be doubted because the church never demanded such spiritual qualifications from the merely poor and destitute before giving them aid.

Ellicott comments:

"The instructions in this passage are so definite, so precise, that it is impossible not to assume in the days of Timothy and of Paul, in some, if not in all the great churches, the existence of an official band of workers, consisting of widows, most carefully selected from the congregation ... (they) were a distinct order."

Ellicott's Commentary, Vol. VIII, p. 202

This special order of women clearly existed as part of the Apostolic Church, and even the heathen made reference to them (J.B. Lightfoot, *Apostolic Fathers*, II, 2, p. 322). That 1 Timothy 5:9-13 is describing this order is the virtually universal opinion of commentators both old and new: Alford, Balsamon, Chrysostom, Conybere and Howson, De Wette, Ellicott, Fritzsch, Grotius, Lock, Lightfoot, Michaels, Mosheim, Meyer, A.T. Robertson, Sadler, Scott, Vincent, Weisinger, Zonarrs, etc.

This order of widows in the Early Church paralleled the "Mothers of the Synagogue" who occupied such a place in intertestamental Judaism (see Holtzman, *Pastoral Briefe*, p. 241).

When we turn to the lexicographical evidence under the word "widow" we find that Lampe, Moulton and Milligan, Bauer, Arndt and Gingrich, etc. all refer to a special order of widows who occupied a special position in the Early Church.

Second, these women should not be viewed as deaconesses or even "head Deaconesses." This would be "quite a mistake" according to Lightfoot (*Apostolic Fathers*, II, 2, p. 322) and would not fit the facts of the text of Scripture or church history according to Alford (III, p. 347).

Paul has already given the qualification for deaconesses in 1 Timothy 3:11. The qualifications for "widow" in 1 Timothy 5:9-13 are more closely paralleled to those required of male elder (3:1-7). The "widows" and deaconesses are always spoken of as two distinct bodies in Scripture and church history. The "widows" sat in the second row behind the male elders, who sat on the first row, while the deacons and deaconesses sat behind the widows (Alford, III, p. 347).

Third, these women functioned in a truly presbyterial capacity. They had charge not only of the other widows but of all the women in the church. They were not "exercising authority over men" (1 Tim. 2:12). They were discipling the women (Tit. 2:4).

In Titus 2:3-5, Paul tells Titus to teach the *presbutidas* (i.e., women elders) to teach the younger women. That he was not simply saying that old age was all that was necessary is clear from the fact that these women teachers had to meet spiritual qualification (v. 3). The subjects in which they were to instruct the other women required spiritual maturity (vs. 4-5). Thus while these women were "older" in age, it is their being spiritually mature that is in view.

This is why Paul says that these women must be *hieroprespestata* (v. 3). This word means according to Vincent,

"... becoming those who are engaged in sacred service. The meaning is the more striking if, as there is reason to believe, the presbutidas represented a quasi-official position in the church" (*Word Studies in the New Testament*, IV, p. 341).

As Moulton and Milligan point out:

"It is sometimes thought that the *presbutidas* of Titus 2:3 ... are the members of a priestly or organized class in view of the *hierprepes* which follows" (p. 533).

Given the distinction between the sexes in the first century, that there arose a need for women elders to counsel and instruct the women in the congregation is no surprise. While Paul tells Titus to teach by verbal instruction (Greek: *lalew*) the women elders, they are to disciple the younger women personally. It would not have been appropriate for Titus to do so.

The women elders were under the authority of the male elders who had oversight over the entire congregation. Just as the deaconic came to include women who could minister to the women in those physical areas where the male deacons could not, the presbytery or eldership came to include women who could minister to other women in spiritual and domestic areas where the male elders could not.

These women elders instructed new female converts and even baptized them (see *Lange's Commentary,* Vol. II, p. 59 on 1 Tim. 5:9).

The following comments from various scholars are given to establish the fact that the existence of women elders in the Early Church has been noted for many years and is not something recently "invented" by feminist scholars.

We then conclude that these "widows" were a distinct and most honorable order, whose duties, presbyteral rather than deaconic, apparently consisted in the exercise of superintendence over and in the ministry of counsel and consolation to, the younger women (*Ellicott's Commentary,* VIII, p. 203).

Such widows, called presbyteresses, seem to have the same relation toward their sex as the presbyters toward the men (*Lange's Commentary,* Vol. II, p. 58).

They supervised the female members in much the same way as the elders were responsible for the men (Scott, *The Pastoral Epistles,* p. 57).

They corresponded in office for their own sex in some measure to the presbyters, sat unveiled in the assemblies in a separate place, by the Presbyters and had a kind of supervision over their own sex (Alford, *The Greek Testament,* Vol. III, p. 347).

"An order of widows is referred to whose duties apparently consisted in the exercise of superintendence over ... the younger women, whose office in fact was, so to say, presbyteral rather than deaconic. The external evidence for the existence ... of such a body, even in earliest times, is so fully satisfactory and so completely in harmony with the internal evidence supplied by 1 Tim. 5:10, e.g., that on the whole we should adopt this view. That the widows here were church officials, who to command respect, must have been foremost in the performance of the duties for which women are looked up to."
(Sadler, *Colossians, Thessalonians and Timothy,* p. 236-237)

Fourth, the documents of the Early Church clearly speak of an order of women elders or disciplers who had a ministry in the church and even a special seat of honor in the congregation.

"The Fathers ... to the fourth (century), recognized a class known as presbyteresses 'aged women' (Tit. 2:3), who had oversight of the female members and a separate seat in the congregation" (Vincent, *Word Studies in the New Testament,* Vol. IV, p. 257).

Stahlin in *Theological Dictionary of the New Testament,* Vol. IX, p. 464f, points out that it is clear that in the Early Church there existed an order of women who ministered on a spiritual level to the other women. It is impossible to reduce their ministry to that of the deaconic.

In Ignatius' Letter to the Symrneans (XIII, 1), he mentions "the virgins who are called widows." While Lightfoot's contention that the order of widows was not primarily made up of unmarried virgins is well taken, yet, it is still clear that some unmarried women were allowed to join the order if they met the spiritual qualifications.

Just as it was no longer thought necessary for men to be married and to be the father of children to be qualified to be an elder, even so it developed that spiritually mature unmarried women could join the female presbytery.

When Polycarp wrote his Letter to the Philippians, he stated the qualifications for becoming a "widow," i.e., woman elder (IV), as well as those for deacons, deaconesses (V) and male elders (VI). The context is clearly dealing with church offices.

Other references to this order have been found in Hermas Vis. II.4; Clem. Hom. XI. 30; Tert. de Pudis 13; Apost. Constitutions VI, 17, 4; Test. Domini. 1.23 and among the heathen, Lucian De Mort. Perezr. 12.

It was not until the Council of Laodicea (A.D. 344) that the order of women elders was officially abolished.

"The appointment of the so-called female elders of presidents shall not henceforth take place in the church" (literal translation of Canon II).

The Canon reveals that certain women were "elders" or "presidents" in the church up to that time. This is the same council that forbade the "laity" from observing the love feast (Canon 28) and in forbidding "lay" intrusions into "clergy" business. It was a council which did much to strengthen the grip of priestcraft on the church and to overturn the last elements of the priesthood of the believer which still survived from Apostolic times.

Fifth, perhaps a dynamic overview of the order's evolution would be helpful at this point.

The Apostolic Church from the very beginning felt a strong responsibility to minister to the poor and destitute in society. Thus there was an emphasis on the care of destitute widows and orphans (Jas. 1:27).

As more of the widows who were receiving financial aid from the Church became Christians, it was probably felt that since they were receiving aid from the church, they should be assigned some work to do in the church.

Those women who were interested in helping with the distribution of aid became involved with the deacons. At first, they were "assistants" to the deacons. But, eventually, they were recognized as deaconesses and the care of destitute women and children was given to them while the male deacons took care of the destitute men and supervised the entire deaconic.

Other women were more spiritually qualified to help the male elders first as "assistants" and then as presbyteresses. The care of the women was given into their hands. They did all the "personal" counseling and discipling needed. Eventually their position became so honorable that spiritually mature younger or unmarried women desired to be involved in discipling other women as well.

When the deaconic was first set up, only seven men were chosen and the qualifications were quite brief (Acts 6:3). As time progressed, the requirements and scope of the deaconic developed beyond its original purpose (1 Tim. 3:8-13).

When the order of widows was first set up, there were age requirements. But as they developed from being "widows" to presbyteresses, such original requirements were dropped. A comparison of 1 Timothy 5:9-10 and Titus 2:3 results in a list of spiritual qualifications for this office and in Titus 2:4-5, the Apostle Paul gives a sevenfold curriculum of instruction.

For several centuries the office of woman elder was fulfilled without disturbing the male's headship in the home and church. All believers were personally discipled and instructed.

It was only the rise of clergyism or priestcraft that led to the extinction of this most noble and biblical office.

Sixth, since we know that God intended for the offices of elder and deacon to continue in the church throughout all ages and cultures—because He placed in Scripture the qualifications and responsibilities of those offices—is it not also true that the office of woman elder is likewise provided for?

In 1 Timothy 5:9-19 and Titus 2:3-5, we find the qualifications and responsibilities for "widow" or *"presbutidas."* Evidently, God intended that elderesses as well as deaconesses should continue in the church throughout the present age.

It is interesting to note that the "widows" in Colonial American Churches were organized as a special group to minister to the women in the churches and in the community. It was such a position of honor and ministry that many widows refused to remarry.

Conclusion

We have a biblical and apostolic solution to the present dilemma of female leadership in the church. It is a third way which avoids feminism and chauvinism at the same time. Given the doctrine of the sufficiency of Scripture, it only stands to reason that God would have made provision in Scripture for the discipling of Christian women. If this biblical program would have been carried out in obedience for the last 1,900 years, we would not have the feminist issue today.

Chapter Seventy-Seven
Head Coverings

Introduction

It is our desire to give a practical exposition of one of the most difficult portions of the New Testament. It has been many years since any significant evangelical labor has been expended on the head-covering issue. Since this practice is largely confined to Catholic or Anabaptist denominations, most evangelicals have never thought through their own position on the subject.

In years past, there has been very little interaction between Anabaptist groups and evangelical churches, but this is changing. Due to several popular family-life seminars, evangelicals and Anabaptists find themselves sitting together. This has led to a natural curiosity on the part of both groups. Evangelicals ask, "Why do your women wear those little caps?" and the Anabaptists ask, "Why don't your women wear head coverings?"

It is in this context of mutual love and respect that we now put forth why evangelical women are not required to wear head coverings. We do this to fulfill the royal mandate found in 1 Peter 3:15, "Be prepared to give a reasonable reply to those who ask you about the hope you harbor in your heart, but do so with humility and respect."

This study is not intended to be an attack on any group but, rather, a practical exposition of the evangelical position on head coverings.

Exegetical Considerations

The first step in exegeting the passage under study is to set forth its literary context, for one of the most fundamental hermeneutical rules is that we must interpret a passage in the light of its context.

As we approach 1 Cor. 11:4-16, the context of this passage becomes crucial. The evangelical position states that the Apostle Paul recommends head coverings as an application of the general principle of the believer's responsibility to conform to the standards of decency, respectability and morality in the culture in which he or she lives. They are to do this in order to preach the Gospel without unnecessary hindrances or offenses to the general populace.

On the other hand, the Anabaptists' position is that Paul commands head coverings as an absolute rule because it is the sign of submission. Thus, head coverings are to be worn in all cultures regardless of that culture's standards of decency and morality.

To the evangelical, Paul is simply recommending that the Corinthians conform themselves to the Corinthian standards of decency and morality. To the Anabaptist, Paul is stating an absolute law which must be obeyed even in cultures where the head coverings imply indecency and immorality. For example, in Germany men wore a head covering while engaged in worship in order to show reverence and respect before God's presence.[1]

To the evangelical, Paul would have written to them that men should wear a head covering, for this would conform to the then existing German standards of decency, morality and respectability. For the Anabaptist, male German Christians would have to be bareheaded, and thus be stigmatized by their culture as being immodest and disrespectful.

With these brief descriptions of both positions, let us lay the text before us.

Since the original Greek does not have the chapter divisions that are present in the English text, we will omit chapter and verse divisions in order to obtain a feel for the literary context, theme and thrust of the passage under study. Please stop and read 1 Cor. 10:32-11:16 for the context.

The Context

In terms of the immediate context, before Paul takes up the subject of head coverings, he lays before the Corinthians his heart's desire that they should follow his example by conforming themselves to the customs of the ethnic group in whose community they live.

Perhaps a paraphrase of 1 Cor. 10:32-11:1 would help to bring out Paul's introduction to his discussion on head coverings:

"Do not create unnecessary stumbling blocks or hindrances (to the free preaching of the Gospel) among Jews, Greeks or even Christians. I conform myself to the social customs of whatever ethnic or national group that I am seeking to evangelize. I do this because I am not selfish. I can reach more people for Christ by my adopting their customs than by my hanging on to my cultural background. So then, you should follow my example in conforming yourselves to the customs of the society in which you live. Remember, even Christ adopted our customs in order to avoid any unnecessary hindrances. Follow me as I follow Christ."

From the context, it is clear that Paul's concern as he approached the issue of head coverings was that of social conformity to cultural customs for the sake of the Gospel. In 1 Cor. 10:32-11:1, the divine principle of rule is set forth. Then in 1 Cor. 11:2-16, Paul applies this principle to the Corinthians in the light of their non-compliance with this very basic principle of the Christian life.

Having stated this principle which he is going to apply, Paul wisely begins by praising them before he chides them. We will paraphrase here and elsewhere to bring out the force of the original.

"I would like to thank you for remembering me personally and for holding firm to the things which I taught you" (v. 2). After his brief "thank you," Paul sets forth a basic theological concept which would provide the common ground between them. Thus, he first begins with what they all agree on and then he proceeds to the area of disagreement.

"Now, one of the things I taught you is that Christ is the 'head' of every man, the husband is the 'head' of his wife and God (the Father) is the 'head' of Christ."

Although Christ as God the Son is not in any way inferior to God the Father in terms of being, essence, glory, nature or person, yet, for the purposes of executing the plan of salvation, there is a voluntary subordination of the Son to the Father. God the Son as "Christ," i.e., the Messiah, the Servant of the Lord, looked to the Father for all things.

In the same way, although women are not inferior to men in any way, for the purposes of marriage harmony, God has ordained that the husband shall be the "head" of the wife. Just as there is a voluntary functional subordination of Christ to the Father, so there is a voluntary functional subordination of the wife to the husband.

A problem in the Corinthian church had arisen because the women had misunderstood Paul's teaching that "in Christ there is neither male nor female" (Gal. 3:28). Paul did teach that women were not inferior to men; but he was speaking in terms of their nature and person. He was not denying a functional subordination which was pragmatically necessary to maintain marriage harmony. Thus he skillfully shows that just as both equality and subordination exist in the divine family of the Trinity, both things can and should exist in the human family as well. It is not either equality or subordination but both equality and subordination. Paul's position is a third way which escapes the women's liberation position and the chauvinistic sexist positions at the same time.

Having clarified his position on equality and subordination in the Divine and human family, Paul now applies the principle of cultural adaptation for the sake of the Gospel in vs. 4-6. Several exegetical observations should be pointed out.

Paul is clearly referring to the attire of men and women when they are personally engaged in taking part in public worship. He envisions both the man and the woman as publicly praying or prophesying. This is so clear that nearly all commentators agree.[2] This leads us to several observations.

A. There is nothing in the text to indicate what a man or woman is to wear outside of the public assembly.

B. To state that a woman should wear a covering at all times means that no man can wear a covering at any time. Since some of the Anabaptists have their women wear caps at all times, they are not consistent, for their men wear hats much of the time.

C. Any deviation from verse four makes any obedience to verse five hypocritical and selective. To gloss over verse four and to dogmatize on verse five reveals faulty exegesis as well as sexist application.

D. It must also be pointed out that since the early church thought of itself as a Body and not a building, it was not entering a "church" building that required the presence or absence of a head-covering. Paul limits his discussion to those who are "up front," i.e., those who are actually taking an active and public role in praying or prophesying.

First, any putting off or on of a head covering merely because one enters a building reveals a faulty concept of the biblical doctrine of the church. To be consistent, the only time you could observe this rule on head coverings is when the people of God meet in small groups or in the assembly and when you are standing up to pray or prophesy publicly before others.

Second, where did the custom of head coverings being put off or on when engaged in public praying or prophesying originate? What are the origins of this practice? The issue as discussed by Paul assumed that the Corinthians knew of the practice. Their problem was non-compliance and not ignorance.

Paul referred to a bald head as "public disgrace." What "public" did he have in mind? Who thought that men with a head covering and women without a head covering when engaged in public praying or prophesying were disgraceful or disrespectful? Did it come from the Bible of their day, the Old Testament? Is there, in the Old Testament, any examples, commands or precepts that it is wrong for a man to pray or prophesy with his head covered or for a woman to do so without her head covered? NO! Indeed, the High Priest, on the most holy day, covered his head with a miter in order to go into the Holy of Holies before the presence of God! There is no Old Testament practice to which Paul would possibly be referring. The practice did not originate in God's Word. This leads us to the following conclusions:

A. The head covering practice was not a Scriptural issue or problem. Paul never once quoted the O.T. or said, "It is written" in reference to the practice of head coverings. There are no O.T. laws to which Paul could appeal.

B. The practice of head coverings cannot be a moral law, for all moral laws were revealed in the Scriptures, and the Jews were forbidden to look elsewhere for any more.

C. The head covering practice was not a part of the essence of worship. If it were, it would have been revealed in the O.T.

D. Thus, while the functional subordination of women was taught in the O.T., the practice of head coverings was not needed to illustrate or support it. Thus, the practice of head coverings is not essential to the concept of subordination. Secondly, did it come from Jewish culture? Did the Jews of Paul's day observe the custom he described to the Corinthians? Answer: NO! According to overwhelming evidence, the Jews practiced exactly the opposite. Jewish men wore a covering and the women went without a covering.[3]

Dr. J.B. Lightfoot comments:

"It was the custom of the Jews that they prayed not, unless first their heads were veiled and that for this reason—that by this rite they might show themselves reverent and ashamed before God and unworthy with an open face to behold Him."[4]

Even T. Edwards admits:

"Among the Jews the men veiled their faces in prayer. The Tallith dates back to the time of Christ and probably earlier" (*Handbook to the Bible*, p. 194).[5]

The Corinthian church was clearly Gentile in composition and origin (1 Cor. 6:9-10). They had little contact with Jewish culture. Even given this fact, it is still remarkable that Paul would abandon his Jewish customs. The only rational explanation of his action must point to his fierce desire to become all things to all men. He stated this desire in 1 Cor. 9:19-23.

Third, did the practice of head coverings described by Paul originate in Greek culture? Was it a Greco-Roman ethnic cultural custom prevalent at Corinth? Does this practice find its origin in the pagan temples of Corinth? YES! What Paul recommended to the Corinthians is that they should follow the head covering practices which were the standards of decency, morality and respectability in the religious culture of Corinth. That this is true is an indisputable fact of archaeology and history. The following references give some of the verification for the Greco-Roman origin of Paul's recommendation.

The International Standard Bible Encyclopedia, vol. II, p. 1348:
"The Pauline injunction as to the veiling of women in public gatherings of the Christians (1 Cor. 11:5), while men were instructed to appear bareheaded, must be mentioned. This is diametrically opposed to the Jewish custom, according to which men wore the head covered by the tallith or prayer shawl, while women were considered sufficiently covered by their long hair. The Apostle here simply commends a Greek custom for the congregation resident among Greek population; in other words, recommends obedience to local standards of decency and good order."

The Expositor's Greek Testament, vol. II, pp. 872-873:
"The argument here appeals to Greek and Eastern sentiment."
"The usage here prescribed seems to be an adoption of Greek customs to Christian concepts."
"(It is) an appeal to social sentiment."

A.T. Robertson, *Word Pictures in the New Testament*, vol. IV, pp. 159-160:
"The Greeks remained bareheaded in public prayer and this usage Paul commends for the men."

Lenski, *The Interpretation of 1 and 2 Corinthians*, pp. 434-435:
"Clearly Paul uses such strong language because of the effect on a woman's reputation in Corinth by such conduct that proclaimed her a lewd woman. Social custom varied in the world then as now, but there was no alternative in Corinth."
Paul now applies the facts which he has stated concerning headship to the customs as they existed in Corinth and elsewhere. Generally speaking, among the Greeks only slaves were covered, and the

uncovered head was a sign of freedom. The Romans reversed this. The free man wore the pileus, the slave went bareheaded. When the latter was emancipated he was said *vocari ad pileum*. Yet the Romans—and we must add the Germans—were accustomed to pray while they were veiled. The Jews had the same custom; and we should not forget that Paul was originally a Jew. This veiling expressed reverence, the proper feeling of unworthiness to appear before God with an open face. Maimonides says: "Let not the Wise Men, nor the scholars of the Wise Men, pray unless they be covered." The Jewish covering was called the tallith.

Vincent, *Word Studies in the New Testament*, vol. III, p. 246:
"The (male) Romans, like the Jews, prayed with the head veiled. The Greeks remained bareheaded during prayer or sacrifice. The Greek usage, which had become prevalent in the Grecian churches, seems to have commended itself to Paul."

Matthew Henry, p. 560:
"Their veils, the common token of subjection to their husbands in that part of the world."

Alford, *The Greek Testament*, vol. II, pp. 564-565:
"(That Paul is talking about or describing) Greek and Roman customs is important."

Poole, M., *A Commentary on the Holy Bible*, p. 577:
"Interpreters rightly agree, that this and the following verses are to be interpreted from the customs of countries. In Corinth the uncovered head was a sign of authority."

Ellicott, *Ellicott's Commentary on the Whole Bible*, p. 327:
"The Greek practice was for men to have their heads uncovered when joining in religious ceremonies. To this practice St. Paul would incline, as being the national custom of the country."

Hodge, C., *Commentary on the First Epistle to the Corinthians*, pp. 204-205:
"Having corrected the more private abuses which prevailed among the Corinthians, the Apostle brings in this chapter to consider those which relate to the mode of conducting public worship. The first of these is the habit of women appearing in public without a veil. Dress is in a great degree conventional. A costume which is proper in one country, would be indecorous in another. The principle insisted upon in this paragraph is, that women should conform in matters of dress to all those usages which the public sentiment of the community in which they live demands. The veil in all eastern countries was and to a great extent still is, the symbol of modesty and subjection. For a woman, therefore, in Corinth to discard the veil was to renounce her claim to modesty and to refuse to recognize her subordination to her husband. It is on the assumption of this significancy in the use of the veil, that the apostle's whole argument in this paragraph is founded."

Lange, *Commentary on the Holy Scriptures*, vol. 10, p. 224:
"According to the usage of the Greeks, men appeared in public religious service with face and head uncovered."

Godet, *Commentary on the First Epistle to the Corinthians*, vol. 1, p. 104:
"The (pagan) ancients in general laid down a difference between the bearing of men and that of women in their appearances in public. Plutarch relates that at the funeral ceremony of

parents, the sons appeared with their heads covered, the daughters with their heads uncovered and their hair flowing. This author adds by way of explanation: 'To mourning belongs the extraordinary, that is to say, what is done on this occasion, is the opposite of what is done in general. What would be improper at an ordinary time becomes proper then. Plutarch also relates that among the Greeks it was customary for the women in circumstances of distress to cut off their hair, whereas the men allowed it to grow: why so? Because the custom of the latter is to cut it and of the former to let it grow.' In Corinthian society, for women to cut their hair or for men to have long hair meant that they were either cultic prostitutes of the fertility rite temples which abounded in Corinth or that they were slaves. Hence, Paul recommended that the Christians in Corinth avoid dressing or looking like immoral or lewd people."

C. Hodge, ibid., p. 204:
      "An unveiled woman, therefore, in Corinth proclaimed herself as not only insubordinate, but as immodest. If she wishes to be regarded as a reputable woman, let her conform to the established usage. But if she has no regard to her reputation, let her act as other women of her class. She must conform either to the reputable or disreputable class of her sex, for a departure from the one is conforming to the other. These imperatives are not to be taken as commands, but rather as expressing what consistence would require."

The Expositor's Greek Testament, vol. II, pp. 872-875:
      "Amongst the Greeks only the (prostitutes), so numerous in Corinth, went about unveiled; slave-women wore the shaven head—also a punishment of the adulterous: with these the Christian woman who emancipates herself from becoming restraints of dress, is in effect identified."

A.T. Robertson, *Word Pictures in the New Testament*, vol. IV, pp. 159-160:
      "Probably some of the women had violated this custom. Among Greeks only the *hetairai*, so numerous in Corinth, went about unveiled; slave-women wore the shaven head." "He does not here condemn the act, but the breach of custom which would bring reproach. A woman convicted of adultery had her hair shorn (Isa. 7:20). The Justinian Code prescribed shaving the head for an adulterous woman whom the husband refused to receive back after two years. Paul does not tell Corinthian Christian women to put themselves on a level with courtesans."

Godet, ibid., p. 104:
      "The Greek slave had her head shaved in token of her servitude; the same was done among the Hebrews to the adulteress."

Matthew Henry, ibid., p. 577:
      "(Cutting the hair) was the practice of those beastly she-priests of Bacchus, who like frantic persons, performed those pretendedly religious rites."

Alford, ibid., p. 565:
      "It was a punishment of adulteresses."

Grosheide, *Commentary on the First Epistle to the Corinthians*, p. 254:
      "Probably prostitutes used to or were compelled to cut their hair and to keep it very short. Paul's argument can be summed up as follows: If immoral women were shaven and if they be-

haved like men, then honorable women should cover their heads ... or else place themselves on a level with immoral women."

Vincent, ibid., p. 247:

"Paul means that a woman praying or prophesying uncovered puts herself in public opinion on a level with a courtesan."

Lange, ibid., p. 224:

"(a shaven head) that is, she assumes the characteristic mark of a disreputable woman."

It is clear that the head covering issue was not just a church issue, but it was a cultural issue that involved the whole Corinthian society. Paul did not feel that Christians should dress in such a way as to bring public scandal and shame on the Gospel. To the Greeks, they should become as Greeks for the sake of the Gospel.

Third, what did these head coverings look like? Charles Hodge comments:

"The veils worn by Grecian women were of different kinds. One and perhaps the most common, was the peplum or mantle, which in public was thrown over the head and enveloped the whole person. The other was more in the fashion of the common eastern veil which covered the face, with the exception of the eyes. In one form or other, the custom was universal for all respectable women to appear veiled in public. The apostle therefore says, that a woman who speaks in public with her head uncovered, dishonoureth her head. Here (it) is used, her own head; not her husband, but herself. This is plain, not only from the force of the words, but from the next clause, for that is even all one as if she were shaven. This is the reason why she disgraces herself. She puts herself in the same class with women whose hair has been cut off. Cutting off the hair, which is the principal natural ornament of women, was either a sign of grief, Deut. 21:12, or a disgraceful punishment. The literal translation of this clause is: she is one and the same thing with one who is shaven. She assumes the characteristic mark of a disreputable woman."

Fourth, in order to show that the Greek customs were acceptable to Christians and not in conflict with Christian thought, Paul argues (vs. 7-15):

A man can have his head uncovered; is not he created in the image and glory of God? But, a woman was created in the (image) and glory of man. So, she can be covered. Remember that Eve was created out of Adam and not Adam out of Eve. Adam was not created to be Eve's help-meet, but Eve was created to be his help-meet. For this reason and because of the angels, a woman can have a head-covering, which (in Corinth) is a sign of being under authority.

This is not to say that men are independent of (or better than) women or that women are independent of (or better than) men. All men are born from women just as Eve came from Adam. Everything in the end comes from God.

So, you decide what is proper with your own sense of propriety: Is it proper (in Corinth) for a woman to pray publicly to God with her head uncovered? Does not (Greek and Corinthian) custom and culture tell you that long hair on a man is shameful, while on a woman, it is her glory? For long hair is given to her as a covering. Now, if anyone really wants to fight about this, let him or her know that we and the other churches do not allow the practice of women publicly praying or prophesying with an uncovered head.

First of all, Paul argues that the Greek custom is adaptable by Christians by stating how it illustrates various facts drawn from O.T. history (vs. 7-12).

At no point does Paul appeal to particular texts, but he bases his argument on events in history. He does not say, "It is written" and then quote Scripture. He is simply showing that the Corinthian custom was adaptable by Christians. The line of argument which Paul is using is the same theological basis for 21st century Christians observing such cultural practices as Father's Day and Mother's Day. While there is no Scripture we can quote to prove that Christians should observe such cultural customs, it is obvious that Christians can adopt such customs in order to show reverence to their parents.

Secondly, Paul appeals to angels in verse 10. What Paul had in mind has been a controversy for the last 1,900 years. The safest interpretation is that the angels are involved in protecting the assembly from satanic attack, and they join with the saints in worship (Psa. 103:20-22; Heb. 12:18-24). These angels who assist us in our worship services would be insulted to see men and women behaving in a lewd and indecent manner. To say more than this enters into pure speculation.[6]

Thirdly, Paul appeals to the Corinthians to examine their own feelings (v. 13). He challenges them to judge the issue for themselves by their own sense of decency or propriety.

Does Paul ever argue for moral laws or absolute truths by appealing to people to examine their feelings? NO! This insight strengthens the evangelical position. Paul is dealing with an application of a general principle. The application is culturally bound and limited. The principle will be applied according to each culture. That this is what Paul is saying in verse 13 is supported by nearly all classic commentaries.

The Expositor's Greek Testament, vol. II, p. 873f:
> "(It is) an appeal to social sentiment."

Matthew Henry, ibid.:
> "Custom is in a great measure the rule of decency."

C. Hodge, ibid., p. 212:
> "This is an appeal to their own sense of propriety."

R.C. Lenski, p. 446:
> "The obligation which Paul points out in v. 7 and v. 10 rests, as he shows, on the facts of creation. It amounts to this: customs that symbolize and reflect these facts are proper. The Corinthians may judge this as far as it applies to them. They need to do no more than to ask the question regarding the propriety of the custom in vogue in their midst..."

Grosheide, p. 239
> "The Apostle appeals to the common sense of the Corinthians."

Alford, p. 568
> "v. 13 appeals to their own sense of propriety."

A.T. Robertson, p. 161:
> "Paul appeals to the sense of propriety among the Christians."

In verse 13, Paul is pointing to a subjective witness in the Corinthians themselves. Their own sense of propriety, shaped by the customs of the culture in which they lived, spoke out in favor of Paul's argument. While engaged in public worship, men should not have their heads covered. Neither should women have their heads uncovered while leading in prayer or publicly prophesying. The cultural upbringing of the Corinthians was a valid witness for Paul's case.

Fourthly, having appealed to a subjective witness within the Corinthians, Paul now appeals to an objective witness in v. 14. He appeals to "nature" as "teaching" them that while it is shameful for men to have long hair, it is the woman's glory to have long hair. What Paul meant by "nature" is a much debated subject. There are as many opinions as there are commentators. Even though a "final" interpretation is perhaps impossible (cf. 2 Pet. 3:16), several things are abundantly clear.

A. Since Paul has just appealed to a subjective witness in verse 13, he is surely not appealing to something subjective again. Whatever he means by "nature," it refers to something external or objective to the Corinthians.

B. This objective witness cannot be based on a Newtonian world view in which there are "natural laws" inherent in the creation. Many commentators have made the fatal mistake of reading 19th, 20th and 21st century scientific world views into this first century text. Thus Paul could not mean "natural law" when he wrote "nature." Any interpretation which claims that Paul is talking about "laws in the creation order" is eisegesis and not exegesis.

C. Since the Greek word translated "nature" is used in various ways in the New Testament, nothing can be "proved" by its etymology. The safest meaning of the word "nature" would be the objective cultural customs of the society in which they lived. This would be the normal everyday meaning of "nature" in any given culture. As Matthew Henry pointed out, "custom is in a great measure the rule of decency."[7] Every culture legislates what is "natural" and "unnatural," i.e., what is against "nature" or in conformity to "nature."

John Calvin comments:

"Paul again sets nature before them as a teacher of what is proper. Now he means by 'natural' what was accepted by common consent and usage at that time, certainly as far as the Greeks were concerned. For long hair was not always regarded as a disgraceful thing in men. Historical works relate that long ago i.e., in the earliest times, men wore long hair in every country. But since the Greeks did not consider it very manly to have long hair, branding those who had it effeminate, Paul conceded that their custom, accepted in his own day, was in conformity with nature.[8] The word 'Nature' refers to what was culturally acceptable."

Charles Hodge points out:

"The form which these feelings assume is necessarily determined in a great measure by education and habit. The instinctive sense of propriety in an eastern maiden prompts her, when surprised by strangers, to cover her face. In a European it would not produce that effect. In writing, therefore, to eastern females, it would be correct to ask whether their native sense of propriety did not prompt them to cover their heads in public. The response would infallibly be in the affirmative. It is in this sense the word nature is commonly taken here."[9]

It was for this reason that the great J. Meyer said: "The instinctive consciousness of propriety on this point had been established by custom and had become nature."[10]

This understanding of nature as custom was held by such commentators as Chrysostom, Calvin, Grotius, Meyer, etc.[11] It is the only position which best conforms to the context of the passage and the line of argumentation that Paul is using.

Paul's fifth witness for his argument is the universal practice of the churches he had established (v. 16). He appealed to the fact that all his other churches adopted the Greek cultural standards of decency in public worship.[12]

Again, we must ask, did Paul ever use *Argumentum ad Populum* to prove a moral law or an absolute truth? NO! Paul is dealing with a practical application of a general principle and not seeking to establish a rule of head coverings.

Summary

Paul has demonstrated that it is the Christian's responsibility to conform himself or herself to the customs of the culture in which they live, as long as these customs are adaptable to Christian ideas and ideals.

We conclude with some closing comments by several noted expositors.

Matthew Poole concludes:

"Interpreters rightly agree, that this and the following verses are to be interpreted from the customs of the countries; and all that can be concluded from the verse is, that it is the duty of men employed in divine ministrations, to look to behave themselves as those who are to represent the Lord Jesus Christ, behaving themselves with a just authority and gravity that belongeth his ambassadors, which decent gravity is to be judged from the common opinion and account of the country wherein they live. Nothing in this is a further rule to Christians, than that it is the duty in praying and preaching, to use postures and habits that are not naturally, nor according to the customs of the place they live, uncomely and irreverent as looked upon."[13]

And to this Lenski adds:

"All of this shows us that Paul is not laying down an absolute rule that is to be observed by Christians of all times in regard to covering the head or leaving it uncovered during worship. Not the custom as a custom is vital but the significance of a custom. If Paul were writing to Jews or to Romans or to Germans, all of whom covered the head during worship because of reverence and shame in God's presence, he would have to tell them that any man among them who violated this custom thereby showed lack of reverence and shame. But to write this to Greeks would be incomprehensible to them. They had an entirely different custom which had an entirely different significance. This significance is sound and good. Hence Paul explains it to the Corinthians at length and bids them to abide by their custom. For to abrogate it and to fly in the face of it means in their case, not only to violate that significance but at the same time to disavow that significance. The fact that Paul sees this significance with a Christian's eye as pertaining to the true God and not with a pagan's eye as pertaining to idol gods should cause no confusion. The fact that he would use the Christian's eye if he were dealing with the opposite custom of other nationalities and not the pagan's eye is again beyond question. By so doing Paul is not introducing into these national customs something that is foreign and unjustifiable of these customs which non-Christians grasped or felt only partially because the glory of the true God was hidden from them."[14]

Practical and Theological Considerations

In the present controversy over head coverings, there are crucial, practical and theological considerations which present great problems to those who feel that 1 Cor. 11 legislates certain special clothing to be worn when engaged in public worship.

First, where in the Spirit or text of the New Testament do we find that certain articles of clothing are designated as being "Christian," i.e., spiritual or holy? Does the New Testament stipulate "priestly" attire for those involved in public worship? Where is it said that an external piece of cloth qualifies a person to worship God?

Second, New Covenant worship in the New Testament is definitely taught to be internal and spiritual, having to do with the attitude of the soul toward God through Christ.

1. Our Lord clearly taught in John 4:19-24 that New Covenant worship has to do with "Spirit and truth" and not with such external things as mountains or, as we believe, clothing. Where in the above passage would head coverings fit? A believer's worship is acceptable to God if it is spiritual and not idolatrous. Christ's answer points to the inner and spiritual character of New Covenant worship. Thus while Old Covenant worship stipulated where, when, how and in what attire to worship God, the liberty of the people of God under the New Covenant leads to a worship of God which centers on the attitudes of the inner-man and leaves much up to the liberty of the Spirit (2 Cor. 3:1-6, 17-18).

2. Paul in Phil. 3:1-3 follows Christ's teaching that New Covenant worship is internal and spiritual in character instead of being concerned with external and carnal things.

The Judaizers taught that external matters determined if your worship was acceptable to God. They "put confidence in the flesh" (v. 3). But New Covenant worship is not involved in placing external things such as circumcision or clothing between God and man. We worship God acceptably because it is rendered through the One Mediator, Jesus Christ, and by the power of the Holy Spirit and in total reliance on these spiritual things alone, thus "putting no confidence in the flesh."

Where would the presence or absence of a hat or veil fit into the spiritual character of New Covenant worship? To think that your worship is acceptable to God if you do or do not have a hat on, is in the last analysis, to threaten the centrality of faith, the singularity of Christ's mediatorship and the effectuality of the Spirit's assistance in worship. God is concerned with the inner soul or spirit and not with the outward person.

"But the Lord said to Samuel, 'Do not look at his appearance or at the height of his stature, because I have rejected him; for God sees not as man sees, for man looks at the outward appearance, but the Lord looks at the heart' " (1 Sam. 16:7).

3. The Apostle Peter also points out where the emphasis of the New Covenant lies in 1 Pet. 3:1-6. Peter places the emphasis not on external things such as clothing, but on inward attitudes and Christ-like character qualities. A Christian's holiness is not something externally visible like a hat or cap, but it should be seen in living a Spirit-filled life.

Third, in our examination of pro-covering articles, we do not find a clear distinguishing between the essential and non-essential elements in biblical worship.

1. The essence of worship resides in those attitudes and activities which are commanded in Scripture as constituting acceptable worship to God. Something is essential to worship if it makes worship acceptable to God.

The pro-covering apologists must clearly declare whether the absence or presence of a head covering is essential to acceptable worship. If a male believer publicly worships the Father through the Son by the Spirit with a hat on, is his worship rejected by God on the sole basis of his having a hat on? If a female believer publicly worships the Father through the Son by the Spirit without a hat on, is her worship rejected or accepted?

To say that it is essential to true worship is to make an external and carnal item essential to worship. This contradicts the character of New Covenant worship which is internal and spiritual.

2. The non-essential elements of worship concern the details of the order of service which are left up to the exercise of Christian liberty within the context of the culture of the local church.

Conclusion

To those who wish to observe the rule on head covering, we say "May God richly bless you." But let them not fall into the assumption that their worship is acceptable because of a hat, cap or scarf. Let them not judge others who do not follow the rule. Let them place the emphasis on the inner and spiritual attitudes and Christ-like character qualities which make a believer's worship acceptable to God. Let them not think that they are more "holy" because of the clothing they wear. According to the New Covenant, our holiness is to be seen in our character—not in distinctive clothing.

To those who do not feel that the rule on head coverings applies to them, we say, "May God richly bless you." But let them not judge those who practice head coverings. Let them not get proud over their "liberty." Let them not scorn the weaker brothers and sisters whose consciences tell them to observe the rule.

In the light of Rom. 14:1-23, let us allow the love of God to temper our passions and the truth of God to guide our convictions. There is no reason why Christians who disagree over this non-essential aspect of public worship cannot dwell together in unity.

References

1. Lenski, R., *The Interpretation of St. Paul's First and Second Epistles to the Corinthians*, Augsburg Publishing House, Minn., 1963, p. 435.
2. Edwards, T., *A Commentary on the First Epistle to the Corinthians*, A.C. Armstrong & Son, N.Y., 1886, p. 268.
   Poole, M., *A Commentary on the Holy Bible*, Banner of Truth Trust, London, 1969, p. 577.
   Calvin, J., *The First Epistle of Paul to the Corinthians*, Wm. B. Eerdmans Publishing Co., Grand Rapids, 1968, p. 227.
   The Expositor's Greek Testament, ed. W. Nicole, Wm. B. Eerdmans Publishing Co., Grand Rapids, 1967, vol. II, p. 870.
   Robertson, A.T., *Word Pictures in the New Testament*, Broadman Press, Nashville, 1931, vol. IV, p. 160.
   Ellicott's Commentary on the Whole Bible, ed., C. Ellicott, Zondervan Publishing Co., Grand Rapids, 1959, vol. VII, p. 327.
   Alford, H., *The Greek Testament*, Moody Press, Chicago, 1968, vol. II, p. 563.
   One Volume New Testament Commentary, Baker Publishing House, Grand Rapids, 1963, N.P., on 1 Cor. 11:1.

Godet, F., *Commentary on the First Epistle of Paul to the Corinthians,* Zondervan Publishing House, Grand Rapids, 1957, vol. II, p. 103.

Henry, M., *Matthew Henry's Commentary,* Fleming H. Revell Co., N.P., N.D., vol. VI, p. 560.

Hodge, C., *Commentary on the First Epistle to the Corinthians,* Wm. B. Eerdmans Publishing Co., Grand Rapids, 1965, p. 204.

Commentary on the Holy Scriptures, ed. J. Lange, Zondervan Publishing House, Grand Rapids, 1960, vol. VI in N.T., p. 223.

3. The evidence is so overwhelming that only the uninformed or prejudiced will not accept it. That the Jews' custom was opposite of what Paul recommends in 1 Cor. 1 is supported by the following sources:

   Vincent, *Word Studies in the New Testament,* Wm. B. Eerdmans Publishing Co., Grand Rapids, 1969, p. 246, 247.

   Lenski, ibid., p. 435.

   Alford, ibid., p. 564.

   Lange, ibid., p. 224.

   One Volume New Testament Commentary, ibid.

   Ellicott, ibid., p. 327.

   Hodge, ibid., p. 207.

   Expositor's Greek Testament, ibid., p. 872.

   Hurley, J., *Did Paul Require Veils or the Silence of Women? A Consideration of 1 Cor. 11:2-16 and 1 Cor. 14:33-36,* W. J. J., vol. XXV, p. 195.

4. *One Volume New Testament Commentary,* ibid.

5. Edwards, ibid., p. 270.

6. Hodge, ibid., p. 209.

7. Henry, ibid., p. 560.

8. Calvin, ibid., p. 235.

9. Hodge, ibid., p. 213.

10. *One Volume New Testament Commentary,* ibid.

11. Edwards, p. 279.

12. The idea that Paul is saying that "controversy" is not practiced in the churches, is unworthy of refutation.

13. Poole, ibid., p. 577.

14. Lenski, ibid., p. 435.

Chapter Seventy-Eight
Church Attendance

I. What are some of the most important questions a Christian can ever ask?

Why do we assemble together on the Lord's Day?
What is our purpose and goal in coming to Church?
Why do we come and what are we supposed to get out of it?

II. These questions force us all to think about our motives and goals in church attendance.

God wants you to examine your heart and find out if your church attendance arises from tradition or the Bible.

A. The Motive Behind Church Attendance

TRADITION	THE BIBLE
1. Habit and custom.	1. Loving obedience to the Lord Jesus.
2. Church attendance is optional. You do not have to attend church.	2. Church attendance is mandatory mandatory (Heb. 10:25; 1 John 2:19).
3. Go, if you feel like it.	3. Go, regardless of feelings.

B. The Purpose of Assembling

	TRADITION	THE BIBLE
Primary Audience	Lost Sinners	The Saints (Acts 2:41, 42)
Primary Focus	How to be Saved	How to Live; what to Believe
Primary Goal	Decisions for Christ	Lives Changed
Primary Emphasis	Services; Altar Calls	God; Individuals; Families
Primary Purpose	Evangelism	Equipping the Saints
Standard of Success	Number of Decisions	Christian Growth and Maturity

III. The Purpose of Assembling Determines the Kind of Material Presented.

The Kind of Material Presented in the Services

TRADITION	THE BIBLE
Emotion-centered, chills and thrills, funny and sad stories, entertainment, pep-talks; you receive a "Blessing" or "Get Saved"; evangelistic to obtain decisions.	Knowledge-centered; the whole man involved (mind, emotions, will); the "How To" of the Christian life, geared to promote growth and maturity.

IV. Knowledge of the Will of God and the Bible is the Key to Christian living.
   A. Knowledge in the Old Testament
      What was the duty of every priest and preacher? 2 Chron. 30:22; Ecc. 12:9-11
      Why was Proverbs written? Pro. 1:1-5
      Fools hate and despise knowledge: Pro. 1:22, 29
      Wise people love knowledge: Pro. 18:15; cf. 11:9
      We should apply our hearts to knowledge: Pro. 22:17
      Knowledge gives stability and strength: Isa. 33:6
      Why do people perish? Hos. 4:6

   B. Knowledge in the New Testament
      What is eternal life? John 17:3
      How are we sanctified? John 17:17
      Paul's concern: Col. 1:9-10
      Paul's command: Phil. 1:9
      Peter's concern: 2 Peter 1:5-9
      Peter's command: 2 Peter 3:18

Conclusion

When the people of God assemble to worship the most high God, they are ushered into the very presence of God to grow in the grace (character) and knowledge (doctrine) of the Lord Jesus Christ.

Chapter Seventy-Nine
Christian Baptism

Introduction

One of the most joyous occasions in the life of a local Church is when a baptismal service is held. It is joyous because of what it symbolizes. It brings a special blessing to the Church as well as to the individual baptized.

Because of its rich biblical meaning, baptism should be viewed with great reverence and received only after serious self-examination. The one baptized must understand the main points of Christian baptism.

I. The Meaning of Baptism
    A. Objectively, baptism is a dramatic portrayal of the death, burial and resurrection of Christ (Rom. 6:1-11). In baptism we are reminded afresh that Jesus died for our sins and was raised for our justification (Rom. 4:25). Thus baptism has as its initial focus the person and work of Christ.
    B. Subjectively, baptism is a dramatic portrayal of union with Christ in His death and resurrection. Baptism thus symbolizes that the person baptized died and rose with Christ (Rom. 6:1-11; Gal. 2:20; 5:24; 6:14; Col. 2:12-13). This is its primary meaning in the New Testament.
    C. In a secondary sense, baptism also symbolizes regeneration, the forgiveness of sins and the coming of the Holy Spirit (Tit. 3:5; Eph. 5:26; 1 Cor. 6:11; Acts 22:16; Mk. 1:8, etc.).
    D. Baptism is thus an outward act that symbolizes an inward reality. And, we must remember, a symbol always points away from itself to the reality it portrays. Just as the symbolic ceremonies of the Old Testament, such as animal sacrifices, could not accomplish what they symbolized (Heb. 10:1-4), even so baptism cannot save, regenerate or wash away sin. We must not confuse symbol and reality.
    E. The confusion of a symbol with the reality it portrays is the basis of all vain and superstitious views of baptism and the Lord's Supper. The bread and the wine are symbols of the body and blood of Jesus and should not be viewed as actually being what they symbolize. While baptism symbolizes salvation, it does not accomplish it. The person baptized may actually not be saved, as in the case of Simon (Acts 8:13; 18-23). Thus baptism has in focus the confession of salvation and is not a magical act guaranteeing the possession of salvation.

II. The Subjects of Baptism
    A. Once the biblical nature of baptism is understood, the question as to who should be baptized is rather obvious. The symbolic nature of baptism requires that the person baptized be viewed as having already experienced the reality which baptism symbolizes. Thus, only those who professed to be saved by faith in the Lord Jesus were baptized in the New Testament. The order was always faith then baptism.
    B. To give baptism to infants, children or adults who do not or cannot confess faith in Christ destroys both the objective and subjective meanings of baptism. To baptize someone who is not in union with Christ, who did not die and rise with Christ, who is not regenerate, whose sins are not forgiven, is a mockery of the Gospel.
    C. Infant baptism, along with forced baptism, was a natural outgrowth of a superstitious view

of baptism in which baptism was thought to accomplish salvation instead of just symboliz-ing it. Infants and unbelieving adults were baptized, because it was believed that the mere act of baptism would save them without faith on their part.

D. There are no examples or commands in the New Testament that infants and unbelieving children or adults are to be baptized. There is no passage in the New Testament that teaches that baptism is proper for unbelievers regardless of their age or condition.

E. The first reference to infant baptism in Church History is by Tertullian, who opposed it! (See Tertullian's work, *On Baptism*, chap. XVII in Ante-Nicene Fathers, vol. III, p. 678.) The baptism of infants and adult unbelievers arose only after the doctrine of baptismal regener-ation was accepted. Even by A.D. 354, infant baptism was still not the norm because Au-gustine himself was not baptized as an infant even though his mother was a devout Christian.

III. The Mode of Baptism

A. Once the primary meaning of baptism is understood, the way it is carried out is also obvious. Immersion is the only mode of baptism that portrays the objective symbolism of Christ's death, burial and resurrection as well as the subjective symbolism of union with Christ and the salvation that results from that union. While sprinkling and pouring can symbolize re-generation, the forgiveness of sins and the coming of the Spirit, both modes fail to point us to the death and resurrection of Christ. They fail to be Christological in essence or practice.

B. If we examine the vocabulary used in the New Testament to describe this ceremony, we find that such words as *bapto, baptizein*, etc. are used. To discover what these words meant, we examined 38 Greek lexicons and dictionaries. All of these works without exception defined *bapto* as meaning "to immerse, to submerge or to dip or to dye." We could not find a single Greek reference work which translated *bapto*, etc., as "sprinkle" or "pour." The Greek language has other words for sprinkle and pour.

C. Immersion is the meaning of these words in the Septuagint. The contrast with sprinkle is plain in such places as Lev. 4:6, etc.

D. All the extra-biblical uses of these words mean to immerse.

E. The usage and context of these words in the New Testament clearly mean to immerse (see Matt. 26:23; Lk. 16:24, etc.).

F. The need for abundant water is only understandable if immersion is the mode in view (see Matt. 3:6; John 3:23; Acts 8:36, etc.)

G. The prepositions "into" and "out of" imply immersion (see Acts 8:38, etc.).

H. The Jews baptized by immersion before Christ was born. The Mishnah and archaeology make this clear. Thus baptism by immersion already existed when John the Baptist started to baptize. There is no evidence of sprinkling or pouring.

I. All Greek Orthodox, Roman Catholic and Protestant scholars admit that immersion was the original mode. Example John Calvin on John 3:23: "Moreover, from these words we may infer that John and Christ administered baptism by total immersion."

IV. The Significance of Baptism

By baptism we publicly identify ourselves with Christ and with His Church. Once baptized, we can join the Church and eat at the Lord's Table along with our brothers and sisters in Christ. Once in the Body, we learn to share the joys and sorrows of the people of God. Baptism is thus the opening of a door to greater fellowship and ministry as well as obedience to the Lord of the Church, who told us to make disciples and then to baptize them in the name of the Father and of the Son and of the Holy Spirit (Matt. 28:19-20).

Chapter Eighty

The Doctrine of the Church as Found in Matthew

The Church is first introduced by Christ in Matthew's Gospel. A careful examination of these introductory statements of Christ concerning the nature and function of the Church are important to those who desire to establish a New Testament Church.

Matthew 16:13-19

1) The Occasion (vs. 13-15):

The confession of Peter comes at a decisive point in the ministry of Christ. The wave of popular indignation at the execution of John the Baptist appears to have been a precipitating factor in the crisis. The feeding of the five thousand marked the crest of both the enthusiasm and the misunderstanding of the masses. John notes the desire of the multitude to make Jesus king by force (John 6:15); Matthew and Mark both stress the dismissal of the crowd and Jesus' solitary prayer (Mt. 14:23; Mk. 6:46). Jesus' refusal to fill the role of a political Messiah, together with His staggering claim to a higher dominion, now alienated many. His withdrawal with His disciples at this time manifested His rejection, even as it avoided the false acclamation. The journeys to Syro-Phoenicia and Caesarea Philippi with the disciples pointed toward the Gentile mission which must begin when Israel's rejection was complete. At the same time, the disciples, as the remnant of Israel, must be confronted with the coming death and resurrection which Christ must accomplish at Jerusalem.... Peter's confession was elicited by Jesus as a decisive step in the constitution of the new Israel by the Messiah.[1]

The above observation of Dr. E.P. Clowney is well put. We must see the confession of Peter in the light of the unfolding of the New Israel. The Messiah came to gather His people as the remnant of the apostate Old Testament Church. The Angel had proclaimed this truth at the very birth of Christ: "He shall save His people from their sin" (Matt. 1:21).

With the rejection of Israel, Jesus would begin to emphasize His flock, His disciples and His Church. It is only natural that at this point in His ministry that He should announce the building of His Church in contrast to the Church of the Pharisees and Scribes.

2) The Confession (v. 16):

In answer to the question of Christ: "But who do you say that I am?" Peter responds, "You are the Christ, the Son of the Living God." Christ had addressed the question to all of His disciples, for He uses the plural form of "you" in His question. Peter's answer, therefore, represented the belief of the apostles.[2]

Peter's confession covered the Person and Work of Christ and forms the basic element in a Christian's view of Jesus. As to His work and office, Jesus was the Messiah. As to His Person, Jesus was the Son of God. Much time could be spent on analyzing this confession, but such a project is not immediately pertinent to our study.

3) The Proclamation (vs. 17-19):
Now Jesus responds to Peter's affirmation of His divinity.

"Blessed are you, Simon Bar-Jonah: for flesh and blood did not reveal it unto you but my Father who is in Heaven. And I say unto you, That you are Peter, and upon this rock I will build my Church and the gates of Hades shall not prevail against it. I will give unto you the keys of the Kingdom of Heaven: and whatsoever you bind on earth shall be bound in Heaven; and whatsoever you shall loose on earth shall be loosed in Heaven."

In order to understand this passage, we must ask several very basic questions.
a) What is "the Church" to which Christ refers?

By the church, is meant not an edifice of wood, stone, etc., but an assembly and congregation of men: and that not of any sort; not a disorderly tumultuous assembly, in which sense this word is sometimes taken; nor does it design the faithful of a family, which is sometimes the import of it; nor a particular congregational church, but the elect of God, the general assembly and church of the first-born, whose names are written in Heaven; and especially such of them as were to be gathered in and built on Christ, from among the Jews and Gentiles.[3]

Even the reference to the "church" is not unseasonable. What more natural than that Jesus, conscious that His labors, outside the disciple circle, have been fruitless, so far as permanent result is concerned, should fix his hopes on that circle and look on it as the nucleus of a new regenerate Israel, having for its *raison d'etre* that it accepts Him as the Christ.[4]

The idea is not that hitherto no Church has existed. His Church should be understood in contrast to the Old Testament Church organization which had now come to an end to make place for the Messiah's Church.[5]

The beginning of its organization is found in Christ's calling of the disciples. The founding of the Church mentioned in Matthew 16 is to be acknowledged as genuine in the full sense of the word, in opposition to the old liberal and the recent eschatological concepts.[6]

The concept (*ekklesia*) occupies an organic and integrating position in the framework of Jesus' preaching of the kingdom of Heaven.[7]

All the commentators agree that Christ is referring to the New Testament Church. But they divide as to the extent of the Church in the mind of Jesus as He uttered the Word.

i) Cotton, Vos, Bruce, Lenski, Bannerman, Henry and Zorn think that Jesus had in mind the church on earth. Jesus said that He would be "building," and this "building" refers to Christ taking out of the world a people for His name. It refers to His gathering His elect on earth. Thus we must see the "Church" in terms of growth, development and process. With this understanding, the "kingdom of Heaven" is not just the church. It may include the church, but the two are not equated here.

ii) Goodwin, Ridderbos, Clowney, Poole, Calvin and Gill feel that Christ is here referring to the universal, mystical, body of Christ in Heaven and on earth. As the other group emphasized the verb "build" and thus saw process, this group emphasizes the noun "Church" and thus sees the end-product of the process in view. Jesus has in mind all the elect gathered into one body. The others see the activity of Jesus, while these see the goal of Jesus. If Jesus would have had the activity of building in mind, He should have said "Churches," which would indicate process and growth. But He said "Church," meaning all the people of God of all ages in Christ.

It seems clear to me that both views are included in the words of Jesus. The verb does imply activity, but the "church" refers to the end-product of all the activity, i.e., all the elect gathered into union with Christ. The scope of the "church" is larger than the earthly manifestation of the Body of Christ. It is important that we see Jesus beginning His concept of the Church as a united body. None of the people of God should be excluded from the Church which Christ shall build. To the Messiah belong a people. To think that Christ is referring to only a part of His people is to go against the whole thrust of the Messianic mission.

Thus Christ refers to the entire Body of believers which shall one day be gathered together in one fold under one Shepherd.

b) What is the Foundation (Rock) of the Church?

By the "rock" on which Christ builds His church, is meant, not the person of Peter; for Christ does not say, upon thee, Peter, but upon this rock, referring to something distinct from him; for though his name signifies a rock or stone and there may be some allusion to it; and he is so-called because of his trust and confidence in the Lord, on whom He was built; but not because he was the foundation on which any others and especially the whole church, were built: it is true, he may be called the foundation as the rest of the Twelve Apostles of the Lamb are, Eph. 2:20; Rev. 21:14, without any distinction from them and preference to them; they and he agreeing in laying doctrinally and ministerially Christ Jesus as the foundation of faith and hope, but not in the same sense as he; neither he nor they are the foundation on which the church is built, which is Christ and Him alone.[8]

Christ is both its Founder and Foundation; He draws souls and draws them to Himself; to Him they are united and on Him they rest and have a constant dependence.[9]

What follows is in form a promise to Peter as a reward of his faith. It is as personal as the most zealous advocates of papal supremacy could desire. Yet it is as remote as the poles from what they mean. Peter, believing that truth, is the foundation and the building is to be of a piece with the foundation.[10]

We must conclude that neither Peter nor his confession can be excluded from the reference of "upon this rock."[11]

The relationship between Peter, his confession, the rock, Christ, the Church and the other apostles is very controversial. Some see that the confession of Peter, "You are the Christ, the Son of the living God," to be the foundational "rock" underlying the church. Others see Christ referring to Himself as the rock or foundation. Then there are those who attempt to put Peter into the picture. The Romanist would find papacy in these words. But it seems clear to me that all of the elements listed form part of the rock mentioned. It is in reference to Peter, confessing Christ, as representing the other apostles, to which Christ refers to by use of the plural pronoun in v. 16, that Christ says "upon this rock I will build my church." But admitting this does not establish the cursed doctrine of the

Roman Antichrist. There are very important considerations to which we must turn our attention.

The Old Testament promises relating to the church were given immediately to particular persons, eminent for faith and holiness, as to Abraham and David; which yet gave no supremacy to them, much less to any of their successors; so the New Testament charter is here delivered to Peter as an agent, but to the use and behalf of the Church in all ages, according to the purposes therein specified and contained.[12]

When establishing the Abrahamic covenant, the Lord changed Abram to Abraham. Abram's wife's name was also changed. Jacob's name was changed to Israel as a reward. God almost dealt exclusively with Moses.

As a matter of fact, all throughout the Old Testament, God gave promises to His church in the form of personal promises. Thus personification of a promise did not mean supremacy of the person. So, is it any wonder that at the institution of the New Testament Church, the promises are given to a person? Peter received the promise for the whole church.

c) Who is the Owner and Builder of the Church?
Christ, the Messiah, is the Owner and Builder of the Church. We must remember the concepts of "a people," "a remnant," "holy seed" and other such rich Old Testament terminology which refer to the people of the Messiah. Jesus is the Owner, "MY church." Jesus is the Builder, "I WILL build." Christ alone is the sovereign Head of the church. He alone can make its laws. No popes, bishops, synods, presbyteries or elders can take the place of Christ.

d) What is "the kingdom of Heaven"?
The "kingdom of Heaven" means the Gospel.[13]

The kingdom of Heaven here means the kingdom of grace, which is the church and the kingdom of glory, which is in the Heavens.[14]

Observe it is not the keys of the church but of the kingdom. The meaning is: Peter, like faith in Jesus as the Christ, admits into the kingdom of Heaven.[15]

We come to a much controverted term when we look at the "Kingdom of Heaven." Some feel that it refers to the Gospel. Others think it is the church. But it is safe to say with Vos and Ridderbos that the term "heaven" is used in the place of "God." Thus the Kingdom of Heaven is the same as the Kingdom of God. The kingdom includes the church, but does not exhaust itself in the church, for the Kingdom rules over all. Thus the kingdom of Heaven includes the Gospel and the church.

e) What are the "Keys"? (Matt. 16:19)
Abilities to open and explain Gospel-truths and a mission and commission from Christ to use of them.[16]

The effect to generalize the function of the keys into preaching authority alone cannot be maintained in the light of the meaning of binding and loosing and of the context of Matt. 18.[17]

"The phrase, 'the keys of the kingdom of Heaven,' occurring in the first passage, is parallel to the power of 'binding and loosing,' spoken of in the second."[18]

It is plain, on an examination and comparison of these statements of Scripture, that our Lord did in them convey to his church a permanent gift of authority and power in the way of discipline that was long to outlast the ministry of the Apostles.[19]

The keys of the kingdom are the ordinances which Christ instituted in the church such as preaching, sacraments, excommunication, prayer, etc.[20]

What is meant is judicial power ... disciplinary, judicial authority.[21]

We now understand that the power of the keys is simply the preaching of the Gospel in those places and in so far as men are concerned, it is not so much power and ministry.[22]

It seems clear that the limitation of the keys to preaching the Gospel is unthinkable in the light of the rest of ch. 16 and the rest of ch. 18 and the reference in John 20:23.

Ridderbos, Henry, Owen, Goodwin, Cotton, Lange, Alford, Vos, Zorn, Clowney and Lenski all see that the keys have reference to the power of church discipline as well as preaching. All see that "binding and loosing" are the function of the keys. There are some minor differences as to labeling of the keys. But at this time I wish to lay out what are the types of the keys which Christ gave. Lenski, Cotton and others have pointed out that there are only two keys.[23]

What these two keys are and what their respective functions are will now be discussed.

i) The Key of Saving Knowledge or Faith (Lk. 11:52):
By this key, one can enter into the kingdom of Heaven, but not alone. By preaching or witnessing, one can help others to enter the kingdom by the same key.

ii) The Key of Order or Discipline:
There are two aspects to this key. Or, if you please, actually two keys under this general heading.

(1) The key of liberty to enter into the church and take part in the sacraments and in the fellowship of the saints.

(2) The key of authority whereby the elders teach and rule in the assembly.
These then are the two main areas where the keys of the kingdom function. (As has been already noticed, "binding and loosing" refer to opening, loosing, remitting and binding, shutting and retaining as function of the keys in the two areas of knowledge and order.)

iii) What objects are said to be loosed or bound in the term "whatsoever"?
The word, "whatsoever" is put into the neuter gender to include things, works and people. John 20:23 shows that sins can be loosed or bound. Matt. 18 shows that people can be bound or loosed. Acts 15 shows that duties or works can be loosed or bound.[24]
Thus the keys have power over people, sins and works. To limit "binding and loosing" to preaching or works is to ignore parallel Scripture which is to cripple the powers of the keys. Even excommunication and the receiving back of repentant sinners are part of the binding and loosing function of the keys of the Kingdom.

f) To whom are the keys given with their respective powers?
That the keys were given to Peter is clear. And that he received them on the behalf of the whole church is also clear from such passages as Matt. 18 and John 20. Peter lived three lives. He was an Apostle, and he received the keys as their representative. Thus the keys were given to the other Apostles (John 20). Peter was an elder (1 Pet. 5:1), and thus the keys are given to all elders (Heb. 13:17; 1

Tim. 5:17). Peter was a believer, and he received on the behalf of all believers (Matt. 18). Thus the keys are to be exercised by the whole church.

The key of saving knowledge is exercised by all believers, for faith in Jesus is the only true admittance into the body of Christ (Heb. 11). All believers have the power to give the Gospel to other people (Acts 1:8; 8:1-4).

The key of liberty is for all believers. Each believer is to live orderly (Acts 21:18). To see to it that his brothers are living orderly lives in accordance with the Bible (1 Thess. 5:14; 2 Thess. 3:6). All believers have the liberty to enter into the fellowship of a local church; to receive the sacraments; to choose and call elders and deacons; to join with the elders in censoring offending brothers (1 Cor. 5:6ff; Gal. 5:9, 13ff; 1 Thess. 5:12-20).

The key of authority is for those believers who are called to be elders by the congregation. They have authority over the circumstances of worship and discipline. For a complete listing of all the powers of an elder in the New Testament, see Cotton.[25]

To lay out all the particular powers and functions of the keys as they relate to believers and elders would require a paper of tremendous size, for the New Testament is quite full of examples of the use of the keys in the life of the church.

Keeping these general questions and answers in mind, we now turn to Matthew 18, where we will find the Lord Jesus giving us a practical view of some of the functions of the keys of the kingdom of Heaven as it relates to church discipline.

Matthew 18:15-20

1) The Context:

Having announced that He will build His church, Jesus "from that time began to show unto His disciples, that He must go unto Jerusalem and suffer many things of the elders and chief priests and scribes, be killed and the third day be raised up" (16:21).

The rejected Messiah-King now commenced to build His church. Christ took Peter, James and John up onto a mountain to behold his transfiguration, glorification and verification by the Father. Jesus' meeting with the Father, Moses and Elijah, with the multitudes gathered below at the foot of the mountain, certainly implies that the church which Jesus is now building is the God-ordained successor to the Old Testament Church of which Moses and Elijah belonged (17:1-23).

Coming down from the mountain, Jesus begins to give some of the basic rules of the new church. We are to pay our taxes and to respect the government (17:24-27).

Chapter 18 opens with a question, "Who then is the greatest in the kingdom of Heaven?" The theme of the entire chapter is going to be concerning the kingdom of Heaven and the church.

In verses 1-3, Christ discusses how to enter the kingdom of heaven. "Except you repent and become as little children, you shall in no wise enter into the kingdom of Heaven." Personal repentance and humility are required of one for his admittance into the kingdom.

Verse 4 reveals that the humility and repentance which are needed for being in the kingdom, are also necessary for "well-being" or prosperity in the kingdom.

Verses 5-55 display the duties, responsibilities and warnings concerning the believer in his personal and interpersonal walk in this world and in the community of the church. We must receive all fellow believers unto our fellowship and friendship (v. 5). We must be careful not to cause them to stumble (v. 6). We must deal with sin in our own lives (vs. 7-9). We must not hate any fellow believer (vs. 10-14). When a brother sins we are to deal with him in love and are to go to him in private to straighten things out. If he refuses to hear us, then we must take two or three brothers with us the next time and try to reason with the offender. If he rejects us, then "tell it to the church." If this fails, then the church will have to use the power of discipline (vs. 15-20). But we must be prepared to forgive our brother seventy times seventy if necessary. We must not lose our compassion, patience or love (vs. 21-34). If we deal unjustly with our brothers and do not forgive them when they repent:

> "So shall also my Heavenly Father do unto you, if you
> forgive not every one His brothers from your hearts" (v. 35).

2) The Text:

In order for us to relate what is said in Matt. 18 to chapter 16 and the rest of the New Testament, we must ask several important questions.

a) Who is designated by the term "brother"?

For the contents of verses 15 and following are concerned in a very general sense with the mutual relations among believers, as appears from the expression "your brother."[26]

This is spoken not to the Apostles as such, but as believers in Christ; and concerns everyone that stands in the relation of a brother or church-member to each other.[27]

But when the term brethren is used, the responsibilities described are clearly those of every member of the fellowship.[28]

"The offender is a brother, one that is in Christian communion, that is baptized, that hears the Word, that prays with thee, with whom thou joinest in the worship of God, stately or occasionally."[29]

As has already been seen by a study of the context, Jesus is discussing the brother to brother relationship. He is not pointing out Apostle-elder or elder-brother relationships. It is strictly one believer to another.

b) What is "the church" to which you appeal for discipline?

From ch. XVI, 18, the term "church" must always be understood as referring to the Christian Church or to the meeting of believers, whether large or small.[30]

That "church" cannot mean the church as represented by her rulers, appears by vs. 19, 20—where any collection of believers is gifted with the power of deciding in such cases. Nothing could be further from the Spirit of our Lord's command than proceedings in what were oddly enough called, "ecclesiastical courts."[31]

For Paul orders (1 Cor. 5:5) that the incestuous Corinthian shall be excommunicated not by a certain chosen number, but by the whole assembly of the godly; and therefore it might appear to be probable that the power of judging is bestowed on the whole of the people.[32]

It is clear from the context (see 18:19ff.) that this promise concerns all the church members and not, say, only the apostles or special office-bearers distinct from the others.[32]

Bring him before the church or congregation to which he belongs.[33]

… evidently the local gathering of believers is referred to.[34]

Therefore in the 17th verse, the church is mentioned as the entity that must intervene if personal and private admonition has no effect.[35]

After several fellow believers have met with you and the offender, you are to take the issue to the congregation. Romanists and others who think that the clergy is the "church" as over against the people of God, can find no support for their theories. That the local congregation is found here is clear from the following considerations.

i) To hold that Christ would announce that He was going to build His "church" and one chapter later not refer to the New Testament church when He uses the same term "church," but is referring to something else, is to fly in the face of all reasonable exegesis. It is clear that Christ was referring to His church in contrast to the Jews' church. Thus the context from chapter 16 to our passages is in favor of a congregational interpretation of the term "church."

ii) The immediate context of the passage is concerned with brother to brother relationship. It is the community of believers living and working things out together. For the thrust of the jump from a brother-brother relationship to one of brother to the Jews or Romans or church leaders would be unnatural. The natural reading of the text conveys the idea of telling the whole church.

iii) The pattern of order is clearly in favor of a congregational hearing. The issue is between one brother and yourself. Then it increases from two people involved to three or four. Then all the believers become involved in the issue. The progression of number is to show the increasing amount of iniquity on the part of the offender. Telling his sin to the church is the climax. But if we try to understand the "church" as its one or two elders or the bishops or the popes, then the pattern of numerical increase corresponding to the increase in iniquity is destroyed. The whole church in its normal worship assembly is to be the last court of appeal.

iv) The "church" disciplines the offender. It would be expected that once the offender has rejected the brother and the "church," the other believers will not treat him as if nothing had happened. They would join into the discipline and break fellowship with the offender. But is it at all reasonable that the congregation could join in the discipline without hearing the issues? In order for any true discipline to be "church" discipline, you need the whole church. So, the entire church must hear if it is to discipline.

v) The rest of the passage makes no sense if the "church" does not mean the local assembly of believers. The place of the "church" is a place of prayer, petition and worship in the name of the Lord. It is a place where Christ is especially present. It is interesting to note that the very commentators who do not hold to the "church" in v. 17 as being the gathering of believers, when they come to vs. 19, 20, they are all for these verses being applied to the local congregation. In this they betray their inconsistency. While they see the "church" in vs. 15, 16, 18, 20, they deny it in verse 17: Yet, the gathering of believers is referred to in vs. 19, 20. And the binding and loosing is a key given to all believers (v. 18).

vi) Other clear New Testament passages confirm a congregational understanding of "the church" (see 1 Cor. 5:2, 4, 5; 6:1-5; 2 Cor. 2:7, 8). The New Testament is full of examples of the whole church choosing or disciplining people.

vii) There are clear extra-biblical examples of a congregational form of discipline among the Jews and sects of our Lord's day.[36] This is mentioned only because some have found examples in extra-biblical materials where issues were rehearsed before the rulers.

viii) The other views as to what the "church" means fall down on examination. We will now deal with some of these views.

  (1) Some feel that Christ was referring to the Sanhedrin, the synagogue or the local civil government. That this idea is false is seen from the following considerations.

    (a) None of these options fit the context of ch. 18. In fact, the context rules out these things. Jesus was not talking about the Jews and their synagogue.

    (b) They are out of accord with the purpose of Christ as stated in ch. 16: "I will build my church." Having stated this, why would Christ send His people to the Pharisees to settle their problems?

    (c) These things are never called "the church" in the New Testament.

    (d) These courts would have been very hostile to the disciples of Christ. That He would be sending His disciples to them at this late date is foolish.

    (e) The civil courts did not hear personal issues which were not of a legal nature. Paul states that Christians should settle problems between believers in the church (1 Cor. 6).

    (f) These ideas are usually founded on one false assumption. Those who assert that Matt. 18:17, "tell it to the church," does not refer to the Christian discipline and that the "church" does not mean the entire body of the assembled people of God, press the idea that the Christian Church did not exist as of yet and thus Jesus could not speak of it. That this is a false assumption is seen from the following.

      (i) The Old Testament spoke of the people of the Messiah and the remnant He would save. This is the church viewed prophetically.

     (ii) Christ refers to the New Testament church in Matt. 16 and 21, as well as in Matt. 18. None of the men who hold to the synagogue idea deny that Jesus refers to the New Testament Church in Matt. 16. Why do they deny it in ch. 18? This is inconsistent.

     (iii) Christ made continual reference to his "flock, sheep, little ones, etc." Is He not speaking of the church?

     (iv) Christ chose the twelve Apostles as the foundation of the New Israel. Were they not His church?

     (v) If their idea were true, it would overthrow the truth that Christ instituted sacraments for the church; that He gave the church the Great Commission; that the teachings of Christ are for the church. If Christ cannot speak of His Church until Pentecost, then nothing in the four Gospels can be applied to the church! Some feel that Christ was referring to elders, presbyteries, synods, bishops, councils or popes. That this is false is clear.

       1. These things are ruled out by a close examination of the context and text.

       2. It would contradict the explicit teaching of Christ that the keys are given to all believers.

       3. It would contradict other plain Scriptures which show the congregation using the key of discipline.

       4. Such teachings would steal the rights of believers and create a class of tyrants in the church.

In summary, the "church" to which Jesus would have us appeal to settle our problems as believers is the local congregation to which we belong. Jesus instituted this order of procedure.

  c) What is the "binding and loosing" spoken of in verse 18?

Nearly all commentators agree that the binding and loosing of ch. 18 is the same as the binding and loosing of ch. 16, and that the binding and loosing of ch. 16 is in reference to the keys of the kingdom of Heaven. In ch. 16, the keys and their functions are in a general sense and are more wide than the particular application in ch. 18. But the power spoken of in ch. 18 is that of excommunication (binding) and the receiving back of penitent sinners (loosing). We have a beautiful example of both the binding and the loosing of a brother in 1 and 2 Corinthians.

I would like to let Lenski summarize up to this point.

> The Church (congregation) is thus the final court of appeal. Those who would place above it a still higher authority: the pope, a bishop, some church board, a house of bishops, a synod composed of clerics or these combined with lay delegates, go beyond the Word of Christ and the teachings of the apostles. In a difficult case the local congregation may seek counsel or advice, but the final jurisdiction in regard to a sinning member belongs to the congregation alone and no one ought either by direct or indirect means to nullify that jurisdiction. Zahn voices the old Christian exegesis, "Die Gemeinde also ist die hoechste kichterliche Instanz auf Erden" [the congregation is the highest authority on earth]. False greatness and authority have often been arrogated to themselves by high officials in the church who have robbed the congregations of their divine authority; and congregations have often been remiss in exercising the Lord's will; but that will stand as it is.[37]

Matthew 21:33-46

This passage is noteworthy because it shows that Jesus did teach that His church took the place of the church of the Jews. The nation Israel is now laid aside and the New Testament church has taken over her privileges, blessings and promises. In the above parable, God is seen as the Owner; the kingdom of God is the vineyard; wicked men are Israel; and the new nation is the church.

> To the Messiah belongs a people.[38]

> With this nation is specified in this context not one or another nations, but the new people of God, that God, with the setting aside of the Old Israel, should grant with the salvation of the Kingdom. Here we thus meet with the concepts "kingdom of God" and "people of God" (in the sense of the Messiah's gathering a new people of God together) in one context. Here is seen that the disclosure of the kingdom establishes itself upon the formation of a people who take the place in sacred history that was Israel's.[39]

National Israel had rejected the Messiah and now the Messiah had rejected her for a new Israel, the true people of God. It is interesting to note that those who state that Christ could not have referred to the Christian "church" in ch. 18 because Pentecost had not yet happened, do not treat the word "church" in chap. 16 the same way. Such inconsistency is its own refutation.

Summary

We have examined three of the clearest places where the Lord Jesus referred to His Church, His Bride which He purchased with His own previous blood. With ignorant and superstitious disciples, Christ had to gently reveal to them that He had come to build a new Israel and to gather a new people of God. There were many things which He wished to tell them but they were not able then to understand or bear these teachings. But He did throughout His ministry speak concerning His church and His mission on earth. He revealed that He was going to build His church. He revealed the basic polity of His church. He revealed the connection His church had with the Old Testament church. He gave principles and sermons regulating the lives of the new people of God. He instituted the Lord's Supper and Baptism. He gave the Great Commission to His church. And He gave many precious promises such as His Second Return.

We must also keep in mind that the didactic portions of the Bible take precedence over the narrative portions. The Acts must be interpreted in the light of the Epistles and didactic portions of the Gospels. With this understanding, we can see that the Church which Jesus set up is the Church which is laid out in the Epistles and narrated in the Acts.[40]

Endnotes

1. Clowney, E.P., *The Biblical Doctrine of the Church*, unpublished paper, pp. 97-99.
2. Henry, M., *Matthew Henry's Commentary*, N.F.C.E., Del., n.d., p. 132.
3. Gill, J., *An Exposition of the New Testament*, by Lassetter, Ga., 1954, p. 150.
4. Bruce, *The Expositor's Greek Testament*, Wm. B. Eerdmans Publishing Co., Mich., 1967, p. 225.
5. Vos, G., *Biblical Theology*, Wm. B. Eerdmans Publishing Co., Mich., 1968, p. 427.
6. Ridderbos, H., *The Coming of the Kingdom*, The Presbyterian and Reformed Publishing Co., Pa., 1962, p. 342.
7. Ridderbos, op. cit., p. 356.
8. Gill, op. cit., p. 150.
9. Henry, op. cit., p. 133.
10. Bruce, op. cit., p. 224.
11. Clowney, op. cit., p. 111.
12. Henry, op. cit., p. 133.
13. Gill, op. cit., p. 150.
14. Cotton, J., *John Cotton on the Churches of New England*, The Belknap Press, Mass., 1968, p. 88.
15. Bruce, op. cit., p. 225.
16. Gill, op. cit., p. 151.
17. Clowney, op. cit., p. 140.
18. Bannerman, *The Church of Christ*, T. & T. Clark, London, 1868, p. 191.
19. Bannerman, op. cit., p. 191.
20. Cotton, op. cit., p. 88.
21. Ridderbos, op. cit., pp. 360.
22. Calvin, J., *Institutes of the Christian Religion*, Wm. B. Eerdmans Publishing Co., Mich., Vol. II, p. 440.
23. Lenski, R.C., *The Interpretation of St. Matthew's Gospel*, The Ausburg Publishing House, Minn., 1965, p. 629.
24. Cotton, op. cit., pp. 89, 90.
25. Ibid., chs. V & VI.
26. Ridderbos, op. cit., p. 364, 365.
27. Gill, op. cit., p. 166.
28. Clowney, op. cit., p. 141.
29. Henry, op. cit., p. 148.
30. Lange, J.P., *Lange's Commentary of the Holy Scriptures*, Zondervan Publishing House, Mich., n.d., p. 329.
31. Alford, H., *The Greek Testament*, Moody Press, Chicago, 1958, p. 188.
32. Calvin, J., *A Harmony of Matthew, Mark, Luke*, Wm. B. Eerdmans Publishing Co., Mich., vol. II, p. 395.

33. Schweizer, E., *Church Order in the New Testament*, Allenson Inc., Ill., 1959, p. 58.

34. Lenski, op. cit., p. 702.

35. Ridderbos, op. cit., p. 365.

36. Goodwin, T., *The Works of Thomas Goodwin*, Nichol, Edinburg, 1865, vol. XL, pp. 65-74.

37. Lenski, op. cit., p. 703.

38. Zorn, R.O., *Church and Kingdom*, The Presbyterian and Reformed Publishing Company, Pa., 1962, p. 34.

39. Ridderbos, op. cit., p. 352, 353.

40. Most Reformed people use this principle against Pentecostals but are reluctant to use this principle for church polity.

Bibliography

Alford, H, *The Greek Testament*, Moody Press, Chicago, 1958.

Bannerman, *The Church of Christ*, T. & T. Clark, London, 1868.

Brown, O., *The Four Gospels*, The Banner of Truth Trust, London, 1969.

Bruce, A., *The Expositor's Greek Testament*, Wm. B. Eerdmans Publishing Co., Mich., 1967.

Calvin, J., *A Harmony of Matthew, Mark, Luke*, Wm. B. Eerdmans Publishing Co., Mich., 1965.

_____, *Institutes of the Christian Religion*, Wm. B. Eerdmans Publishing Co., Mich., 1962.

Clowney, E.P., *The Biblical Doctrine of the Church*, unpublished, n.p.

Cotton, J., *John Cotton on the Church of Christ*, The Belknap Press, Mass., 1968.

Gill, J., *An Exposition of the New Testament*, Lassetter, Ga., 1954.

Goodwin, T., *The Works of Thomas Goodwin*, Nichol, Edinburg, 1865.

Henry, M., *Matthew Henry's Commentary*, N.F.C.E., Del., n.p.

Lange, J.P., *Lange's Commentary on the Holy Scriptures*, Zondervan Publishing House, Mich., n.d.

Lenski, R.C., *The Interpretation of St. Matthew's Gospel*, The Ausburg Publishing House, Minn., 1965.

Owen, J., *The Works of John Owen*, The Banner of Truth Trust, London, 1968.

Poole, M., A Commentary on the Holy Bible, The Banner of Truth Trust, London, 1969.

Ridderbos, H., *The Coming of the Kingdom*, The Presbyterian and Reformed Publishing Company, Pa., 1962.

Schweizer, E., *Church Order in the New Testament*, Allenson Inc., Ill., 1958.

Vos, G., *Biblical Theology*, Wm. B. Eerdmans Publishing Co., Mich., 1968.

Zorn, R., *Church and Kingdom*, The Presbyterian and Reformed Publishing Company, Pa., 1962.

Chapter Eighty-One
Evangelism

God's Goal—Matthew 16:18

I. God wants His church to grow (Dan. 2:35; Matt. 13:32; Acts 2:47).

II. True church growth is by conversions, not by transference.

The Problem: Matthew 15:2, 6, 9

Evangelism

	TRADITION	THE BIBLE
Who?	The pastor is supposed to do it.	Every believer and every member (Matt. 28:18-20; Acts 1:8; 8:1-4; 1 Thess 1:7-10).
Why?	He is paid to do it. It is his job.	Christ commands all His disciples to reproduce themselves by converts (Matt. 28:19).
Where?	Within the walls of the church building by the pastor in his sermons.	Outside the walls of the church, in homes, at work, i.e., everywhere (Acts 2: homes; 8: roadside; 16: jail; 17: marketplace).
The people's responsibilities?	Invite sinners to church to hear the pastor's sermon.	To lead sinners to Christ and to disciple them in the things of God (Matt. 28:19-20).
The pastor's responsibility?	To make the church grow.	To equip the saints that they will make it grow (Eph. 4:11-13).
If few are converted?	The pastor is at fault. Trade him in for a new man.	The people are at fault if the pastor has taught them the truth.
Origin and motivation	The duty, responsibility and salary of the pastor.	Maturity and growth (Eph. 4:14-15; Heb. 5:11-14; 1 Pet 2:1-3).
How is it to be carried out	The pastor is to preach, teach and visit.	The believers are to witness, teach and visit (Acts 8:4; Matt. 25:34-40; James 1:27; 2:14-26).

Summary

The goal of the church's evangelistic program is to equip all believers to be faithful evangelistic priests. While the word "preaching" is almost always used to describe the evangelistic activities of all believers, the church's primary responsibility is summed up in the New Testament by the word "teaching."

While sinners are called to receive Christ as an aspect of the teaching ministry of the Church, evangelism is not the "Alpha and Omega" of the mission of the Church. Evangelism needs to be viewed as a responsibility of all Christians and not just the task of "paid" professionals.

Chapter Eighty-Two
Social Action

Introduction

God's plan of salvation includes the body as well as the "soul." Some have mistakenly thought that once a person's "soul" was saved, this ended the Church's responsibility to that person. It has been assumed that the Church is to minister to the spiritual needs while the state is to take care of all physical or material needs. But these assumptions, which come out of tradition, are unscriptural and rob the church of its God-ordained responsibility.

The Church is viewed by God as being a family. Just as we seek to meet all the needs of our children (physical as well as spiritual), even so the Church should seek to meet all the needs within the Body.

This implies that the Church must help people on a financial level as well as on a spiritual level. While the church works primarily to meet the needs of its members, it also bears a responsibility to do what it can in the community. The Church is to minister to the Body and to the world.

1) The Church's responsibility to meet the material and financial needs of its members:
   a) The Concept and Practice:
   The Church is to function as a true Body of believers by meeting each other's needs in material and financial matters as well as in spiritual things. The Body has a God-given responsibility to minister to the material needs of its members. Thus every local Church should be providing financial assistance and counseling to its members in order that the entire Body may experience financial freedom and prosperity. In this way, each Church will have the joy of experiencing Acts 4:34: "There was not a needy person among them."
   i) The Biblical Basis for This Practice
      (1) The Apostolic history gives us a Scriptural precedent for this practice (Acts 2:44-45; 4:34-37).
      (2) The Epistles provide us with the Scriptural principles and precepts for this practice (1 Cor. 12:20-27; 2 Cor. 8:9; Gal. 6:10; James 2:14-16; 1 John 3:17).
   ii) The Early History of This Practice
      (1) It arose spontaneously in the early Church as an expression of the love of the brethren (John 13:34-35; Acts 2:41-47; 4:32-37).
      (2) The abuse of this practice soon followed.
      (3) The early Church tried to meet 100 percent of all the needs of all the members at the same time. This led to the liquidation of all the assets of all the members (Acts 4:34). They began to experience financial bondage and poverty instead of financial freedom and prosperity.
      (4) Hypocrisy soon set in (Acts 5:1-11).
      (5) Division and strife arose in the Church because of favoritism and racial discrimination (Acts 6:1-2).
      (6) People began to criticize the way the leaders gave out financial or material assistance (Acts 6:1).
   iii) The practice was not totally abandoned, for the abuse of a biblical principle does not mean it should be negated or ignored.

(1) The Apostles put a stop to the abuse by ordaining deacons to oversee the distribution of money or material things to meet the needs of people (Acts 6:7).

(2) Those chosen to be deacons were believers whose honesty and integrity could not be questioned by anyone inside or outside the Church (Acts 6:3-7; cf. 2 Cor. 8:18-21).

iv) Financial assistance was not limited only to one local Body, but Churches helped each other out when the needs became too much for one congregation to handle by itself (1 Cor. 15:1-3).

v) The early Christians took their responsibility seriously. They attempted to maintain the balance between individual and corporate giving.

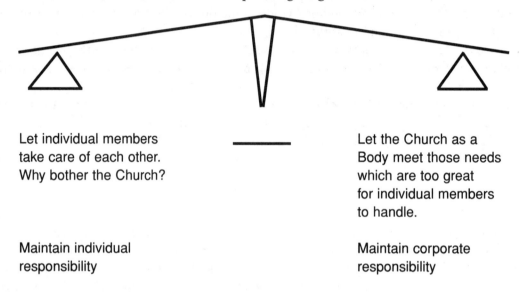

Let individual members take care of each other. Why bother the Church?   ———   Let the Church as a Body meet those needs which are too great for individual members to handle.

Maintain individual responsibility   Maintain corporate responsibility

b) Guiding Principles for this Practice

i) The person in need has the responsibility to make his need known to the deacons. If someone is too proud to obey this principle, he is generally the first one to get bitter because the members and the Church did not help him (James 4:6; 5:14).

ii) The deacons are to investigate all requests for assistance, judging each request on its own merits (Acts 6:3).

iii) The deacons should report to the elders any requests and their assessment of what the church should do to help.

iv) The elders should follow biblical and practical guidelines in their judgments (1 Tim. 5:9-16).

v) The Church is not to supplant or substitute for the responsibility of family members for each other (1 Tim. 5:8).

vi) When a special need arises, special offerings (above and beyond the regular tithes and offerings) should be taken (1 Cor. 16:1-2).

vii) To attempt to meet 100 percent of all the needs of all members at one time would lead to financial bondage and poverty. Great care must be taken to discern what need qualifies and what percentage of the need should be given.

viii) Building character qualities in the lives of people should be the guiding principle in determining whose need qualifies. The Church may loan small amounts instead of giving money. They may give a percentage of the need instead of the entire amount. The reasons for such actions are as follows:

(1) The "prodigal Son principle" (Lk. 15:11-24). God wants some people "to reap what they have sown" (Gal. 6:7). When a person has brought himself into repeated financial problems by not obeying the directives and counsel of the elders, the Church may relinquish all future financial responsibility for this person.

(2) With certain kinds of people, loaning them money will build character qualities in their lives, whereas merely giving it to them would not do so. Such qualities as responsibility, creativity and thriftiness can be enhanced in this way.

ix) Whenever possible, instead of giving money, the entire Body should be mobilized to meet the needs of its members. This action would build character qualities such as unity, sacrifice and perseverance in the corporate life of the Body. This would be a greater witness to the heathen than the mere giving of money.

x) This practice and concept in no way negates the right of private ownership. The Church cannot Scripturally demand that any member must turn over his possessions to the Church. All giving is voluntary and cannot be under necessity (Acts 5:4; 2 Cor. 9:7).

c) God's Blessing on This Practice

i) The promises of God that He will meet our financial needs are, in Scripture, often tied to our faithfulness in meeting the needs of others (2 Cor. 9:6; Phil. 4:14-19).

ii) As we "do unto others what we would have them do unto us," when we are in need, they will come to our aid (2 Cor. 8:13-15).

Conclusion

Amazing growth takes place when the people of God realize their duty to care for each other. When the Church of God meets the needs of those around her, the world sits up and takes notice.

Chapter Eighty-Three
Revival

Introduction

There is an obvious need for a mighty revival of true biblical religion to sweep across the country and the world. The moral and religious decline in America necessitates a revival in order to avoid a mighty judgment of God upon us. Christians should be deeply concerned about the subject of revival.

I. What is Revival?
   A. We must distinguish between true and false religious revivals.
      1. A true revival is a sovereign moving of God in a community or nation wherein there suddenly appears: (1) a general and gripping conviction of sin and God's judgment; (2) a turning to the biblical Gospel for salvation; (3) an overwhelming sense of God, his glory, power, love, grace, truth and presence; and (4) the local Bible-believing churches are increased and strengthened.
      2. A false revival is an emotional outburst, usually the result of sensational and fanatical measures used by man to stir up the emotions of people. The mind is not addressed with biblical truth, but the emotions are manipulated by various psychological techniques. It centers in strange physical manifestations and is of a temporary nature. In the end it leaves the churches "burned-over," divided and weakened in number and influence. It results in death and not life.

II. What are the Signs of a True Revival?
   A. It manifests the sovereign moving of God. People are convicted of sin and turned to salvation without the necessary presence of preaching. God works with and without preaching.
   B. It is preceded and accompanied by much prayer on the part of the believers in general.
   C. It often begins with the low and humble and with ordinary Christians.
   D. A deep conviction of man's sinfulness and God's judgment sweeps across the community.
   E. It centers in the great doctrines of the Bible, particularly the doctrines of sin, judgment, salvation, the new birth, justification, the doctrines of grace, heaven, hell, etc.
   F. The population is subjected to an overwhelming sense of God: that He really exists; that He is Holy and angry with our sin; that Christ is the only way of salvation, etc.
   G. Aggressive evangelism is carried on by the people of God. A true revival is not carried on by the sole labors of one man or a group of pastors. All the people of God are active.
   H. It produces permanently transformed lives. Notorious sinners become fervent saints. There is no falling away or let down.
   I. It increases and strengthens the local evangelical churches.

III. How to Labor for Revival
   A. While we state that true revivals are the sovereign work of God, this does not mean that we must negate the responsibility of man to labor for such a revival. There are no formulas to produce instant revival. We cannot coerce God to send one. But we must do all we can to obey those Scriptures which speak of the people of God humbling themselves and

seeking revival. We should pray knowing that revival is a sovereign work of God, and labor as if we can bring it about.

B. What can we do as individuals?
1. Pray regularly for revival.
2. Regain our lost love.
3. Renew our dedication to Christ.
4. Read books on past revivals.
5. Seek the filling of the Spirit.
6. Set apart special days of fasting and prayer for revival.

C. What can we do as a Church?
1. Pray with and for one another.
2. Give book reports on revival literature.
3. Have special messages, seminars and visiting speakers on revival.
4. Set up regular times of fasting and praying for revival.

Conclusion

We are told in 2 Chron. 7:14 how to labor for revival. It is our responsibility to do all we can, and it is God's responsibility to send a mighty revival.

Chapter Eighty-Four

How to Give a Public Testimony

I. A verbal confession of Christ as Savior and Lord in the presence of others is always assumed to be part of the salvation process in the N.T. (Matt. 10:32-33; Rom. 10:9-11; 1 Cor. 12:3).

Why? (Matt. 12:34)

II. The Scriptures teach us the importance of giving a testimony in the congregation.
   A. To give public thanks to God (Psa. 35:18).
   B. To give public praise to God (Psa. 111:1).
   C. To bless God publicly (Psa. 26:12).
   D. To share with God's people what God has been doing in your life (Psa. 66:16-20).

   AS A MATTER OF FACT, PSALM 107 IS ENTIRELY GIVEN OVER TO CALLING US TO BEAR PUBLIC TESTIMONY IN THE CONGREGATION.

III. Public testimonies result in:
   A. Praise and thanks given to God.
   B. Sinners being saved.
   C. Saints being encouraged and stirred up to walk in holiness.

IV. Some practical guidelines on giving a testimony:
   A. BE GOD-CENTERED: Always make God the principle actor and the main point of attraction. Let all glory go to Him—not you.
   B. DON'T BE AFRAID OR ASHAMED: Ask for the filling of the Spirit for boldness.
   C. DON'T COMPETE WITH OTHERS BY:
      1. embellishing
      2. exaggerating
   D. Strive to end your testimony with the people praising God for His greatness instead of praising you for your "greatness."
   E. Learn to exhort, admonish, encourage, or even rebuke one another in your testimony.

Chapter Eighty-Five

Twelve Rules for Public Prayer

One of the great blessings of the gathered people of God is public prayer. Throughout the Old and New Testaments God's people have met to pray together. Most churches still have a Wednesday night "Prayer Meeting" as a legacy of the last great revival in 1904. Yet, the art of public prayer has fallen on hard times. The following suggestions are intended to enrich the public prayers of God's people.

I. **Do not have private devotions during public prayer:** When people use the prayer meeting as a time to confess their personal sin and to catch up on personal needs, they are usually guilty of neglecting private prayer. The prayer meeting is not "your" time to catch up on personal devotions.

II. **Do not confess the details of personal sin.** Public prayer is primarily the time to lift up the united needs and concerns of the Church and the nation. It is not the time to confess your dark deeds. No one can pray "with" you in such prayers.

III. **Do not use singular pronouns:** When you pray in public, you are representing all the people. The use of such singular pronouns as "I," "me" and "my" means that you are leaving everyone else out of your prayer. In public prayer, you are leading the people in prayer. If you pray with singular pronouns, everyone ends up "listening" to "your" prayer instead of joining with you in praying.

IV. **Do not wait for your turn to pray:** When someone prays with singular pronouns, the other people "wait" for their turn to pray instead of praying along with the person. Public prayer is to be the united prayer of God's people. Enter into the prayers of others.

V. **Do not repeat requests:** People who "wait" for "their" turn to pray repeat the same requests all over again because they were only listening to others pray. They did not enter into the prayers of others. So, they ended up repeating the same requests over and over again. But God is not deaf and once something has been publicly prayed for, it need not be repeated. You should lead the people in prayer for a new request.

VI. **Be specific in your requests.** A public prayer request must be specific in that it is:
   (1) attainable: Do not pray for something you cannot get in this life. For example, do not pray for perfection. Do not promise God that you will never sin again;
   (2) measurable: People should be able to ask you next week if your request was answered;
   (3) Scriptural: We should pray for those things found in Scripture. If a request does not have any biblical warrant, then it will not be answered (1 John 5:14).

VII. Do not pray for vague generalities. Do not ask God for "holiness," "humility" or any other such vague terms as if God was going to send it down in a bolt of lighting. Those who are most proud are usually the first to pray loudly for "humility."

VIII. Do not pray in a "funny" voice. You should talk to God in the same way you talk to anyone else. Use your normal speaking voice and not some "churchy" tone. Be yourself.

IX. Do not use "thee" and "thou" unless you are too old to change. There is nothing sacred about 1611 English.

X. Do be brief in your prayer. Do not drone on and on as if God and everyone else will be impressed by your much speaking.

XI. Do use plural pronouns: When you pray say, "We thank you, O Lord" instead of saying, "I thank you, O Lord." The use of "we," "us" and "our" allows people to pray with you. Fake language and fake prayers tend to go together.

XII. Do include praise and thanksgiving in your prayers (Phil. 4:6). Do not approach prayer as a "shopping list" for God to magically grant. We should thank God for what we have before asking for more.

Chapter Eighty-Six

Biblical Principles for Building Projects

When a church decides to build a permanent house of worship, the following guidelines should be followed:

1. All building projects should follow the principles laid down in Scripture (Psa. 127:1). In the Bible, building projects were always completed by Spirit-motivated giving from believers and unbelievers (Exo. 35:20-29; Ezra 1:1-5) and by Spirit-led workers (Exo. 28:3; 31:1-5; 35:30-35; 36:1-3). When the Holy Spirit is behind a project, enough funds and workers will be supplied (Exo. 35:3-7).

2. It would be wrong to adopt any carnal, deceptive or manipulative fund-raising practices (2 Cor. 10:3-5). We must not be conformed to the world when it comes to fund-raising (Rom. 12:1-2). We cannot in good conscience trick or argue anyone into giving to the Lord's work. If someone's wallet is closed to God, so is his heart.

3. Therefore all giving and working must be:
   a. unto the Lord (2 Cor. 8:5).
   b. willing (Exo. 35:29; 2 Cor. 8:11-12).
   c. cheerful and enthusiastic (2 Cor. 9:2, 7).
   d. sacrificial and generous (2 Cor. 8:1-3; 9:5).
   e. not reluctant or under compulsion (2 Cor. 9:7).
   f. as a test of sincerity and love to the Lord (2 Cor. 8:8-9; 9:6-8).
   g. honest in the sight of God and man (2 Cor. 8:18-21).
   h. trusting the Lord to supply your future needs (2 Cor. 9:10-11).

4. Raising funds above tithes and offerings for special projects has always been part of church life (example: 1 Cor. 16:1-3).

5. The deacons were delegated such projects by the elders of the church (Acts 6:1-4).

6. We should build in view of the future needs of our children, grandchildren and great-grandchildren. We must not make the mistake of building only in the light of the present circumstances. If the Lord does not return in our lifetime, whatever we build will hopefully be around a hundred years from now!

7. The elders and deacons must review relevant biblical principles of finance and guidance throughout the project.

8. The congregation's response to the plan set forth by the officers of the church should be one of approval and not controversy, nitpicking, slander, backbiting or gossip (Acts 15:6, 12, 22-28).

Conclusion

God is more concerned with the way we build than with what we build. A large and beautiful house of worship that is built by evil means will not be blessed by His presence.

Chapter Eighty-Seven

The Structures and Goals of the Evangelism Committee

1) Central Goal
    a) To plan programs and activities with the overall purpose of promoting the evangelization of our communities and the world.
    b) To motivate, instruct and equip every believer in the church to be an effective evangelist of his or her relatives, friends and neighbors.
2) Structural Goals
    GOAL: In order to implement the central goal, the committee must set up and supervise programs and activities in the church.

    a) SEMINARS
        i) To set up seminars on "How to Witness" in which Christians are motivated and instructed.
            (1) When is the best time?
            (2) Where would be the best place?
            (3) A live presentation?
            (4) Videotapes or film?
            (5) Should it be a series given in Sunday School?
        ii) Should they be publicized and open to be public?
        iii) If so, where and at what cost should they be publicized?
        iv) What policies should govern the expense incurred if videotapes or films are rented?
        TASK: Develop a statement of purpose for seminars.

    b) LITERATURE
        i) What role should literature on evangelism play in the instructing and motivating of Christians?
        ii) What is the best way to encourage people to read good books on evangelism? Example: Book of the month; book table.
        iii) There needs to be an authorized selection of recommended tracts, booklets and books to be used in evangelism. A book table should be set up and an explanation given.
            Who?   When?   Where?
        iv) Should the church provide free tracts?
        v) What policies concerning literature should be set up?
        TASK: Develop a statement of purpose on literature.

c) SPECIAL MEETINGS
    i) Should we hold a special week or series of evangelistic services?
    ii) How often?
    iii) When?
    iv) Where?
    v) The details of publicity must be worked out.
    TASK: Develop a statement of purpose on evangelistic meetings.

d) OUTREACH MINISTRIES
    i) What outreach ministries should be developed in the church?
        (1) Jail meetings
        (2) Teams for ministering to other churches
        (3) Homes for foster care
        (4) Half-way house for counseling
        (5) Divorce counseling
        (6) Coffee-cup evangelism, etc.

e) What are the qualifications for leading or participating on a ministry team?

3) What role should videotapes and films have in instructing people on outreach ministries?
   TASK: Develop a statement of purpose on outreach ministries.

Chapter Eighty-Eight

Developing Mission-Mindedness in Young People

The task and duty of world evangelism passes from one generation to another much like a baton is passed from runner to runner in a relay race. The runner who starts the race depends upon the second runner, and the second runner depends on the third runner, who in turns depends upon the fourth runner to cross the finish line in victory. Each runner must be in good shape, and he must be prepared to run with the baton when it is passed to him. If he is not prepared, the race will not be run or won.

The question before us as a church is this: "Are we preparing the next generation to run the race for world evangelism? Are we training them to pick up the baton?"

Unless we begin to develop mission-mindedness in our young people, we will not see a mighty army of young people prepared to serve the Lord as missionaries. If they are not groomed to think missions, eat missions and even dream missions, what hope is there that they will offer their lives for missionary service?

We must make the task and calling of the missionary something valued very highly in the minds of our young people. They must feel the romance of it. The idealism of it must grab hold of their imagination. They must feel that to be a missionary is one of the most wonderful things a Christian can ever be.

In order to implement a strong missions program in a church, there are various steps which can be taken.

Step No. 1: Make sure that you are mission-minded yourself. Have you in the past and do you in the present read books and articles on missions and missionaries? Are you willing to correspond with missionaries to find out their needs and requests? Do you pray for the specific needs of specific missionaries? (No, it is not enough to simply pray, "God, bless all the missionaries. Amen.") Do you sacrificially give to support missions above and beyond your regular tithes and offerings?

As the missions committee, it is your unique privilege and responsibility to keep missionaries and their needs before the church. But if you yourself are not missions-minded, how in the world do you think the church will become mission-minded? Make sure that you have caught the vision of world evangelism.

Step No. 2: You should set up a monthly newsletter or bulletin which will keep the church informed as to what is happening to foreign and home missionaries. Their needs and requests can be given at that time. The important thing is not to let your people forget your missionaries.

Step No. 3: We need to have annual missionary conferences which will involve the entire church. A full week of special meetings will be sufficient. There should be a mixture of speakers, slide presentations and exciting films.

Step No. 4: Develop programs aimed at the youths of the church.
   A. Have a missionary story read or told once a month during opening exercises.
   B. After the story, have a special prayer for missionaries.
   C. Take a special missions offering beyond the regular offerings. Obtain a large globe and make it into a "piggy bank" for missions. Whenever there is a birthday, let the birthday child put as many pennies into the globe as his age. If the child is 13 years old, 13 pennies are to be put into the globe.
   D. Show mission films during Sunday School.
   E. Set up a missions library for the children to check out books and read. Encourage children to check out a book and then give a report to their class about it. This will get others to read books as well.

Title	Publisher
Knight of the Snows: Wilfred Grenfell	Christian Literature Crusade
Trail Maker: David Livingstone	Christian Literature Crusade
To Be a Pilgrim: John Bunyan	Christian Literature Crusade
Friend of the Chiefs: Robert Moffat	Christian Literature Crusade
The Doctor Who Never Gave Up: Ida Scudder	Christian Literature Crusade
The Man Who Freed the Slaves: William Wilberforce	Christian Literature Crusade
Young Man in a Hurry: William Carey	Christian Literature Crusade
The Missionary Heroine of Calabar: Mary Slessor	Christian Literature Crusade
Saint in the Slums: Kagawa of Japan	Christian Literature Crusade
The Monk Who Shook the World: Martin Luther	Christian Literature Crusade
On the Clouds to China: Hudson Taylor	Christian Literature Crusade
Wizard of the Great Lake: Alexander Mackay	Christian Literature Crusade
God's Madcap: Amy Carmichael	Christian Literature Crusade
Horseman for the King: John Wesley	Christian Literature Crusade
Ann H. Judson of Burma	Christian Literature Crusade
Never Say Die: Gladys Aylward	Christian Literature Crusade
Queen of the Dark Chamber: Christiana Tsai	Moody Press
Words Wanted:	Wycliffe Bible Translators
Gladys Alward: The Little Woman	Wycliffe Bible Translators
Gipsy Smith	Wycliffe Bible Translators
George Muller: Young Rebel in Bristol	Wycliffe Bible Translators
The Life of David Livingstone	Wycliffe Bible Translators
Firebrand of Flanders	Wycliffe Bible Translators
Heroes of the Faith	Wycliffe Bible Translators
One Hour to the Stone Age	Wycliffe Bible Translators
Five Pioneer Missionaries	Banner of Truth
John Paton: Missionary to the New Hebrides	Banner of Truth
Jeannette Li	Banner of Truth
God Made Them Great	Banner of Truth

Five Christian Leaders	Banner of Truth
Five English Reformers	Banner of Truth
The Korean Pentecost	Banner of Truth
The Unlisted Legion	Banner of Truth
Men of Purpose	Henry E. Walter
Twelve Reformation Heroes	Pickering & Inglis

Step No. 5: Set up a map display in the sanctuary, with red pins pointing out where missionaries are laboring for the Lord. This will once again keep the missionaries in the minds of the people of God.

Step No. 6: Be prepared to raise special support to send young people on summer missionary tours. As your youths become interested in missions, give them the opportunities to see mission work from firsthand experience.

Step No. 7: Set up a special fund to give financial aid to students in Bible college or seminary. We must show that we are really behind our young people who plan to go into the ministry.

Chapter Eighty-Nine

The Missionary and the Poor

When a Western missionary goes to a Third World country, one of the first things that creates an enormous cultural shock is the visible presence of the poor. Robert Kreider relates his experience.

> We visited the Bihari refugee camp on the edge of Dacca, Bangladesh. Three hundred refugees live together in an area no larger than a small basketball court. As we entered the area, dozens of thin, but bright-eyed, curious children crowded around to see, to touch, to hear. Adults came up and angrily tried to chase them away. Approached by beggars on the ferry boat, in the street, literally everywhere, we were haunted by the admonition of our Lord: "Give to him that asketh." The hundreds of people sleeping on the concrete floor of Hawrath Railroad Station in Calcutta evoked the image of the Son of Man having no place to lay His head.
>
> We saw people carrying enormous loads on their heads and backs and heard the Scriptural injunction: "Bear ye one another's burdens." And in noting others carrying heavy loads from a yoke borne on the shoulders, we remembered Christ's words: "Take my yoke upon you."[1]

The sadness at seeing the poor and the sick everywhere is soon overwhelmed by a sense of utter helplessness. What can one missionary do to help the poor and the sick? Should he spend his time organizing relief programs? Should he petition the national government to redistribute the wealth in that society? Should he give away his own food and clothing? What should he do?

The obvious but hard answer is that Christ did not call him or her to fight poverty per se, but to preach the Gospel. One person cannot solve all the problems of the poor. As soon as he has met the needs of a few, the many come looking for what has already been given away. To put it bluntly, there are too many poor for poverty to vanish from the face of the earth. Did not Jesus say, "Ye have the poor always with you" (Matt. 26:11)?

The utopian dream of a world free of hunger, poverty and injustice is one of humanism's optimistic leaps into the dark. The Bible tells us that poverty and injustice will continue as long as sinners live on earth. Only at the Second Coming of Christ shall a new earth be created where there will be no place for sorrow, death or pain.

Even though biblical Christians do not entertain vain utopian hopes and dreams, they have done more to erase poverty, hunger and injustice than any other force in history. Those nations which embraced biblical Christianity during the Reformation have developed the highest living standards and the freest societies on earth. The sociological benefits of having a Reformation basis or background have been pointed out by Dr. Lorraine Boettner.[2] He demonstrates that a nation's religion will affect its standard of living.

India's problems are not rooted in having too many people. Other countries, such Holland, have more people per square mile than India! India's problems are rooted in its false religion. Its poverty and starvation flow out of its Hinduism. Her religion is the greatest hindrance to her prosperity.

The same can be said for Latin America's ignorance and poverty. Such things flow out of Roman Catholicism. A nation's theology will directly affect its living standard.

This is why those who are concerned with the poverty and injustice on the mission field feel that the greatest need in the Third World is a massive turning to Reformation Christianity. Only upon this base could these nations overcome poverty and injustice, as did the Western Protestant nations. Without a Christian basis, a Third World country may be doomed to international panhandling (i.e. foreign aid).

Thus, the Gospel missionary who feels with the poor will realize that salvation is what Third World people need most of all. The Gospel will do more for the poor than bread, clothing or bullets. Did not Jesus say that He came to "preach the Gospel to the poor" (Lk. 4:18)?

Jesus did not build houses for the homeless or overthrow governments by violence. He knew that the root of injustice could be cured only by the preaching of the Gospel; for wherever the Gospel is received, there follows godliness, cleanliness and prosperity.[3]

Even though a religious and moral explanation of the Third World's poverty is obvious, the non-Christian world (including the World Council of Churches) is furious at even the slightest suggestion that biblical Christianity produces a superior lifestyle and standard of living. In an age in which the World Council of Churches is trying to convince everyone that all religious are one, the superiority of Christianity over the pagan religions is absolutely rejected as not even being a consideration.

The non-Christian community, in league with the World Council of Churches and Marxist ideology, has sought to place the full blame of the world's poverty and injustice on the Western countries and, in particular, the United States. The Marxists reject religion and morals as being the explanation of the ills of this world and, instead, point to world economics. One non-communist but Marxist influenced church leader put it this way: 10,000 persons died today because of inadequate food. One billion people (more than one fourth of all persons living today) are mentally or physically retarded because of a poor diet. The problem, of course, is that the world's resources are not evenly distributed. We in the West are an affluent island amid a sea of starving humanity. North America, Europe and Australia have only one fourth of the world's population, but they greedily consume one half of the world's available food. The average income per person in India is about $70 per year; in the U.S. about $4,000. We now have almost 60 times as much as our brothers over there and the difference will continue to widen.[4]

Such people evidently assume that a "redistribution of wealth" is the answer to poverty. This is an old Marxist theory that has never worked even in communist countries. It is interesting to note that those people who talk about "redistributing wealth" never distribute their wealth. They always want us to give away what we worked hard for while they continue to be the idle rich. Jane Fonda, the Kennedys and many other idle rich come readily to mind as an example. Until they "redistribute" all their wealth, their words are hollow.

Harold B. Kuhn points out the Marxist thinking behind much of the "liberation theology" being developed in Latin America.

Latin liberation theology appeals largely to Marxist models. This accounts for its simplistic assumption that all human ills grow out of the misdoings of one class, which is regarded as the bearer of all evil. In the radical form of this theology, North American capitalism is seen as the sole cause of injustice and misery in Latin America. Its advocates can thus easily adopt the myopic stances of the United Nations World Population Conference in Bucharest and the World Food Conference in Rome, both held in 1974, and close their eyes to the problems raised by burgeoning populations and tradition-hindered ways of agriculture. This is a source of great confusion.[5]

Anyone who understands the doctrine of total depravity or human psychology knows that if all the wealth of the world was redistributed, within one year there would once again exist the poor, the middle class and the rich. Some people will not work and are addicted to poverty. Others are unscrupulous and will heap dishonest wealth to themselves. Others will prosper through honest toil.

Of course, when Marxist-influenced missiologists, theologians and politicians began screaming about "the American fascist capitalist pigs" who are single-handedly responsible for the poverty and injustice in this world, they completely ignore the fact that communism generates immense poverty and injustice through its totalitarian denial of basic human rights.[6]

Are we then to do nothing for the poor? No, we are not saying that. Just because the Gospel gets to the heart of the problem because it deals with the hearts of the people is no excuse for individual Christians and churches not to do what they can to help the poor, heal the sick and feed the hungry.[7] The Gospel has the first place but not the only place.

Ministering to the poor in material things is a handmaid to the Gospel. Missionaries have always done what they could to raise the living standard and lengthen the life-expectancy of the people to whom they ministered. Even though they have been accused of being "culture-busters," they have done for the Third World what it could not do for itself. In the past, missionaries have helped people climb out of their poverty by teaching them better agricultural techniques. Mission hospitals and schools were built to deal with body and mind. Even things like concrete factories or exporting of native art objects have been developed by concerned missionaries. The half has yet to be told of all the wonderful and tremendous things which fundamental Bible-believing missionaries have done to raise the living standards of the poor for the cause of Jesus Christ. The love and compassion of Jesus moved missionaries in the past and will move them in the future to take pity on the poor and the oppressed.

What definite steps have missionaries taken to deal with the poor?

Step No. 1: They have won disciples to Jesus Christ and planted local national churches. As Glasser put it: "There is but one acid test that should be applied to all activities that claim to represent obedience in mission. Do they or do they not produce disciples of Jesus Christ?"[8]

Step No. 2: They have worked with these disciples in developing proper attitudes and skills which will help them become self-supporting. Why work with Christians and not just non-Christians at large? The Bible tells us to do good "especially to those of the household of faith" (Gal. 6:10).

Biblical Christians reject the present popular doctrine of universalism, which is the motivation of most of the World Council of Churches projects. Some have assumed that the poor and the oppressed belong to the church or that all men are the children of God.[9]

Kuhn points out:

One peril that shows through the literature of liberation theology is an uncritical use of biblical models. The major model currently in use is that of the Exodus. Rather too easily, in my opinion, Latin American theologians assume that today's oppressed people are the heirs of God's Exodus—that they are the present-day counterparts of the Israelitish people in Egypt. Attempts to domesticate God have not been particularly successful in the past and there is little reason to suppose that this current form will be any more effective. It is precisely this form of idolatry that emerges as any group assumes for itself a "people of God" role. It is disturbing that liberation theologians do not give more attention to building a set of common values and adequate symbols among their peoples. Without these, any liberation by violence will probably lead only to a change of oppressors. Mere oppression neither makes any people to be "the people of God" nor guarantees that a victory by force will produce lasting liberation. A second peril grows out of the first. Some liberation theologians suggest that the Exodus is a model by which all oppressed peoples, regardless of their plight, find deliverance from their miseries. It may be questioned whether the Bible can be used indiscriminately to justify all political and economic struggles.

A third peril lies hidden in the rationale advanced for this position. Hugo Assmann, who with Gustavo Gutierrez and Juan Luis Segundo, may be regarded as a spokesman for Latin liberation theology, highlights this aspect of the problem. In his *Theology for a Nomad Church*, Assmann makes clear the movement's assumption that the purely "salvationist" understanding of the Christian mission has been rendered obsolete by what Gutierrez calls "the unvarnished affirmation of the possibility of universal salvation."[10]

Step No. 3: Once the national church becomes self-supporting and self-ruling, it can begin its own deaconate ministry in which it will attempt to meet the needs of its own community. The nationals can become involved in political appeal and in the struggle to overcome injustice. The missionaries should be a moral force only and not political activists.

Poverty can be overcome, not by theft, which is the true meaning of the "redistribution of wealth," but by Third World people becoming evangelical Christians.

Endnotes

1. Robert Kreider, "To Give But to Receive," pp. 3-4.
2. Loraine Boettner, *Roman Catholicism*, Presbyterian Reformed Publishing Co., Philadelphia, 1969.
3. The difference between the Hindu and Christian sections of India are like night and day. The Christian sections of India are clean and prosperous, while the Hindu sections are filled with filth and poverty.
4. Ron Sider, "The Graduated Tithe," Partners in Mission.
5. Harold B. Kuhn, "The Evangelical's Duty to the Latin American Poor," *Christianity Today*, Feb. 4, 1977, pp. 537-538.
6. Kuhn, ibid., p. 537.
7. Howard A. Snyder, *The Problem of Wine-Skins*, InterVarsity Press, Downers Grove, Ill., 1977, p. 46.
8. Arthur F. Glasser, Mission Trends, No. 1, editors Gerald H. Anderson, Thomas F. Stransky, Paulist/Eerdmans, 1974.
9. One example of the heresy of universalism is found in Feeding the Hungry: Mission by Congressional District (Bread for the World, Christian Citizens' Movement).
10. Kuhn, ibid., p. 538.

Chapter Ninety
Heathen Religions

The Lausanne Covenant

The Urgency of the Evangelistic Task

More than 2.7 billion people, which is more than two-thirds of mankind, have yet to be evangelized. We are ashamed that so many have been neglected; it is a standing rebuke to us and to the whole church. There is now, however, in many parts of the world an unprecedented receptivity to the Lord Jesus Christ. We are convinced that this is the time for churches and para-church agencies to pray earnestly for the salvation of the unreached and to launch new efforts to achieve world evangelization. A reduction of foreign missionaries and money in an evangelized country may sometimes be necessary to facilitate the national church's growth in self-reliance and to release resources for unevangelized areas. Missionaries should flow ever more freely from and to all six continents in a spirit of humble service. The goal should be, by all available means and at the earliest possible time, that every person will have the opportunity to hear, understand and receive the good news. We cannot hope to attain this goal without sacrifice.

It was estimated in 1977 that the task of reaching those who have never heard the Gospel was growing at such a rate that 200,000 missionaries would be needed to reach the 4.7 billion unevangelized in A.D. 2000.[1]

With the 2.7 billion unevangelized then, growing to more than 4.7 billion by A.D. 2000, what can we do to meet this problem?

What should our attitude be toward the heathen religions of this world? Should we adopt the universalist's code that all religions are just different roads to the same God and that all religions are worshiping "God" under different names?

Kosuke Koyama evidently likes the universalist's answer. To him, anyone who accepts the biblical teaching that all heathen religionists are worshiping demons (1 Cor. 10:20) and cannot be saved unless they turn from their idols to worship and serve the Christian God (1 Thess. 1:9-10), is full of "super-arrogance" and "super-ignorance." He states:

> One day some years ago, I met a missionary couple from the West in Bangkok International Airport. They had just arrived in Bangkok. There they expressed the view that Thai Buddhism is a manifestation of demons! How simple! Thirty million people in the Buddhistic tradition of seven hundred years were brushed aside in one second. The remark betrayed super-arrogance and super-ignorance. More than this, I heard that the People's Republic of China with her seven hundred million are all "atheistic," therefore "not saved," and even positively the enemy of the Gospel! This calamity of super-arrogance and super-ignorance derives from the inability to appreciate the complexity of the living man in the living history.[2]

The universalist assumes that he is humble because he exalts human reason and human religions and degrades the Scriptures as being just one revelation of God among many other "Bibles" of other religions. The Bible-believing missionary who lovingly confronts paganism for what it really is—man's attempt to cover up his rebellion against God—is labeled "super-arrogant" and "super-ignorant."

The truth of the matter is that the "ecumaniacs" and universalists are "super-arrogant" and "super-ignorant." They are arrogant in that they think their own opinion is more valuable than what God teaches in His Word. They are "proud" of what pagan religions have produced, for they assume this proves the superiority of man's reason. They are ignorant of both the Scriptures and the power of God (Matt. 22:29).

The Third World is rushing to embrace syncretism. Byang H. Kato points out five reasons why Third World missiologists and leaders are accepting the old liberal lie that all men will eventually be saved. He states:

> Incentives for syncretism in Africa are not hard to see. The incentive for universalism (i.e., the idea that all will be saved in the end) are the same for syncretism since only a thin line separates the two ideologies. The reason for growing syncretism tendencies may be summed up briefly as follows:
>
> (1) The prevailing wind of religious relativism in the older churches is carried abroad by the liberal missionaries in person and through literature.
>
> (2) Emotional concerns for the ancestors who died before the advent of Christianity force some theologians to call for a recognition of religious practices of pre-Christian idol worshipers.
>
> (3) Inadequate biblical teaching has left the average Christian with inability to "rightly divide the Word of truth." Syncretistic or neo-orthodox teachers bring their views, and even Christian leaders fail to discern what is right according to the teaching of God's Word.
>
> (4) Liberal Christianity has done a thorough job in picking up key brains from the Third World and grooming them in liberal schools in the Western world.
>
> (5) The study of comparative religions without the effort to assert the uniqueness of Christianity has helped produce theologians of syncretistic persuasion.[3]

To those who love Jesus and His Gospel, the present flood of liberal theology onto the mission field and into mission theology breaks the heart. To see a denial of the uniqueness of Christ and His Gospel; to be told that Peter was wrong in Acts 4:12 because there are plenty of other names by which men will be saved; to be persecuted by these liberal ecumaniacs because you believe the Bible, is hard to accept. But liberals have never been liberal toward Bible-believing Christians. The universalists have never been universalistic enough to include Bible-believing Christians.

The time has come for Christians to restate Machen's thesis that liberal theology is not Christian theology but belongs to the religion of humanism. Universalism is not "Christian" because it is not biblical. Bible-believing Christians can accept and proclaim the statements in the Lausanne Covenant and the even clearer statements of the Frankfurt Declaration.

The Lausanne Covenant

The Uniqueness and Universality of Christ

We affirm that there is only one Savior and only one Gospel, although there is a wide diversity of evangelistic approaches. We recognize that all men have some knowledge of God through His general revelation in nature. But we deny that this can save, for men suppress the truth by their unrighteousness. We also reject as derogatory to Christ and the Gospel every kind of syncretism and dialogue which implies that Christ speaks equally through all religions and ideologies. Jesus Christ being Himself the only God-man, who gave Himself as the only ransom for sinners, is the only mediator between God and man. There is no other name by which we must be saved. All men are perishing because of sin, but God loves all men, not wishing that any should perish but that all should repent. Yet those who reject Christ repudiate the joy of salvation and condemn themselves to eternal separation from God. To proclaim Jesus as "the Saviour of the world" is not to affirm that all religions offer salvation in Christ. Rather it is to proclaim God's love for a world of sinners and to invite all men to respond to Him as Saviour and Lord in the wholehearted personal commitment of repentance and faith. Jesus Christ has been exalted above every other name: we long for the day when every knee shall bow to Him and every tongue shall confess Him as Lord.

The Frankfurt Declaration

We recognize and declare:

Jesus Christ our Savior, true God and true man, as the Bible proclaims Him in His personal mystery and His saving work, is the basis, content and authority of our mission. It is the goal of this mission to make known to all people in all walks of life the gift of His salvation.

We therefore challenge all non-Christians, who belong to God on the basis of creation, to believe in Him and to be baptized in His name, for in Him alone is eternal salvation promised to them,

We therefore oppose the false teaching (which is circulated in the ecumenical movement since the Third General Assembly of the World Council of Churches in New Delhi) that Christ Himself is anonymously so evident in world religions, historical changes and revolutions that man can encounter Him and find salvation in Him without the direct news of the Gospel.

We therefore oppose the universalistic idea that in the crucifixion and resurrection of Jesus Christ all men of all times are already born again and already have peace with Him, irrespective of their knowledge of the historical saving activity of God or belief in it. Through such a misconception the evangelizing commission loses both its full, authoritative power and its urgency.

Unconverted men are thereby lulled into a fateful sense of security about their eternal destiny.

We recognize and declare:

The offer of salvation in Christ is directed without exception to all men who are not yet bound to Him in conscious faith. The adherents to the non-Christian religions and world views can receive this salvation only through participation in faith. They must let themselves be freed from their former ties and false hopes, in order to be admitted by belief and baptism into the body of Christ. Israel, too, will find salvation in turning to Jesus Christ.

We therefore reject the false teaching that the non-Christian religions and world views are also ways of salvation similar to belief in Christ.

We refute the idea that "Christian presence" among the adherents to the world religions and a give-and-take dialogue with them are substitutes for a proclamation of the Gospel which aims at conversion. Such dialogues simply establish good points of contact for missionary communications.

We also refute the claim that the borrowing of Christian ideas, hopes and social procedures—even if they are separated from their exclusive relationships to the person of Jesus—can make the world religions and ideologies substitutes for the Church of Jesus Christ. In reality they give them a syncretistic and therefore anti-Christian direction.

It is not unloving, unkind, proud or vain to believe the biblical teaching that salvation comes only to those who believe in Jesus (Jn. 3:16). To accept the Scriptures is to love God and humbly to receive God's truth. The heathen shall all perish in Hell (Psa. 9:17; Rom. 2:12). This is true even though we may not like it.

What About the Heathen?

The following answers are suggestions which have been formed over many years of involvement in mission-related studies. Some of the things which I will share with you may seem radical, but in light of the urgency of reaching the lost, I do not believe that they are radical enough.

1. The doctrine of Hell needs to be revived.

It is a fact beyond dispute that there is a correspondence between the doctrine of Hell and missionary vision. When churches go liberal and jettison this doctrine, there is no missionary vision left.

I took a brief survey of my friends in the ministry and discovered that not one of them had preached an entire message on the subject of Hell. Pastors shy away from this doctrine because they are afraid of having a "fire and brimstone" reputation.

In the various books and articles which I have read on the subject of missions, virtually none of them remind the reader that the heathen are being cast into Hell every second of the day.

Without a revival of the preaching and defense of the biblical doctrine of Hell, the average layman will not feel the urgency of the task. He will not weep for the lost who have never heard. He will not have compassion on the heathen. He will not sacrificially give to missions.

Let pastors and seminary professors preach "fire and brimstone" sermons with tears streaming down their faces. Let them inspire those who hear them to give themselves and everything they have to reach the lost. Let the fire of missionary passion and vision spread from pulpits and lecterns, and then we shall see our generation evangelized for Christ (see Robert Morey, *Death and the Afterlife*, Bethany House).

2. We need to receive the Power of the Holy Spirit to get the job done.

Pentecost was the endowment of the church with POWER to evangelize the world for Christ (Lk. 24:49; Acts 1:8).

Only to the degree we begin to receive and exercise the power of the Spirit, can the church arise to the mission challenge.

We need to preach and teach on the doctrine of the Holy Spirit. We see in Latin America what Spirit-filled missionaries and churches can do. Let us seek the Spirit's power and experience true revival.

3. Creeping Universalism needs to be challenged and refuted.

Once again, the pernicious doctrine of neo-universalism has raised its ugly head in evangelical circles. One self-proclaimed "thinker" has openly denied the historic Christian doctrine that the heathen are lost and will go to Hell.[4] He proposes the heretical idea that those who have never heard the Gospel are saved by being sincere in their pagan religion. This is wicked as well as anti-Scriptural.

The failure to accept the biblical doctrine of the lost condition of the heathen will do great harm to missionary vision. Let us then affirm the historic truth, "Outside of the church, there is no salvation." Without faith, no one can be saved. Without the Gospel, no faith is possible (Rom. 10:17). This teaching is hard but biblical.

4. Mission theorists need rebuking and debunking.

Most missiologists remind me of those who were concerned about rearranging the deck furniture on a sinking ship. The ship is going down, people are dying, and yet they are concerned with rearranging theological furniture!

The time for a moratorium has come—a moratorium, i.e., on the fruitless infighting of mission theorists. The heathen are perishing while missiologists spend their time criticizing each other's theories.

To those who are Bible-believing Christians, the heart issues are very clear.

No. 1: All who have never received or heard about Jesus Christ and His salvation will be cast into Hell.

No. 2: The Church's mission is to preach the Gospel to every human being (Mk. 10:15) and to make disciples in every nation, baptizing and gathering them into local churches (Matt. 28:19, 20).

No. 3: The issue is: "We want to reach the most people in the shortest time. How can we do it?" Regardless of the cost, our duty is to preach the Gospel to every man and woman on this planet. This is the heart issue.

Things have gotten out of balance to such a degree that only a radical turning to Scripture can put things back in focus.

For example, cultures shall pass away, but the souls of men live on forever. Thus we should be more concerned with the salvation of immortal souls than with saving cultures. Is it more important to see a pagan culture "saved" than to get the pagans saved? Or, is it more important to see sinners saved even if it destroys a pagan culture?

In Heaven, no saved pagan will complain about losing his pagan culture to gain Christ! Paul did not complain about losing his culture. He rejoiced instead (Phil. 3:1-9).

5. The urgency of the task casts doubt on the present "brick and mortar" mentality of most missionaries.

Dr. Ralph Winter points out:

> We will also note the appalling, counter-balancing fact that, while missions have been successful in planting churches almost everywhere, nevertheless, do not look now, but 95 percent of all missionaries today are embedded in work with those same national churches, doing only local outreach at best. This success-stagnation development is all the more disturbing in the face of the astounding fact that 84 percent of the non-Christians of the world are beyond the outreach of 95 percent of all existing church and mission efforts.[5]

With 2.7 billion who have never heard, what in the world are we doing with 95 percent of our missionaries involved in situations where minimum contact with the unevangelized is guaranteed? Is it not true that at the rate mission hospitals and schools are being "liberated" by the communists and "nationalized" by other totalitarian nations, the putting of money into buildings which in a few years will serve antichrist forces, is a waste and a misuse of the Lord's money? The communists and the cults do not put their money into "brick and mortar," and are growing at a rate far surpassing Christian missions. They put their money and energy into literature and radio to evangelize multitudes with their false gospels.

6. The Third World must become involved in missions.

The Western missionary cannot carry the entire task of world evangelism on his shoulders alone. Every church should be involved in local evangelism and in foreign missions. As the Lausanne Covenant states:

The Church and Evangelism

> We affirm that Christ sends His redeemed people into the world as the Father sent Him and that this calls for a similar deep and costly penetration of the world. We need to break out of our ecclesiastical ghettos and permeate non-Christian society. In the church's mission of sacrificial service, evangelism is primary. World evangelization requires the whole church to take the whole Gospel to the whole world. The church is at the very center of God's cosmic purpose and is His appointed means of spreading the Gospel.

Cooperation in Evangelism

> We affirm that the church's visible unity in truth is God's purpose. Evangelism also summons us to unity, because our oneness strengthens our witness, just as our disunity under-

mines our Gospel of reconciliation. We recognize, however, that organizational unity may take many forms and does not necessarily forward evangelism. Yet we who share the same biblical faith should be closely united in fellowship, work and witness. We confess that our testimony has sometimes been marred by sinful individualism and needless duplication. We pledge ourselves to seek a deeper unity in truth, worship, holiness and mission. We urge the development of regional and functional cooperation for the furtherance of the church's mission, for strategic planning, for mutual encouragement and for the sharing of resources and experience.

When national churches begin to evangelize, the church growth is phenomenal.[6]

7. We Need to Adopt Radical Programs to Reach the Lost

One radical program is to adopt the strategy of successful cults like the Mormons. *Eternity* magazine reports that:

> The real key to reaching the goal reports MARC, is for evangelicals to adopt the mission strategy of Mormons. The Mormons expect that every Mormon young man will serve a two-year mission assignment, supported by himself and/or his family before he begins a vocation. If we estimate that there are 10 million mission-minded Christian families in the U.S. alone and that each one has one son under 21, 10 percent or 1,000,000 would be short-term missionaries today.[7]

We need to train our young people to look toward a short-term missionary term if not full-time service. Missionary vision must begin in the home and be nurtured in the church before it can be exported to the world.

Conclusion

Heathen religions are the result of man's flight from God and not man's search for God (Rom. 1:18-25). The only hope of any sinner anywhere on this planet is Jesus Christ and His Gospel.

Endnotes

1. *Eternity,* Vol. 20, No. 7, July 1977, p. 7.

2. Kosuke Koyama, *What Makes a Missionary?,* Mission Trends No. 1, ed. Anderson & Stransky, Paulist, 1974, p. 122.

3. Byang H. Kato, *The Gospel, Cultural Context and Religions Syncretism, Let the Earth Hear His Voice,* World Wide Publications, 1975, pp. 1218, 1219.

4. Clark Pinnock, *Eternity,* Vol. 27, No. 12, Dec. 1976, p. 13. See also: Pinnock, *A Case for Faith* (Bethany House Pub., Minn., 1986) pp. 109-111. For a refutation of his view see Robert Morey's *Death and the Afterlife,* Bethany House).

5. Ralph Winter, "Where's the Scoreboard," *Eternity,* Vol. 28, No. 7, July 1977, p. 40.

6. See John Worrall, "Why Christianity Is Thriving In a Turbulent Black Africa," *U.S. News & World Report,* Vol. LXXXII, No. 7, May 2, 1977, p. 63.

7. *Eternity,* Ibid., p. 61.

Chapter Ninety-One

Christian Education Committee

1) CENTRAL GOAL

To plan programs and activities with the overall purpose of promoting the spiritual maturity of the members of this church and their families.

TASK: As a group, discuss and then give a definition of:

"Spiritual Maturity"

"Every area of life"

"Members and families"

2) STRUCTURAL GOALS

GOAL: In order to implement the central goal, this committee must set up and supervise programs and activities in this church.

a) SUNDAY SCHOOL

i) Contrast the traditional concept with a "Body Life" concept of Sunday School.

    (1) When was Sunday School invented?

    (2) Why was it invented?

    (3) How has Sunday School developed since then?

    (4) What is the purpose of Sunday School according to tradition?

    (5) Does Sunday School lead to the father's neglect of the religious education of his children?

    (6) Can this abuse of Sunday School be overcome?

    (7) How can Sunday School be restructured to reflect the central goal?

ii) Teachers

    (1) Where, when and how can teachers be trained for Sunday School?

        (a) Literature

        (b) Seminars

            (i) Live

            (ii) Videotape

            (iii) Films

        (c) Classes

        (d) Retreats

    (2) What standards and qualifications should be used in selecting teachers?

iii) Class Structure

    (1) Teacher-pupil ratio

(2) Age or maturity classification?

iv) Literature
(1) Denominational
(2) Independent
(3) Written by someone in church

v) Sunday School and the Family
(1) How can we structure Sunday School to strengthen family religious education?
(2) Can Sunday School help "Family Night"?
(a) Take-home paper
(b) Work with family

vi) Sunday School and Modern Media
(1) Musical instruments
(2) Videotapes
(3) Films
(4) Flannel board
(5) Puppets

vii) Sunday School choir and special programs

viii) Sunday School and training people to memorize Scripture.
(1) How many Scriptures?
(2) What method?
(3) Parent participation?
(4) Rewards as incentives
(5) Material for memorizing Scripture
(a) Flash cards
(b) Literature
(c) Cartoons
(d) Songs
(e) Etc.
TASK: Develop a statement of purpose for Sunday School.

b) SEMINARS
i) How do seminars fit into the central goal?

ii) What seminars should be promoted in this church?

iii) Seminars (kinds of)
(1) Live
(2) Videotape
(3) Film
(4) Retreats

iv) What Topics Should Be Covered in a Seminar Format?
    (1) How To Discipline Your Children
    (2) How to Manage Your Money
    (3) Etc.

v) How Often Should the Church Sponsor a Seminar?

vi) What Responsibilities Should Be Fulfilled by the Christian Education Committee?
    (1) Selecting Seminars
    (2) Scheduling
    (3) Publicity
    (4) Travel
    (5) Etc.

vii) Should the Adult Sunday School Be Used for Seminars?

viii) What About House Churches?

TASK: Develop a statement of purpose for seminars.

c) Tape Ministry
    i) Review structure and demands of tape ministry with a view to seeing to it that one person does not have to bear the entire burden.
    ii) What equipment is needed?
    iii) What is the total cost?
    iv) How can this ministry be publicized?
    v) What policies should be set forth as guidelines?
    vi) If someone must use large amounts of time in this activity, should they be paid? What does "the laborer is worthy of his wages" (1 Tim. 5:18) mean? If the ministry ultimately requires a full-time worker, is this biblical?

TASK: Develop a statement of purpose for the tape ministry.

d) Videotapes and Films
    i) Review catalogs to see if there are any interesting tapes/films.
    ii) What tapes/films meet specific needs in the church?
    iii) What are those specific needs?
        (1) Church growth
        (2) Discipline of children
        (3) Training for Sunday School teachers
        (4) Etc.
    iv) Where and when should they be shown?
        (1) Sunday School
        (2) Worship service, Agape Feast, etc.
        (3) Enrichment groups
        (4) Friday or Saturday evening in homes, halls, etc.
        (5) Wednesday evening

    v) What policies should be set up on the rental fees involved?
    vi) Should they be open to the public?
    vii) Where, how, when and at what cost should they be publicized?
TASK: Develop a statement of purpose for videotapes and films.

e) Retreats
    i) Define what a retreat is.
    ii) Discuss its place in the local church.
    iii) Can the entire church go off to a retreat?
       Over a weekend?
    iv) When can different groups in the church hold a retreat?
       Youths, Women, Men
    v) What place can a men's or women's breakfast have in the program of the church?
    vi) How often can the church as a whole hold a retreat?
    vii) What policies should be set up to cover the cost, schedule, etc.
TASK: Develop a statement of purpose for retreats.

f) Literature
    i) What place can literature have in promoting spiritual maturity?
    ii) Should a church library be set up?
    iii) What programs can be set up to promote reading of good books?
       Book of the month, Handouts, Newsletter, Book table, etc.
TASK: Develop a statement of purpose for literature.

g) The Public School System
Given the humanism, drugs and immorality often found in the public school system, there are only two options open to Christians. Either they get busy and clean up the public schools or they take their children out of the system. If there are problems in the school district such as the teaching of secular humanism, New Age religion, communism, witchcraft, the occult, ESP, etc., Christian parents should get involved at once:

Immediate Goals
a. Bring the issue to the attention of the administration.
b. If not resolved, bring it to the attention of the parents.
c. When the parents are organized, present the issue to the school board.
d. If not resolved, bring it to the attention of the media by public protests.
e. If not resolved, get a lawyer and sue the school district.

Long Range Goals
a. Christian parents must attend and run the local PTA.
b. They must elect a Christian majority on the school board and see to it that school and its teachers are not promoting anti-God, anti-Christian and anti-family values. There are districts where the local school system is free from the evils of this age and able to give a good education to children because enough Christians are on the school board. Christians must become involved.
    If the public school system is totally corrupt, and this is often the case with inner-city schools, and there are not enough Christians to clean it up, then parents must take their

children out of the public school system. They can either send them to a local Christian school or do home schooling.

TASK: Motivate the parents of public school students in the church to clean up the local schools. Have some of them run for the local school board.

h) The Christian School

Since the humanists and occultists in the public school spend their time giving "therapy" to the students, Johnny cannot read. At the same time, they are painfully aware that the average student in a Christian school is one to two grades ahead of public school students. Christian school students are making the highest scores on the SATs. This means that the next generation of "educated" people will be the products of the Christian school system! This explains the anger that is focused against the Christian school movement by the National Education Association.

The federal government may pass a plan in which school taxes go to whatever school your children attend regardless if it is public or private. This will create thousands of new Christian schools.

If we are going to retake our culture for Christ, then our children must become artists, lawyers, doctors, politicians, etc., in order to influence the public. They will not be able to do this with the low level of education they receive in public schools.

Whenever the funds and the students are sufficient, a Christian school should be started.

If one is started, the parents must be prepared to pay enough to give a living wage to the teachers. Quality education will cost a great deal of money.

TASK: Organize the parents who want to start a Christian school. See how much they are willing to pay. Contact Christian school societies for literature and advice.

i) What if the public school is corrupt or there is not a Christian school near to you or you cannot afford to send your children there? Then consider home schooling. It has been repeatedly demonstrated that for many, the BEST education possible is home schooling. Home school students take the top honors in academic tests and become aggressive leaders. Because they are not subjected to the peer pressure of the ungodly and they do not have to waste half of the school day in transportation, discipline problems, "mickey mouse" courses, home room, study hall and ignorant teachers, they get a superior education.

TASK: Give a presentation on home schooling. Contact the home school groups and get their literature and advice.

Chapter Ninety-Two

How to Respond to Gossip

(Prov. 10:18; 26:4)

If someone comes to you and begins to slander someone in the church, what should you do?

1. Some people do nothing at all.

They do not want to get involved. But the fact is that they are now involved whether they like it or not. They have already sinned against God by listening to the slander. This is true even if the person attacked is an elder (1 Tim. 5:19). Their attitude has been affected for the worse and the seeds of bitterness have been sown (Pro. 17:4; 18:8). A whisperer can drive a wedge even between best friends (Pro. 16:28).

2. Stop the person immediately.

Don't let him proceed any further. Tell him: "If you are upset with someone, you must personally go to him to find out if your problems have any merit. Maybe you misunderstood the situation or you do not have all the facts. Don't go with accusations. Go with questions. How do you know until you go directly to the person?" (Matt. 18:15)

3. Exhort him about his sin.

He has already sinned against God and the person in question by complaining and grumbling in the presence of others (1 Thess. 5:14). Tell him, "If you do not go, I will have to go and tell the person that you are running around gossiping about him" (Gal.6:1).

4. Exhort him to check Scripture to see if his complaints have any biblical merit.

Ask him: "Where in the Bible do you find the basis for your accusations? Your 'feelings' are not enough" (Pro. 28:26).

5. Be prepared for the typical excuses for disobeying Scripture.
   a. "I am too angry to go."
      Answer: The fact of your anger reveals that you should have gone a long time ago (Eph. 4:26).
   b. "He will not listen."
      Answer: How do you know if you have not gone? Do you have a crystal ball to peer into the future?
   c. "I feel intimidated by his high IQ."
      Answer: If he is not deliberately intimidating you, he bears no guilt. We often feel intimidated

before people more intelligent than we are because they do know more than we do. But the problem is in us and not in them.

d. "I am afraid of his knowledge of the Bible."
Answer: If he is not deliberately making you afraid, he bears no guilt. If your slander is not based on Scripture, of course you will be afraid of him! He will no doubt examine your accusations by the Bible and reject whatever is not biblical.

e. "I have already made up my mind and nothing can change it. He could show me a thousand Bible verses and it will not make any difference."
Answer: Your attitude is proof that the Holy Spirit is not with you (James 3:6).

f. "You go to him for me. Let me tell you all my accusations and then you go to him."
Answer: To go to anyone else (even to an elder or a deacon) instead of going to the person you are upset with is sin. No one can go for you.

g. "I have gone to him in a way. I told him that there was a group of people upset with him."
Answer: It was dishonest to mislead the person into thinking that you were not part of the "group." You should have confessed that it was you who was running around slandering him.

h. "I will not go alone. I will talk to others until I find some people with the same gripes and then we will go as a group."
Answer: You must go alone according to Matt. 18:15. To talk to others is gossip and slander.

6. Explain that his slander is a "log" in his eye which he must deal with before he can point out the "splinter" in someone else's eye (Matt. 7:3-4).

The sin of gossip is usually far more evil than the problems gossipers complain about. Gossipers always hurt more people and do greater damage to the Body of Christ (Pro. 6:14, 16-19)! Even if the issues raised were valid, their gossiping is almost always the greater evil.

7. Tell him that he must go to the person he has slandered and ask him to forgive him.
He must also ask those who heard him for their forgiveness (Pro. 28:13; Matt. 5:23-24).

8. Explain to him that if he will not repent, he will be publicly disciplined by the elders of the church (Matt. 18:17; Rom. 16:17; 2 Cor. 12:20; Jude 16).

9. Warn him that if his accusations are non-moral and non-doctrinal and are actually attacks on someone's personality, he is the one at fault (Matt. 7:1).

10. Finally, ask him, "Are the accusations so serious that you are willing to destroy the peace and unity of the church?"

Chapter Ninety-Three
Baptism and Salvation

1) Heb. 5:9 tells us that Jesus saves those who OBEY Him.
2) What does this mean? It means to do what Christ has commanded.
3) But does this mean that in order to be saved we have to keep EVERY commandment in the Bible? Of course not!
   a) Since there are HUNDREDS of commandments in the Bible, no one would ever be saved.
   b) The Bible clearly says that salvation is by grace apart from obedience to the law (Rom. 3:19-22; Eph. 2:8-9).
4) The only possible solution is to divide all the commands of Scripture into two groups:

Things to Obey		
Before Salvation		**After Salvation**
Unrepentant	S	Repentant
Unbelievers	A	Believers
Justification	L	Sanctification
Conversion	V	Christian Life
Repent from Sin	A	Baptism
Believe in Jesus (Acts 20:21)	T	Church Membership
	I	Attending Church
	O	Giving Offerings
	N	Loving Your Wife
		Submitting to Your Husband
		Disciplining Your Children, etc.

5) Repenting and believing are usually mentioned together in the Bible because they are two sides of the same act which takes place in the heart (1 Thess. 1:9). When one is mentioned alone, the other is assumed (examples: John 3:16; Acts 2:38).
   repent = to turn from [one action]   believe = to turn to
6) While God's grace is the GROUNDS of salvation, the action of repenting and believing is always said to be the MEANS by which that salvation is received (John 6:27-29; Acts. 16:30-31; Eph. 2:8-9).
7) Baptism in the Bible is something that REPENTANT BELIEVERS do. Obviously, since the Bible ALWAYS places repentance and faith BEFORE baptism, then the only people who can be baptized are REPENTANT BELIEVERS. It is thus something that a child of God does as part of his obedience in the Christian life.
8) This is why there is no reference to baptism in Romans chapters one to five, where God's plan of salvation is set forth. It is first introduced in chapter six, which deals with the Christian life. In chapter six, Paul asks: "How shall we live AFTER we are saved? Shall we continue in sin AFTER we have been saved?"

One clear proof that Christians are baptized is found in Acts 10:44-48.
a) Notice the order of events:
   i) Peter preaches the Word.
   ii) Cornelius hears the Word.
   iii) He repents and believes (Rom. 10:17).
   iv) He is now a child of God.
   v) He is then baptized by the Holy Spirit.
   vi) He speaks in tongues.
   vii) He is baptized.
b) Was Cornelius a repentant believer who was filled with the Holy Spirit just like the Apostles were and spoke in tongues BEFORE he was ever baptized? Or, was he a still a "child of the devil" UNTIL he was baptized? Can a "child of the devil" be "filled by the Holy Spirit" and speak in tongues? That is absurd!

An Analysis of Matthew 3:11

1) Matt. 3:11: "baptize unto repentance" (KJV). What does the Greek word *eis* translated "unto" in the KJV mean?
   a) Were unrepentant people baptized so that they could obtain repentance? This would be against the biblical order of "repent and be baptized" as found in Acts 2:38 and elsewhere.
   b) We do not baptize unrepentant sinners. We baptize those who have already repented. Thus baptism is not the basis of repentance, but repentance is the basis of baptism!
   c) *Eis* when used in connection with baptism in this passage must mean that they were baptized with a view to the fact that they had already repented.

2) Modern Translations
   Many modern translations have interpreted the Greek word *eis* as meaning that repentance was the basis of their baptism.
   Amplified: "*because of* repentance"
   Renaissance: "*because of* repentance"
   Phillips: "*as a sign of* your repentance"
   Goodspeed: "*in token of* your repentance"
   Williams: "*to picture* your repentance"
   Twentieth Century: "*to teach* repentance"
   Living Bible: "baptize *those who repent* of their sins"

3) Greek Lexicons
   a) *Thayer's Greek Lexicon* (p. 184): *Eis* can be used: "of reference or relation; with regard to, in reference to; as regards."
   b) *An Intermediate Greek-English New Testament* (Liddell & Scott) p. 23: "in regard to."
   c) *A Greek-English Lexicon of the New Testament* (Green) p. 54: "in accordance with."
   d) *A Greek-English Lexicon of the New Testament* (Arndt & Gingrich) p. 229. Under the heading "other uses of eis," we find, "the causal use because of ... and perhaps Mat. 3:11."

4) Greek Scholars
   a) *A Manual of the Greek New Testament* (Dana & Manty): According to these Greek scholars, *eis* can be used in the sense of: "(7) because of. Rom. 4:20, but because of the promise of

God he did not waver in unbelief" (cf. Matt 3:11; Mk. 2:18; Rom. 11:32; Tit. 3:14). The sentence in Matt. 12:41 and Lk. 12:32 is forceful for a causal use of this preposition. What led to their repentance? Of course, it was John's preaching. Matt 3:11 furnishes further evidence: Did John baptize that they might repent, or because of repentance? If the former, we have no further Scriptural confirmation of it. If the later, his practice was confirmed and followed by the apostles, and is in full harmony with Christ's demand for inward, genuine righteousness. In connection with this verse we have the testimony of a first-century writer to the effect that John the Baptist baptized people only after they had repented.

An Analysis of Matthew 12:41

1) We are told in this verse that the people of Nineveh "repented [*eis*] the preaching of Jonah." What does eis mean in this passage?
   a) Does this mean that they repented in order to obtain Jonah's preaching? That would be absurd.
   b) Obviously, the people repented "because of" or "in the light of" or "in accordance with" what Jonah had already preached to them. Their repentance looked back to something already done; i.e. the preaching of Jonah.

2) Modern Translations
   a) Renaissance: "they repented *because of* the preaching"
   b) Wuest: "they repented *as a result of* the proclamation"
   c) RSV and many others: "they repented *at* the preaching"

3) Greek Lexicons
   a) *Thayer's Greek Lexicon* (pgs. 184-185): "with respect to, in reference to; as regards ... out of regard to the substance of his preaching, Mt. xii.41."
   b) Arndt and Gingrich (p. 229): "the causal use because of ... Mt. 12:41."
   c) Green (p. 54): "in accordance with Matt. 12:41."

4) Greek Scholars
   a) *Dana and Manty's Greek Grammar* (p. 104): "The sentence in Mat. 12:41 and Lk. 12:32 is forceful evidence for a causal use of this preposition. What led to their repentance? Of course, it was Jonah's preaching."
   b) *Dr. Randy Yeager* on Matt. 12:41: "This is an interesting example of *eis* with the accusative in a causal sense."

An Analysis of Acts 2:38

1) What does "baptized [*eis*] remission of sins" mean in Acts 2:38?
   a) Thesis No. 1
      There is an exact parallel between Matt. 3:11: "baptize [*eis*] repentance," Matt. 12:41: "repented [*eis*] preaching," Acts 2:38: "baptize [*eis*] forgiveness."
   b) Thesis No. 2
      Eis in Matt. 3:11 means that these people were baptized with a view to or in the light of the fact that they had already repented.
   c) Thesis No. 3
      Eis in Matt. 12:41 means that they repented with a view to or in the light of the fact of the preaching of Jonah which had already taken place.

2) Logical Conclusions
   a) Then *eis* in Acts 2:38 means that these people were baptized with a view to or in the light of the fact that their sins had already been forgiven.
   b) We are to baptize people who have already repented of their sins, believed in Jesus and have had their sins washed away by His blood.
   c) The idea that we should baptize unrepentant, unbelieving, unforgiven sinners is nowhere found in the New Testament. Faith and repentance must PRECEDE baptism according to the N.T. The order is always "believe and be baptized" and "repent and be baptized"—never the reverse.

3) Modern Translations
   a) Wuest: "baptized in relation to the fact that your sins have been put away"
   b) Renaissance: "baptized because of forgiveness"
   c) Weymouth: "baptized with a view to"
   d) Marshall's Greek-English Interlinear: "baptized with a view to"

4) Greek Scholars
   a) A.T. Robertson: "Another usage exists which is just as good Greek as the use of *eis* for aim or purpose. It is seen in Matt. 10:41 in three examples *eis onoma prophetou, dikaiou, mathetou* where it cannot be purpose or aim, but rather the basis or ground, on the basis of the name of prophet, righteous man, disciple, because one is, etc. It is seen again in Matt. 12:41 about the preaching of Jonah (*eis to kerugma Iona*). They repented because of (or at) the preaching of Jonah. The illustrations of both usages are numerous in the N.T. and the Koine generally (Robertson, *Grammar*, p. 592). So I understand Peter to be urging baptism on each of them who had already turned (repented) and for it to be done in the name of Jesus Christ on the basis of the forgiveness of sins which they had already received.

   b) Dr. Randy Yeager: Just as *eis* with the accusative can be telic when the context demands, it can also be causal, as we have translated in Acts 2:38. The men of Nineveh repented—"because of the preaching of Jonah" (Mat. 12:41). Such true believers, made thus by the supernatural ministry of the Holy Spirit, who have truly repented and who have definitely made the leap of faith to Christ are immersed because their sins are forgiven, not in order that their sins may be forgiven.

Conclusion

If we let Scripture interpret Scripture, then Acts 2:38 will be interpreted in the light of Matt. 3:11 and Matt. 12:41.

Once this is done, it is clear that salvation is by grace alone, through faith alone, in Christ alone, apart from the works of the law such as baptism.

Part Four
The Nation

Chapter Ninety-Four

The Christian's Attitude Toward the State

Introduction

One of the most practical questions which a child of God should ask is: "What should be my attitude toward and my responsibilities to the government which rules over my country?"

Since we are living in the age of revolution and violence, Christians must think through their relationship to the state. We can no longer assume that America will always be a land of freedom. Slowly but surely, the government is taking away our freedoms. If someone one hundred years ago said that the day would come when the government would outlaw the voluntary exercise of religious activities in public schools and on public land, the response would have been:

"IT WILL NEVER HAPPEN HERE"

Today we lament in grief and say:

"WHY HAS IT HAPPENED HERE?"

Why are our freedoms slowly but surely being taken away? Why do we look with concern—and fear—toward the future?

EXTERNAL No. 1: The Success of Islamic terrorism.

In every country where Islam has triumphed, the Church is under persecution. Examples: Sudan, Indonesia, etc.

INTERNAL No. 2: The Success of Secular Humanism.

The humanists now control the media, the government and the schools. They have declared war on the Christian Church.

What Is Secular Humanism?

Secular humanism is the philosophy which says that "Man is the measure of all things." Man is his own god. There is no supreme God. God did not create us. We evolved by chance. There are no absolutes in ethics. The state legislates ethics and morality according to the exercise of arbitrary power. "Might makes right." In this light, the "freedom" and "dignity" of man must be refuted by viewing people as having worth only insofar as they benefit the State. Political and religious freedoms must be taken away. An elite group of humanists must control the nation. Any individual or any economic, racial, religious, political or educational group which will not teach the religious creed of humanism must be exterminated. Parents who teach their children Christianity will be punished by the taking away of their children in the name of child abuse laws. The state will be supreme in all things. In the name of "morality" the state can liquidate anyone or any class of people (abortion, infanticide, euthanasia, mercy killings and the "termination" of unteachables).

IS THIS AMERICA'S FUTURE?

A CHRISTIAN VIEW OF THE STATE

I. General Principles:

    A. All authority resides in God. He is the origin and source of all authority (Dan. 4:28-37; Matt. 28:18).

    B. All human authority is delegated authority.
       "Delegated authority" means that God will hold the person or institution accountable to Him for the way they used the authority given to them (Rev. 20:11-15).

    C. It also means that no person or institution has absolute or intrinsic authority. They cannot do as they please (John 19:10-11).

    D. Delegated authority is valid only when it operates according to Scriptural guidelines and functions within Scriptural limits.

    E. The Scriptures recognize four sovereign spheres of authority.

CHURCH	STATE	FAMILY	BUSINESS
1 Thess. 5:12-13 Heb. 13:17, 24 etc.	Rom. 13:1-7 1 Pet. 2:13-17 etc.	Eph. 5:22-29 Eph. 6:1-4 etc.	Eph. 6:5-9 1 Pet. 2:18-19 etc.

    F. While the spheres are interrelated and do interact with each other, they must not invade each other in an attempt to take over the authority or responsibilities which God delegated to the another spheres. Example: State vs. Church or State vs. Business

II. A Christian View of Government (the State)

    A. The origin of the state as a human institution is to be found in the image of God within man. Government is the natural result of man's creation by a personal and orderly Deity. The state is part of God's plan for man (versus evolutionary theories).

    B. The authority of the state is delegated and limited by God in Scripture (Rom. 13:1-7) (versus absolute and arbitrary power theories).

C. The functions and responsibilities of the state according to Scripture are:

> Rom. 13:1-7
> 1 Tim. 2:1-2
> 1 Pet. 2:13-17
> etc.

(1) To protect and promote the welfare of the citizens.
(2) To punish evildoers.
(3) To reward the good.
(4) To promote unified cultural tasks.
(5) To administer justice.
(6) To implement, as God's ministers, Scripturally based civil law for the good of all.
(7) To keep unity and order in society.
(8) To ensure religious freedom.

D. The state is not to intrude into the other sovereign spheres and take over their authority or responsibilities.

1. The state has no Scriptural authority to dictate who can preach or what is to be believed.

2. The state has no Scriptural authority to pass legislation which makes the father's headship illegal or to make all children the wards of the state.

3. The state has no Scriptural authority over the education of children. The parents bear that responsibility.

4. The state should not be nationalizing and running all businesses. Neither should the state forbid private ownership or enterprise. The more the state interferes with and regulates the business community, the poorer the economy and the lower the living standards become. Socialism has always been a disaster.

III. The Responsibilities of Christians to the State

A. To recognize the priority of their heavenly citizenship over their earthly citizenship (Phil. 3:20; Heb. 11:13-16). (Versus blind nationalism: "My country right or wrong.")
National racism
Militaristic Imperialism

B. Pray for the leaders (1 Tim. 2:1-2).
C. Pay taxes (Rom. 13:6).
D. Show respect to officials (Rom. 13:7; 1 Pet. 2:17).
E. Obey all valid laws (1 Pet. 2:13-17).
F. Support "law and order" (1 Tim. 2:2).
G. Work for freedom (religious rights, civil rights, etc.).
H. Work for justice for the oppressed (widows, orphans, etc., James 1:27).
I. Obey ordinances (salute flag, etc.) (1 Pet. 2:13).
J. Put righteous people in office by getting involved in politics (voting, campaigning, etc.).
K. Use all available legal means to secure freedom or protection (Acts 22:25-29; 25:11).
L. Preach the Gospel to leaders (Matt. 28:19).

M. Be involved in the defense of your country or when it is involved in a just war (Judges 2:16; 3:12-30).

N. Be prepared to overthrow an evil government or alien power who takes over your country. When a state no longer functions according to Rom. 13:1-5, that government is no longer ordained of God. This is particularly relevant when a government persecutes the church. A Christian as a good citizen will have to revolt against corrupt governments.

Examples:

Reformation wars by Christians

Attempted assassination of Hitler by Christians

Freedom movements in communist countries

O. For a detailed study see Robert Morey, *When Is It Right To Fight?*

Chapter Ninety-Five
A Biblical View of Peace

1) The word "PEACE" appears approximately 415 times in the KJV. It usually refers to:
   a) "Holding one's peace," i.e., not speaking (example: Gen. 24:21).
   b) "Peace offering," i.e., Levitical sacrifices (example: Lev. 3:1).
   c) "Peace" with God. Justification based on Christ's righteousness (example: Rom. 5:1).
   d) The inner "peace" of God. Comfort and calmness given in sanctification (example: Phil. 4:7).

2) Only rarely does "peace" refer to "national peace" as opposed to civil or international war.
   O.T.: 26 times (example: Lev. 26:6)
   N.T.: two times (example: 1 Thess. 5:3; Rev. 6:3-4)
   a) National peace could be preserved and war avoided by making treaties (example: Gen. 26:29). But there were times when treaties were forbidden by God because God wanted His people to go to war (example: Deut. 23:6).
   b) National peace could also be obtained by going to war! (example: Lev. 26:3, 6-8; Josh. 11:23; 14:15; 21:43, etc.) The purpose of war was peace!
   c) National peace could also be used as a weapon to conquer a nation (example: Dan. 8:25 KJV: "by peace [He] shall destroy many.").
   d) The antichrist will use international peace as a way to seduce mankind (1 Thess. 5:3).
   e) Christ shall send war to disrupt Satan's worldwide peace (Rev. 6:3-4).
   f) Permanent, universal peace awaits the eternal Kingdom which is set up on a new earth after the final judgment (example: Isa. 65:17-25; Rev. 21:1-8). There is peace because all the wicked have been removed (Matt. 25:46).
   g) All attempts to arrive at universal, permanent peace in this age are doomed to failure (example: Matt. 24:6-8).

3) The Bible and historic Christianity are always quite realistic about human nature and government. Idealism and biblical Christianity are always enemies. The Bible never presents a romantic view of man. The Bible describes man as he really is.
   a) Idealistic and romantic views of man in which man is viewed as good or neutral by nature, instead of totally depraved, lead to rule by mob or tyrants. Truth, morality, justice and beauty are not determined by a majority vote or by the arbitrary decrees of tyrants.
   b) We will be ruled either by God's Law or we will be ruled by the tyranny of the majority or the arbitrary laws of tyrants.
   c) All utopian views of man are doomed to failure because man is sinful by nature.
   d) America was set up as a republic and not as a democracy because our fathers had a realistic view of man. We are to be governed by law—not by the majority.
   e) Because man is sinful by nature, a system of checks and balances was placed in the Constitution. Just as we cannot trust the majority of the people to choose what is right or just, neither can we trust their representatives to choose what is right or just. Man, as man, cannot be trusted because he is sinful by nature.
   f) Universal peace is possible only after the righteous are perfected and the wicked removed at the return of Christ and the setting up of His eternal Kingdom (Matt. 25:46).

g) Where in the Bible is pacifism taught or enjoined, by precept, command or example? Answer: NOWHERE!

4) The justice of wars fought for righteous causes such as self-defense, to overthrow tyrants, to deliver people from oppression, etc., is found in the N.T. as well as the O.T.
O.T.: Gen. 14
N.T.: Matt. 21:33-41

Part II Introduction

Is the Bible a "Book of War" or a "Book of Peace"? Does it give a romantic view of man's nature and history, or is it filled with realistic descriptions of human depravity and violence? In other words, does the Bible manifest that its authors were pacifists, or does it manifest an attitude toward war and peace reflecting the "just war" position?

1) What Should We Expect to Find in the Bible?
   a) If the biblical authors were pacifists, we would expect to find more references to peace than war. Warfare would never be honored or glorified. Warriors would never be praised or lifted up as heroes. There would be clear condemnations of all wars, including wars involving God's people. God would not be pictured in a warlike manner. His people would never use force against evil. Peace would be exalted above war. Treaties would be more frequent than war. Slavery under tyranny would be viewed as more moral and desirable than war or revolution. God would never command or allow war in any situation whatsoever.

What Does the Record Show?

   b) The Bible was written by the hands of men who viewed the use of force to overcome evil as a just cause for war or revolution. War and its warriors are glorified and exalted as righteous and holy before God. God Himself commanded His people to go to war. He is pictured as a God of War. His armies in Heaven and on earth are using force against evil and Satan's kingdom.
      i) War is referred to 256 times, while peace in the sense of an absence of war is referenced only 28 times.
      ii) Treaties are mentioned 18 times. Most of them were condemned by God because they were appeasements of aggressors. Israel learned by hard experience that all their treaties with Assyria, Babylon and Egypt ended in war. While peace treaties do work at times (Gen. 26:29), God generally took a dim view of treaties to appease tyrants (Deut. 23:6).

   c) God at times commanded His people to go to war in order to achieve peace; i.e., the purpose of such wars was peace! (Lev. 26:3-8).

   d) Christ Himself is pictured as a warrior (Rev. 19:11-21), and He sends war to disrupt the peace" arranged by Satan to aid the antichrist (Rev. 6:1-8; 1 Thess. 5:3).

   e) "Peace" can be used as a weapon to destroy a nation (Dan. 8:25). "By peace [He] shall destroy many."

   f) Permanent and universal peace will only be realized on earth when Jesus returns, the wicked are removed and the righteous perfected (Isa. 65:17, 25; Rev. 21:1-8).

g) Wars, i.e., the use of force to overcome evil, will be a part of human history until Jesus returns (Matt. 24:6-8).

h) All Utopian hopes of peace on earth are doomed to failure as long as man is sinful by nature.

2) How Do Pacifists Try to Establish Their Position in Scripture? "The Tricks of the Trade."

Step No. 1: Avoid all passages which speak directly to the issue of the state using force to punish criminals and an army to protect the nation. Particularly avoid Rom. 13.

Step No. 2: Appeal to passages which in their contexts deal with the church or with the individual. Establish that the N.T. Church should not use physical force in its discipline. Show that on a day-to-day basis we should "go the second mile" and "turn the other cheek" (example: Matt. 5).

Step No. 3: Make a jump from individual ethics to national ethics. Apply to the State what was only applied to the Church or individual in Scripture.

Step No. 4: Take general ethical statements which in their contexts apply to non-life-threatening situations (peacetime/not a war situation) and apply them to national times of war or times when your life or the lives of others are threatened (example: Rom. 12:17-21).

Step No. 5: Always keep to vague generalities or statements. Do not pay any attention to exegesis or to the Greek or Hebrew. Merely quote the text and give it a pacifist slant.

Step No. 6: Apply the same methods to the writings of the early church fathers.

ONCE YOU UNDERSTAND THESE SIX TRICKS, YOU CAN HANDLE ANY PACIFIST ARGUMENT OR BOOK.

3) How Does the "Just War" Position Argue Its Case?
  a) By starting out with a commitment to theism, i.e., God in His revelation is the origin, basis and judge of truth, morals, justice and beauty. We must begin with God, not man.

  b) By a rejection of rationalism, mysticism and empiricism.

  c) Since God Himself has always used force to overcome evil, this means it is in principle moral and just to use force.

Examples:

The Flood	The Plagues	The Tower of Babel
The Conquest	Sodom	The Judgment Day

  d) God has commanded His people to use force. He would never command something immoral or unjust in principle.

  e) Nowhere in the O.T. or N.T. is the State told to disarm. Nowhere in Scripture is the use of force in war or self-defense condemned.

f) Christ and the Apostles appealed to just war situations with approval.

g) God gave the sword to the State to punish the wicked and protect the righteous.

h) The early Christians remained in the military, and nowhere in the N.T. is war in principle condemned.

Conclusion

"There is a time for war and a time for peace" (Ecc. 3:8).

For further details see Robert Morey's book, *When Is It Right to Fight?*

Chapter Ninety-Six

An Introduction to Christian Apologetics

I. WHAT IS IT?

A. The word "apologetics" is a Greek word transliterated into English. It is found in the New Testament in such places as 1 Pet. 3:15. Its basic meaning is:

> to give a logical defense of what you believe
> when someone questions or challenges you

B. The subject of apologetics is that branch of Christian theology/philosophy which seeks to defend Christianity when it is attacked by hostile religions, philosophers or critics. This requires the apologist to do three things:
1. To articulate the Christian position on various theoretical and practical issues.
2. To set forth arguments which demonstrate the validity of the Christian position.
3. To refute other positions which contradict or challenge the Christian position.

II. WHY BOTHER WITH APOLOGETICS?

A. We must defend the Faith in obedience to the command of Christ (1 Pet. 3:15; Jude 3).

B. We need to help people remain in the Christian Church (Gal. 6:1).

C. We are to evangelize people with the Gospel (Matt. 28:19-20; Acts 17:16-34).

III. WHERE SHOULD WE GET OUR APOLOGETICS?

A. We should not simply adopt the current popular philosophies as our defense. Some Christian thinkers in the past have unwisely adopted whatever philosophy was popular in their day.

Examples:		adopted	
	Origen		Platonism
	Augustine	→	Neo-platonism
	Aquinas	→	Aristotle
	Hodge	→	McCoshism
	Finney	→	Taylorism
	Shedd	→	Kantianism
	Dooyeweerd	→	Husseralism
	Barth	→	Neo-Kantianism
	Tillich	→	Eastern Philosophies
	Bultmann	→	Existentialism
	Liberation Theology	→	Marxism

B. We should strive to be biblical in our philosophy. This means that we should have exegetical reasons for the positions which we claim to be "Christian." If we do not, then we have no right to claim that we have a "Christian" view.

Example: Dooyeweerd in *New Critique of Theoretical Thought* (four volumes) claims to be the ultimate Christian philosophy. Yet, he refers only to one or two verses from the Bible. He begins his philosophy with his own experience, i.e., man. He does not begin with God. (See R.A. Morey's book, *The Dooyeweerdian Concept of the Word of God*, Pres. & Ref. Pub. Co.)

IV. **HOW SHOULD WE PREPARE TO DO APOLOGETICS?**
  A. Sanctify Christ as Lord in terms of salvation (1 Pet. 3:15).
  B. Sanctify Christ as Lord in terms of sanctification (1 Pet. 3:15).
  C. Learn to think and not just feel when it comes to Truth. Never let human reason, emotion or experience be the final arbitrator of Truth. God's revelation in Scripture is the ultimate judge of all Truth. Paul reasoned with people on the basis of Scripture (Acts 17:2, 3, 16-34; 1 Cor. 15:3-4).
  D. The Bible and Christianity are not to be viewed as irrational or mystical. Christian beliefs and experiences can be defined, explained and defended.
  E. The Bible and Christianity are not to be viewed as nonrational or "upper story." The Greeks started the philosophic tradition of viewing life as a dichotomy. Kant's usage of this dichotomy in his noumenal vs. phenomenal levels of thought has given Western Man the idea that truth can be found on one of two levels or stories.

upper-story: non-rational, non-factual, feeling, belief, religion, ideas, free-will
lower-story: rational, factual, knowledge, science, matter, determinism

  1. The Greeks developed a philosophic dichotomy as a reaction to the contradictory philosophies of the pre-Socratic philosophers.

    a. Parmenides (Sixth-Fifth Century B.C.). "The Father of Rationalism." He believed that all was Static Being. He denied that things changed, decayed or moved. Static Being was real while change was illusion.

    b. Heraclitus (Sixth-Fifth Century B.C.). "The Father of Empiricism." He believed that all was Becoming, i.e., in a state of constant flux. Change was real while Static Being was illusion.

    c. The history of Western Philosophy is simply the attempt to put Parmenides and Heraclitus together. All the great philosophers attempted to build a system which resolved the conflict between rationalism and empiricism.
      (1) Plato $\dfrac{\text{Mind}}{\text{Matter}}$

      (2) Aristotle $\dfrac{\text{Essence}}{\text{Form}}$

2. The Middle Ages saw a return to dichotomistic thought as Aquinas embraced Aristotle's philosophy.

$$\frac{\text{Essence}}{\text{Form}} \quad \text{became} \quad \frac{\text{Grace}}{\text{Nature}}$$

3. During the Renaissance, philosophers such as Jean Rousseau (1712-1778) continued on the dichotomy.

$$\frac{\text{Freedom}}{\text{Nature}}$$

4. The Age of Enlightenment saw the development of the dichotomy in the philosophy of Emmanuel Kant (1724-1804).

$$\frac{\text{Noumenal}}{\text{Phenomenal}}$$

5. German Liberal Theology followed the Kantian dichotomy.

$$\frac{\text{Belief}}{\text{Knowledge}} \quad \frac{\text{Faith}}{\text{Facts}} \quad \frac{\text{Religion}}{\text{Science}} \quad \frac{\text{Myth}}{\text{Truth}}$$

6. Neo-orthodox theologies such as Karl Barth (1886) carried on the dichotomy tradition.

$$\frac{\text{Salvation-history (Bible, Faith, etc.)}}{\text{history} \quad \text{(Science, Facts, etc.)}}$$

F. We must avoid the basic humanistic assumptions of "Human Autonomy" and "Ontological Thinking."

1. Human Autonomy is the assumption or presupposition that man, starting from himself, with himself, by himself, rejecting any outside or special revelation, can construct a unified field of knowledge within which he can understand himself, the world around him and all the interrelationships involved. "Man is the measure of all things" (Protagoras). "Might makes right" (Thrasymachus).

2. The following diagram illustrates "human autonomy."

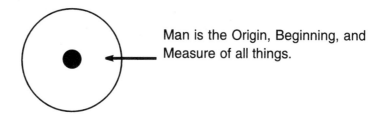

Man is the Origin, Beginning, and Measure of all things.

3. There are three areas of life which have traditionally been used as the basis of humanistic thought. A philosopher will rely on his reason, his experience or his feelings.

4. "Ontological thinking" is the assumption that reality must conform to what I think it is. Any idea which I view "unthinkable" cannot be true. Any object including "God" which I deem "unthinkable" cannot exist.

5. There is a unity and diversity in humanistic thought. The unity is found in the twin assumptions of human autonomy and ontological thinking. The diversity arises as different areas of life are absolutized and viewed as the origin of meaning.

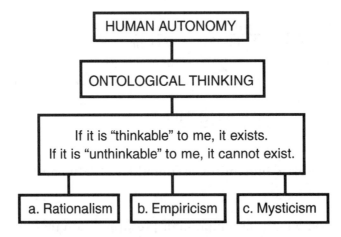

a. RATIONALISM: The assumption that reality and truth will correspond to what human "reason" thinks them to be. The Real is the Rational and the Rational is the Real.

b. EMPIRICISM: The assumption that reality and truth will correspond to what human "experience" finds them to be. All knowledge comes by way of the five senses.

c. MYSTICISM: The assumption that reality and truth will correspond to what human "emotion" feels them to be. Truth is found by looking within one's self.

6. There is another assumption which nearly all humanistic philosophies embrace: Ultimate Monism
   The assumption that Ultimate Reality (i.e., that which underlies "Reality" or makes up the "stuff" or "substance" of the universe) is One Being. Everything must be viewed in terms of a scale of Being in which there are no qualitative differences between things be-

cause everything participates in this One Being. Differences are due to different quantitative arrangements of Being.

Answer: There are TWO levels of Being:
a. God's infinite, self-sufficient, eternal being.
b. Creation's finite, dependent, temporary being. The "being," "substance" or "existence" of the universe does not participate in or flow out of the being of God. We are not a part of God in His essence or being.

7. Let us examine the ideas and concepts of "god" which arose in Greek philosophy. Greek philosophy illustrates the assumptions of human autonomy, ontological thinking and ultimate monism. Notice the gradual process from empiricism to idealism.
   a. "God" was thought to be a material substance which could be known through the senses. "God" was an empirical God.
      (1) Thales: water
      (2) others: earth, fire, air
   b. "God" was thought to be a material substance which could not be known through the senses but had to be logically perceived as that substance which made up earth, air, fire and water. Anaximander put forth "Apeiron" as "God" or "Ultimate Reality."
   c. "God" was thought to be non-material and ideal, i.e., not matter but idea. God can only be perceived logically. "God" was a Rational God. Parmenides' One, Heraclitus' Logos, Anaxagoras' Nous, Plato's World of Ideas or Idea of the Good, Aristotle's Unmoved Mover or Thought Thinking Itself, and Plotinus' One are all examples.
   d. "God" was thought to be mystically perceived. "God" could not be known through the senses or reason. Only the inner emotions could come into contact with ultimate reality or God.
      Example: The popular occultic religions of the masses in which the oracle or demon-possessed medium would give answers to all questions.

Conclusion

Because humanistic philosophers assumed human autonomy, ontological thinking and ultimate monism, while they disagreed with each other as to what area of man should be viewed as the basis of knowledge, no true critical work could be done. The basic assumptions of humanistic thought end in skepticism because you cannot start with man and end up having any knowledge of truth or morals.

I. DIFFERENT APPROACHES TO APOLOGETICS
   A. Two basic approaches to apologetics have developed in the present evangelical world.
      1. Evidentialism: the belief that the only way to defend Christianity and to defeat anti-Christian thought is to use arguments drawn from three areas:
                              "Brute Facts"
         a. Scientific facts (geology, archaeology, etc.)
            (Facts of science)
         b. Logical arguments (reason/logic)
            (Facts of reason)
         c. Personal experience (Livability)
            (Facts of experience)

Evidentialists will use one, two or all three of these areas as the basis for their apologetics. They want to deal with the "facts." Some of them are empiricists, rationalists and mystics.

    2. Presuppositionism: the belief that the only way to defend Christianity and to defeat anti-Christian thought is to deal with the presuppositions, assumptions, "first principles" or starting points of philosophical systems. It is useless to deal with science, logical arguments or personal experience until you first deal with the foundational ideas or assumptions. They want to deal with the underlying "ideas." Some of them have fallen into mysticism and fideism.

  B. Nearly all present popular apologists can be placed in one of these two approaches. They are hostile to any other approach and often seek to discredit any approach other than their own. The seminaries usually line up behind one approach.

  C. We should not continue the in-fighting of these people, but seek to put them together in a synthesis. Do not choose either/or, but both. The biblical principle is clear that we can use all these apologists (1 Cor. 3:4-5, 21-23).

    1. Notice that they have the same goals: to defend Christianity and to refute non-Christian systems.

    2. Notice that the difference between the two approaches may reveal that they have fallen into the basic dichotomy of non-Christian philosophy.

Upper: presuppositionalism, ideas, philosophy, pre-logic, etc.
Lower: evidentialism, facts, science, logic, etc.

    3. If we reject the basic dichotomy, we can absorb both into one system.

II. BASIC DIAGRAM OF SYNTHESIS

  A. This diagram avoids the Greek dichotomy of truth.

  B. It includes all aspects of philosophic inquiry.

  C. It questions a system at every level. Most apologists usually concentrate on one level.

  D. The whole is greater than the sum of the parts.

  E. It takes into account "ideas" and "facts," because the Bible does this.

    Example: presupposition: Gen. 1:1
                 fulfilled prophecy: Isa. 41:21-29; 42:9; 46:10
                 empirical evidence: John 20:27; Acts 1:3
                 reason: Isa. 1:18; Acts 17:2
                 miracles: John 20:30-31, etc.

  F. What apologetic approach you use with someone should be determined on the basis of what kind of person you are dealing with.

III. THE IMPORTANCE OF ASKING THE RIGHT QUESTION AT THE RIGHT LEVEL

  A. Asking the right question is the name of the game.

  B. Most philosophers and theologians limit their questions to one aspect or level of a philosophic system.

  C. We need to ask questions at every level in order to deal with a system in its entirety.

IV. THE PLIABILITY OF THIS SYNTHESIS

A. We can conform our apologetics to the person's temperament, education, interest and desires.

Example: Concrete thinkers: fulfilled prophecy (Facts)

Abstract thinkers: logic/presuppositions (Ideas)

Existential thinkers: livability (life)

B. Traditional apologists are not pliable, and hence often only appeal to certain kinds of people.

the philosophic people—Van Til

the scientific people—Montgomery

the existential people—Schaeffer

the logic people—Clark

C. The Bible confronts people at every level of their lives and thoughts. It is God's whole revelation for the whole man for the whole of life.

D. The Bible is pliable and meets people where they are to take them to where they should be. Should not our apologetics do the same?

E. The Bible was written for all people: rich/poor, high I.Q./low I.Q., educated/uneducated, etc. Should not our apologetics do the same?

F. We need to be pliable enough to give the appropriate apologetic that will mean the most to the person to whom we are witnessing. We can use books by Schaeffer, Clark, Van Til, Montgomery, etc. They are all ours in Christ.

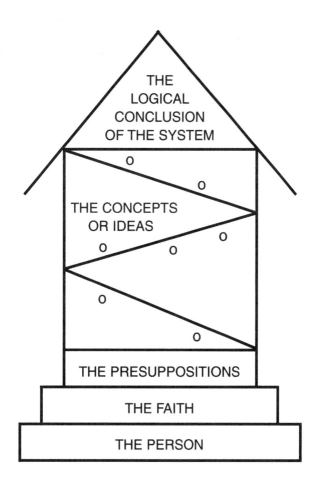

(1) The person is the foundation of any system, for the nature of the person determines the precepts. Who and what we are determines who and what we can know or understand. Too often we forget that we are dealing with a person and not just with a position. The nature of the person determines our methods in apologetics.

(2) The faith which underlies the presuppositions needs to be examined, for at the bottom of every system there is faith.

(3) We must examine the presuppositions which underlie a system and from which the concepts are developed.

(4) Next comes the individual concepts or ideas which make up the bulk or substance of the system.

(5) In the last section we come to the logical conclusion of the system, for if we are consistent, the system will take us somewhere. Where it will take us is the crucial question.

For more details see Robert Morey's book, *An Introduction to Defending the Faith.*

Chapter Ninety-Seven

What Is Apologetics?

Introduction

This question should concern us all, for God has called us to do the work of apologetics (1 Pet. 3:15; Jude 3).

I. We do three things in apologetics:
   A. We **DEFINE** a doctrine.
   B. We **DOCUMENT** it from Scripture and Church History.
   C. We **DEFEND** it by refuting all opposing views and answering those who attack it.

II. There are two ways of doing apologetics:
   A. Theoretical Apologetics: Developing a Christian world and life view of everything in life.

metaphysics	science	mathematics
epistemology	psychology	human sexuality
ethics	biology	history
aesthetics	zoology	etc.

   B. Applied Apologetics: Refuting modern systems of unbelief:
   1. The things which are under attack today:

theism	Christianity	morals
mono-theism	the historical Jesus	truth
personal/infinite God	absolute values	miracles
Creation ex nihilo	hetero-sexuality	significance
uniqueness of man	marriage	the supernatural
the Bible	meaning	etc.

   2. Groups that are on the attack:

atheists	cultural relativists	satanism
agnostics	existentialists	ethical relativists
free-thinkers	politically correct	liberals
skeptics	pagan religions	evolutionists
know-it-alls	cults	magic users
secular humanists	occult	witchcraft
Marxists	New Age	feminists
socialists	neo-paganism	etc.

III. The way that Jesus taught his disciples to do apologetics:
   A. PRECEPT: He taught them what to say and how to do it.
   B. EXAMPLE: Then He showed them how to do it by debating the Scribes, Pharisees, etc.

IV. What must Christians do to prepare themselves and their children apologetically? Every church and school should do the following:

A-ppropiate the funds needed

P-rovide the resources required (books/tapes)

O-bligate teachers to use those materials

L-earn the Christian world and life view

O-bserve those who have already done this

G-rab people's attention (skits/mock debates)

E-ducate them about apologetics

T-rain them to debate the heathen (precept and example)

I-dentify the movements on the attack today

C-ritique modern apostate thinkers and systems

S-ystematically refute them one by one

V. The Big Picture:

A. Your apologetics should flow out of the Christian world and life view. You are merely applying the biblical view of life to all of life when you do apologetics.

B. What are the essential concepts of the Christian world and life view?
   1. Creation
   2. Fall
   3. Redemption

C. These three concepts form the glasses through which all of life must be interpreted. If you examine all my books, you will discover that all of them are consciously written from the standpoint of Creation, Fall and Redemption.

VI. Apologetics Sunday: Just as many churches across this land observe "Missions Sunday," why not begin to observe "Apologetics Sunday"? One Sunday out of the year should be set aside and placed on the church's calendar as Apologetics Sunday. On that day the pastor or a guest speaker will preach on the subject of defending the faith. Special "apologetic" projects could be presented, and the people made aware of the great need today for Christians to "stand up for Jesus." Ask your pastor if you can observe Apologetics Sunday in your church.

Conclusion

Apologetics is every Christian's obligation as well as privilege (Jude 3). Since we are living in a post-Christian age, we must be steadfast in defending the Faith once and for all delivered to the saints.

Chapter Ninety-Eight

Christianity and Humanism

PART ONE

The Ten Fundamental Principles of the Christian World and Life View

1. A person's beliefs, values, morals, etc., will be reflected in the way he or she lives (Prov. 23:7; Matt. 12:33-37).

2. We can judge someone on the basis of how he lives (John 7:24; Matt. 7:6, 15-20; Gal. 5:19-21; 1 John 2:4).

3. A nation's culture reflects the beliefs, values, morals, etc., of those involved in the culture-forming process (philosophers, artists, teachers, politicians, lawyers, judges, doctors, wealthy people, and media people).

4. We can judge a culture on the basis of its laws, which are simply codified beliefs, values, and morals (Jer. 6:22-23; Tit. 1:12-13).

5. Pre-Christian Greek and Roman pagan cultures codified anti-biblical laws supporting abortion, infanticide, child abuse and rape, suicide, incest, murder for entertainment, etc.

6. When enough Christians became involved in the culture-forming process in the Roman Empire, pagan laws were repealed and biblical laws legislated.

7. Throughout the rest of Western History, the West in terms of its culture was basically "Christian," since its laws reflected the beliefs, values, morals, etc., of the Scriptures.

8. American Christians during the Fundamentalist-Liberal debate in the 1920s, developed an inward focus on personal piety to the exclusion of any concern for the culture-forming process. It was thought to be unspiritual to be involved in law, medicine, education, art, politics, etc. They ignored the culture and went "soul-winning."

9. Since the Christians abandoned the culture-forming professions, the non-Christians moved into the vacuum. The modern pagans are now repealing biblical laws and reinstating the old pagan laws in favor of abortion, infanticide, etc.

10. The only hope is for Christians to once again enter the culture-forming process, and when they are in places of influence, to repeal the pagan laws and to reinstate the biblical laws. If they do not do this as soon as possible, the modern pagans will be in a position to begin the same kind of persecution that their forefathers in the Roman Empire had done to the Christians.

PART TWO

The Christian Viewpoint

Because man is created in the image of God, each human being from the moment of conception to the oldest age has intrinsic worth. The intrinsic worth and dignity of man is immutable and cannot be affected by lack of acquired worth or economic considerations. The utility of a person has no bearing on the intrinsic worth of man as the image-bearer of God. The sanctity of human life in all of its stages from conception to old age leads to the following conclusions:

1. No genetic experimentation on fertilized human eggs can be allowed. The destruction of such eggs is the killing of human life.

2. It is wrong to manipulate the DNA code to determine the sex, race or physical characteristics of human beings.

3. Abortion is always wrong, except where the life of the mother is threatened.

4. All forms of infanticide are wrong (either passive or active).

5. All so-called "mercy killing" is actually murder, whether it is done through passive or active means.

6. Active or passive euthanasia is always wrong.

7. There should be no age limit for medical care. This would be a form of murder.

8. Suicide should not be legalized. Neither should "suicide clinics" or "death pills."

9. No "final solutions" for "undesirables."

10. No "liquidation" of those who think differently.

PART THREE

The Humanist Viewpoint

Human life is the result of a chance governed evolutionary process in a closed natural system. There is no intrinsic value to human life for it is no different from animal life. Human life has only acquired worth in terms of its utility and function. When a person's utilitarian worth is over so far as society is concerned, the person has no "right" to life but only the privilege of life. Thus, abortion, infanticide, euthanasia, etc., are perfectly alright. The following arguments prove this point.

1. Economic considerations may lead to the termination of a person. It is cheaper to abort than to give welfare.

2. The fact of or possibility of a "miserable life."

3. "Unwanted children" should be aborted.

4. "Inconvenient" pregnancies can be terminated.

5. "Responsibilities" outweigh "rights."

6. Overpopulation will lead to the need of terminating useless life.

7. Future food and fuel shortages mean planned terminations.

8. The few (unwanted, handicapped, elderly) should be willing to sacrifice for the many.

9. People in a miserable condition "want to die."

10. "Parasites" are people who no longer have any contribution to make to the economic health of the state. They do not produce any goods or services. Thus they should be terminated.

Conclusion

Humanism is a love affair with death. It means death to morality, truth, justice and freedom. It brings death to the unborn, the aged and the handicapped. It turns beauty into ugliness and order into chaos. It has never produced anything that speaks of life.

Chapter Ninety-Nine
Biblical Anthropology

Introduction

Humanity's origin, nature, attributes, uniqueness, abilities, significance, dignity, meaning, worth, greatness, nobility, purpose, destiny, place in the universe, sexuality, politics, gender issues, and aesthetic qualities are more controversial today than in the past. Why is this true?

Secular humanism has become more consistent in following its *a priori* presuppositions to their logical conclusions. For example, in his book, *Beyond Freedom and Dignity,* Prof. B.F. Skinner of Harvard came to the conclusion that if "God" as a concept is dead, then "man" as a concept is dead as well. Thus, the concepts of the dignity and freedom of man are dead as well.

God

↓

angels

↓

man

↓

animals

↓

things

Modern evolutionists assume that man should now be classified as just one primate among many. Zoology must take the place of anthropology. Man must not be viewed as distinct from or superior to the other animals on the planet. Some animals are more important than man.

The practical implications of a humanistic definition of man are seen in the individual and collective depravity of those who assume that since man is only an animal, then they can live as animals, die as animals and treat other people as animals. The idea of "human" rights is a myth! The end result can be seen in the Nazi concentration camps and the Soviet Gulags, where human beings were treated as disposable junk.

Given these grim realities, the Christian is the only one today who has a solid basis for the unity and dignity of man. But today too many "Evangelicals" have adopted many of the presuppositions of humanism and, as a result, have a defective view of man. It is thus necessary to define and to defend the biblical view of man in opposition to errant Christians as well as to anti-Christians.

Prolegomena

Before we define and defend our view of man, it is necessary to set forth certain principles that will guide us in our search for truth.

1. We must decide which question to ask:

What is man according to God?	What is man?
Theistic question	Humanistic question
Theocentric worldview	Anthropocentric worldview
God is the Origin of truth	Man is the Origin of truth
God is the measure of all things	Man is the measure of all things
Man is whatever God says he is	Man defines himself

2. We must decide on the method by which we find the truth about man:

Theistic Worldview	Humanistic Worldview
Special revelation in Scripture	Human reason, experience, feelings, faith, etc.
Revealed anthropology	Natural anthropology
Revealed theology	Natural theology
Revealed philosophy	Natural philosophy
Historical/grammatical exegesis	Rationalism, empiricism, mysticism, fideism, etc.
Sola Scriptura	Sola ratione
Objective	Subjective
Absolute	Relative
Supra-temporal	Temporal
Supra-cultural	Cultural

3. We should look at man as he is and does in the real world instead of trying to find some abstract "ideal" man that no one has ever seen or heard.

4. We should view the evil men do as part of man's essence instead of trying to find some "hidden" or "higher" nature that is intrinsically good.

5. Man cannot be understood except in the context of his relationship to God.

6. It is impossible to understand man apart from and independent of the Bible.

7. When man is viewed apart from God, he loses all uniqueness and meaning.

8. There is no divine self in man to find.

9. Humanism is based on an abstract and idealized view of man that is naive in its optimistic view of the ability of human reason to understand itself apart from and independent of God's revelation.

10. Arminianism is based on an *a priori* abstract and idealized view of man that was derived from ancient Greek philosophy and the humanistic ideals of the Renaissance.

11. Biblical theology is the queen of the sciences and is dominant over all other disciplines. The Bible is thus to be preferred to the theories of man.

12. The concept of "free will" is based on a naive view of human nature that is as abstract as it is pagan.

The Biblical View of Man

A. Did God create man or did he evolve from lower life forms?
1. The "days" of Genesis 1 are normal 24 hour days.
2. The age of universe is far younger than claimed.
3. The fatal flaws of theories of evolution:
   a. time + chance + matter = 0
   b. "Survival of the fittest" versus DNA
   c. Everything came from nothing?
   d. Life from non-life?
   e. Order from chaos?
   f. The personal from the non-personal?
   g. Morality from non-moral?
   h. Consciousness from non-consciousness?
   i. Beauty and meaning from survival of the fittest?
   j. Theories with no hard evidence versus a "fact"

B. How did God create man?
1. Body and soul (Matt. 10:28; 2 Cor. 4:16; 3 John 2)
2. Two errors to avoid:
   a. Materialism: you are only matter.
   b. Spiritualism: you are only mind.
3. Matter and mind constitute man.

C. In what sense is man created in the image of God?
    1. Special Revelation is the only basis for understanding what the "image of God" means.
    2. Beware of philosophical or psychological answers to this question. Why go to pagan philosophers to find out what man is? (Isa. 8: 19-20).
    3. Silly answers:
        a. Man stands on two feet.
        b. Man has a free will.
        c. Man's reason.
        d. Man's personality.
        e. Male/female sexual relationship.
        f. Immortality of the soul.
        g. Man is a trinity of body, soul and spirit.
        h. God has a male body.
    4. The Reformed answer:
        a. Where in the Bible is the "image of God" mentioned?
            Gen. 1:26-27; 9:6   Eph. 4:24
            1 Cor. 11:7   Col. 1:15; 3:10
            2 Cor. 4:4   James 3:9

        b. What can be gleamed exegetically from those passages?
            1. The "image" has a *functional* sense of dominion over the earth. Man stands over the earth (Gen. 1:28; cf. Psa. 8:6-8).
            2. The "image" has a *relational* sense of man has a relationship to God, to other humans, to the animals, and to the world (Gen. 1-3).
            3. The "image" has a *unique* sense of man being distinct from the rest of the creation. Man stands apart from the world (nature). (Gen. 1-3).
            4. The "image" has a *noetic* sense in that man was created with intrinsic knowledge (Col. 3:10).
            5. The "image" has a *positional* sense of righteousness in the sight of God (Eph. 4:24).
            6. The "image" has an *ethical* sense of true holiness (Eph. 4:24),

D. What happened to the image of God at the Fall?
    1. Man lost his innate knowledge of God, himself and the world and now produces idolatry and wickedness (Rom. 3:10-18; 1 Cor. 2:14).
    2. Although corrupted, polluted, and enslaved to sin, the image-bearing capacity remains within man (James 3:9).
    3. Original sin means that man is "conceived in iniquity" and "born in sin" in the sense that:
        a. He is now unrighteous in his position;
        b. He is now unholy in his condition.
E. What are the four states of the Christian?

Before the Fall	After the Fall	After Regeneration	The Eternal State
Perfect freedom to obey God.	No freedom to obey God.	Growing freedom to obey God.	Perfected freedom to obey God.

Natural Theology Versus Revealed Theology

Do not be bound together with unbelievers; for what partnership have righteousness and lawlessness, or what fellowship has light with darkness? Or what harmony has Christ with Belial, or what has a believer in common with an unbeliever? Or what agreement has the temple of God with idols? (2 Corinthians 6:14-16)

Introduction

The conflict between Natural and Revealed Theologies existed long before Jesus was born. There were those Jews, such as Philo, who felt that Greek philosophy was so superior to the prophets that it would be better if Judaism abandoned its sole dependence on divine Revelation and appealed to Greek philosophic "Reason" as the Origin of truth. They were called "Hellenistic Jews" because they were more "Greek" than Jewish.

Orthodox Jews viewed Hellenistic Jews as traitors because they had turned their backs on the Torah and embraced Greek philosophy in its place of Scripture. Many of the books written during the intertestamental period record the violent conflicts between Hellenized Jews and Orthodox Jews. 1 and 2 Maccabees record how the conflict unfolded in the life of the Jewish people. Dr. H.W. Hoehner explains:

> Hellenism is the devotion to ancient Gk. thought, customs, and life style.... Alexander the Great, who was taught by Aristotle, devoting his life to conquering the world for the spread of Gk. culture.... The entrenchment of Hellenism can more readily be seen among the Alexandrian Jews, esp. among some of their philosophers such as Philo, who adopted the allegorical interpretation which led to the sacrificing of the truth in the OT on the altar of pagan philosophy.[1]

The "Sadducees" mentioned in the NT were the Hellenistic Jews of Jesus' time. They were theological liberals who followed Natural Theology in denying miracles, angels and demons, the immortality of the soul, the resurrection of the body, and the life everlasting (Acts 23:8).

The Sadducees were the bitter enemies not only of the Orthodox Jews but also of Jesus. They confronted Him with trick questions and evasive answers. In one brilliant exchange between the Sadducees and Jesus, He put them to shame by saying: "You are in error, not understanding the Scriptures nor the Power of God! (Matt. 22:29).

The Pharisees were the Orthodox Jews of the NT. They did not accept the Sadducees as fellow Jews but as sell-outs to pagan Greek philosophy. Paul used their mutual hatred of each other when he announced that he was on trial for being a Pharisee, who believed in the resurrection:

> But perceiving that one part were Sadducees and the other Pharisees, Paul began crying

out in the Council, "Brethren, I am a Pharisee, a son of Pharisees; I am on trial for the hope and resurrection of the dead!" And as he said this, there arose a dissension between the Pharisees and Sadducees; and the assembly was divided. For the Sadducees say that there is no resurrection, nor an angel, nor a spirit; but the Pharisees acknowledge them all. And there arose a great uproar; and some of the scribes of the Pharisaic party stood up and began to argue heatedly, saying, "We find nothing wrong with this man; suppose a spirit or an angel has spoken to him?" And as a great dissension was developing, the commander was afraid Paul would be torn to pieces by them and ordered the troops to go down and take him away from them by force, and bring him into the barracks (Acts 23:6-10).

The Apostle was clearly on the Orthodox side and had no use for the liberals and their Natural theology. As a matter of fact, Paul never appealed to man's "reason" as the basis for doctrine and morals. He based his theology on Scripture alone (1 Cor. 15-3-4).

Later, a full-scale theological war erupted in the Apostolic Church between those who followed Greek philosophy (Natural Theology) and those who followed Scripture (Revealed Theology). Such NT books as Colossians and 1 John were written to refute the invasion of Greek philosophy into the early church.

Paul passionately warned Timothy not to listen to the siren call of human philosophy in 1 Tim. 6:20:

O Timothy, guard what has been entrusted to you, avoiding worldly and empty chatter and the opposing arguments of what is falsely called "knowledge."

With rigorous thrusts of his verbal sword, the Apostle dismisses Greek philosophy (Plato, Aristotle, et al) as nothing more than mere "chatter," i.e. foolish and frivolous talk that is a waste of time. Philosophic "chatter" is described by Paul as:
a. "worldly": finding its Origin in the world, i.e. Nature, instead of in God's Revelation. Hence it is godless and profane.
b. "empty": pointless, i.e. devoid of anything of profit to the Christian.
c. "falsely called knowledge": Paul dismisses all of Greek philosophy as "pseudo knowledge," which is actually the "antithesis" of real knowledge.

As an Orthodox Jew, Paul's hostility to Greek philosophy is quite caustic and severe:

See to it that no one takes you captive through philosophy and empty deception, according to the tradition of men, according to the elementary principles of the world, rather than according to the Messiah (Colossians 2:8).

Natural philosophy is dismissed by Paul as:
a. "empty deception": foolish and pointless lies.
b. "the traditions of men": finding its Origin in man and his traditions rather than in God and His Revelation.
c. "the elementary principles of the world": Paul uses the technical Greek term for the "first principles" of Greek philosophy. He knew exactly what he was saying. These "first principles" were abstracted from "the world," i.e. Nature, instead of from divine Revelation.
d. "not according to the Messiah": A.T. Robertson explains:
    And not after Christ. Christ is the yardstick by which to measure philosophy and all phases of human knowledge. The Gnostics were measuring Christ by their philosophy

as many men are doing today. They have it backwards. Christ is the measure for all
human knowledge since he is the Creator and the Sustainer of the universe.[2]

When some of the saints at Corinth fell into the error of following Greek philosophy instead of following Scripture, Paul reminded them that the philosophers of this world never found God by human
reason, experience, faith or feelings.

> For it is written, "I will destroy the philosophy of the philosophers, and the cleverness of
> the clever I will set aside." Where is the philosopher? Where is the scribe? Where is the de-
> bater of this age? Has not God made foolish the philosophy of this world? For since in the phi-
> losophy of God the world through its philosophy did not come to know God, God was well-
> pleased through the foolishness of the message preached to save those who believe. For indeed
> Jews ask for miracles, and Greeks search for philosophy (1 Corinthians 1:19-22).

The Greek lexicons are unanimous that the Greek word "wisdom" in the passage above is a clear
attack of Paul upon Greek philosophy in general and Greek rhetoric in particular. Thayer states that
"wisdom" here refers to:

> the empty conceit of wisdom which men make a parade of, a knowledge more specious
> than real of lofty and hidden subjects: such as the theosophy of certain Jewish Christians, Col.
> 2:23; the philosophy of the Greeks, 1 Cor. 1:21f; 2:1; with "of this world" added, 1 Cor. 1:20;
> 3:19; "of this age," 1 Cor. 2:6; "wisdom of this age," 1 Cor. 1:19; "wisdom of the wise," 1 Cor.
> 2:5 (in each of these last passages the word includes also the rhetorical art, such as is taught in
> the schools), cf. Fritzsche, Romans, vol. i, p. 67f; the wisdom which shows itself in speaking
> (R. V. wisdom of words), the art of the rhetorician, 1 Cor. 1:17; … (so R in 1 Cor. 1:4 and all
> texts in 1 Cor. 1:13) … discourse conformed to philosophy and the art of rhetoric, 1 Cor.
> 2:4,13.[3]

When the Apostle Paul mocks the vaunted claims of Greek philosophy as mere "foolishness," he is
only voicing the same attitude displayed by the prophets and the Apostles. To put it bluntly, the Bible
from Genesis to Revelation is absolutely hostile to Natural religion, philosophy, and theology.

It must also be pointed out that nowhere in the Bible do we ever find anyone at anytime encouraging the people of God to listen to the philosophers. No one in the Bible ever appealed to human reason, experience, feelings or faith as the basis of doctrine or morals.

Even though many today do not want to hear this, the Bible does not give one kind word about
Natural theology or philosophy. The attempt to discover truth, justice, morals, meaning, and beauty
apart from and independent of Scriptures is everywhere declared a miserable failure due to the sinful
nature of man (1 Cor. 1:25-31).

In this study we will explore the origin, nature, and history of Natural Theology and how it has
been the mother of every heresy and false doctrine that has ever plagued the Christian Church.

We will follow the example of the prophets, apostles, and our Lord Himself in looking to Special
Revelation as the Origin of truth, justice, morals, meaning, and beauty. The God who is there, is not
silent, but has spoken in Scripture that we might know who He is and who we are and how we can
come into His presence with acceptance.

Part One

The following propositions come from 40 years of research on and study of the biblical philosophy
of religion. I will set forth the results of my research in a series of propositions.

Proposition No. 1: Just as the philosophy of science is prior to the discipline of science, the philosophy of religion is prior to the practice of religion. Before you choose a religion, you must first decide what is the nature, origin, attributes, and results of "religion."

Proposition No. 2: Religion, like science, law, politics or medicine, is to be discussed under the categories of Truth and Morals. Thus a particular religion is either true or false, good or evil, just or unjust, right or wrong, helpful or harmful.

Proposition No. 3: All religions make truth claims. A "truth claim" is a "propositional statement," which is a declarative sentence that gives a statement of fact the meaning of which is either true or false. Such declarative sentences constitute the belief system of a religion.

Proposition No. 4: There are no universal, self-evident or intuitive religious truth claims that are embraced by all religions. Instead, religions often contradict each other in their truth claims. Thus, while all religious truth claims can be false or one claim can be true and all the others false, they cannot all be true.

Proposition No. 5: Religious truth claims cannot be reduced to mere personal preference. Stating a truth claim (i.e. "God created the world") is not the same as announcing your favorite ice cream flavor. It is not just a matter of personal taste or prejudice but is either true or false, good or evil.

Proposition No. 6: Religious truth claims cannot be reduced to emotive statements or exclamatory sentences, which are only psychological expressions indicating the emotional state of a person.

Proposition No. 7: It is self-contradictory to say, "All religious truth claims are emotive statements expressing personal preferences that are exempt from Truth and Morals," because the person who is making this statement expects you to accept the religious truth claim he just stated as "true" and "good."

It is like the man who announced, "Everything I say is a lie." If he is speaking the truth, then not everything he says is a lie. But if he is lying, then he does speak the truth. Either way he is wrong.

Part Two

Proposition No. 8: In the end, there are actually only two religions in the world.

A. Natural religion:
  1. Man-made: arises out of some aspect of his being:
    a. human reason
    b. human experience
    c. human faith
    d. human feelings
  2. Man-centered:
    a. Man is the Origin of all things:
      (1) Truth
      (2) Justice
      (3) Morals
      (4) Meaning
      (5) Beauty
      (6) God
    b. Man is the Measure of all things:
      (1) Truth
      (2) Justice
      (3) Morals
      (4) Meaning
      (5) Beauty
      (6) God

    c. Man is the Judge of all things:

      (1) Truth

      (2) Justice

      (3) Morals

      (4) Meaning

      (5) Beauty

      (6) God

  3. Autonomous: independent of God and any information from Him.

  4. Foundational: the basis of Natural Theology, which is Natural Religion expressed in Christian terminology.

B. Revealed Religion:

  1. God-made religion: arises out of some aspect of His being:

    a. divine reason

    b. divine experience

    c. divine faith

    d. divine feelings

  2. God-centered:

    a. God is the Origin of all things:

      (1) Truth

      (2) Justice

      (3) Morals

      (4) Meaning

      (5) Beauty

      (6) God

    b. God is the Measure of all things:

      (1) Truth

      (2) Justice

      (3) Morals

      (4) Meaning

      (5) Beauty

      (6) God

    c. God is the Judge of all things:

      (1) Truth

      (2) Justice

      (3) Morals

      (4) Meaning

      (5) Beauty

      (6) God

  3. Autonomous: Independent of man and any information from him (Rom. 11:34-35).

  4. Foundational: Revealed Religion is the basis of Revealed Theology, which is the exposition of God's special revelation found solely in Holy Scripture (Sola Scriptura).

Footnotes

1. *The Zondervan Pictorial Dictionary of the Bible* (Grand Rapids: Zondervan, 1976), 3:117.

2. Archibald Thomas Robertson, *Word Pictures in the New Testament* (Nashville: Broadman, 1931) IV:491.

3. Joseph Henry Thayer, *Greek-English Lexicon of the New Testament* (Grand Rapids: Zondervan, 1965) p. 582.

The Cost of Discernment

In an age in which discernment is viewed as a vice and gullibility as a virtue, there is a price to be paid if one decides to be "picky" about what to believe and how to live.

We are constantly told not to judge others, but to be positive and accepting of all beliefs and lifestyles. "Something is true if you believe it" seems to be the greatest dogma of the 21st century. This queer notion dominates much of the church as well as much of the world today.

The spirit of this age is a gullible spirit. This is the root reason why the cults are flourishing today and why gurus, psychics, channelers, self-proclaimed deities and messiahs are able to amass millions of dollars. It seems that the more ridiculous the belief, the more successful it becomes!

Those of us who have decided to swim against the tide of relativism that has engulfed our culture are made out to be the "bad guys." We are told that it is "unloving," "unkind," "critical" and "conceited" to judge other people's religious beliefs or practices. Of course, it would be "unkind" for us to point out to them that they are hypocrites, because they are doing exactly what they are condemning us for doing! They are judging us in the name that it is wrong to judge!

This should not surprise us in the least. If we are the friends of God, the world will view us as its enemies (James 4:4). Discerning people are never as popular as the typical non-judgmental conformist who plays for the applause of the world. Indeed, Jesus warned us that too much popularity is a sign of being a false prophet (Lk. 6:26)!

In John 15:19, Jesus said that the world loves its own. This is why it is perfectly proper at a cock-tail party to speak of one's love for Maharishi Yogi, but it is not proper to speak of your love for Jesus Christ. Reincarnation is an acceptable topic, but woe to that person who dares to bring up the subject of hell. As one Universalist-Unitarian said to me, "All religions are true—except yours."

We accept the fact that since the world hated Jesus, it will hate us because we represent Him and His kingdom (John 15:18). This is part of the cost not only of apologetics but of Christian discipleship itself.

Because we know this, we are perfectly content to bear with "the slings and arrows of outrageous foes" in the world. We have even come to expect it. When someone gives us an encouraging word, it is like a breath of fresh air. But this does not happen too often. We have all been crucified many times over by bigoted humanists, cultists and occultists. It goes with the territory. The proverb, "If you can't take the heat, you better stay out of the kitchen," is most apropos for counter-cult evangelism.

But what we will never accept is the same kind of treatment by people in the church who should know better. I for one am quite tired of being rebuked by little old ladies who think that the Mormons are Christians because their church is called, "The Church of Jesus Christ of Latter-day Saints!" If I had a dollar for every time I have been told, "Judge not lest ye be judged," I could retire to the Bahamas.

I remember one woman in Cape May, New Jersey, who came up after my lecture series on the cults and said: "Why do you claim that the Mormons are false prophets? I asked the Mormon missionaries who live next to me if they were false prophets and they said, 'No!' Aren't you bearing false witness against them?" Evidently, gullibility has no limits!

We have all had countless experiences with ignorant people who think that "all roads lead to God," "all truth is God's truth," "everyone worships the same God under different names" and "all healing comes from God." We bear patiently with them, instructing them in the hope that God will grant them repentance unto the acknowledging of the truth (2 Tim. 2:24-26).

But what can we say about all those pastors who oppose our work and think that they are doing God a favor by putting us down as negative thinkers? Educating their people about the cults is a waste of time to them. Money, buildings and numbers seem to be their only concern.

It is sad to say, but most pastors are not interested in teaching their people to be discerning. Their sermons are often based on stories, jokes and illustrations. They tell their people to accept their doctrines by faith. They do not encourage in-depth Bible study. As one pastor told me, "You cannot have a big church and get too deep into the Bible or doctrine, because you are bound to offend too many people and they will leave." He was committed to shallow preaching as a principle!

These pastors can be as vicious as cultists. And when they get in charge of a Bible college or seminary, they will hunt down "unbelief" and root it out with a zeal that can only be equaled by the Inquisition. I was raised in a non-Christian home by a father who was an agnostic when sober and an atheist when drunk. I started reading philosophy while still in high school. After my conversion to Christ, I joined the most prominent evangelical church in New York City. I assumed that the pastor and Sunday School teachers would answer my questions. And, since I read constantly, I had lots of questions.

Now, I was not mean or nasty about issues. I just wanted to know why I was supposed to believe this or that doctrine. What was wrong with asking, "Where is this taught in the Bible?"

I soon ran into all kinds of trouble. I was told to "let go and let God" have His way with me by accepting things by faith. I was counseled that a "spirit of unbelief" lay behind all my questions. Why couldn't I be like everyone else and just accept what the pastor said? Why did I stir up trouble by asking questions? Why was I reading all those books? It was not normal to be so interested in the cults. What was a 16-year-old kid doing studying Greek and Hebrew?

The man who led me to Christ warned me that "much learning will make you mad." It was dangerous to study theology, philosophy, the cults and the occult.

Finally, my pastor graciously told me that I should go to a Bible college where such questions could be answered. So, upon graduation from high school, I went to a Bible college. And boy, was I excited. At last I would find answers to my questions. At last I would be free to ask questions without someone accusing me of unbelief.

I wish I could tell you that my expectations were realized at this Bible college. But not only were my questions not answered, I was severely condemned for the sin of asking questions, which they said was rooted in the sin of intellectualism.

One student came up after our New Testament Introduction class in which I had asked the professor how to answer the arguments of form criticism, and said: "Bob, I hate you! Why do ask questions? You are getting everyone upset. Why can't you just accept the truth without questioning it?"

I tried to explain that asking questions was the way I discovered the truth to accept. I had read much of liberal theology and I needed to know how to answer their arguments against the Bible. That is why I came to a Bible college.

Some of the professors simply did not have any answers, and this caused some hard feelings. I was sent to see the dean to try and work out the problem.

The dean asked me: "Bob, have you ever asked Jesus to take away your questioning mind and to give you a believing heart instead? Are you willing to get on your knees right now and ask Jesus to take your mind away and give you a heart for God?" We got on our knees and prayed for Jesus to take my mind away and give me a heart instead.

It did not work. I could not stop asking why we should believe this or that. Like bubbles of air rising in water, the questions kept surfacing. I could not stop. I will never forget one chapel talk in which a professor took the text, "Open thy mouth wide and I will fill it," and interpreted it to mean that we must accept without question what God has revealed through his teachers at the Bible college. He made all of us sit there with our mouths open during his talk!

Finally, I was brought before the president of the college, who tried one last line of reasoning with me. He asked, "Bob, am I a man of God?" Of course I had to answer, "Yes." He responded, "Do I preach the Word of God by the power of God in the Spirit of God?" Again, what could I have answered but "Yes"? "Then how can I be wrong? If I by the power of God preach the Word of God in the Spirit of God, how can I be wrong?" To this I had no answer but silence.

Even though I had not broken any rules, and they admitted that I did not have a bad attitude, I was thrown out of that Bible college for the sin of asking too many questions.

I was forced to come to the conclusion that evangelical Christianity had no answers. Their doctrines were based on mysticism and a gullible spirit that accepted whatever the pastor or the professor said. A discerning spirit was not welcome in such circles. A questioning mind would not be tolerated. To ask questions would rock the boat and make waves—which is never allowed in such circles. Faith was an existential leap.

With a deep sense of disillusionment, I began to drift toward Neo-orthodoxy. The president had told me that he had never met anyone with a Ph.D. who loved God. The choice was set before me. If I wanted to love Jesus, then I could not think. If chose to think, I could not love Jesus!

I left that "Bible" college deeply hurt by my experience. Several of my friends who also got kicked out left the Christian faith altogether. One even became an atheist! But God had mercy on me and brought me into contact with discerning thinkers such as Francis Schaeffer, Gordon Clark, Walter Martin and John Montgomery. Humanly speaking, I would have been lost to the evangelical church if it were not for them.

Schaeffer was willing to sit down and answer my questions, and he did not put me down for asking them. He came up with solid answers to my questions. I remember one time telling him with tears: "You mean that I not crazy for asking such questions? It is not wrong to wonder why? I can be a Christian and think at the same time?"

While I was delivered from apostasy, many students have been lost to the church forever. They could not take the anti-intellectualism and the gullible spirit that they found in far too many evangelical circles. The lack of discernment has driven many thinking people out of the church.

I must ask why are so many Christians gullible? Why is there such a lack of discernment today? Why are people still sending checks to PTL and Jimmy Swaggart? Why would anyone in his right mind buy into the "blab it-grab it" theology? Why would someone claim to be an evangelical and at the same time openly deny the inspiration of Scripture, the miracles recorded in the Bible, the need to hear of and believe in Jesus for salvation and the reality of a conscious afterlife in heaven or hell?

The following is a short list of some reasons why so many people are undiscerning today.

1. A misunderstanding of what Jesus meant when He said in Matt. 7:1, "Judge not, lest ye be judged."

From Matt. 7:5, it is clear that Jesus was rebuking hypocrites who publicly condemn people for doing something that they themselves are doing in secret. Standing up and condemning someone for adultery while being engaged in an adulterous affair is what Jesus was condemning. Thus, the passage has nothing to do with the non-judgmental, positive-thinking relativism of today.

Later on in the same passage, Jesus tells us to judge certain kinds of people as being wild savage dogs and pigs (v. 6). He even commands us to judge certain people as being false prophets (v. 15).

In John 7:24, Jesus tells us to "judge with righteous judgment." Indeed, no one could be baptized unless he was "judged" converted. No one could join a church unless he was "judged" qualified. Neither could there be any church officers without someone being "judged" as satisfying the requirements laid out in the Pastoral Epistles.

2. A wrong understanding of "love."

Modern "luv" cannot compare to the richness of biblical love. Sappy sentimentalism and a gullible spirit do not constitute true love. It is not loving to affirm deviant doctrines or lifestyles.

Biblical love is sometimes confrontational and means that we will tell someone the truth even if it will make him our enemy (Eph. 4:25; Gal. 4:16). The truth will often offend people (1 Cor. 1:18). It cannot be avoided.

3. Assuming that something is true if you believe it.

Truth is made to conform to what we want it to be. It is subjectivized and relativized until it is no longer truth. This is the theme of the New Age. Everyone has his own truth!

But the Bible tells us to believe something if it is true. For example, Luke asks his readers to believe in the bodily resurrection of Christ because there is convincing evidence to demonstrate that it is true (Acts 1:3).

4. Assuming that personal piety guarantees doctrinal purity.

While I was doing a show on a prominent Christian television network, I found that they were considering having a guest whom I knew to be a member of a large cult. When I pointed out the deviant doctrines of the man, the host replied: "You must be mistaken! He is too nice to be a heretic!" "Niceness" does not guarantee truthfulness!

5. They were never trained to check Scripture to see if something is true before they believe it (Acts 17:11).

It is the pastor's job to train his people to be discerning (Eph. 4:12; Heb. 5:14). I love to preach in churches where I can hear the pages of Bibles being turned as people are looking up in Scripture to see if what I am saying is true. I love to see people taking notes. Their pastor has trained them well.

Just as the cults are the unpaid bills of the church, the lack of discernment today must be laid at the feet of the clergy. But they are victims, too.

The Bible colleges and seminaries which trained them must share the blame. While there are a few exceptions, most pastors were never trained to be discerning. They were never encouraged to ask questions. Some kind of existential faith was pushed on them. A mystical basis for faith cannot survive in apologetics. Is it any wonder that they themselves cannot discern truth from error?

Conclusion

The cost of discernment is high. You will not be the most popular guy in town. You will have to take your lumps as you expose heresy. You will have to endure the resulting anger of people who do not want to be "judged."

But the cost of being gullible is even higher, for it pushes thinking people right out of the church! For the cause of God and Truth and the immortal souls of men, we must be discerning, regardless of the cost.

Chapter One Hundred Two

The Divine Use of Ridicule and Humor in the Bible

The Apostle Paul warned Christians not to allow the world to squeeze them into its mold (Rom. 12:1). Instead, we need to be transformed by the renewing of our minds by allowing the Scriptures to equip us for every good work (Rom. 12:2; 2 Tim. 3:16-17). One of the devices of Satan (2 Cor. 2:11) that has molded many Christians today is the heresy of "political correctness."

This heresy teaches that we should never judge the doctrines or lifestyles of others. Any Christian who boldly stands up for Jesus and the gospel today is condemned as being unkind, unloving and judgmental. Of course, when someone condemns you for condemning others, they are hypocrites because they are condemning you! If they really believe it is wrong to judge others, why are they judging you?

One recent attack on biblical Christianity is the idea that it is wrong to ridicule, mock or scorn false religions and false prophets. Indeed, the only heresy that political correctness allows is the heresy of calling anything a heresy.

Political correctness teaches that the supreme evil is to offend people by hurting their feelings. Thus, if you say anything that hurts the feelings of a false prophet or his followers, you have sinned. This idea is so ingrained in people today that they assume that the use of humor, scorn and mockery is a vice. But is this assumption itself wrong?

If we give heed to Scripture, we will find that use of humor, ridicule, and scorn to mock false religion is a virtue and not a vice. It is one of the works of God and Christ and was practiced by prophets and apostles. The Church Fathers and the Reformers used scorn and ridicule to mock the heresies of their day. They were not neutered like most church leaders today. They commanded the allegiance of real men because they were not wimps or cowards.

God mocks, scorns and ridicules the absurd attempts of the heathen to overthrow His sovereignty in Psa. 2:4: He that sits enthroned in the heavens scornfully laughs at them. The LORD will mock them.

The Lord laughs at the wicked in Psa. 37:13, because He knows that their day of doom is drawing near. Psa. 59:8 is translated variously:

But Thou, Jehovah, wilt laugh at them; Thou wilt mock at all the nations (ABPS).

And all the while thou, Lord, makest light of them (Knox).

But you, Lord, simply laugh at them: You ridicule all the pagan nations (Harrison).

Yahweh, you laugh at them, You make fun of these pagans (Jerusalem).

If mockery and ridicule are wrong, then God is guilty of sin. But the Holy One hates false religion and ridicules it as "stupid" in Jer. 10:8:

But they are altogether stupid and foolish; In their discipline of delusion—their idol is wood! (NAS).

The whole lot of them are brutish and stupid: The teachings given by these Nothings is void of sense (Jerusalem).

No wonder Divine wisdom mocks at them in Pro. 1:26:
I also will laugh at your calamity; I will mock when your fear comes (KJV).
I will laugh at your calamity; And mock when your destruction cometh (Septuagint).
I, for my part, will laugh at your distress; I will jeer at you when calamity comes (Jerusalem).
So in the day of your trouble I will be laughing: I will make sport of your fear (Basic English Bible).

"But," someone may argue, "even though God can mock and ridicule, surely it would still be wrong for us to do so." But Psa. 52:6 says: "The righteous … shall mock him."
This is what Elijah did on Mt. Carmel. "At midday, Elijah mocked them" (1 Kgs. 18:26).

When we turn to the prophets, they all mocked and ridiculed the wicked. This is why they were often murdered! Amos hurt the feelings of people when he mocked them saying:
Listen to me, you "fat cows" of Bashan living in Samaria—you women who encourage your husbands to rob the poor and crush the needy—you who never have enough to drink!" (Amos 4:1).

In case some may think that Spirit-inspired mockery is an Old Testament thing, when we turn to the New Testament, what do we find? John the Baptist no doubt hurt people's feelings when he called them "a brood of snakes" and warned them of judgment to come (Lk. 3:7). Jesus mocked the Pharisees, the Sadducees and others until they became so angry that they tried to murder him on different occasions. Read Matt. 23 to see Jesus ridicule them. The crowd roared with laughter as He scorched His enemies. The apostles ridiculed apostates and other enemies of the gospel (2 Pet. 3). Paul even used sexual humor in Gal. 5:12 to ridicule the legalists.

The Balance
Does this teaching mean you have a right to be rude and offensive to people in general? No! We are warned not to be mockers and scoffers in everyday life. The use of argumentum ad ridiculum is reserved for the refutation of false religions and the defense of the gospel. A mocking attitude is wrong when directed against God, the things of God, the Church, and God's people. It is thus not to be used against fellow Christians. As much as lies within you, give no offense except the offense of the cross.

Conclusion
If we want to walk in the footsteps of the prophets, the apostles and Jesus Himself, then we cannot buy into the politically correct heresy that dominates the world today. Ye fearful saints, obey the Word and ignore the cavils of wimps and cowards. Let God be true even if this means that you will have to say that every man is a liar (Rom. 3:4).

Chapter One Hundred Three
Introduction to the Cults

I. The Biblical Mandate

All Christians are commanded by God to defend the Christian Faith (Jude 3). Thus, we should not to be ignorant of Satan's devices (2 Cor. 2:11). Jesus foretold the coming of false Christs and false prophets (Matt. 24:4-5, 11, 23-27). He said that we will be able to know them (Matt. 7:15-23).

II. The Amazing Growth of the Cults

One hundred years ago there were only five or six cults in the United States with only a few thousand followers. Today there are over five thousand cults with more than 50 million people involved. New cults are being incorporated every day.

Why did the major cults arise in the 19th century?
    A. There was a crisis in religious authority.
    B. Unparalleled natural catastrophes occurred.
    C. An "End of the World" mania gripped the population.
    D. Prophets and prophetesses appeared by the dozens.
    E. Occult beliefs and practices became popular.

Part One

I. Definition of the word "Cult"
A religious organization founded upon the authority and teaching of one or more individuals whose authority is viewed as being equal to or greater than the authority of Scripture and whose teaching contradicts the theology of biblical and historic Christianity.

II. Scope of the word "Cult"
    1. A cult is an organization whose authority structure rests upon some human authority. This authority figure may be viewed as a prophet, messiah or god. He or she may even be called "pastor" or "elder." The crucial point is that in a cult, the authority structure does not allow for any disagreement or individuality. The members must conform every area of life to the wishes of those over them. The power of the authorities is absolute.
    2. In a cult, the authorities contradict biblical truth by teaching things that are heretical in nature. Most cults deny essential biblical teachings such as the Trinity, the Deity and bodily resurrection of Christ, etc.

III. How to Identify a Cult
There are thus two key elements in all cultic groups:
    1. Misplaced Authority
In a cult, the authority of the leadership is viewed as being equal to or greater than the Bible. The leadership speaks as God's "prophet" and has absolute authority over every aspect of life.

True Authority	False Authority
God	God
The Bible	The Leader
The Clergy/Laity	The Membership

2. Doctrinal Errors

In a cult, while they may claim to be "Christian" and even the true church, they actually deny historic Christianity.

Key questions to ask religious groups/churches:

Is the Bible the final authority in faith and practice?

Is God a personal "I AM" or an impersonal "it"?

Is there only one God?

Is man a god or a god-in-the-making?

Is God infinite, eternal, omnipresent, omniscient, omnipotent, immutable, perfect, incorporate, invisible, good, etc.?

Is God a Trinity?

Did Jesus Christ come in the flesh?

Was He the Christ or only a Christ?

Was He born of a virgin?

Did He die on the cross for our sins?

Did He rise bodily from the grave?

Did He ascend to the right hand of the Father?

Is He coming back personally, bodily and visibly?

Is salvation by grace or by works?

Is Jesus Christ the only way of salvation?

Does man have an immortal soul?

Does this soul survive the death of the body?

Do we go to Heaven or Hell at death?

Will all men be raised bodily at the Judgment Day?

Does eternal conscious punishment await the wicked?

Part Two

I. How to Witness to Cultists

   A. Realize that the initial problem is the authority issue. Until you can refute this authority, the cultist will be closed-minded.

   B. The use of the false prophecies made by the cultic leader or leaders has been used by God to bring many people out of the world. Once this prophecy fails, they must be viewed as false prophets according to Deut. 18:21-22.

II. Application of Method

   A. Jehovah's Witnesses: *How to Answer a Jehovah's Witness* (Bethany House Publishers)

   B. Mormons: *How to Answer a Mormon* (Bethany House Publishers)

C. Reincarnation: *Reincarnation and Christianity* (Bethany House Publishers)

D. Astrology: *Horoscopes and the Christian* (Bethany House Publishers)

E. See chapters on Seventh-day Adventists and Moonies.

Conclusion

These steps can be quickly grasped, easily retained and readily used by the average person because they do not require a great deal of memorization or knowledge. This method not only successfully cult-proofs a church but it has also been used by God to bring thousands of cultists to a saving knowledge of Jesus Christ.

Chapter One Hundred Four

How to Witness to Mormons

Remember that we are not to argue over doctrine or Scripture. The authority of Joseph Smith as a "prophet" of God is the real issue.

Establish the following points:

Step No. 1: Joseph Smith was only one of many 19th century "prophets." There was nothing unique about his claims.

Step No. 2: He was a part of a movement called "Restorationism" in which many people claimed to be "restoring" a gospel that had been "lost" since the first century: Alexander Campbell, Charles Russell, Ellen G. White, Joseph Smith and many others claimed to be "God's latter-day prophet."

Step No. 3: Down through the ages, thousands of people have claimed to be "God's prophet." Either they are all false or only one is right. How can we know if someone is a false prophet?

    a. Circular reasoning proves nothing:
       Mormon: "Joseph Smith was a prophet of God."
       Christian: "How do you know that?"
       Mormon: "Because God spoke to him."
       Christian: "But how do you know that?"
       Mormon: "Because he was a prophet of God."
    b. Subjective feelings prove nothing:
       Mormon: "Joseph Smith was a prophet of God."
       Christian: "How do you know that?"
       Mormon: "Because I feel it in my heart."
       Christian: "But do not all religions claim that?"
    c. We need a way to find out the truth that is:
       1. objective, not subjective.
       2. neutral, not biased.
       3. based on facts, not circular reasoning.
       4. found in historic documents, not speculation.

Step No. 4: Deut. 18: 20-22 gives us the answer.
       If someone claims to be a prophet,
       Examine his prophecies.
       If they failed to happen,
       Then he is a false prophet.

Step No. 5: Since Joseph Smith claimed to a prophet, there are only two options:

    a. He was a false prophet. Thus he was either a liar or a nut.

    b. He was a true prophet. Then we must join one of the Mormon denominations. But which one? All of them claim to be the "true" followers of Joseph Smith!

The only way to know is to examine his prophecies.

The following are only five of the many prophecies made by Smith. Just one false prophecy is enough to discredit him. These prophecies come from such Mormon documents as Doctrine and Covenants, The Pearl of Great Price, History of the Church, Journal of Discourses, and Mormon newspapers, magazines, sermons, diaries, etc.

1. Smith prophesied that people live on the moon, dress like Quakers, live to be a thousand years old and are six feet in height. Brigham Young also claimed that people live on the sun!

2. Smith prophesied that the ten lost tribes of Israel are living in a tropical valley at the North Pole. The Apostle John is still alive and lives with them there.

3. Smith prophesied that the Second Coming of Christ and the end of the world would take place in 1891.

4. Smith prophesied that a temple would be built on the "temple lot" in Independence, Missouri, within the generation of those living in 1832.

5. Smith prophesied that he would return from Salem, Massachusetts, with "many people" and "much treasure."

These are only five of 64 false prophecies given by Smith.

Step No. 6: Be prepared for the following tricks.

1. "I do not care what you show me. Smith could not have said these things, because he was a prophet of God."

2. "So what if Smith did say these things! Moses, Jonah and Jesus were 'false' prophets, but we still believe in them."

3. "But I have a burning witness in my heart."

Conclusion

Fact No. 1: Smith claimed to be a prophet.

Fact No. 2: His prophecies were false.

Therefore he was a false prophet.

How to Witness to Jehovah's Witnesses

Remember not to argue over doctrine or Scripture. The only real issue is the authority of the Watchtower Society as God's prophet and God's organization on earth.

Step No. 1: Before you begin, ask them if they will promise not to lie to you. In *Aid to Bible Understanding* (p. 1060), they are told that they can lie to those "who do not deserve the truth."

Step No. 2: Tell them that the historic documents and facts have the final say.

Step No. 3: Establish the following facts:

Fact No. 1: The Society has claimed to be God's prophet (*Watchtower*, 4/1/72, pp. 197, 200, etc.).

Fact No. 2: The only way to prove it is to examine the record of the prophecies made by the Society (*Watchtower*, 4/1/72, p. 197).

Fact No. 3: Deut. 18:20-22 tells us that if someone gives a false prophecy, he is a false prophet (*Aid to Bible Understanding*, p. 1348).

Fact No. 4: The Society has used this method to refute other groups (*Awake*, 10/8/68, p. 23).

Step No. 4: Beware of the following tricks:
a. "The Watchtower never claimed to be a prophet."

b. "OK. I admit that the Watchtower claimed to be a prophet and made some mistakes. But we all make mistakes."

c. "A false prophet is someone who does not admit his false prophecies."

d. "This is old light. Let us discuss new light, for the Bible says the light gets brighter and brighter."

e. "I do not care about all this. It is not important. Let us study the Trinity."

Be firm that the issue of the authority of the Watchtower must be resolved before going on to study what it teaches.

Step No. 5: Ask them what happened on the following dates, and then present the Watchtower documents. Be prepared for some Jehovah's Witnesses to deny that the Watchtower ever said anything about these dates.

1799 The beginning of the time of the end.

1874 Christ's invisible return to earth.

1878 Christ's kingly office begins.
     The power of the Kingdom begins.
     God rejects all the churches.

1914 Armageddon (the end of the world).
     6,000 years since Adam completed.

1915 Armageddon.

1918 Armageddon and the destruction of the churches.

1925 Armageddon and the Resurrection.
     Beth Sarim built.

1931 Christ's return switched from 1874 to 1914.

1975 Armageddon and the end of the world.
     6,000 years since Adam switched from 1914 to 1975.

1986 The time of peace and safety.
     Armageddon.

Conclusion

Since the Society claims to be God's prophet, but its prophecies failed to happen; then the Society is a false prophet. Since the Society is a false prophet, it has no authority to speak for God—so, why follow it? Look to the Bible instead!

Campbellism and the Church of Christ

Part One

The Restoration Movement

The "Restoration" Movement began in the 19th century under the leadership of Thomas Campbell, Barton Stone, Walter Scott and Alexander Campbell (1788-1866).

The importance of these "Restorers" was based on their claim that:

1. The Christian Church disappeared in the first century. The "true" Gospel was lost at that time.

2. The Roman Catholic Church and all Protestant Churches are apostate organizations, and are not to be viewed as "Christian" churches.

3. All the historic creeds and confessions are worthless and should be ignored.

4. God raised up Alexander Campbell to "restore" the "true" Gospel and to re-establish the Christian Church. He restored the pure "Apostolic" Church.

5. The Millennium was going to be ushered in during their lifetime by the "Restoration" Movement.

6. The "true" Gospel teaches that "baptism unto remission of sins" is essential for salvation. The "Restorers" spoke of this as "baptismal regeneration."

7. The "baptism" given by all other churches is not saving. You have to be re-baptized in accordance with the Campbellite doctrine of baptism to be saved.

8. Only Bible names should be used in the name of a church. It is wrong to use such names as Baptist, Catholic, Presbyterian, etc. Even though they first called themselves "Reformed Baptists," they later took up such names as "Disciples of Christ," "the Churches of Christ" and "The Christian Church."

9. Nothing should be allowed in the Church unless there is a "book, chapter and verse" for it. On this basis the "Reformers" were opposed to the use of musical instruments in worship, missionary societies, etc. This point has led to thousands of church fights and splits. The "Churches of Christ" split off from the "Disciples of Christ" over such issues, and have never stopped splitting since that time.

10. Some Campbellite theologians have denied the omniscience of God by teaching that God does not know the future. (For example see *The Gospel Plan of Salvation,* by T.W. Brents, published by the Gospel Advocate Company in Nashville, Tennessee).

Significant Dates in Campbellite History:

1809: Thomas Campbell censured by the Presbyterian Church for false teaching.

1809: Thomas Campbell writes "Declaration and Address" for the "The Christian Association of Washington." It functioned as a "creed" for the young movement.

1809: Alexander Campbell arrives in America and joins his father's association.

1811: The Association becomes an independent church after being rejected by the Presbyterians once again.

1812: The Campbells are re-baptized by a Baptist preacher at Buffalo Creek. This was 15 years before Scott originated the doctrine of "baptism unto remission of sins."

1813: The Campbells join the Redstone Baptist Association.

1820: Alexander Campbell represents the Baptist Church in a debate with John Walker, a Presbyterian.

1823: August: The Redstone Baptist Association prepares to censure the Campbells for false doctrine but they resign and set up an independent Baptist Church.

1823: October: Alexander Campbell debates McCalla, still claiming to represent Baptists. The Campbells now call themselves "Reformed Baptists."

1827 November: Walter Scott preaches "baptism unto remission of sins." William Amen was the first one "baptized unto remission of sins." Scott's followers call themselves the "Christians."

1832: Campbell's "Disciples of Christ" openly unite with Scott's "Christians."

1849: Controversy over missionary societies splits the "Restoration" Movement.

1860: Controversy over musical instruments splits the movement.

1906: The Churches of Christ listed as a separate denomination apart from the Disciples of Christ and the Christian Church. The Campbellites popularize Scott's doctrine of "baptism unto remission of sins."

1920: Over a hundred controversies split the movement on such issues as musical instruments, head coverings, communion cups, schools, orphanages, Sunday School, divorce, re-marriage, etc.

Part Two

The Campbellite Origin of the Major Cults

I. Campbellism and Mormonism

The evidence is clear that Mormonism arose out of the Campbellite "Restoration" Movement.

1. The leading figures in early Mormonism were originally preachers in Campbellite churches, and many of them had personally worked with Alexander Campbell: Sidney Rigdon, Parley Pratt, Oliver Crowdery, Orson Hyde, Lyman Wight, Edward Partridge, John Corril, Isaac Morely, John Murdock, etc.

2. So many thousands of "Disciples of Christ" joined the Mormons that Alexander Campbell called Mormonism "Satan's counterfeit" of the Disciples of Christ

3. Joseph Smith was taught the "Restoration" concept and its peculiar doctrines by Sidney Rigdon. When Joseph Smith adopted most of the points of the "Restoration" Movement, he put himself as the "Restorer" of the Gospel and the Church in the place of Alexander Campbell.

a. The Church and the "true" Gospel were lost in the first century.

b. All subsequent churches are apostate.

c. Joseph Smith "restored" the Church and the Gospel.

d. A church should use Bible names. The Mormons first called themselves the "Church of Christ." Most Mormon denominations still use such names.

e. You must be baptized "unto remission of sins" by a Mormon priest to be saved.

f. Smith challenged Alexander Campbell to a public debate on the issue of who was the true "Restorer."

Bibliography

1. Mormon Sources:

History of the Church (by Joseph Smith) vol. I:120-125, 188. vol. II:268, 269n, 270.

Journal of Discourses, vol. II:17, 18; vol. XI:3.

Joseph Smith: An American Prophet (by John Evans) 211, 214-216.

2. Anti-Mormon Scholars:

Shadow or Reality (by the Tanners) pp. 66-68.

Origin of Campbellism (by J. Milburn)

3. Campbellite Sources:

Memoirs of Alexander Campbell, vol. II:344-347

II. Campbellism and Christadelphianism

Dr. John Thomas, a prominent "Disciple of Christ" and personal friend of Alexander Campbell, decided that if we should throw out the creeds and use only Bible names, then why should we believe in the Trinity? He went on to deny the deity of Christ, the personhood of the Spirit, the bodily resurrection of Christ, Christ's physical return to this world and the immortality of the soul. He taught "soul sleep" and denied the doctrine of Hell. He did not believe in a paid clergy, but each member was viewed as a minister.

He was able to persuade many other "Disciples" to join him in establishing the "Christadelphians," or "Brethren in Christ." His movement was composed of Campbellite and Millerite churches.

Bibliography

Cyclopedia of Biblical, Theological and Ecclesiastical Literature (by McClintock and Strong), vol. XI: 937- 938.

III. Campbellism and Jehovah's Witnesses

Benjamin Wilson was a "Disciple of Christ" who followed Dr. Thomas into Christadelphianism. Although he never studied Greek, he published a Greek-English interlinear called *The Emphatic Diaglott*.

It was Wilson who introduced Charles Taze Russell to those very doctrines which have become the central theology of the Jehovah's Witnesses. The Watchtower Society even published and used Wilson's interlinear for many years. Campbellism through Christadelphianism is the origin of the Jehovah's Witnesses.

Bibliography

Cyclopedia of Biblical, Theological and Ecclesiastical Literature (by McClintock and Strong), vol. XI:937-938; vol. XII:868-869.

Apostles of Denial (Ed Gruss) pp. 14-16, 193-196.

Part Three

The Doctrinal Errors of Campbellism

While there are many doctrinal issues that divide the evangelical from the Campbellite, the greatest point of controversy is their view of baptism. The evangelical believes that salvation is by grace alone, through faith alone, in Christ alone. Human works such as baptism, church membership, etc., are not necessary for salvation. While obedience to God's Law has a role to play in assurance of salvation, it has no role to play in salvation. Baptism, like circumcision, is a outward rite which symbolizes an inner state. While both ceremonies symbolize regeneration, they do not accomplish it.

In opposition to evangelical doctrine, Campbellite theology teaches "baptismal regeneration." It is claimed that water baptism by immersion of adults only unto remission of sins does not merely symbolize regeneration, but it actually accomplishes it. Faith is not enough. Obedience to God's Law must also take place, or salvation is not possible. Unless you are baptized in the exact way they dictate (immersion, adults only), for the exact purpose they have in mind (unto remission of sins), and by the right person (a Campbellite preacher), not only is your baptism invalid but you are not yet saved no matter how sincerely you believe in Jesus Christ as your Savior!

To add baptism to faith is nothing more than adding works to grace, which is impossible according to Rom. 11:6. The attempt to evade this by claiming that baptism is part of faith is not linguistically or grammatically possible. If obedience to God's commands such as baptism is what "faith" is, then why stop with baptism? What about all the other commands of God, such as "love your wife"? A works-salvation can never say when enough works have been done!

The Reasons Why Baptism Is Not Essential for Salvation

1. If the Campbellite doctrine is true, then the Restorers were not saved men! Thomas Campbell, Alexander Campbell, Walter Scott and Barton Stone were never baptized "unto the remission of sin." While they repudiated their infant baptism when they were baptized by the Baptists, they never repudiated their Baptist baptism and were re-baptized according to Campbellite baptism.

2. Jesus never baptized anyone. If baptism is essential for salvation, then Jesus never saved anyone.

3. Paul did not view baptism as part of the Gospel (1 Cor. 1:14-17).

4. John's baptism did not save anyone, even though it was "unto remission of sins" (Mk. 1:4; cf. Acts 19:1-5).

5. Since there is only one God, there is only one way of salvation (Rom 3:28-30). This means that whatever is necessary for salvation today was also necessary during O.T. times.

6. The Gospel of justification by faith alone apart from obedience to God's commands is taught in both O.T. and the N.T. (Rom 1:1-2).
    Abraham: before the Law (Rom. 4:1-5)
    David: after the Law (Rom. 4:6-8)
    Habakkuk: in the Prophets (Rom. 1:17)

7. Baptism is the N.T. parallel of circumcision, just as the Lord's Supper is the parallel of the

Passover (Col. 2:11-12). Since circumcision was not essential for salvation, then neither is baptism.

8. Abraham was saved before he was circumcised in order to emphasize that salvation was by faith alone apart from obedience to God's commands, and that the Gentiles would be saved by faith alone apart from obedience to any command such as baptism (Rom. 4:9-11, 16, 23-5:2).

9. Cornelius was saved and baptized by the Holy Spirit before he was baptized (Acts 10:44-48). This passage clearly refutes baptismal regeneration.

10. Baptismal regeneration:
    a) makes salvation depend on the availability of water
    b) makes salvation depend on the availability of a Campbellite preacher
    c) confuses the symbol with the reality
    d) makes faith and obedience the same thing
    e) is based on a superstitious and magical view of baptism.

11. The thief on the cross was saved without baptism. The Campbellite argument that he was saved under the O.T. way of salvation is not possible, seeing that Christ had already died on the cross and finished the atonement before the thief died. The thief belongs on the N.T. side of the cross, and not on the O.T. side.

12. Campbellites claim that the word "unto" in Acts 2:38 (*eis* in the Greek) always means "in order to obtain," and is always "forward looking." In this way they make remission of sins follow the act of baptism in a cause and effect relationship. Baptism causes forgiveness of sins.

The problem with this idea is that Greek scholars do not see this as the meaning of "eis." Liddell and Scott, Thayer, A.T. Robertson, Dana and Manty, Vine, etc. state that "eis" is often used in the sense of "in reference to something already previously existing or accomplished." In this sense, baptism is done after and because of remission of sins. Once your sins are forgiven, then you should be baptized.

That the Greek scholars are correct is seen from the way "eis" is used in the N.T.:
1. Matt. 3:11: "baptism unto (*eis*) repentance"
   You get baptized because you have repented. You do not get baptized so you can obtain repentance. The order is, "repent and be baptized."

2. Matt 12:41: "they repented at (*eis*) the preaching of Jonah"
   Obviously, the preaching came first and then the people repented in response to that preaching.

3. Matt. 28:19: "Baptizing them in (*eis*) the name of the Father and of Son and of the Holy Ghost"
   The Triune God exists before one is baptized.

4. Mk. 1:9: "baptized of John in (*eis*) Jordan"
   Jesus did not come into possession of the Jordan River as He was baptized. The Jordan existed long before baptism was invented.

5. 1 Cor. 10:2: "baptized unto (*eis*) Moses"
   Moses existed before the "baptism" in the Red Sea. The people were not "baptized" in order to obtain Moses. Their "baptism" was in response to his leadership.

Conclusion

As long as the Campbellites teach that baptism is essential for salvation, they will be viewed as a cult by evangelical Christians. Salvation is by grace alone, through faith alone, apart from obedience to any of God's commands. Works are the evidence of salvation instead of the basis for it.

Chapter One Hundred Seven

The Sacred Books
of Mormonism

Introduction

To understand Mormonism, we must study the primary sources of Mormon teaching. *The Book of Mormon, The Pearl of Great Price,* and *Doctrines and Covenants* are the unique sacred books of the Mormon Church. These books are held by Mormons to be inspired by God and superior to the Bible.

We are going to examine these books as to their genuineness, truthfulness and authenticity in the light of the Bible, orthodox theology, history and the sciences. Many Mormons claim that only the doctrinal portions of their sacred books are important, and the other portions which deal with history and related subjects are not important or relevant to an examination.

In response to this, we must point out that while doctrine is very important, if the historical parts are inaccurate and false, these books could not have come from God because a perfect God could not give an imperfect revelation. Any religion that does not let its books of authority be logically examined does not have any books of authority.

One Mormon leader, Dr. Ross T. Christianson of Brigham University, stated concerning *The Book of Mormon:*

> Let me say that it makes a great deal of difference whether the events recounted actually happened. If the book's history is fallacious, its doctrine cannot be genuine.[1]

In *How to Answer a Mormon* (Minn.: Bethany House, 1983), we examined the false prophecies of Joseph Smith. Since this as been done elsewhere, we will omit any references to false prophecies in this study.

Part I

The Book of Mormon

A. The Story

The Book of Mormon is the purported history of the origins of two great civilizations which existed in the Americas before 1492. According to the book's account, there have been two great ancient migrations to the New World. The first one was about 2,250 B.C.

These people originally lived around the tower of Babel. The Lord told a prophet to build barges for a transoceanic trip to a New World. The Lord gave the prophet a complete blueprint for the barges and they were built accordingly.

After the barges were finished, the people complained to the Lord that He had forgotten to put something in the design of the barges. God had forgotten to put windows or holes in the barges and the people knew that once they closed the door, they would suffocate.

The Lord commanded two round windows to be cut in the barges. One was to be cut in the roof and one in the bottom of each barge. The people again complained that the water would rush in the barge if a hole was cut in the bottom. The Lord then commanded them to plug up the hole in the bottom of the barges.

The people then left the Old World, and after 340 days at sea all the barges landed in the same place at the same time on the west coast of Central America. Here the Jeredites built a large civilization. Unfortunately, the Jeredites were extremely warlike and they exterminated themselves.

The second and more important of the two migrations occurred around 600 B.C. This migration was headed by Lehi and his sons. The Lord told Lehi to leave Jerusalem and to come to the New World. God again gave the blueprints for the ship. The ship was constructed, and they crossed the ocean and landed in Central America. There they built a large and industrious civilization. Laman, a son of Lehi, was so rebellious and wicked that God cursed him with a black skin (2 Nephi 5:21). His descendants are the American Indians. These people were called the Lamanites. Nephi, the other son of Lehi, and his descendants became the Nephites. These two civilizations were constantly at war with each another.

After His resurrection, Jesus came to the Nephites, preached the Gospel to them, instituted baptism, the Lord's Supper and other church institutions. The Lamanites proved too strong for the Nephites, and after several great battles the Nephites were annihilated except for one man by the name of Mormon. He is the one who collected the history of his people and engraved them on golden plates. He then took the plates and hid them in a hill in Palmyra, New York. He was killed after this.

In 1827, Mormon, who was now called Moroni because he had become an angel after death, revealed the location of the plates to Joseph Smith. Smith found the plates and translated the "Reformed Egyptian" with the aid of a pair of magical spectacles. His translation of these golden plates is the present-day *Book of Mormon*.

B. The Origin of *The Book of Mormon*

There are several different theories as to its origin. Some scholars believe that Smith wrote the book himself,[2] but this is no longer held by most scholars.

Most scholars have come to the conclusion that the *Book of Mormon* was originally a romantic novel written by Solomon Spalding.[3] Smith and Rigdon had the clear opportunity to steal it and then reworked it by inserting the "religious" material. The evidence for this has been gathered by Crowdrey, Davis and Scales in their book, *Who Wrote the Book of Mormon?* (Santa Ana, CA: Vision House, 1977).

As the above authors demonstrate, a handwriting analysis of the original text of the *Book of Mormon* reveals that the bulk of the manuscript is in the handwriting of Spalding, and not Smith. The evidence seems to be conclusive to anyone with an objective view.

Mormons have claimed at times that the ideas in *The Book of Mormon* were so new and startling that they could not be part of a previously existing work. But this is not true. The idea that Jews had migrated to the New World was not a new idea. The idea was first mentioned by Menasseh Ben Israel in his book *The Hope of Israel* in 1650. His book was printed in Latin, Spanish and English and stirred up a great deal of controversy. Menasseh was involved in the cabalistic and occultic arts of his day. Historical research has revealed that there is nothing in the book that had not already appeared in print long before it came out.

C. The Bible and The Book of Mormon

My purpose in this section is to demonstrate that *The Book of Mormon* contradicts the Bible. A person must choose between these two books, and he must label one false and the other true. One foundational principle is the older revelation always judges any supposed newer revelation.

1. Micah 5:2 and Matt. 2:1 state that Jesus Christ was born in Bethlehem. But *The Book of Mormon* in

Alma 7:9, 10, clearly states, "the Son of God ... shall be born of Mary at Jerusalem." Jerusalem is a city (1 Nephi 1:4), and the contradiction is irreconcilable.

2. The prophet Jeremiah and Lehi were contemporary prophets according to *The Book of Mormon*. Jeremiah said that there were no prophets preaching the truth in his day. Lehi contradicts Jeremiah in 1 Nephi 1:4 by stating, "There came many prophets prophesying unto the people that they must repent or the great city Jerusalem must be destroyed." Is the Bible or *The Book of Mormon* true? This is a clear contradiction.

3. In Num. 21:5-9, Moses says God sent "fiery serpents" into the camp of Israel to punish them. But *The Book of Mormon* in 1 Nephi 17:41 states God sent "fiery flying serpents" among the Israelites. *The Book of Mormon* not only contradicts the Bible, but who has ever seen a "fiery flying serpent"?

4. Immediately after God created Adam and Eve, He commanded them to have children and to fill the earth with mankind (Gen. 1:28). *The Book of Mormon* in 2 Nephi 2:22-25 states that Adam and Eve had to sin in order to have children. They sinned in order to obey God's command! *The Book of Mormon* further states that Adam and Eve knew no joy and did no good until they had sinned. The original sin was the first good thing Adam ever did! Not only does this teaching contradict the Bible, but it is a glorifying of the first sin.

5. 3 Nephi 12:2 and Moroni 8:11 state that remission of sins is the result of baptism, while the Bible states that remission of sins is by faith alone (Acts 10:43; 16:30, 31). Salvation by baptism is salvation by works, and the Bible emphatically says salvation is "not of works" but "through faith" (Eph. 2:8, 9). The gospel of *The Book of Mormon* is not the gospel of the Bible (Gal. 1:6-9).

6. Not only does *The Book of Mormon* contradict the Bible, but it also plagiarizes over 27,000 words from the 1611 King James Version.[5] Compare 2 Nephi 12-14 with Isa. 2-14; 3 Nephi 13:1-18 with Matt. 6:1-23; Mosiah 14 with Isa. 53. The important thing that should shake every Mormon is the question, "How did Joseph Smith happen to translate *The Book of Mormon's* Reformed Egyptian into perfect King James English?" The only logical conclusion one can believe is that whoever wrote *The Book of Mormon* did it after 1611 and quoted extensively from the King James Version. Another damaging observation about *The Book of Mormon* is that whoever quoted the King James quoted some verses modern scholars now reject.[6] The Mormons are hard put to answer this one.

We have found *The Book of Mormon* directly contradicting the Bible as well as orthodox theology. *The Book of Mormon* must be rejected, for it could not be a revelation from God anymore than the Muslim Qur'an.

D. Scientific Evidence Against The Book of Mormon
The scientific mistakes in *The Book of Mormon* are abundant. We have selected a few of the clearest ones for examination.

1. Joseph Smith claims in *The Pearl of Great Price* that a Professor Charles Anthon of Columbia University, saw the characters on the golden plates and identified them as being "Egyptian, Chaldie, Assyriac and Arabic; and said they were true characters."[7] If this were true it adds significant evidence for the genuineness of *The Book of Mormon*. But this is not true! Professor

Anthon denies his authenticating the characters. Walter R. Martin, has reproduced the letter sent by Professor Anthon to Mr. Howe.
In the letter, Anthon says, "The whole story ... is perfectly false."[8]
Furthermore, he states the whole Mormon claim is a scheme to get people's money. To disregard the testimony of Professor Anthon is irrational.

2. After traveling for three days from Jerusalem along the Red Sea, Lehi and his family found a large valley and a river that emptied into the Red Sea. There they rested and refreshed themselves.[9]

   The story is delightful, but false. There was no such valley in history and there was no river anywhere along the shore of the Red Sea.[10] If there had been a large river in the area described by *The Book of Mormon*, there would have been a large prosperous civilization there. If not, it would have been a stopping place for all the desert caravans. It would be found in some ancient records, and there should be some evidence still extant.[11] But the fact is, it never existed and thus *The Book of Mormon* is historically and geographically false.

3. The archaeological evidence against *The Book of Mormon* is overwhelming. According to *The Book of Mormon*, the people in the Old World were using steel weapons and tools before 600 B.C. In the New World, steel weapons, tools and machines were in use before 399 B.C.[12] But steel was not invented or processed until 1856![13] This must be acknowledged as a mistake in the book.

4. The civilizations in the Americas are described in the following terms by *The Book of Mormon:* "The whole face of the land was covered with buildings—people as the sands of the sea" (Mormon 1:7); "silks, fine linen, oxen, cows, sheep, swine, goats, horses, asses, elephants" (Ether 9:17-19; Alma 1:29); "two million men plus their wives and children are killed" (Ether 16:2); "ships, temples like Solomon's synagogues, sanctuaries all built after the manner of the Jews" (Heldman 3:14; 2 Nephi 5:15, 16; Alma 16:13); "swords, cimeters, breast plates, head plates, armor" (Alma 43:18-21; Ether 15:15); "houses and chariots" (Alma 18:9; 20:6; 3 Nephi 3:22; 21:14). Thirty-one large cities are named in the book. Metal coins were used as money in 82 B.C. (Alma 11:1-19). All the people were literate and bilingual.[14] The Smithsonian Institute and the archaeological department of Columbia University have gone on official record stating *The Book of Mormon's* descriptions of the civilizations in America are false from beginning to end. There were no elephants, cows, pigs, goats, horses, chariots, silk, etc. in America before 1492.[15]

5. There were no remains or traces of Jewish temples or anything that could be identified with the civilization described in *The Book of Mormon.*[16]

6. The weapons of warfare mentioned in the book included bows and arrows. The interesting thing is that bows and arrows were not in America until after A.D. 1000. *The Book of Mormon* gave bows and arrows to the Indians 600 years too early.[17]

7. The language of *The Book of Mormon* and its people was supposedly Reformed Egyptian. The truth is that the language never existed. This fact is conclusive evidence against accepting the book.[18]

8. The American Indian is Jewish, and his skin is black according to *The Book of Mormon* (2 Nephi 5:21). Anthropology has established that the Indians are Mongoloid in origin and their skin is not black.[19] If the Mormon Church cannot prove that the American Indian is Jewish or Semitic in origin and their skins are black, they will have to recognize that *The Book of Mormon* is false.

9. More scientific pieces of evidence against *The Book of Mormon* are the corrections, additions and subtractions in the text of the book. When you compare the 1830 edition with the present edition, you will find over 3,000 changes.[20] The changes are in grammar and theology. Truth in 1830 is truth today because truth does not change. If the 1830 edition was inspired, the present edition, which is radically different from it, cannot be inspired.

Examine the following examples:

  a. The title page of the 1830 edition said that Joseph Smith was the author. The present edition says he only translated it. Why the change in the authorship of the book?

  b. 1 Nephi 11:18 in 1830 read, "The virgin thou seest is the mother of God." The present editions read, "The virgin thou seest is the mother of the Son of God." (The Roman Catholic Church would prefer the 1830 edition!)

  c. 1 Nephi 11:21 in 1830 read, "Behold the Lamb of God, yea, even the Eternal Father." It now reads, "Behold the Lamb of God, yea, even the Son of the Eternal Father."

  d. In 1 Nephi 19:16-20, there are more than 50 changes.

  e. Mosiah 21:28 read "King Benjamin" in 1830. It now reads "King Mosiah." The two names are vastly different; thus the editions contradict each other.

Summary

We have found *The Book of Mormon* to be false biblically, geographically, archaeologically, anthropologically, historically and linguistically and to have internal contradictions as evidenced by the corrections in the book since 1830. *The Book of Mormon* is spurious and a gross miscarriage of the truth.

Part II

Doctrines and Covenants

This sacred book of the Mormon church is a collection of the revelations given to Joseph Smith and his successors. Each revelation has an introduction with the date, place and a summary of the message. While *The Book of Mormon* is mainly historical in nature, *Doctrine and Covenants* is mainly doctrinal. Since we are dealing with doctrine, our sole guide for this examination is the Bible.

Judaism, Christianity and Mohammedanism are the three great monotheistic faiths. Polytheism is considered paganism by each of these faiths. In *Doctrine and Covenants*, Mormonism reveals itself as a polytheistic religion. This makes Mormonism paganism by definition. The following evidence is given to prove that polytheism is a part of Mormon teaching.

  I. "Gods exist and we had better strive to prepare to be one with them."
     Discourses of Brigham Young, page 351.[21]

II. "In the beginning the head of the Gods called a council of the Gods and they came together and concocted a plan to create the world and people it."
The Journal of Discourses, Volume VI, page 3.[22]

III. "Each of these gods, including Jesus Christ and His Father, being in possession of not merely an organized spirit but a glorious body of flesh and bone..."
Key to the Science of Theology, page 42, by Parley Pratt.[23]

IV. "Many men say there is one God; the Father, the Son and the Holy Ghost are only one God! I say this is a very strange God anyhow ... all are to be crammed into one God." *Joseph Smith's Teaching*, page 55, by E.F. Parry.[24]

V. "We believe in the plurality of Gods."
Brigham Roberts in *Mormon Doctrine of Deity*, page 11.[25]

VI. In the Mormon *Catechism for Children*, page 13, you find this question and answer: "Are there more Gods than one?
Yes, many."[26]

VII. "The Gods organized and formed the Heavens and the earth."[27]

The evidence is conclusive that Mormonism is a polytheistic religion. As a matter of fact, it is very much like the old pagan religions of Greece and Rome. The ancient gods and goddesses had human bodies and used sex to have divine children. See Dr. Morey's book, *The Battle of the Gods*.

Mormonism is not Christian, but pagan. The Bible emphatically declares there has always been only one God and there will never be any more gods in the future.[28] Mormonism, being polytheistic, must deny the Trinity, and it does.[29] Not only does Mormonism deny the Trinity, but it denies the spiritual nature of God the Father.

"The Father has a body of flesh and bone as tangible as man's."[30]

"God Himself was once as we are now and is an exalted man..." *The Journal of Discourses*, Volume VI, page 3.[31]

"As man is, God once was; as God is, many may become." *Millenial Star*, Volume 54, by Lorenzo Snow, former president of the Mormon Church.[32]

"Therefore we know that both the Father and the Son are in form and stature perfect men; each of them possesses a tangible body, infinitely pure and perfect and attended by transcendent glory, nevertheless a body of flesh and bones."[33]

Not only is God the Father an exalted man, but according to the original doctrines of Mormonism, this man is Adam! That modern Mormons are either ignorant or deceptive about this doctrine does not negate the fact that this is what was taught by both Smith and Young.

"When our father Adam came into the Garden of Eden, he came into it with a celestial body and brought Eve, one of his wives, with him... He is our father and our God and the only

God with which we have to do." Brigham Young, in *The Journal of Discourses*, Volume I, page 50.34

In *Doctrines and Covenants,* Adam is declared to be:
  "The Father"
  "The Prince of All"
  "The Ancient of Days"
  "The possessor the keys of salvation"35

  In opposition to this, the Scriptures state:
  "God is not a man; God is Spirit; A Spirit hath not flesh and bones; Before me there was no God formed; Neither shall there be after me; For I am God and not a man; There is none else; There is none like unto me."36

If Adam could make Godhood, cannot others make it? The answer is yes! Section 132 of *Doctrine and Covenants* is titled "Essentials for the Attainment of the Godhood." Man can become a god!37 The only essential requirement is that you have a celestial marriage.38 If you do not, upon death you will become an angel.39

Space does not permit me to bring forth the more bizarre doctrines which we found in *Doctrine and Covenants.* These revelations are not true to God's Word and are to be considered "another Gospel which is not another" (Gal. 1:6-9). God's eternal anathema rests on this book.

Part III

The Pearl of Great Price

The Pearl of Great Price is a collection of the revelations and Bible translations of Joseph Smith. This book is doctrinal in nature. The doctrines presented are anti-biblical and spurious. Here are a few examples of its bizarre teachings.

1. Polytheism is taught in Abraham 4. This chapter is a paraphrase of Gen. 1 and 2 with a notable difference—everywhere Genesis says "God," Abraham 4 says "Gods!" These "Gods" are eternal (Abra. 3:18). They were the preexistent souls of men (Abra. 3:23). Abraham is declared as one of these "gods" who took part in the creation work (Abra. 3:23).

2. The creation was not *ex nihilo* (literally "out of nothing"), but the forming and organizing of already existing materials.40 Matter is eternal, according to Section 93:33 of *Doctrine and Covenants.*
   Therefore the creation could not be *ex nihilo.* Needless to say, the universe is not eternal and the creation was *ex nihilo.*
   Many proofs show the universe is not eternal.41
   The Bible definitely teaches creation *ex nihilo* in Gen. 1:1.

3. The "seed" of God referred to in His promise to Abraham was Christ, according to Gal. 3:16. *The Pearl of Great Price* in Abraham 2:11 states the "seed" was the Mormon priesthood. This is a clear contradiction of the Bible.

4. The most shocking example of false teaching found in this book is that not only is God a man,

but God is a sinful man! According to Abraham 2:22-25, God told Abraham to deceive Pharaoh and to tell him that Sarah was not his wife but his sister. God was the author of the deception! The biblical account states the author of this sinful deception and scheme was Abraham (Gen. 12:10-20). The teaching of Abraham 2:22-25 is a slam against the character and nature of God. The Scriptures teach that God cannot lie, and He cannot tell others to do so.[42]

5. Perhaps the greatest refutation of *The Pearl of Great Price* is the so-called "Book of Abraham." Smith had staked his inspiration and prophetic authority on his ability to translate certain Egyptian scrolls that he had purchased from a traveling show. He claimed that they were some long-lost works of Abraham. But these same exact scrolls were rediscovered and then translated by modern scholars who have all stated that the scrolls are part of the Egyptian Book of the Dead, and do not even mention Abraham. Thus Smith's "inspired" translation is a fraud. For a full discussion of the details of this fascinating story, contact Modern Microfilm Company (Box 1884, Salt Lake City, Utah, 84110) for their literature on the subject.

From the foregoing examples, it can be seen that *The Pearl of Great Price* cannot be a revelation from God, because it contradicts God's eternally revealed Word, the Bible. This book is spurious and must be rejected.

Summary

The Book of Mormon, Doctrine and Covenants and *The Pearl of Great Price* have been examined in the light of Scripture and have been found to be false. Not only do these books contradict the Bible, but also secular science such as archaeology, anthropology, linguistics, geography and history. The Mormon claim of inspiration for these books is therefore rejected. To the Christian, there is only one divinely inspired book, the Bible. It alone can claim absolute infallibility. It alone demands absolute obedience. From the evidence printed in this research paper, we can only say, with Martin Luther of old, "Sola Scriptura!"

Appendix I

Mormonism View of the Bible

From the following statements it will be evident that Mormonism downgrades the trustworthiness, truthfulness and value of the Bible.

1. "From sundry revelations which had been received, it was apparent that many important points touching the salvation of man had been taken from the Bible or lost before it was completed" (Joseph Smith, Section 70, *Doctrine and Covenants*).

2. "Because ye have a Bible ye need not suppose it contains all my words or need ye suppose that I have not caused none to be written" (*Book of Mormon* 101:10).

3. "We believe the Bible to be the Word of God as far as it is translated correctly" (Section 8 of the *Articles of Faith*).

4. "Guided by *The Book of Mormon, Doctrine and Covenants* and the Spirit of the Lord, it is not difficult for one to discern the errors in the Bible" (*Doctrines of Salvation*, Volume III, p. 191.)[43]

5. "There are many plain and precious things taken away from the book ... and also many covenants of the Lord" (*Book of Mormon* 23:26-28)

6. "Let the Bible then be read reverently and with prayerful care, the reader ever searching the light of the Spirit that He may discern between truth and the errors of men" (*Articles of Faith*, p. 237, by J.E. Talmage).

Appendix II

The Mormon Priesthood

Sections 13 and 107 of *Doctrine and Covenants* teach that the priesthood of Melchizedek was conferred on Joseph Smith and will be conferred on his successors. The Bible states that the Melchizedekian priesthood was given to Christ and He will not pass it on to anyone. Heb. 7:24 states, "But this man, because He continueth ever, hath an unchangeable priesthood."

The word "unchangeable" in the KJV is a mistranslation of the Greek word *aparbatos*, which means literally, "not liable to pass to a successor"[44] or "untransferrable."[45] Modern translators have made the correction.

Goodspeed: "But He continues forever, so His priesthood is untransferrable."

Phillips: "Priesthood that needs no successor."

Williams: "Because He Himself lives on forever, enjoys the only priesthood that has no successor."

Wuest: "the priesthood which is untransferrable."

Weymouth: "but He, because He continues forever, has a priesthood which does not pass to any successor."

The evidence is conclusive that the doctrine which teaches the passing on of the Melchizedek priesthood to Joseph Smith or anyone else is false according to Heb. 7:24.

Endnotes

1. Ross T. Christianson, University Archeological Society News Letter, No. 64, January 30, 1960 (Provo, Utah: Brigham Young University). Quoted by Gordon H. Fraser, *What Does the Book of Mormon Teach?* (Chicago: Moody Press, 1964), p. 12.

2. For this view see Gordon H. Fraser, *What Does the Book of Mormon Teach?* (Chicago: Moody Press, 1964), pp. 102-109.

3. For this view see:
   Eber D. Howe, *Mormonism Unvealed* (Painesville: published by the author, 1834).
   G.B. Arbaugh, *Revelations in Mormonism* (Chicago: University of Chicago, 1932).
   James D. Boles, *The Book of Mormon* (Rosemead, CA: Old Path Book Club, 1958).
   James H. Snowsen, *The Truth About Mormonism* (New York: George Durant, Co., 1926).

4. Jer. 2:8, 26; 4:9; 5:31; 14:13-15, etc.

5. Hoekema, *The Four Major Cults* (Grand Rapids: Wm. B. Eerdmans, 1963), p. 85.

6. Walter R. Martin, *The Maze of Mormonism* (Grand Rapids: Zondervan, 1962) pp. 51-53.

7. P.G.P.:2:62-64.

8. Walter R. Martin, *The Kingdom of the Cults* (Grand Rapids: Zondervan, 1965) pp. 160-161.

9. *Book of Mormon:* 1 Neph. 2:5-10.

10. Fraser, ibid., p. 33.

11. Ibid., pp. 33-38.

12. *Book of Mormon:* 1 Neph. 4:9; Jasom 1:8; 2 Neph. 5:15.

13. T.W. Wallbank and A.M. Taylor, *Civilization Past and Present* (Chicago: Scott, Foresman and Co., 1956), pp. 327-328.

14. Hoekema, ibid., p. 78.

15. Martin, *The Kingdom of the Cults,* ibid., pp. 162-163.

16. Ibid.

17. Fraser, ibid., pp. 62, 63.

18. Hoekema, pp. 75-87.

19. Fraser, pp. 39-50.

20. Martin, *The Maze of Mormonism,* pp. 49-50; Hoekema, ibid., pp. 23, 82-87.

21. Martin, ibid., p. 80.

22. Ibid.

23. Ibid.

24. Ibid., p. 81.

25. W.E. Biederwolf, *Mormonism Under the Searchlight* (Grand Rapids: Wm. B. Eerdmans, n.d.) p. 28.

26. Ibid.

27. P.G.P.: Abra. 4:1.

28. Isa. 43:10, 11; 44:6, 8; 45:5, 18, 22; 46:9; 1 Cor. 8:4-6.

29. J.E. Talmage, *Articles of Faith* (Salt Lake City: The Church of Jesus Christ and the Latter-day Saints Publishing Co., 1962) pp. 40-41.

30. *Doctrines and Covenants:* 130:22.

31. Martin, ibid., p. 60.

32. Ibid.

33. Talmage, ibid., p. 42.

34. Martin, ibid., p. 80.

35. *Doctrines and Covenants:* 27:11; 78:16; 107:54; 116.

36. Num. 23:19; 1 Sam. 15:29; Job 9:32; Hos. 11:9; John 4:24; Col. 1:15; John 1:18; 1 John 4:12; Isa. 43:10; 46:9.

37. *Doctrines and Covenants:* 76:58; 132:20, 21, 37; 132.

38. *Doctrines and Covenants:* 132.

39. *Doctrines and Covenants:* 7:6; 128:21; 129's introduction to sections 2 and 13.

40. P.G.P.: Abra. 3; 4; 5.

41. See "Just How Old Is the Universe," chapter 40.

42. Rom. 3:4; Heb. 7:18; Prov. 6:16-18; Rev. 21:8.

43. Hoekema, ibid., p. 23.

44. J.W. Thayer, *Greek-English Lexicon of the New Testament* (Grand Rapids: Zondervan, 1962), p. 54.

45. J.S. Strong, *The Exhaustive Concordance of the Bible* (New York: Abingdon Press, 1963), p. 13 of Greek dictionary.

A Fact Sheet for Seventh-day Adventists

There is only one fundamental issue between evangelicals and Seventh-day Adventists: Was Ellen G. White a prophetess of God? She was either who she claimed to be, or she was a liar or a nut case. There are no other logical options.

I. Her Claims

"God was speaking through clay. In these letters which I write, in the testimonies I bear, I am presenting to you that which the Lord has presented to me. I do not write an article in the paper expressing merely my own ideas. They are what God has opened before me in vision—the precious rays of light shining from the throne." E.G. White, *Testimonies,* vol. 3, p. 63.

"When I send you a testimony of warning and reproof, many of you declare it to be merely the opinion of Sister White. You have thereby insulted the Spirit of God." E.G. White, *Testimonies,* Vol. 5, p. 661.

"Those who are reproved by the Spirit of God should not rise up against the humble instrument. It is God and not an erring mortal, who has spoken to save them from ruin." *Testimony for the Church,* Vol. 3, p. 257.

"Seventh Day Adventists hold that Ellen G. White performed the work of a true prophet during the seventy years of her public ministry. As Samuel was a prophet, as Jeremiah was a prophet, as John the Baptist, so we believe that Mrs. White was a prophet to the church of Christ today." *The Adventist Review & Herald* (Oct. 4, 1928).

II. The Evidence

What of White's prophecies? Did she predict the Second Coming of Christ? Yes she did!

1843: "I have seen that the 1843 chart was directed by the hand of the Lord and that it should not be altered, that the figures were as he wanted them." *Early Writings,* p. 64, 1882 edition.

1844: "We heard the voice of God like many waters, which gave us the day and hour of Jesus' coming." *A Word to the Little Flock,* p. 14, 1847 edition.

1845: "It is well known that many were expecting the Lord to come at the 7th month, 1845. That Christ would then come we firmly believed. A few days before the time passed ... Ellen was with the band at Carver, Mass., where she saw in vision, that we should be disappointed." *A Word to the Little Flock,* p. 22, 1847 edition.

1849: "Now time is almost finished and what we have been 6 years learning they will have to learn in months." *Early Writings*, p. 57.

1856: "I was shown the company present at the conference. Said the angel: 'Some food for worms, some subjects of the seven last plagues, some will be alive and remain upon the earth to be translated at the coming of Jesus.'" *Testimonies for the Church*, vol. I, pp. 131-132.

1862: "The system of slavery, which has ruined our nation, is left to live and stir up another rebellion." *Early Writings*, p. 256.

Since White's predictions of the return of Christ did not come true, we must conclude on the basis of Deut. 18:21-23 that she was a false prophet.

III. What About White's Visions?

The biblical and historical material that White claimed to receive by way of visions was actually stolen from dozens of books. (See Walter Rea, *The White Lie*, M&R Publications, 1982, Box 2056, Turlock, California, 95381.)

The health and nutrition visions were also stolen from medical books of that period. (See Ronald Numbers, *Prophetess of Health*, Harper & Row, N.Y., 1976.)

Conclusion

The only conclusion possible is that Ellen G. White was not only a dishonest woman who plagiarized the works of others, but she was also a false prophet.

Chapter One Hundred Nine

How to Deal With Moonies

Introduction

When coming to a conclusion about the man who calls himself Rev. Moon, we must remember two important principles:

I. We must not focus on nonessential issues, but on the words and works of Moon himself.

II. We must realize that we are dealing with an occult leader as well as with a cultic group.

"REVEREND" MOON AND HIS UNIFICATION CHURCH	
AN OCCULT LEADER	A CULTIC GROUP
Moon claims to have been a spiritistic clairvoyant from his childhood. He "sees" the spirits of living people and can talk with the spirits of the dead and other spirit beings. He claims to have had conversations with the spirit of Buddha, Noah, Moses, etc. His "visions" are spiritistic in nature.	Moon's authority is above Scripture. He is the true mediator, while Jesus was a failure. Moon's teachings are in opposition to biblical and historic Christianity. His followers are willing to kill for him. He has absolute control of every aspect of the lives of his followers.

First, focus on Moon's witchcraft:

The following is an actual dialogue with a Moonie that led to his leaving the Unification Church and becoming a Christian.

Ask No. 1: Do you believe in witchcraft? "NO."

Ask No. 2: You mean that you do not believe in seances, table rapping and communicating with the spirit of dead people? "YES."

Ask No. 3: You agree with the Bible that the occult is condemned by God? Do you agree with Deut. 18:9-12? "YES."

Ask No. 4: Then you would agree that no witch or spiritistic medium can be viewed as a prophet of God? "OF COURSE."

Ask No. 5: On the basis of what the Bible clearly teaches, what do you say about Moon's claim that he talks to the spirits of the dead? He even went to the medium Arthur Ford! How then can you follow someone who is a "witch" according to the Bible? "CAN YOU PROVE TO ME THAT MOON IS IN-VOLVED IN THE OCCULT?" Are you willing to look in the *Divine Principle*? "YES." For Moon's in-volvement with the occult see his *Divine Principle* (pgs. 16, 58, 60, 77, 88, 163, 181-182).

Second, focus on Moon's cultic character.

Ask No. 1: Turn to Deut. 13:1-5. If someone who claims to be a prophet teaches us to worship other gods and contradicts what God has revealed in Scripture, we are to reject him. Do you agree with the Bible? "WE ACCEPT THE BIBLE, BUT GREATER LIGHT HAS COME."

Ask No. 2: But surely you recognize that "greater" does not mean "contradictory" but "fuller" or "richer?" "YES."

Ask No. 3: Moon clearly contradicts what the Bible says about many things. Thus Moon is a false prophet. "PROVE TO ME THAT MOON CONTRADICTS THE BIBLE."

In his book *Divine Principle*, Moon:
1. denies that Christ was God (pgs. 209ff).
2. says that the world is eternal, i.e., never created. There is thus no biblical Creation (pgs. 114-116).
3. denies Christ's and our bodily resurrection (pgs. 212, 116, 170f).
4. claims that the Bible is not for today. He even says that Jesus' words are not the truth (pg. 131).
5. rejects the Trinity (pgs. 217f).
6. teaches that Christ's death was not predestined by God, and thus Jesus' death on the cross does not take away our sins (pgs. 142-145).
7. says that Christ's body was invaded by Satan (pg. 148).
8. claims that the "Holy Spirit is a female spirit" (pg. 215).
9. says that there is no eternal Hell and that all will be saved (pgs. 190, 360).

Third, emphasize that Moon is a false prophet.

Ask No. 1: Did you know that the Bible tells us how to identify a false prophet? "NO."

Ask No. 2: Well, in Deut. 18:20-22, Moses says that if someone claims to be a prophet but he gives a prediction that fails, he is a false prophet. Is this what Deut. 18 is saying? "YES."

Ask No. 3: What did Moon predict or prophesy about President Nixon? "I DO NOT KNOW." Moon predicted that Richard Nixon would remain the president (*San Francisco Chronicle*, Jan. 19, 1974). Moon later said: "I am sure there is a communistic power working behind the scenes. They came to threaten to kill him if he did not resign, and that is what compelled him to do so" (*San Francisco Chronicle*, Dec. 10, 1975). Since Moon was wrong about Nixon, he is false prophet. "I WILL HAVE TO CHECK THIS OUT." Check it out all you want, but in the end you will see that he made a false prophecy about Nixon.

Ask No. 4: 1981 is the watershed for Moon. Do you know what he prophesied about 1981? "NO." Well, the Lord of the second advent was to be revealed in 1967. When this prophecy failed, 1981 was announced by Moon as the time when the world would recognize the Lord of the second advent and the Kingdom of Heaven would begin. "I DID NOT KNOW ABOUT THIS." 1981 was chosen because of its being the end of three 21-year periods. Since the 1981 date failed, Moon is a false prophet.

Conclusion

According to the Bible, Moon must be labeled as a false prophet, a witch, a medium, a heretic, an infidel, a pagan, and a cult leader. We call upon him and his followers to repent of their sins and to accept Jesus Christ as the only true Lord of the first and second advent. Moon is only one more pathetic false prophet and false Christ that Jesus warned us would be coming to deceive people (Matt. 24:24). May God be pleased to open his blind eyes to the truth of the glorious Gospel that Christ died for our sins and arose bodily on the third day for our justification (1 Cor. 15:3-4; Rom. 5:25).

Chapter One Hundred Ten

Jehovah's Witnesses and the Resurrection of Christ

Introduction

Have you ever wondered why nearly all the cults deny the bodily resurrection of Christ? Why is Satan so interested in denying the resurrection of Christ? The reason why Christ's resurrection is a special target of Satan's attack is that salvation is impossible for the one who denies it!

"If you confess with your mouth that Jesus is Lord (i.e. Jehovah) and believe in your heart that God raised Him from the dead, you shall be saved" (Rom. 10:9-10).

You cannot be saved if you deny the Deity or the resurrection of Christ! Since these two doctrines concern who Christ is and what He did, Satan attacks these central doctrines of the Gospel.

"For I delivered to you as of first importance what I also received, that Christ died for our sins according to the Scriptures and that He was buried and that He was raised on the third day according to the Scriptures" (1 Cor. 15:3-4).

"and if Christ has not been raised, your faith is worthless; you are still in your sins. Then those also who have fallen asleep in Christ have perished. If we have hope in Christ in this life only, we are of all men most to be pitied" (1 Cor. 15:17-19).

We must be set for the defense of the Gospel (Phil. 1:16) and contend for the faith which was once for all of time delivered to the saints (Jude 3). This means that we must defend the bodily resurrection of Christ against all those who would seek to deny it.

It is no surprise that the Watchtower Society denies the bodily resurrection of Christ, as they also deny His Deity. They reject all essential Christian truths, such as the Trinity. They believe that the man Jesus died and was never raised back to life in His body. For them there is no Easter. We have the biblical responsibility to answer their arguments against the bodily resurrection of Christ and to go on to prove that Christ is now alive in His resurrection body at the right hand of the Father in heaven.

This can be done in several steps.

I. The first thing that must be recognized is that there are three different Jesuses in Watchtower Theology (2 Cor. 11:3-4):

JESUS No. 1	JESUS No. 2	JESUS No. 3
Michael the Archangel was the first creation of Jehovah God. "First creation of God" p. 282 "known as Michael" *Make Sure All Things*	He is a man, i.e., a human being. When he died, he went into non-existence. His body probably dissolved into gas. "The man Jesus is dead, forever dead." C.T. Russell, Vol. 5, p. 454	After three days, Jehovah called into existence a spirit creature named Jesus. "In his resurrection, he was no more human. He was raised a spirit creation." *The Kingdom Is at Hand*, p. 258

II. How to Answer a Jehovah's Witness

   A. Carefully define the Christian position:

   The body which was born of Mary, grew into manhood, was crucified on the cross and laid in the tomb, was revived and glorified as the Spirit of Jesus re-entered it. That same body is now seated at the right hand of the Father in Heaven and will return one day to resurrect all the bodies of humanity for the Judgment Day.

BEFORE		AFTER	
(HUMBLE BODY)	Natural Earthly Mortal Perishable	Supernatural Heavenly Immortal	(GLORIFIED BODY) Imperishable

   B. Demonstrate the possibility of Christ's bodily resurrection by pointing out all the bodily resurrections recorded in Scripture.

Old Testament	New Testament
1. 1 Kings 17:17-24 2. 2 Kings 4:18-20, 31-37 3. 2 Kings 13:20-21	1. Matt. 9:18-25 2. Matt. 27:52-53 3. Lk. 7:11-17 4. John 11:38-45 5. Acts 9:40-42 6. Acts 20:9-12

C. Demonstrate the probability of Christ's bodily resurrection.

Hermeneutical principle: "The meaning of a word is determined by its usage."

1. All references in Scriptures to someone being "raised from the dead" refer to bodies coming back to life.
2. No reference in Scripture is ever made of resurrecting "spirits" or "souls."
3. The Scriptures refer to Christ as being "raised from the dead."
4. The logical conclusion is that Christ's body was brought back to life. He was not "raised" a spirit because the words for "resurrection" such as "raise," etc., always refer to the body.

D. Demonstrate the actuality of Christ's resurrection on the basis of the following arguments.

1. Christ's body could not be destroyed (Acts 2:25-27).
2. His body was not in the tomb (Lk. 24:1-8).
3. Where is His body? What natural conclusion do we draw? Answer: His body got up and "walked" out.
4. Christ explicitly stated that He would raise His body (John 2:18-22).
5. Christ had the power to take back His life (John 10:17-18).
6. After His resurrection, Christ proved that His body was raised by "many proofs" (Acts 1:3).
   a. He showed the wounds inflicted on His body when crucified (Lk. 24:39, 40).
   b. He ate and drank before them. A "Spirit" cannot eat or drink (Lk. 24:41-43; Acts 10:40-41).
   c. He explicitly denied that He was a "Spirit" creature (Lk. 24:37-39).
   d. He demonstrated to Thomas that His body was alive (John 20:24-29).
   e. Over 500 people saw His resurrection body (1 Cor. 15:3-8).
   f. Our resurrection is to be bodily. It is based on the bodily resurrection of Christ (Rom. 8:11; Phil. 3:21; 1 Cor. 15:4-19, 35- 44, 49-50).
   g. 2 John 7 states that Christ will return in His body.

E. Be prepared to answer typical Watchtower arguments.

WATCHTOWER ARGUMENT	BIBLICAL ANSWER
1. "1 Pet. 3:18 teaches that Christ was raised a Spirit creature."	1. 1 Pet. 3:18 does NOT say "Christ became a Spirit," but that He was made alive "by the (Holy) Spirit." Peter is merely echoing what Paul taught in Rom. 8:11.
2. "1 Cor. 15:50 says that no flesh and blood shall inherit the kingdom of God, i.e., no bodies can enter Heaven. So Christ could not have a body because He ascended into Heaven."	2. a. "Kingdom of God" does not refer to Heaven but to the eternal state after Christ returns (v. 35) b. "Flesh and blood" in the context refers to a "mortal" body which will perish. The kind of bodies which will go into the eternal state will be immortal bodies which will not perish (v. 35, 42-44, 50). c. Christ did not have a mortal "flesh and blood" body after His resurrection. It was "flesh and bones" (Lk. 24:39) i.e., immortal and incorruptible.

Watchtower Argument	Biblical Answer
3. "1 Cor. 15:45 states that Christ became a Spirit after His resurrection."	3. a. If the second half of the verse means that Christ did not have a body, then the first half means that Adam did not have one either. b. Adam's becoming a "soul" had reference to his creation, when God breathed into Adam's dead body and it became alive (Gen. 2:7). c. Christ's becoming a "Spirit" had reference to His resurrection when His Spirit was placed inside His body once again and it became alive. d. The contrast between Adam and Christ, in the context, is the contrast of the kind of body each received. e. Examine the contrasts: v. 35: "What kind of body will be resurrected?" **Adam's Body vs. Christ's Body** v. 42 Perishable vs. Imperishable v. 43 Dishonor vs. Honor v. 43 Weakness vs. Power v. 44 Natural vs. Spiritual v. 45 Living vs. Life-giving v. 46 First vs. Second v. 47 Earthly vs. Heavenly v. 49 Image of earthly vs. Image of Heavenly v. 50 flesh and blood vs. flesh and bones v. 50 Perishable vs. Imperishable v. 53 Perishable vs. Imperishable v. 53 Mortal vs. Immortal f. The passage proves that Christ was given an immortal, imperishable, glorious, Heavenly body which is what we will get at our resurrection.
4. "If Christ's Body was raised, would not His disciples recognize Him? Since they did not, He was not bodily raised" (Lk. 24:17-30; John 20:14)	4. Christ was instantly recognized by His disciples except in the cases where He kept them from doing this. The problem was in the eyes of the disciples, not in the body of Jesus (Lk. 24:16, 31; John 20:19-20, 26)

Watchtower Argument	Biblical Answer
5. "If Christ's body was raised, how could it go through locked doors and walls?	5. a. God can do anything He pleases to do. You mean to say you can lock God out of a house? b. Christ did not go "through" doors or walls. He was supra-dimensional and could "pop" from place to place.
6. "What about Mark 16:12? Christ simply manufactured bodies as angels do."	6. The last section of Mark 16 is not a part of Scripture.

Conclusion

Christ's resurrection was bodily in nature. Thus, the future resurrection of all men on the Judgment Day will be bodily as well.

Chapter One Hundred Eleven

The Occult and Parapsychology

Introduction

The occult has to do with the rites, ideas, practices and miraculous feats connected with witchcraft. The word "occult" itself means "hidden" or "unseen." It was used to describe those satanic rites which were forbidden by civil law during the Middle Ages. Those who desired to practice witchcraft did so while "hidden" or "unseen" to escape prosecution.

I. The 19th century witnessed the revival of witchcraft in the West. It was renamed "spiritualism" or "spiritism." Later, Theosophy renamed it pseudo-scientific "psychic forces." With the beginning of the Society for Psychical Research (SPR), witchcraft was viewed as an issue of the scientific investigation of the natural mental abilities of man. It became popular to study psychic phenomena.

It was J.B. Rhine in the 1950s who took psychical research and renamed it as ESP (i.e., Extra-sensory Perception).

Such terms as "parapsychology" were later developed to describe the miraculous feats which psychics could do such as Uri Geller's bending of spoons or levitating objects.

II. Why do people get involved in the occult?
  1. To contact the dead.
  2. To see the future.
  3. To obtain power.
  4. To contact Satan or demons.
  5. To satisfy curiosity or the need for excitement gained through frightening experiences.

III. Satan and the occult

  A. Satan is an extra-dimensional energy being composed only of "mind," having no body or material essence.

  B. Satan, and those energy beings who rebelled against God, fled to this world. They were the first "ETs."
    1. Satan has always tried to counterfeit God's miracles by producing His own supernatural feats (Matt. 24:24; 2 Thess. 2:9; Rev. 13:11-17).
    2. God has always condemned occult practices as demonic (see chart).

IV. Parapsychology and the Bible

Modern parapsychologists claim that all supernatural feats are the result of natural human abilities. There is thus no difference between "satanic" and "divine" miracles. Jesus is viewed as a great psychic who healed people by His own mental abilities or powers. But both the prophets (Gen. 41:16), Jesus (John 5:19, 30) and the apostles (Acts 3:12-13) stated that these miraculous feats did not come from their own power but from God. On the other hand, they clearly stated that there are demonic forces who could also do supernatural feats such as fortune telling (Acts 16:16-18). Those in contact with the demonic forces can do miraculous feats (Matt. 24:24).

V. Satanic Counterfeits of Divine Miracles

Modern occultists redefine biblical miracles by using parapsychological terminology. For example, what the Bible calls "prophecy," an occultist would call "precognition." In the following chart there is a contrast between divine and satanic miracles and the parapsychological terms that are used today to describe events which seem to parallel biblical miracles.

Miracle	Divine	Satanic
1. precognition	Biblical prophecies (example Micah 5:2; 2 Pet. 1:20-21)	fortune tellers, psychics, false prophets, astrologers, etc. (Deut. 13:1-4; Isa. 47:9-14)
2. levitation	2 Kings 6:6; John 6:16-21; Acts 1:9	Matt. 4:5, 8
3. teleportation	Gen. 5:24; 2 Kings 2:11; John 6:21; Acts 8:39-40	Matt. 4:5, 8
4. molecular transformation	Exo. 7:14-21 John 2:1-11	Exo. 7:22
5. creation of matter out of nothing	2 Kings 4:1-7 John 6:1-13	apportation possible but not creation *ex nihilo*
6. manipulation of weather	1 Kings 17-19 Exo. 9:13-26 Mk. 4:35-41; etc.	Job 1:19; Mk. 4:37
7. spontaneous human combustion (SHC)	2 Kings 1:9-12 Num. 16:35	Job 1:16 Rev. 13:13

Miracle	Divine	Satanic
8. manipulation of animals and insects	Exo. 8-9; 1 Kings 17:6; Mk. 11:1-7	Exo. 8:7
9. telepathy	Matt. 9:4; Acts 5:1-11	Satan can blind the mind (2 Cor. 4:4), put ideas in it (Matt. 16:22-23), or take ideas out of it (Matt. 13:19).
10. dream interpretation	Gen. 40:4-22 41:15-32	Gen. 41:8 Dan. 4:6-7
11. visions and revelations	Ezk. 40:2 2 Cor. 12:7	Matt. 4:8
12. out of body experiences (OBE)	Ezk. 37:1; 40:1-2 2 Cor. 12:2-4 Rev. 4:1	T.M., Yoga, drugs, near death experience
13. power to cause sickness and death	Exo. 9:1-12; 11:1-8	Job 2:7; Mk. 9:17-29
14. power to heal sickness	Acts 3:6-13	Christian Science, T.M., Psychic healers, etc.
15. creation of life from non-life	Exo. 8:16-17	cannot really do this (Exo. 8:19). hallucinations possible (Exo. 7:11; Rev. 13:13-15)
16. exorcism of demons	Acts 16:16-18	Matt. 12:27
17. signs, wonders, miracles	Heb. 2:4	2 Thess. 2:9 Rev. 13:13

VI. The Tools of the Occult
   A. One list of occult tools is 108 pages.
   B. Present popular tools
      1. Ouija Board
      2. Fortune Telling (palm reading, crystal ball, tea leaves, tarot cards, psychic games, etc.)
      3. Seances (trumpets, drums, balls, table rapping, etc.)
      4. Levitation
      5. Psychic Phenomenon (dream interpretation, dowsing, psychometry, healing, etc.)
      6. Apportation (teleportation of people or objects from one place to another)
      7. Satanism (church of Satan)
      8. Materializations (ectoplasmic manifestations)
      9. Astral-Projection (out of body experiences)
     10. Transcendental Meditation (T.M., Yoga)
     11. Drug abuse
     12. Astrology

VII. The Bible and the Occult
   The following chart reveals that all occult practices are condemned in Scripture as being satanic in origin and power. Thus, they are an abomination to God and forbidden to His people.

DIVINATION	SORCERY	ASTROLOGY	ENCHANTER	MEDIUM
The use of occult tools to discern the future, answer questions or to interpret dreams.	The practice of the occult arts.	Looking to the stars for the future and for daily guidance.	The caster of spells and curses. The use of hypnotic trances to find answers in the spirit world. The use of magic	A demon possessed person who serves as the contact to the spirit world.
Gen. 30:27 44:5, 15 Lev. 19:26 Num. 22:6-7 23:23 Deut. 18:9, 10, 14, 15 1 Sam. 6:2 2 Kgs. 17:17 2 Chron. 33:6 Isa. 44:25 Jer. 14:14 27:9; 29:8	Exo. 7:11 Isa. 47:9, 12 57:3 Jer. 27:9 Dan. 2:2 Mal. 3:5 Acts 8:9, 11 12:6, 8 19:19 Gal. 5:20 Rev. 21:8 22:15 2 Chron. 33:5	2 Kgs. 17:16 23:5 Isa. 47:13 Dan. 2:2-10, 20-28 4:7 5:7, 11, 15 Amos 5:26 Acts 7:40-43 Deut.4:19 Jer. 8:1-2 19:13	Exo. 7:11, 22 8:7, 18 Lev. 19:26 Num. 24:1 Deut. 18:10 2 Kings 17:17 21:6 2 Chron. 33:6 Isa. 47:9, 12 Jer. 27:9 Dan. 1:20	Lev. 19:31 20:6, 27 Deut. 18:10 1 Sam. 28:3-9 2 Kgs. 21:6 23:24 1 Chron. 10:13 2 Chron. 33:6 Isa. 8:19 19:3

DIVINATION	SORCERY	ASTROLOGY	ENCHANTER	MEDIUM
Ezk. 12:24 13:6, 7, 23 21:21-23, 29 22:28 Mic. 3:6, 7, 11 Zech. 10:2 Acts 16:16				
31 Times	13 Times	17 Times	14 Times	11 Times

WIZARD	HUMAN SACRIFICES	SOOTHSAYING	WITCH OR WITCHCRAFT	MONTHLY PROG-NOSTICATORS
A male medium.	The appease-ment of occult forces by human sacrifices often connected with astrology.	Magicians who perform psychic acts.	Female medium or spiritists.	Predicting the events of the forthcoming month by the moon and astrology.
Lev. 19:31 20:6, 27 Deut. 18:10 1 Sam. 28: 3, 9 17 2 Kings 21:6 23:24 2 Chron. 33:6 Isa.8:19 19:3	Lev. 18:21 20:2-5 Deut. 18:9-10 2 Kings 16:3, 31 21:6 23:10 2 Chron. 28:3; 33:6 Jer. 7:31 19:5 32:35 49:2 Ezk. 16:21 20:31	Josh. 13:22 Isa. 2:6 Dan. 2:27 4:7 5:7, 11 Mic. 5:12 Acts 16:16	Exo. 22:18 Deut. 18:10 2 Kings 9:22 2 Chron. 33:6 Mic. 5:12 Nahum 3:4	Isa. 47:13 1 Sam. 15:23
11 Times	18 Times	8 Times	7 Times	1 Time

Conclusion

The Christian cannot have anything to do with the world of the occult. While modern humanists call it "E.S.P." or "psychic experiments," Christians must avoid it at all costs. The satanic origin and power behind the occult must be boldly pointed out by Christians. The present occult revolution may be the preparation of the world for the coming of the anti-Christ, who will produce "psychic miracles" to deceive the world (2 Thess. 2:9-12; Rev. 13:13). The Christian does not fear the occult because "greater is He that is in us than he that is in the world" (1 John 4:4). While we do not "fear," we do have a healthy respect of occult powers.

Chapter One Hundred Twelve
The New Age Movement

Introduction

The New Age Movement (NAM) is in the news today because of its fantastic claims.

"Christ" has returned!

We are all gods and Christs!

A "New Age" has dawned!

The following are popular: astrology, reincarnation, crystal balls, tarot cards, seances, ouija boards, channeling, psychics, gurus, astral-travel, pagan groups, witchcraft, satanism, devil worship, ESP, UFOs, numerology, good luck charms, crystals, transcendental meditation, Eastern religions, "mind" cults and gnostic mystery religions.

We must look beyond the surface to the underlying concepts, political goals and programs of the NAM. We must not spend too much time on nut cases or con artists. The NAM is far more serious than gurus, Zen-masters and psychics ripping off the gullible and the naive. The success of the NAM constitutes a clear and present threat not only to the Church but also to the nation. We must look beyond its surface sensationalism to its underlying concepts/goals/programs.

I. The Terminology of the NAM.

    A. The NAM is not new in the sense of not previously known. The concepts of the NAM are very old. The same ideas and practices were called the occult or witchcraft not too long ago. For example, what once was called "mediumship by a witch" is now called "channeling by a psychic friend."

    B. "New" as opposed to "Old":

Age of Pisces	Age of Aquarius
The Old	The New
Christianity	New Age Movement

    C. "New Age" in sense of an idealistic utopianism: the belief that history is moving toward an ideal age in which harmony and peace will prevail over all the earth. This was originally a biblical concept involving the return of Christ, the resurrection and judgment day. But instead of Jesus making a "new Heavens and a new earth," the NAM says man will bring it about by his own powers.

Utopianism	
Christian	Humanistic
Jesus at His return to earth	Man will bring it about

Humanistic Utopianism	
secular	religious
materialistic	spiritualistic
Marxism	NAM
dialectic	event/evolution

Both Marxism and the NAM are Christian heresies in this sense.

II. What is the NAM?

It is a religious form of Humanism: the belief that man is the measure of all things and thus the Origin and Judge of truth, justice, morals and beauty. Man is his own "god" literally or figuratively.

Humanism	
secular	religious
no God	no God
no absolutes	no absolutes
relativism	relativism
autonomy	autonomy
subjectivism	subjectivism
materialism	spiritualism
all is matter	all is mind
rationalism	mysticism
"science"	parapsychology
anti-Christian	anti-Christian

III. The NAM is religious atheism:

It denies the existence of an infinite/personal God who exists outside of and independent of the universe.

IV. The NAM Misuses the word "God."

The NAM takes the word "God" and applies it to the universe. The problem with this is that the attributes of the universe and God are opposites.

God	The Universe
infinite	finite
eternal	limited by time
omnipresent	limited by space
omnipotent	limited in power
omniscient	limited in knowledge
sovereign	limited in control
immutable	mutable
perfect	flawed/imperfect
good	evil/good
independent	dependent

V. The NAM's solution:

It denies the existence of the universe! The world we see around us is an illusion! Our bodies do not exist. Evil does not exist. Pain, sickness and death are all illusions! We are not limited or finite in any way. "Mind" or "consciousness" is all that really exists.

VI. The NAM's worldview leads to:

A. solipsism, egoism, selfishness

B. no concern, compassion or help for the sick, handicapped, old or dying. The NAM does not build hospitals or nursing homes.

VII. When did the NAM begin?

It began in the 1950s with J.B. Rhine. It became popular in the 1960s and led to drugs, rebellion, the Beatles, Gurus, free sex, Cayce, Dixon, cults, ESP, etc.

VIII. Why did it become popular?

A. The failure of secular humanism to provide a materialistic basis for truth, justice, morals or beauty. Man was reduced to an animal, machine, a meaningless accident in a backwater without dignity/worth/meaning.

$$\text{Man} \longrightarrow \text{a dog}$$

B. Because of the failure of secular atheism, many '60s humanists became religious atheists. Example: John Denver.

C. Humanism has always swung between two poles:

materialism	spiritualism
"man is a dog"	"man is a god"

D. Humanism is doomed to swing back and forth because it is reductionistic, i.e., man is reduced to only one element: body/mind, matter/spirit.

E. When humanism is the dominant worldview in any culture, the culture swings back and forth from materialism to spiritualism.

Ancient Greece	
materialism	spiritualism
Heraclitus	Parmenides
matter	mind
empiricism	mysticism
Aristotle	Plato

19th Century	
Early: materialism	Late: spiritualism

20th Century	
Early: materialism	Late: spiritualism

F. The popularity of humanistically based religions depends on whether the culture is in a materialistic or spiritualistic phase.

Popular Forms of Materialism	
secular	religious
atheism	Neo-orthodoxy
agnosticism	Paul Tillich
skepticism	"God is dead"
Marxism	soul sleep
anti-miracle	annihilationism
anti-ESP	Seventh-day Adventists
anti-God	Watchtower
rationalism	Armstrong

Popular Forms of Spiritualism	
secular	religious
ESP	spiritualism
Parapsychology	occult
SPR	witchcraft
Psychics	NAM

F. This explains why the NAM is so popular at this time. Western humanistic culture is swinging toward its spiritualistic pole.

IX. Only when a culture is dominated by the Christian worldview does it escape from both materialism and spiritualism.

The Biblical World View	
Reality is matter/visible	spirit/invisible.
Man is body/flesh	mind/spirit.

X. The NAM will lose its popularity when the culture swings back to its materialistic pole. Psychism always becomes boring. The rip-offs, con-games and frauds run it into the ground. You can only pretend that there is no pain until you are in pain! To say "there is no death" never stopped anyone from dying! Example: Mary Baker Eddy. The mere act of stubbing one's toe tends to vanquish all claims to divinity! When you have kids, you find out that you are not omniscient or omnipotent. Is it any wonder that the NAM is primarily composed of affluent singles!

XI. How widespread is the NAM?
It has invaded every area of society and has thousands of organizations in an international network:

religion	sports	music	sales	military	UN
science	psychology	art	business	medicine	
education	cartoons	movies	police	politics	

XII. Is the NAM dangerous? Yes!
    1. It is psychologically damaging.
    2. It is socially worthless.
    3. It is financially disastrous.
    4. It is scientifically fraudulent.
    5. It is spiritually delusive.
    6. It is biblically satanic and demonic.

XIII. Why should we be concerned?

The goals of the NAM call for the destruction not only of the Church but also the nation. In search of its monistic ideal of "oneness," the NAM wants three things:

A. A one-world government run by a charismatic leader trained in the occult arts of psychism. The NAM names Hitler as their first attempt! The U.S. Constitution must be destroyed, and the UN must take over.

B. A one-world religion run by a New Age Christ who will be forced on all religions. There will be no freedom of religion.

C. A centralized control of money, food, goods, jobs and births. If you do not accept their one-world government or religion, you will be denied money, food, jobs, goods and the right to have children. "Illegal" babies will be murdered, as they are in China. People who resist "re-education," i.e., NAM teaching, will be denied work. There will be no human or civil rights: No freedom of religion, speech, assembly or of the press! This is the dark side of the New Age movement.

XIV. Our greatest fear:

The NAM is the final fulfillment of the biblical prophecies about the anti-Christ and the end of the world. What is scary is that there is a direct correspondence between the biblical anti-Christ and the NAM!

A. NAM doctrines: 1 John 2:18-23; 4:1-4; 2 John 7-11; 2 Thess. 2:1-5.

B. NAM miracles: 2 Thess. 2:9-12; Rev. 13:12-15.

C. NAM goals: A one-world government and religion dedicated to the destruction of the Bible and Christianity: Rev. 13:3-18.

Conclusion

Since the essence of Humanism is rebellion against God, it has always sought to destroy the people and worship of God. Be it materialistic Marxism in the Communist World or the spiritualistic New Age Movement in the West, the Church faces its greatest challenge today as it proclaims the Gospel to a lost and dying world.

An Open Letter to Witches

I see from the pentagram you wear and all your other magical charms that you believe in the power of magic. Perhaps you have attended a Wiccan gathering or you have participated in magic rituals. I don't know.

But so many questions fill my mind. Have you "drawn down the moon" yet? Have you ever felt a power come upon you? Do you worship a particular goddess? Have you been initiated? Do you have a Wiccan name? Have you gone sky-cladding? Are you in the outer or the inner circle? Have you used blood in your rituals? Have you ever called forth a familiar spirit?

The reason I am writing to you is that I have studied the occult for more than 30 years and I have come to certain conclusions. I know that you will disagree with some of my conclusions because we have traveled different paths. But I have the added benefit of the testimonies of those who used magic in the highest levels possible such as the Golden Dawn and the O.T.O. (Ordo Templi Orientis) and then, having come to faith in Christ, have now renounced magic.

All I ask is that you have an open mind and give serious attention to the things I now bring up. Remember an unexamined faith is a worthless faith.

1) The fact is that magic does not work. After all the talk about the "power" that people can get from magic, I have never known a more powerless group of people.

Many of those who use magic are sick all the time. They go through multiple marriages. They have money problems. Their cars get flat tires. They get their share of the flu and colds. Even more seriously, they cannot beat their own drug or sex addiction. They are usually in bondage and totally powerless to change their lives for the better.

If magic really worked, they would never be sick. They would win every horse race in town! They would own Wall Street by now! They would be able to maintain successful marriages. Witches would be picking the winning lottery numbers every week. But the fact is, when the "rubber meets the road," magic simply does not work. You can waste a lot of money and time on magic and be no better off. In fact, you will end up worse off.

2) Their lame duck excuses as to why they are sick or why they can't keep their marriage together or why they aren't rich are weak and feeble. One psychic "healer" (a relative of mine) is sick all the time. Her first husband is dying of cancer! When she boasted to me of her magical powers, I confronted her with the rather obvious fact that her magic did not work for her or for her ex-husband. She replied that her magic will not work for herself.

But who says that you cannot heal yourself by magic? Where is this written down? And who says that your husband or wife cannot use magic to heal you? If her magic cannot help herself or her husband, then what good is it?

I could not help but also point out that she is always crying about money problems. What use is her magic if it cannot make her rich?

3) A magical world view is internally contradictory and hypocritical.
   a) To say, "There are no moral absolutes" is to give an absolute.
   b) To say, "Do what thou wilt, this is the whole of the law" has been used to justify everything from black magic to human sacrifice. If there are no standards, then on what grounds can witches condemn child abuse, Hitler, murder, etc? They can't.
   c) To say "Everything is relative" and "There is no evil," and then to turn around and say that Christianity is "evil" is contradictory.
   d) To say, "Everyone has the right to believe what they want" and then to condemn Christians for what they believe is contradictory.
   e) To say, "Do what thou wilt" and then to tell Christians not to do what they wilt is hypocritical.
   f) To say, "It is wrong to judge/condemn others," and then to judge/condemn Christians is contradictory.

4) A magical view of life does not correspond to reality.
   a) No magic is going to make you thin if you do not stop eating. No magic will make you rich if you do not get up and go to work.
   b) The claim of modern witches that they are reviving pre-Christian paganism is not historically true. The rituals and beliefs of modern day magic are of recent origin.
   c) A close relative of mine who is into the occult told me that he was going to use magic to get himself a parking space in New York City. I in turn told him that I would ask Jesus to get me a space. He drove around for four hours before finding a place, while I found one at once and did not have to go around the block even once! His magic was not even good enough to find him a parking space!

5) A magical view of life is a cop out and it breeds irresponsibility. Instead of taking responsibility for their lives, those who use magic always blame "bad luck" or claim that someone is using black magic against them. The truth is that you are responsible for the choices you make in life—not magic.

6) It attracts people with mental problems. Sad but true. I have seen this many, many times. The state mental hospitals are filled with people who were users of magic. It appeals to nut cases.

7) They live in constant fear of the powers they draw down. Hence they need the occult protection of the circles, towers, shields, charms, etc. What a terrible religion of fear!

8) If you depend upon trinkets such as pentagrams to protect you, you do not have any real power. To think that a stupid piece of metal or glass is going to protect you from a demon is just plain stupid.

9) The lust for blood is evil. It has led to horrible crimes. Killing animals and people for their "energy" is wicked as well as criminal.

10) Sex magic is filthy and gross beyond words and involves child abuse, bestiality, sodomy, etc. You will never have a normal satisfying sex life once you debase yourself in sex magic.

11) Magic is for losers. The greatest magicians all ended up broke, alone and miserable. Check to see what happened to people such as Crowley. They were all losers.

12) Whenever a true Christian challenges them, the magicians always lose. I have challenged occultists to take their best shot and they always failed. On one occasion, a coven sent demons to kill me, but I did not even get a headache!

13) While there is a lot of hate and lust in magic, there is no love. If you leave the group or reveal the secrets, they will try to kill you. I helped to move a girl from Philadelphia to Florida to escape her former occult friends. If they really loved her, why did they try to kill her? If she wanted to leave the group, why did they object to her "doing what she wilt"?

14) There is no forgiveness, comfort or salvation in magic. It has no Savior or God who loves and cares for you. The occult is lonely, sad, cold and sterile.

15) The Bible says that the true power behind the magical arts is Satan. Those who deny this are the dupes of the devil.

Conclusion

These are just a few things that came to mind as I thought about what I have learned in 30 years of research in the occult. The Lord Jesus Christ has broken the power of the magic and has brought life, love and immortality to light through the Gospel. Jesus is Victor!

The occult has nothing to offer that compares with the love of Jesus. Turn to Him in repentance. Renounce your witchcraft as the works of the devil. Burn your magic books and smash your altars. Turn ... or burn. Repent ... or perish! Jesus is Victor!

Chapter One Hundred Fourteen

The Riddle of Reincarnation

Introduction

One of the most popular beliefs in the world concerning death is the transmigration or reincarnation of the soul. This belief is the main competitor today to the Christian concept of heaven and hell.

Hollywood stars such as Shirley Maclaine have given reincarnation great popularity. One finds increasing references to it in television shows and movies. The tabloids at grocery store checkouts run sensational stories "proving" it every week. What is reincarnation all about, and how should Christians respond to it?

1) Eastern transmigration

The orthodox Hindu idea of reincarnation teaches that when you die, your soul does not go to heaven or hell. Instead, your soul goes into some other kind of body here on earth.

This body can be an insect, fish, animal or human body. This is why they practice vegetarianism and will not even kill the pests that destroy their harvests.

2) Western reincarnation

When occultists such as Edgar Cayce realized that the concept of reincarnating into animal and insect bodies would not be attractive to Westerners, they decided to alter the concept.

Using the Western concepts of evolution and progress, they taught that through reincarnation the soul always progressively evolves up the scale of being. Thus you cannot regress back into an insect or animal body once you have reached the human stage. You are either born into another human body, or you fly off the wheel of karma and are absorbed back into oneness.

3) The theory of karma

In Hindu theology, there is no personal god who hands out rewards and punishments like in the Bible. Instead, there is the non-personal principle of karma, which decides on the basis of the good and evil you have done in previous lives if you will be reborn as rich or poor, healthy or handicapped, slave or master, etc.

4) Good and bad karma

Karma teaches that you are either suffering or prospering in your present life because of the evil or good you did in a previous life.

If you are born as a poor little black "crack" baby in Harlem with terrible physical and mental sufferings, you are only getting what you deserve. You must have done some really evil things in a past life to have such "bad" karma. But if you are born into a rich white family with health and wealth all your days, then you too are only getting what you deserve. You must have done some really good things in a past life to have such "good" karma.

5) The arguments for reincarnation
    a) It solves the problem of evil
       Karmic reincarnation solves the problem of evil by viewing it in terms of punishment and reward. If you are suffering in this life, it is because of the evil you did in a past life. If you prospering, it is because of the good you did in a past life. Everyone is only getting what they deserve. Answer: Karmic reincarnation does not solve the problem of evil.
       1. You ultimately arrive at a "first" life in which there was no previous life to explain the evil in it.
       2. Or, you end up making evil eternal, which only extends the problem, not solves it.
    b) Reincarnational recall proves it.
        i) Deja vu recall.
        ii) Spontaneous recall.
        iii) Hypnotic recall.
        iv) Psychic recall.

Answer: These arguments are erroneous.

No. 1: Deja vu can be "felt" with things built in your lifetime, such as a house or a city as well as with people.

No. 2: Logically speaking, when more than one person at the same time claims to be the present reincarnation of Jesus, Buddha, Elvis, etc., either one is right and the others are liars, or they are all liars. But they can't all be right.

No. 3: Spontaneous recall never happens under scientific conditions. Thus it is worthless as evidence.

No. 4: Hypnotic recall is highly unreliable. Example: Bridey Murphy.

No. 5: Psychic recall is plagued with the problem of fraud. How can you tell if they really know who you were in a past life?

No. 6: Why are recalls usually of important people?

No. 7: Why is it that all recall experiences teach Hindu doctrine? In all the hundreds of cases I have researched, I did not find a single instance where orthodox Christians were recalled. Where are the recalls of Calvin, Spurgeon, Edwards, etc.?

    c) The Bible teaches it. John the Baptist was a reincarnation of Elijah. Jesus told us that we must be "born again" into a new body at death.
       Answer: Since Elijah never died, he cannot be reincarnated. The "new birth" has to do with spiritual regeneration in this life.
    d) Christianity once taught it. But it was later removed by church councils.
       Answer: What council? When? Where? There is no evidence of this in church history. The early church fathers all wrote against it.

The Christian answer
    1. The atonement of Christ makes reincarnation unnecessary.
    2. The resurrection of the body makes reincarnation impossible.

Chapter One Hundred Fifteen
Astrology

Introduction

Astrology is big business today. There are more than 10,000 full-time astrologers and more than 175,000 part-time astrologers in the United States. More than 2,000 newspapers carry daily astrological readings. Zodiac jewelry has become popular. Even restaurant table mats have horoscopes! We must understand the occult art of astrology because we face it all the time.

1) The History of Astrology

    a) The Tower of Babel (Gen. 11:3-9) is the first mention in Scripture.

    b) Ancient Babylonian, Egyptian, Chinese forms of Astrology: The future of nations and kings was determined by the stars.

    c) Greek Astrology: through Ptolemy (A.D. 150) it became a "science" and was applied to all men—not just kings.

    d) The Apostles and the Early Christian Church greatly weakened the influence of astrology by condemning it as a tool of Satan and an occult art.

    e) Astrology in the Middle Ages became a popular superstition as people grew ignorant of the Bible and true Christianity.

    f) The impact of Copernicus and later astronomers: Astrology and its earth-centered universe did not appeal to people once they knew that the planets circled the sun and not the earth. Astronomy took the place of astrology.

    g) The occult revolution of the late 1800s: Astrology returned along with such things as seances, palm reading, Ouija boards and other occult practices.

    h) Present day astrology:

        i) "Slop" astrology is found in newspapers and on table mats. It is not worth the paper it is printed on.

        ii) "Pop" astrology is found in astrological magazines or books. It is written for the masses, and is worthless so far as any astrological predictions are concerned.

        iii) "Serious" astrology is only for those who have enough faith in it to pay huge sums of money to have their personal horoscope drawn up by a "professional" astrologer. Some of the popular big name astrologers charge around $10,000 for each horoscope.

    i) Pertinent Historical Facts

        i) It is an ancient pagan religion which involved the worship of the stars (2 Kings 17:16-17; 23:4-5; Amos 5:26; Acts 7:39-43).

        ii) It has always gone "hand in glove" with the other occult arts (Isa. 47:12-14).

        iii) Astrologers have always been hostile to biblical Christianity. There are no "Christian astrologers" (2 Kings 17:16-17; Acts 13:6-12).

2) Our Judgment of Astrology.

    a) The Scriptures condemn it as an abomination before God and an occult tool of satanic origin and power (2 Kings 17:16; 23:5; Isa. 47:13; Amos 5:26).

    b) Astrology is not a science, but only a superstition; i.e., a fraud. The scientific evidence against astrology is irrefutable.

        i) Present day astrologers are still using Ptolemy's earth-centered horoscope. The facts are that this solar system is heliocentric. The contradiction is irrefutable.

ii) Ptolemy assumed the flat earth theory and thus developed the belt of signs in the Zodiac. The earth is a sphere.

iii) Ptolemy developed a Zodiac with seven signs. These signs included the sun and moon as "stars." Present day charts still use Ptolemy's basic Zodiac.

(1) Such planets as Pluto, Neptune and Uranus were not originally included because they were not discovered until the invention of the telescope. Without all the "stars" of this solar system, all the horoscopes have been off. What about all the other constellations now known? Why and how is astrology accurate if it does not take into account modern astronomy?

(2) Above the latitude 66 degrees, we cannot calculate what point of the Zodiac is ascending on the horizon. This renders astrological predictions impossible for those living above the latitude 66 degrees.

Conclusion

The romance of the stars is a dangerous game. Christians must have nothing to do with any occult tools of satanic power and origin.

Chapter One Hundred Sixteen
The Ouija Board

1) What Are Witchcraft and Magic?

The attempt to do, know or control things which man does not normally do, know or control. Example: control the weather, know the future, make someone die or love you.

2) What Are the Ways It Is Done?
   a) Speech: incantations, spells, chants, etc.
   b) Feats: dancing, jumping, rocking, etc.
   c) Pain: fire walking, beds of nails or glass, fish hooks, cuts, burns, etc.
   d) Divination: messages from the spirit world—mediums, seances, crystal ball, a table, stars, hand, head, ears, eyes, feet, tea leaves, pendulums, dice, talking boards, etc.

3) What Is a "Talking Board"?
   A board used to receive messages from the spirits.
      a) The board has letters, numbers and words (yes/no).
      b) A pointer spells out the messages: pendulum, planchette, pencil, etc.

4) When Were They Invented?
   a) Ancient pagan religions used them: Asia, Africa, Middle East, Europe.
   b) Reintroduced in the 19th century.
      i) In France: 1853 a spiritualist invented the "planchette" as a tool for mediums.
      ii) In the United States: 1892 William Fuld invented the "Ouija" board.
      iii) Other talking boards: witch board, finger of fate, mystic voodoo, ESP, psychic, aye-see, etc.

5) What Does Quija Mean?
   a) Fuld asked the board to name itself. It spelled out "Ouija."
   b) It combines two words for "yes"—French "oui" and German "ja."

6) Did Fuld use the Board for Directions?

   a) Yes. Major business deals were determined by "ouija." Fuld became a millionaire.

7) Is It Only a Game?
   a) Fuld's company went to court in 1920 to establish it as a religious device to contact the spirit world. They denied that it was a "game." They went all the way to the Supreme Court, where it was acknowledged as a mediumistic tool.
   b) Witches, psychics, and parapsychologists view it as a mediumistic tool for automatic writing.
   c) Serious users of it claim it is not a game.
   d) Christian scholars do not think it is "just a game."
   e) Psychologists and doctors do not view it as a harmless game.

    f) Who views it as a game?
       i) ignorant parents
      ii) silly teens
     iii) uneducated pastors

8) Is It Dangerous?
    a) Spiritualists, psychologists, psychiatrists, medical doctors, theologians and scholars all say it can be very harmful.
    b) Earnest Turley and Nellie Hurd would say so, if they were alive. They were murdered through it.
    c) Francisco Madero used it to justify overthrowing the Mexican government in 1910. Revolution came through it.
    d) Fraud, immorality, drugs, divorce, assault, etc. have been traced back to a message from Ouija.
    e) Demon possession can happen! "The Exorcist" was based on a true story, which began with Regan playing with Ouija.
    f) Psychics say so.
    g) Christian scholars say so.
    h) Psychiatrists/doctors say so.
    i) Dr. Kurt Kock compiled hundreds of case histories.

9) Is It Always Demonic?
No. 80 to 90 percent of the time someone is making it work as a joke, or it is the result of involuntary muscle movement. But in 10 to 20 percent of the cases contact is made with demons. Paranormal knowledge is given which cannot be explained.

10) What Does God Say About It?
He calls it an "abomination" in Deut. 18:9-14. It was forbidden by the Old Testament and New Testament and was always condemned by Jews and Christians as satanic in origin.

Conclusion

What Must We Do?
    1. Confess it as sin.
    2. Renounce Satan and all his works.
    3. Throw it away or burn it.
    4. Never play with it again.

Chapter One Hundred Seventeen
The Gnostic Gospels

Introduction

It has become quite popular on college campuses for atheistic professors to attack Christianity by stating that Gnosticism was the "original" Christianity. Thus, the Christian student today has to have a basic understanding of Gnosticism in order to defend the faith (Jude 3).

1. The Early Christian Church rejected various fake gospels produced by a Greek mystery religion called Gnosticism, which attempted to absorb Christianity. The Apostle Paul attacked Gnosticism directly in Colossians while John attacked it in 1 and 2 John and Revelation. Every subsequent Church Father and council attacked the Gnostics. At no point did the Christian Church accept Gnosticism.

2. The Gnostics denied the existence of the biblical personal/infinite God, monotheism, the Trinity and that Jesus was human and divine. They even denied that He was Christ! Jesus, to them, was simply a link in the chain of Being. They also denied that Jesus died for our sins, and His bodily resurrection. The Gnostics rejected the Old Testament and New Testament and drew upon Eastern ideas such as Reincarnation and pantheism.

3. While the New Testament began within 10 to 15 years of the death of Jesus (A.D. 33), and we have a fragment of Mark which can be dated A.D. 50 and Luke A.D. 57, the vast majority of the Gnostic gospels were not written until late into the third and fourth centuries.

4. The Gnostics had a stronghold in Egypt, and some fourth century manuscripts have been found in Nag Hammadi. These false gospels contained historical and literary blunders which reveal that they were not written in the first century. Their literary style is drastically different from the New Testament, and they exalt absurd stories of Jesus' childhood such as:
   (a) Jesus would make clay birds and change them into real ones.
   (b) While playing hide and seek, Jesus searched for some children in a particular house into which they had run. When He came to the door and asked the mother if there were any children inside she said, "No, only kids." Outraged, Jesus turned all of the children into goats.
   (c) Jesus had a twin brother.
   (d) Jesus had sexual involvement with various women.

5. In John 2:11, the Apostle John stated that the first miracle Jesus did was turning the water into wine at the wedding of Cana. The Gnostic materials, which are filled with absurd miracles of the child Jesus, cannot be viewed as valid in the light of John 2:11.

6. Certain newspaper writers sensationalized the finding of the Gnostic gospels as they did the finding of the Dead Sea Scrolls. Once scholars had a chance to translate these works, nothing new was discovered that was not already known from the writings of the early Church Fathers. The Early Church never said or pretended that these fake gospels did not exist. The Church never hid anything from anybody. They showed that these were spurious works.

7. While the New Testament is organically linked to the Old Testament, the Gnostic works reject the existence of God, the creation of the world out of nothing, the goodness of matter and flesh, the necessity of a substitutionary blood atonement, etc. Whereas Christianity is an extension of Old Testament Judaism, Gnosticism is an extension of Eastern religions, such as Buddhism.

8. No biblical scholar today feels that there is any significance to the Gnostic works beyond that of historical curiosity as to what this mystery religion believed. Since none of them were written in the first century, and they did not appear until several hundred years after Christ, they are worthless as a guide to Jesus' life. The first century New Testament, written by the Apostles who were eyewitnesses and friends of Jesus Christ, is logically and historically a superior guide to the life and teaching of Jesus.

9. Christianity triumphed over Gnosticism because of the superiority of the biblical Gospel. While such writers as Pagels try to prove that Christianity triumphed because of its political structure, this is a very superficial position. We must ask on what basis did the early Fathers have political authority in the Church? The Orthodox position won out because it was in harmony with the Old Testament and New Testament, and descended from the Apostles and other eyewitnesses. It was rooted in the historical bodily resurrection of Jesus Christ as a real space/time event which was verified by over 500 eye-witnesses. Gnosticism was built on myth and subjectionism.

10. Modern forms of Gnosticism attempt to discount the New Testament and appeal to the Nag Hammadi texts as "Lost Bibles." This is historically and theologically absurd. The attempt to identify Gnosticism as a part of Early Christianity is doomed to failure once it is understood that Gnosticism existed before Christianity appeared, and that it tried to absorb all the religions it encountered. It was clearly denounced as "antichrist" by the Apostles and Church Fathers. It never represented biblical or historic Christianity. Since the Gnostic "Gospels" attack the New Testament, it is obvious that the New Testament existed before them.

11. There is but one eternal personal infinite God who created the world out of nothing. This God eternally existed in three centers of consciousness or personality, which the New Testament identifies as the Father, the Son and the Holy Spirit. This Triune God has done all that is necessary for man's forgiveness and salvation. Jesus Christ was incarnate as a real man and died a real death. He was bodily raised from the dead, having paid off all the punishment that God's Law demands. Christ's death makes Karmic reincarnation unnecessary. Jesus has paid it all. Our responsibility is to repent of our sin and to accept Jesus Christ as the Lord of all of life.

Conclusion

Gnosticism was never part of Christianity. It was always viewed as a pagan religion. The so-called Gnostic "Gospels" are obviously frauds.

Chapter One Hundred Eighteen
Atheism and Absolutes

Introduction

The problem of "absolutes" has plagued philosophy from the very beginning. Theists have always argued that unless you begin with God as the Infinite Reference Point which gives meaning to all the particulars of life, it is impossible to have any absolutes. Some modern atheists have denied this, and claim instead that they can have "absolutes" without God. That they are in error at this point can be shown by the following points.

1. Modern atheists boldly proclaim, "Everything is relative." We have all heard this claim many, many times. They applied this idea first to morals and then to all areas of life such as science, art, etc. (see Robert Morey, *The New Atheism and the Erosion of Freedom*).

2. An "absolute" refers to some kind of standard by which we understand or judge something as being either true/false, right/wrong, black/white, hot/cold, helpful/harmful, etc.

3. Human language cannot exist without distinctions drawn from such "absolutes." For example, "I am writing to you." The law of non-contradiction means in this case that I am not you.

4. Atheists commit the fallacy of equivocation at this point. When the theist uses the word "absolute," he is referring to those standards which are:

infinite	not finite,
universal	not cultural
objective	not subjective
perfect	not imperfect
immutable	not mutable
eternal	not temporal

5. The atheist's claim to be able to have "absolutes" without God rests upon a very basic error in logic. He has switched the meaning of the word "absolutes" without mentioning this to the theist. The so-called "absolutes" of the atheist are finite, cultural, subjective, imperfect, mutable and temporal. This is, of course, a contradiction of terms because the atheist's "absolute" is a non-absolute!

    Such relative "absolutes" would be useless so far as ethics is concerned, because we can make up whatever so-called "absolutes" we want, Hitler included. Thus the so-called "absolutes" of the atheist are only the subjective projections of his personal feelings, ideas, biases, etc.

6. In logic, we cannot have a universal in our conclusion if we do not have one in our premises. Thus a finite creature such as man can never make the leap to a universal if all he has are his own limited and biased feelings and ideas, which are all particulars.

7. An infinite universal can only come from an infinite Being. Thus only the infinite God of Scripture can give us a sufficient basis for absolutes. The finite gods of paganism cannot generate any basis for universals in truth, justice, morals or beauty. (See Robert Morey, *Battle of the Gods.*)

8. While some modern atheists claim to be able to have "absolutes" and "universals" without God, what they really mean are relative absolutes and finite universals. This is the same as claiming to be able to draw a round square or a square circle! Philosophically and logically speaking, it is impossible to have relative absolutes or finite universals.

9. The atheists are using the old "pea and shell" game to confuse people. They redefine such words as "absolute" to mean the exact opposite of what the word means. Thankfully, some of them are a little more honest and state that there are no absolutes in logic, mathematics, history, and science.

When Albert Einstein was asked how he knew that the speed of light in a vacuum was the same everywhere in the universe, he replied, "God does not play dice with the universe." Even such principles as the speed of light require the existence of God.

Conclusion

Without God nothing in life can have meaning, because there would be no standards by which we could discern the difference between good and evil, truth and error, justice and injustice, and right from wrong. Morality and civilization vanish once man is reduced to a hairless ape.

An Evangelical Appraisal of Greek Philosophy in General and Aristotle in Particular

Introduction

Evangelical Christians have historically held fast to the principle of sola scriptura as defined by the Protestant Reformers. The truth about God, man, sin and salvation has been revealed in the Bible alone. The self-revelation of God in Scripture is thus the final court of appeal in all matters of faith and practice. To "go beyond what is Written" leads to conceit and pride (1 Cor. 4:6).

While Roman Catholics base their theology on a combination of the Bible and pagan philosophers, particularly Aristotle, the Reformers were men of the Book. They knew that Romans 1 and 2 teach that natural theology is useless because sinful man suppresses any truth he might have derived from the creation around him or the conscience within him. Man shuts his eyes and plugs his ears and then wonders why he does not see the light or hear the music of God's existence and attributes. Thus, sinful man naturally goes into idolatry as Paul illustrates in Romans.

Evangelicals follow the same path as the Early Church Fathers who denounced Greek philosophers (such as Plato and Aristotle) as demon-possessed. They boldly proclaimed that Christ and Jerusalem had nothing to do with Baal and Athens. As I demonstrated in the book, *Battle of the Gods*, the early Christians had nothing but contempt for pagan theology and philosophy.

The Early Church was Jewish in origin and reflected the orthodox Jewish hostility toward heathen religions. One will search in vain to find a single prophet of God in the Old Testament who showed any appreciation for heathen religions or philosophies. The Gentiles and their religions were all condemned as idolatrous and demonic in worship (Deut. 32:17; Psa. 106:36-37). The apostles followed the prophets and thus repeated the same condemnation (1 Cor. 10:20; Gal. 4:8; Rev. 9:20).

What about the Lord Jesus? Surely He must have said something to indicate that God appreciated all the pagan philosophers. Alas, Jesus was just as exclusive as the prophets before Him and the apostles after Him. His words to the Samaritan woman, "Salvation is from the Jews" (John 4:22), clearly mean that salvation is not from the Greeks, Romans, Indians, Chinese, Africans, Europeans, as well as the Samaritans. Jesus' words in John 14:6: "I am the way, the truth, and the life. No one comes to the Father but through me," forever doom all the ecumenical delusions of such apostates as Peter Kreeft.

While modern Romanists, Protestant liberals, Witches, and New Agers join in an ecumenical frenzy of exalting pagan philosophy, Evangelicals exalt the Word of God. They know that we are saved by grace alone, through faith alone, in Christ alone, according to the Bible alone.

With these few introductory words, the following statement represents the historic Evangelical position:

> Since no one seeks after the God who is there, all natural religion has its origin in man's suppression of and rebellion against natural revelation. Greek philosophy is just as apostate as Hinduism, Buddhism, Islam or Animism. The gods of the Greek philosophers were demonic in ori-

gin and idolatrous in nature. The Greek philosophers never found the true God. Their theology sprang from their worship of the creation instead of the Creator, who is blessed forever. Their foolish hearts were darkened as they gave themselves to vain speculations and immoral practices. Their so-called "proofs" for the existence of their false deities do not lead to the one true God of Scripture. Since they do not speak according to the Law and the prophets, they have no light.

The Pagan Philosopher Aristotle

What then shall we say about Aristotle (387-322 B.C.)? He is rightly called, "The High Priest of Empiricism" (John Gates, *Adventures in the History of Philosophy: An Introduction From a Christian Viewpoint*, Zondervan, 1961, p. 27). Any standard reference work on the history of philosophy, secular or Christian, will document that Aristotle believed that all knowledge comes to us via the five senses. This automatically excludes any and all forms of supernaturalism, Christianity included.

Not only is his epistemology anti-Christian, Aristotle's views on all other subjects are just as pernicious. His metaphysical dichotomy of "form/essence" produced the heresy of the secular/sacred dichotomy that kept papist priests in power for centuries. The idea that the form of something need not correspond to its essence, not only renders knowledge impossible, but it provided the philosophic framework in which the blasphemy of the popish error of transubstantiation in the Mass developed. His ethical relativism was based on a pleasure/pain sliding scale that has no room for the Ten Commandments.

Humanistic "evangelical" philosophers pretend that Aristotle believed in the one true God found in the Bible. But anyone who actually reads the works of Aristotle knows that he was a polytheist. Among the gods and goddesses he worshiped, Aristotle paid homage to a supreme deity whom he defined as "thought thinking itself."

How anyone can confuse the Triune God of Scripture with an abstract principle of "thought thinking itself" is beyond us. Aristotle's supreme deity thinks only on itself. How one can reconcile this god with the God revealed in John 3:16 remains a mystery.

Any Christian who is under the delusion that we can find the basis of Christian theology and philosophy in the works of Socrates, Plato, Aristotle or pagan philosophy in general, is either ignorant or deceptive. No philosopher ever found the true God by human reason, experience, feelings or faith. There is no other foundation for truth, justice, morals, meaning and beauty than Jesus Christ!

Chapter One Hundred Twenty

Roman Catholicism Today

Introduction

What was the Reformation all about? What was so terrible with the Roman Catholic Church that the Protestant Reformers went off and started their own churches? Why did they protest, and what did they protest?

Today as never before there is a growing feeling among many mainline Protestants that the time has come for Roman Catholics and Protestants to unite into one church. This is the goal of the National Council of Churches (NCC) and the World Council of Churches (WCC). To see this happen, two things must be done.

First, the history of the Reformation must be rewritten:

1. to omit any reference to the three million Protestants killed by torture during the Inquisition run by the Jesuits

2. to omit any reference to the millions who died during the Thirty Years War

3. to describe the Reformers as crazy and as villains

4. to remake Romanist villains into heroes or martyrs, such as the recent rewrite of history to clear "Bloody Mary" of her crimes

Second, the issues which created the Reformation must be:

1. completely excluded and never studied even in seminary

2. downplayed as unimportant

3. viewed as resolved because the Church of Rome has supposedly changed

In reality, the issues are still important enough to make any union with the Church of Rome impossible. Furthermore, the WCC not only wants all Protestant and Catholic Churches to unite into one super-church, but they want to form all religions into a one world religion! This is a direct fulfillment of Bible prophecy that in the last days when the false prophet and the anti-Christ will rule the world, there will be a one-world religion as well as one-world government. It is for this reason that evangelical Christians do not join the NCC or the WCC. In this light, it is important to remember why we are Reformed and not Roman Catholics.

The Essential Issues Between Catholics and Protestants

Issue No. 1
The Roman Catholic Church is structured according to O.T. Judaism instead of N.T. Christianity.

Old Testament Judaism	Roman Catholicism
1. The High Priest	The Pope
2. Jewish Priests	Catholic Priests
3. Continuous Sacrifices (Animal)	Continuous Sacrifices (The Mass)
4. The Temple	The Cathedral
5. The Holy City (Jerusalem)	The Holy City (Rome)
6. Physical Discipline Even Unto Death	Physical Discipline Even Unto Death
7. Passive Laity	Passive Laity
8. Under Law/Good Works	Under Law/Good Works
9. O.T. Worship with incense, altar, etc.	Worship with incense, altars, etc.
10. Church/State As One	Church/State As One

Why should we continue to follow an old covenant of law/works when Christ has established a New Covenant of grace/faith? The book of Hebrews tells us that the Old Covenant with its priesthood, altars, ceremonies, sacrifices, etc., have all been fulfilled in the work of Christ. Hence they are forever gone.

Issue No. 2
The Issue of Religious Authority
The central burning issue that divides the Reformed from the Romanist is the issue of religious authority; i.e., what is the final court of appeal and the ultimate judge of truth, justice and morals? This is where the line is drawn with every cult. In a cult, the leadership always views itself as having equal or greater authority than the Bible. On this basis, we must conclude that the Church of Rome is a cult.

Now we recognize that some people do not view the Church of Rome as a cult because of its size and age. But the size or age of a religion cannot erase the fact of it being a cult if its authority structure is cultic.

To put it simply, the Church of Rome is the oldest and the biggest "super-cult" of all time. It has killed multiple millions—more than the Christian Scientists, Mormons, Jehovah's Witnesses, Hare Krishnas, Jim Jones and all the killer cults put together. It has burned more Bibles, destroyed more Protestant churches, and murdered more Gospel preachers than the Communists! For a thousand years it succeeded in burying the Gospel under a mountain of false doctrines and superstitious ceremonies. If it were not for the brave men and women of the Reformation, we might still be in bondage to the Church of Rome.

The following diagram contrasts the Romanist and Reformed views of authority.

Religious Authority	
Romanist	Reformed

1. The Church:
  a. the pope
  b. the council of bishops
  c. tradition and practice.
	The Bible is the only
	and final authority
	in all matters of faith

2. The Bible	

The Chief Problem: The Claim of Infallibility

While the Church of Rome has changed some of the minor details of its ceremonies, its doctrines have not changed since the Council of Trent (1545 to 1563). Indeed, the Roman Church cannot change its doctrines because it claims to be infallible in doctrine. Thus, if it ever admitted that it was at any time wrong on any doctrine, it could no longer claim to be infallible!

Since Romanists base their faith on the infallibility of the Pope and the Church, no one can doubt or question Catholic dogma. While the Bible is mentioned as being one of the sources for its authority, the Roman Church is actually the only and final authority because it will allow only its interpretation of Scripture. Thus, when a doctrine is in conflict with Scripture, the Scripture is conformed to the doctrine!

The Bible has become a piece of putty which can be molded by the priests into anything they want it to be. When pressed, modern priests will often attack the infallibility of the Bible in order to defend the infallibility of the Pope and the Church!

True Religious Authority

Principle No. 1: There can be only one ultimate final authority.

The attempt to have two, three or more "final" authorities is impossible. Ultimately one will win out over the others. Just as there can be only one captain of the ship or one head of the home, even so there is only enough room in this universe for One Final authority (Matt. 6:24).

Principle No. 2: God is this one ultimate final authority. God has authority over all of life because He is the Creator and Sustainer of all things (Matt. 28:18).

Principle No. 3: God has revealed His mind and will in Scripture, and thus Scripture is the ultimate final authority. The Bible is not to be viewed as a collection of funny religious ideas from thousands of years ago. It is the present revelation of the heart and mind of the Creator toward man, His image bearer. It is the last court of appeal, the final judge, the ultimate arbitrator, the absolute standard of truth, justice, morals and beauty:

    a. Isa. 8:20
    b. Acts 17:2, 10-12
    c. 2 Tim. 3:16
    d. 2 Pet. 1:19-21

Principle No. 4: Nothing can override the authority of Scripture. Churches, popes, bishops, pastors, priests, human traditions, kings, presidents, congresses, civil judges, supreme courts and all human authorities must bow before the eternal Word of the Almighty. Nothing is to be added to or subtracted from the Word of our God.

    a. Deut. 4:2; 12:32
    b. Pro. 30:5-6
    c. John 10:35
    d. Rev. 22:18-19

Issue No. 3
The Holy Scriptures

The leaders of the Church of Rome, such as its priests, have always viewed themselves as "the Church," and the congregation as "the laity." This radical distinction has given them much power over the people.

When the priests say, "Only the Church can interpret the Bible," they are claiming exclusive rights to the Bible. In every cult, the leadership cannot stand the idea of "the laity" interpreting the Bible on their own. If they do, they will find things in the Bible which clearly contradict the doctrines and authority of the leadership. Historically, how did the priests of Rome prevent this?

First, they kept the Bible away from the people:

    a. They kept the Bible in languages which people could not understand: Latin, Greek or Hebrew.
    b. They outlawed any vernacular translations.
    c. They destroyed any translations by burning them.
    d. They put to death all who dared to translate it.
    e. They made it illegal to have or read a Bible.
    f. They substituted other books in its place:
       examples: prayer books, missals, devotionals, etc.

Second, they kept the people away from the Bible.

    a. They told them that the Bible was far too difficult for people to read.
    b. They warned them that the Bible was dangerous.
       It could destroy their faith and damn their soul.
    c. They discouraged people from learning how to read.
    d. They spoke out against the printing press. Why?
       1. The Reformation followed the invention of the printing press. The resulting accessibility of Scripture posed a tremendous threat to "the Church." This is why various Popes condemned the printing press as a work of the devil.
       2. Those countries where there was a high rate of literacy became Protestant. Thus, "public" education was denounced by "the Church" as evil.

3. While the Protestant countries became centers of education and industry, Catholic countries were kept ignorant and poor.

e. They threatened them with death if they did read it.

But has not "the Church" changed? Does it not now allow people to read the Bible?

Yes, in Protestant countries such as the United States, where there is freedom of religion and where Bibles can be purchased in every bookstore, it cannot do otherwise. But they cannot just let people read the Bible per se.

They have produced their own translations which:

1. Like the Jehovah's Witnesses mistranslate the original text to safeguard their doctrines (example Gen. 3:15).
2. place notes in the text which give the "official" interpretation (example: Rom. 5:1).

In "Catholic" countries the story is different. The Bible is still shunned as "dangerous." As documented by the Hefleys in their book, *By Their Blood: Christian Martyrs of the 20th Century* (Mott Media, 1979), wherever the Church of Rome has political power, it still does all it can to keep the Bible away from the people. The Roman Church has never retracted its official denial of religious freedom and its right to use violence to force people to accept its doctrines.

Issue No 4: Salvation

How can sinners find acceptance before a Holy God? On what basis can they have any hope of escaping His just wrath?

Romanist	Reformed
God accepts us on the basis of our performance of certain religious duties such as baptism, confirmation, confession, attending mass, good works, etc., as well as by grace.	God accepts us solely on the basis of the performance of Jesus Christ in His sinless life, good works, death and resurrection. Salvation is by grace alone through faith alone … in Christ alone.

Salvation—Not by Works but by Grace

The idea that our salvation depends on our participation in certain religious ceremonies and living a life of good works is the basis of all false religions past or present. The ancient Egyptian priests taught their people that their good deeds and their bad deeds would be weighed at death and that if the good outweighed the bad, they could go to paradise. This works mentality is the basis of all major religions, such as Buddhism, Hinduism and Islam. It is the basis of all the cults, such as Mormonism and the Jehovah's Witnesses. It is the basis of all liberal religion as found in mainline churches, such as the United Methodist churches.

If you search the history of religion from the beginning of time, you will discover that the religion of the Bible is the only religion that has ever taught that salvation is by the unmerited free grace of God. It is the only religion that teaches that God became a man in order to die in man's place and to do all that is necessary for man's salvation. It is the only religion that points man away from his own works to the works of Christ.

It is on this basis that we cannot view the Church of Rome as a Christian Church. It has always made salvation dependent on participation in its religious ceremonies and the doing of good works. It thus has the same view of religion that all pagan religions have.

What can we say about the issue of works vs. grace?

1. One problem with trying to earn your salvation by good works is that you can never know if you have done enough to tip the scales in your favor. Does one big sin outweigh a hundred small good deeds? What if you are one good deed short? What if you piled up a lot of good deeds all your life, but did a big sin just before you died?

2. The main problem with a works mentality is that it contradicts the plain teaching of Scripture.
   a. John 3:16
   b. John 6:28, 29
   c. Rom. 3:9-28
   d. Rom. 4:1-8, 16
   e. Rom. 5:1,2, 6-11
   f. Rom. 11:6
   g. Gal. 2:21; 5:4
   h. Eph. 2:1-10
   i. Tit. 3:4-7
   etc.

Issue No. 5: The Finished Work of Christ vs. the Mass
A. The O.T. Sacrifices (Leviticus)
   1. Numerous in number and kind.
   2. Continuously offered on altars by priests.
   3. The death of the sacrifice accomplished each time.
B. The Catholic Sacrifices (The Mass)
   1. Numerous in number and kind.
   2. Continuously offered on altars by priests.
   3. The death of the sacrifice accomplished each time.
C. The N.T. View of Christ's Death
   1. O.T. sacrifices were numerous and continuous because they did not spiritually or morally cleanse or save anyone (Heb. 10:1-4, 11).
   2. Their purpose was to predict, not to save (Col. 2:17).
   3. The book of Hebrews says that Christ's sacrifice was better than the O.T. sacrifices. Why?
      a. His sacrifice was singular, not numerous (Heb. 10:12, 14). One sacrifice.
      b. His sacrifice was final, not continuous (Heb. 9:24-28; 10:10, 18). For all of time.
      c. His death was accomplished once, not repeatedly (Heb. 9:26-28; Rom. 6:9-10). He will never die again.

Issue No. 6: The Priesthood of the Believers

In Catholic theology, the "priesthood" is composed of the officials of the Church such as the Pope, the bishops, cardinals, priests, etc. The congregation is called the "laity" or laymen and they are not viewed as priests.

Thus a Catholic priest is a mediator between God and His people. The priest is to hear their confession of sin and he is the one who "forgives" (absolves) them of sin and decides what works of penance they must perform. He is the one you must pay to get a suffering loved one out of purgatory. He can even sell you an "indulgence" or "time off" from suffering in purgatory—if the price is right.

At the Reformation, the Reformers revived the biblical doctrine of the priesthood of the believer. Once the common people understood this doctrine, the power of Rome was broken. The people realized that:

> They were the church.
> They were priests.
> Christ was the only mediator between God and man.
> They should confess their sins to God alone.
> Only God can forgive sins.
> Purgatory was a myth.
> Indulgences were a con-game.
> Only God decides who goes into Heaven or Hell.
> The Catholic priests could no longer rule by fear and intimidation. The people rose up and drove them out of the church!
> This historic doctrine of the Reformation must be clearly emphasized today as one of the chief issues between Romanists and Christians.

I. Basic Theological Definition
    Under the New Covenant, every Christian is a priest of the most High God (Isa. 61:1-6; 1 Pet. 2:5, 9; Rev. 1:6; 5:8, 9). All Christians have immediate access to God's presence through Christ, and thus have no need for human priests or mediators. There is now only one High Priest who is the mediator of the New Covenant, Jesus Christ our Lord (1 Tim. 2:5).

The High Priest and only Mediator is Jesus Christ (Heb. 2:17; 1 Tim. 2:5).	All Believers are priests and ministers of God (1 Pet. 2:5)

II. The Basic New Testament Principle
    All the privileges and responsibilities of the Old Testament priests now belong to all believers—except those privileges and responsibilities fulfilled or abrogated by Christ or delegated to the officers of the New Testament Church or explicitly denied them by the New Testament itself.

III. The Old Testament Priesthood

    A. The Privileges of Being a Priest
        1. Immediate access to God (2 Chron. 26:16-21)
        2. Enjoying the dignity of the office (2 Chron. 26:16-21)
        3. Exercising the authority of the office (Lev. 13:1-8)

    B. The Responsibilities of Being a Priest
        1. Offering up sacrifices (Lev. 1-7)
        2. Worshiping God (Heb. 9:6)
        3. Interceding on behalf of others (Lev. 16:17)
        4. Church discipline (Neh. 8:13-18)
        5. The ministry of the Word (Neh. 8:1-8)
        6. Seeing to it that the ceremonies were properly observed (Neh. 8:13-18)

IV. The Priesthood of the Believer in the New Testament

   A. Our Privileges as Priests

      1. Immediate access to God's presence (Matt. 27:51; Heb. 10:19-22)

      2. Enjoying the dignity of our office (1 Pet. 2:5, 9)

      3. Exercising our authority over:

         a. Sin (Matt. 16:19; cf. John 20:23; Acts 8:20-23)

         b. Satan (Lk. 10:17; Rom. 16:20; Acts 16:18)

   B. Our Responsibilities as Priests

      1. Offering up sacrifices to God:
        "Spiritual" not animal sacrifices (1 Pet. 2:5)

         a. The sacrifice of obedience (Psa. 4:5)

         b. The sacrifice of thanksgiving (Psa. 50:14, 23)

         c. The sacrifice of a broken spirit, a broken and contrite heart (Psa. 51:16-17)

         d. The sacrifice of our body and mind (Rom. 12:1-2)

         e. The sacrifice of the people we win to Christ (Rom. 15:16)

         f. The sacrifice of our gifts to support the Gospel Ministry (Phil. 4:18)

         g. The sacrifice of praise and thanksgiving (Heb. 13:15)

         h. The sacrifice of good works; i.e., sharing with others in need (Heb. 13:16)

      2. Worshiping God (Jn. 4:23, 24; Phil. 3:3)

      3. Interceding for others (1 Tim. 2:1; James 5:16)

      4. Church discipline (Matt. 18:15-17; 1 Cor. 5:4, 7, 11; 2 Thess. 3:14; Rom. 15:14)

      5. The ministry of the Word:

         a. To the Unsaved: Matt. 28:19, 20; Acts 8:4

         b. To the Saved: Col. 3:16; Rom. 14:19

      6. Participation in the New Testament sacraments

         a. Baptism: Receiving: Acts 2:41

                     Giving: Acts 8:12; 36-38

         b. Lord's Supper: Receiving: Acts 2:46; 20:7

                          Giving: Acts 2:46; 20:7

   C. The Significance of Our Priesthood

      It overthrows the Romish doctrines of prayers to the "saints" (and Mary), and of the priest being our mediator before God. It establishes once and for all time the believer's right to read and interpret the Bible and to pray directly to God through Christ as the only mediator between God and man (note: see the chapter on the Priesthood of the Believer for a fuller treatment).

Conclusion

The Reformation was not a mistake. It was not based on insignificant issues. The truths for which our Protestant fathers lived and died are just as important today as when they were first preached.

While we love Roman Catholics and do not hold any animosity against them personally, we must still say that their religion is not true according to the Bible. The only way for them or us or anyone to be saved is to trust in the person and work of Jesus as providing all that is necessary for our salvation. All other ground is sinking sand.

Chapter One Hundred Twenty-One

An Open Letter to Roman Catholic Apologists

Dear Catholic Apologists:

The *New Catholic Catechism* in Section 847 states that non-Catholics who "seek God with a sincere heart" and "try in their actions to do his will as they know it through the dictates of their conscience" will "achieve eternal salvation."

The *Catholic Catechism* in Sections 839-845 says that sincere people from non-Christian religions such as Jews, Hindus, Buddhists, Muslims, Taoists, animists, etc., will make it to heaven without the necessity of hearing of or believing in Catholicism. As long as they are sincere in their faith and live a good life, they will make it to heaven.

Various modern popes have also publicly stated that this means that sincere people who have no religious convictions such as agnostics, atheists, skeptics, etc., will make it to heaven without the necessity of hearing of or believing in Catholicism. As long as they are sincere and live a good life, they will make it to heaven.

The *Catholic Catechism* also says in Section 838 that the Orthodox, Evangelicals, Pentecostals, Lutherans, Presbyterians, Baptists, etc., will also make it to heaven without hearing of or believing in the Roman Catholic Church. As long as they are sincere in their faith and live a good life, they will make it to heaven.

Peter Kreeft, a well-known Catholic scholar, in his book, *Ecumenical Jihad* (Ignatius, 1996), describes an out-of-body experience during which he met Buddha, Confucius, and Muhammad in heaven (pgs. 79f). He also sees the Orthodox, Jews and Evangelicals making it to heaven without believing in the Roman Catholic Church. This has a profound impact on the question of the legitimate existence of Catholic apologetics. Since your church teaches that non-Catholics can make it to heaven without converting to Catholicism, we non-Catholics request that you stop trying to convert us. Why?

1. We do not need to hear of or believe in your church to make it to heaven. There is thus no rational basis for your existence.
2. Our "ignorance" of Catholicism is our salvation according to your Catechism. Thus, if you try to convert us, you will endanger our souls! Your Catechism in Section 846 states that people go to hell if they come to believe that the Roman Catholic Church is the true religion but "refuse to enter it." Thus, you may cause us to lose our salvation if you convince us that your religion is true. So, please leave us alone. We are doing fine without you.
3. Section 846 also states that people who believe that the Roman Catholic Church is the true religion but "refuse to remain in it," will go to hell. Those who leave the Roman Church and then are sincere in their new beliefs and live a good life will still make it to heaven. But, if you con-

vince them that the Roman Catholic Church is the true church, you will endanger their immortal soul! So, leave them alone! As sincere ex-Catholics, they are going to heaven. Don't damn them by trying to convert them back to popery.

4. Section 856 of the Catechism states that a "respectful dialogue" with non-Catholics may be done. But you have failed to be "respectful." Instead, you have repeatedly engaged in rude and offensive "Protestant bashing." If Evangelicals are only "separated brethren," then stop demonizing them.

Conclusion

Since, according to your church, we non-Catholics can get to heaven without becoming Roman Catholics, there is no need for you to exist. And, since we are quite happy in our own religion, we do not want you to try to convert us. Catholic apologetics will do more harm than good. It is thus time for you to seek gainful employment elsewhere. We suggest you put your talents to work selling insurance, cars or shoes.

Ten Reasons Why I Am Not a Roman Catholic

Having been invited on several occasions to become a Roman Catholic, I have thought deeply on this issue for many years. Now, it is not my intent to offend sincere Roman Catholics. All of us are traveling on our own spiritual road. But, for people like me, all roads do not lead to Rome!

While there are many more reasons why I cannot convert to Catholicism, the following 10 reasons are of a practical nature drawn from my personal experience. Your experience may be different. But I can only speak to what I have seen and heard over 50 years of life.

Reason No. 1: Since the modern Roman Catholic Church clearly teaches that it is not necessary to become a Roman Catholic to go to heaven, why then should I bother joining it? If popes, priests, Mary, the saints, the mass, statues, novenas, etc., are not essential for salvation, and I can make it to heaven through my own sincere faith in whatever I choose to believe, I simply don't see why I should waste my time converting to Romanism. I am OK where I am!

Reason No. 2: The authority of the Roman Catholic Church seems completely arbitrary to me. I am old enough to remember Catholic friends telling me that they were in danger of hell fire if they ate meat on Friday. Then the rule was dropped.

"Outside of the Church, there is no salvation" was a big doctrine at one time. A lot of Protestants were killed during the Inquisition under that dogma. But that has been changed to: "Outside of the Church, there is lots of salvation." Which is right?

I remember how my Catholic landlady had a royal fit when the pope announced that her favorite saint, for whom she and her local church were named, was no longer listed as a saint. They even changed the name of her church!

Obviously, the Bible and Catholic tradition cannot be cited as the authority for the above changes. So, when push comes to shove, the supposed twin authority of Scripture and Tradition is a myth. The true authority lies in the "Church," conceived of as the contemporary leaders beginning with the Pope at the top and working itself down to the local parish priest.

What this means is that the present generation of Catholic leaders can do whatever they want. They don't need any higher authority because they are the highest authority on earth. If the present pope wished, he could declare Mary to be the fourth member of the Godhead. Past popes did not need Scripture or Tradition to teach that she was sinless or that she ascended into heaven. Arbitrary authority produces arbitrary laws and doctrines.

Reason No. 3: The Roman Catholic Church cannot give me an infallible list of infallible papal decrees. Those Catholic apologists who come up with a list cannot get their list declared infallible by the Magisterium. Without an infallible list drawn up by the infallible Church, "infallibility" means nothing.

Reason No. 4: The Roman Church cannot give me an infallible list of infallible interpretations of specific passages in the Bible. Thus all the interpretations given by popes, bishops, prelates, priests, and apologists are not "infallible" per se, but only their own private opinion of what a specific passage means. Why then, is the Protestant condemned for doing the same thing?

Reason No. 5: It always amused me to no end when a Catholic apologist asked the people in the audience to turn to a passage in their Bible as proof for some Catholic doctrine. How Protestant of him! Are not such appeals nothing more or less than the practice of sola scriptura? If you appeal to the Bible as your authority for popery, this means the Bible is a higher authority than popery.

Reason No. 6: The doctrine of papal infallibility is an exercise in circular reasoning. A pope is infallible whenever he is infallible. As soon as you catch a pope in error, he is excused because he was fallible at that time. Thus you cannot prove or disprove papal infallibility.

Reason No. 7: Most Catholics do in fact worship and adore the statues and relics of Mary and the saints. Thus, they are guilty of idolatry. It does not matter if a theologian uses different Latin words to defend the practice. The average Catholic does not know of or care about such fine distinctions in Latin. They kiss and adore the statues of the Virgin Mary or the saints as sincerely and fervently as a Hindu does the idols of his gods and goddesses.

Reason No. 8: I have never heard the Gospel preached in a Roman Catholic Church. In 40 years, I have not found a single Roman Catholic apologist who understood the grace of God. All their hope of heaven is based on their being a loyal Catholic and a good person. Either the Roman Church does not preach the Gospel or it has utterly failed to teach it to the average member. I choose to go where the Gospel is preached with clarity.

Reason No. 9: The pagan rituals and superstitious practices of Catholicism are a big turnoff to me. They are not only tolerated but encouraged and defended.

> Candles, incense, beads, and bells,
> Priests, nuns and popes from hell;
> All these things mean naught to me,
> For Sovereign grace has set me free.

Reason No. 10: I am complete in Jesus Christ (Col. 2:10). Thus I find no need for popery in any way. Since Jesus died for my sins, rose for my justification, and intercedes for me in heaven, I do not need the pope, priests, masses, Mary, the saints, indulgences, pilgrimages, etc.

> Jesus paid it all!
> All to Him I owe.
> Sin had left a crimson stain;
> But Jesus washed it white as snow.

Chapter One Hundred Twenty-Three
The Challenge of Islam

Introduction

The following material is to be used in conjunction with Robert Morey's book *Islamic Invasion*. These supporting documents are taken from the Qur'an and the Hadith, which are viewed by Muslim authorities as the "first" and "second" inspiration.

According to Muslim traditions, Allah wrote the Qur'an in pure Arabic in heaven on a large stone table. The angel Gabriel took the table of the Qur'an and made Muhammad recite it. His recitations were memorized or written down by others on whatever objects were on hand such as sticks, stones, bones, palm leaves, etc.

After Muhammad died, various conflicting Qur'ans were produced. It was the Caliph Uthman who made his own version of the Qur'an the official one (see Bukhari's Hadith, Vol. 1, pg. 56, No. 63). He later burned all the other conflicting Qur'ans. The Qur'an sold today is the Uthman version.

The Hadith is the record of the teachings and examples of Muhammad not found in the Qur'an and are thus authoritative for all Muslims. To deny the Hadith is to be guilty of apostasy under Islamic Law. The greatest of all Hadith scholars was Bukhari.

Since most people do not have access to the Qur'an or the Hadith, we have supplied some of the material here. It would be impossible to supply all the supporting documents as this would run into hundreds of pages. For more details on the history of the Qur'an and the Hadith, see the book *Islamic Invasion*.

The Challenge

Surah 2:23: And if you are in doubt as to what we have revealed from time to time to our servants, then produce a Sura like unto it.

The Doctrine of Abrogation

Surah 2:106: None of our revelations do we abrogate or cause to be forgotten, but we substitute something better or similar.

Muslim Terms Before Islam

Surah 2:127-128: And remember Abraham and Ishmael raised the foundations of the House (with this prayer) … "Our Lord! Make of us Muslims…"

Surah 2:132: And this is the legacy that Abraham left to his sons, and so did Jacob; "Allah has chosen the Faith for you; then die not except in the Faith of Islam."

Jihad

Surah 2:190-194: Fight in the cause of Allah against those who fight you … and kill them wherever you catch them … if they fight you, kill them. Such is the reward of those who suppress the Faith…. And fight them on until there is no more tumult or oppression, and there prevail justice and faith in Allah.

Surah 2:216: Fighting is prescribed for you.

Surah 2:244: Fight in the cause of Allah.

Surah 4:74: Let those who fight in the cause of Allah, who sell the life of this world for the

Hereafter, to him who fighteth in the cause of Allah.... Soon shall We give him a reward of great value.

Surah 4:89: If they turn apostates, seize them and kill them wherever you find them.

Surah 4:91: Seize them and kill them wherever you get them.

Surah 5:33: The punishment of those who wage war against Allah and his apostle ... they shall be slaughtered, or crucified, or their hands and feet shall be struck off alternately, or they shall be banished from the land.

Surah 5:51: O ye who believe! Take not the Jews and the Christians for your friends.

On Jesus

Surah 5:72-73: They do blaspheme who say: Allah is Christ the son of Mary.... They do blaspheme who say: Allah is one of three (gods) ... Christ the son of Mary was no more than an apostle.

Ask No Questions

Surah 5:101: Ask not questions about things which, if made plain to you may cause you trouble.... Some people before you did ask such questions, and on account lost their faith (in Islam).

The Greatest Deceiver

Surah 3:54: The greatest Deceiver (Makara) of them all is Allah.

Beating Wives

Surah 4:34: Men are the managers of the affairs of women ... those you fear may be rebellious admonish; banish them to their couches, and beat them.

People Turning Into Monkeys, Rats and Pigs

The Qur'an

Surah 2:65: And you know well those among you who transgressed in the matter of the Sabbath: We said to them: "Become apes! Despised and rejected."

Surah 7:163-166: Ask them about the town which stood by the sea shore. Behold! They sinned in regard to the Sabbath. On their Sabbath day, the fish swam up to them and stuck their heads out of the water [to tempt the people to catch them]. But the fish did not do this on the day that was not the Sabbath. In this way We tempted them because they were devoted to sinning. When some of them said, "Why do you bother preaching to people whom Allah will destroy or inflict with a terrible punishment?" The preachers responded, "To fulfill our obligation to their Lord and they might yet fear Him." When they ignored the warnings given to them, We saved those who avoided evil, but We punished the evil-doers with a grievous punishment because they were devoted to sinning. When in their insolence they transgressed the warnings, We said to them, "Become monkeys! Despised and rejected."

The Hadith

Bukhari, Vol. IV, chapter 32, p. 415: The statement of Allah: And ask them (O Muhammad) about the town that was by the sea, when they transgressed in the matter of the Sabbath (1) when their fish came to them only on the Sabbath day and did not come... "Become monkeys! Despised and rejected."

Bukhari, Vol. IV, No. 524, pg. 333: The Prophet said, "A group of Israelites were lost. Nobody knows what they did. But I do not see them except that they were cursed and transformed into rats, for if you put the milk of a she-camel in front of a rat, it will not drink it, but if the milk of a sheep is put in front of it, it will drink it.

(1) It was illegal for the Israelites to eat the meat or drink the milk of camels, while they were allowed to eat the meat and drink the milk of sheep. The prophet inferred from the rat's habit that some of the Israelites had been transformed into rats.

(2) Later on the prophet was informed through Inspiration about the fate of those Israelites: They were transformed into pigs and monkeys.

Mohammed's Inspiration

The Hadith

Mohammed would hear ringing in his ears; his heart would beat rapidly; his face turn red; his breathing would become labored; he would fall to the ground or lie down; he would shake; his eyes would open wide; his lips tremble; spit drool from the corners of his mouth; he would sweat profusely; he saw and heard things no one else ever saw or heard; he would sometimes make a snoring noise like that of a camel; and he would be covered with a sheet.

Vol I, Nos. 1, 2, 3, 4
Vol. II, chapter 16 (pg. 354), 544
Vol. III, Nos. 17, 829
Vol. IV, Nos. 95, 438, 458, 461
Vol. V, Nos. 170, 462, 618, 659
Vol. VI, Nos. 447, 448, 468, 478, 481, 508

A Test of Prophethood

The Hadith

Bukhari Vol. IV, No 546: When Abdullah bin Salam heard of the arrival of the Prophet at Medina, he came to him and said, "I am going to ask you about three things which nobody knows except a prophet:

1. What is the first sign of the Hour (i.e. the end of the world)?
2. What will be the first meal taken by the people of Paradise?
3. Why does a child resemble its father and why does it resemble its maternal uncle?"

Allah's Apostle said, "Gabriel just now told me of their answers."

Abdullah said, "He (i.e. Gabriel), from amongst all the angels, is the enemy of the Jews."

Allah's Apostle said, "The first sign of the Hour will be a fire that will bring together the people from the East to the West; the first meal of the people of Paradise will be extralobe of fish-liver. As for the resemblance of the child to its parents: If a man has sexual intercourse with his wife and gets his discharge first, the child will resemble the father, and if the woman gets her discharge first, the child will resemble her."

The Seal of Prophethood

The Quran

Surah 33:40: Mohammed is not the father of any of your men, but (he is) the Apostle of Allah and the Seal of the Prophets (rests upon him).

The Hadith

Bukhari Vol. I, No. 189; No. 741: Narrated As-Sa'ib Yazid: ... I stood behind him (i.e.

Allah's Apostle) and saw the Seal of Prophethood between his shoulders, and it was like the "zir-al-Hijla" (the size of a button on a small tent or a partridge egg.

Bukhari Vol. IV, No. 741: Narrated As Sab'ib bin Yazid: ... standing behind him (i.e. Allah's Apostle) I saw the Seal (of the Prophets) between his shoulders.

Muslim Vol. IV, No. 5790-5793; Chapter CMLXXIX: The Fact Pertaining to the Seal of His Prophethood, Its Characteristic Feature and Its Location on His Body.

Jabir b. Samura reported: "I saw the Seal on his back as if it were a pigeon's egg." This hadith has been narrated on the authority of Simak with the same chain of transmitters.

As-Sa'ib b. Yazid reported: My mother's sister took me to Allah's Messenger and ... I stood behind him and I saw the Seal between his shoulders.

Abdullah b. Sarjis reported: I saw Allah's Apostle and ate with him bread and meat.... I then went after him and saw the Seal of Prophethood between his shoulders on the left side of this shoulder having spots on it like moles.

The Story of a Giant She-Camel Prophet

The Qur'an

Surah VII:73: To the Thamud people.... This she-camel of Allah is a sign unto you: So let her graze on Allah's earth and do not let her come to any harm, or you will be seized by a terrible punishment.

Surah VII:77: Then they ham-strung the she-camel and insolently defied the order of their Lord ... so the earthquake took them unawares and they lay prostrate in their homes in the morning.

Surah LIV:23: The Thamud rejected their Warners.

Surah LIV:27: For We sent the she-camel as a trial for them.

Surah LIV:29: But they called to their companion and he took a sword in his hand and ham-strung her.

Surah LIV:30-31: Ah! How terrible was my penalty and my warning! For We sent against them a single mighty blast and they became like the dry stubble used by one who pens cattle.

Surah XCI:11: The Thamud people rejected their prophets through their inordinate wrongdoing.

Surah XCI:13-14: But the apostle of Allah said to them, "It is a she-camel of Allah! Do not hinder her from drinking." But they rejected him and ham-strung her. So their Lord, on account of this crime, destroyed the traces of them and made them all suffer equally.

The Companions of the Cave

The Qur'an

Surah XVIII:9-25: Do you understand that the Companions of the Cave and of the Inscription were wonders among our signs? Behold, the youths entered the Cave and said, "Our Lord, bestow upon us your mercy and deal with us in the right way." We drew a veil over their ears for a number of years in the Cave. Then we awakened them in order to test which of the two parties was best at calculating the number of years they had stayed in the Cave. We relate to you their story in truth.... So they stayed in their Cave three hundred years and some add nine more years to that.

The Man Who Died for a Hundred Years

The Qur'an

Surah II:259: Or take the similitude of one who passed by a village in ruins to its roofs. He said, "Oh! How shall Allah restore it to life after its death?" But Allah caused him to die for 100 years. The he raised him up and said, "How long have you stayed here?" He said, "A day or a part of a day." He said, "No, you have been here for 100 years! But look at your food and your drink, they show no signs of age. And look at your donkey! We have made you a sign unto the people. Look further at the bones (of your body) how We clothed them with flesh."

A 90 Foot Adam

The Hadith

Bukhari Vol. IV, No. 543: Narrated Abu Huraira: The Prophet said, "Allah created Adam, making him 60 cubits tall."

No Dogs or Cats Allowed!

The Hadith

Bukhari Vol. IV, No. 539: Narrated Abu Talha: The Prophet said, "Angels do not enter a house which has either a dog or a picture in it."

Bukhari Vol. IV, No. 540: Narrated Abdullah bin Umar: Allah's Apostle ordered that the dogs should be killed.

Muslim Vol. I, No. 551: Ibn Mughaffal reported: The Messenger of Allah ordered killing of the dogs, and then said: "What about them, i.e. other dogs?" and then granted concession to keep the dog for hunting and the dog for the herd and said: "When the dog licks the utensil, wash it seven times and rub it with dirt the eighth time."

Muslim Vol. I, No. 552: A hadith like this has been narrated from Shu'ba with the same chain of transmitters except for the fact that in the hadith transmitted by Yahya those words are: "He (the Holy Prophet) gave concession in the case of the dog for looking after the herd, for hunting and for watching the cultivated land," and there is no mention of this addition (i.e. concession in case of watching the cultivated lands) except in the hadith transmitted by Yahya.

Footnote No. 486: The dog is one of the unclean beasts according to Islam and eating its flesh is forbidden and its keeping in the house as a pet is also prohibited for the Muslims. They have, however, been permitted to keep dogs for hunting, herding and watching.

Chapter DCXVIII: The Price of a Dog ... and the Selling of a Cat Forbidden

Muslim Vol. III, No. 3803: Abu Mas'ud al-Ansari reported that Allah's Messenger forbade the charging of price of the dog.

Muslim Vol. III, No. 3806: Khadji reported Allah's Messenger as saying: "The price of a dog is evil."

Muslim Vol. III, No. 3808: Abu Zubair said: I asked Jabir about the price of a dog and a cat; he said, "Allah's Messenger disapproved of that."

Muslim Vol. III, No. 3809: Ibn 'Umar reported Allah's Messenger giving command for killing dogs.

Muslim Vol. III, No. 3810: Ibn 'Umar reported: Allah's Messenger ordered us to kill dogs and he sent men to the corners of Medina that they (i.e. the dogs) should be killed.

Muslim Vol. III, No. 3813: Abu Zubair heard Jabir b. Abdullah saying: Allah's Messenger ordered us to kill dogs and we carried out this order so much that we also killed the dog coming with a woman from the desert.... He said, "It is your duty to kill the jet-black dog having two spots, for it is the devil."

(See also Muslim Vol. III, Nos. 3814-3829)

Satan in the Nose Overnight

The Hadith

Bukhari Vol. IV, No. 516: "Satan stays in the upper part of the nose all night."

Footnote (1) We should believe that Satan actually stays in the upper part of one's nose, though we cannot perceive how, for this is related to the unseen world of which we know nothing except what Allah tells us through his Apostle Mohammed.

Muslim Vol. I, No. 462: Abu Huraira reported: The Apostle of Allah said, "When any one of you awakes from sleep and performs ablution, he must clean his nose three times, for the devil spends the night in the interior of his nose."

Playing Chess Forbidden

The Hadith

Muslim Vol. IV, No. 5612, Chapter CMXLVI: It Is Prohibited to Play Chess

Allah's Apostle said, "He who played chess is like one who dyed his hand with the flesh and blood of swine."

Non-Muslims Have Seven Intestines!

The Hadith

Muslim Vol. III, Nos. 5113, Chapter DCCCLXII: A Believer Eats in One Intestine Whereas a Non-Believer Eats in Seven Intestines.

Ibn Umar reported Allah's Messenger as saying that a non-Muslim eats in seven intestines while a Muslim eats in one intestine.

(See also Nos. 5114-5120)

Don't Pray Looking Up

The Hadith

Muslim Vol. I, Nos. 863, Chapter CLXXIII: It Is Forbidden to Lift One's Eyes Toward the Sky in Prayer

Abu Huraira reported Allah's Apostle saying: "People should avoid lifting their eyes towards the sky while supplicating in prayer, otherwise their eyes would be snatched away."

The Wondrous Wings of a Fly

The Hadith

Bukhari Vol. IV, No. 537: Narrated Abu Huraira: The Prophet said, "If a house fly falls into the drink of anyone of you, he should dip it (into the drink) because one of its wings has a disease and the other wing has the cure (for that disease).

Bukhari Vol. VII, No. 673: Narrated Abu Huraira: Allah's Apostle said, "If a fly falls in the vessel of any of you, let him dip all of it into the vessel and then throw it away, for in one of its wings there is a disease and in the other wing there is healing."

The Qur'an Forgotten by the Prophet

The Hadith

Bukhari Vol. VI, No. 558: Narrated Aisha: Allah's Apostle heard a man reciting the Qur'an at night, and said, "May Allah bestow His mercy on him, as he has reminded me of such and such verses of such and such Suras, which I was caused to forget."

Bukhari Vol. VI, No. 562: Narrated Aisha: The Prophet heard a reciter reciting the Qur'an in the mosque one night. The Prophet said, "May Allah bestow his mercy on him, as he has reminded me of such and such verses of such and such Suras, which I missed."

The Setting of the Sun

The Qur'an

Surah 18:86: When he (i.e. Zul-qarnain) reached the setting of the sun, he found that it set in a pond of murky water.

Mohammed Bewitched!

The Hadith

Bukhari Vol. VII, No. 658: Narrated Aisha: A man called Labid bin al-A'sam from the tribe of Bani Zaraiq worked magic on Allah's Apostle until Allah's Apostle started imagining that he had done a thing that he had not really done.

Bukhari Vol. VII, No. 660: Narrated Aisha: Magic was worked on Allah's Apostle so that he used to think that he had had sexual relations with his wives while he actually had not.... "He is under the effect of magic."

Bukhari Vol, VII, No. 661: Narrated Aisha: Magic was worked on Allah's Apostle so that he began to imagine that he had done something although he had not.

The Prophet Had Lice

The Hadith

Bukhari Vol. IX, No. 130: One day the Prophet visited her (i.e. the wife of Ubada bin As-Samit) and she provided him with food and started looking for lice in his head.

Drinking Camel Urine

The Hadith

Bukhari Vol. I, No. 234: The Prophet ordered them to go to the herd of camels and to drink their milk and urine.

The Crying Palm Tree

The Hadith

Bukhari Vol. II, No. 41: Narrated Jabir bin Abdullah: The Prophet used to stand by a stem of a date-palm tree. When the pulpit was placed for him we heard the stem crying like a pregnant she-camel till the Prophet got down from the pulpit and placed his hand over it.

Bukhari Vol. IV, No. 783: Narrated Ibn Umar: The Prophet used to deliver his sermons while standing beside the trunk of a date-palm. When he had the pulpit made, he used it instead. The trunk started crying and the Prophet went to it, rubbing his hand over it (to stop its crying).

The Fingers of Life

The Hadith

Bukhari Vol. I, No. 170: He put his hand in that pot and ordered the people to perform ablution from it. I saw the water springing out from underneath his fingers.

Bukhari Vol. IV, No. 773: I saw water flowing from underneath his fingers.

Bukhari Vol IV, No. 776: So he placed his hand in that pot and the water started flowing among his fingers like springs.

Shouting Food

The Hadith

Bukhari Vol. IV, No. 779: ... no doubt, we heard the meal glorifying Allah, when it was being eaten (by Allah's Apostle).

600 Wings

The Hadith

Bukhari Vol. VI, No. 380: Mohammed has seen Gabriel with six hundred wings.

The Devil Urinates Into the Ear

The Hadith

Bukhari Vol. II, No. 245: If one sleeps and does not offer the prayer, Satan urinates in his ears. Narrated Abdullah: The Prophet said, "Satan urinated in his ears."

No Garlic or Onions Allowed

The Hadith

Bukhari Vol. I, No. 812: What has been said about uncooked garlic or onion. And the statement of the Prophet: "Whoever has eaten garlic or onion because of hunger or otherwise should not come near our mosque" (see also Nos. 813-815).

Bukhari Vol. VII, No. 362: Narrated Abdul Aziz: It was said to Anas, "What did you hear the Prophet saying about garlic?" Anas replied, "Whoever has eaten garlic should not approach our mosque."

Bukhari Vol. VII, No. 363: Narrated Jabir bin Abdullah: The Prophet said, "Whoever has eaten garlic or onion should keep away from us."

Yawning Comes From Hell

The Hadith

Vol. IV, No. 509: Narrated Abu Huraira: The Prophet said, "Yawning is from Satan."

Hell-Fire for Women

The Hadith

Bukhari Vol. I, No. 28: The Prophet said, "I was shown the Hell-fire and that the majority of its dwellers were women who were ungrateful."

Bukhari Vol. I, No. 301: Allah's Apostle ... said, "O women! Give alms, as I have seen that the majority of the dwellers of Hell-fire were you women.... I have not seen anyone more deficient in intelligence and religion than you."

Bukhari Vol. II, No. 161: The Prophet then said ... "I also saw the Hell-fire and I had never seen such a horrible sight. I saw that most of the inhabitants were women."

No Assurance of Salvation

The Hadith

Bukhari Vol. V, No. 266: The Prophet said, "By Allah, even though I am the Apostle of Allah, yet I do not know what Allah will do to me."

What Made the Prophet Afraid?

The Hadith

Bukhari Vol. II, No. 167: The sun eclipsed and the Prophet jumped up terrified that it might be the Hour [of Judgment].

Healing Palm Leaves

The Hadith

Bukhari Vol. II, No. 443: The Prophet passed by two graves and those persons (in the graves) were being tortured.... He then took a green leaf of a date-palm tree, split it into two pieces and fixed one on each grave. The people said, "O Allah's Apostle! Why have you done so?" He replied, "I hope that their punishment may be lessened until they (i.e. the palm leaves) became dry."

What Color was Mohammed?

The Hadith

Bukhari Vol. 1, No. 63: While we were sitting with the Prophet in the mosque, a man came riding on a camel. He made his camel kneel down in the mosque, tied its foreleg and then said, "Who among you is Mohammed?" At that time the Prophet was sitting among us leaning on his arm. We replied, "The white man reclining on his arm."

Bukhari Vol. II, No. 122: Mohammed is described as "a white person."

Bukhari Vol. II, No. 141: When the Prophet raised his arms in prayer "the whiteness of his armpits became visible."

Bukhari Vol. IV, No. 744: Narrated Ismasil bin Abi Khalid: I heard Abu Juhaifa saying, "I saw the Prophet and Al-Hasan bin Ali resembled him." I said to Abu Juhaifa, "Describe him (i.e. Allah's Apostle) for me." He said, "He was white and his beard was black with some white hair in it. He promised to give us 13 young she-camels, but he died before we got them."

What Color Was the Apostle's Hair?

The Hadith

Bukhari Vol. I, No. 167: About the dyeing of hair with henna. Without a doubt I saw Allah's Prophet dyeing his hair with it and that is why I like to dye my hair with it (see also Vol. IV, No. 747 and Vol. VII, No. 785).

A Child Bride

The Hadith

Bukhari Vol. V, No. 234: Narrated Aisha: The Prophet was engaged to me when I was a girl six years old.... I was playing in a swing with some of my girl friends.... Unexpectedly Allah's Apostle came to me in the afternoon and my mother handed me over to him. At that time I was a girl of nine years of age.

Bukhari Vol. V, No. 236: The Prophet ... married Aisha when she was a girl of six years of age and consummated that marriage when she was nine years old.

Chapter One Hundred Twenty-Four
Fact Sheet for Muslims

Introduction

The teachings of Muhammad are making their way into Western society. In years past, contact between Muslims and Christians was limited to Black Muslims selling newspapers on a street corner or Muslim students coming here to study. But two things have radically changed this situation.

First, every year thousands of Muslims are immigrating to the West from such places as Pakistan. They are here to stay and they need our respect and acceptance.

Second, oil-rich Middle Eastern countries such as Saudi Arabia are using billions of oil dollars to convert Westerners to Islam. They have been building thousands of mosques all over the United States, England and Europe in anticipation of millions of converts. They are giving a thousand dollars to any South African black who converts to Islam, and then pay him even more for each person he brings with him!

The Issues

The issues which divide Christianity and Islam are very clear. When the historical and factual errors of the Qur'an and the shortcomings of Muhammad are pointed out by scholars, this should not be taken as a personal insult by Muslims. When Muslims contradict the Bible and state that Jesus Christ was not the Son of God, that Jesus was never crucified and that Jesus cannot save anybody, should their attacks on Christianity be taken as a personal insult by Christians? We hope not! After all, to disagree with someone is not the same as to insult someone.

I. Muhammad taught that Christians believe in three gods named the Father, the Mother (Mary), and the Son (Jesus) (Sura 116). Yet, the truth is that no Christian church has ever taught such a doctrine. Christians have always believed in one God eternally existing in three persons: the Father, the Son and the Holy Spirit. How can Muhammad be an infallible prophet and the Qur'an inspired by God when they make such a blunder remains one of the great problems facing Islam.

II. Muhammad also denied that Jesus was the Son of God, that Jesus died on the cross and that Jesus was the Savior. He taught that Jesus was only one of many prophets of which he, Muhammad, was the greatest. Yet, how could he be greater than Jesus Christ? Jesus was born of a virgin and was sinless in nature and the doer of mighty miracles such as raising the dead. But there was nothing superior about Muhammad's birth or life. He never made the lame to walk, the blind to see or the dead to live. Allah even commanded him to repent of his many sins. How then can he be greater than the Christ?

III. The contrast between Jesus and Muhammad could not be greater. While Jesus forbade the use of force to convert people (Matthew 26:51-54), Muhammad commanded his followers in the Qur'an (Sura IX.5) to force people to accept Islam by war, plunder, slavery or the threat of death!

IV. The Qur'an itself is filled with every kind of self-contradiction, historical and scientific error known to man. In Sura XVIII.82-98, the Qur'an tells us that Alexander the Great was a believer in the one true God, and that he lived through two generations of men. Since Alexander was a pagan and died when only 33 in 323 B.C., the Qur'an is obviously in error.

The use of circular reasoning on the part of Muslims cannot erase these errors. To argue, "the Qur'an is inspired, therefore it cannot contain any errors," is to put the cart before the horse.

A rational person cannot accept the Qur'an or any other "bible" if it has historical and factual errors. This holds for Christians, Mormons, Jews or Hindus as well as for Muslims. Thus our Muslim friends should be willing to let the evidence decide the Truth.

V. Most Western scholars have always stated that Muhammad had mental problems. He was given to fits and spells as a child, during which he claimed to have seen and talked to desert spirits including a goddess.

VI. He married over a dozen women, including taking another man's wife under "divine" command (Sura XXXIII.37-38). He even married a little girl 6 or 7 years of age.

That Muhammad had 13 wives is not denied by Muslim scholars. That Muhammad took a girl 6 or 7 years old as one of his wives is admitted by such Muslim historians as:

> Ibn Hisham (vol. iii, p. 94)
> Ibn Athir (vol ii, pp. 117,118)
> Mishkat (pp. 262, 272)

As to taking another man's wife, Muslim writer Kausar Niazi admits: "The Holy Prophet never married another man's wife except that of Zayd" (*Islam and the West*, p. 17).

VII. In terms of his beliefs, Muhammad held a strange combination of ideas from the Old Testament, the New Testament and his own pagan background. He never freed himself from such pagan rituals as running seven times around the "Black Stone" in Mecca. This stone is a rock which the pagans in Muhammad's day worshiped as a god who "fell" from Heaven. This is not known by most Muslims.

Haykal's *The Life of Mohammed*, which is a Muslim work, states that the "black rock" or Ka'bah was "a pantheon full of statues for idol worship." The rocks "appeared to have fallen from Heaven" and were "worshipped as divinities" (p. 30).

The pagan ceremony included a pilgrimage to the rock, running around it seven times and praying toward it. This is what all Muslim scholars admit. That Muhammad took a pagan ceremony and changed its meaning does not alter the fact of the pagan origin of why Muslims pray toward Mecca, make a pilgrimage to it and run around it seven times. This is also stated in the *Encyclopedia Britannica*, vol. 15, p. 152, under "Mecca."

VIII. While a Muslim must work his way to paradise by repeating the Muslim prayer five times a day, fasting, giving money and going on a pilgrimage to Mecca, the Christian believes he is saved by grace alone through faith alone in Christ alone.

IX. The United States is a great country because it has a Constitution which guarantees civil rights to all beliefs. Islamic law does not recognize non-Muslims as having any civil rights. This is why the death penalty is mandated for any Muslim who chooses to convert to some other religion. This is why Jews and Christians are often put to death and their goods plundered in many Muslim countries such as Egypt as well as Iran.

Conclusion

America has room for all religions as long as they respect the lives, properties and rights of others. The conflict between Christ and Muhammad cannot be ignored. Either Jesus is Lord or Muhammad was a false prophet. But Muhammad is dead, while Jesus is alive forevermore.

An Open Letter to Muslims

Dear Muslim Friend,

In an age when most people do not believe that Truth exists or that it is worth their time and effort to seek it, the mere fact that you have sought us out reveals that you want to know the Truth about who and what God is and how to find acceptance before Him.

The Truth is important because it sets us free from ignorance and superstition. And, once free from these things, Truth can then set us free from the fear of death and bondage to sin.

We too share the same desire and love of the Truth that you have. Let us then search for the Truth together as fellow travelers on the road of life.

Religious Truth Claims

All religions make Truth claims, i.e. they all claim to tell us the Truth about God, man, salvation, and the universe. Yet, they do not make the same claims. One religion may claim that man is God or that the universe is God, while another religion may claim that man and the universe were created by God and are not God or gods at all. One religion may claim that there is only one God while another religion may claim that there are millions or even billions of gods.

Obviously, the religions of this world make different Truth claims. In fact, they contradict each other on almost every point. This is a sad but true fact of life that we both already understand and believe.

Yet, we all know people who claim: "All religions worship the same God." How foolish! How naive! The Hindu who worships millions of gods and goddesses is not worshiping the Allah of the Muslims. The Christian who worships one God in three Persons: the Father, the Son and the Holy Spirit, is not worshiping the Allah of the Muslims either. Each religion makes its own unique claim about the nature of deity.

What Is a Religion?

By definition, a religion is a worldview that tells us what to believe and how to live. It is composed of ideas, i.e. doctrines, and values, i.e. morals. A religion wants us to accept certain ideas as the True explanation of all that is. Intellectual assent to these ideas is what constitutes "faith."

But a religion not only wants our intellectual assent that certain ideas or concepts are true, it also wants us to obey a list of commands and prohibitions. In other words, a religion expects us to obey its laws and observe its rites and rituals.

Is Islam a Religion?

Is Islam a religion? Of course it is. It puts forth various ideas that it claims to be the Truth, and it demands that all men believe them. It also demands that all men obey its laws and observe its rituals.

Common Ground

In order for us to dialogue, we have to begin with ideas that we both accept as true. The common ground that we have is the truth that "Islam is a religion." Do you accept that statement? We do. It seems self-evident to us that Islam is a religion. If you do not accept this first point, then the rest of this letter will be a waste of time.

Question No. 1: Is Islam a religion? Yes ____ No____

Islam's Truth Claims

Since we all agree that Islam is a religion, then we must also agree that it asks us to believe certain ideas or concepts as the truth. These ideas are its Truth claims. In other words, the teachings of Islam are either true or they are false. There is no middle ground. They are either one way or the other.

Question No. 2: Does Islam put forth various teachings that it expects us to accept as the Truth? Yes____ No____

Blind Faith Will Not Do

Truth claims should not be accepted by blind faith. The issues are far too important for us to make a "leap into the dark" and just believe something because we were told to believe in it by our parents, some religious leader or the state or our culture.

If we are all supposed to maintain whatever religion our parents taught us, then no one should convert from it to any other religion. But no one really believes this. Hindus accept converts from other religions just as Muslims do. As a matter of fact, people are changing religions all the time. We personally know Muslims who became Christians, Christians who became Jews, Hindus who became Buddhists, etc. Some people go from one religion to another as easily as they change cars.

Question No. 3: Do you know of people who left the religion they were raised in and converted to a different religion? Yes____ No____

People can and do change their religion. This is simply a fact of life that we must all deal with. Our own children may leave our religion and convert to another religion. It happens all the time. Only a fool would deny this.

Why would someone convert to another religion? Some people change religions because of marriage. They fall in love with a person of a different religion and they give up their religion to marry that person. It happens all the time.

Other people change religions due to coercion, such as threats of violence or bribes of money, sex or political advantage. If you change your religion because someone threatens to kill you if you do not accept their religion, this is not good. If you convert to a religion in order to obtain money, sex or a job, this is not good either.

The only moral reason to change your religion is on the basis of the Truth. If you find out that your former religion was not telling you the Truth, then you should leave it. To continue to believe in a religion that you know to be false is to live an intellectually dishonest life.

If you find that another religion is telling you the Truth, then you should be willing to join it no matter the price or consequences. To find and follow the Truth is the only way to get to ultimate reality.

The issue is thus reduced to whether you really care about the Truth. To believe in a religion for any other reason than it is the Truth is to cheat yourself. Convenience, habit, upbringing, fear or greed do not constitute a sufficient basis for belief in any religion. Something is not true simply because you believe it. You should believe in something because it is true.

Question No. 4: Is your desire for Truth so strong that you would be willing to leave your present religion if the Truth led you to do so? Yes ___ No___

This is where the "rubber meets the road." This is the ultimate test of your character and love of the Truth. If you are not willing to follow the Truth if it leads you to leave your present religion, then you do not really care about the Truth. If your attitude is, "Don't confuse me with the facts, my mind is already made up," then you do not really want the Truth at all.

If you feel that you must blindly follow what your parents taught you until the day you die, then you will never know if what they taught you is really true or a lie. Why? For you it is irrelevant if it is true or a lie. It doesn't really matter to you. You were born a Muslim and you will die a Muslim. That is all you care about.

How sad to live your entire life without ever seeking the Truth, to have a closed mind that will not accept anything that contradicts what you want to believe. An unexamined faith is a worthless faith. It is no better than no faith at all for it comes from prejudice and ignorance instead of the joyous search for and the acceptance of the Truth.

Question No. 5: Could Islam be false in its teachings and rituals? Yes___ No___

This question lays all the cards on the table. "All things are possible." This means that you must accept the fact that what you have believed all your life could be a lie.

If this is not even a possibility to you, then why pretend that you want the whole Truth and nothing but the Truth? A deep commitment to finding and following the Truth regardless of where it takes you is the only attitude consistent with intellectual honesty and integrity.

Face it, Islam could be a false religion. Two thirds of the people on this planet think so. Are you even open to this fact of logic? If not, then why are you reading this letter? It is addressed to open-minded Muslims who are willing to examine the evidence against Islam with objectivity and intellectual honesty.

Question No. 6: Are you willing to examine the Truth claims of Islam? Yes ___ No___

Question No. 7: Are you willing to entertain the possibility that Allah is a false god, Muhammad a false prophet and the Qur'an a false book? Yes___ No___

If you react to these questions by getting angry, what does this reveal about you? Are you open or closed to the Truth? If Islam is false, why in the world would you want to continue to believe in it?

If you are still with us at this point, hopefully you feel the same as we do: There is nothing more important in this life than the Truth. It is worth whatever price we have to pay. We will follow it wherever it leads us.

The Importance of Questions

How can we test the Truth claims of Islam to see if they are true or false? By honestly seeking the answers to crucial questions we can find out if Islam is true or false. Remember, the Truth is never afraid of the light of research.

The following questions require you to think objectively about Allah, Muhammad and the Qur'an.

Don't just answer them off the top of your head without doing any research. Cheap answers will always cheat you out of the Truth. Instead, go to a library and look up the answers in encyclopedias and dictionaries. Find history books on Arabia and on Islam that answer these questions. We found them, so can you.

The following propositions will test your knowledge of the historical origins of the rituals of Islam found in the Qur'an. Mark each answer with a check mark.

1. The Qur'an refers to people, places, things, and events which are nowhere explained or defined within the Qur'an itself. True____ False____

2. These things were not explained because it was assumed that the people hearing the Qur'an already knew of them. True____ False____

3. Some passages in the Qur'an would be unintelligible without recourse to pre-Islamic history. True____ False____

4. All Islamic scholars use pre-Islamic history to explain parts of the Qur'an. True____ False____

5. Thus, it is both legitimate and proper to use pre-Islamic history to explain the Qur'an. True____ False___

6. Yusuf Ali does this when it comes to such things as the she-camel, the elephant army, the 12 springs, the youths in the cave, the blind man, and many other things found in the Qur'an. True___ False___

7. Mecca was a pre-Islamic pagan center of worship. True___ False___

8. The Kabah in Mecca was a pagan temple filled with 360 idols. True____ False ____

9. Archaeologists have found three other ancient Kabahs in Arabia. True___ False ____

10. The pre-Islamic pagans prayed by bowing down toward Mecca several times a day. True___ False___

11. The pre-Islamic pagans made a pilgrimage to Mecca. True___ False____

12. When the pre-Islamic pagans got to Mecca, they ran between two hills. True____ False____

13. The pre-Islamic pagans ran around the Kabah seven times. True____ False___

14. The pagans kissed and caressed a large black stone on the wall of the Kabah. True____ False___

15. The pre-Islamic pagan idolators sacrificed an animal. True___ False___

16. The pre-Islamic pagans threw a magical number of stones at a pillar of the devil. True___ False____

17. The pagans held their public meetings on Friday instead of Saturday or Sunday. True___ False____

18. The pre-Islamic pagans fasted during the day and feasted at night for one month. True___ False____

19. The pre-Islamic pagan fast began and ended with the moon in its crescent phase. True____ False____

20. The pre-Islamic pagans gave alms to the poor. True___ False___

21. The pre-Islamic pagans performed ritual washings before prayers. True___ False___

22. As one of their washings before prayer, the pre-Islamic pagans snorted water up and then out of their nose. True___ False____.

23. The pre-Islamic pagans cut off the hands of thieves. True___ False___

24. The pre-Islamic pagans forbade marrying sisters. True___ False___

25. The pre-Islamic pagans forbade the eating of swine's flesh. True___ False___

26. In pre-Islamic Arabian genealogies, Ishmael is nowhere mentioned as the father of the Arabs. True___ False___

27. Abraham, the father of Ishmael, was not an Arab. True___ False___

28. Hagar, the mother of Ishmael, was an Egyptian and not an Arab. True___ False___
29. Since his mother and his father were not Arabs, Ishmael was not an Arab. True___ False___
30. Ishmael could not be the "father" of the Arabs because they already existed before he was born. True___ False___
31. According to the historical and literary evidence, Abraham and Ishmael lived in Palestine. True___ False___
32. They never lived in Mecca. True___ False___
33. They never built the Kabah. True___ False___
34. They never established the rituals connected with the Kabah such as the pilgrimage. True___ False___
35. According to Arab history, the Kabah at Mecca was built by Kosia, the pagan great-grandfather of Muhammad. True___ False___
36. The title "Al-Ilah" was used by pagan Arabs in reference to one of the gods worshiped at the Kabah. True___ False___
37. The word "Al-Ilah" was shortened into "Allah." True___ False___
38. The moon-god was called "Al-Ilah" and then "Allah" by some Arab pagans in southern Arabia. True___ False___
39. Al-lat, Al-uzza and Manat were worshiped by the pagan Arabs as "the daughters of Allah." True___ False___
40. Muhammad's father lived and died as a pagan and yet the word "Allah" was part of his name. True___ False___
41. Yusuf Ali points out in his translation of the Qur'an that pre-Islamic pagan Arabs worshiped the moon as a god. True___ False___
42. Many of the pre-Islamic pagan rituals associated with the worship of Allah and his daughters were incorporated into the Qur'an and are now part of Islam. True___ False___
43. The religion of Islam has adopted the name, the rituals, and the crescent moon symbol of the pagan Arab moon-god. True___ False___
44. Some of the material found in the Qur'an can be traced back to pre-Islamic pagan Arabian religions. True___ False___
45. Infidels are recorded in the Qur'an as saying that Muhammad took old wives' tales and myths and put them into the Qur'an. True___ False___
46. The Qur'an warns against asking questions about Islam because if the answers are revealed, you will lose your faith in Islam. True___ False___

The Key to the Answers

All the above propositions are true. If you got all 46 right you are a genius. But if you answered false on any of the propositions, you do not know the truth about Islam.

Concluding Remarks

We have discussed together some very important issues which touch upon the origins of the rituals and beliefs found in the religion of Islam. The burning question that confronted us was whether Islam was created out of pre-existing pagan rituals and beliefs or was it revealed from heaven.

After studying the standard reference works on Islam, we must conclude that the rituals and beliefs of Islam are clearly earthly in origin, i.e. they were not brought down by Gabriel to Muhammad. The question of origins is the key to whether Islam is true or false. Your willingness to research this issue is an indication that you really do care about the Truth. Thank you for caring.

The Problem of Sin

While the issue of the origins of Islam is an intellectual question that can be answered only by research into the historical evidence, there is another issue that confronts us all. Regardless of your religion, there is the inescapable fact that we have all failed to live up to our religious convictions. Muslim, Christian, Buddhist, etc., it doesn't really matter. We have all violated whatever moral standards we have adopted.

This means we have to find a way to be forgiven or cleansed of our sins. Why? If you believe in an afterlife and that there is a hell to escape and a paradise to gain, how can you gain entrance into heaven?

Two Problems We All Face

Our problem is twofold. First, our hearts are prone to evil. Thus we find it very easy to feel lust, jealousy, hatred, anger, and greed. Even when we try to be good, our own heart will betray us.

Question: Do you admit that your heart is prone to evil? Yes____ No____

Second, God is keeping a record of all our evil thoughts, words and deeds. He will hold us accountable for these evils on the Day of Judgment. On that Day we will have to face the reality of our own failures and sins.

Question: Do you recognize that you will be held accountable for all your sins on the Day of Judgment? Yes____ No____

How can you change your heart and clear your record in heaven? In order to come before a holy God with acceptance, you have to do these two things. Well, how are you going to do them?

Will Good Works Do the Job?

Some people think that if they do good deeds that this will change their hearts and clear their record. But can good works really change anyone's heart? We tried it and found that no matter how much good we did, evil was still present in our hearts.

Question: Haven't you found this true of your own heart? Yes____ No____

No matter how many good deeds you perform, your heart still has evil thoughts and motives. No, doing good deeds will never stop your heart from thinking or feeling evil things.

The same problem confronts us if we think that we can erase the divine record of our sins by doing good deeds. How many good deeds are necessary to balance out our bad deeds? It all depends on whether you are thinking of the evil that God sees or the evil we see in ourselves.

When we look at our own lives, we all tend to cut ourselves some slack. We like to think that we are not as bad as some and better than most. We don't come off so bad as long as we compare ourselves to other people.

But what if we compare ourselves to a holy and righteous Deity? If we think in terms of all the sins that an all-knowing Deity sees and hears us do, we do not come off so well. Our sins are like the sand on the seashore—too many to count!

Question: Can doing a few good deeds really clear away the mountain of sin that is against us? Yes____ No____

Question: Haven't you found it true that even when you do a good deed, you had evil motives such as pride? Yes___ No___

Question: Can evil motives cancel out a good deed? Yes___ No___

When we give money to be seen of men, this cancels out the good deed. Thus good deeds will never change your heart or clear your record.

A Mediator Needed

Since we have sinned, we are not allowed to come into the presence of a holy God. But if we cannot go to God for forgiveness, how will we obtain forgiveness? If good deeds will not work, how will we ever enter paradise?

What if someone went before God on our behalf? What if there was a mediator who could intercede on our behalf?

Question: Wouldn't a mediator solve our problem with sin? Yes___ No___

Now, such a mediator must be sinless and without blame. Otherwise, he could not go before a holy God either. The mediator must be as righteous and as holy as God Himself or he cannot stand before God.

Even if this mediator could enter God's presence, how could he clear the record of all our sins? He would have to pay off our debt to justice somehow. One obvious way is for him to take upon himself the punishment due to us. In other words, in order for us to escape the fires of hell, he would have to smother the flames of hell in his own bosom.

This mediator would have to be the bridge between heaven and earth and between God and man. A mediator who is not quite God or not quite man is a bridge broken at either end. We need someone to represent God to us and us to God. This mediator has to be both God and man at the same time or salvation is not possible.

The Gospel

Have you ever heard the word "Gospel"? What is it all about? It is a word which means "good news." What is the good news? The good news is that Jesus Christ is the only mediator between God and man. He did what we could not do. He entered into the presence of God on our behalf to obtain forgiveness for us.

How could he do this? On what basis? He bore our sins and iniquities in his own body on the cross. He died for our sins according to the Gospel. This is why salvation is a gift of God's grace.

Jesus paid the price for our salvation. Thus God now offers us eternal life free of charge. We become a Christian simply by asking Jesus to be our Mediator—our Savior—our Redeemer. You don't become a Christian by joining a church, getting baptized or doing some other good deed. No, salvation is by grace alone through faith alone in Christ alone. He brings us into the very presence of God.

Question: Haven't you ever wondered why the God of Islam seems so distant—so far off? Yes___ No___

Without a mediator, God is far off and distant. A distant God is only feared, not loved. He is unapproachable and seems far away.

Question: Don't you see the need for a mediator to pay off your sins and clear your record? Yes___ No___

Question: Does Islam offer you a mediator to take away your sins? Yes___ No__

Question: If Islam has no mediator and no atonement, does it have any gospel, i.e. good news? Yes___ No___

The End of the Matter

Dear Friend, Islam leaves you high and dry with no way to deal with the corruptions of your heart here on earth or the record of your sins in heaven. It does not build a bridge between you and God. It does not have a mediator who is both God and man. With no Savior and no atonement, it can never give you any sure hope of heaven.

But all these things are found in the Gospel. Stop right now and ask Jesus to be your Mediator. Ask Him to come into your heart as your Lord and Savior. Receive forgiveness through His atoning work. Pray this simple prayer:

Lord Jesus, I ask you to reveal Yourself to me. Save me and cleanse me of my sins. Pay off my debt to God. Come into my heart and save me from hell and make a home in heaven for me. I acknowledge that you are the Son of God and that you died on the cross for me and rose from the dead on the third day.

If you sincerely prayed this prayer, you have become a child of God by faith in Jesus Christ. Jesus has now cleared your record in heaven and the Holy Spirit will now come into your heart to deal with the corruptions found in it. God is no longer distant and far off. He is your Father and you are his child. Welcome to the family of God! Contact us so we can share your joy.

Chapter One Hundred Twenty-Six

Are the Arabs the Descendants of Ishmael?

Introduction

The Middle East will never have peace until the above question is honestly answered according to the historical facts. Myths and legends are fine as stories for children, but in the real world we must have facts and documentation.

Part One

The Arab Claim

The Arabs' claim to the land of Israel rests entirely on three false assumptions:

1. All Arabs are the descendants of Abraham through Ishmael.
2. Ishmael and his descendants were included in the covenant God made with Abraham.
3. Since the Abrahamic covenant included the land of Israel, the Arabs have a legitimate claim to it.

Ten Historical Facts

1. According to the Torah, when Abraham left Ur of the Chaldees, he went west to what is now called Israel (Gen. 12ff). He became a dweller in tents in that land. It was in Israel that God made a covenant with him for the land in which he was living at that time. It was in Israel that he fathered Isaac, Ishmael, and many other sons and daughters. Isaac was the only son of Abraham chosen by God to be the heir of the covenant. Abraham took Isaac to Mt. Moriah to be offered up as a sacrifice to God.

2. The Torah is contradicted by Qur'an at nearly every point. According to Surah 2:119-121, Abraham and Ishmael did not dwell in tents in Israel but in the city of Mecca in Arabia. Together they rebuilt the Kabah and placed the black stone in the wall. It was Abraham who started the tradition of an annual pilgrimage to Mecca, throwing stones at the devil, etc. Abraham took Ishmael (not Isaac) to nearby Mt. Mina to offer as a sacrifice to God.

3. Ishmael's 12 sons were named Nebaioth, Kedar, Adbeel, Mibsam, Mishma, Dumah, Massa, Hadad, Tema, Jetur, Naphish, and Kedemah (Gen. 12:11-16) They intermarried with the local population in North Arabia and produced several nomadic tribes know as the Ishmaelites.

4. It was prophesied in the Torah that Ishmael and his family would "live to the east of all his brothers" (Gen. 16:12). "And they settled from Havilah to Shur which is east of Egypt as one goes toward Assyria" (Gen 25:18). This broad area is the desert section east of Egypt in Northern Arabia toward the kingdom of the Assyrians.

5. The Ishmaelites are mentioned as a distinct tribe in the Assyrian records. They later intermarried with and were absorbed by the Midianites and other local tribes. In Gen. 37:25-28; 39:1, the Ishmaelites are called the Midianites and in Judges 8:22-24; cf. 7:1f, the Midianites are called the Ishmaelites. The identification cannot be made any stronger.

6. Arabia was already populated by the descendants of Cush and Shem long before Abraham or Ishmael were born (Gen. 10:7). Their cities and temples have been well documented by archaeologists.

7. If all the Arab people descended from Ishmael as Muhammad claimed, where did all the original Arabs go? What happened to them? Who did Ishmael marry if the Arabs did not already exist? If Arabia was unpopulated, who built Mecca? Since he lived there, obviously it existed before he was born. The facts speak for themselves. The Arab people existed before, during, and after Ishmael started roaming the wilderness of North Arabia.

8. The descendants of Ishmael were scattered in Northern Arabia from the wilderness of Shur to the ancient city of Havilah. They were absorbed by the local tribes such as the Midianites (Gen. 37:25-28; 39:1; Judges 8:24). There is no historical or archaeological evidence that Ishmael went south to Mecca and became the "Father" of the Arab race. Some modern Arab scholars admit that before Muhammad, Qahtan was said to be the "Father" of the Arab people, not Ishmael.

9. The Abrahamic Covenant was given only to Isaac and to his descendants. Ishmael and the other sons of Abraham were explicitly excluded by God from having any part of the covenant made with Abraham (Gen. 18:18-21).

10. Therefore the descendants of Ishmael and the other sons of Abraham do not have any claim to the land of Israel, because they are not included in the covenant God made with Abraham. Only the Jews have any claim to the land of Israel.

Part II

Islam's Claim

Muslims like to claim that Islam give them the right to claim the land of Israel as their own. This claim rests upon two false assumptions:

1. All Arabs are the descendants of Ishmael.
2. Muhammad went to Jerusalem.

Three Historical Facts

1. The first assumption has already been proven false. The Arab people are not all the descendants of Ishmael, and hence they are not the heirs of the patriarchs, the prophets, the Scriptures or the land of Israel.

2. The claim that Muhammad went to Jerusalem is false. According to the Qur'an and the Hadith, Muhammad had a dream in the middle of the night in which he traveled through the sky, visited seven heavens, met great people like Jesus, and visited the Jerusalem. Since this was only a dream, he was never actually in Jerusalem. The mosque on the temple site in Jerusalem is a hoax built on the lie that Muhammad stood on the site.

3. Nowhere in the Qur'an does it state that Ishmael is the progenitor of the Arab race. Since it is not taught in the Qur'an, it cannot be a true Islamic belief.

Conclusion

The Arab people are not the children of Ishmael. Even if they were, they would still have no claim to Israel, because Ishmael was excluded by God Himself from having any part in the covenant made with Abraham. Isaac was the only heir of the Abrahamic covenant. Thus, the Arabs as a people have no claim to the land of Israel.

The Muslims have no claim to the land of Israel either. Muhammad never went to Jerusalem except in a dream. The only ones with a spiritual and biblical claim to the land of Israel are the descendants of Isaac, the Jews.

Documentation

Arabian literature has its own version of prehistoric times, but it is entirely legendary (*Encyclopedia Britannica*, Vol. 2:176).

The pure Arabs are those who claim to be descended from Joktan or Qahtan, whom the present Arabs regard as their principle founder.... The 'Arabu 'l-Musta'ribah, the mixed Arabs, claim to be descended from Ishmael ... they boast as much as the Jews of being reckoned the children of Abraham. This circumstance will account for the preference with which they uniformly regard this branch of their pedigree, and for the many romantic legends they have grafted upon it.... The Arabs, in their version of Ishmael's history, have mixed a great deal of romance with the narrative of Scripture (*A Dictionary of Islam*, pgs. 18-19).

Muhammad was not informed about the family of Abraham" (*Encyclopedia of Islam*, I:184). See also pages 544-546.

There is a prevalent notion that the Arabs, both of the south and north, are descended from Ishmael; and the passage in Gen. xvi.12, "he (Ishmael) shall dwell in the presence of all his brethren," is often cited as if it were a prediction of that national independence which, upon the whole, the Arabs have maintained more than any other people. But this supposition is founded on a misconception of the original Hebrew, which runs literally, "he shall before the faces of all his brethren," i.e., (according to the idiom above explained, in which "before the face" denotes the east), the habitation of his posterity shall be "to the east" of the settlements of Abraham's other descendants.... These prophecies found their accomplishment in the fact of the sons of Ishmael being located, generally speaking to the east of the other descendants of Abraham, whether of Sara or of Keturah. But the idea of the southern Arabs being of the posterity of Ishmael is entirely without foundation, and seems to have originated in the tradition invented by Arab vanity that they, as well as the Jews, are of the seed of Abraham—a vanity which, besides disfiguring and falsifying the whole history of the patriarch and his son Ishmael, has transferred the scene of it from Palestine to Mecca (McClintock and Strong, *Cyclopedia of Biblical, Theological, and Ecclesiastical Literature*, Vol. I:339).

In the Qur'an, "Gen. 21.17-21 ... are identified with Mecca" (*The Concise Encyclopedia of Islam*, p. 193). It also states that the southern Arabs come from Qahtan, not Ishmael (p. 48).

See also:
The Encyclopedia of Religion, Vol. 7, pg. 296, where the connection between the Midianites and the Ishmaelites is noted.
The Shorter Encyclopedia of Islam, pgs. 178-179.
A Popular Dictionary of Islam, p. 127.

Chapter One Hundred Twenty-Seven
Judaism

Introduction

The first thing we must understand is that Judaism is not a race but a religion. In fact, most Jews today are not believers in or members of any of the various sects of Judaism. Almost 80 percent of the Jews in America do not belong to any Jewish religious organizations.

Part 1

The Biblical View

The second error we must correct is the idea that "Judaism" does not accept Jesus as the Messiah. This is erroneous because what we call "Christianity" is actually "Messianic Judaism." The early Christian Church was only one of many Jewish sects. They even met in the synagogue (James 2:2).

Acts 24:5: "For we have found this man a real pest and a fellow who stirs up dissension among all the Jews throughout the world, and a ringleader of the sect of the Nazarenes."

Acts 24:14: "But this I admit to you, that according to the Way which they call a sect I do serve the God of our fathers, believing everything that is in accordance with the Law, and that is written in the Prophets."

Acts 28:21: "And they said to him, 'We have neither received letters from Judea concerning you, nor have any of the brethren come here and reported or spoken anything bad about you.' "

Acts 28:22: "But we desire to hear from you what your views are; for concerning this sect, it is known to us that it is spoken against everywhere."

Acts 28:23: "And when they had set a day for him, they came to him at his lodging in large numbers; and he was explaining to them by solemnly testifying about the kingdom of God, and trying to persuade them concerning Jesus, from both the Law of Moses and from the Prophets, from morning until evening."

The third fact to remember is that if you are a Gentile who has accepted Jesus as the Messiah, then you are a believer in Messianic Judaism. This means that you are now Jewish in religion.

Rom 2:28: "For he is not a Jew who is one outwardly; neither is circumcision that which is outward in the flesh."

Rom 2:29: "But he is a Jew who is one inwardly; and circumcision is that which is of the heart, by the spirit, not by the letter; and his praise is not from men, but from God."

Phil. 3:2: "Beware of the dogs, beware of the evil workers, beware of the false circumcision."

Phil. 3:3: "For we are the true circumcision, who worship in the Spirit of God and glory in Christ Jesus and put no confidence in the flesh."

Gentiles must remember that they are wild branches grafted on the tree of Judaism, while those Jews who reject Jesus are broken off the tree and are thus no longer part of Judaism.

Rom. 11:13: "But I am speaking to you who are Gentiles. Inasmuch then as I am an apostle of Gentiles, I magnify my ministry."

Rom. 11:14: "If somehow I might move to jealousy my fellow countrymen and save some of them."

Rom. 11:15: "For if their rejection be the reconciliation of the world, what will their acceptance be but life from the dead?"

Rom. 11:16: "And if the first piece of dough be holy, the lump is also; and if the root be holy, the branches are too."

Rom. 11:17: "But if some of the branches were broken off, and you, being a wild olive, were grafted in among them and became partaker with them of the rich root of the olive tree."

Rom. 11:18: "Do not be arrogant toward the branches; but if you are arrogant, remember that it is not you who supports the root, but the root supports you."

Rom. 11:19: "You will say then, Branches were broken off so that I might be grafted in."

Rom. 11:20: "Quite right, they were broken off for their unbelief, but you stand by your faith. Do not be conceited, but fear."

Rom. 11:21: "For if God did not spare the natural branches, neither will he spare you."

The tree = Biblical Judaism
The Jews = the natural branches in the tree
The Gentiles = branches from wild trees
Unbelieving Jews = branches broken off the tree
Believing Jews = branches still in the tree
Believing Gentiles = branches grafted on the tree

Part 2

The Modern Meanings of 'Judaism'

The word "Judaism" has many definitions. Not even the Jews have a unified definition. If you ask two Jews, they will give you three opinions! The following definitions of Judaism reflect the massive confusion that exists on the subject.

1. The original religion of mankind. Judaism is thus the first and oldest religion. Adam, Eve, Abel, Seth, and all true believers in God before the Flood were part of Judaism.

2. The covenant with Noah. The present day Jewish cult called B'nai Noah, the Noahides or Sons of Noah, led by J. David Davis, reduces Judaism to the laws established by Noah after the Flood.

3. The covenant with Abraham. The blessings, promises and curses connected with the Abrahamic covenant are sometimes identified as Judaism.

4. The covenant with Moses. We now come to what most people assume to be Judaism. The Mosaic laws governing the civil, ceremonial, and cultic aspects of the national and religious life of the nation of Israel are often what people think when they hear the word "Judaism."

5. Jewish life during the diaspora. After the destruction of the temple, the synagogue became the center of Jewish religious life instead of the temple. The rabbi instead of the temple priest became the teacher of the Law. Many different Jewish sects arose that contradicted each other on fundamental doctrines:

Scribes	The Apocrypha
Pharisees	The Pseudepigrapha
Sadducees	The Targums
Herodians	The Septuagint
Zealots	The Midrash
Hellenists	The Dead Sea Scrolls
Apocalypticists	
Essenes	

6. The Talmudic period. After the temple was destroyed in A.D. 70, the oral traditions had to be written down or they would be lost. The Mishnah, the Jerusalem Talmud, and the Babylonian Talmud were written. Since without a temple or its ceremonies, the Mosaic covenant was impossible, a system of legalistic rules about food, drink, etc., were substituted for the Mosaic covenant.

7. The Cabalistic occult period. During the Middle Ages in Europe, many Jews practiced witchcraft, magic, and the occult sciences called the Cabal. Much of modern witchcraft is derived from the Cabal. The Golem is an example of this occult brand of Judaism.

8. The Rationalistic period. After the Industrial Revolution, many European Jews adopted a secular humanistic worldview. A rationalistic Judaism arose that was anti-supernatural in nature. The Mosaic authorship of the Pentateuch and the historicity of miracles were rejected.

9. The Zionistic period. When the Jews returned to Israel, there was a small revival of Talmudic Judaism. But most Israelis are still secular humanistic in outlook. Yet many of these secular Jews feel that the old geographical boundaries of biblical Israel should be set up again.

10. The Messianic period. As more and more Jews accept Yeshua as the Messiah, there is a growing movement to reclaim Jesus as a Jewish prophet.

Part 3

How to Graft Broken Branches Back on to the Tree

1. Don't assume that the Jew you are talking to believes in God.

2. If he does believe in "God," realize that he is usually pantheistic in outlook.

3. If he believes in a personal God, don't assume that he believes in the Bible.

4. If he says he believes in the Holy Scriptures, realize he only means the five books of Moses, the Torah. He does not believe the Writings or the Prophets are inspired.

5. Realize that he believes that Christianity was created by Paul—not Jesus, and that Paul derived it from Greek paganism—not Judaism.

6. Understand that he believes that the Catholic Inquisition killed millions of Jews and that this is what Christians do: kill Jews. He blames Christianity for the crimes of Roman Catholicism.

7. Once you get through all these hurdles, share with him that true Christianity is Jesus. Show him that Jesus fulfilled the Old Testament:

Old Testament	New Testament
Unfulfilled prophecies	fulfilled
Unsatisfied longings	satisfied
Incomplete destiny	completed
Unexplained ceremonies	explained

Is Historic Judaism in its Rabbinic and Messianic Forms Exclusive or Inclusive of Other Religions?

Introduction

A rabbi once confronted me with great anger: "How dare you say that Jesus is the only way! We Jews do not believe that our religion is exclusive. Jesus is OK for Gentles but not for Jews. You are intolerant if you say that your religion is the only true religion. To say that means you are anti-Semitic and a hatemonger."

While the rabbi was in line with the popular relativism of the day, he was out of line with the historic Judaism found in the Hebrew Scriptures and in the writings of Rabbinic Judaism. In effect, he had denied what his religion has always stood for and was no longer a "Jew" theologically.

When Christians say that there is only one way to heaven, they are simply repeating what the Law and Prophets and the rabbis taught. We must remember that the word "Christian" was invented by Gentiles who did not understand who we were. All Christians regardless of ethnic background or color are actually Messianic Jews who have accepted the long-awaited Messiah in the person of Jesus.

Proposition 1: The Torah (Law), the Prophets, the Rabbis, Rabbi Yeshua and the Apostles were all exclusive of other religions.

a. The Torah: No other gods!
   "You shall have no other gods before Me (Exo. 20:3).
b. The Prophets: No other Savior!
   "I, even I, am the LORD; And there is no savior besides Me (Isa. 43:11).
c. The Rabbis were united on this point:
   "In virtue of the commandment, 'Thou shalt have no other gods' Israel will have a claim to be remembered favorably as exterminators of idolatry" (Midrash Rabbah [IX.45] Numbers I, Vol. V., p. 320).
   "Know this day, and lay it to thy heart, that the LORD, he is God in heaven above and upon the earth below beneath; there is none else (ib. iv, 39). Not only that, but we have sworn to our God that we will not exchange Him for any other god" (Midrash Rabbah [I.16] Deut., Vol. VII, p. 131).
d. Rabbi Yeshua (Jesus): No other Way!
   Jesus said to him, "I am the way, and the truth, and the life; no one comes to the Father, but through Me (John 14:6).

e. The Apostle Peter: No other Name!
"And there is salvation in no one else; for there is no other name under heaven that has been given among men, by which we must be saved" (Acts 4:12).

f. The Apostle Rabbi Saul: No other Mediator!
"For there is only one God, and only one mediator also between God and men, the man Christ Jesus (1 Tim. 2:5).

Proposition 2: All the gods of other religions are either nothing or demons.

a. The Torah:
"They sacrificed to demons who were not God, To gods whom they have not known, New gods who came lately, Whom your fathers did not dread" (Deut. 32:17).

"And they shall no longer sacrifice their sacrifices to the goat demons with which they play the harlot. This shall be a permanent statute to them throughout their generations" (Lev. 17:7).

b. The Prophets:
"For all the gods of the peoples are idols, But the LORD made the heavens" (1 Chron. 16:26).

"They have cast their gods into the fire, for they were not gods but the work of men's hands, wood and stone. So they have destroyed them (2 Kings 19:18).

Have you not driven out the priests of the LORD, the sons of Aaron and the Levites, and made for yourselves priests like the peoples of other lands? Whoever comes to consecrate himself with a young bull and seven rams, even he may become a priest of what are no gods" (2 Chron. 13:9).

"Has a nation changed gods, When they were not gods?" (Jer. 2:11).

"Why should I pardon you? Your sons have forsaken Me And sworn by those who are not gods" (Jer. 5:7).

"But they are altogether stupid and foolish In their discipline of delusion—their idol is wood! Beaten silver is brought from Tarshish, And gold from Uphaz, The work of a craftsman and of the hands of a goldsmith; Violet and purple are their clothing; They are all the work of skilled men. But the LORD is the true God; He is the living God and the everlasting King (Jer. 10:8-9).

"Can man make gods for himself? Yet they are not gods!" (Jer. 16:20).

c. The Rabbis were united on this point:
"I am not called 'the god of idolaters,' but 'the God of Israel' " (Rabbah Midrash, Exo. 29:4-5).

"But is not burning incense to a demon idolatry?" (b. Talmud, San. 65a).

"And they shall no more offer their sacrifices unto demons" (b. Talmud, San. 61a).

d. Rabbi Yeshua (Jesus):
"that they may know Thee, the only true God" (John 17:3).

e. The Apostles:
"No, but I say that the things which the Gentiles sacrifice, they sacrifice to demons, and not to God; and I do not want you to become sharers in demons" (1 Cor. 10:20).

"However at that time, when you did not know God, you were slaves to those which by nature are no gods (Gal. 4:8).

Proposition 3: To worship any God other than YHWH was a capital crime in Israel to be punished by death.

a. The Torah:
"He who sacrifices to any god, other than to the LORD alone, shall be utterly destroyed" (Exo. 22:20).

"You shall also say to the sons of Israel, 'Any man from the sons of Israel or from the aliens so-journing in Israel, who gives any of his offspring to Molech, shall surely be put to death; the people of the land shall stone him with stones" (Lev. 20:2).

"As for the person who turns to mediums and to spiritists, to play the harlot after them, I will also set My face against that person and will cut him off from among his people" (Lev. 20:6).

"You shall not allow a sorceress to live" (Exo. 22:18).

"Moreover, the one who blasphemes the name of the LORD shall surely be put to death; all the congregation shall certainly stone him. The alien as well as the native, when he blasphemes the Name, shall be put to death" (Lev. 24:16).

"If your brother, your mother's son, or your son or daughter, or the wife you cherish, or your friend who is as your own soul, entice you secretly, saying, 'Let us go and serve other gods' ... you shall surely kill him; your hand shall be first against him to put him to death, and after-wards the hand of all the people" (Deut. 13:6-9).

"You shall bring out that man or that woman who has done this evil deed, to your gates, that is, the man or the woman, and you shall stone them to death" (Deut. 17:5).

"Seize the prophets of Baal; do not let one of them escape." So they seized them; and Elijah brought them down to the brook Kishon, and slew them there" (1 Kgs. 18:40).

"But rather, you are to tear down their altars and smash their sacred pillars and cut down their Asherim" (Exo. 34:13).

b. The Rabbis were united on this point:
"Our Rabbis taught: Seven precepts were the sons of Noah commanded: social laws; to refrain from blasphemy; idolatry; adultery; bloodshed; robbery; and eating flesh cut from a living ani-mal" (b. Talmud, San. 56).

Footnote (1), p. 382: "These commandments may be regarded as the foundation of all human and moral progress. Judaism has both a national and a universal outlook in life ... it recognizes that moral progress and its concomitant Divine love and approval are the privilege and obligation of all mankind. And hence the Talmud lays down the seven Noachian precepts, by observance of which all mankind may attain spiritual perfection, and without which moral death must inevitably ensue. That perhaps is the idea underlying the assertion that a heathen is liable for death for the neglect of any of these."

"R. Huna, Rab Judah, and all the disciples of Rab maintained: A heathen is executed for the violation of the seven Noachian laws" (b. Talmud, San. 57a).

"He who sacrifices to any god, other than to the LORD alone, shall be utterly destroyed" (B. Talmud, Gittin 57b).

"The Torah decreed that such a charmer is to be stoned" (b. Talmud, San. 65a).

"There is no severer penalty than incurred for idolatry, for God himself is jealous of it, as it is said, 'Thou shalt have no other gods before me, etc.' (Exo. xx, 3); as it is written, 'For the LORD thy God is a devouring fire, a jealous God' (Deut. iv, 24) ... the penalty for idol worship is so severe..." (Midrash [II.18] Deut., Vol. VII, p. 45).

"He who engages in idol worship is executed. It is all one whether he serve it, sacrifice, offer incense, make libations, prostrate himself, accept it as a God, or say to it, 'Thou art my God' " (Mishnah 60b).

"The necromancer and the charmer are subject to the death penalty of stoning, so is a sorceress also subject to the penalty of stoning" (b. Talmud, Yebamoth 4a).

"Our Rabbis taught: Thou shalt not suffer a witch to live: this applies to both man and woman.... How are they executed? ... stoning.... The sorcerer who insists on exact paraphernalia works through demons" (b. Talmud, San. 67a).

"Our Rabbis taught.... The inclusion of heathens, to whom blasphemy is prohibited just as to Israelites, and they are executed by decapitation; for every death penalty decreed for the sons of Noah is only by decapitation" (b. Talmud San. 56a).

Conclusion

Rabbi Yeshua and the Apostles taught that no physical violence was to be used in evangelism or church discipline. The Church set up by Jesus can only exclude from her membership rolls: idolaters, pagans, cultists, occultists, homosexuals, lesbians, heretics, apostates, and those commit bestiality.

When the Roman Catholic Church used violence to force pagans, Jews and Protestants to convert and then tortured and killed those who refused, this was not New Testament Christianity. There is no historical evidence of Evangelical Christians using violence in this way. We use the moral persuasion found in the Gospel instead of brute force. We believe in missions, not missiles; Bibles not bullets. Messianic Jews believe in religious freedom for all.

Chapter One Hundred Twenty-Nine
The Pharisees

Since the New Testament mentions the Pharisees frequently, it is necessary to understand who they were and what they taught.

1) The origin of the Pharisees is a mystery that has not been completely solved. From the historical evidence we have, it can safely be said that the Pharisees came into being around the time of the Maccabean revolt.

2) Their Divisions:
   a) The Talmud says there are seven types of Pharisees:
      i) Schechemites: who keep the law for what it will profit them.
      ii) Tumblers: always hanging down the head and dragging the feet.
      iii) Bleeders: who, to avoid looking at women, shut their eyes and so bump their heads.
      iv) Mortars: wearing caps in the form of mortar, covering the eyes from seeing impurities.
      v) What-am-I-yet-to-doers: who soon as one law is kept, ask what is next.
      vi) Fearers: who keep the law out of a fear of judgment.
      vii) Lovers: who obey Jehovah because they love Him with all their hearts.

   b) The Jewish Encyclopedia lists these seven types:
      i) The "shoulder" Pharisee, who paraded his good deeds before men like a badge on the shoulder.
      ii) The "wait-a-little" Pharisee, who would ask someone to wait for him while he performed a good deed.
      iii) The "blind" Pharisee, who bruised himself by walking into a wall because he shut his eyes to avoid seeing a woman.
      iv) The "pestle" Pharisee, who walked with hanging head rather than observe alluring temptations.
      v) The "ever-reckoning" Pharisee, who was always counting his good deeds to see if they offset his failures.
      vi) The "God-fearing" Pharisee, who like Job, was truly righteous.
      vii) The "God-loving" Pharisee, like Abraham.

3) Their Beliefs:
   a) Their Orthodoxy:
   They believed in the inspiration of the entire Old Testament; the existence of the supernatural; the existence of angels, Satan, evil spirits and demons; life after death; a concept of a Heaven and a Hell; a personal coming Messiah; immortality and the resurrection of the body.

   b) Their Unorthodoxy:
   They believed in an allegorical method of interpreting the Bible; the ancient traditions and laws were just as binding as those of the Scripture; an extreme legalism; salvation by the works of the law.

4) Their Power:
   a) Politically:
      The Pharisees grew to such power that they ruled the entire nation. They were a radical group that wanted out of the Roman Empire. The common people supported them because of this.
   b) Religiously:
      The Pharisees were in the majority and they usually held the highest offices in Judaism. Because of their orthodoxy, the common people supported them and followed their teachings.

5) Their Legacy:
   They were the only ancient sect of Judaism to survive. The Orthodox Jew of today is, practically speaking, a Pharisee. He still practices the legalism of his fathers.

Bibliography

The Jewish Encyclopedia
Life and Times of Jesus the Messiah by A. Edersheim
New Testament Survey by M. Tenny
The International Standard Bible Encyclopedia, ed. by J. Orr
Smith's Bible Dictionary by W. Smith
Zondervan Pictorial Dictionary, ed. by M. Tenny

Hinduism Exposed

Introduction

Hinduism is one of the oldest pre-Christian pagan religions still viable in the world today. While we think of it as the faith of Mother India, it actually traces it origins to a mysterious tribe of Europeans called the Aryans, who invaded and conquered Northern India from 1500 B.C. to 500 B.C. The light-skinned Brahmins of Northern India claim to be their physical and spiritual descendants.

The Aryans

The Aryans brought with them their sacred writings called the Vedas. They were originally fire worshipers, and this is why they believed in cremation instead of burying their dead. They also invented the theory of soul-transmigration in which at death you do not go to heaven or to hell but you are reborn into another body on earth. This next body could be animal, vegetable or human depending on whether you were good or bad. Your past behavior catches up with you in your present life due to the law of karma.

You could in your next reincarnation end up a clam, a carrot, a bush or a human being. The highest rebirth you could wish for was to be born as one of the white-skinned Brahmins who by virtue of their color were considered the "higher" class.

The Ugly Reality of Racism

The inherent racism of historic Hinduism is thus blatant. You were judged by the color of your skin, not the content of your character, skills or talents. The darker your skin, the lower your caste and rank in Hindu society. The whiter your skin, the higher your caste and rank. The Brahmins prided themselves on their white skin while despising the darker skinned untouchables who were often viewed and treated as sub-humans.

This explains why Hindu gurus are more than willing to travel to the West to convert rich white Europeans to Hinduism, but never travel to black Africa to make converts. The truth is, they don't want black people whose skin color is an indication of bad karma. As long as they can sucker rich white people into giving them money ("Money is evil. So give it all to me.") why bother with darker skinned people?

This can be documented by the statements of many of the gurus who have reaped riches in the West. When one guru was asked on television what he was doing to help the poor, he responded, "Let the Christians take care of them. I am here to help the rich."

The Caste System

The terrible caste system was invented in order to protect the white Brahmins from polluting their sacred whiteness with black blood. You had to marry and to labor in the caste into which you were born. The lines were clearly drawn and no one was allowed to move from one caste to another by marriage or trade.

The mechanism of the caste system is tied to the Hindu theory of soul-transmigration in which your rebirth determines your caste. Your rebirth was predetermined by your karma. Your karma in turn was determined by how you lived in your past life. For example, if you were born with a dark skin to untouchable parents, your life of misery and poverty is your punishment for being evil in your previous life. In other words, you are getting what you deserved.

The poor, the sick, the disabled, the dark-skinned, etc. are what they are because of their own fault. The deserve their suffering because they did something bad in a previous life, and their karma has caught up with them. We should not interfere with their suffering because if we do, we will doom them to experience it in the next life. Thus the kindest thing to do is to let them alone so they get their suffering over and hopefully have a better rebirth the next time around.

On the other hand, if you were born with white skin to Brahmin parents, your life of wealth and pleasure is your reward for good deeds done in your previous life. You deserve to be rich and white. You earned it. Thus you have no moral obligation to help those less fortunate them you.

The social inequities of Hinduism ultimately led millions of lower caste Indians to abandon Hinduism for Buddhism, Islam, Sikhism or Christianity because those religions did not lock them into a rigid caste system. Social and financial mobility required a change of religion. Of course, if you were a rich white Brahmin, why would you convert to a religion that would strip you of your social status and wealth?

Social Evils

Being originally fire worshipers, Hindus developed the grisly practice of burning a widow alive on the funeral pyre of her husband (suttee). If a widow did not willingly jump into the fire, she was often thrown into it by the mob gathered to watch her burn to death.

Child sacrifices to animal gods such as sacred crocodiles were common until this Hindu practice was criminalized by the British. The ritual murder and burial of travelers by the Kali cult (the thugees) is another example of Hinduism's inherently demonic nature and inspiration.

Other immoral practices of Hinduism included using children as sex slaves in Hindu temples. They not only served the sexual perversions of the priests and gurus but were used as prostitutes to bring in money. The poorest of the poor who often could not afford to keep a new child, left the baby in a temple assuming that the child would have a better life with the priests than with its parents. They doomed their child to a life of pain and misery.

The tourist who travels to India's many temples is often shocked by wall art that depicts sodomy, child sex, orgies and bestiality of the grossest kind. Yet, all this is part of what lies at the core of Hinduism.

The same shock is received when tourists see Hindus drinking urine from animals and humans and smearing dung in their hair and on their body. The smell that emanates from the gurus, monks and holy men of Hinduism is enough to warn us that Hinduism is rotten to the core. .

Why are we beginning our discussion of Hinduism with such ugly topics as racism, the caste system, burning of widows, ritual child abuse and gross immorality? To see the true nature of Hinduism we must study what it produces in those societies where it is the dominant religion. Thus, a mere abstract philosophic presentation of Hinduism in the classroom will give a false view of it. Hinduism is far more than a list of abstract dogmas. It is actually a social program that seeks to organize a culture according to Hindu concepts of soul-transmigration, karma, race and caste.

The Philosophic Failures of Hinduism

1. Hinduism denies the existence of the infinite/personal triune God of the Bible who exists independent of and apart from the universe He created out of nothing. It is atheistic in this sense.

2. Hinduism never solved the problem of the One and Many or the infinite/personal dichotomy.

3. Those Hindus who emphasize the One over the Many, teach Monism (All is One) and pantheism (All is God), erasing any distinction between Creator and creation. "God" is an impersonal infinite force or power which manifests itself as the universe around us. The "things" we see around us do not really exist per se. They are only illusions of the One. This is what the high caste Hindus teach the Westerners who come to India in search of "enlightenment."

4. The vast majority of Hindus do not follow the Brahmin doctrine of monism. Instead of emphasizing the One over the Many, they emphasize the Many over the One and practice the most vile forms of polytheism imaginable in which they worship millions of gods and goddesses. It is said that the Hindus worship more gods and goddesses than the total number of Hindus who exist today. They worship snakes, monkeys, elephants, crocodiles, cats, insects and other absurdities.

5. As a worldview, Hinduism fails to answer crucial questions:

   a. Why does the Universe exist as opposed to not existing? Since it cannot answer this question, Hinduism simply denies the existence of the world around us. It is an illusion (maya) or dream.

   b. Is the universe eternal or did it have a beginning? Hinduism has always taught that the universe is eternal. But this has been successfully refuted by modern science. This also exposes an inherent contradiction within Hinduism. If the universe does not exist but is illusionary in nature, how then is it eternal? How can Hinduism speak of the universe going through eternal cycles if the universe does not exist?

   c. Why does the Universe exist in such a form that predictability and science are possible? By denying the existence of the world around it, Hinduism did not develop science and cannot explain why the universe works.

   d. What is evil? Once again, since Hinduism could not answer this question, it simply denied that evil existed.

   e. Why does evil exist? Hinduism cannot answer this question.

   f. What is man? Hinduism denies that we actually exist.

   g. How can we explain the uniqueness of man? Hinduism cannot explain why man is distinct from the world around him.

   h. Why do we do evil? Hinduism cannot answer this question.

   i. What is sin? Because it does not have a concept of a personal/infinite Creator, Hinduism has no concept of "sin" per se.

   j. How do we obtain forgiveness for our sins? There is no forgiveness in Hinduism. You will have to suffer in the next life for the evil you do in this present life. This answer exposes an inescapable contradiction within Hindu philosophy. If the universe, evil, and man do not actually exist but are only illusions (maya), then on what grounds does karma exist? If it does not actually exist either, then on what grounds does reincarnation happen?

   k. On what basis can we explain man's desire for meaning, significance, justice, morals, truth and beauty? Hinduism has no answer to these questions.

   l. How can we provide a sufficient basis for meaning, significance, justice, morals, truth and beauty? Hinduism cannot provide a philosophic basis for any of these things.

Conclusion

Hinduism cannot answer the essential philosophic questions that always arise wherever and whenever the human intellect matures. It has been weighed in the scales of truth and has been found lacking.

Even more importantly, Hinduism has no concept of a Creator God, the Creation, the Fall of man into sin and guilt, a Day of Judgment, atonement or forgiveness, or a Savior who redeems us from our sins by the sacrifice of Himself in our place.

It did not produce democracy, science or equality among different races and ranks of mankind. Instead it produced great social evils that afflict the Indian people to this day. As a religion and a philosophy, Hinduism is a complete failure and cannot provide a basis for meaning, significance, justice, morals, truth and beauty.

Buddhism Unmasked

Introduction

Buddhism is an Eastern religion that has gained many followers in the West especially among movie stars. It is only appropriate that we examine this ancient pagan religion.

The Buddha

Buddhism is supposedly built upon the teachings and example of a Hindu guru who was called the "Buddha," i.e. Enlightened One. The problem we face is that this guru did not write down any of his teachings. Neither did any of his early disciples. A few manuscripts appear four to five hundred years after his death! But most of the manuscripts do not appear until nearly 1,000 years after his death. This gives plenty of time for legends and myths to arise that falsify the life and teachings of the guru.

This problem is further complicated by the development of two contradictory literary traditions: Pali and Sanskrit. These divergent literary traditions produced hundreds of Buddhist sects that disagree with each other on many major points.

No Primary Sources

Because of the lack of primary source materials for the history of Buddhism, modern scholars seriously doubt the reliability of the traditional legends about the Buddha. As a matter of fact, if he were alive today he would not recognize the religion that bears his name! Since Buddhists themselves disagree on the "facts" of the life and teachings of their guru, there is more than adequate reason to cast doubt on the entire history of the "Buddha."

What We Know

There are only a few facts about this Hindu guru that are agreed upon by most scholars. He was born around 563 B.C. in what is now called Nepal. His name is not known for certain. The ones that history preserved are spelled differently. One variation is Siddhartha Gautama. Although this name is doubted by many scholars, we will use it for lack of a better alternative.

It is universally agreed that Siddhartha did not intend to start a new religion. He was born a Hindu. He lived as a Hindu. And he died a Hindu in 483 B.C. The myths and legends that gradually built up around him over the centuries are no safe guide to what he really believed or practiced.

As Buddhism evolved over the centuries, many different authors from varying cultures set forth their own ideas in the name of the Buddha. As a result, Buddhism developed inherent contradictions. When this was realized, Buddhism embraced these contradictions as a badge of honor. Thus the making of self-contradictory statements has become one of the pronounced features of Zen and other esoteric forms of Buddhism.

The Myths

The many conflicting and fascinating legends about his early life, marriage, wanderings and enlightenment are unreliable. Siddhartha was supposedly born into a wealthy family and grew up isolated from the poverty and suffering in the surrounding culture. Some legends exaggerate the wealth of his family and even make them into royalty. But these legends are obvious embellishments and there is no historical evidence to back them up.

He was married and had one infant child by the age of 29. Disobeying his father's wishes, he went out into the world and for the first time saw the pain and suffering of the unwashed poor and the untouchables. Their suffering made him feel guilty over his life of ease and luxury.

As he became psychologically obsessed with guilt, instead of doing something positive to alleviate human suffering, like setting up a hospital or giving food to the hungry, Siddhartha decided to increase human suffering by abandoning his family and taking up the life of a Hindu beggar/monk. By making his family suffer as well as himself, he only added to human suffering. This is one of the great defects of both Hinduism and Buddhism. They increase human suffering with their belief systems.

For six years Siddhartha wandered around the countryside begging and abusing his body in the attempt to purify his soul. But his suffering did not profit anything for anyone including himself. The legends state that he was sitting under a fig tree when it dawned on him that the source of all his suffering was his failure to find a Middle Way between pleasure and pain, wealth and poverty, etc. He had gone from one extreme to another and both experiences had left him dissatisfied with life.

Then a new idea came into his mind. His real problem was that he had DESIRES. When his desires were not met, he became dissatisfied. Thus the way to avoid frustration and the suffering it caused, is to arrive at the place where he had no desires for anything, good or evil. For example, he should have no desire to see his wife or child or to help the poor and needy. Desire *qua* desire must be eradicated.

With these insights (sic), Siddhartha was proclaimed a "Buddha," i.e. an Enlightened One. Did this mean he went back to his family and fulfilled his moral obligation to his wife and child? No, his wife and child remained abandoned. Siddhartha's so-called "enlightenment" was intensely self-centered and inherently selfish. This is still one of the main problems of Buddhism.

Now that he was a "Buddha," he should not have any desires to be or do anything. We would therefore expect him to withdraw to a cave and die in isolation. But his desire to preach sermons and make converts was apparently alive and well. He set forth preaching his new message to all who would hear him.

According to the legends, from his enlightened lips came the Four Noble Truths, the Eightfold Path, the Ten Perfections, and many other sophisticated teachings. But Siddhartha never really taught any of these things. They were developed many centuries after his death and his name was invoked in order to give them the air of authority.

No God

Siddhartha never taught that he was a god or that he should be worshiped as a god. He did not even claim to be a saint or an avatar. As a Hindu, he believed in millions of finite gods and goddesses. But being finite deities, they were of little consequence and could be ignored except when you needed their assistance. Thus most Buddhists call upon the gods only when they need something.

The Evolution of Buddhism

The starting point for any analysis of Buddhism is Hinduism. Scholars have long pointed out that Buddhism was intended to be a reform movement within Hinduism, not a separate religion. Indeed, much of Buddhism is a reaction to the sociological evils spawned by the Hindu commitment to such things as the caste system with its millions of untouchables. The following charts summarize the unity and diversity between Hinduism and Buddhism.

Unity	
Hinduism	Buddhism
1. human autonomy 2. monism 3. idealism 4. karma 5. enlightenment 6. reincarnation	

Diversity	
Hinduism	Buddhism
1. Brahmanism	rejected
2. caste system	rejected
3. The Vedas	rejected

4. enlightenment
   for only a few
	enlightenment
	   for all

5. group	individual
6. polytheistic	atheistic
7. eternal soul	no soul per se

Christianity and Buddhism

Buddhism is inferior to Christianity in many ways:

A. "Southern" Buddhism is polytheistic involving the worship of idols including the Buddha (a huge, fat, smiling, pot-bellied man sitting in the lotus position). Some rub his stomach for good luck. Sacrifices are presented to him.

B. The OT prophets pointed out the defects of polytheism and the folly of worshiping what we make with our own hands. My book *Battle of the Gods* has two chapters on the philosophic defects of polytheism.

C. "Northern" Buddhism is more atheistic than polytheistic. If any god is acknowledged, it is the "god" within us. Buddhists deny the existence of the personal/infinite Maker of heaven and earth. They are atheistic in this sense.

D. Having no infinite/personal Creator, Buddhism cannot provide any basis for truth, justice, meaning, morals or beauty. It cannot answer the riddles of the origin or goal of life.

E. Its inward orientation made the development of science impossible.

F. Its concept of suffering prevented them from alleviating human suffering.

G. Their concept of karma and reincarnation compounded the problem of evil by adding more suffering to it.

H. Because Buddhism teaches that man's problem is primarily ignorance, it never developed a way to gain forgiveness for sin.

I. Because it strives only for enlightenment, Buddhism offers no plan of salvation.

J. Its goal is not to glorify God or to make a positive contribution to humanity but the extinction of individual consciousness in the ocean of nothingness called Nirvana. Its failure to find a purpose and meaning for life that is greater than life itself is one of its greatest defects.

K. Because of its narcissistic and self-centered nature, Buddhism appeals to those who seek justification for living a selfish lifestyle. This is why Hollywood movie stars are drawn to it.

L. Buddhism fails the test of history by being based on groundless myths and legends. It thus has no basis in history and is built on lies and deceptions set forth in Buddha's name.

The Answer to Buddhism

1. The Biblical Doctrine of Creation: The universe is not eternal as Buddhism teaches. It had a beginning and will have an end. Man is created in the image of an infinite/personal Creator. God created matter as well as mind, and both are good. Buddhism fails the test of science with its idea of an eternal universe.

2. The Biblical Doctrine of the Fall: Man's problem is moral and not metaphysical. He has sinned against God's law by violating its commands and failing to live up to it standards. Our problem is not that we have a body or that we are conscious of our individual existence. Our problem is that we are sinners in need of salvation. Buddhism fails the test of morals because it fails to address the sin problem.

3. The Biblical Doctrine of Redemption: God so loved us that He sent His Son to die for our sins on the cross. His atoning work renders karma and reincarnation unnecessary. The goal is to retain our individual consciousness for all eternity in service to God and others. Buddhism fails the test of salvation because it provides none.

Conclusion

Buddhism is legendary while Christianity is historical. Buddhism is irrational and attempts to escape logic and reason. But Christianity is the very essence of logic and reason. Buddhism is a death-wish philosophy and is not mentally healthy. It does not really enable people to cope with the real world but tries to escape reality and live according to illusion and fantasy. In every respect it fails the tests of truth. Jesus Christ alone is the Way, the Truth and the Life. We cannot go to the Father without Him.

Chapter One Hundred Thirty-Two

Is Sunday the Christian Sabbath?

Introduction

The doctrine of sabbatarianism comes in two forms: Christian and cultic. In its Christian form, sabbatarianism teaches that the Sabbath was changed from Saturday to Sunday. Thus, the "Christian Sabbath" is on Sunday and not on Saturday. This was the position of the Puritans and the Pilgrims. They legislated various civil laws called "blue laws," which forced everyone to observe Sunday as a day of rest. It was illegal to conduct business on Sunday.

The Puritan view of the Sabbath was a radical departure from the theology of the European Reformers, such as Calvin, who believed that the Sabbath and all other Jewish ceremonial laws were fulfilled by Christ and were thus no longer in force.

In its cultic form, sabbatarianism claims that Saturday is the true Sabbath and that it is the only valid day of worship for Christians as well as for Jews. They do not believe that the Sabbath was changed by God from Saturday to Sunday.

Such cults as the Seventh-day Adventist Church, etc., claim that it was the Roman Catholic Church that changed the day from Saturday to Sunday. Some early Adventist writers went so far as to claim that anyone who went to church on Sunday had the mark of the beast on his forehead, and would be destroyed on the Judgment Day.

While the Christian and cultic forms of sabbatarianism disagree on which day the Sabbath should be observed, they use the exact same arguments to prove that we should keep a Sabbath. Thus it does not really matter if we are dealing with followers of the Puritans or the Adventists, they will both argue that the Sabbath is a creation ordinance, a moral law, etc. A refutation of the basic arguments which underlie all forms of sabbatarianism is the focus of this study.

The following treatment of the subject reveals that both views are erroneous. The Sabbath was swept away along with all the other ceremonial laws when the veil of the temple was ripped from top to bottom. We can no more keep the Sabbath today than offer animal sacrifices. Christ has come, and all things are new.

The Study Outline

PART I
The Sabbatarian Position Outlined

PART II
An Examination of Sabbatarian Arguments:
1. The "Creation Ordinance" Argument
2. The "Moral Law" Argument
3. The "Sabbath Made for Man" Argument
4. The Hebrews 4:9 Argument

Part I

The Sabbatarian Position Outlined

The utmost care has been taken to research Christian Sabbatarianism in order to give it a fair and positive presentation. The classic literature, such as the works of John Owen, has been carefully examined. The modern expositions of sabbatarianism, such as John Murray, were consulted. The following presentation of Christian sabbatarianism, therefore, is not a straw man. It is a factual exposition of the doctrine and the arguments given to support it.

The cultic writings of Ellen G. White, Herbert Armstrong, etc., have been carefully researched to document their arguments for sabbatarianism as well. (Note: The Worldwide Church of God, founded by Herbert W. Armstrong, abandoned sabbatarianism in 1994, eight years after Armstrong's death.)

Sabbatarianism stated

God instituted a seven-day week for all mankind and his domesticated animals. This was instituted at Creation and is to be observed in all ages by all men until the end of the world. A week composed of less or more than seven days is sinful and in violation of the will of the Creator.

In this seven-day week, man is to sanctify or set apart one day out of seven. This sanctification of one-seventh of his time is to be composed of:
- Physical cessation from all labor, except works of necessity, charity, or mercy.
- Wholly giving oneself to the worship of God through the use of the public and private means of grace.
- Abstaining from all activities which center in self-pleasure or recreation that tend to distract the mind from spiritual worship and contemplation. This includes sexual pleasure for married couples.

According to cultic sabbatarianism, the seventh day, i.e. Saturday, is the only day that God ever sanctified and appointed as a day of rest for all mankind. Sunday is a pagan day of worship, and is not to be viewed as a Sabbath.

According to Christian Sabbatarianism, the Sabbath was appointed by God to be observed on the seventh day from Adam to Christ. But God Himself has now changed the Sabbath to the first day of the week, i.e. Sunday, from Christ's resurrection to the end of the world. The Lord's Day is now the Christian's Sabbath.

The Sabbatarian Arguments Set Forth

1. God commanded Adam and Eve to keep one day out of seven as a Sabbath rest. This means that Sabbath-keeping is a "creation ordinance." As a creation ordinance, it is binding on the entire human race throughout all generations. The Sabbath creation ordinance consists of three parts:

   a. God instituted a seven-day week for man and his domesticated animals.

   b. God commanded man to keep one day out of seven as a Sabbath.

   c. God instilled into the very being of man and his animals a physical, psychological, spiritual and social need to observe a one day out of seven biological cycle within man and his animals. Thus the seventh day was observed as the Sabbath by man at creation.

2. In the Ten Commandments, God commanded Israel to keep one day out of seven as a Sabbath rest. Since the Sabbath command is in the Decalogue, it must be a "moral law." As such, it is binding on all mankind until the end of the world.

While the cultic Sabbatarian would restrict the fourth commandment to the seventh day, the Christian Sabbatarian would state that the seventh day is not part of the moral law, but is a positive or ceremonial law. The day can be changed without breaking the Fourth Commandment.

3. The Fourth Commandment begins with the word, "Remember." This proves that Moses was calling upon the Jews to remember what they already knew of and practiced, namely, the Sabbath. Moses was not introducing something new, but, rather, he was reminding them of the Sabbath-keeping which had been practiced since man was created.

4. Christ said, "The Sabbath was made for man" (Mark 2:27). This means that the Sabbath is a moral law because it was made for man, i.e., mankind as a whole. The Greek word means all of humanity.

5. Hebrews 4:9 states that the Christian is still to observe a Sabbath day of rest.

6. The Sabbath was practiced before the Fourth Commandment was given (Exodus 16). Therefore it was observed since the Creation itself.

7. In Matthew 24:20, Christ prophesied that Christians would be observing the Sabbath even at the end of the world.

8. The silence of the New Testament as to the Christian's obligation to keep the Sabbath proves that they were all keeping it.

   a. Since it had been commanded in the Old Testament, and it is nowhere abrogated in the New Testament, it is still in effect.
   b. The early church was Jewish and kept it automatically.
   c. There were "pastoral reasons" for the silence.

Part II

An Examination of the Sabbatarian Arguments

The Creation Ordinance Argument

The Sabbatarian Position
God instituted Sabbath-keeping as a creation ordinance.
Examination of This Argument

1. What is a creation ordinance? Answer: An activity or institution which God set up at creation for all mankind to observe perpetually until the end of the world. Some of the obvious creation ordinances are activities, such as work (Gen. 1:28; 2:15, 20) and the cultural mandate (Gen. 1:28), or institutions, such as marriage (Gen. 2:8) and the family (Gen. 2:24).

2. What is needed exegetically to prove that Sabbath-keeping is a "creation ordinance?" Answer: To prove that Sabbath-keeping is a creation ordinance, you must find in the creation account itself one or more of the following things:
   a. A command given to man to keep a seven-day week.
   b. A command given to man to rest on the seventh day.
   c. An example of man resting the seventh day.
   d. An explanation as to why man should rest on the seventh day.

   The hard exegetical facts are that there is not a single command, example or explanation for Sabbath-keeping in the creation account. There is absolutely nothing in Genesis 1 to 3 or elsewhere to warrant the assumption that Sabbath-keeping was a creation ordinance. This Sabbatarian argument is not based on Scripture.

3. "But isn't the Sabbath creation ordinance found in Genesis 2:1-3?" Answer: No, the word "Sabbath" does not appear in the text. A biblical-theological approach would show that Genesis 2:1-3 is Moses' comment looking back to the creation period within the context of his own understanding of the Ten Commandments, and not a reference to Adam's understanding at the beginning of history.
   It does not say in the text that "man" or "animals" sanctified the day, or that they rested. It is a simple statement that God's immediate creative acts were over. That God "rested" is clearly an anthropomorphic (i.e. attributing human characteristics to God) statement, for God does not get tired and hence does not need rest.

4. "But the seventh day is mentioned. Doesn't this prove that it is a creation ordinance?" Answer: Not necessarily. Nudity and vegetarianism are also a part of the creation account. But who would claim these elements as creation ordinances just because they are mentioned. Besides, the seventh day was hallowed, not the first day after the Sabbath (Greek, *mia sabbaton*), which is Sunday.

5. "But doesn't Genesis 2:1-3 serve as a pattern or model for us to follow?" Answer: We hope not. After God worked six days, He rested on the seventh day and He has been "resting" to this very time (Hebrews 4:10-11). God did not begin another cycle of six days' work and one day of rest.

Thus, if man is to follow God's example, then he would have to work six days at the beginning of his "career" and then rest until the end of his life!

At any rate, to prove that Sabbath-keeping is a creation ordinance, we must be shown an example of man's keeping of it. Since this is true for any other creation ordinance, why should Sabbath-keeping be exempt from this rule of faith?

Also, Adam would have never been able to observe a proper Sabbath because God's seventh day was only Adam's second day, whereas Adam's seventh day was God's fifth day. Which seventh day did Adam observe?

If Genesis 2:1-3 is a creation ordinance, then the seventh day is the permanent Sabbath, for the text does not say, "God sanctified one day out of seven," but, "God blessed and sanctified the seventh day." Christian Sabbatarians always overlook this fact.

All the biblical passages, such as Nehemiah 9:5-38 (cf. vs. 13-14), which give us a summary of redemptive history, always place the beginning of the Sabbath with Moses and not Adam. If Sabbath-keeping began at creation, surely the Scripture would have placed it there when surveying the history of the world, but it does not.

There is no mention of a seven-day week as being commanded or observed in the Genesis account of creation. No example, command or precept can be given from Genesis 1-3. While a seven-day week appears later on in redemptive history, there is no evidence that Adam or Eve observed such a measurement of time.

6. "I was told that all ancient cultures followed a seven-day week. Is this true?" Answer: No, it is not true. Anthropology and archaeology have proven conclusively that various ancient cultures used different ways of measuring time (13 day week, nine day week, etc.). If the Sabbath were a creation ordinance, surely it would have been observed by ancient cultures just as they observed all other valid creation ordinances. A true creation ordinance is universal, but Sabbath-keeping is not.

7. "But don't men and animals have a natural seven-day cycle?" Answer: No, they don't. Various psychological tests have also shown that there is no biological time rhythm or clock for a seven-day week in man or animals. Extensive tests have been done with isolated men and animals to see if there is a built-in time clock. The evidence is conclusive that neither man or animals are Sabbath-keepers by nature or being.

Sabbath-keeping does not have anything to do with the psychological or physiological well-being of man. Men and animals normally rest in their work instead of from their work. The classic Sabbatarian argument which claimed that Sabbath-keeping is physically constituted in men and animals should be laid to rest forever.

The Moral Law Argument

The Sabbatarian Position
Sabbath-keeping is a part of God's moral law, and thus is binding on all men.

Examination of This Argument
The diagram on the following page illustrates the differences between moral laws and ceremonial laws, which reveal that the Sabbath command is a ceremonial law. If the Sabbath has the attributes of a ceremonial law, is treated like a ceremonial law, and is listed with ceremonial laws, the only rational conclusion one can make is that it is a ceremonial law.

Moral Laws	Ceremonial Laws	Sabbath
1. It reflects some aspect of the moral character of God, i.e., a moral law tells us what God is like.	1. It is not a reflection of God's character. It is didactic in the prophetic sense of prefiguring the work of Christ.	1. It does not reflect some aspect of the moral character of God. It pointed backward to the creative work of God and pointed forward to the redemptive work of Christ.
2. It is an aspect of the image of God in man, i.e., part of man's moral character as created by God. A moral law tells us how and in what ways we can bear God's moral likeness. It is a part of man's humanity. It makes man man.	2. It is not a part of the image of God in man. It is not a part of man's humanity. It is a tool used by God to teach man spiritual truth.	2. It is not a part of God's image in man. It is not a part of man's humanity. It is a tool to teach men spiritual truth.
3. General revelation from the creation and the conscience reveal a moral law. Special revelation is not needed to know a moral law. It will be anthropologically universal, since it is rooted in man's nature and conscience.	3. General revelation from creation and conscience cannot give us ceremonial laws. They must be known by special revelation. There is nothing in God, man or the world to indicate a ceremonial law.	3. Nine of the Ten Commandments are anthropologically universal. Only the Fourth Commandment depends on special revelation. There is nothing in God, man or the world to indicate a seven-day week or one Sabbath-day out of seven days.
4. It is eternally true and it will never be done away with. It will be obeyed in the eternal state because man will always be in God's image.	4. It is instituted for a specific period of time and then it is fulfilled.	4. It began with Moses, and was fulfilled by Christ. As a day of rest, it is not observed in Heaven now, and neither will it be observed in the eternal state.
5. It is unchangeable and immutable because God's character and the image of God in man cannot change.	5. Ceremonial laws change from age to age, according to God's appointment.	5. Christ, as the Lord of Sabbath, fulfilled it and set it aside. Christian Sabbatarians admit that it changed from the seventh day to the first day of the week. It is thus neither unchangeable nor immutable.
6. It is universally binding on all men in all ages.	6. It is binding only on those to whom it is given. Usually it is directed only to the people of God, and not binding on the Gentiles.	6. It was binding only for Israel. No Gentiles were ever commanded or condemned concerning the Sabbath law. It was not universally binding on all men in all ages. It was a covenant sign to Israel.
7. A moral law always has precedence over a ceremonial law.	7. It is always subservient to a moral law if any contradiction arises (i.e., David's eating of the shewbread, Matt. 12:16).	7. The Sabbath command was subservient to moral laws (Matt. 12:9-12). It was subservient even to other ceremonial laws (John 7:22-23).
8. Since God's character is harmonious, moral laws never contradict each other in that you must break one to obey the other.	8. There will be conflict at times between moral and ceremonial laws.	8. There have been occasions when the Fourth Commandment was broken in order to keep the Sixth (Mark 2:23-28). It cannot, therefore, be a moral law.
9. A moral law is valid regardless of the situation because it is a moral absolute. We can never deal with it from the perspective of situational ethics. 1 Cor. 10:13 teaches that we never have to sin.	9. Whether you obey or disobey a ceremonial law depends on the situation (Matt. 12:16).	9. The priests "broke" or desecrated the Sabbath. But because of the circumstance and the situation, they were declared innocent (Matt. 12:5). No moral law has "except" clauses. If the Sabbath is a moral law, why is it a situational law?
10. A consistent violation of moral law is inconsistent with a Christian profession and must be dealt with by church discipline, even unto excommunication.	10. The punishment depends on the situation and circumstances surrounding the violation of a ceremonial law.	10. Sabbath-breaking depends on the situation. There are all sorts of "I had to" exceptions for breaking the Fourth Commandment. They are called "works of mercy, charity, or necessity." No moral laws have such exceptions.
11. A moral law does not assume man's fall into sin. God's and man's nature at creation is sufficient to account for a moral law.	11. It assumes the fall and prefigures redemption. Thus, it is eschatological in character.	11. The Sabbath was eschatological in that it pointed forward to the Messianic age of the rest of faith (Heb. 4). We cease trying to work for salvation, and rest instead in Christ's work.

One of the most telling reasons for rejecting the Sabbath as a moral law is that few modern Sabbatarians treat "violations" of the Fourth Commandment as constituting serious sin. You would be excommunicated for consistently breaking the other nine commandments. But to break the Fourth Commandment does not lead today to any church discipline. Indeed, we know of situations where the pastor is a strict Sabbatarian, but his fellow elders go out to eat on Sundays!

If it is a moral law, why is it not applied like one? Since the punishment for Sabbath-breaking was death in the Old Testament, on what grounds can anything less than excommunication be done to those who consistently "break" the Fourth Commandment today?

We might also add that what constitutes a "violation" of proper Sabbath-keeping is determined in a variety of ways and ends up in "dos" and "don'ts" which are purely subjective and arbitrary. Thus, what constitutes Sabbath-breaking in one church will be found to be acceptable in another church.

"But," the Sabbatarian replies, "regardless of all that you have said, it is still found in the Ten Commandments, and this means it must be a moral law or it wouldn't be found there."

In reply, we must observe the following points:

Is everything in the Ten Commandments moral? Is there not a mixture of ceremonial and moral law within the Decalogue itself?

Fifth Commandment—Obey your parents and "you will live long on the land which God has given to you." Who would say that living in the land of Israel is a moral law? Even the Puritans pointed this out as a ceremonial element in the Decalogue.

Fourth Commandment—"The seventh day is the Sabbath." Who, besides those who view Saturday as the Sabbath, would say that this is a moral law? Christian Sabbatarians such as Ezekiel Hopkins pointed out this ceremonial element.

Since Christian Sabbatarians admit that there is a mixture of moral and ceremonial law in the Decalogue, the fact that the Jews were commanded in the Decalogue to keep the seventh day as a Sabbath cannot prove it to be a moral law.

Archaeology helps us to understand why in the midst of the covenant Decalogue you find a ceremonial law. In the covenant treaties of the great kings in the ancient Near East, a ceremony would be given in the midst of the treaty to act as a sign of covenantal obedience and submissiveness by the vassal slave to the conquering king.

The covenant servants could break the other parts of the covenant and find forgiveness. But if they forsook the ceremonial sign of covenantal obedience to the king, then the covenant as a whole was viewed as broken.

The structure of the Decalogue is like the treaties of the great kings (Meredith Kline, *The Treaty of the Great King* (Eerdmans, 1963, pp. 27-44).

The Sabbath was the sign of Israel's covenantal obedience and submission (Exodus 31:12-17; Isaiah 56:47; Deuteronomy 5:11).

Once Israel abandoned the Sabbath, God abandoned them (Ezekiel 20:12, 20-24).

The Ten Commandments as written by the hand of God were only 10 short and brisk commands. People have always confused Moses' exposition of these commands with the commands themselves. For example, the Tenth Commandment according to Paul in Romans 13:9 is, "You shall not covet." It was Moses who added several illustrations of the kinds of things we should not covet: house, wife, servants, etc. (Exodus 20:17).

The Ten Commandments are as follows:

You shall not have any other gods before me.
You shall not make for yourself any idol.
You shall not take the name of Yahweh your God in vain.
Observe the Sabbath day.
Honor your father and your mother.
You shall not murder.
You shall not commit adultery.
You shall not steal.
You shall not bear false witness.
You shall not covet.

Moses would read the sentence and then expound on it for the benefit of his hearers. For example, in Exodus 20:17, we read "You shall not covet." The same words are found in Deuteronomy 5:21.

But when Moses illustrates what kinds of things we should not covet, the words are not the same. The following chart reveals that some words were added or omitted, and the order is not the same. Obviously, Moses was not reading what God wrote on the tablets of stone.

Exodus 20:17	Deuteronomy 5:21
house	wife
wife	house
male slave	field
female slave	male slave
ox	ox
donkey	donkey

When it comes to the Fourth Commandment, the only words God wrote on the tablet of stone were, "Observe the Sabbath day." All the other words were from Moses, who tried to explain to the people what the commandment meant. For example, the Sabbath day is to be a day of rest. But who is to rest on that day? God did not say. Thus Moses had to illustrate who was to rest on that day. That this is true is seen from the fact that when Moses illustrated in Exodus and in Deuteronomy who was to rest, the lists are not the same. He adds some words in Deuteronomy not found in Exodus.

Exodus	Deuteronomy
you	you
son	son
daughter	daughter
male slave	male slave
female slave	female slave
cattle	ox
sojourner	donkey
	cattle
	sojourner

The idea that Moses would add new words to what God had written with His own finger is absurd. Moses probably added oxen and donkeys to the list because some Jews had limited resting to only those animals specifically mentioned by Moses in Exodus 20. Thus they were making their oxen and donkeys work on the Sabbath, but not their cattle.

When Moses tried to explain to the Jews why they should keep the Sabbath, he gives a different reason in Deuteronomy 5 than what he gave in Exodus 20. While in Exodus 20 Moses referred to the creation week, in Deuteronomy 5 he omits any reference to the creation week and instead refers to the Exodus out of Egypt. If God had written the words in Exodus 20 about the creation week, Moses would not have substituted them with a reference to the Exodus. The following chart reveals that the creation reference was not part of the Ten Commandments, but was Moses' added commentary.

Exodus 20:11	Deuteronomy 5:15
For in six days the LORD made the heavens and the earth, the sea and all that is in them, and rested on the seventh day; therefore the LORD blessed the seventh day and made it holy.	And you shall remember that you were a slave in the land of Egypt, and the LORD your God brought you out of there by a mighty hand and by an outstretched arm, therefore the LORD your God commanded you to observe the Sabbath day.

What does this mean? The reference to the creation week in Exodus 20 was not part of the original Ten Commandments. Thus, it was not part of the "moral" law!

This insight pulls the rug out from beneath both Christian and cultic Sabbatarians. Most of their rhetoric is based on the idea that the reference to the creation week was part of the Ten Commandments. The fact that Moses omitted any reference to it in Deuteronomy 5 and substituted the Exodus instead forever dooms their argument.

These observations also refute the argument that since Moses referred to the creation in Exodus 20, this means that the Sabbath began at the creation. If this argument was valid, then since Moses only mentions the Exodus out of Egypt in Deuteronomy 5, we would have to conclude that the Sabbath began with the Exodus. But, in the context, Moses was not dating the inception of the Sabbath, but rather he was motivating people to obey it.

Many other arguments show that the Sabbath was a ceremonial law.
1. Old Testament and New Testament writers consistently place the Sabbath in the lists of the other ceremonial laws. No moral law is grouped or listed with ceremonial laws (1 Chron. 23:31; 2 Chron. 2:4-8, 13; 31:3; Neh. 10:33; Ezek. 45:17; Hos. 2:11; Col. 2:16; Heb. 4).

2. How could God despise Sabbath-keeping and put an end to it if it were a moral law (Isa. 1:10-14; Hos. 2:11)?

3. If it is a moral law, why is it never repeated in the New Testament like the other nine commandments?

4. The author of Hebrews treats the Sabbath like all other ceremonial laws, i.e., as a type or shadow of Christ's work of salvation (Heb. 4; cf. Col. 2:17).

5. Jesus clearly equated "Sabbath" with the ceremonial "sacrifice" in Matthew 12:7. Thus, He taught that it was a ceremonial law.

6. The Jerusalem Council in Acts 15 was faced with a direct question which certainly bears on the Sabbath issue: "How much of Mosaic law should the Gentile Christians keep?"

   If Sabbath-keeping was a moral law binding on Gentiles, then they would have included it in their decision. But they did not bind the Gentiles to obey the Sabbath. Thus it was only a ceremonial law fulfilled in Christ.

7. If it were a moral law, then the apostle Paul would never leave its observance up to Christian liberty as he taught in Colossians 2:16.

8. If Sabbath-keeping was binding on New Covenant believers as a part of the moral law, then why did the early Christians:
   - work on Sundays without complaint.
   - never call the "Lord's Day" a "Sabbath."
   - consistently teach that the Fourth Commandment was a ceremonial law fulfilled by Christ, and as such no longer binding? Centuries went by before anyone talked about a "Christian Sabbath." Why? Where is the apostolic and historical pedigree for the Sabbatarian doctrine? It has no such pedigree.

9. It is geographically impossible for all men to keep the Sabbath. What would those in cold climates do without heat (Exo. 35:13)? In the far North, where there are six months of day and six months of night, how can the Sabbath be kept? Is it not true that a moral law can be kept anywhere? But the Sabbath cannot be kept universally across this planet, which has days of different lengths. What will colonies on Mars or on space stations do about the Sabbath? These are issues that Sabbatarians will have to face in coming years, if the Lord tarries.

10. The Jewish Sabbath lasted from Friday sundown to Saturday sundown. If the Fourth Commandment is still in effect as a creation ordinance, then why do Christian Sabbatarians not begin their Sabbath Saturday evening and end it Sunday evening? How can they brush aside the "sundown" to "sundown" structure of the Old Covenant Sabbath?

11. It is economically impossible to shut down our modern industrial society every Sunday. If the steel mills turned off their furnaces one day out of the week, it would be impossible to produce steel, for it takes a week for them to heat up sufficiently to begin production (cf. Gary North, "The Economics of Sabbath Keeping," in *The Institutes of Biblical Law*, pp. 824-836).

The 'Sabbath Made for Man' Argument

The Sabbatarian Position:
Christ clearly taught that the Sabbath was a moral law in Mark 2:27 on two grounds:
1. The Sabbath was made for man, i.e., it is a moral law.
2. It was made for man, i.e., not for Jews only, but mankind considered as a whole.

Examination of This Argument
1. An examination of the context (vs. 23-28) reveals that instead of seeking to establish the Sabbath as a moral law, Christ clearly equates it with the ceremonial law concerning the shewbread. The Pharisees made too much of the Sabbath, and Christ now instructs them as to a proper view of the ceremonial nature of the Sabbath. Christ and His disciples could "break" the

Sabbath, just as David and his men could "break" the law about shewbread because both were ceremonial laws.

2. Christ's statement, "the Sabbath was made for man and not man for the Sabbath," plainly reveals the ceremonial nature of the Sabbath. Ceremonial laws are "made for man," i.e., for man's assistance, help, ignorance, etc. Thus Christ was teaching that just as the law regarding shewbread was "made for man" and could not be used against the health and welfare of people, so the Sabbath law was also "made for man." That is, it is no more a moral law than the law for shewbread. It is clear that the Pharisees had twisted the Sabbath all out of proportion and Jesus here puts it in proper perspective.

3. As to the argument that since Christ said "for man," instead of "for Israel," that this means "all mankind who ever lived or will live in all ages and places," we make the following observations:
   a. An examination of the usage of the Greek word translated "man" reveals that it rarely means "all mankind." In fact, in many places, such as 1 Timothy 2:1, it is impossible to understand it as "all mankind."
   b. Most Sunday Sabbatarians are strict Calvinists who go to great lengths when discussing the atonement to prove that this Greek word does not mean "all mankind." They rightly point this out in such places as Rom. 5:18, 1 Tim. 2:4, Titus 2:11, etc.

It seems quite strange to us that the very same theologians who dogmatically state that "man" in Mark 2:27 must mean "all mankind," are equally strong in other passages as cited above that the word cannot mean "all mankind"!

The Hebrews 4:9 Argument

The Sabbatarian Position

In this chapter the author of Hebrews clearly states that there remains for the Christian a Sabbath day of rest.

Examination of This Argument

1. This argument's greatest proponent was the Puritan, John Owen. But the exegetical evidence against his Sabbatarian position is so great that no classic commentator can be cited who agreed with his interpretation. Even some of the Puritans, such as John Brown, rejected Owen's interpretation.
   With almost all the classic commentaries and exegetes against the Sabbatarian position on Hebrews 4, this at once makes us suspicious of its validity.

2. A careful exegesis reveals that Hebrews 4 is teaching the exact opposite of the Sabbatarian position. The context is clear on the following points:
   a. God's "rest" in Hebrews 3:18 stands symbolically for the promised land. Because of unbelief, most of the generation died in the wilderness instead of entering His "rest" (3:16-19).
   b. From this Old Testament example, the author now informs his audience that the promise of a greater "rest" stands before them (4:1a).
   c. This "rest" is of such a nature that:
      ● We can fall short of it (v. 1b).
      ● We fall short if we do not believe the Gospel (v. 2).
      ● It is entered into by faith (v. 3).
   d. This "rest" is now drawn from another Old Testament example: God's Sabbath rest (v. 4).
   e. The author combines God's Sabbath rest with the "rest" of the promised land (v. 5), and

states that disobedience to the Gospel hinders anyone from entering "rest" (v. 6).

   f. Even now in the age of salvation, the age of "Today" (v. 7; cf. 2 Cor. 6:2), God calls us to enter a "rest"; a rest like God's Sabbath rest; a rest like that in Canaan (v. 9).
The only reason for putting the word "Sabbath rest" (Greek, *sabbatismos*, v. 9) instead of just "rest" as in the rest of the context is that the author had just used God's "Sabbath" as an illustration or example.

   g. The nature of the "rest" or "Sabbath rest" of v. 9 is explained in verses 10-11.

- Just as God ceased forever from His works, even so we are to cease from depending upon or trying to produce works to merit salvation. The works we produce are elsewhere called "dead works" (6:1).
- Let us enter the "rest of faith" in the Gospel and persevere to the end. We must not fall into or rest upon dead works.
- The danger to which the author was addressing himself was apostasy, not which day was to be observed by Christians. The audience was tempted to return to Judaism, thus the author exhorts them to persevere in the faith, and he warns them of condemnation if they become disobedient to the Gospel.

The fact that this is the theme of the entire book and the thrust of chapter four is accepted by nearly all commentators. Why do the Sabbatarians ignore this broader and immediate context? The emphasis in Hebrews 4 is on a future rest that yet awaits all who persevere to the end in faith (cf. 10:38-39), and the author's fear that by moving back under the Old Covenant they would fall short of that *sabbatismos.*

The conclusion of the author's argument is given in vs. 14-16. In order to enter God's rest, we must "hold firmly to the faith" (v. 14) in Christ's meritorious priestly atonement. Therefore, let us "approach the throne of grace with confidence" (v. 16) in view of Christ's work for us.

Conclusion

Hebrews 4 is a passage which shows that God's Sabbath and the Promised Land were an eschatological foreshadowing of the believer's rest of faith in the Gospel of salvation, accomplished by the sealing of the New Covenant by the blood of Christ. Heb. 4:9 does not say "Sabbath day" but rather "Sabbath-like rest" (*sabbatismos*). The context rules out the Sabbatarian interpretation, because the emphasis falls not on a day to be observed in this age, but on an eternal rest awaiting all who live by faith until the end (cf. 3:14).

The 'Remember' Argument

The Sabbatarian Position

The word "remember" in the Fourth Commandment points us to the past observance of the Sabbath since the creation.

Examination of This Argument

1. The Hebrew word *zachar* in Exodus 20:8 is in the Kal infinitive form and not in the imperative. The *Brown, Driver and Briggs Lexicon* does not place the word as found in Exodus 20:8 in the section under "recalling something or someone you already knew about" (sections 1-2). Rather, it means to recall to mind from now on, i.e., "to observe or commemorate" a certain day.
2. An examination of the *Englishman's Hebrew and Chaldee Concordance* reveals that in many cases "remember" has the meaning of a future calling to mind. Thus, Moses was saying, "From now on, recall to mind and sanctify..."

3. When *zachar* is used for observing a ceremonial day, it is usually combined with and is synonymous with *shamar*, which means to observe or preserve (cf. Deut. 16:1, 3).

The Exodus 16 Argument

The Sabbatarian Position

The Sabbath was observed before Moses, starting with the creation. This can be shown in Exodus 16, where the people started resting on the seventh day as a Sabbath before the Ten Commandments were given. Thus, it was already being observed by the people of God.

Examination of This Argument
1. Exodus 16 is still during the lifetime of Moses. There is nothing to indicate a pre-Mosaic origin of the Sabbath in Exodus 16. This is further borne out when we remember the "sign" nature of the Sabbath in Israel's covenant relationship with God.

2. On the contrary, the following points are clear:
   a. It is doubtful that the Egyptians allowed the Jews a Sabbath day during their 400 years of bondage. Thus, it was not the practice of the people of God to rest the seventh day when they were Egyptian slaves.
   b. Special revelation is not needed for a moral law or for something already observed. If something is going to be introduced for the first time, there must be a special revelation and a training period so that the people can adapt to the new practice or ceremonial law.
   c. In Exodus 16:45, God sets forth a new test for the people of God. He would give manna six days, with a double portion on the sixth day.
   d. When the sixth day arrived, the people gathered a double portion. But they did not know why a double portion was given. It is obvious in verse 22 that the people asked Moses what a double portion meant.
   e. Moses responds in verses 22 to 26 with his interpretation of the revelation/test given in verses 4 and 5. "Since God gives us a double portion on the sixth day, He does not plan to give us any manna on the seventh. It is a day of rest. So, cook up your extra manna to eat tomorrow and stay home."
   f. Some of the people still did not understand this new test of a day of rest. Thus, they went out on the seventh day for manna but found none (v. 27).
   g. Since the previous revelation of this new regulation had been ignored by many people, God once again revealed to Moses that this new test of obedience was to be strictly observed (vs. 28-29).
   h. So, the people finally gave in to the new law and rested on the seventh day (v. 30).

Conclusion

An accurate exegesis of Exodus 16 reveals that the Lord was foreshadowing the Fourth Commandment by giving a new test or commandment in Exodus 16. The purpose of this incident was to introduce the people of God to a new concept and a new law which had not been previously known or observed. Consequently, this passage cannot be used as proof that Sabbath-keeping began at Creation.

The Matthew 24:20 Argument

The Sabbatarian Position

Christ prophesied that Christians would be observing the Sabbath even at the end of the world when He returns—"pray that your flight be not on the Sabbath day."

Examination of This Argument

1. In verse 20 Christ is discussing what believers should do in A.D. 70 when Titus would come to destroy the Temple and Jerusalem. Jesus is not dealing here with the end of the world, but with the end of the Temple (v. 12).

2. Jesus was simply saying, "Since the Jews forbid travel on their Sabbath, pray that you as Christians do not have to escape to the hills on that day, for the Jews will hinder you."

3. The "Sabbath" referred to in this verse is the Jewish Saturday Sabbath and obviously has no reference to the "Lord's Day." And it is certainly stretching the point to suggest that Christ had in view a time when the "Sabbath" would be transferred to Sunday.

4. Christ was simply referring to things which would hinder escape from Jerusalem's destruction:
   a. Greed for material possessions (vs. 17-18).
   b. Pregnancy or nursing babies (v. 19).
   c. Winter time (v. 20).
   d. Jewish Sabbath (v. 20).

The Argument From Silence

The Sabbatarian Position

The New Testament is silent about the Sabbath, and this silence proves that they observed it. We do not need a command, example or precept in the New Testament to prove that the Sabbath is to be kept. They go on to argue that:

● Since God had already commanded people to observe the Sabbath as a creation ordinance and as a moral law in the Old Testament, it is obviously still in force in the New Covenant age. Anything commanded in the Old Testament and not explicitly abrogated in the New is still in effect.

● The early church was Jewish and they kept the Sabbath, even though they changed it to the first day after the Sabbath. No one contested this practice or the change from the seventh to the first day. Thus, it was never an issue of controversy to be mentioned in the New Testament.

● There were also "pastoral concerns" for not mentioning the Sabbath in the New Testament. Why would the New Testament writers bring up something which was already assumed? To be silent on the Sabbath would not cause controversy, but to discuss it would do so.

Examination of This Argument

Many Sabbatarians readily admit that the New Testament neither repeats the Fourth Commandment or applies it to Christians. Virtually all sides agree that there is a conspicuous silence in the New Testament about any present obligation of the Christian to observe the Sabbath. No rules or regulations are ever set forth for keeping the Sabbath. No examples of Christians keeping the Sabbath can be found. No one is ever disciplined for breaking the Sabbath. The only perceptual passages seem to abrogate the Sabbath (Col. 2:16-17). Why is the New Testament silent?

It is interesting to note that Baptists upbraid the Presbyterians for their use of the argument from silence to justify infant baptism, and yet these same Baptists will often employ this same argument to defend sabbatarianism! The following comments refute the argument from silence.

1. The argument from silence can be valid when it is used to demonstrate that in principle all ceremonial laws have been abrogated, and if something is not reinstated, it is no longer binding. This is using silence in a Scriptural manner.

2. That the argument from silence can be used against the Sabbath can be seen from an exegesis of Hebrews 7:14. Here the author builds his argument for the unique priesthood of Christ on the silence of the Old Testament.

3. The early church was not made up exclusively of Jews or Jewish proselytes. The missionary

labors of Paul and others brought in pagan converts. These Gentiles had no Jewish background, and were never instructed to keep a Sabbath after becoming Christians.

4. The history of the early church clearly shows that they did not observe the Lord's Day as a Sabbath, or refer to the Fourth Commandment as binding on Christians. They taught that the Sabbath command was a ceremonial law fulfilled by Christ.

5. That the early Christian Jews could change the Sabbath from the seventh to the first day and not get involved in a controversy with the Jews or Judaizers is so foolish as to be self-refuting.

6. There were no "pastoral reasons" for the silence of the New Testament. The pastoral concerns of the apostle Paul led him to state clearly that the Sabbath was a "shadow" ordinance (Col. 2:17).

No one, therefore, can condemn you for not observing dietary laws, feast days, or the weekly Sabbath (Col. 2:16). It is clear that Paul is dealing with the Jewish seventh-day Sabbath and not the so-called "Christian Sabbath" because he also speaks of dietary laws and "new moons." The New Testament, therefore, is not silent on the matter, but specifically indicates its passing away with the coming of Christ.

Conclusion

While the New Testament never reinstitutes the Sabbath, it positively abrogates its significance as a day to be observed. The Sabbath found its fulfillment in Christ, who is the Lord of the Sabbath. Thus, Paul declared it "nailed to the cross." Christ alone in His Word can bind the conscience of the child of God.

The practical fruits of sabbatarianism have historically led to many evils such as:

- Legalism: Church leaders making up arbitrary rules and regulations to govern the Sabbath.
- Anarchy: Each Sabbatarian sets forth his own rules of what can be and cannot be done on Sunday.
- Party spirit: It breeds pride and an air of superiority.
- It fosters a critical and judgmental spirit.
- It kills the joy of the Christian's worship day by fostering a gloomy, morbid and even fearful attitude.
- It hurts families by forbidding laughter, play and, historically, even sexual relations between husband and wife.
- It has divided churches and split communities.
- It has brought about a state of bondage by taking away Christian liberty and imposing the "beggarly elements" from the Old Covenant upon the Christian's conscience.

Part III

A Biblical-Theological Approach to the Sabbath

1. The Sabbath is a concept revealed in the context of the Mosaic covenant. Thus, the Sabbath did not appear until Moses' time.

The creation ordinance argument obscures the covenantal "sign" nature of the Sabbath. This is why Sabbatarians have yet to develop the distinctively covenantal character of the Sabbath as a test or sign of covenantal obedience to God (cf. Exo. 31:12-17; Isa. 56:47; Deut. 5:11).

2. When the concept of the Sabbath was first introduced, it only signified physical rest. It did not have any spiritual overtones at all (Exodus 16).

As the history of redemption unfolded, the concept of the Sabbath deepened in its meaning and began to have spiritual significance. The worship of God in private and public slowly became part of the Sabbath.

3. If the Sabbath had been instituted since the creation of man, it would have deepened beyond

mere physical rest by the time of Exodus 16. Since the Sabbath did not develop spiritual overtones until the later prophets, this reveals that it could not have been observed from the beginning of history. The dynamic unfolding and deepening process of biblical truth would not have been stagnant from Adam to Moses.

4. As the unfolding spiritual character of the Sabbath developed, it came to signify a day of "rest in God," a rest of faith in God and a day spent in the worship of God.

5. But the Pharisees in our Lord's time externalized the Sabbath and made it a day of gloominess. They manifested a legalistic zeal and attention to the strict outward observance of the day. They sought to undo and to reverse the unfolding dynamic spiritual meaning of the day. They did not see that the Sabbath was essentially eschatological in nature and that it prefigured the Messianic age in which believers would rest from dead works by having a conscience void of offense due to Christ's perfect work on the cross (Heb. 4:1-16; 10:1-25; Col. 2:14-17).

6. The Lord of the Sabbath has ushered in the age of the Sabbath. The shadow of a weekly Sabbath is no longer needed, because that which it prefigured has come.

7. Weekly Sabbath-keeping is part of the Old Testament "promise" and has no place in the New Testament "fulfillment." Sabbath-keeping has served its purpose and, just as the scaffolding around a building is taken away once the building is completed, so the weekly Sabbath has been done away by Christ, the Master Builder of the New Temple, which is the new Israel of God, the Church.

8. We look forward to a greater fulfillment of the Sabbath age. It prefigures the saints' rest in Heaven and the eternal state.

9. Sabbatarianism is retrogressive and reactionary. It tries to stop the unfolding dynamic of the eschatological character of the Sabbath. It attempts to turn back the hands of the clock of redemptive history by keeping the shadow, and ignoring the reality which cast the shadow. Let us go on in faith and embrace the reality which cast the shadow of the weekly Sabbath.

Conclusion

The Sabbatarian position cannot stand up under close exegetical scrutiny. In its place we need to develop a practical theology of our corporate Gospel duties in the light of passages like Hebrews 10:25.

Part IV

A Brief Theology of Corporate Christian Worship

1. The "Lord's Day" has historically been identified with Sunday, called in the New Testament "the first day of the week," which is the day Christ rose from the dead.

That this is true has been demonstrated to such a degree in debates against the Adventists by such writers as Walter Martin, that we will not here develop the argument (Walter Martin, *The Truth About Seventh-Day Adventism* (Zondervan, 1965).

The fact that Sunday is specifically referred to in the New Testament as *mia sabbaton* (literally, "the first after the Sabbath") should raise serious questions about the wisdom of identifying Sabbath and Sunday. The New Testament clearly designates Sunday as a day other than the "Sabbath."

2. On Sunday morning, Christians historically have assembled for worship, fellowship, instruction and the ordinances of baptism and the Lord's Supper. This is obvious from the post-resurrection appearances of Christ (all of which took place on "the first after the Sabbath"), the data in the book of Acts and the subsequent history of the early church.

3. What we are to do when we assemble is given in the New Testament by way of example and command. The examples and commands found in Acts 2:41-42; 20:7; 1 Cor. 5:4; 11:2, 23ff.; 14:26; 16:2; and Heb. 10:25. These passages delineate the essentials. We must attend the gathering together

of the saints to hear preaching, participate in the ordinances, give offerings, and minister to each other in the context of the Body of Christ.

In the light of these New Testament teachings, there are several theological reasons (such as the first day being the time of the resurrection and Pentecost) for Christians preferring to meet on Sunday. But there are no biblical directives which state that it is sin for the brethren to meet together on some other day.

The truth is that the New Testament emphasizes our corporate duties, not a day on which those duties must be fulfilled. Sin is committed if these duties are not fulfilled in the Christian's life; but there is no indication that sin is committed by fulfilling these duties on the "wrong" day.

4. If you faithfully fulfill your corporate New Covenant duties on the day of worship in the local church where you are a member, then you are free to do whatever God leads you to do. No one has the right to set up extra-Scriptural rules regarding what can and cannot be done on the worship day (Col. 2:16). Your conscience is to be under God and His Word, and not in bondage to the traditions or laws of men.

5. Our assembling together should be a time of great joy and rejoicing, for Christ has ushered in the "Year of Jubilee," and has proclaimed liberty throughout the earth. Our times together should be filled with joy and Christian fellowship. The resurrection of Christ signifies hope, life and joy. These things—not fear or gloom—should characterize our corporate gatherings.

6. Since Christian liberty (with reference to the observance or non-observance of days) is clearly to regulate such external matters, no Christian should judge another Christian in areas of personal freedom (Rom. 14:4-23; Col. 2:16; Gal. 5:1).

Part V

Sabbath-Keeping In Church History

1. The early Church did not see any relationship between the Lord's Day and the Fourth Commandment. The Sabbath was viewed as a ceremonial law fulfilled in Christ (Phillip Schaff, *The History of the Christian Church*, Vol. 1, pp. 477-479; Vol. II, pp. 202-205; Vol. III, pp. 378-385).

2. The Middle Ages saw the union of church and state, beginning with Constantine. The Sabbath was introduced by theocratically-minded religious and civil leaders who drew civil laws from the Old Testament. Sabbatarianism had its greatest day in the scholastic period of Roman Catholic theology (R.A. Morey, *Exclusive Psalmody*, Research and Education Foundation, 1975, pp. 41-56).

3. The pre-Reformers and early Reformers threw out the medieval Catholic Sabbath and returned to the theology of the early church (Dr. Richard Gaffin, *Calvin and the Sabbath*, Westminster Theological Seminary thesis).

4. The Puritan period continued the tradition of church-state union, and in this context the Sabbath was re-established in their 17th century theocracies. It was a return to scholastic Catholic thinking.

5. Today, only within the Reformed community is there any serious attempt to revive the Christian Sabbatarian position. To some, it has become a sacred cow or a theological shibboleth. At the same time, Reformation studies on the position of the early Reformers are reviving the Continental Reformed position, which is the position of this author.

6. Cultic Sabbatarians often make seventh-day Sabbath-keeping essential for salvation. This reveals that they are preaching salvation by works instead of by grace. They, like the Pharisees, go about seeking to establish their own righteousness. Their judgment is just.

Conclusion

The Sabbath was a ceremonial law which pointed backward to creation and forward to salvation by faith. It was ceremonial in nature, function and attributes. The Continental Reformed position is thus confirmed as the best understanding of the biblical data.

Suggested Reading

John Calvin, *Institutes of the Christian Religion,* Book 11, Chapter 8, section 28-34.

From Sabbath to Lord's Day, ed. D.A. Carson (Grand Rapids: Zondervan, 1982).

Richard Gaffin, *Calvin and the Sabbath,* unpublished Th. M. thesis at Westminster Theological Seminary.

James Hessey, *Sunday: Its Origin, History and Present Obligation* (London: Cossell, 1889).

Gary North, "The Economics of Sabbath Keeping" in R.J. Rushdoony's *The Institutes of Biblical Law* (P&R, 1976) pp. 824-836.

Hiley Ward, *Space-Age Sunday* (Macmillan, 1960).

Robert Morey, *An Examination of Exclusive Psalmody* (New Life, 1974).

Chapter One Hundred Thirty-Three
Conclusion

A local church is like a ship at sea. While it may have carefully mapped out where it wants to go, the winds of adversity and conflict often drive a church where it did not intend to go. Every church experiences the good, the bad, and ugly. It is part of spiritual warfare and cannot be avoided.

The material found in this work can be adapted for sermons, Sunday School classes, and group Bible studies. Indeed, the manuscript was tested in Baptist, Presbyterian, and Pentecostal churches with great success. The pastors loved the fact that most of the material is in the form of sermon outlines and can be used for overheads or PowerPoint. Teachers found the materials that handle difficult issues such as head coverings very helpful. It is our prayer that you will spiritually profit in your private life as well as church experience.

To God Alone be the Glory.